Lecture Notes in Computer Science 12612

More information about this subseries at http://www.springer.com/series/7410

Yongdong Wu · Moti Yung (Eds.)

Information Security and Cryptology

16th International Conference, Inscrypt 2020 Guangzhou, China, December 11–14, 2020 Revised Selected Papers

Editors
Yongdong Wu
Jinan University
Guangzhou, China

Moti Yung
Computer Science Department
Columbia University
New York, NY, USA

ISSN 0302-9743 ISSN 1611-3349 (electronic)
Lecture Notes in Computer Science
ISBN 978-3-030-71851-0 ISBN 978-3-030-71852-7 (eBook)
https://doi.org/10.1007/978-3-030-71852-7

LNCS Sublibrary: SL4 – Security and Cryptology

This Springer imprint is published by the registered company Springer Nature Switzerland AG
The registered company address is: Gewerbestrasse 11, 6330 Cham, Switzerland

Preface

The 16th International Conference on Information Security and Cryptology (Inscrypt 2020) was held in Guangzhou, Guangdong, from December 11 to 14, 2020. It was co-organized by the State Key Laboratory of Information Security, the Chinese Association for Cryptologic Research, and the College of Cyber Security of Jinan University, and in cooperation with the IACR. Due to the COVID-19 pandemic, it was held as a hybrid of physical and online components.

Inscrypt is an annual conference held in China, targeting research advances in all areas of information security, cryptology, and their applications. The 2020 conference instance received a total of 79 submissions from Russia, Korea, Australia, China Hong Kong, and China mainland. The two PC chairs were supported by 45 Program Committee (PC) members and 13 sub-reviewers, who were leading experts on cryptology and security from 13 countries or regions. The PC team selected 24 papers as Full Papers, and 8 papers as Short Papers. In the selecting process, the papers were bid for by the PC members and then automatically assigned to them for reviewing. The reviewing process was conducted using a double-blind peer review process, and each paper was reviewed by at least three PC members or sub-reviewers. All the accepted papers were included in the conference proceedings.

The program of Inscrypt 2020 included six excellent invited academic keynote talks by Professors Danfeng (Daphne) Yao (USA), Yang Liu (Singapore), Aggelos Kiayias (United Kingdom), Orr Dunkelman (Israel), Giuseppe Persiano (Italy), and Chuanming Zong (China), as well as one industrial keynote talk by Dr. Qisen Huang (Nsfocus, China). In addition, the program included nine regular presentation sessions on AI Security, Asymmetric ciphers, Post-quantum Cryptology, Systems security, Privacy Protection, Digital Signatures, etc.

It would have been impossible to have a successful Inscrypt 2020 conference without the significant contribution of many people. First, we would like to thank all the authors for submitting their research results to the conference. We were also very grateful to the PC members and external reviewers for contributing their knowledge and expertise and for their hard reviewing work. Second, we were greatly indebted to the Honorary Chairs, Weiqi Luo and Dongdai Lin, and General Chairs, Jian Weng and Robert H. Deng, for their overall and organization efforts. Third, we thank Kaimin Wei and Shanxiang Lyu for organizing the online and offline conference program, Boyu Gao for checking all the latex files and for assembling the files for submission to Springer, and Mr. Chen and the IACR for setting up and maintaining the Web Submission and Review software for the paper submission and review process. Last but not least, we thank Alfred Hofmann, Anna Kramer, and their Springer colleagues for handling the publication of the conference proceedings.

December 2020

Yongdong Wu
Moti Yung

Preface

Organization

Inscrypt 2020

16th China International Conference on Information Security and Cryptology

Guangzhou, China
December 11–14, 2020

Sponsored and organized by

State Key Laboratory of Information Security
(Chinese Academy of Sciences) Jinan University

in cooperation with

International Association for Cryptologic Research
Chinese Association for Cryptologic Research

Honorary Chairs

Weiqi Luo	Jinan University, China
Dongdai Lin	Chinese Academy of Sciences, China

General Chairs

Jian Weng	Jinan University, China
Robert H. Deng	Singapore Management University, Singapore

Technical Program Chairs

Yongdong Wu	Jinan University, China
Moti Yung	Google and Columbia University, USA

Organizing Chairs

Kaimin Wei	Jinan University, China
Shanxiang Lyu	Jinan University, China

Steering Committee

Feng Bao	Huawei International, Singapore
Kefei Chen	Hangzhou Normal University, China

Dawu Gu	Shanghai Jiao Tong University, China
Xinyi Huang	Fujian Normal University, China
Hui Li	Xidian University, China
Dongdai Lin	Chinese Academy of Sciences, China
Peng Liu	Pennsylvania State University, USA
Zhe Liu	Nanjing University of Aeronautics and Astronautics, China
Wen-Feng Qi	National Digital Switching System Engineering and Technological Research Center, China
Meiqin Wang	Shandong University, China
XiaoFeng Wang	Indiana University at Bloomington, USA
Xiaoyun Wang	Tsinghua University, China
Jian Weng	Jinan University, China
Moti Yung	Google and Columbia University, USA
Fangguo Zhang	Sun Yat-sen University, China
Huanguo Zhang	Wuhan University, China

PC Members

Binbin Chen	Singapore University of Technology and Design, Singapore
Kai Chen	Chinese Academy of Sciences, China
Yu Chen	Shandong University, China
Jorge Cuellar	University of Passau, Germany
Hong-Ning Dai	Macau University of Science and Technology, China
Jérémie Decouchant	University of Luxembourg, Luxembourg
Muhammed Esgin	Monash University, Australia
Liming Fang	Nanjing University of Aeronautics and Astronautics, China
Dawu Gu	Shanghai Jiao Tong University, China
Jian Guo	Nanyang Technological University, Singapore
Chunpeng Ge	University of Wollongong, Australia
Shoichi Hirose	University of Fukui, Japan
Shujun Li	University of Kent, UK
Yingjiu Li	University of Oregon, USA
Kaitai Liang	University of Surrey, UK
Feng Lin	Zhejiang University, China
Jingqiang Lin	Chinese Academy of Sciences, China
Joseph Liu	Monash University, Australia
Zhe Liu	Nanjing University of Aeronautics and Astronautics, China
Peng Liu	Pennsylvania State University, USA
Jiqiang Lu	Beijing University of Aeronautics and Astronautics, China
Xiapu Luo	The Hong Kong Polytechnic University, China
Di Ma	University of Michigan-Dearborn, USA

Weizhi Meng	Technical University of Denmark, Denmark
Neetesh Saxena	Cardiff University, UK
Hwajeong Seo	Hansung University, Korea
Ling Song	Jinan University, China
Chunhua Su	The University of Aizu, Japan
Willy Susilo	University of Wollongong, Australia
Qiang Tang	New Jersey Institute of Technology, USA
Ding Wang	Nankai University, China
Long Wang	IBM Watson, USA
Zhuo Wei	Huawei Technologies Research, Singapore
Jinming Wen	Jinan University, China
Wenling Wu	Chinese Academy of Sciences, China
Hongjun Wu	Nanyang Technological University, Singapore
Shouhuai Xu	University of Texas at San Antonio, USA
Wenyuan Xu	Zhejiang University, China
Wun-She Yap	Universiti Tunku Abdul Rahman, Malaysia
Tsz Hon Yuen	The University of Hong Kong, China
Lu Zhou	Nanjing University of Aeronautics and Astronautics, China
Fan Zhang	Zhejiang University, China
Kehuan Zhang	The Chinese University of Hong Kong, China Hongkong

Sub-reviewers

Zhenzhen Bao
Chun Guo
Zhaoyang Han
Feiran Huang
Zhuotao Lian
Meicheng Liu
Yaobin Shen
Siang Meng
Yi Tu
Xueqiao Xue
Zhichao Yang
Haibin Zheng

Sponsors

NSFOCUS

NSFOCUS

HUAWEI

Contents

AI Security

Asymmetric Cipher

Post-quantum Crypto

Secure Sequence

Digital Signature

Mathematical Fundamental

Symmetric Cipher

AI Security

Polytopic Attack on Round-Reduced Simon32/64 Using Deep Learning

Heng-Chuan Su, Xuan-Yong Zhu(✉), and Duan Ming

State Key Laboratory of Mathematical Engineering and Advanced Computing, Information Engineering University, Zhengzhou 450001, China
xuanyong.zhu@263.net

Abstract. In CRYPTO 2019, Gohr uses the residual network technology of artificial intelligence to build a differential distinguisher, and attacks the reduced-round Speck32/64. We tried this method to recover the keys for ten-round Simon32/64. In this paper, we have three innovations. First, we construct polytope neural network distinguisher. On eight-round Simon32/64, polytope neural network distinguisher could increase the success rate of three neural network distinguishers with 0.76 success rate to 0.92. Second, we propose an attack on Simon32/64 based on the combination of the probability of differential path and polytope neural network distinguisher. This method can only increase the computational complexity of the chosen data as the number of rounds increases. Nine-round polytope neural network distinguisher is used to filter out data, whether it is what we want. Eight-round neural distinguisher is used to recover the final round key. The computational complexity of key recovery on the final key of eleven-round Simon32/64 is $2^{33.4}$. Third, we propose an attack called Bayesian Key Research with Error. With this attack, the computational complexity of key recovery on the final key of eleven-round Simon32/64 is $2^{30.9}$.

In our paper, the main idea is combining polytope differences with neural networks. By constructing polytope differential neural network distinguisher, we make a key recovery attack. In order to increase the number of rounds, we first used brute force attack and then proposed Bayesian Key Research with Error. We think this idea can be applied to many cryptographic algorithms.

Keywords: Deep learning · Polytopic attack · Simon32/64

1 Introduction

Cryptography is the core foundation of current information security, and sequence cipher and block cipher are the primary means of modern data security. For the attack and analysis of the cryptographic algorithm, it is mainly to mine the inherent non-random characteristics of the algorithm and design and construct the corresponding attack methods. The typical attack methods include linear attack, differential attack, and algebraic attack, and the application of

Y. Wu and M. Yung (Eds.): Inscrypt 2020, LNCS 12612, pp. 3–20, 2021.
https://doi.org/10.1007/978-3-030-71852-7_1

multi attack methods. In practical use, the non-random feature is to construct a distinguisher with a probability advantage. Based on sufficient data, the distinguishers allow to determine the correct key, to attack the cryptographic algorithm. At present, differential attack and its various deformation attack methods are among the main theoretical methods of algorithm attack. The main basis of the attack method is: the input vector is different in some specific positions, and the output vector changes unevenly; that is to say, there is a high probability differential pair. In the actual algorithm attack process, the high probability differential pairs of multiple series links are connected to form a high probability differential path, based on which a differential divider is constructed. It is one of the core tasks of cryptanalysis and attack to find a high probability differential path and construct an efficient distinguisher.

With the rapid development of high-performance computing and big data in recent years, artificial intelligence technology based on deep learning has made incredible achievements in speech recognition [17], machine translation [18], and many other fields. Artificial intelligence technology has inherent advantages in detection and recognition based on fixed weak features. Based on this, cryptography researchers try to introduce artificial intelligence into the cryptanalysis.

In 2011, Hospodar et al. Proposed a side-channel attack method for AES using deep learning technology [1]. In 2012, Alani proposed a known-plaintext attack method based on neural network technology [2], decrypting the ciphertext through the trained neural network when the key is unknown. In 2019, Gohr uses the residual network technology of artificial intelligence to build a differential distinguisher [3], and attacks the reduced-round speck encryption algorithm.

In this paper, we use neural networks to construct the differential distinguisher and the key recovery attack of Simon32/64 [5,6,13]. First, we use our nine-round differential neural network distinguisher to recover the keys for ten-round by wrong key randomization and Bayesian optimization. In this experiment, choosing 2^{14} plaintext pairs, statistics based on 50 results we could know that the attack was successful in 50 out of 50 trials; our implementation outputs a key guess in approximately half a quarter of a minute on average (measured average in 100 trials: 14.36 s) when running on a single thread of our machine with no graphics card usage. Second, we propose an attack on Simon32/64 based on the combination of the probability of differential path and polytope neural network distinguisher. This method can only increase the computational complexity of the chosen data as the number of rounds increases. Nine-round polytope neural network distinguisher is used to filter out data, whether it is what we want. Eight-round neural distinguisher is used to recover the final round key. The computational complexity of key recovery on the final key of eleven-round Simon32/64 is $2^{33.4}$. Third, we propose an attack with Bayesian Key Research with Error on Simon32/64. In our attack, we consider the affect of the bad points in building wrong key randomization table. The computational complexity of key recovery on the final key of eleven-round Simon32/64 is $2^{30.9}$.

The second section of this paper introduces the Simon algorithm and some properties of Simon; the third section is to construct differential distinguisher based on neural networks; the fourth section is the result of differential neural network distinguisher and polytope differential neural network distinguisher; the fifth section is key recovery attack on Simon32/64 on the final round with three method. First, Bayesian key research. Second, brute force polytopic attack. Third, Bayesian Key Research with Error; the sixth section summarizes the work of the paper and future work.

2 The Simon Family of Block Ciphers

2.1 Notations

Bitwise addition will in the sequel be denoted by $\oplus$, bitwise and will in the sequel be denoted by $\wedge$, and bitwise rotation of a fixed-size word by $\lll$ for rotation to the left.

2.2 A Short Description of Simon

Suppose the left half of input texts to the i-th round is L^{i-1}, and the right half is R^{i-1}. The subkey is K^{i-1}. The round function is

$$\left(L^i, R^i\right) = \left(R^{i-1} \oplus F\left(L^{i-1}\right) \oplus K^{i-1}, L^{i-1}\right) \tag{1}$$

where

$$F(x) = ((x \lll 1) \wedge (x \lll 8)) \oplus (x \lll 2) \tag{2}$$

2.3 Some Properties of Simon

Here, we introduce some properties of Simon [5,6,13].

Proposition 1. *Let ΔL^{i-1} and ΔR^{i-1} is the input differential of r-round Simon. We assert $\Delta R^i = \Delta L^{i-1}$.*

From Simon's encryption algorithm, this can be easily found.

Proposition 2. *Assume that E is any Simon variant with a free key schedule and that Eve is an attack that tries to recover the Simon key used purely differential methods, i.e., assume that it gets as input plaintext differences $P_0 \oplus P_1$, $P_0 \oplus P_2$, ..., $P_0 \oplus P_n$ as well as ciphertexts $C_0, C_1, ..., C_n$. Then the full key recovery can never be successful with a success rate beyond 50%.*

Proof. To see this, consider any pair of ciphertexts (C_0, C_1) and a Simon subkey k. Suppose that $E_k^{-1}(C_0) \oplus E_k^{-1}(C_1) = \delta$, where E_k denotes single-round encryption under the subkey k. Flip the most significant bit of k and call the resulting new subkey k'. Then it is straightforward to verify that $E_{k'}^{-1}(C_0) \oplus E_{k'}^{-1}(C_1) = \delta$ as well. The proposition follows by applying this reasoning to the first round of E.

3 Differential Distinguisher Based on Neural Network

In this section, we will use neural networks to make a distinguisher on Simon32/64. There are many kinds of neural networks, such as Artificial Neural Network [7], Convolutional Neural Network [7–9], Recurrent Neural Network [7], Residual Network [10] and so on. Integrated computing resources and model success rate, here we only report results on neural models we used. It takes a lot of time to find and train a good neural network. We do experiments on a machine equipped with a GTX 1060 Ti graphics card. After a series of experiments, we chose the Residual Network to construct our differential distinguisher.

3.1 Model Structure

In this section, we introduce our model structure.

Training Data. We chose a pair (C_0, C_1) of ciphertexts for Simon 32/64 can be written as a sequence of four words (w_0, w_1, w_2, w_3), each words has sixteen bits. In our work, the w_i are directly interpreted as the row-vectors of a 4×16-matrix and the input layer consists of 64 units likewise arranged in a 4×16 array. The value of output layer is zero or one. Zero corresponds to random data and one corresponds to differential data.

Network Structure. Our network is a residual tower of two-layer convolutional neural networks preceded by a single bit-sliced convolution and followed by a densely connected prediction head. The input layer is connected in channels-first mode to one layer of bit-sliced, e.g., width 1, convolutions with 32 output channels. Batch normalization is applied to the output of these convolutions. Finally, rectifier nonlinearities are applied to the outputs of batch normalization, and the resulting 32×16 matrix is passed to the main residual tower. Each convolutional block consists of two layers of 32 filters. Each layer applies first the convolutions, then a batch normalization, and finally, a rectifier layer. At the end of the convolutional block, a skip connection then adds the output of the final rectifier layer of the block to the input of the convolutional block and passes the result to the next block. The prediction head consists of two hidden layers and one output unit. The first and second layers are densely connected layers with 64 units. The first of these layers is followed by a batch normalization layer and a rectifier layer; the second hidden layer does not use batch normalization but is simply a densely connected layer of 64 Relu units. The final layer consists of a single output unit using a sigmoid activation.

3.2 Training Model

In this section, we introduce how to train the network and some of its parameters.

Data Generation. Training and validation data were generated by using the Linux random number generator ($\backslash dev \backslash urandom$) to obtain uniformly distributed keys K_i and plaintext pairs P_i with the input differential $\Delta = 0x0000\backslash 0x0008$ as well as a vector of binary-valued real\random labels Y_i. To produce training or validation data for k-round Simon32/64, the plaintext pairs P_i was then encrypted for k-rounds if Y_i was set. Otherwise, the second plaintext of pair was replaced with a freshly generated random plaintext.

In this way, data sets consisting of 10^7 samples were generated for training; 10^6 samples were generated for validation.

Loss Function. Because the output label is 0 or 1, the neural network output will become a floating-point number from 0 to 1 through the *Sigmoid* function. We use *binary accuracy* function to evaluate the accuracy of training and testing. The middle boundary is 0.5. We think of the output of the network as 0 when it less than 0.5. Opposite, we think of the output of the network as 1 when it greater than 0.5. Based on the reason for the accuracy, we chose *mean-squared-error* as the loss function.

Learning Rate and Optimizer. Optimization was performed against *mean-squared-error* loss plus a small penalty based on L2 weights regularization (with regularization parameter $c = 10^{-5}$) using the Adam algorithm with default parameters in Keras. A cyclic learning rate schedule was used, setting the learning rate l_i for epoch i to $l_i = \alpha + \frac{(n-i) mod (n+1)}{n}(\beta - \alpha)$ with $\alpha = 10^{-4}, \beta = 2{\cdot}10^{-3}$ and $n = 9$.

4 Polytope Distinguisher Based on Neural Network

4.1 Polytope Differential Neural Network Distinguisher

Differential Neural Network Distinguisher. The differential neural network distinguisher can be regarded as an extension of the traditional differential distinguisher. The traditional techniques and methods can not describe the non-random characteristics of the differential distribution of multi-round cipher algorithm, while the deep learning can.

Polytope Neural Network Distinguisher. To improve the success rate of differential neural network distinguisher, we propose the fusion of polytope difference [14–16] and neural network. That we call it *Polytope Neural Network Distinguisher.*

A Brief Introduction For Polytope. Similar to differential cryptanalysis, we are not so much interested in the absolute position of these texts but the relations between the texts. If we choose one of the texts as the point of reference, the relations between all texts are already uniquely determined by only considering their differences with respect to the reference text. If we thus have $d+1$ texts, we can describe their relative positioning by a tuple of d differences. It can be see from Fig. 1.

As a convention we will construct a d-difference from a $(d+1)$-polytope as follows:

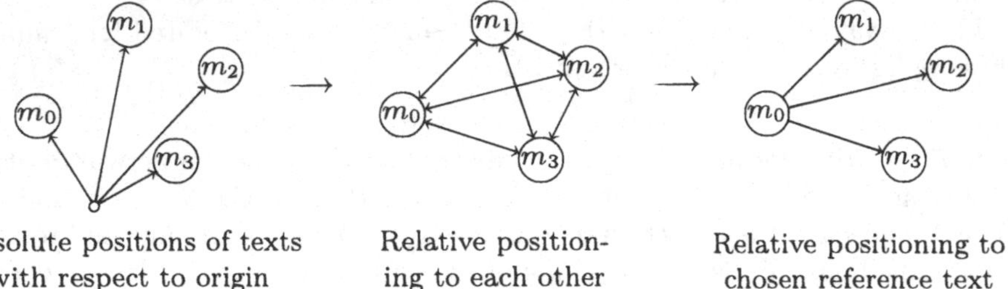

Fig. 1. Depiction of three views of a polytope with four vertices.

Convention. For a (d+1)-polytope $(m_0, m_1, \cdots, m_d)$, *the corresponding d-difference is created as* $(m_0 \oplus m_1, m_0 \oplus m_2, \cdots, m_0 \oplus m_d)$.

This means, we use the first text of the polytope as the reference text and write the differences in the same order as the remaining texts of the polytope. We will call the reference text the *anchor* of the d-difference. Hence if we are given a d-difference and the value of the *anchor*, we can reconstruct the corresponding $(d+1)$-polytope uniquely.

Using the idea, we try to establish the neural network distinguisher of non-random characteristics of polytope difference distribution.

Compared to Sect. 3, the differences between polytope differential neural network distinguisher and differential neural network distinguisher are the input data and dense layers. In polytope differential neural network distinguisher, we make the input data is (C_0, C_1, C_2, C_3) with $\Delta_i = C_0 \oplus C_i, i = 1, 2, 3$. C_i represents a differential with C_0. The first and second layers are densely connected layers with 160 units.

4.2 Result

Result in Differential Neural Network Distinguisher. After we build and train the model, we had already obtained a neural network distinguisher for a certain differential. With the input differential $\Delta = 0x0000\backslash 0x0008$ we choose the depth of residual block is one on six-round Simon32/64. The training was run for 200 epochs on the dataset of size 10^7. One epoch takes about 57 s with a GTX 1060 Ti graphics card. The datasets were processed in batches of size 5000. The last 10^6 samples were withheld for validation. We could draw the picture of the accuracy, and the loss for training data and testing data named Fig. 2.

From Fig. 2, we can easily find out the differential distinguisher what we constructed based on neural network had a very good accuracy on 6-round Simon32/64. With the increase of the number of rounds and keep the input differential unchanged, the success rate of the neural network distinguisher decreases gradually. On 10-round Simon32/64, the success rate will be close to 0.5 with the input differential $\varDelta = 0\backslash 0x0008$. Here we made a table about the number of rounds and the success rate with the two different input differential. One is $0\backslash 0x0008$, the other one is $0x0008\backslash 0$. The results are shown in the following table.

As can be seen from Table 1, we can find a very interesting situation. The r-round accuracy of $\varDelta_2 = 0x0008\backslash 0$ is almost equal to $r-1$-round accuracy of $\varDelta_1 = 0\backslash 0x0008$. We can easily get the reason for this result from Proposition 1.

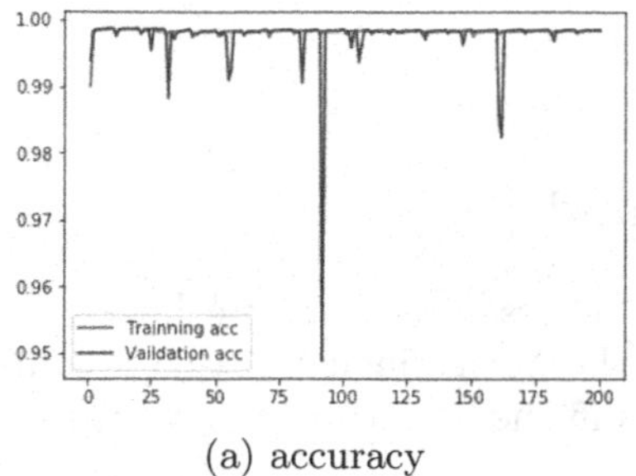

(a) accuracy

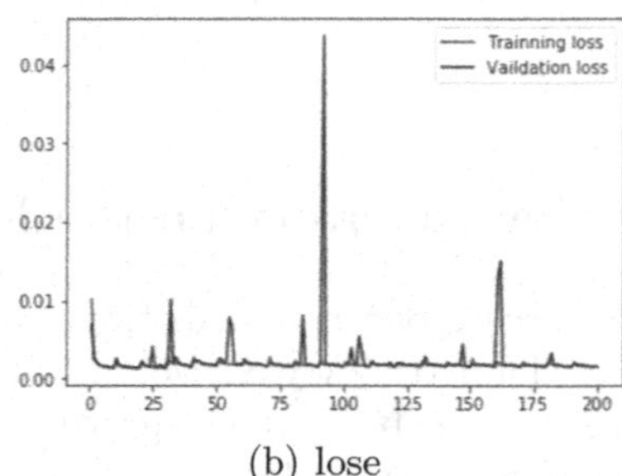

(b) lose

Fig. 2. Training a neural network to distinguish 6-round Simon32/64. Output for the input differential $\varDelta = 0\backslash 0x0008$ from random data.($left$)Training and validation accuracy by epoch.($right$)Training and validation loss by epoch

Table 1. The number of rounds and the best success rate with the two different input differential.

Nr	$\varDelta_1 = 0\backslash 0x0008$	$\varDelta_2 = 0x0008\backslash 0$
Six round	0.9985	0.9671
Seven round	0.9661	0.7768
Eight round	0.7664	0.6277
Nine round	0.6277	0.5007
Ten round	0.5007	0.5009

Result in Polytope Differential Distinguisher Based on Neural Network. The polytope difference we choose is $(0, 0008)$, $(0, 0004)$, $(0, 0002)$. Here, we give the result of three differences and their polytope difference on eight-round to ten-round directly. The results are shown in the following table.

As can be seen from Table 2. The accuracy of polytope neural network distinguisher is greater than differential neural network distinguisher. The order of differential does not affect the success rate.

Table 2. The result of three differences and their polytope difference on seven-round to ten-round.

Nr	(0, 0008)	(0, 0004)	(0, 0002)	Polytope difference
Seven round	0.9661	0.9655	0.9659	0.9944
Eight round	0.7664	0.7659	0.7661	0.9251
Nine round	0.6277	0.6279	0.6263	0.6373
Ten round	0.5007	0.5002	0.5004	0.5017

5 Key Recovery on the Final Round

To showcase our neural distinguishers' utility as research tools, we have constructed a partial-key recovery attack based on the $N9$ distinguisher that is competitive to the best attacks previously known from the literature on Simon32/64 reduced to ten rounds.

5.1 Wrong Key Randomization

When we decrypt ciphertext (C_0, C_1) of Simon32/64 for one round. We could have $\left(C_0{}', C_1{}'\right) = E_k^{-1}(C_0, C_1)$, here we define k is the key and E is encryption algorithm. The basic idea of wrong key randomization is that the expected response of our distinguisher upon wrong key decryption [3] will depend on the bitwise difference between the trial key and the real key.

Let (C_0, C_1) be a ciphertext pair and k be the real subkey used in the final round of encryption. Let $\delta \in F_2^{16}$ and let $k' = k \oplus \delta$ be a wrong key. Denote the response of our distinguisher D to decryption by the key k' by $R_{D,\delta} = D\left(E_{k'}^{-1}(C_0, C_1)\right)$. $R_{D,\delta}$ was a random variable depending on δ induced by the ciphertext pair distribution and compute its mean μ_δ and standard deviation σ_δ.

We calculated the wrong key response profile for our nine-round distinguishers for Simon32/64. For each δ, we generated 5000 random keys and message input pair (P_0, P_1) and encrypted for ten-round to obtain ciphertexts (C_0, C_1). Denoting the final subkey of each encryption operation by k, we then performed single-round decryption to get $E_{k\oplus\delta}^{-1}(C_0), E_{k\oplus\delta}^{-1}(C_1)$, and had the resulting partially decrypted ciphertext pair rated by a neural distinguisher. μ_δ and σ_δ were then calculated as empirical mean and standard deviation over these 5000 trials. The wrong key response profile is shown in Fig. 3.

It can be seen from the figure above that, the mean value is larger when there are fewer error bits. We can use this property to recover key.

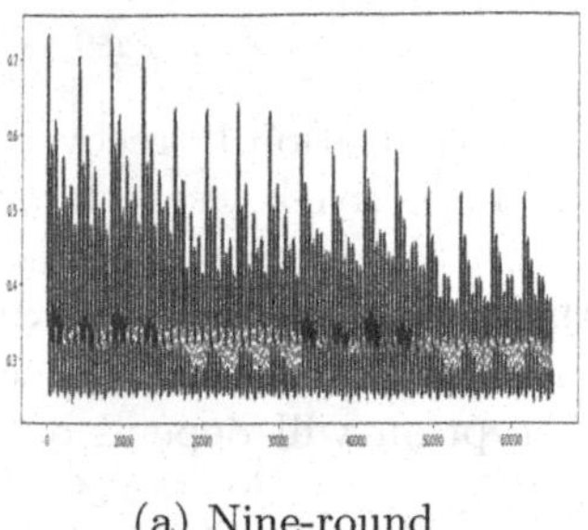

(a) Nine-round

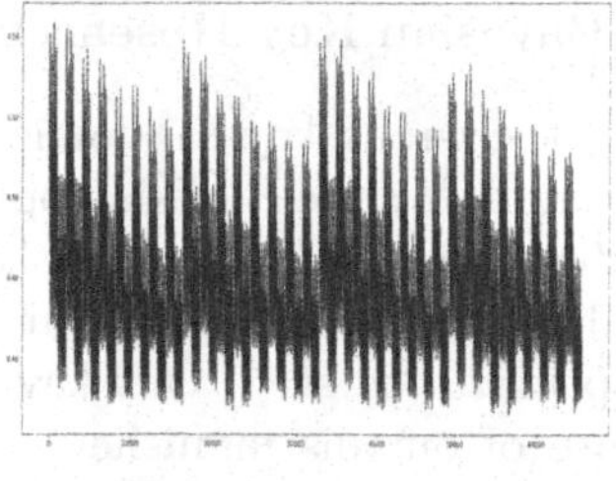

(b) Eight-round

Fig. 3. Wrong key response profile (only μ_δ shown) for Simon32/64. $(left)\mu_\delta$ for nine-round Simon32/64 and our eight-round neural distinguisher.$(right)\mu_\delta$ for 10-round Simon32/64 and our 9-round neural distinguisher

5.2 Bayesian Optimization

Bayesian optimization [11] is a method that is commonly used for the optimization of black-box functions f that are expensive to evaluate. Examples are found in many domains; the tuning of hyperparameters of machine learning models is one common example. It uses prior knowledge about the function to be optimized to construct a probabilistic model of the function that is easy to optimize. According to Bayesian statistics, unknown models or parameters are uncertain and conform to a certain probability distribution.

To judge whether a sample conforms to a certain distribution, we need to start from the n-dimension distribution of the sample and make full use of the information provided by the probability density of the multivariate normal distribution to calculate the posterior probability. So the sample is expected to obey the normal distribution. Just right the average of the neural distinguisher response approximately follow an n-dimension normal distribution with mean μ_δ and standard deviation $\sigma_\delta/\sqrt{n}$, and it also can be precomputed. After that, the candidate keys can be selected by the maximum score and probability of the observed distinguishing responses.

In particular, we will first guess this probability distribution according to subjective judgment or experience, which is called prior distribution; then we will modify the guess on this probability distribution according to more and more observations (new data or new evidence), and the final probability distribution is called posterior distribution.

Suppose we have an unknown quantity to estimate θ, and there is a prior distribution $P(\theta)$ for this variable. Make D as a series of observations or evidence. We hope to modify the cognition of θ distribution through D. According to Bayesian theorem, we have:

$$P(\theta) = \frac{P(D \mid \theta)\, P(\theta)}{P(D)} \tag{3}$$

It can be seen that by using Bayesian inference, we can reasonably combine the prior cognition with the actual evidence to get an updated posterior cognition.

5.3 Bayesian Key Research

We use the wrong key randomization and Bayesian optimization to recover the final rounds. We use Bayesian optimization to build an effective key search policy for reduced-round Simon. This key search policy drastically reduces the number of trial decryptions used by our basic attack, at the cost of a somewhat expensive optimization step. Our key search policy's basic idea is that the expected response of our distinguisher upon wrong key decryption will depend on the bitwise difference between the trial key and the real key.

Step 1. To decrypt the final round, we need some random key $K = (k_0, k_1, \cdots, k_{n-1})$, neural distinguisher N, ciphertext structure $C = C_0, \cdots, C_{m-1}$. We choose key at random without replacement from the set of all subkey candidates. The wrong key response profile for next to final round distinguishers is μ and σ.

Step 2. For $k_j, j \in \{0, 1, \cdots, n\}$, we decrypt C_i with k_j for all $i \in \{0, 1, \cdots, m-1\}$ to have P_{i,k_j}. Use our neural distinguisher N,

$$v_{i,k_j} = N\left(P_{i,k_j}\right) \quad for \quad all \quad i. \tag{4}$$

We make a change for

$$s_{i,k_j} = log_2\left(v_{i,k_j} / \left(1 - v_{i,k_j}\right)\right) \tag{5}$$

We called s_{i,k_j} is score. $s_{k_j} = \sum_{i=0}^{m-1} s_{i,k_j}$ is the score of k_j. Let

$$m_{k_j} = \sum_{i=0}^{m-1} s_{i,k_j} / m \tag{6}$$

m_{k_j} is the mean of k_j.

Step 3. For $\delta, \delta \in \left(0, 1, \cdots, 2^{16} - 1\right)$, we use Bayesian optimization to infer m_{k_j} belong to which μ_δ and σ_δ. It is easy to see that the probability density at the observed values are maximised by minimizing the weighted Euclidean distance $\varepsilon_\delta = \left(m_{k_j} - \mu_{\delta \oplus k_j}\right)^2 / \sigma^2_{\delta \oplus k_j}$. When the minimum $\varepsilon_{\delta'}$ was selected, The Corresponding is δ', so the new key $k_{new} = k_j \oplus \delta'$.

Step 4. Now we have some new keys, the number is n. Replace these new keys and repeat *step*2 and *step*3 for some iterations l. All keys tried, and their scores s_{k_j} on the current ciphertext structure are stored.

Step 5. Return the key corresponding to the maximum score.

Experiment. Bayesian key research is used with a nine-round differential neural network distinguisher and its associated wrong key response profile. Before we return a key, we perform a small verification search with a hamming radius of final around the subkey candidates currently best. Hamming radius removes remaining bit errors in the key guess.

As we chose the Δ is $(0, 0x0008)$. First, we want know what value for chosen plaintext pairs, so we make an experiment to encrypt data for ten-round Simon32/64. Then we used nine-round neural distinguisher to try to recover the ten-round key. The variable is the number of plaintext pairs we choose.

Table 3. Key recovery on ten-round Simon32/64 with increase the number of choose plaintext pair in fifty trials.

	2^8	2^9	2^{10}	2^{11}	2^{12}	2^{13}	2^{14}
The number of error bits is 0	32	28	34	44	46	49	50
The number of error bits is 1	16	20	16	6	4	1	0
The number of error bits is 2	2	2	0	0	0	0	0

It is easy to see from Table 3 that as the number of data increases, the more correct number of keys recover. According to the results of the table, we chose 2^{14} for our experiment. In the trials subsequently described, an iteration count for the Bayesian key search policy of $1 = 5$ and candidate number $n = 32$, our implementation outputs a key guess in approximately a quarter of a minute on average (measured average in 100 trials: 1436.51 s) when running on a single thread of our machine with no graphics card usage.

5.4 Polytopic Attacks on Simon32/64

In this section, we propose an attack on Simon32/64 based on Polytope neural network distinguisher.

Overview. The idea of our attack is to extend neural distinguisher with the differential path. We define $p, p < 1$ is the probability of the differential path from $\Delta_1 \xrightarrow{r} \Delta_2$ for r round Simon32/64. We use Δ_2 to construct a neural network distinguisher D. Assume the accuracy of neural network distinguisher is an array Acc with a number of rounds. We can assert that the values in the array are decreasing to 50%. We can set a threshold C_1 for distinguisher. Let $Acc\,[j] \geq C_1, for \quad max(j)$. We called the j round neural distinguisher is D_j. We try key recovery attack $r + j - 1$-round of Simon32/64.

Improved Attack. This basic attack can be accelerated in various ways. Here, we focus on the following ideas:

First, we consider $D_p[j]$ is an j-round polytope neural network distinguisher. The r-round polytope differential of a path is $\Delta_1 \xrightarrow{r} \Delta_2$. $p, p < 1$ is the probability of the differential path. Then we choose M pairs of plaintext.

$$M > (1/p) \times m \tag{7}$$

m is the number of attack data.

Second, we use the $D_p[j]$ to filter out the m data we want from M. After that, we use $D_p[j-1]$ to determine which key has the highest score. That is the answer. Algorithm 1 sums up the algorithm.

Algorithm 1. Polytopic Key Recovery on the Final Round

Require: j-round Polytope Neural Network Distinguisher D^j, $j-1$-round Polytope Neural Network Distinguisher D^{j-1}, Ciphertext structure $C = C_0, \cdots, C_{M-1}$

for all i such that $0 \le i \le M-1$ **do**
  $v_i \leftarrow D^j(C_i)$ for all i
end for
$C = C_0, \cdots, C_{m-1} \leftarrow$ *select top m for M*
for $key = 0$ to $2^{16}-1$ **do**
  $C^{j-1} = C_0^{j-1}, \cdots, C_{m-1}^{j-1} \leftarrow Decrypt((C = C_0, \cdots, C_{m-1}), key)$
  $v_{key}^{j-1} \leftarrow D^{j-1}(C_i^{j-1})$ for all key
end for
$K \leftarrow Maximum(v^{j-1})$
return K

Experiment. We make an attack in ten-round and eleven-round of Simon32/64 with $D_p[9]$ filter out data and $D_p[8]$ give the score. The polytope difference we choose is $(0, 0008)$, $(0, 0004)$, $(0, 0002)$. Because the weight of difference is smaller, the lower the probability of the differential path in the previous rounds. The order of polytope difference does not affect the experimental results.

$$(0020, 0088) \xrightarrow{2^{-2}} (0008, 0020) \xrightarrow{2^{-2}} (0000, 0008) \tag{8}$$

$$(0010, 0044) \xrightarrow{2^{-2}} (0004, 0010) \xrightarrow{2^{-2}} (0000, 0004) \tag{9}$$

$$(0008, 0022) \xrightarrow{2^{-2}} (0002, 0008) \xrightarrow{2^{-2}} (0000, 0002) \tag{10}$$

In the experiment, $m = 256$ is our choice. So we could use p and m to compute M. We only recover key on the final round because the result of the last round is enough to show the effect of our attack. The average error of guess key and the true key is 1-bit on the ten-round. The average error of guess key and the true key is 2-bit on the eleven-round. To clear the error bit, the best way is to increase m. Here, we make experiments on eleven-round Simon32/64. We give Table 4 to show our result.

Table 4. Key recovery on Eleven-round Simon32/64 with increase the number of choose plaintext pair in fifty trials.

	2^8	2^9	2^{10}	2^{11}	2^{12}	2^{13}
The number of error bits is 0	5	20	35	38	44	50
The number of error bits is 1	15	12	10	12	6	0

Computational Complexity. We used 11 rounds of attacks to calculate the computational complexity [12].

First, we choose $m = 2^{13}$, so $M = m \times \frac{1}{p^3} = 2^{25}$, we regard the computational complexity of polytope differential neural network distinguisher as four times because the length of input data is 128 bits.

$$MakeScore : 2^{25} \times 4 = 2^{27} \tag{11}$$

$$SelectM \to m : nlog_2^n = 2^{25} \times 25 \tag{12}$$

$$m \to key : 2^{16} \times m \times 4 \times 4 = 2^{33} \tag{13}$$

$$Max : 2^{16} \times m + 2^{16} = 2^{29} + 2^{16} \tag{14}$$

$$Finalkey : 2^{27} + 2^{25} \times 25 + 2^{33} + 2^{29} + 2^{16} \approx 2^{33.4} \tag{15}$$

$$Fullkey : 2^{27} + 2^{25} \times 25 + (2^{33} + 2^{29} + 2^{16}) \times 4 \approx 2^{35.2} \tag{16}$$

The computational complexity of key recovery attack on the final round was $2^{33.4}$. The computational complexity of full key is $2^{35.2}$. It can be seen from the formula that with the increase of the number of rounds, the increase of computational complexity is only related to formula (11) and (12).

5.5 Analysis

Error Bits. There are two reasons for the presence of error bits.

First, the accuracy of polytope neural network distinguisher was not 1. As we extend the round with polytope difference and data volume. In fact, after the r round encryption, we can't guarantee that all the data are accord with $(0, 0008)$, $(0, 0004)$, $(0, 0002)$. In our experiment, $D_p[r]$ is used to filter out the data we want. Although we chose the data with the highest scores, we still can't guarantee that every data conforms to this differential.

Second, Proposition 2 is the reason. As we use distinguisher to give the data a score. The score based on how many probabilities does this data belongs to $D_p[r-1]$. In theory, more than one *key* satisfies this condition.

For these two reasons, there will be some error bits in the key recovery attack.

The Limitations of Bayesian Key Research. In our attack, we do not use Bayesian Key Research. The accuracy of polytope neural network distinguisher is greater than differential neural network distinguisher. So as we use polytope neural network distinguisher to filter out data, the fewer bad points we have. From Fig. 3 we could know the mean value of some wrong keys is almost the same as that of correct keys. In the experiment, it is easy to produce error bits. In order to carry out comparative experiments on polytope neural network distinguisher, we generate an wrong key randomization table of the distinguisher based on 8-rounds of polytope neural network distinguisher. The table is shown in Fig. 4. From Fig. 4, it is easy to see that only the correct key has a unique peak value. Although there are still some wrong keys with a high average value, there is a certain gap between them and the peak value. This is a good information for us no matter what kind of key recovery attacks.

Whether using polytope neural network distinguisher or neural network distinguisher can not guarantee that the filtered data meet the difference conditions we set, that is, the filtered data has some bad points, which are very destructive to Bayesian Key Research algorithm. When there are some bad points in data, the value generated by the points does not belong to the correct distribution. It can be clearly known from Bayesian statistics that this destructive effect is fatal to Bayesian Key Research algorithm.

Therefore, Bayesian Key Research algorithm is not used in the experiment, but the idea of brute force attack is used. On simon32/64, the complexity of simple differential attack is not high. And the most important thing is that it has strong anti-interference ability for bad points. With the increasing of m, the number of error bits will gradually reduce to 0; Bayesian Key Research is not, with the continuous increase of m, error bits will still exist.

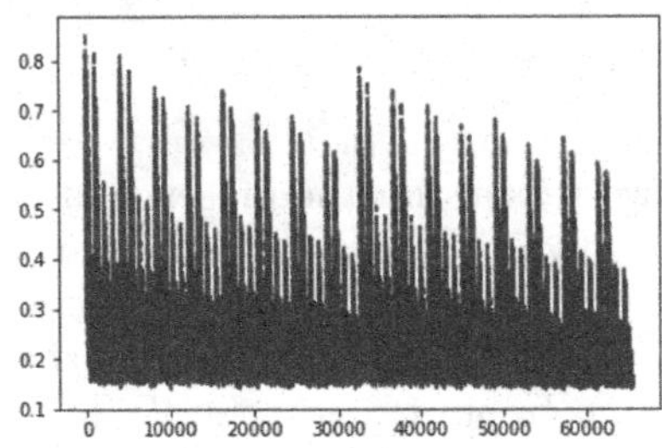

Fig. 4. μ_δ for nine-round Simon32/64 and eight-round polytope neural distinguisher

5.6 Bayesian Key Research with Error

Wrong Key Randomization with Error. After the analysis in Sect. 5.5, we can see that the Bayesian Key Research algorithm cannot be used because of the bad points. Compared with brute force solution, Bayesian Key Research needs less keys, which can greatly reduce the computational complexity. However, it takes a long time to construct the wrong key randomization table. Therefore, Bayesian Key Research is a very good technical means in the case of decoding of cryptographic algorithm normalization.

In this part, we consider constructing wrong key randomization with error. Next, we will take the single difference case as an example to describe the algorithm. Compared with the normal knowledge, a filter function is added to the error key filtering algorithm with bad points.

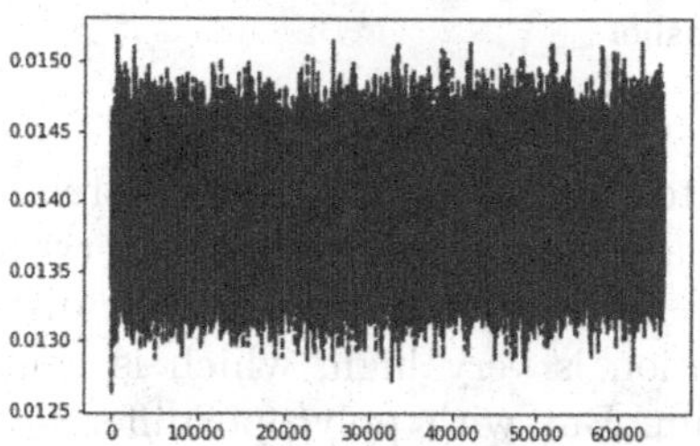

Fig. 5. Wrong key randomization with μ_δ for nine-round Simon32/64 and eight-round differential neural distinguisher

According to (8), select the difference (0008, 0020), and the probability of 0.25 after one round of encryption is (0000, 0008).

First chose n data for ten-round encryption with difference (0008, 0020).

Second select m data from n with nine-round differential neural network distinguisher.

Third use eight-round differential neural network distinguisher to build wrong key randomization with m data.

According to the above three steps, we can construct an wrong key randomization table. Through the table, we can also intuitively see why the key recovery attack can not be carried out by increasing the number of rounds in the case of single differential. Figure 5 show the table.

As can be seen from Fig. 5, in the case of single difference, the dominance of cryptographic features is not obvious, so it is easy to make wrong judgment when using neural network distinguisher. Because the success rate of the 9-round neural network distinguisher is only 0.6277. Compared with the polytope neural network distinguisher, the results are not satisfactory. The wrong key randomization with error table constructed according to polytope neural network distinguisher is shown in Fig. 6.

It can be clearly seen from Fig. 6 that compared with the case of single difference, the wrong key randomization with error table constructed by polytope differences has clear advantages. This result explains why brute force attacks can be used to increase the number of rounds on the polytope neural network distinguisher.

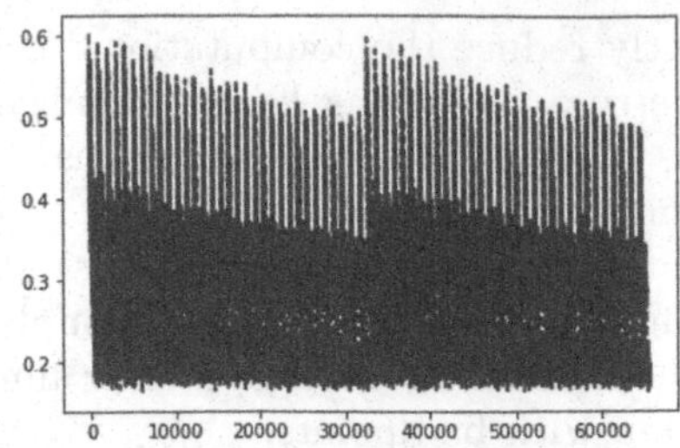

Fig. 6. Wrong key randomization with μ_δ for nine-round Simon32/64 and eight-round differential neural distinguisher

In order to conform to one data of 9-round differential neural network distinguisher. Then, it has a probability of p, after decryption by the wrong key, conforms to the 8-round differential neural network distinguisher. In fact, the probability of this situation is very high, which is caused by the encryption mode of Simon algorithm. But with polytope differences even if one data is filtered out from the 9-round polytope neural network distinguisher. The probability of meeting the 8-round polytope neural network distinguisher after one round of decryption by the wrong key is not more than p^3.

Therefore, it brings a result that the polytope neural network distinguisher has stronger anti-interference performance for bad points. This is also the main reason why it can attack Simon algorithm by increasing the number of rounds.

Bayesian Key Research with Error. Compared with Bayesian Key Research, wrong key randomization with error table is replaced by the wrong key randomization table. No other part of the algorithm needs to be changed. Here we directly give the result that the attack against 11-rounds of Simon32/64 is the same as the parameters selected in 5.4. For how much computational complexity can be reduced, we perform a calculation, because the table has been constructed, so the complexity of finding data in table can be counted as 1.

$$MakeScore : 2^{25} \times 4 = 2^{27} \tag{17}$$

$$SelectM \rightarrow m : nlog_2^n = 2^{25} \times 25 \tag{18}$$

$$m \rightarrow key : 160 \times m \times 4 \times 4 = 160 \times 2^{17} \tag{19}$$

$$Max : 160 \times \left(m + 2^{16}\right) = 160 \times \left(2^{13} + 2^{16}\right) \tag{20}$$

$$Finalkey : 2^{27} + 2^{25} \times 25 + 160 \times \left(2^{17} + 2^{13} + 2^{16}\right) \approx 2^{30.9} \tag{21}$$

$$Fullkey : 2^{27} + 2^{25} \times 25 + 160 \times \left(2^{17} + 2^{13} + 2^{16}\right) \times 4 \approx 2^{31} \tag{22}$$

The computational complexity of key recovery on the final round was $2^{30.9}$. The computational complexity of full key is 2^{31}.

For the results of key recovery using the Bayesian Key Research with Error, about 1 to 2 error bits will be generated on average. This is due to the uncertainty of the number of bad points. Therefore, a hamming distance of 2-length can be searched for the key after the key search. This ensures the correctness of the key.

6 Conclusion

In this paper, we use neural networks to construct the differential distinguisher and the key recovery attack of Simon32/64. First, we use our nine-round differential neural network distinguisher to recover the keys for ten-round by wrong key randomization and Bayesian optimization. In this experiment, chosen 2^{14} plaintext pairs, statistics based on 50 results we could know that the attack was successful in 50 out of 50 trials; our implementation outputs a key guess in approximately half a quarter of a minute on average (measured average in 100 trials: 14.36 s) when running on a single thread of our machine with no graphics card usage. Second, we propose a brute force attack on Simon32/64 based on the combination of the probability of differential path and polytope neural network distinguisher. This method can only increase the computational complexity of the chosen data as the number of rounds increases. Nine-round polytope neural network distinguisher is used to filter out data, whether it is what we want. Eight-round neural distinguisher is used to recover the final round key. The computational complexity of key recovery on the final key of eleven-round Simon32/64 is $2^{33.4}$. Third, we propose an attack with Bayesian Key Research with Error on Simon32/64. In our attack, we consider the affect of the bad points in building wrong key randomization table. The computational complexity of key recovery on the final key of eleven-round Simon32/64 is $2^{30.9}$.

As the increase of memory, we only do our experiment on eleven-round Simon32/64. But we believe this idea could have rich uses in cryptanalysis. We consider that there is still work to be done in the next step. First, try to increase the success rate of neural network distinguisher so that could reduce data. Second, use a better data filtering algorithm to filter the data that matches the differential. Third, attempts to summarize and analyze the rules of the differential distribution table of the output rounds of the neural network distinguisher, and try to extend the number of cipher rounds after the neural network distinguisher. Last, try to combine neural networks with other cryptanalysis methods.

References

1. Hospodar, G., Gierlichs, B., Mulder, D.E., Verbauwhede, I., Vandewalle, J.: Machine learning in side-channel analysis: a first study. J. Cryptogr. Eng. **1**(4), 293 (2011)
2. Alani, M.M.: Neuro-cryptanalysis of DES and triple-DES. In: Huang, T., Zeng, Z., Li, C., Leung, C.S. (eds.) ICONIP 2012. LNCS, vol. 7667, pp. 637–646. Springer, Heidelberg (2012). https://doi.org/10.1007/978-3-642-34500-5_75
3. Gohr, A.: Improving attacks on round-reduced Speck32/64 using deep learning. In: International Cryptology Conference, pp. 150–179 (2019)
4. Beaulieu, R., Shors, D., Smith, J., et al.: The SIMON and SPECK Families of Lightweight Block Ciphers. IACR Cryptology ePrint Archive (2013)

5. Abed, F., List, E., Lucks, S., et al.: Differential cryptanalysis of round-reduced Simon and speck. In: Fast Software Encryption, pp. 525–545 (2014)
6. Qiao, K., Hu, L., Sun, S., et al.: Differential analysis on Simeck and SIMON with dynamic key-guessing techniques. In: International Conference on Information Systems Security, pp. 64–85 (2016)
7. Lecun, Y., Bengio, Y., Hinton, G.E., et al.: Deep learning. Nature **521**(7553), 436–444 (2015)
8. Howard, A., Zhu, M., Chen, B., et al.: MobileNets: efficient convolutional neural networks for mobile vision applications. Arxiv: Computer Vision and Pattern Recognition (2017)
9. Zhang, X., Zhou, X., Lin, M., et al.: ShuffleNet: an extremely efficient convolutional neural network for mobile devices. In: Computer Vision and Pattern Recognition, pp. 6848–6856 (2018)
10. He, K., Zhang, X., Ren, S., et al.: Deep residual learning for image recognition. In: Computer Vision and Pattern Recognition, pp. 770–778 (2016)
11. Pelikan, M., Goldberg, D.E., Cantupaz, E., et al.: BOA: the Bayesian optimization algorithm. In: Genetic and Evolutionary Computation Conference, pp. 525–532 (1999)
12. Lawler, B.: Computational complexity: a conceptual perspective written by Oded Goldreich, and published by Cambridge University Press, 606 p. (2008). ISBN 978-0-521-88473-0. ACM SIGSOFT Softw. Eng. Notes **35**(1), 37–38 (2010)
13. Wang, N., Wang, X., Jia, K., et al.: Differential attacks on reduced SIMON versions with dynamic key-guessing techniques. Sci. China Ser. F: Inf. Sci. **61**(9), 1–3 (2018)
14. Tiessen, T.: Polytopic cryptanalysis. In: International Cryptology Conference, pp. 214–239 (2016)
15. Tiessen, T.: From higher-order differentials to polytopic cryptyanalysis. In: Phan, R.C.-W., Yung, M. (eds.) Mycrypt 2016. LNCS, vol. 10311, pp. 544–552. Springer, Cham (2017). https://doi.org/10.1007/978-3-319-61273-7_29
16. Wang, J., Wu, Q., Fu, C., Zhou, G., Duan, M.: Improved impossible polytopic attacks on round-reduced DES. In: Journal of Physics: Conference Series, vol. 1486 (2020). https://doi.org/10.1088/1742-6596/1486/3/032010
17. Graves, A., Mohamed, A.R., Hinton, G.: Speech recognition with deep recurrent neural networks. In: IEEE International Conference on Acoustics. IEEE (2013)
18. Bahdanau, D., Cho, K., Bengio, Y.: Neural machine translation by jointly learning to align and translate. Computer Science (2014)

DAS-AST: Defending Against Model Stealing Attacks Based on Adaptive Softmax Transformation

Jinyin Chen[1(✉)], Changan Wu[1], Shijing Shen[1], Xuhong Zhang[1], and Jianhao Chen[2]

[1] College of Information Engineering, Zhejiang University of Technology, Hangzhou, China
{chenjinyin,wuchangan,shenshijing,2111903214}@zjut.edu.cn

[2] College of Control Science and Engineering, Zhejiang University, Hangzhou, China
xuhongneverg@gmail.com

Abstract. Deep Neural Networks (DNNs) have been widely applied to diverse real life applications and dominated in most cases. Considering the hardware consumption for DNN and large amount of labeled training data to support the performance, machine-learning-as-a-service (MLaaS) came into being. However, malicious attacker takes the opportunity to launch possible deep model stealing attacks via black-box access, leading to a great security threat to the interests of the model agency. Addressing to the problem, defensive methods are designed, mainly categorized to truncated-based and perturbation-based, to reduce the stealing efficiency or increase the attack cost, i.e. more queries. Essentially, it is still a challenge to fully defend the deep model stealing attack. In the paper, we propose a novel defense algorithm based on adaptive softmax transformation by introducing posterior probability perturbation, namely DAS-AST. We evaluate the proposed defense against several state-of-the-art attack strategies, and compare the performance with other defense methods. The experiment results show that our defense is effective across a wide range of challenging datasets and performs better than the existing defenses. More specifically, it can degrade the average accuracy of the stolen model at least 30%, without affect the accuracy of target DNN model on original tasks.

Keywords: DNN models · Model stealing attack · Model security

1 Introduction

Deep neural network (DNN) has been successfully applied to machine translation, image recognition, auto-driving, natural language processing and other fields. To reduce the burden of GPU demand and large amount labeled training data, commercial cloud APIs such as machine-learning-as-a-service (MLaaS) become more and more popular, i.e. AmazonLM[1] and AzureML[2]. Models in

[1] 'Amazon machine learning,' https://aws.amazon.com/aml/.

[2] 'Azure machine learning,' https://azure.microsoft.com/en-us/overview/machine-learning.

Y. Wu and M. Yung (Eds.): Inscrypt 2020, LNCS 12612, pp. 21–36, 2021.
https://doi.org/10.1007/978-3-030-71852-7_2

such applications are valuable intellectual property of their owners, as training these models requires plenty of manpower and material resources, owners can monetize their models by claiming clients pay to use the prediction APIs. Consequently, the deep model represents business value and it is necessary to keep it confidential.

The deep model also becomes the target of theft for its commercial value. Model stealing attacks are mainly categorized into three classes according to their motivations. The first category is violating model privacy, named prior attack, including adversarial attack [2,7,23], model inversion attack [1,5,6] and membership attack [24,26]. Attackes can launch a confrontational attack better on the premise of obtaining the internal knowledge of the model among the various attacks mentioned above. The second attack is stepping stone to evasion, in other word, the adversary may achieve evasion of detection, i.e. malware spam [27] classification successfully if the attackers gain full knowledge of the detection model. The third attack is reducing query charges, that is attacker steals the function of the model by querying prediction APIs repeatedly and obtains substitute models with similar functions [20,29].

Ever since the model stealing attacks captured most attentions, there are also a dozen of available defense methods proposed against them, which are mainly categorized as detect abnormal query patterns [10,11] and predicted posterior output limitation [14,21,29]. The mainstream methods of defense are either hiding part of the posterior probability or adding perturbation to the posterior probability. The former method is truncated-based defense which just preserve the most-confident part of posterior probabilities, or rounding posteriors probabilities to decimals. The latter method is perturbation-based defense by adding disturbance to the posterior probability. The common consideration of such defensive measures is posterior perturbation to maintain accuracy, such as manipulating posterior perturbation while retaining top one probability confidence [14,21]. More specifically, we find the truncated-based defense can slow down the stealing processing and enforce the attackers take more charge budgets. However, such defense cannot always satisfy absolute accuracy reduction in model stealing performance. It is also a challenge for the perturbation-based defense since it easily leads into extra restrictions in order to maintain the accuracy with posterior perturbation.

In our view, the attacker can effectively steal the model through the output confidence distribution of the model. In addition, when the attacker can only obtain the highest confidence of the model output under extreme conditions, they can still complete the stealing of the model well, this is why truncated-based defense cannot complete the absolute defense of the model shown in Fig. 1. It leaks the confidence distribution or the highest confidence value. On the other hand, in the Fig. 1, perturbation-based defense can effectively defend against model stealing attack, which introduce noise in the output of model confidence. Because the introduced noise changes the distribution of confidence, and makes the value with the highest output confidence change to a certain extent. However DAS-AST is not only to add disturbance noise to posterior probability

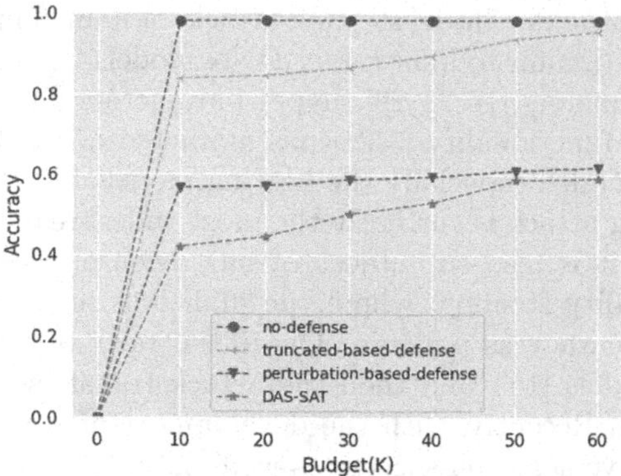

Fig. 1. The accuracy comparison of stealing models under different defenses on MNIST [4]. We apply Lenet [13] to train target models and attack models. The model stealing attack is 'knockoff' [20]. The x-axis represents the number of queries made by the attacker during the attack, i.e. attack budgets, and the y-axis represents the accuracy of the model stolen by the attacker. We use the average of preserving the most-confident probabilities [20] and rounding posteriors probabilities [29] as the truncated-based defense result, and use the average of reversesigmoid [14] and mad [21] as the perturbation-based defense result. In the Fig. 1, it can be observed that truncated-based defense is ineffective against such attack, and DAS-AST is more effective than recent perturbation-based defense.

as truncated-based defense, but also to intervene the distribution of posterior probability to defend against model stealing attack under the premise that the maximum confidence distribution remained.

In our work, we propose a new defense against model stealing attack based on adaptive softmax transformation (DAS-AST). We conclude the main contribution as follows.

- Aiming at the model stealing attack, we propose a novel accuracy-preserving defense for DNNs, namely DAS-AST. It is constructed based on adaptive softmax transformation, which can realize effective defense without accuracy decline of the target model on original task.
- Through extensive experiments, we find that DAS-AST consistently mitigate various attacks and additionally outperform benchmarks.
- Compared with other defense methods, the proposed DAS-AST is a light-weighted defense method, in other word, without adding burden on the model.

2 Related Work

In this section, we briefly review the existing model stealing attacks and defense methods.

Model Stealing Attacks. Model stealing attack, or named model extraction in some literature [17,31], aims to infer target DNN models information with black-box access, i.e. parameters [16,21,29], hyper-parameters [30], architecture [19]. Additionally, model functionality [3,21] has attracted a lot of attention due to the value of DNNs model, especially the hosting models in MLaaS APIs. Model functionality stealing attack is currently the most widespread and the most concerned attack, and it is also the object of our defense. Most works focus on the model functionality stealing, where the malicious attackers aim to obtain the target model accuracy as possible. The initial work of model stealing aims at simple linear models [15], and then the attack transfers to simple machine learning models [29]. Recently, with the development of DNNs, model stealing attacks on DNNs have achieved success as well [3,10,20,22].

Model Stealing Defenses. Model stealing defense developed along two directions. Existing defense work aims to either detect model stealing attacks [10,11, 18,32], or defend against attackers through output perturbation of the black-box DNNs, i.e. posterior prediction [9,27]. Among the defense methods, perturbation-based defenses are especially effective. In particular, classic defensive approaches are consisted of rounding probabilities [29], retaining probabilities only of top-k classes [20], introducing perturbation in posteriors probabilities [14,21]. These aforementioned defenses sacrifice original task accuracy for model confidentiality, while our proposed DAS-SAT introducing softmax adaptive transformation mechanism in the output layer, which can effectively promise the accuracy performance of original task. Consequently, DAS-AST is not only more effective in protection of the deep model, but also can promise that it will not negatively affect the model on the original task.

3 Method

Before we introduce the proposed method in detail, we formerly give out some critical definitions and formulate the problem.

3.1 Preliminary

Deep Neural Network Basics. A DNN model is a computational function $F(x)$ with hierarchical structures. In general, a DNN model consists of three parts: input layer with input $x_i \subseteq X^{H \times W \times C}$, where H, W, C represent the height, width and channel number of the input respectively, output layer with output $y_i \subseteq Y^{1 \times c}$ over c classes and several middle layers. Each part is a layer of neurons that apply activation functions to the weighted output of the precious layer. Mathematically, DNN can be abstracted as Eq. (1).

$$F(x_i, \Theta) : x_i \rightarrow y_i \, (x_i \in R^n, y_i \in R^m) \tag{1}$$

where Θ represents its parameters.

Model Functionality Stealing. Model stealing is an interactive process between attack model F_A (stealing model) and target model F_T (victim model) via black-box queries. The attack is implemented by two steps. (1) Transfer set construction: the attacker A queries input $x \subseteq P_A(X)$ and target model returns a posterior probability $y = P(y|x_A) = F_T(x_A)$. In this way, attacker constructs a 'transfer set' of input-prediction pairs $D_{transfer} = (x_A, y_T)$. (2) Attack model training: the attacker trains the attack model F_A in $D_{transfer}$ by minimizing the cross-entropy (CE) loss as Eq. (2).

$$L_{CE}(y, \hat{y}) = -\sum_k p(y_k) \cdot \log(\hat{y}_k) \tag{2}$$

The end-goal of the attack is to obtain accuracy as high as possible in the same test set D_{test} of the target model.

Defense Objectives. In DAS-AST, it introduces noise into the model in order to perturb predictions of target model, represented as Eq. (3).

$$\tilde{y} = F_T^{\delta}(x) = y + \delta \tag{3}$$

The defense against model stealing has two objectives. The first is accuracy, after introducing noise disturbance, it will inevitably affect the accuracy of the model on D_{test}. Essentially, it is designed to keep the target model work correctly on original task. Consequently, extra condition for keeping the most confident probability is necessary. The second one is non-duplication, which is used to measure the decline in model stealing. DAS-AST uses the decline of attack model accuracy on the test set D_{test} in defense.

3.2 Framework Structure

The most important point for model stealing is to obtain the posterior output distribution of the target model by means of querying as Fig. 2 of the 'output' shows. In our work, we introduce adaptive softmax transformation into posterior probability, and aim to change the distribution of posterior probability rather than simply add noise to hide certain confidence information. DAS-AST mainly adopts the adaptive softmax transformation mechanism which can make the distribution of transfer set far away from the boundary of the target model as Fig. 3 shows.

3.3 Adaptive Softmax Transformation

Softmax Definition. The forward propagation process of DNN can be expressed as: f: $R^M \longrightarrow R^N$, where M represents the dimension of the input, N represents the dimension of the output. Input the sample $x \subseteq X$ into the DNN models for prediction, after the last layer of full connection, a vector $Z(x, i)$ will be obtained, $i \subseteq 0, 1, 2, 3...., c-1$, c represents the total number of categories of

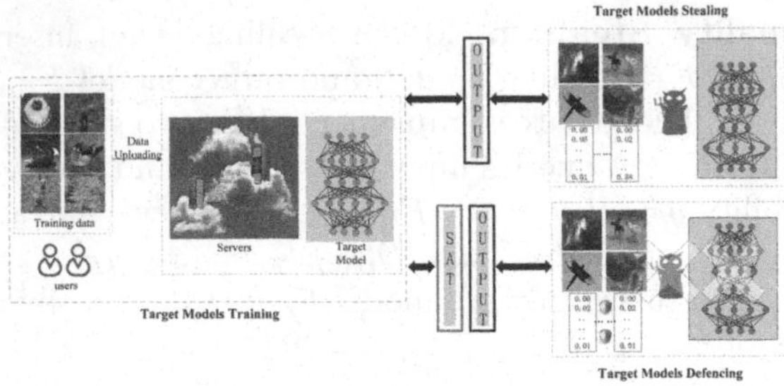

Fig. 2. The framework of DAS-AST. In the target models training phase, users upload training data with labels to severs for model training. After training of target models, the server performs proxy management on the models and provide users with APIs access models. The attackers obtain the posterior probability of the target model by inputting queries and making transfer set, they use the transfer set to train the attack model, and complete the model functionality stealing of the target model. In order to protect the target models, we introduce adaptive softmax transformation before the output of target models, which can effectively protect the output probability distribution of the target models.

the dataset, and the vector $Z(x,i)$ represents the weight value when the input is classified into the i-th category, i.e. the score. This vector is called the logical output (logits) of the target model. In order to normalize the logits value of each category, use the softmax function to activate it, and obtain a normalized probability vector $f(x)$ containing various logits values. The vector represents the probability of the input being classified into each category, and the probability value of the largest category is the model classification result. The logits vector $Z(x,i)$ is converted into a probability vector $f(x)$ by the softmax activation function, and the calculation method is as follows:

$$f_i(x) = \frac{e^{z(x,i)}}{\sum_{i=0}^{C} e^{Z(x,i)}} \tag{4}$$

where e represents the natural base, x is the input of the target model, and $f_i(x)$ represents the probability of the input being classified into the i-th category.

Softmax Definition. Inspired by the exponential mechanism of differential privacy protection, we transform the softmax function and adaptively optimize the transform factor. The transformed softmax function expression is that:

$$f_i'(x) = \frac{\mathrm{e}^{\varepsilon Z(x,i)/2\, s(H,\|\cdot\|)}}{\sum_{i=1}^{C} \mathrm{e}^{\varepsilon Z(x,j)/2\, s(H,\|\cdot\|)}} \tag{5}$$

where $f_i(x)$ represents the transformed softmax function, ε is the transform factor, H is the score function of exponential mechanism , j represents the number of all elements, i represents the i-th element and s is the sensitivity function of

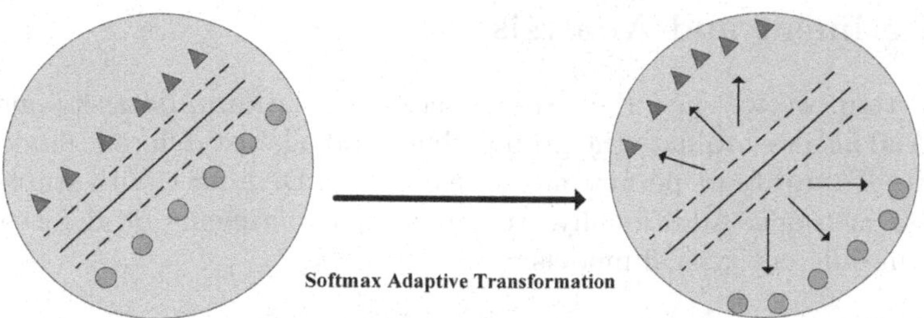

Fig. 3. The damage of transfer set distribution. The carefully crafted transfer set approach the boundary of the target model (the left side of Fig. 3). After introducing adaptive softmax transformation, the sample distribution of the transfer set becomes messy and far away from the target model boundary.

H, the definition formula of s is as follows:

$$s(H, \|\cdot\|) = \max_{D,D:D\neq D'} \|H(D,r) - H(D',r) \tag{6}$$

where D represents the input and $H(D,r)$ represents the score function that D is classified as r class, D' represents the adjacent data set of D, and there is at most one data difference between them, $||\cdot||$ represents the norm calculation symbol, which is used to measure the difference between $H(D,r)$ and $H(D',r)$. Optimizing ε through adaptive algorithm, the goal of optimization is the accuracy of the target model in Fig. 4.

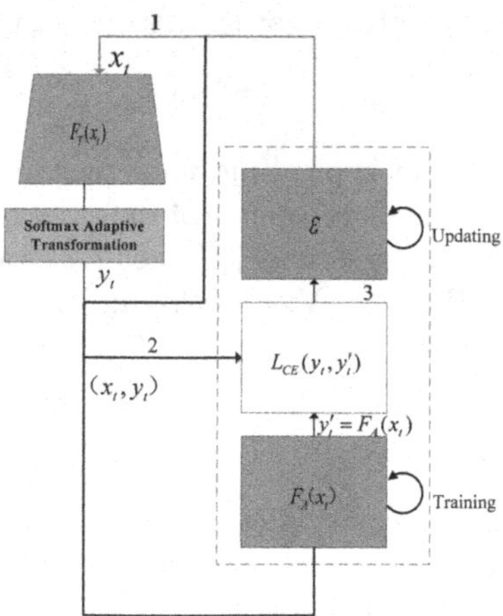

Fig. 4. The flow chart of adaptive softmax transformation. DAS-AST can reduce the accuracy of the attack model through adaptive transformation optimization of transformation factor.

4 Experiment and Analysis

In this section, we will introduce the experiment platform, datasets and DNN models. And also we evaluate the proposed method against different model stealing attacks. To testify its performance, we compare DAS-AST with state-of-the-art defense methods. Additionally, we carry out experiments on defense transferability in different typical models.

4.1 Experiment Setup

Platform. The specific configuration of the experimental environment is as follows: i7-7700K 4.20GHzx8 (CPU), TITAN Xp 12GiBx2 (GPU), 16GBx4 DDR4 (Memory), Ubuntu 16.04 (OS), Python 3.6, Pytorch1.1.0, Tensorflow-gpu-1.3.

Datasets. We evaluate model stealing attack and defense on five public datasets, including MNIST[3], Fashion-MNIST[4], CIFAR10[5], CUBS200 and Caltech-256. We show some sample images of each dataset in Fig. 5. MNIST includes 70,000 gray-scale images of handwritten digits. Among them, 60,000 are used as the training set, 10,000 are used as the test set for 10 classes. Fashion-MNIST is made of a training set of 60,000 examples and a test set of 10,000 examples. Each example is a 28×28 grayscale image, associated with a label from 10 classes. The CIFAR10 dataset consists of 60,000 colored images with sizes of 32×32, belonging to 10 classes with 6,000 images per class and training set of 50,000 images, while the test set is consisted of 10,000 images. CUBS200 includes 200 bird sub-categories, the training set has 5994 images and the test set has 5794 images. Each image provides image class tag information. Caltech-256 contains 30608 images, 256 object categories, at least 80 images per category and a maximum of 827 images.

DNN Model. We use different typical model structures for different datasets. In order to better evaluate the effectiveness of defense, the structure of stealing model is consistent with the target model: Lenet [13] for MNIST and Fashion-MNIST, Alexnet [12] for CIFAR10, Vgg16 [28] and ResNet34 [8] for CUBS200 and Caltech-256.

4.2 Defense Evaluation

Attack Strategies. We use the most effective model stealing attacks to evaluate defense method. Specifically, in our experiments we use the following attacks: (1) Jacobian-based Data Augmentation 'JBDA' [22]; (2,3) 'JB-self' and 'JB-top3' [10]; and (4) 'knockoff' [20], as Table 1 shows.

[3] MNIST can be download at: http://yann.lecun.com/exdb/mnist/.
[4] Fashion-MNIST can be download at: https://www.worldlink.com.cn/en/osdir/fashion-mnist.html.
[5] CIFAR10 can be download at: https://www.cs.toronto.edu/kriz/cifar.html.

(a) MNIST

(b) FashionMNIST

(c) CIFAR10

(d) CUBS200

(e) Caltech-256

Fig. 5. Examples of images from different datasets.

Table 1. The accuracy of undefended target models.

Datasets	Acc (F_T)	Acc (F_A)			
		JBDA	JB-self	JB-top3	knockoff
MNIST	98.7%	89.0%	87.0%	94.7%	**98.4%**
Fashion-MNIST	92.1%	45.3%	56.4%	77.8%	**69.0%**
Cifar10	91.5%	37.4%	33.6%	78.6%	**81.0%**
CUBS200	80.4%	8.0%	3.90%	21.7.0%	**67.3%**
Caltech-256	79.6%	15.5%	16.0%	35.4%	**76.5%**

Defense Effect. We evaluate effectiveness of DAS-AST on five different datasets under four model stealing attacks, the defensive results is showed in Fig. 6.

As shown in Fig. 6, DAS-AST has a good defensive effect under the all types of attacks. Model stealing attacks increase with the increase of queries (budget), DAS-AST can not only force the attacker to increase the number of queries, but also make the accuracy of the stealing model absolutely drop. DAS-AST maintain at least 20% average accuracy reduction in attacker performance on small datasets. Take CIFAR10 as an example, DAS-AST reduces accuracy of the JBDA attacker by 25.6% (37.4%⟶11.8%), JB-self attacker by 21.4% (33.6%⟶18.3%), JB-top3 attacker by 60.3% (78.6%⟶18.3%) and knockoff attacker by 62.3 % (81.0% ⟶16.7%) and achieves better performance in large datasets, which has more realistic meaning.

4.3 Defense Comparison

We compare DAS-AST with the state-of-the-art method in the in the strongest attack 'knockoff', in which budget = 40k.

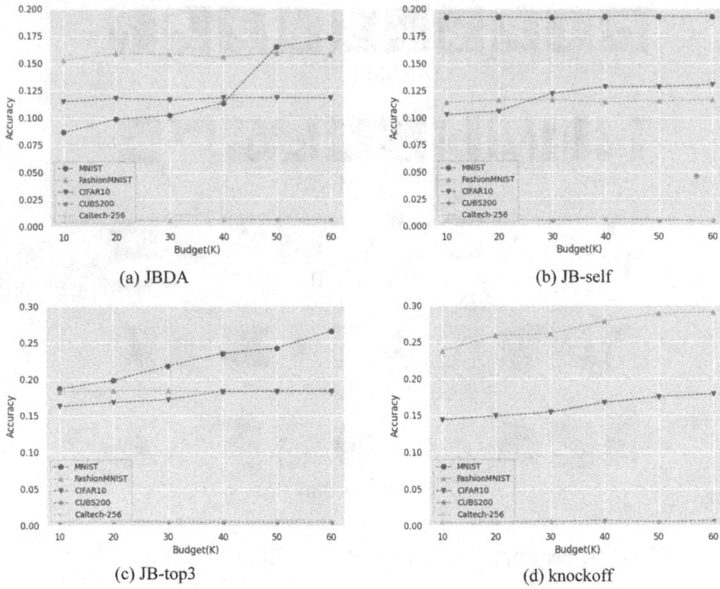

Fig. 6. The accuracy of defended target models with different budgets in different attacks. The accuracy in Fig. 6 denotes the classification accuracy of the model stolen by the attacker under the defense method, the lower the accuracy, the better the defense effect.

Table 2. knockoff attack vs. DAS-AST + Baseline Defenses.

		MNIST	Fashion-MNIST	CIFAR10	CUBS200	Caltech-256
Acc (F_A)	Without defense	97.8%	66.7%	79.0%	66.8%	75.4%
	Rounding	90.2% (↓7.6%)	60.5% (↓6.2%)	72.8% (↓6.2%)	57.2% (↓9.6%)	68.7% (↓6.7%)
	Top-k	88.5% (↓9.3%)	63.0% (↓3.7%)	75.0% (↓4.0%)	55.3% (↓11.5%)	70.5% (↓4.9%)
	Random noise	74.4% (↓23.4%)	43.8% (↓22.9%)	42.2% (36.8%)	11.4% (↓55.4%)	22.5% (↓52.9%)
	Mad	59.6% (38.2%)	35.4% (↓31.3%)	47.6% (↓31.4%)	29.2% (↓37.6%)	53.8% (↓21.6%)
	Reverse_sigmoid	58.8% (↓39.0%)	45.7% (↓21.0%)	59.7% (↓19.3%)	7.5% (↓59.3%)	11.2% (↓64.2%)
	DAS-AST	**53.1% (↓44.7%)**	**27.8% (↓38.9%)**	**16.7% (↓62.3%)**	**0.7% (↓66.1%)**	**0.4% (↓75.0%)**

In Table 2, we find that DAS-AST is better than other defense benchmarks. Especially in high-dimensional complex datasets, i.e. CUBS200 and Caltech-256. We can observe from Table 2 that DAS-AST reduces accuracy of the knockoff attacker by 66.1% (67.3%⟶0.7%) on CUBS200, 75.0% (76.5%⟶0.4%) on Caltech-256. The superior performance on complex datasets makes our method more realistic significance. Model training on complex datasets is more complicated and the cost is larger, therefore, the models of complex datasets contain

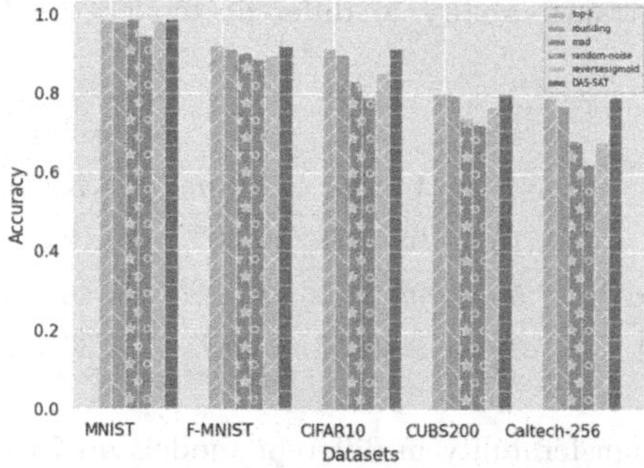

Fig. 7. The accuracy of target model after defense. The accuracy in Fig. 7 denotes the classification accuracy of the model on the original task after adding defense measures, the higher the accuracy, the smaller the negative impact of the defense method on the original model.

more value. DAS-AST can invalidate model stealing attacks on complex datasets as Fig. 6 shows. At the same time, it can be found in the comparison of Fig. 7 that DAS-AST will not affect the original accuracy of the target model. DAS-AST does not simply introduce noise, but desensitizes the output information through the adaptive change of the output layer activation function, so that the attacker cannot obtain enough information to steal models.

4.4 Defense Transferability

Model Structures. In order to verify the transferability of DAS-AST on different models, we use different model structures in experiments for each data set: CNN_A, Lenet [13] and Alexnet [12] for MNIST and Fashion-MNIST in Table 3; Alexnet [12], Vgg16 [28] and Resnet34 [8] for CIFAR10, CUBS200 and Caltech-256 in Table 4. The network structure of CNN_A is in the Table 5. We keep the target model and attack model consistent structure.

The experimental results in Table 4 show that DAS-AST has good defense transferability with different models. In different models, DAS-AST can achieve a good defense effect. During the experiment, we found that the complexity of the attack model is correlated with the stealing effect, however, increasing the complexity of the model means increasing the cost of stealing. Therefore, the structure of the model is also one of the key points of model privacy protection.

Model Complexity. Under normal circumstances, the attacker cannot obtain the structural information of the model. We assume that the attacker is in a black box of the target model and adopts different model structures for model stealing attacks. The structures of target model for each data set: Lenet [13] for MNIST and Fashion-MNIST in Table 6, Vgg16 [28] for CIFAR10, CUBS200 and Caltech-256 in Table 7.

Table 3. The defense transferability in different models on MNIST and Fashion-MNIST.

Dataset	MNIST			Fashion-MNIST		
Model	CNN_A	**Lenet**	Alexnet	CNN_A	**Lenet**	Alexnet
Acc (F_T)	98.10%	98.70%	99.40%	89.10%	92.10%	91.80%
Acc (F_A) (undefensed)	97.50%	98.60%	99.30%	65.40%	69.20%	76.50%
Acc (F_A) (defensed)	57.30%	59.00%	59.00%	14.30%	29.10%	32.10%

Table 4. The defense transferability in different models on CIFAR10, CUBS200 and Caltech-256.

Dataset	CIFAR10			CUBS200			Caltech-256		
Model	Alexnet	**Vgg16**	Resnet34	Alexnet	**Vgg16**	Resnet34	Alexnet	**Vgg16**	Resnet34
Acc (F_T)	68.90%	91.50%	72.40%	71.30%	80.40%	81.30%	74.90%	81.60%	78.40%
Acc (F_A) (undefensed)	58.50%	78.70%	60.10%	52.70%	67.3%	68.70%	64.90%	79.60%	78.40%
Acc (F_A) (defensed)	10.20%	17.90%	12.10%	0.50%	0.50%	0.50%	0.40%	0.40%	0.50%

Table 5. The network structure of CNN_A.

Layer Type	CNN_A
Conv+ReLu	$5 \times 5 \times 32$
Max Pooling	2×2
Conv+ReLu	$5 \times 5 \times 64$
Max Pooling	2×2
DenseFully Connected	1024
Dropout	0.5
DenseFully Connected	10
Softmax	10

Table 6. The influence for defense of attack model in different complexity on MNIST and Fashion-MNIST.

Dataset	MNIST			Fashion-MNIST		
Model	CNN_A	**Lenet**	Alexnet	CNN_A	**Lenet**	Alexnet
Acc (F_T)	98.70%			92.10%		
Acc (F_A) (undefensed)	97.30%	98.60%	98.80%	63.20%	69.20%	76.50%
Acc (F_A) (defensed)	57.10%	59.00%	59.00%	14.30%	29.10%	32.10%

We observe from Table 6 and Table 7 that the stealing effect of the model is the best when the target model and the attack model have the same structure. At the same time, DAS-AST maintain a good defense effect especially in CUBS200 and Caltech-256.

Table 7. The influence for defense of attack model in different complexity on CIFAR10, CUBS200 and Caltech-256.

Dataset	CIFAR10			CUBS200			Caltech-256		
Model	Alexnet	**Vgg16**	Resnet34	Alexnet	**Vgg16**	Resnet34	Alexnet	**Vgg16**	Resnet34
Acc (F_T)	91.50%			80.40%			81.60%		
Acc (F_A) (undefensed)	52.90%	78.70%	63.70%	41.50%	67.3%	63.10%	58.10%	79.60%	75.20%
Acc (F_A) (defensed)	10.20%	17.90%	12.10%	0.30%	0.50%	0.80%	0.40%	0.40%	0.50%

4.5 Defense Visual Analysis

We use the method of feature visualization Grad-cam [25] to display the sample features before and after the defense in the form of heat maps in Fig. 8.

In the Fig. 8, we can see that after defense of DAS-AST, the sensitive features of the sample are obscured to a certain extent, the salient points of the heat map change from partial features to overall outlines, which is consistent with the idea of DAS-AST. We can infer from this that DAS-AST can reduce the leakage of sensitive information in the sample, thereby protecting the privacy of the models. As Fig. 8 shows, on the small dataset, i.e. MNIST and FashionMNIST, due to the relatively small size of the data sample, it can be seen that the focus area of the heat map overlaps in important parts before and after the defense. On the contrary, on CIFAR10, CUBS200 and Caltech-256 datasets, the difference before and after defense is obviously. The visualized results explain the differences in defense under different scale samples, e.i. better defense on complex samples.

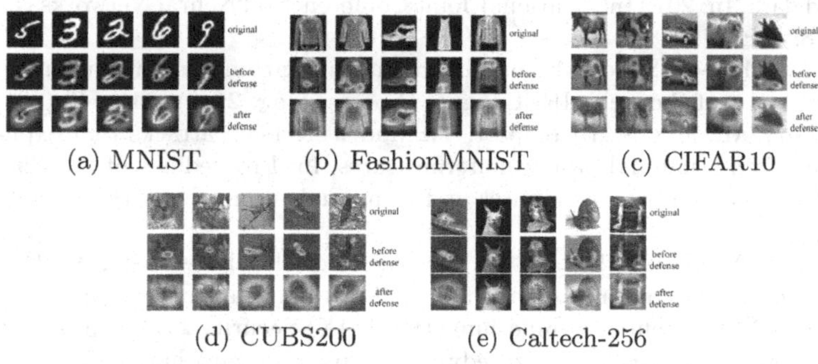

Fig. 8. The feature visualization results.

5 Conclusion and Future Works

In this work, we were motivated by limited success of existing defenses against DNN model stealing attacks. We proposed the first defense strategy with AST, and found DAS-AST is effective in defending a variety of target models and against various attack strategies. In particular, we find DAS-AST can reduce the average accuracy of the adversary at least 30% in all kinds of datasets, without significantly affecting target model accuracy. Despite this, there are also serval shortcomings that need to be resolved urgently for DAS-AST. On the one hand, if attacker launches an adaptive attack on the premise that the attacker has the defense knowledge of DAS-AST, it is different for us to achieve successful defense. On the other hand, when attacker only uses the output label for training stealing model, DAS-AST becomes useless, and this problem is also need to be solved in the current defense of model stealing attack. These will become the focus of our future work.

Acknowledgments. This research was supported by the Zhejiang Provincial Natural Science Foundation of China under Grant No. LY19F020025, the Major Special Funding for Science and Technology Innovation 2025 in Ningbo under Grant No. 2018B10063, the National Key Research and Development Program of China under Grant No. 2018AAA0100800.

References

1. Ateniese, G., Mancini, L.V., Spognardi, A., Villani, A., Vitali, D., Felici, G.: Hacking smart machines with smarter ones: how to extract meaningful data from machine learning classifiers. Int. J. Secur. Netw. **10**(3), 137–150 (2015)
2. Athalye, A., Carlini, N., Wagner, D.: Obfuscated gradients give a false sense of security: circumventing defenses to adversarial examples. arXiv preprint arXiv:1802.00420 (2018)
3. Correia-Silva, J.R., Berriel, R.F., Badue, C., de Souza, A.F., Oliveira-Santos, T.: Copycat CNN: stealing knowledge by persuading confession with random non-labeled data. In: 2018 International Joint Conference on Neural Networks (IJCNN), pp. 1–8. IEEE (2018)
4. Deng, L.: The MNIST database of handwritten digit images for machine learning research [best of the web]. IEEE Signal Process. Mag. **29**(6), 141–142 (2012)
5. Fredrikson, M., Jha, S., Ristenpart, T.: Model inversion attacks that exploit confidence information and basic countermeasures. In: Proceedings of the 22nd ACM SIGSAC Conference on Computer and Communications Security, pp. 1322–1333 (2015)
6. Fredrikson, M., Lantz, E., Jha, S., Lin, S., Page, D., Ristenpart, T.: Privacy in pharmacogenetics: an end-to-end case study of personalized warfarin dosing. In: 23rd {USENIX} Security Symposium ({USENIX} Security 2014), pp. 17–32 (2014)
7. Goodfellow, I.J., Shlens, J., Szegedy, C.: Explaining and harnessing adversarial examples. arXiv preprint arXiv:1412.6572 (2014)
8. He, K., Zhang, X., Ren, S., Sun, J.: Deep residual learning for image recognition (2016)
9. Höhna, S., Coghill, L.M., Mount, G.G., Thomson, R.C., Brown, J.M.: P3: Phylogenetic posterior prediction in RevBayes. Mol. Biol. Evol. **35**(4), 1028–1034 (2018)
10. Juuti, M., Szyller, S., Marchal, S., Asokan, N.: Prada: protecting against dnn model stealing attacks. In: 2019 IEEE European Symposium on Security and Privacy (EuroS&P), pp. 512–527. IEEE (2019)
11. Kesarwani, M., Mukhoty, B., Arya, V., Mehta, S.: Model extraction warning in MLaaS paradigm. In: Proceedings of the 34th Annual Computer Security Applications Conference, pp. 371–380 (2018)

12. Krizhevsky, A., Sutskever, I., Hinton, G.E.: Imagenet classification with deep convolutional neural networks (2012)
13. LeCun, Y., et al.: LeNet-5, convolutional neural networks, vol. 20, no. 5, p. 14 (2015). http://yann.lecun.com/exdb/lenet
14. Lee, T., Edwards, B., Molloy, I., Su, D.: Defending against machine learning model stealing attacks using deceptive perturbations. arXiv preprint arXiv:1806.00054 (2018)
15. Lowd, D., Meek, C.: Adversarial learning. In: Proceedings of the Eleventh ACM SIGKDD International Conference on Knowledge Discovery in Data Mining, pp. 641–647 (2005)
16. Milli, S., Schmidt, L., Dragan, A.D., Hardt, M.: Model reconstruction from model explanations. In: Proceedings of the Conference on Fairness, Accountability, and Transparency, pp. 1–9 (2019)
17. Murphy, G.C., Notkin, D.: Lightweight source model extraction. ACM SIGSOFT Softw. Eng. Notes **20**(4), 116–127 (1995)
18. Nelson, B., et al.: Misleading learners: co-opting your spam filter. In: Yu, P.S., Tsai, J.J.P. (eds.) Machine Learning in Cyber Trust, pp. 17–51. Springer, Boston (2009). https://doi.org/10.1007/978-0-387-88735-7_2
19. Oh, S.J., Schiele, B., Fritz, M.: Towards reverse-engineering black-box neural networks. In: Samek, W., Montavon, G., Vedaldi, A., Hansen, L.K., Müller, K.-R. (eds.) Explainable AI: Interpreting, Explaining and Visualizing Deep Learning. LNCS (LNAI), vol. 11700, pp. 121–144. Springer, Cham (2019). https://doi.org/10.1007/978-3-030-28954-6_7
20. Orekondy, T., Schiele, B., Fritz, M.: Knockoff nets: stealing functionality of black-box models. In: Proceedings of the IEEE Conference on Computer Vision and Pattern Recognition, pp. 4954–4963 (2019)
21. Orekondy, T., Schiele, B., Fritz, M.: Prediction poisoning: towards defenses against DNN model stealing attacks. In: International Conference on Learning Representations (2019)
22. Papernot, N., McDaniel, P., Goodfellow, I., Jha, S., Celik, Z.B., Swami, A.: Practical black-box attacks against machine learning. In: Proceedings of the 2017 ACM on Asia Conference on Computer and Communications Security, pp. 506–519 (2017)
23. Papernot, N., McDaniel, P., Sinha, A., Wellman, M.: Towards the science of security and privacy in machine learning. arXiv preprint arXiv:1611.03814 (2016)
24. Salem, A., Zhang, Y., Humbert, M., Berrang, P., Fritz, M., Backes, M.: ML-leaks: model and data independent membership inference attacks and defenses on machine learning models. arXiv preprint arXiv:1806.01246 (2018)
25. Selvaraju, R.R., Das, A., Vedantam, R., Cogswell, M., Parikh, D., Batra, D.: Grad-CAM: why did you say that? Visual explanations from deep networks via gradient-based localization (2016)
26. Shokri, R., Stronati, M., Song, C., Shmatikov, V.: Membership inference attacks against machine learning models. In: 2017 IEEE Symposium on Security and Privacy (SP), pp. 3–18. IEEE (2017)
27. Siciliano, R., Aria, M., D'Ambrosio, A.: Posterior prediction modelling of optimal trees. In: Brito, P. (ed.) COMPSTAT 2008, pp. 323–334. Springer, Heidelberg (2008). https://doi.org/10.1007/978-3-7908-2084-3_27
28. Simonyan, K., Zisserman, A.: Very deep convolutional networks for large-scale image recognition. In: International Conference on Learning Representations, May 2015

29. Tramèr, F., Zhang, F., Juels, A., Reiter, M.K., Ristenpart, T.: Stealing machine learning models via prediction APIs. In: 25th {USENIX} Security Symposium ({USENIX} Security 2016), pp. 601–618 (2016)
30. Wang, B., Gong, N.Z.: Stealing hyperparameters in machine learning. In: 2018 IEEE Symposium on Security and Privacy (SP), pp. 36–52. IEEE (2018)
31. Yoshida, K., Kubota, T., Shiozaki, M., Fujino, T.: Model-extraction attack against FPGA-DNN accelerator utilizing correlation electromagnetic analysis. In: 2019 IEEE 27th Annual International Symposium on Field-Programmable Custom Computing Machines (FCCM), pp. 318–318. IEEE (2019)
32. Zheng, H., Ye, Q., Hu, H., Fang, C., Shi, J.: BDPL: a boundary differentially private layer against machine learning model extraction attacks. In: Sako, K., Schneider, S., Ryan, P.Y.A. (eds.) ESORICS 2019. LNCS, vol. 11735, pp. 66–83. Springer, Cham (2019). https://doi.org/10.1007/978-3-030-29959-0_4

Bidirectional RNN-Based Few-Shot Training for Detecting Multi-stage Attack

Bowei Jia, Yunzhe Tian, Di Zhao, Xiaojin Wang, Chenyang Li, Wenjia Niu(✉), Endong Tong(✉), and Jiqiang Liu

Beijing Key Laboratory of Security and Privacy in Intelligent Transportation, Beijing Jiaotong University, 3 Shangyuan Village, Haidian District, Beijing 100044, China
{Jiabowei,Tianyunzhe,Dizhao,Xiaojinwang,Licheny,Niuwj,Edtong,Jqliu}@bjtu.edu.cn

Abstract. Feint attack, as a combination of virtual attacks and real attacks of a new type of APT attack, has become the focus of attention. Under the cover of virtual attacks, real attacks can achieve the real purpose and cause losses inadvertently. However, to our knowledge, all previous works use common methods such as Causal-Correlation or Cased-based to detect outdated multi-stage attacks. Few attentions have been paid to detect the feint attack, because of the diversification of the concept of feint attack and the lack of professional datasets. Aiming at the existing challenge, this paper explores a new method to construct such dataset. A fuzzy clustering method based on attribute similarity is used to mine multi-stage attack chains. Then we use a few-shot deep learning algorithm (SMOTE&CNN-SVM) and bidirectional recurrent neural network model (Bi-RNN) to obtain the feint attack chains. Feint attack is simulated by the real attack inserted in the normal causal attack chain, and the addition of the real attack destroys the causal relationship of the original attack chain. So, we used Bi-RNN coding to obtain the hidden feature of feint attack chain. In experiments, we evaluate our approach through using the LLDoS1.0 and LLDoS2.0 of DARPA2000 and CICIDS2017 of Canadian Institute for Cybersecurity.

Keywords: Multi-stage attack · Feint attack · Fuzzy clustering · Bi-RNN model · Few-shot learning

1 Introduction

Under the background of the rapid development of global network informationization, the hidden, pervasive and targeted Advanced Persistent Threat (APT) poses a growing threat to various high-level information security systems [14]. APT attacks are increasing which target to national and enterprise network information systems and data security faces severe challenges. In March 2011, at the 6th International Conference on Information Warfare and Security (ICIW), three security researchers at Lockheed Martin proposed an Intrusion Kill Chain (IKC) [4]. From the perspective of intrusion detection, they decomposed the attack process into seven steps: reconnaissance, weaponization,

Y. Wu and M. Yung (Eds.): Inscrypt 2020, LNCS 12612, pp. 37–52, 2021.
https://doi.org/10.1007/978-3-030-71852-7_3

delivery, exploitation, installation, command and control (C2), and actions on objectives. This model redefines the kill chain in the military field to cyberspace security, providing us with new ideas for solving APT attacks [9, 19].

However, at the end of 2017, Trend Micro pointed out that there has been a new type of APT attack named feint attack [10]. It not only uses the same attack, but also makes full use of two separate malware attacks. One attack (Virtual attack) is responsible for distracting and masking the malicious activity of another attack (Real attack) to provide a way to further infect or steal data and intellectual property. Enterprise IT Security Risk Survey Report pointed out that the above-mentioned virtual attacks are often distributed denial of service (DDoS) attacks [5]. Through analysis of security experts, these DDoS attacks are only "smoke bombs" that attackers use to cover their real attacks. Some enterprises that have suffered from DDoS attacks find that DDoS attacks are only part of the overall network attack, accounting for only 29% of the total attack time. When a DDoS attack occurs, the enterprise's security department must try to quickly restore normal access services because the normal external access of the enterprise is denied or interrupted. Therefore, during the DDoS attack, security departments are often required to go all out to solve the DDoS attack problem, and then the attacker "make a feint to the east but attack in the west" causing security departments cannot take into account the other intrusion. After the feint attack, 25% of companies will lose important data at the same time. As it turns out, in order to improve the efficiency of attack, an attacker often launches a variety of other forms of attack when launching a DDoS attack. Therefore, once a company is found to be attacked by DDoS, it must understand the full threat situation and be ready to handle multiple types of network attacks, otherwise it is likely to suffer greater losses. The Trend Micro report predicted that such attacks will become more common in 2018.

The feint attack mode has received extensive attention in the field of cyberspace security. However, in the face of the special attacks, how to carry out related detection and defense work is still a problem. The detection of multi-stage attack mode at home and abroad is currently in the key research stage. This paper mainly focuses on the special attack mode of feint attack, and proposes a detection model based on fuzzy clustering in alert correlation and Bi-RNN algorithm. The main contributions are as follows:

1. Replaying the traffic packet of the LLDoS 1.0 and LLDoS2.0 of DARPA2000 intrusion detection attack scenario [13] and the traffic packet (.pcap) of Intrusion Detection Evaluation Dataset (CICIDS2017) [18] through snort, generating the raw alert data, and further based on the five-tuple (*AttackType, S_IP, D_IP, S_Port, D_Port*) performing alert aggregation. The main purposes are to reduce the duplicate alert data of the same attack event, and use the fuzzy clustering based on attribute similarity to process the raw alert after aggregation. Multi-stage attack chains are mined in the attack scenario to form a multi-stage attack mode comparison library.
2. We improve the traditional deep learning algorithm and CICIDS2017 dataset in our experiment is preprocessed by the imbalanced learning strategy. Specifically, we used the deep convolutional neural network to learn the new feature representation of the dataset. Then the few-shot learning is performed by the hierarchical SVM classifier. The classification result was divided into the virtual attacks and real attacks with

the confidence level. Finally, we constructed the dataset of virtual attacks and real attacks, which is the basic element library of the feint attack chain.

3. Using the multi-stage attack and element attack event library obtained in the first and second stages, our method of attack chain recovery technology based on Bi-RNN was proposed. According to the method, feint attack is simulated by the real attack inserted in the normal causal attack chain, and the addition of the real attack destroys the causal relationship of the original attack chain. The hidden feature is obtained by Bi-RNN coding. Further we classified the two types of trainable samples. Finally, our work achieved the purpose of detecting the feint attack accurately.

The structure of this paper is organized as follows. Section 2 will discuss the related work in this field. Section 3 will present feint attack chains construction and detection methods through feint attack chains model. Section 4 gives experimental and results. Finally, conclusion is showed in Sect. 5.

2 Related Work

Causal Correlation Analysis The causal alert correlation method associates the alert information according to the causal dependence between the attacks. If the result of one attack behavior creates a precondition for another attack behavior, it is considered that there is a causal dependence between the two attack behaviors, and the causal relationship is utilized. Nguyen et al. [15] conducted an empirical game analysis of the multi-stage interaction between the attacker and the defender to obtain a heuristic strategy under the Bayesian attack graph model. Haas et al. [8] proposed a graph-based alert association (GAC) algorithm to isolate attacks, identify attack scenarios, and assemble multi-stage attacks from a large set of alerts. Pei et al. [16] proposed a method which models multi-stage intrusion analysis as a community discovery problem analysis system, and discovers all "attack communities" embedded within the graphs. A novel method based on the Hidden Markov Model is proposed to predict multi-stage attacks using IDS alerts by Holgado et al. [11] They consider the hidden states as similar phases of a particular type of attack. Katipally et al. [12] use data mining to process alarms and input the processed data into the hidden Markov model (HMM), ultimately achieving the purpose of analyzing and predicting the behavior of the attacker.

Cluster Correlation Analysis The clustering alert correlation method associates alert information with some identical or similar features, that is, clustering by the similarity between alert attribute values, such as the same destination address, the same attack source, attack means, etc. Ahmadianramaki et al. [1] proposed a three-layer processing framework that uses causal knowledge to correlate alerts, automatically extracts causal relationships between alerts, builds the attack scenario using Bayesian networks. And further predicting the most likely next attack behavior. Barzegar et al. [3] proposed approach reconstructs attack scenarios by reasoning based on the evidences in the alert stream. The main idea of the proposed approach is to identify the causal relation between alerts using their similarity. Alvarenga et al. [2] proposed approach applies process mining techniques on alerts to extract information regarding the attackers behavior and the multi-stage attack strategies they adopted. The strategies are presented to the network administrator in friendly high-level visual models. Large and visually complex models that are difficult to understand are clustered into smaller, simpler and more intuitive models using hierarchical clustering techniques.

The multi-stage attack detection based on causal correlation requires a large amount of expert knowledge. The acquisition of expert knowledge is very difficult, and can not discover new attack behavior. In this paper, the fuzzy clustering method based on attribute similarity is used to mine the multi-stage attack mode. The previous work of detection of the multi-stage attack chain does not consider the special type of feint attack chain, and the length of the constructed attack chain is too long, which makes it difficult to retain its inherent causal relationship in further analysis and pre-processing. Therefore, based on previous work, our research mainly defines and divides virtual attacks and real attacks, builds the attack chain based on causal correlation and Bi-RNN model, further obtains the trainable attack sample set, and finally obtains the attack chain detection classifier through training.

3 Feint Attack Chains Construction and Detection Method

In order to achieve the feint attack chain detection based on the virtual attack chain and real attack chain, we propose a new detection method in this section which mainly utilizes fuzzy clustering and Bi-RNN algorithm. The input to our model is raw data stream (The packet format is.dump and.pcap) of LLDoS1.0 and LLDoS2.0 of DARPA2000 and CICIDS2017 of Canadian Institute for Cybersecurity, and the output is the result of the classifier for detecting feint attack, that is, whether there is a feint attack behavior in a multi-stage attack sequence. We will describe in detail the implementation of each algorithm proposed in this paper, and show how to utilize our model to construct and

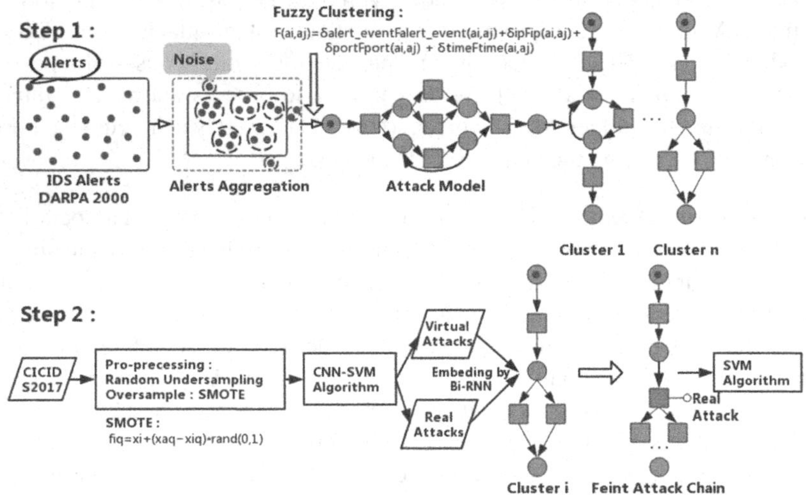

Fig. 1. Framework of feint attack chains construction and detection method

detect the feint attack chain. Framework of bidirectional RNN based few-shot training for detecting multi-stage attack is shown in Fig. 1.

Using the captured real-time data packet or replaying the classical attack dataset by snort to obtain the raw alerts. The multi-stage attack mode is mined by the fuzzy clustering method based on attribute similarity, and the virtual attack and real attack are defined and divided by the few-shot deep learning model [6]. The real attack is embedded into the attack chain by Bi-RNN coding, and the feint attack chain is constructed. Further we classified the two types of trainable samples. Finally, our work achieved the purpose of detecting the feint attack accurately.

3.1 Alert Correlation Based on Fuzzy Clustering

Definition 1. ***IDS alert****is a kind of alert generated when attack operations occur. It shows security situation of the entire network. We represent IDS alert as alert* $= a_1$, a_2,..., a_n*where* a_i*indicates the* i_{th}*alert and is a nine-tuple:*

$$a_i = (Timestamp, Protocal, S\_IP, D\_IP, S\_Port, D\_Port, AttackType, Classification, Priority)$$

Definition 2. ***Raw alert****refers to a single attack action performed by the attacker in the network. It may be an alarm generated directly by the IDS after the scan of the host service or the exploitation of a vulnerability of the host, without any processing.*

Definition 3. ***Attack sequence****is a sequence of IDS alerts that is produced by an attacking process. We represent the attack sequence as* $AS = \{a_1, a_2, ..., a_n\}$.

Alert Aggregation. We found that there are many attack type, source IP, destination IP, source port and destination port with the same or similar alerts in a certain time window, which are recorded as five-tuple (*AttackType, S_IP, D_IP, S_Port, D_Port*). According to the specific circumstances of the alert, this paper divide them into the following modes:

- *If* (*AttackType, S_IP, D_IP, S_Port, D_Port*) is the same, then it means the same attack event is alerted multiple times.
- *If* (*AttackType, S_IP, D_IP, S_Port*) is the same, then it means an attacker scans the ports of another host and queries the services it runs.
- *If* (*AttackType, S_IP*) is the same and *D_IP* is on the same network segment, then it means the attacker scans the target network segment to query the surviving hosts.
- *If* the *AttackType* is different as well as *S_IP* and *D_IP* are same, then it means the attack is belongs to the springboard attack.

By merging multiple alerts caused by the same security event into one alert record, the alert aggregation can greatly reduce the number of raw alerts and reduce the number of alerts to be associated, which can greatly reduce the time required for alert correlation. The complexity of the resulting multi-stage attack model is also greatly reduced, which is more conducive to us to explore the phenomenon of feint attack.

We defined the *Alert Aggregation Rate* as follows:

$$Alert\ Aggregation\ Rate = (Raw\ Alerts - Output\ Alerts)/Raw\ Alerts \quad (1)$$

Attribute Similarity Calculation. In this section, the basic attack chain needed in the virtual and real attack chain is constructed by using fuzzy clustering alarm association algorithm based on attribute similarity. The correlation of attack events is analyzed by using similarity function of different attributes from a large number of alarm events. This method can be used to connect multiple seemingly isolated security events in the attack scenario.

Attack Event. The attack events in the IDS alerts are classified based on the IKC model. From the attacker's point of view, the attacks in the subsequent stages are more complex and more purposeful, and the acquired rights are higher. In the attack event dimension, the similarity formula for a_i, a_j belonging to an attack sequence is as follows:

$$F_{alert\_event}(a_i, a_j) = \begin{cases} 1, \Delta\alpha = 0 \text{ or } 1 \\ e^{-(\Delta\alpha - 3/2)}, \Delta\alpha > 1 \\ 0, else \end{cases} \tag{2}$$

$$\Delta\alpha = \alpha(a_i.alert\_event) - \alpha(a_j.alert\_event)$$

Δa represents the stage difference between two alarms. If the stage difference is 0 or 1, it indicates that two alarms are in the same stage or in two adjacent stages, and have the most greatest similarity. The upper limit of similarity is 1, and the minimum is 0.

IP Address. H represents two IP addresses in binary form that are consecutively the same number of bits from high to low. We use the method of comparing the same number of bits of two IP addresses to measure the similarity of IP addresses.

$$F_{\mathrm{IP}}(a_i, a_j) = N/32 \tag{3}$$

where $N = \max\{H(a_i.sIP, a_j.dIP), H(a_i.sIP, a_j.sIP), H(a_i.dIP, a_j.dIP)\}$.

Port. The maximum value of the port is 65535, so the port difference value can be normalized to represent.

$$F_{\mathrm{Port}}(a_i, a_j) = 1 - |p1 - p2|/65535 \tag{4}$$

Timestamp. In a multi-stage attacking process, the time interval is relatively short when two attacks are in the same phase, and the time interval may be longer when two attacks occur in different phases, or there is a long latency following the previous access. For this reason, we do not set time window for alert logs. The similarity function of the timestamp property is as follows:

$$F_{Time}(a_i, a_j) = e^{-\Delta t}$$
$$\Delta t = a_i.time - a_j.time \tag{5}$$

The complete similarity is calculated using the following function:

$$F(a_i, a_j) = \delta_{alert\_event} F_{alert\_event}(a_i, a_j) + \delta_{ip} F_{ip}(a_i, a_j) + \delta_{port} F_{port}(a_i, a_j) + \delta_{time} F_{time}(a_i, a_j) \tag{6}$$

δ is the weight of the attribute value.

Scan the alert sets after aggregating, analyze each alert a_i in turn, and calculate the membership degree of each classified result of a_i.The specific calculation method is to calculate the similarity of all alerts in a_i and an existing cluster. The membership degree of a_i belonging to a cluster is the highest similarity between a_i and the alerts in the cluster. Before calculating the similarity, we first determine the attack event of the alert with the latest timestamp in the cluster and the attack event of a_i, and judge whether the number of stages corresponding to the latter attack event is less than the number of stages corresponding to the former attack event. If Δa is greater than or equal to -1, we calculate the similarity of two alerts using a similarity function with multidimensional attributes. If less than -1, we calculate the membership of a_i belonging to the next cluster. The largest membership degree of a_i belonging to the existing clusters is r. Assuming that, the largest membership degree of ai belonging to an existing cluster is r. When r is greater than the threshold value λ, it is considered that the alerts in this cluster and the alerts a_i are triggered by the same attack process. If r is less than the threshold value λ, a_i is used as a new cluster, which may be the beginning of a new attack process.

3.2 Building the Virtual-Real Lib

Definition 4. ***Virtual attack and Real Attack****: A virtual attack is defined as an attack that is accurately identified by IDS or an attack classifier. A real attack is a more concealed attack (which may be a normal behavior) or a new type of attack, which neither cause the IDS to generated alert nor is judged as an attack behavior by the classifier.*

The input to this section is the CICIDS2017 dataset, which has 83 statistical features such as duration, number of packets, number of bytes, packet length and so on. The output is the classification result of the attack, which lays the foundation for the next step of dividing the virtual attacks and real attacks. We mainly studies existing attack detection algorithms and improves traditional deep learning methods for attack detection. Based on deep learning and few-shot deep learning algorithms, the raw alerts are preprocessed by unbalanced learning strategies, such as random downsampling and SMOTE oversampling techniques. Then, combining with the feature extraction in deep convolution neural network and the classification in SVM classifier to build the optimal CICIDS2017 classifier.

Considering that when the attacker launches a feint attack, the virtual attack actually plays the role of attracting the attention of the defense side, and the real attack adopted later is of strong concealment and not easy to be detected. Thus, the attacker should use virtual attacks can be accurately detected by defenders. Combined with such characteristics, this paper simulates the process of being deceived, and filters the results of model classification by using a classifier trained with intrusion detection data. In order to enhance the confidence of virtual and real attacks, attacks that have been missed eight or more times in the test results of ten models obtained from ten cross-validation are selected as the real attack sample set. Attacks that have been classified correctly ten times are selected as a virtual sample set.

Less class-sample combining oversampling technique are referred as SMOTE algorithm, which is proposed by Sáez J et al. [17] Assuming that in the training data S, x_i is a sample belonging to the minority class. The first step in SMOTE is to calculate the k-nearest neighbors set P_i of x_i. From P_i, we randomly select a sample x_a. And the difference between the x_i and x_a corresponding to the attribute q is denoted as $diff(q) = x_{aq} - x_{iq}$. The mathematic formula of the synthesis of new sample f_{iq} belonging to the minority class as follows:

$$f_{iq} = x_i + \left(x_{aq} - x_{iq}\right) * rand\ (0,\ 1) \tag{7}$$

where rand (0,1) is a random number in (0,1). Then the above process is repeated according to the predefined oversampling rate, and the synthetic new sample is added to the initial training sample to increase the number of samples belonging to the minority class. In this way, the degree of imbalance is greatly reduced and there is a relative balance between majority classes and minority classes in the new training data set. Finally, the new training data set are classified by the classifier and the classification results are obtained.

3.3 Feint Attack Chain Construction and Detection Model

Definition 5. ***Feint Attack Chains:****By analyzing the various situations of feint attacks, it is summarized as a multi-stage attack mode of virtual attacks and real attacks.*

The attacker hides the attack trajectory, and sometimes uses the policy of "make a feint to the east but attack in the west" to perform a large number of attacks on the vital host A, such as DDoS attacks, causing a large number of alerts, while the real target host is B. Due to the security personnel processing the DDoS attack against host A, there is no way to deal with the alarm caused by the real attacks on host B.

The attacker uses a highly concealed attack in some steps of the multi-stage attack sequence, or uses an advanced attack to prevent the IDS system from generating an alert to confuse the operation and maintenance personnel. The lack of some processes in the multi-stage attack process, resulting in the inability to completely restore the entire attack path (such as using DNS queries in LLDoS2.0 instead of IPsweep in LLoS1.0).

Our attack chain recovery technique is based on Bi-RNN. We use the attack chain established in the first stage and the real attack in the second stage to embed the atomic attack event into the attack chain through Bi-RNN coding. The forward RNN records the information of the attack chain from the cause to the result, and the reverse RNN records the information of the attack chain from the result to the cause, ensuring the maximum retention of the correlation information. The process is shown in Fig. 2.

Finally, we label the sample set of feint attack and non-feint attack chains, and further train the model to automatically classify the attack chain samples. Based on the machine learning algorithm, a special attack detection model for the virtual attack and real attack chain is constructed by training the feint attack and non-feint attack chain samples, and the model parameters are determined. Furthermore, the learning model integration of specific weight enhancement is carried out by voting method to improve the detection accuracy of model. In this way, the purpose of accurately identifying the feint attack is achieved.

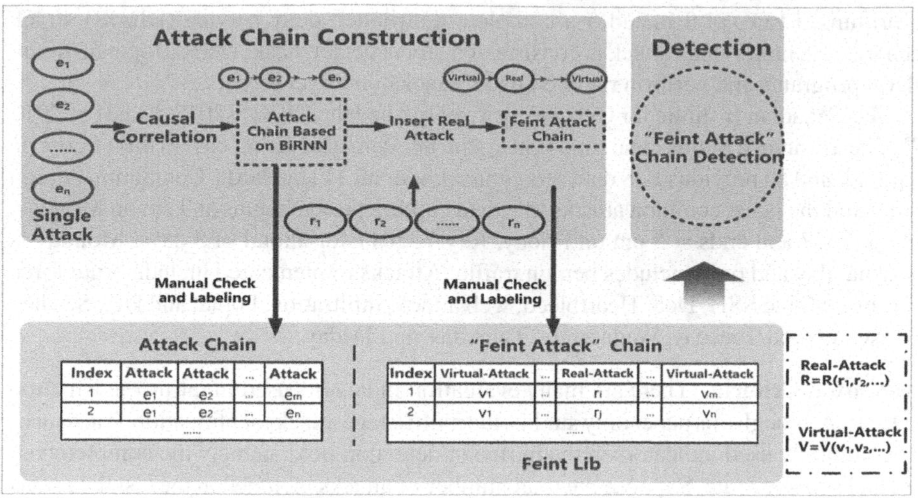

Fig. 2. Feint attack chains construction

4 Experimental and Results

4.1 Experimental Setup

Experimental Environment We choose same hardware and software configurations when carrying out the experiments. Our experiment is conducted on the windows 10 operating system with the hardware environment Intel(R) Core(TM) i7-7500U CPU, 8 GB RAM and IT hard disk. We utilize the programming language python 3.5. The main items of our hardware and software configuration can be found in Table 1.

Table 1. Hardware and software configuration

No.	Hardware or software	Type
1	Operating system	Windows 10
2	Programming language	Python3.5
3	Development environment	JetBrains PyCharm 2018.1.4
4	CPU	Inter(R) Core(TM)i7-7500U
5	RAM	8GB
6	Disk	IT hard disk

The DARPA2000 dataset is a collection of intrusion scenario correlations from MIT Lincoln lab. It is widely used to verify the effectiveness of various alert event correlation algorithms. LLDOS1.0 includes a complete distributed deny service (DDOS) attack scenario, the multi-stage attack is consists of 5 steps: detect, hack, install trojan mstream DDoS programs and perform remote DDoS attacks on target servers.

The Canadian Institute for Cybersecurity published the CICIDS2017 dataset in 2017 [7]. The advantage of this data: time is near, the benchmark data set covers the 11 criteria required, and all previous IDS data sets cannot cover all 11 standards. Containing benign traffic and the latest common attacks, the data capture period begins at 9 am on Monday, July 3, 2017 and ends at 5 pm on Friday, July 7, 2017 for a total of 5 days. Monday is a normal day and only includes benign traffic. Attacks implemented include brute force FTP, brute force SSH, DoS, Heartbleed, web attack, infiltration, botnet and DDoS. They are executed on Tuesday, Wednesday, Thursday and Friday.

Evaluation Criteria. There are many evaluation indicators used in intrusion detection systems. Although this paper only studies the multi-stage attack identification, it also uses the commonly used indicators in the intrusion detection field, namely the completeness rate and accuracy rate. Suppose the total number of attacks included in the test data set is N, the number of attacks identified by the recognition method is RN, and the number of attacks identified in these test data sets is actually R. The definitions of these indicators are as follows:

1. *Completeness Rate:* The completeness rate is the completeness of the description method, that is, whether all attacks can be found. The calculation method for multi-stage attack recognition completeness rate is:

$$Completeness\ Rate = R/N \tag{8}$$

2. *Accuracy Rate:* Accuracy rate is the correctness of the description method, that is, how many of the identified attacks are correct. The calculation method for multi-stage attack recognition accuracy is:

$$Accuracy\ Rate = R/RN \tag{9}$$

4.2 Experimental Result and Evaluation

Alert Correlation Based on Fuzzy Clustering. Use the snort's command sudo snort-r /LLS DDOS 1.0-inside.dump -l/home-A fast-c/etc/snort/snort.conf in Linux to replay the original traffic packets from LLDoS1.0 and LLDoS2.0 of DARPA2000 and CICIDS2017.

Through the network traffic packet analysis software Wireshark, we analyzed all traffic packets (including normal background traffic) in the DMZ and Inside areas of LLoS1.0, and the packets containing only attack traffic in each of the five attack phases of the DDoS attack.

We tracked the TCP flow of the key attack steps and found that the attacker performed a large number of *IP sweep* (ICMP echo request) on the target network segments, among which 18 hosts survived (ICMP echo reply). The next step is *Sadmind ping*, querying the Sadmind vulnerability and verifying whether the service is running on the surviving host.

There are 6 hosts that meet this condition. Buffer overflow attacks on these 6 hosts invaded the host, and 3 hosts are successfully invaded, namely: 172.16.115.20, 172.16.112.10 and 172.16.112.50. Log in to these three hosts using the rsh service telnet, upload and install the DDoS Daemon (including mstream server and mstream master). Among them, the attacker installed server and master on 172.16.115.20, and only installed server on 172.16.112.10 and 172.16.112.50. It can be seen that 172.16.115.20 is the jump host of the attacker in the internal network. Finally, log in to 172.16.115.20, check the port mstream daemon port 6723, execute the mstream command, set the target IP to 131.84.1.31, and use the forged IP to initiate the DDoS attack for 5 s.

Combine the two-part alerts (DMZ: 7024 and Inside: 10145) obtained by using snort, and perform alert aggregation on 17169 raw alerts to obtain 3222 alerts. The alert aggregation rate reaches 81.23%. The result is shown in Table 2.

Table 2. The performance of alert aggregation

Raw alerts	Amount	Aggregation rate (%)
DMZ	7024	–
Inside	10145	–
Total	17169	–
Alert aggregation	3222	81.23

Using the fuzzy clustering algorithm proposed in Sect. 3.1, 3222 alerts are clustered, and a total of 944 attack sequences are obtained. It contains a large number of sequences of length 1, indicating that there are a large number of fragmentation alerts in the alert clustering.

After deleting the sequence of length 1, a total of 195 multi-stage attack sequences are obtained. After extracting the multi-stage attack mode, nine sequence patterns are obtained.

Building the Virtual-Real Lib. By using the down-sampling and SMOTE algorithms, the number of samples in our datasets is as shown in Table 3.

The performances of the model using only CNN and the model using few-shot deep learning are shown in Fig. 3. It can be seen that CNN is easy to cause over-fitting, while the model of few-shot deep learning effectively avoids over-fitting.

The result of few-shot deep learning model is shown in Table 4. We can see that our method has significantly improved the detection rate of Minority class-sample (U2R and R2L).

We find that CNN-SVM with SMOTE gets better recall and precision. CNN model without SMOTE has quite lower recall when classifying U2R and R2L traffic. The reason is that the amount of U2R and R2L packages is too lower than that of other packages what we have mentioned above. But the recall to U2R and R2L traffic has been greatly improved by introducing SMOTE. The results are shown in Fig. 4.

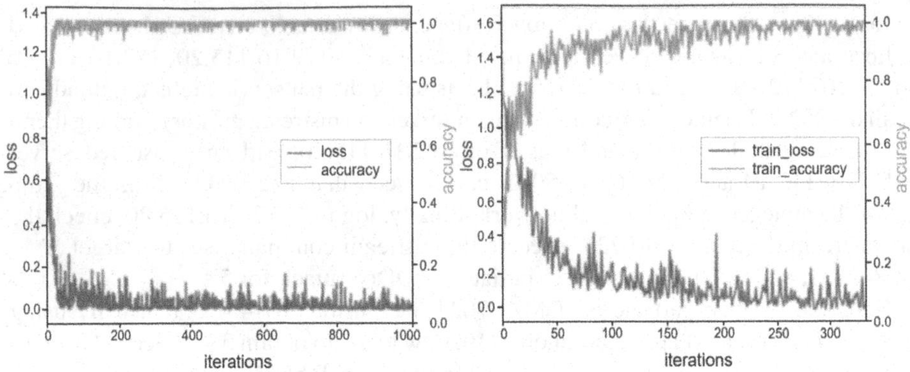

Fig. 3. The performances of the CNN model (left) and the few-shot deep learning model (right)

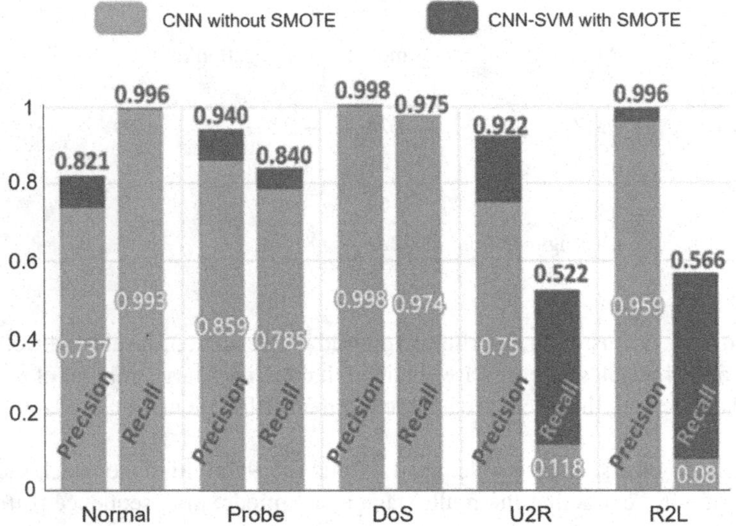

Fig. 4. Precision and recall comparison between the CNN without SMOTE and the CNN-SVM with SMOTE

The Virtual-Real Lib contains 20,718 real attacks and 189,826 virtual attacks. In order to verify the reliability of our results, we take all of real attacks and *Normal* to test, and the results show that more than 95.6% of the real attacks are missed as normal.

Build Feint Lib and Detect the Feint Attack. Feint Lib contains 11758 records of feint attack chains, and there are 20 attacks in each record. The number of training set is 9408 and the number of testing set is 2350. Some samples in the dataset are shown in Table 5. Label 1 means the chain is a feint attack chain and Label 0 means the chain is a common chain.

The number of real attacks in the attack chain are 1 to 7. Among them, the number of attack chains containing one real attack is 3371, the number of attack chains containing

Table 3. The statistics of datasets before and after down-sampling and SMOTE

Dataset name	Number of train data before down-sampling and SMOTE	Number of train data after down-sampling and SMOTE
Benign	1886428	17965
DoS Hulk	184858	12323
PortScan	127144	8476
DDoS	33468	6693
DoSGoldenEye	8234	8234
FTP-Patator	6350	6350
SSH-Patator	4717	4717
DoS slowloris	4636	4636
DoS Slow-httptest	4399	4399
Bot	1572	1572
Brute Force	1205	1205
XSS	521	521
Infiltration	28	280
SQL Injection	16	160
Heartbleed	8	80

Table 4. The confusion matrix of the few-shot deep learning model

Confusion matrix		Predicted category					Recall
		Benign	Probe	Dos	U2R	R2L	
Actual	Benign	60352	123	103	9	6	0.996
	Probe	387	3501	260	0	18	0.840
	Dos	5686	82	224081	0	4	0.975
	U2R	73	13	17	119	6	0.522
	R2L	7018	4	6	1	9160	0.566
Precision		0.821	0.940	0.998	0.922	0.996	Acc:95.6%

two real attacks is 3248, the number of attack chains containing three real attacks is 1811, the number of attack chains containing four real attacks is 672, the number of attack chains containing five real attacks is 200, the number of attack chains containing six real attacks is 50, the number of attack chains containing seven real attacks is 11, and the number of attack chains containing eight real attacks is one.

Finally, we chose $c = 0.5$ and $g = 1$ which can get the best *acc*(78.8764%) in cross validation and got 75.23% accuracy on the test set, which is shown in Fig. 5.

Table 5. Samples of the feint lib

Features									Label	
0	tcp	telnet	REJ	0	…	1	0	0	neptune.	0
0	icmp	ecr_i	SF	520		0.73	0.23	0.27	neptune.	1
0	icmp	ecr_i	SF	1032		0	0	0	smurf.	1
0	icmp	ecr_i	SF	1032		0	0	0	smurf.	1
0	icmp	ecr_i	SF	1032		0	1	1	neptune.	1
0	icmp	ecr_i	SF	1032		0	0	0	smurf.	1
0	icmp	ecr_i	SF	1032		0	1	1	neptune.	1
0	tcp	private	S0	0		0	0	0	smurf.	0
0	icmp	ecr_i	SF	520		0	1	1	neptune.	1
0	icmp	ecr_i	SF	1032		1	0	0	neptune.	1
0	tcp	other	REJ	0		0	0	0	smurf.	1
0	icmp	ecr_i	SF	1032		0	0	0	smurf.	1
0	icmp	ecr_i	SF	1032		0	0	0	smurf.	1
0	icmp	ecr_i	SF	18		0	0	0	smurf.	1

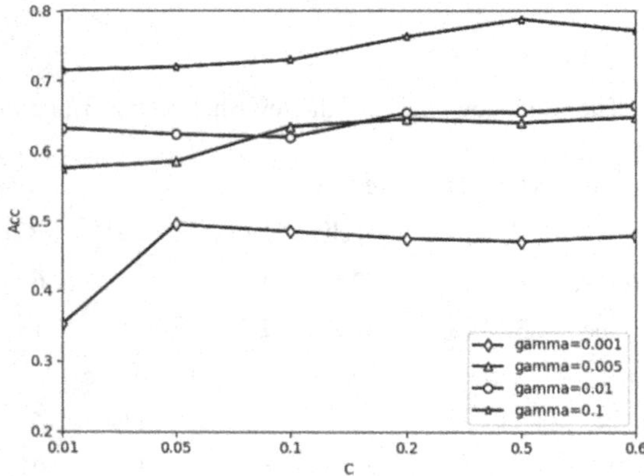

Fig. 5. The feint attack chain detection performances of models with different gamma and c

5 Conclusion

In this paper, aiming at the feint attack mode in APT attack, we proposed a new detection method which mainly utilizes fuzzy clustering and Bi-RNN algorithm. Firstly, by analyzing the existing feint attacks, we defined virtual attacks and real attacks as the basic attack events that constitute the feint attack chains. In the attack scenario, the fuzzy clustering method based on attribute similarity is used to mine multi-stage attack chains. A multi-stage attack mode comparison library is formed, and a few-shot deep learning model is proposed and divides attacks into virtual attacks and real attacks to construct a dataset of atomic attack events. Then, the atomic attack event is embedded into the attack chain through Bi-RNN coding, and the feint attack chain is constructed to form the feint attack dataset. Finally, the attack chain samples containing the feint attack behavior and the non-feint attack behavior are further classified to achieve the purpose of accurately identifying the feint attack. Our innovation lies in the first use of bidirectional RNN coding to construct the attack chain, ensuring maximum retention of causal information. We verified our method by using the LLDoS1.0 and LLDoS2.0 of DARPA2000 and CICIDS2017 of Canadian Institute for Cybersecurity. The experimental results show that our method can derive the multi-stage attack sequence from the alert correlation by fuzzy clustering, and the feint attack behavior is mined from the attack chains. The attack sequence is encoded by Bi-RNN, and achieve 75.23% accuracy to identify feint attack. We research on the key technologies of behavior detection, and realize the prototype system based on the virtual attack and real attack chain, achieving zero breakthrough in detecting such attacks.

Acknowledgement. This work was supported by the National Natural Science Foundation of China (61972025, 61802389, 61672092, U1811264, 61966009), the Fundamental Research Funds for the Central Universities of China (2018JBZ103, 2019RC008), Science and Technology on Information Assurance Laboratory, Guangxi Key Laboratory of Trusted Software (KX201902).

References

1. Ahmadian Ramaki, A., Rasoolzadegan, A.: Causal knowledge analysis for detecting and modeling multi-step attacks. Secur. Commun. Netw. **9**(18), 6042–6065 (2016)
2. De Alvarenga, S.C., Barbon, S., Jr., Miani, R.S., et al.: Process mining and hierarchical clustering to help intrusion alert visualization. Comput. Secur. **73**, 474–491 (2018)
3. Barzegar, M., Shajari, M.: Attack scenario reconstruction using intrusion semantics. Expert Syst. Appl. **108**, 119–133 (2018)
4. Bhatt, P., Yano, E.T., Gustavsson, P.: Towards a framework to detect multi-stage advanced persistent threats attacks. In: 2014 IEEE 8th International Symposium on Service Oriented System Engineering, pp. 390–395. IEEE (2014)
5. Bhuyan, M.H., Bhattacharyya, D.K., Kalita, J.K.: Information metrics for low-rate DDoS attack detection: a comparative evaluation. In: 2014 Seventh International Conference on Contemporary Computing (IC3), pp. 80–84. IEEE (2014)
6. Chowdhury, M.M.U., Hammond, F., Konowicz, G., et al.: A few-shot deep learning approach for improved intrusion detection. In: 2017 IEEE 8th Annual Ubiquitous Computing, Electronics and Mobile Communication Conference (UEMCON), pp. 456–462. IEEE (2017)
7. Panigrahi, R., Borah, S.: A detailed analysis of CICIDS2017 dataset for designing intrusion detection systems. Int. J. Eng. Technol. **7**(3.24), 479–482 (2018)
8. Haas, S., Fischer, M.: GAC: graph-based alert correlation for the detection of distributed multi-step attacks. In: Proceedings of the 33rd Annual ACM Symposium on Applied Computing, pp. 979–988 (2018)
9. Hahn, A., Thomas, R.K., Lozano, I., et al.: A multi-layered and kill-chain based security analysis framework for cyber-physical systems. Int. J. Crit. Infrastruct. Prot. **11**, 39–50 (2015)
10. He, D., Chan, S., Zhang, Y., et al.: How effective are the prevailing attack-defense models for cybersecurity anyway? IEEE Intell. Syst. **29**(5), 14–21 (2013)

11. Holgado, P., Villagrá, V.A., Vazquez, L.: Real-time multistep attack prediction based on hidden markov models. IEEE Trans. Dependable Secure Comput. **17**(1), 134–147 (2017)
12. Katipally, R., Yang, L., Liu, A.: Attacker behavior analysis in multi-stage attack detection system. In: Proceedings of the Seventh Annual Workshop on Cyber Security and Information Intelligence Research, p. 1 (2011)
13. Lee, K., Kim, J., Kwon, K.H., et al.: DDoS attack detection method using cluster analysis. Expert Syst. Appl. **34**(3), 1659–1665 (2008)
14. Li, M., Huang, W., Wang, Y., et al.: The study of APT attack stage model. In: 2016 IEEE/ACIS 15th International Conference on Computer and Information Science (ICIS), pp. 1–5. IEEE (2016)
15. Nguyen, T.H., Wright, M., Wellman, M.P., et al.: Multi-stage attack graph security games: heuristic strategies, with empirical game-theoretic analysis. In: Proceedings of the 2017 Workshop on Moving Target Defense, pp. 87–97 (2017)
16. Pei, K., Gu, Z., Saltaformaggio, B., et al.: Hercule: attack story reconstruction via community discovery on correlated log graph. In: Proceedings of the 32nd Annual Conference on Computer Security Applications, pp. 583–595 (2016)
17. Schuster, M., Paliwal, K.K.: Bidirectional recurrent neural networks. IEEE Trans. Signal Process. **45**(11), 2673–2681 (1997)
18. Sharafaldin, I., Lashkari, A.H., Ghorbani, A.A.: Toward generating a new intrusion detection dataset and intrusion traffic characterization. In: ICISSP, pp. 108–116 (2018)
19. Yadav, T., Rao, A.: Technical aspects of cyber kill chain. In: Abawajy, J.H., Mukherjea, S., Thampi, S.M., Ruiz-Martínez, A. (eds.) SSCC 2015. CCIS, vol. 536, pp. 438–452. Springer, Cham (2015). https://doi.org/10.1007/978-3-319-22915-7_40

An Illumination Modulation-Based Adversarial Attack Against Automated Face Recognition System

Zhaojie Chen[1], Puxi Lin[1], Zoe Lin Jiang[2,3], Zhanhang Wei[1], Sichen Yuan[1], and Junbin Fang[1,2](✉)

[1] Guangdong Provincial Engineering Technology Research Center on VLC, The Guangzhou Municipal Key Laboratory of Engineering Technology on VLC, and The Department of Optoelectronic Engineering, Jinan University, Guangzhou 510632, China
tjunbinfang@jnu.edu.cn

[2] Cyberspace Security Research Center, Peng Cheng Laboratory, Shenzhen 518055, China

[3] Harbin Institute of Technology, Shenzhen 518055, China

Abstract. In recent years, physical adversarial attacks have been placed an increasing emphasis. However, previous studies usually use a printer to physically realize adversarial perturbations, and such an attack scheme will meet inevitable disadvantages of perturbation distortion and low concealment. In this paper, we propose a novel attack scheme based on illumination modulation. Because of the rolling shutter effect of CMOS sensor, the created perturbation will not be distorted and completely invisible. According to the attack scheme, we have proposed two novel attack methods, denial of service attack (DoS attack) and escape attack, and offered a real scene to apply the attack methods. The experimental results show that both of two attack methods have a good performance against AFR. DoS attack has an attack success rate of 92.13% and escape attack has an attack success rate of 82%.

Keywords: Physical adversarial attack · Automated face recognition · Illumination modulation · Denial of service attack · Escape attack

1 Introduction

The vulnerability of artificial intelligence (AI) system exposes against adversarial attacks. In the digital domain, the effectiveness of adversarial attacks has been proven and consecutively improved [1–3]. The scheme and performance of physical adversarial attacks are being explored and some physical adversarial attacks have been designed and developed recently. However, most of the studied physical adversarial attacks usually use a printer to physically realize adversarial perturbations [4–9], which leads to two disadvantages: a) the adversarial perturbations will be distorted from printing the perturbations to capturing the printed perturbations by a camera, and b) the visible attacks lead to the low concealment.

Y. Wu and M. Yung (Eds.): Inscrypt 2020, LNCS 12612, pp. 53–69, 2021.
https://doi.org/10.1007/978-3-030-71852-7_4

This paper proposed a novel attack scheme by modulating illumination. Because of the rolling shutter effect of CMOS cameras, the perturbations will be achieved while taking pictures under modulated illumination. Utilizing the proposed attack scheme, the perturbations will not be distorted and will be invisible to humans. The invisibility contributes to the high concealment. Furthermore, we proposed two practical and novel attack methods against the AI system based on the proposed scheme, denial of service attack (DoS attack), and escape attack. The experimental results show that the DoS attack has an attack success rate of 92.13% and the escape attack has an attack success rate of 82%.

The main contributions of this paper are:

(1) We propose a novel attack scheme to physically realize perturbations of adversarial examples. Utilizing the proposed attack scheme, the practical issues of previous physical adversarial attacks can be overcome. The perturbation will not be distorted and will be invisible to humans, so the concealment will be higher than using a printer.
(2) We propose two novel attack methods based on the proposed attack scheme facing to automated face recognition (AFR) system, DoS attack and escape attack. The experimental results show that they are effective. Besides, we offer a scene to threat the AFR system in real-world.

2 Related Work

In 2014, Christian et al. [1] found some "intriguing properties of neural networks". After the carefully constructed imperceptible perturbations were mixed into digital images, deep neural networks could be misled. They named such a technology "adversarial attack". After the concept was defined, the effectiveness of adversarial attacks has been consistently improved [2, 3]. However, these researches focused on the digital domain, and the efficiency of adversarial attacks in the physical world is still questionable [6].

Recently, many studies have developed their physical adversarial attacks [4–10]. In [5], a crafted adversarial eyeglass frame can fool an AFR. In [6], they proposed "adversarial stickers" placed on the hat to deceive an AFR. In [4], the image classification system was attacked by black or white stickers attached to a stop sign. In [7], the crafted adversarial stickers are placed at the lens of a camera to fool an image classifier. In [8], a novel adversarial patch is proposed to attack person detection. In [9], a kind of adversarial T-shirt is designed to deceive a person detector.

Previous adversarial attacks usually used a printer to physically realize adversarial perturbations. However, using such an attack scheme, many studies ignore the concealment of attacks, which reduces practicability.

The most relevant study to ours is [10]. They utilized the invisibility of infrared light, projected infrared light to real faces, and created perturbation while face images were captured by the camera of AFR. Compared to the traditional attack scheme, its concealment is higher.

3 Proposed Method

We proposed a novel attack scheme by modulating illumination and utilizing the rolling shutter effect of CMOS cameras. Furthermore, we propose two novel practical attacks against AFR.

3.1 Rolling Shutter Effect

There are two common image sensors, CCD and CMOS. The COMS has the advantages of low cost and high quality, which leads to its university in industry. A CMOS sensor usually uses a rolling shutter as exposure mode, and a CCD sensor uses a global shutter. A rolling shutter scans and activates the same row or column of pixels, so pixels are exposed line by line. There is a short time interval between adjacent rows and columns.

Aiming to a rolling shutter, we modulate the LED using on-off keying intensity modulation (OOK IM) at a very high frequency. To reduce the influence of other light sources, such as the ambient light, we set the exposure of CMOS sensor at a low level.

In the short time interval, the on/off state of LED may change, so different columns may be exposed in very different brightness. Finally, there are many black fringes in the captured picture. Because the LED flashes at a very high frequency, it is beyond the limit frequency of the human eyes and invisible to humans.

The width of black fringes is determined by the following formula.

$$w_{fringe} = \frac{T_{LED}}{T_{col}} = \frac{1}{f_{LED}T_{col}}, 1 < w_{fringe} < w_{image}$$

w_{fringe} is the width of captured black fringes, w_{image} is the width of image size, T_{LED} is the flashing time of LED, f_{LED} is the modulated frequency of LED, and T_{col} is the exposure time of each column (Fig. 1).

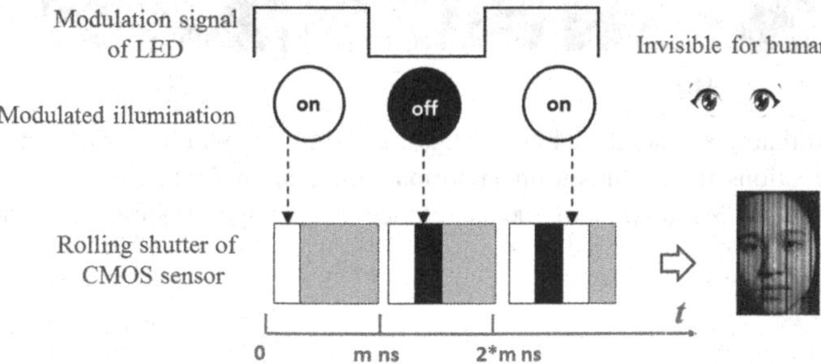

Fig. 1. This picture describes the exposure process of a rolling shutter under high speed modulated illumination. The "on/off" state of LED could change in a short time interval (for instance, 100 ns). When the LED luminaire is on, the bright pixels are stored at the activated row or column of pixels. When it is off, because of the low exposure of camera, the black fringe is stored at the activated row or column of pixels.

3.2 Attack Scheme

A novel attack scheme by modulating illumination is proposed in this paper. The invisible perturbations of black fringes will be achieved under modulated illumination and low exposure. By modulating its flashing frequency, the width of black fringes can be controlled, and different width of fringes stands for different degrees of perturbation. Therefore, if an adversarial attack restricts its perturbations as black fringes, we can physically realize the perturbations by utilizing the rolling shutter effect.

The proposed attack scheme has two advantages compared to the traditional attack scheme.

(a) The perturbations created by the rolling shutter effect will not be distorted. When using a printer as the attack scheme, the perturbations may be distorted from printing to shooting, which may reduce the adversarial property of attacks. However, the fringes created are black, and a black pixel will not be distorted. So if an attack limits the perturbations as black fringes, the perturbation will not be distorted.

(b) Concealment of the proposed attack scheme makes great progress compared to use a printer. The illumination is modulated at a high frequency, so it is beyond the limit frequency of human eyes and completely invisible to humans.

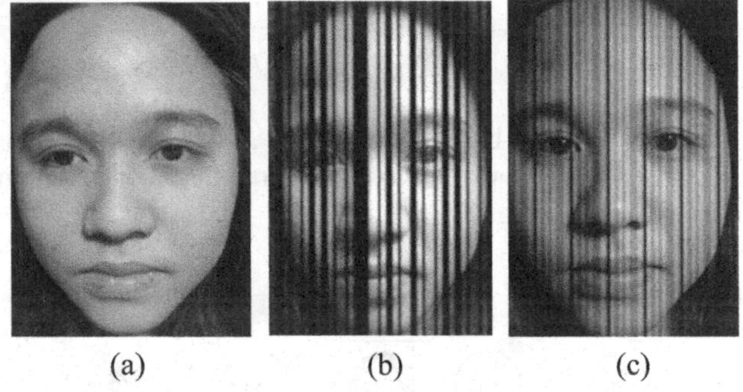

(a) (b) (c)

Fig. 2. The perturbations created are black fringes, and different width of fringes means different degrees of perturbations. (a) face image under normal illumination; (b) face image under modulated illumination using the flashing time of 300 ns; (c) face image under modulated illumination using the flashing time of 85 ns

3.3 Attack Methods

After modulating illumination and setting low exposure, we cover face images with wide and narrow black fringes to develop two attack methods respectively.

After we add wide black fringes to pictures, as it is shown in Fig. 2(b), the important facial features may be covered, for instance, eyes or nose. Because of the absence of key facial features, face detection of AFR system may be ineffective under the strong interference. The subsequent process of face recognition, such as face alignment or feature extraction, will be invalid, and the AFR system will be paralyzed.

After the narrow black fringes are added to pictures, as it is shown in Fig. 2(c), the key facial features are not completely covered, and face detection may work. However, the narrow black fringes will still influence the normal face recognition. First, the mutated pixels in the edges of fringes add lots of repetitive and useless gradient information. Second, the fringes usually pass through key facial features, which will add lots of repetitive and useless gradient information to the facial features. If there are two interfered face images from two different people, useless gradient information their facial features contained is the same, so the difference between two different faces may decline. AFR system may distinguish two different people with a low difference and may judge them as the same person.

We propose two attack methods facing to AFR, denial of service attack (DoS attack) and escape attack. Attacking the face detection unit of AFR, Dos attack uses quite wide black streaks and makes the whole AFR paralyze. Attacking the feature extraction unit of AFR, escape attack uses narrow black streaks and lets the AFR system lack the ability to distinguish two different people.

3.4 Threat Model

We offer a real scenario to apply the proposed two attacks. To use a remote AFR system, users stay in a special space, use camera of their smartphones to capture facial data, and upload the facial data to the remote face recognition system. In such a scene, it is possible for attackers to modulate illumination and control the exposure of camera in smartphone.

Before attacking, attackers install a modulated LED over the attacked area, and own a soft to remotely control the exposure of camera in smartphone, which are implementable.

When a user wants to pass the verification of AFR system, a DoS attack is launched. Because of DoS attack, the whole AFR system is paralyzed, so the user can not pass the verification.

When a user wants to upload his/her facial data to dataset as a baseline face image, an escape attack is launched. The face image of user in backend will be interfered.

When an attack wants to invade an AFR system, an escape attack is launched. An attacked face image will be captured by camera of attack's phone. After compared to the user's interfered face image in backend, AFR will judge the attacker and the user as the same person, and the attacker invade the AFR system successfully.

4 Experiments and Results

4.1 Experiment Scheme

A. *Experimental physical environment*

The experimental physical environment is a 3 m × 3 m × 3 m space. The high-speed modulated LED is installed in the center of the room, 2 m above the ground, so that the modulated illumination can fully and uniformly illuminate the whole space. The used LED is a common commercial LED, with a modulator to control the frequency of LED. During the experiment, we turn off other light sources and only use high-speed modulated LED to provide illumination (Fig. 3).

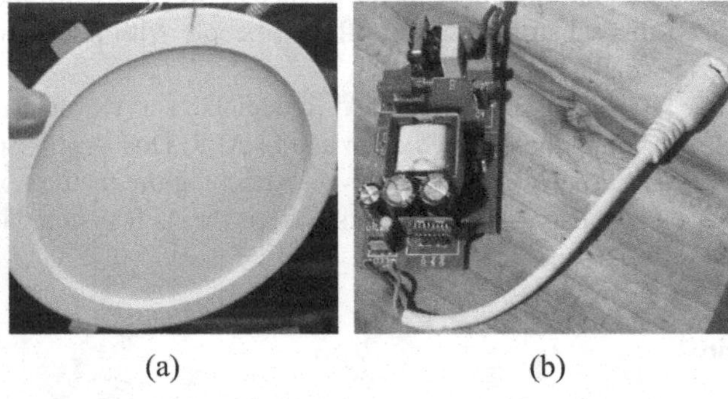

(a) (b)

Fig. 3. (a) The used common commercial LED; (b) the modulator installed to modulate the flashing interval of the LED

B. *Image sensor*

We use the rear camera of HUAWEI-nova4e as the image sensor of AFR system. We set the shutter speed of camera to 1/4000 s to implement a low exposure while attacking (Table 1).

Table 1. The parameters of used camera

Name	Value
Vendor	HUAWEI
Type of phone	Nova 4e
Image size	24 MP(4224 * 5632)
Type of shutter	Rolling shutter

C. *Face recognition system*

We choose the face recognition algorithm in Dlib library [11]. Dlib is an open-source library providing machine learning algorithms. There are three processes in the established Dlib face recognition system, face detection, face alignment, feature extraction.

In face detection, histogram of oriented gradient (HOG) algorithm [12] is used. HOG thinks that the information of images is stored in gradients and the HOG feature can be formed by calculating the amplitude and direction of gradients.

In face alignment, the Dlib library provides two trained models. One model extracts 5 feature points from face image, and the other extracts 68 feature points. Face alignment with 68 points is used in this paper.

In feature extraction, the Dlib library provides the feature extraction model of ResNet. Using the ResNet model, it returns a 128-dimensional feature vector, which represents the input face (Fig. 4).

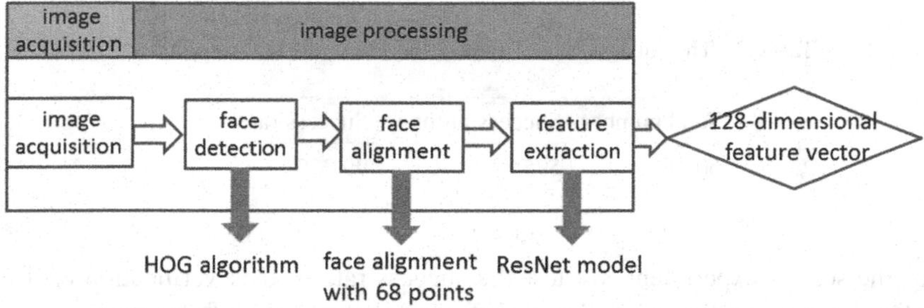

Fig. 4. The processes of Dlib face recognition system.

D. *The method of taking face images*

We use two model faces to in experiments. During experiments, the model faces are kept in a well-lit area. To avoid the poses or facial expressions influence face recognition, when taking pictures, the poses or expressions of model faces should be consistent.

Besides, the width of black fringes is only related to the inherent character of CMOS. But the size of face images is related to the distance between CMOS and faces. So we classify face images according to their size. To those faces make up more than 80% of the images, we classify them as "short-distance" face images; to those faces make up less than 80% but more than 40% of the images, we classify them as "medium-distance" face images; to the rest, we classify them as "far-distance" face images (Fig. 5).

4.2 Experiment for Dlib Face Recognition System

First, we should verify the effectiveness of Dlib face recognition system under normal situations. The proposed two methods attack face detection and feature extraction, so we set up two experiments to verify the effectiveness on face detection and feature

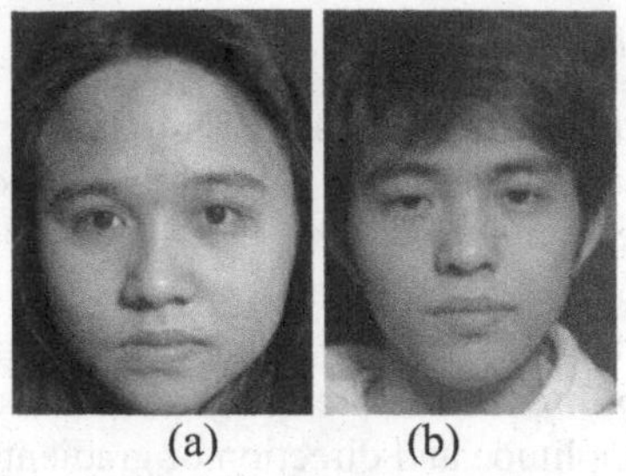

Fig. 5. Two model faces used in experiments. (a) model face 1, (b) model face 2

extraction respectively. Labeled faces in wild (LFW) dataset [13] is used to evaluate its performance.

For the first experiment, we test the success rate of face detection on LFW. On the provided 6000 face images, there are only 45 face images undetected (Table 2).

Table 2. The success rate of face detection on LFW using Dlib

Total number	Success number	Success rate
6000	5955	99.25%

For the second experiment, we test the success rate of face verification on LFW. A verification needs a threshold, and if difference between two face images is below threshold, two face images will be judge as the same person.

After using the default threshold of 0.6 and compared the provided 3000 pairs of faces, the accuracy of 98.63% is computed if two face images belong to different people (Table 3).

Table 3. Using the threshold of 0.6 and testing on LFW, the confusion matrix is computed. The overall accuracy is 98.2833%, and when two face images belong to the same person, the accuracy is 97.9333%, and when two face images belong to different people, the accuracy is 98.6333%.

TP = 2938	FP = 41
FN = 62	TN = 2959

To increase the accuracy when two face images belong to different people, we use the threshold of 0.5 and retest. The improved accuracy is 99.1% if two face images belong to different people (Table 4).

Table 4. Using the threshold of 0.5, when two face images belong to different people, the accuracy is 99.1%.

TP = 2411	FP = 27
FN = 589	TN = 2973

4.3 Experiment for DoS Attack

To set up a controlled experiment, we compute the success rate of face detection under normal illumination, and the captured face images are like Fig. 2(a). We test 15 face images for each model face, and every face in the picture was detected.

For the main experiment, we test 178 face images, and they are like Fig. 2(b). The average success rate of face detection is 7.87% under attack. When the distance decreases, the success rate also decreases. For far-distance face images, the success rate is 13.11%; for medium-distance images, the success rate is 8.1%; for short-distance images, the success rate is 1.81%. A shorter distance means a higher proportion of face in images, and more black fringes on the face, so it is more likely for black fringes to cover key facial features (Fig. 6 and Tables 5, 6).

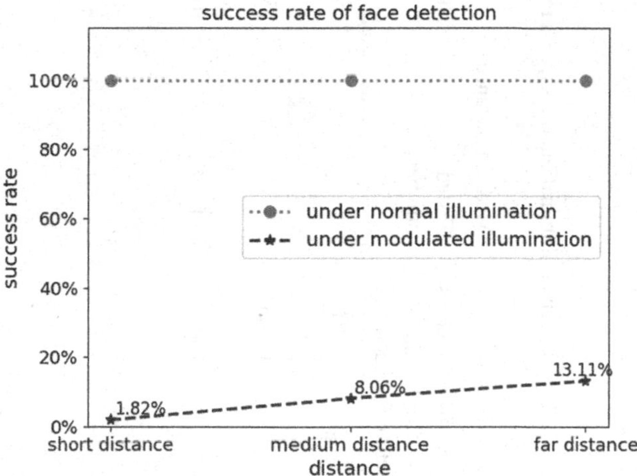

Fig. 6. Under normal illumination, every face in image is detected. However, under DoS attack, the success rate of face detection drops sharply.

Table 5. Under normal illumination, the success rate of face detection is always 100%.

Normal face detection	Short-distance			Medium-distance			Far-distance		
	Tested number	Number of successful detection	Success rate of detection	Tested number	Number of successful detection	Success rate of detection	Tested number	Number of successful detection	Success rate of detection
Model face 1	5	5	100%	5	5	100%	5	5	100%
Model face 2	5	5	100%	5	5	100%	5	5	100%
Average success rate	10	10	100%	10	10	100%	10	10	100%

Table 6. Under modulated illumination, the average success rate of face detection is 7.87%.

Attacked face detection	Short-distance			Medium-distance			Far-distance		
	Tested number	Number of successful detection	Success rate of detection	Tested number	Number of successful detection	Success rate of detection	Tested number	Number of successful detection	Success rate of detection
Model face 1	25	1	4%	32	3	9.34%	31	3	9.68%
Model face 2	30	0	0%	30	2	6.67%	30	5	16.67%
Average success rate	55	1	1.81%	62	5	8.1%	61	8	13.11%
Totality	Model face 1			Model face 2			Totality		
	Tested number	Number of successful detection	Success rate of detection	Tested number	Number of successful detection	Success rate of detection	Tested number	Number of successful detection	Success rate of detection
	88	7	7.95%	90	7	7.78%	178	14	7.87%%

4.4 Experiment for Escape Attack

To set up a controlled experiment, we compute the success rate of face verification under normal illumination. We take 30 face images, which are like Fig. 2(a), and do 75 comparisons using the threshold of 0.5. Experimental result shows a high success rate of 100% under normal illumination.

For the main experiment, we take 60 face images and do 300 comparisons. The average difference between two face images drops from 0.6 to 0.45, which is below the threshold 0.5. So the average success rate of face verification under attack is 18%.

Besides, under normal illumination, a farther distance means a lower difference. However, it is contrary to escape attack. Under escape attack, a shorter distance leads to a lower difference. A shorter distance means a bigger face in image, so there are more black fringes passing through the key facial features, and more useless gradient information will be added to the key facial features, which leads to a lower difference (Figs. 7, 8, 9 and Tables 7, 8).

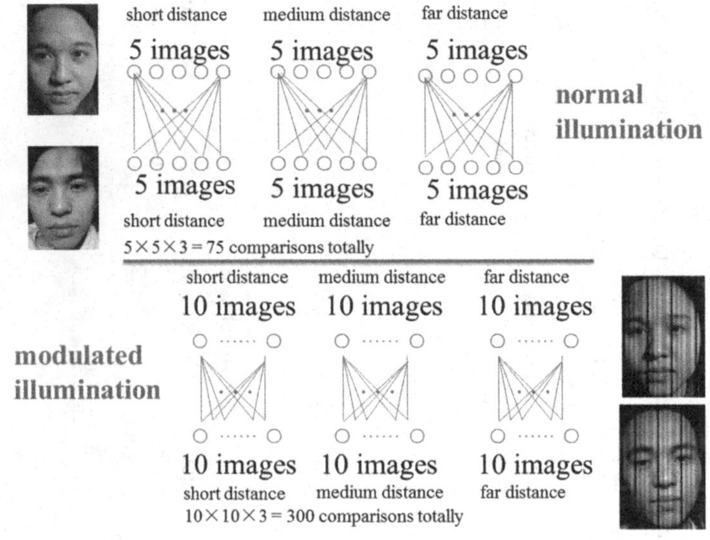

Fig. 7. This picture describes the method of face verification.

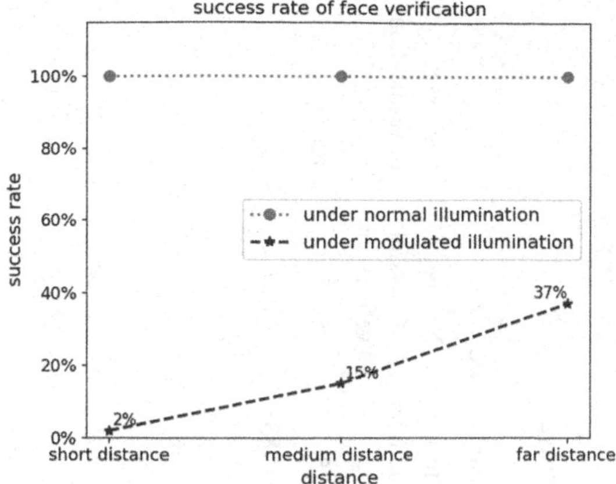

Fig. 8. Under normal illumination, face verification has a success rate of 100%. However, under escape attack, the success rate of face verification drops sharply, and the average success rate is 18%.

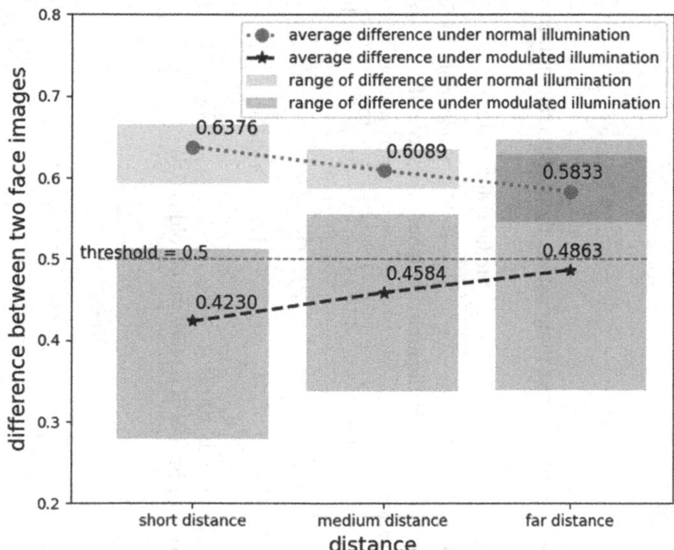

Fig. 9. i) Under normal illumination, the average difference between two face images are about 0.6. However, the average difference under modulated illumination is about 0.45, which is below the threshold, 0.5. ii) Under normal illumination, a shorter distance means a higher difference. However, it is contrary to modulated illumination. It reveals the availability of escape attack.

Table 7. Under normal illumination, the success rate of face verification is always 100%.

Normal face verification	Short distance			Medium distance			Far distance		
	Tested number	Number of successful verification	Success rate of verification	Tested number	Number of successful verification	Success rate of verification	Tested number	Number of successful verification	Success rate of verification
	25	25	100%	25	25	100%	25	25	100%
Difference between two face images	0.6376			0.6089			0.5833		
Total average success rate of face verification is 100% Total average difference between two face images is 0.6099 (threshold is 0.5)									

Table 8. Under escape attack, the average success rate of face verification is only 18%.

Attacked face verification	Short distance			Medium distance			Far distance		
	Tested number	Number of successful verification	Success rate of verification	Tested number	Number of successful verification	Success rate of verification	Tested number	Number of successful verification	Success rate of verification
	100	2	2%	100	15	15%	100	37	37%
Difference between two face images	0.4230			0.4584			0.4863		
Total average success rate of face verification is 18% Total average difference between two face images is 0.4559 (threshold is 0.5)									

5 Conclusion

In this paper, we propose a novel attack scheme based on illumination modulation to physically realize perturbations of adversarial examples. Utilizing the rolling shutter effect of CMOS camera, the created perturbations will not be distorted and can achieve a higher concealment than traditional attack scheme for using a printer do.

According to the attack scheme, we have proposed two novel attack methods based on illumination modulation. The experimental results show that both of these two attack methods get a good performance facing the established AFR. DoS attack has an attack success rate of 92.13% and escape attack has an attack success rate of 82%.

In future, we will control the illumination more rigorous to realize the stronger attack.

Acknowledgments. This work was partially supported by National Natural Science Foundation of China (61771222, 61872109), Key research and Development Program for Guangdong Province (2019B010136001), Science and Technology Project of Shenzhen (JCYJ20170815145900474), Peng Cheng Laboratory Project of Guangdong Province (PCL2018KP004), The Fundamental Research Funds for the Central Universities (21620439), Natural Scientific Research Innovation Foundation in Harbin Institute of Technology (HIT.NSRIF.2020078).

References

1. Szegedy, C., et al.: Intriguing properties of neural networks. arXiv preprint arXiv:1312.6199 (2013)
2. Goodfellow, I.J., Shlens, J., Szegedy, C.: Explaining and harnessing adversarial examples. arXiv preprint arXiv:1412.6572 (2014)
3. Su, J., Vargas, D.V., Sakurai, K.: One pixel attack for fooling deep neural networks. IEEE Trans. Evol. Comput. **23**(5), 828–841 (2019)
4. Eykholt, K., et al.: Robust physical-world attacks on deep learning visual classification. In: Proceedings of the IEEE Conference on Computer Vision and Pattern Recognition (CVPR), pp. 1625–1634 (2018)
5. Sharif, M., Bhagavatula, S., Bauer, L., Reiter, M.: Accessorize to a crime: real and stealthy attacks on state-of-the-art face recognition. In: Proceedings of the 2016 ACM SIGSAC Conference on Computer and Communications Security, pp. 1528–1540 (2016)
6. Komkov, S., Petiushko, A.: AdvHat: real-world adversarial attack on ArcFace Face ID system. arXiv preprint arXiv:1908.08705 (2019)
7. Li, J., Schmidt, F., Kolter, Z.: Adversarial camera stickers: a physical camera-based attack on deep learning systems. In: International Conference on Machine Learning, pp. 3896–3904 (2019)
8. Thys, S., Van Ranst, W., Goedemé, T.: Fooling automated surveillance cameras: adversarial patches to attack person detection. In: Proceedings of the IEEE Conference on Computer Vision and Pattern Recognition Workshops (2019)
9. Xu, K., et al.: Adversarial t-shirt! Evading person detectors in a physical world. In: European Conference on Computer Vision (2020)
10. Zhou, Z., Tang, D., Wang, X., et al.: Invisible Mask: Practical Attacks on Face Recognition with Infrared. arXiv preprint arXiv:1803.04683 (2018)

11. Rosebrock, A.: Facial landmarks with dlib, OpenCV, and Python. https://www.pyimagesearch.com/2017/04/03/facial-landmarksdlib-opencv-python/. Accessed 19 Oct 2020
12. Dalal, N., Triggs, B.: Histograms of oriented gradients for human detection. In: IEEE Computer Society Conference on Computer Vision and Pattern Recognition, pp. 886–893 (2015)
13. Huang, G.B., Ramesh, M., Berg, T., Learned-Miller, E.: Labeled Faces in the Wild: A Database for Studying Face Recognition in Unconstrained Environments. https://vis-www.cs.umass.edu/lfw/. Accessed 19 Oct 2020

Asymmetric Cipher

Generic Construction of Server-Aided Revocable Hierarchical Identity-Based Encryption

Yanyan Liu[1,2,3(✉)] and Yiru Sun[1,2,3]

[1] State Key Laboratory of Information Security, Institute of Information Engineering, Chinese Academy of Sciences, Beijing 100093, China
{liuyanyan,sunyiru}@iie.ac.cn

[2] State Key Laboratory of Cryptology, P.O. Box 5159, Beijing 100878, China

[3] School of Cyber Security, University of Chinese Academy of Sciences, Beijing 101408, China

Abstract. In this paper, we extend the notion of server-aided revocable identity-based encryption (SR-IBE) to the hierarchical IBE (HIBE) setting to obtain the definition of server-aided revocable hierarchical IBE (SR-HIBE), and consider a stronger security called SSR-a/sID-CPA security. Specifically, the security required that the challenge identity ID^* is revoked when both the private key for ID^* or some ancestors of ID^* and the public key for ID^* are revealed, or both the private key and the secret key for ID^* or some (may be different) ancestors of ID^* are revealed. And the adversary can have access to the transformation keys oracle. Then, we propose a generic construction of SR-HIBE schemes from any L-level revocable HIBE scheme and $(L+1)$-level HIBE scheme. The security of our generic SR-HIBE scheme inherits those of the underlying building blocks. Furthermore, when the maximum hierarchical depth is one, we obtain a generic construction of SR-IBE schemes from *any* IBE scheme and two-level HIBE scheme.

Keywords: Generic construction · Server-aided revocation mechanism · Hierarchical identity-based encryption

1 Introduction

Identity-based encryption (IBE), which was proposed by Shamir [12] in 1984, provides a public key encryption mechanism that an arbitrary string representing user's identities (e.g., email address, ID number) can be used as public keys. As an extension of IBE, hierarchical identity-based encryption (HIBE) supports key delegation functionality. It has been well studied on (H)IBE [1,3,5–7,13–15] since after Boneh and Franklin [4] gave the first IBE scheme in 2001. As for many multi-user cryptosystems, adding an efficient revocation mechanism to

Y. Wu and M. Yung (Eds.): Inscrypt 2020, LNCS 12612, pp. 73–82, 2021.
https://doi.org/10.1007/978-3-030-71852-7_5

the (H)IBE scheme to revoke the malicious user is a necessary problem. In 2008, Boldyreva et al. [2] introduced the notion of revocable IBE (RIBE). In their definition, each user can issue a long-term secret key corresponding to his identity, but only using this secret key cannot decrypt the ciphertext. In their work, the size of the key update in each time period is logarithmic in N (i.e., $\mathcal{O}(r\log\frac{N}{r})$, where r is the number of the revoked users).

In order to reduce the workload of the users and capture decryption key exposure resistance (DKER) property, Qin et al. [11] introduced server-aided RIBE (SR-IBE)and defined semantic security against adaptive-identity security chosen plaintext security (SR-aID-CPA). In the SR-IBE scheme, almost all the workloads of users are outsourced to an untrusted server, and the users need no communication with the KGC during key updating and can compute their decryption keys at any time period by themselves. The server can be untrusted since it does not keep any secret, and the only requirement is computing correctly.

Cheng and Meng [10] revisited Qin et al.'s security model [11] and proposed a stronger one called SSR-sID-CPA security where ID^* should be revoked before t^* if both the private key $\mathsf{privk}_{\mathsf{ID}^*}$ and the public key $\mathsf{pk}_{\mathsf{ID}^*}$ are all revealed to the adversary. Besides, the adversary is allowed to have access to the transformation key oracle since the untrusted server could be operated by anyone, including the adversary.

Motivations. Observe that the RHIBE scheme supports both key revocation and key delegation functionalities, the secret key of a user can be divided into two parts: one part is its own secret key which used to realize key revocation by combining with the key update while the second part is used to realize key delegation for its descendants. Thus, the workloads of users in RHIBE are much heavier than that in RIBE. So it has practical interest to add a server-aided revocation mechanism to the RHIBE setting to reduce the user's heavy workload. Besides, note that [9] and [10] also considered the generic construction of SR-IBE. In their works, the server gains and sends a random chosen message to the recipient. While the server may be untrusted, if he sends a random string which is not what he obtained, then the recipient cannot obtain the real message and may have no idea of that.

For security aspect, the security model of SR-IBE in [10] considered a stronger security called SSR-a/sID-CPA security to capture both DKE attacks on the local decryption key and TKE attacks on the transformation key. In order that the security definition be as close to the practical scenarios as possible, it is needed to consider the corresponding stronger security of the SR-HIBE scheme.

Our Contributions. In this paper, we add a server-aided revocation mechanism to the HIBE scheme and propose a generic construction of SR-HIBE scheme. Our contributions are as follows:

First, we extend the notion of SR-IBE to the SR-HIBE case and give a formal definition of SR-HIBE scheme. We also give a stronger security definition of SR-HIBE by extending that of SR-IBE in [10]. Specifically, the challenge identity ID^* is revoked when both the private key $\mathsf{privk}_{\mathsf{ID}^*}$ for some $\mathsf{ID} \in \mathsf{prefix}(\mathsf{ID}^*)$ and the public key $\mathsf{pk}_{\mathsf{ID}^*}$ are revealed, or both $\mathsf{privk}_{\mathsf{ID}}$ for some $\mathsf{ID} \in \mathsf{prefix}(\mathsf{ID}^*)$ and the secret key $\mathsf{sk}_{\mathsf{ID}'}$ for some $\mathsf{ID}' \in \mathsf{prefix}(\mathsf{ID}^*)$ are revealed. Besides, the adversary also can have access to the transformation keys oracle. To the best of our knowledge, it is the first time to realize the server-aided revocation mechanism in the HIBE setting.

Second, we propose a generic construction of SR-HIBE scheme from any L-level RHIBE with DKER and a $(L+1)$-level HIBE. In our construction, the decryption key size is equal to that of the underlying HIBE scheme, and the ciphertext size is the same as that of the underlying RHIBE scheme. Our generic construction inherits those of the underlying building blocks.

Third, our construction implies a generic transformation from any IBE and two-level HIBE to SR-IBE scheme by combining with Ma and Lin's work [9] that the generic construction of RIBE with DKER from any IBE and a two-level HIBE. Compared with the SR-IBE scheme with DKER in [9], our construction can guarantee both the integrity and privacy of messages. If the server sends something that is different from what he obtained, then the recipient cannot decrypt and thus can detect this dishonest behavior.

2 Preliminaries

Notations. Let λ be the security parameter, $\mathsf{negl}(\lambda)$ represents a negligible function. For positive integer $n \in \mathbb{N}$, $[n]$ represents the set $\{1, \cdots, n\}$. PPT is the abbreviation for probabilistic polynomial time. In (R)HIBE, $\mathsf{ID} = (\mathsf{id}_1, \cdots, \mathsf{id}_\ell)$, $\mathsf{id}_i \in \mathcal{ID}$, denotes a ℓ-level user with identity ID, where id_i and $\mathcal{ID}$ are called as element identity and element identity space. For $\ell \in \mathbb{N}$, define $(\mathcal{ID})^{\leq \ell} := \bigcup_{i \in [\ell]} (\mathcal{ID})^i$ and the hierarchical identity space $\mathcal{ID}_h := (\mathcal{ID})^{\leq L}$, where L is the maximum depth of the hierarchy. The level-0 user is denoted as kgc, i.e., the key generation center. For a ℓ-level identity $\mathsf{ID} = (\mathsf{id}_1, \cdots, \mathsf{id}_\ell)$, $\mathsf{ID}_{[i]} := (\mathsf{id}_1, \cdots, \mathsf{id}_i)$ represents the length-i prefix of ID, $i \in [\ell]$, define $\mathsf{pa}(\mathsf{ID}) := (\mathsf{id}_1, \cdots, \mathsf{id}_{\ell-1})$ as the direct ancestor of ID, and $\mathsf{prefix}(\mathsf{ID})$ denotes the set that consisting of itself and all of its ancestors, i.e., $\mathsf{prefix}(\mathsf{ID}) := \{\mathsf{ID}_{[1]}, \cdots, \mathsf{ID}_{[|\mathsf{ID}|]} = \mathsf{ID}\}$. Furthermore, $\mathsf{ID} \| \mathcal{ID} \subseteq (\mathcal{ID})^{\ell+1}$ represents the subset that contains all the nodes who have ID as its direct ancestor.

2.1 Revocable Hierarchical Identity-Based Encryption

In this paper, we adopt the syntax definition of the RHIBE scheme in [8] with a little change. Specifically, we separate the secret key $\mathsf{sk}_{\mathsf{ID}}$ into two parts: $(\mathsf{sk}_{\mathsf{ID}}, \mathsf{msk}_{\mathsf{ID}})$, where $\mathsf{sk}_{\mathsf{ID}}$ is the actual secret key for ID which used in GenDK algorithm to generate the decryption key, and $\mathsf{msk}_{\mathsf{ID}}$ which is used in GenSK and KeyUp algorithms for delegation functionality when ID worked as a "delegate KGC" for its children. Note that this modification does not change the syntax definition of RHIBE since it is just a change in form. Due to the space limit, we omit the syntax definition here, and the reader can get more details in [8].

2.2 Server-Aided Revocable Hierarchical Identity-Based Encryption

In this section, we give a definition of SR-HIBE by extending that of SR-IBE in [10] to the HIBE setting and consider a stronger security definition which called SSR-a/sID-CPA secure. As in [10], the "revoke" algorithm also not explicitly mentioned as part of the syntax.

Definition 1 (Server-Aided Revocable Hierarchical Identity-Based Encryption, SR-HIBE).

$\mathsf{Setup}(1^\lambda, L) \rightarrow (\mathsf{mpk}, \mathsf{sk_{kgc}})$. *This algorithm is run by the KGC. On input the security parameter* 1^λ *and the maximum depth of the hierarchy* $L \in \mathbb{N}$*, output a public parameter* mpk *and the KGC's secret key* $\mathsf{sk_{kgc}}$ *(also called the master secret key).*

$\mathsf{UserKG}(\mathsf{mpk}, \mathsf{sk_{pa(ID)}}, \mathsf{ID}) \rightarrow (\mathsf{pk_{ID}}, \mathsf{sk_{ID}}, \mathsf{sk'_{pa(ID)}})$.[1] *This algorithm is run by a parent user* $\mathsf{pa(ID)}$ *when a user* $\mathsf{ID} \in \mathcal{ID}_h$ *registers to the system. On input the public parameter* mpk*, the parent's secret key* $\mathsf{sk_{pa(ID)}}$ *and an identity* ID*, output a public key* $\mathsf{pk_{ID}}$*, a secret key* $\mathsf{sk_{ID}}$ *and the updated parent's secret key* $\mathsf{sk'_{pa(ID)}}$*. The public key* $\mathsf{pk_{ID}}$ *is sent to the server through public channel and the secret key* $\mathsf{sk_{ID}}$ *is sent to the user* ID *by secret channel.*

$\mathsf{UpdKG}(\mathsf{mpk}, \mathsf{sk_{ID}}, \mathsf{t}, \mathsf{RL_{ID,t}}, \mathsf{uk_{pa(ID),t}}) \rightarrow (\mathsf{uk_{ID,t}}, \mathsf{sk'_{ID}})$. *This algorithm is run by the user with* $\mathsf{ID} \in \mathcal{ID}_h$*. It takes the public parameter* mpk*, the secret key* $\mathsf{sk_{ID}}$*, the time period* t*, the revocation list* $\mathsf{RL_{ID,t}} \subseteq \mathsf{ID}||\mathcal{ID}$ *and the parent's update key* $\mathsf{uk_{pa(ID),t}}$ *as inputs, outputs an update key* $\mathsf{uk_{ID,t}}$ *and the updated secret key* $\mathsf{sk'_{ID}}$*. The update key* $\mathsf{uk_{ID,t}}$ *is sent to the server by public channel.*

$\mathsf{TranKG}(\mathsf{mpk}, \mathsf{pk_{ID}}, \mathsf{uk_{pa(ID),t}}) \rightarrow \mathsf{tk_{ID,t}}$. *This algorithm is run by the server. It takes the public parameter* mpk*, a public key* $\mathsf{pk_{ID}}$ *of a user with* $\mathsf{ID} \in \mathcal{ID}_h$ *and a parent's update key* $\mathsf{uk_{pa(ID),t}}$ *as inputs, outputs a transformation key* $\mathsf{tk_{ID,t}}$ *for time period* t*.*

$\mathsf{PrivKG}(\mathsf{mpk}, \mathsf{privk_{pa(ID)}}, \mathsf{ID}) \rightarrow \mathsf{privk_{ID}}$.[2] *This algorithm is run by the user with* $\mathsf{pa(ID)} \in \mathcal{ID}_h$*. It takes the public parameter* mpk*, a parent's private key* $\mathsf{privk_{pa(ID)}}$ *and* $\mathsf{ID} \in \mathcal{ID}_h$ *as inputs, outputs a private key* $\mathsf{privk_{ID}}$*.*

$\mathsf{DecKG}(\mathsf{mpk}, \mathsf{privk_{ID}}, \mathsf{t}) \rightarrow \mathsf{dk_{ID,t}}$. *This algorithm is run by the recipient. On input the public parameter* mpk*, a private key* $\mathsf{privk_{ID}}$ *of user with* $\mathsf{ID} \in \mathcal{ID}_h$ *and a time period* t *as inputs, output a decryption key* $\mathsf{dk_{ID,t}}$ *for time period* t*.*

$\mathsf{Enc}(\mathsf{mpk}, \mathsf{ID}, \mathsf{t}, M) \rightarrow \mathsf{ct_{ID,t}}$. *This algorithm is run by the sender. It takes the public parameter* mpk*, the recipient's identity* $\mathsf{ID} \in \mathcal{ID}_h$*, a time period* t *and a message* M*, outputs a ciphertext* $\mathsf{ct_{ID,t}}$*, which is sent to the server.*

$\mathsf{Transform}(\mathsf{mpk}, \mathsf{ct_{ID,t}}, \mathsf{tk_{ID,t}}) \rightarrow \mathsf{ct'_{ID,t}}$. *This algorithm is run by the server. It takes the public parameter* mpk*, a ciphertext* $\mathsf{ct_{ID,t}}$ *and a transformation key* $\mathsf{tk_{ID,t}}$*, outputs a partially decrypted ciphertext* $\mathsf{ct'_{ID,t}}$*, which is sent to the recipient by the public channel.*

---

[1] When $L = 1$, i.e. for the RIBE case, $\mathsf{sk_{pa(ID)}} = \mathsf{sk_{kgc}}$, thus $\mathsf{UserKG}(\mathsf{sk_{kgc}}, \mathsf{ID}) \rightarrow (\mathsf{pk_{ID}}, \bot, \mathsf{sk'_{kgc}})$.

[2] When $\mathsf{pa(ID)} = \mathsf{kgc}$, $\mathsf{privk_{pa(ID)}} = \mathsf{sk_{kgc}}$, thus $\mathsf{PrivKG}(\mathsf{mpk}, \mathsf{sk_{kgc}}, \mathsf{ID}) \rightarrow \mathsf{privk_{ID}}$.

$\mathsf{Dec}(\mathsf{mpk}, \mathsf{ct}'_{\mathsf{ID},\mathsf{t}}, \mathsf{dk}_{\mathsf{ID},\mathsf{t}}) \rightarrow M/\bot$. *This algorithm is run by the recipient* $\mathsf{ID} \in \mathcal{ID}_h$. *It takes the public parameter* mpk, *a partially decrypted ciphertext* $\mathsf{ct}'_{\mathsf{ID},\mathsf{t}}$ *and a decryption key* $\mathsf{dk}_{\mathsf{ID},\mathsf{t}}$, *outputs a message* M *or a symbol* $\bot$.

Correctness. We require that for all $\lambda \in \mathbb{N}$, $L \in \mathbb{N}$, $(\mathsf{mpk}, \mathsf{sk}_{\mathsf{kgc}}) \leftarrow \mathsf{Setup}(1^\lambda, L)$, $\ell \in [L]$, $\mathsf{ID} \in \mathcal{ID}_h$, $\mathsf{t} \in \mathcal{T}$, $\mathsf{M} \in \mathcal{M}$, $\mathsf{RL}_{\mathsf{ID}_{[\ell-1]},\mathsf{t}} \subseteq \mathsf{ID}_{[\ell-1]} \parallel \mathcal{ID}$, if $\mathsf{ID}' \notin \mathsf{RL}_{\mathsf{pa}(\mathsf{ID}'),\mathsf{t}}$ holds for all $\mathsf{ID}' \in \mathsf{prefix}(\mathsf{ID})$, and all parties follow the above prescribed algorithms $\mathsf{Setup}, \mathsf{UserKG}, \mathsf{UpdKG}, \mathsf{TranKG}, \mathsf{PrivKG}, \mathsf{DecKG}, \mathsf{Enc}, \mathsf{Transform}$ to generate $\mathsf{mpk}, \mathsf{ct}'_{\mathsf{ID},\mathsf{t}}, \mathsf{dk}_{\mathsf{ID},\mathsf{t}}$, then $\mathsf{Dec}(\mathsf{mpk}, \mathsf{ct'}_{\mathsf{ID},\mathsf{t}}, \mathsf{dk}_{\mathsf{ID},\mathsf{t}}) = M$.

Security Definition. We give a stronger security definition for SR-HIBE called SSR-a/sID-CPA secure by combining that of SR-IBE in [10] and that of RHIBE in [8]. Specifically, ID^* is revoked before t^* when both the private key $\mathsf{privk}_{\mathsf{ID}}$ for some $\mathsf{ID} \in \mathsf{prefix}(\mathsf{ID}^*)$ and the public key $\mathsf{pk}_{\mathsf{ID}^*}$ are revealed, or both $\mathsf{privk}_{\mathsf{ID}}$ and the secret key $\mathsf{sk}_{\mathsf{ID}'}$ for some (may different) ancestors of $\mathsf{prefix}(\mathsf{ID}^*)$ are revealed. The adversary has access to the transformation keys oracle. The following game is played between an adversary $\mathcal{A}$ and the challenger $\mathcal{C}$.

At the beginning, $\mathcal{A}$ announces the challenge identity/time period pair $(\mathsf{ID}^*, \mathsf{t}^*) \in \mathcal{ID}_h \times \mathcal{T}$ and sends them to $\mathcal{C}$. After that, $\mathcal{C}$ runs $(\mathsf{mpk}, \mathsf{sk}_{\mathsf{kgc}}) \leftarrow \mathsf{Setup}(1^\lambda, L)$, prepares a table SKList to store the new generated identity/public key/secret key tuple $(\mathsf{ID}, \mathsf{pk}_{\mathsf{ID}}, \mathsf{sk}_{\mathsf{ID}})$ or update this tuple during the game, and a list $\mathsf{PrivKList}$ to store new generated identity/private key pairs $(\mathsf{ID}, \mathsf{privk}_{\mathsf{ID}})$ and identity/decryption key pairs $((\mathsf{ID}, \mathsf{t}), \mathsf{dk}_{\mathsf{ID},\mathsf{t}})$. We will not explicitly mention those addition/update. Then $\mathcal{C}$ executes $(\mathsf{uk}_{\mathsf{kgc},1}, \mathsf{sk}'_{\mathsf{kgc}}) \leftarrow \mathsf{UpdKG}(\mathsf{mpk}, \mathsf{sk}_{\mathsf{kgc}}, \mathsf{t}_{\mathsf{cu}} = 1, \mathsf{RL}_{\mathsf{kgc},1} = \emptyset, \bot)$. After that, $\mathcal{C}$ sends mpk and $\mathsf{uk}_{\mathsf{kgc},1}$ to $\mathcal{A}$. From this point on, $\mathcal{A}$ may adaptively issue any of the following queries to $\mathcal{C}$:

User's key generation query: When $\mathcal{A}$ issues a query $\mathsf{ID} \in \mathcal{ID}_h$, $\mathcal{C}$ first checks if $(\mathsf{ID}, *, *) \notin \mathsf{SKList}$ and $(\mathsf{pa}(\mathsf{ID}), \mathsf{pk}_{\mathsf{pa}(\mathsf{ID})}, \mathsf{sk}_{\mathsf{pa}(\mathsf{ID})}) \in \mathsf{SKList}$ for some $\mathsf{pa}(\mathsf{ID})$. If not, return $\bot$. Otherwise, $\mathcal{C}$ runs $(\mathsf{pk}_{\mathsf{ID}}, \mathsf{sk}_{\mathsf{ID}}, \mathsf{sk}'_{\mathsf{pa}(\mathsf{ID})}) \leftarrow \mathsf{GenSK}(\mathsf{mpk}, \mathsf{sk}_{\mathsf{pa}(\mathsf{ID})}, \mathsf{ID})$. Furthermore, if $\mathsf{ID} \in (\mathcal{ID})^{\leq L-1}$, $\mathcal{C}$ then executes $(\mathsf{uk}_{\mathsf{ID},\mathsf{t}_{\mathsf{cu}}}, \mathsf{sk}'_{\mathsf{ID}}) \leftarrow \mathsf{UpdKG}(\mathsf{mpk}, \mathsf{sk}_{\mathsf{ID}}, \mathsf{t}_{\mathsf{cu}}, \mathsf{RL}_{\mathsf{ID},\mathsf{t}_{\mathsf{cu}}} = \emptyset, \mathsf{uk}_{\mathsf{pa}(\mathsf{ID}),\mathsf{t}_{\mathsf{cu}}})$ and returns $\mathsf{uk}_{\mathsf{ID},\mathsf{t}_{\mathsf{cu}}}$ to $\mathcal{A}$.
In the following, we require all identities ID appearing in the following queries must have been queried in this query, namely, $(\mathsf{ID}, \mathsf{pk}_{\mathsf{ID}}, \mathsf{sk}_{\mathsf{ID}}) \in \mathsf{SKList}$.

Public key reveal query: When $\mathcal{A}$ queries on $\mathsf{ID} \in \mathcal{ID}_h$, $\mathcal{C}$ obtains the entry $(\mathsf{ID}, \mathsf{pk}_{\mathsf{ID}}, \mathsf{sk}_{\mathsf{ID}})$ and returns $\mathsf{sk}_{\mathsf{ID}}$ to $\mathcal{A}$.

Secret key reveal query: When $\mathcal{A}$ queries on $\mathsf{ID} \in \mathcal{ID}_h$, $\mathcal{C}$ retrieves $\mathsf{sk}_{\mathsf{ID}}$ and returns it to $\mathcal{A}$.

Revoke and update key query: When $\mathcal{A}$ queries on $\mathsf{RL} \subseteq \mathcal{ID}_h$ (the set of identities that will be revoked), $\mathcal{C}$ first checks if the following condition holds:

- $\mathsf{RL}_{\mathsf{ID},\mathsf{t}_{\mathsf{cu}}} \subseteq \mathsf{RL}$ for all $\mathsf{ID} \in (\mathcal{ID})^{\leq L-1} \cup \{\mathsf{kgc}\}$ that appear in SKList.
- For all identities ID such that $(\mathsf{ID}, *, *) \in \mathsf{SKList}$ and $\mathsf{ID}' \in \mathsf{prefix}(\mathsf{ID})$, if $\mathsf{ID}' \in \mathsf{RL}$, then $\mathsf{ID} \in \mathsf{RL}$.
- If $\mathsf{t}_{\mathsf{cu}} = \mathsf{t}^* - 1$ and $\mathcal{A}$ has issued the private key reveal queries on some $\mathsf{ID} \in \mathsf{prefix}(\mathsf{ID}^*)$, and public key reveal query on ID^*, then $\mathsf{ID}^* \in \mathsf{RL}$.

– If $\mathsf{t_{cu}} = \mathsf{t}^* - 1$ and $\mathcal{A}$ has issued the private key reveal queries on some $\mathsf{ID} \in \mathsf{prefix}(\mathsf{ID}^*)$ and secret key reveal queries on some $\mathsf{ID}' \in \mathsf{prefix}(\mathsf{ID}^*)$, then $\mathsf{ID}, \mathsf{ID}' \in \mathsf{RL}$.

If not, return $\perp$. Otherwise, $\mathcal{C}$ increments $\mathsf{t_{cu}} \leftarrow \mathsf{t_{cu}} + 1$. Then, $\mathcal{C}$ executes the following two steps for all identities that have been issued a secret key generation queries and not been revoked, i.e., $\mathsf{ID} \in (\mathcal{ID})^{\leq L-1} \cup \{\mathsf{kgc}\}$, $(\mathsf{ID}, *, *) \in \mathsf{SKList}$ and $\mathsf{ID} \notin \mathsf{RL}$, in the identity hierarchy order:

1. Set $\mathsf{RL}_{\mathsf{ID},\mathsf{t_{cu}}} \leftarrow \mathsf{RL} \cap (\mathsf{ID} \| \mathcal{ID})$, where $\mathsf{kgc} \| \mathcal{ID} := \mathcal{ID}$.
2. Run $(\mathsf{uk}_{\mathsf{ID},\mathsf{t_{cu}}}, \mathsf{sk}'_{\mathsf{ID}}) \leftarrow \mathsf{UpdKG}(\mathsf{mpk}, \mathsf{sk}_{\mathsf{ID}}, \mathsf{t_{cu}}, \mathsf{RL}_{\mathsf{ID},\mathsf{t_{cu}}}, \mathsf{uk}_{\mathsf{pa}(\mathsf{ID}),\mathsf{t_{cu}}})$. When $\mathsf{ID} = \mathsf{kgc}$, $\mathsf{uk}_{\mathsf{pa}(\mathsf{kgc}),\mathsf{t_{cu}}} := \perp$.

Finally, $\mathcal{C}$ sends all the generated update key $\{\mathsf{uk}_{\mathsf{ID},\mathsf{t_{cu}}}\}_{(\mathsf{ID},*,*)\in\mathsf{SKList}}$ to $\mathcal{A}$.

Transformation key reveal query: When $\mathcal{A}$ issues a query $(\mathsf{ID}, \mathsf{t}) \in \mathcal{ID}_h \times \mathcal{T}$, $\mathcal{C}$ first checks if the conditions that $\mathsf{t} \leq \mathsf{t_{cu}}$, $\mathsf{ID} \notin \mathsf{RL}_{\mathsf{pa}(\mathsf{ID}),\mathsf{t}}$, $(\mathsf{ID}, \mathsf{t}) \neq (\mathsf{ID}^*, \mathsf{t}^*)$ hold. If not, return $\perp$. Otherwise, $\mathcal{C}$ retrieves $\mathsf{pk}_{\mathsf{ID}}$), runs $\mathsf{tk}_{\mathsf{ID},\mathsf{t}} \leftarrow \mathsf{TranKG}(\mathsf{mpk}, \mathsf{pk}_{\mathsf{ID}}, \mathsf{uk}_{\mathsf{pa}(\mathsf{ID}),\mathsf{t}})$ and returns $\mathsf{tk}_{\mathsf{ID},\mathsf{t}}$ to $\mathcal{A}$.

Private key generation query: Upon a query $\mathsf{ID} \in \mathcal{ID}_h$, $\mathcal{C}$ checks if $(\mathsf{ID}, *) \notin \mathsf{PrivKList}$ and $(\mathsf{pa}(\mathsf{ID}), \mathsf{privk}_{\mathsf{pa}(\mathsf{ID})}) \in \mathsf{PrivKList}$ for some $\mathsf{pa}(\mathsf{ID})$. If not, return $\perp$. Otherwise, $\mathcal{C}$ runs $\mathsf{privk}_{\mathsf{ID}} \leftarrow \mathsf{PrivKG}(\mathsf{mpk}, \mathsf{privk}_{\mathsf{pa}(\mathsf{ID})}, \mathsf{ID})$ and returns nothing to $\mathcal{A}$.

Similarly, we require that all identities ID appearing in the following queries must have been queried by this query and hence $(\mathsf{ID}, \mathsf{privk}_{\mathsf{ID}}) \in \mathsf{PrivKList}$.

Private key reveal query: Upon a query $\mathsf{ID} \in \mathcal{ID}_h$ from $\mathcal{A}$, $\mathcal{C}$ finds $(\mathsf{ID}, \mathsf{privk}_{\mathsf{ID}}) \in \mathsf{PrivKList}$ and returns $\mathsf{privk}_{\mathsf{ID}}$ to $\mathcal{A}$.

Decryption key reveal query: Upon a query $(\mathsf{ID}, \mathsf{t}) \in \mathcal{ID}_h \times \mathcal{T}$ from $\mathcal{A}$, $\mathcal{C}$ first checks the conditions that $((\mathsf{ID}, \mathsf{t}), *) \notin \mathsf{PrivKList}$, $\mathsf{t} \leq \mathsf{t_{cu}}$, and if $\mathsf{ID} \notin \mathsf{RL}_{\mathsf{pa}(\mathsf{ID}),\mathsf{t}}$, then $(\mathsf{ID}, \mathsf{t}) \neq (\mathsf{ID}^*, \mathsf{t}^*)$ are all holds. If not, return $\perp$. Otherwise, find $\mathsf{privk}_{\mathsf{ID}}$ from $\mathsf{PrivKList}$, run $\mathsf{dk}_{\mathsf{ID},\mathsf{t}} \leftarrow \mathsf{DecKG}(\mathsf{mpk}, \mathsf{priv}_{\mathsf{ID}}, \mathsf{t})$ and return $\mathsf{dk}_{\mathsf{ID},\mathsf{t}}$ to $\mathcal{A}$.

Challenge phase: Once the adversary $\mathcal{A}$ submits two messages M_0, M_1 with equal length, $\mathcal{C}$ chooses a random bit $b \in \{0, 1\}$, computes and sends the challenge ciphertext $\mathsf{ct}_b^* \leftarrow \mathsf{Enc}(\mathsf{ID}^*, \mathsf{t}^*, M_b)$ to $\mathcal{A}$.

Guess. $\mathcal{A}$ make a guess b' for b and wins the game if $b' = b$.

Definition 2 (SSR-sID-CPA security). *A SR-HIBE scheme $\mathcal{SR\text{-}HIBE}$ is SSR-sID-CPA secure if for any PPT adversary $\mathcal{A}$, its advantage denoted as $\mathbf{Adv}^{\mathsf{SSR-sID-CPA}}_{\mathcal{SR-HIBE},\mathcal{A}}(1^\lambda) = \left|\Pr[b' = b] - \frac{1}{2}\right|$ is negligible in λ.*

Adaptive-Identity Security. In the adaptive security game, $\mathcal{A}$ chooses $(\mathsf{ID}^*, \mathsf{t}^*)$ along with two messages M_0, M_1 at the challenge phase with the restrictions that (1) If $\mathsf{t}^* \leq \mathsf{t_{cu}}$, then $\mathcal{A}$ has not submitted a decryption key reveal query on $(\mathsf{ID}^*, \mathsf{t}^*)$, (2) If $\mathcal{A}$ has issued both the private key reveal query on some $\mathsf{ID} \in \mathsf{prefix}(\mathsf{ID}^*)$ and the public key reveal query on ID^*, or both the private key reveal query and the secret key reveal queries on some $\mathsf{ID} \in \mathsf{prefix}(\mathsf{ID}^*)$, then $\mathsf{ID}^* \in \mathsf{RL}_{\mathsf{pa}(\mathsf{ID}),\mathsf{t}^*}$. $\mathcal{SR\text{-}HIBE}$ is adaptive-identity secure if for any PPT adversary $\mathcal{A}$, its advantage denoted as $\mathbf{Adv}^{\mathsf{SSR-aID-CPA}}_{\mathcal{SR-HIBE},\mathcal{A}}(1^\lambda) = \left|\Pr[b' = b] - \frac{1}{2}\right|$ is negligible in λ.

3 Generic Construction of Server-Aided Revocable HIBE with DKER

In order to satisfy the security guarantee, we assume that if $\mathcal{ID} = \{0,1\}^n$, then for the identity $\mathsf{ID} = (\mathsf{id}_1, \cdots, \mathsf{id}_i) \in \mathcal{ID}_h$, $i \leq [L]$, $\mathsf{id}_i \in \mathcal{ID}' = \{0\} \times \{0,1\}^{n-1}$, and the time period space $\mathcal{T} = \{1\} \times \{0,1\}^{n-1}$. Namely, it should keep that $\mathcal{ID}' \cap \mathcal{T} = \emptyset$. The generic construction of SR-HIBE are as follows.

$\mathsf{Setup}(1^\lambda, L)$: It takes the security parameter 1^λ and the maximum depth of the hierarchy $L \in \mathbb{N}$ as inputs, the algorithm runs $(\mathsf{r.mpk}, \mathsf{r.msk_{kgc}}) \leftarrow \mathsf{r.Setup}(1^\lambda, L)$ and $(\mathsf{h.mpk}, \mathsf{h.msk_{kgc}}) \leftarrow \mathsf{h.Setup}(1^\lambda)$. Then, output the public parameter $\mathsf{mpk} := (\mathsf{r.mpk}, \mathsf{h.mpk})$ and the KGC's secret key $\mathsf{sk_{kgc}} := (\mathsf{r.msk_{kgc}}, \mathsf{h.msk_{kgc}})$.

$\mathsf{UserKG}(\mathsf{mpk}, \mathsf{sk_{pa(ID)}}, \mathsf{ID})$: On input the public parameter $\mathsf{mpk} = (\mathsf{r.mpk}, \mathsf{h.mpk})$, the parent's secret key $\mathsf{sk_{pa(ID)}} = (\mathsf{r.msk_{pa(ID)}}, \mathsf{h.sk_{pa(ID)}})$ and identity $\mathsf{ID} \in \mathcal{ID}_h$, the parent $\mathsf{pa(ID)}$ runs $((\mathsf{r.sk_{ID}}, \mathsf{r.msk_{ID}}), \mathsf{r.msk'_{pa(ID)}}) \leftarrow \mathsf{r.GenSK}(\mathsf{r.mpk}, \mathsf{r.msk_{pa(ID)}}, \mathsf{ID})$, Then, output the public key $\mathsf{pk_{ID}} := \mathsf{r.sk_{ID}}$, the secret key $\mathsf{sk_{ID}} := \mathsf{r.msk_{ID}}$ and the parent's updated secret key $\mathsf{sk'_{pa(ID)}} := \mathsf{r.msk'_{pa(ID)}}$.

$\mathsf{UpdKG}(\mathsf{mpk}, \mathsf{sk_{ID}}, \mathsf{t}, \mathsf{RL_{ID,t}}, \mathsf{uk_{pa(ID),t}})$: On input $\mathsf{mpk} = (\mathsf{r.mpk}, \mathsf{h.mpk})$, the secret key $\mathsf{sk_{ID}} = (\mathsf{r.msk_{ID}}, \mathsf{h.sk_{ID}})$, the time period $\mathsf{t} \in \mathcal{T}$ and a revocation list $\mathsf{RL_{ID,t}} = \mathsf{r.RL_{ID,t}}$ and the parent's update key $\mathsf{uk_{pa(ID),t}} = \mathsf{r.ku_{pa(ID),t}}$, run $(\mathsf{r.ku_{ID,t}}, \mathsf{r.msk'_{ID}}) \leftarrow \mathsf{r.KeyUp}(\mathsf{r.mpk}, \mathsf{r.msk_{ID}}, \mathsf{t}, \mathsf{r.RL_{ID,t}}, \mathsf{r.ku_{pa(ID),t}})$. Then, output an update key $\mathsf{uk_{ID,t}} := \mathsf{r.ku_{ID,t}}$ and the updated secret key $\mathsf{sk'_{ID}} := \mathsf{r.msk'_{ID}}$.

$\mathsf{TranKG}(\mathsf{mpk}, \mathsf{pk_{ID}}, \mathsf{uk_{pa(ID),t}})$: On input the public parameter $\mathsf{mpk} = (\mathsf{r.mpk}, \mathsf{h.mpk})$, a public key $\mathsf{pk_{ID}} = \mathsf{r.sk_{ID}}$ and the update key $\mathsf{uk_{pa(ID),t}} = \mathsf{r.ku_{pa(ID),t}}$, the server runs $\mathsf{r.dk_{ID,t}} \leftarrow \mathsf{r.GenDK}(\mathsf{r.mpk}, \mathsf{r.sk_{ID}}, \mathsf{r.ku_{pa(ID),t}})$, and outputs a transform key $\mathsf{tk_{ID,t}} := \mathsf{r.dk_{ID,t}}$ for identity ID in time period t.

$\mathsf{PrivKG}(\mathsf{mpk}, \mathsf{privk_{pa(ID)}}, \mathsf{ID})$: On input the public parameter $\mathsf{mpk} = (\mathsf{r.mpk}, \mathsf{h.mpk})$, the private key $\mathsf{privk_{pa(ID)}} = \mathsf{h.sk_{pa(ID)}}$ and the identity $\mathsf{ID} \in \mathcal{ID}_h$, the user $\mathsf{pa(ID)}$ runs $\mathsf{h.sk_{ID}} \leftarrow \mathsf{h.Delegate}(\mathsf{h.mpk}, \mathsf{h.sk_{pa(ID)}}, \mathsf{ID})$[3] and outputs the private key $\mathsf{privk_{ID}} := \mathsf{h.sk_{ID}}$.

$\mathsf{DecKG}(\mathsf{mpk}, \mathsf{privk_{ID}}, \mathsf{t})$: On input the public parameter $\mathsf{mpk} = (\mathsf{r.mpk}, \mathsf{h.mpk})$, the private key $\mathsf{privk_{ID}} = \mathsf{h.sk_{ID}}$ and the time period t, the user $\mathsf{ID} \in \mathcal{ID}_h$ runs $\mathsf{h.sk_{ID,t}} \leftarrow \mathsf{h.Delegate}(\mathsf{h.mpk}, \mathsf{h.sk_{ID}}, \mathsf{t})$ and outputs a decryption key $\mathsf{dk_{ID,t}} := \mathsf{h.sk_{ID,t}}$.

$\mathsf{Enc}(\mathsf{mpk}, \mathsf{ID}, \mathsf{t}, M)$: On input the public parameter $\mathsf{mpk} = (\mathsf{r.mpk}, \mathsf{h.mpk})$, an identity $\mathsf{ID} \in \mathcal{ID}_h$, a time period $\mathsf{t} \in \mathcal{T}$ and a message $M \in \mathcal{M}$, the algorithm runs $\mathsf{h.ct_{ID,t}} \leftarrow \mathsf{h.Enc}(\mathsf{h.mpk}, (\mathsf{ID}, \mathsf{t}), M)$ and $\mathsf{r.ct_{ID,t}} \leftarrow \mathsf{r.Enc}(\mathsf{r.mpk}, \mathsf{ID}, \mathsf{t}, \mathsf{h.ct_{ID,t}})$. Finally, output the ciphertext $\mathsf{ct_{ID,t}} := \mathsf{r.ct_{ID,t}}$.

$\mathsf{Transform}(\mathsf{mpk}, \mathsf{ct_{ID,t}}, \mathsf{tk_{ID,t}})$: On input the public parameter $\mathsf{mpk} = (\mathsf{r.mpk}, \mathsf{h.mpk})$, a ciphertext $\mathsf{ct_{ID,t}} = \mathsf{r.ct_{ID,t}}$ and a transform key $\mathsf{tk_{ID,t}} = \mathsf{r.dk_{ID,t}}$ for identity ID in time period t, run $\mathsf{h.ct'_{ID,t}} \leftarrow \mathsf{r.Dec}(\mathsf{r.mpk}, \mathsf{r.dk_{ID,t}}, \mathsf{r.ct_{ID,t}})$. Output a partial decrypted ciphertext $\mathsf{ct'_{ID,t}} := \mathsf{h.ct'_{ID,t}}$.

---

[3] When ID is level-1 user, $\mathsf{pa(ID)} = \mathsf{kgc}$, then $\mathsf{privk_{pa(ID)}} = \mathsf{sk_{kgc}}$.

$\mathsf{Dec}(\mathsf{PP}, \mathsf{ct}'_{\mathsf{ID},\mathsf{t}}, \mathsf{dk}_{\mathsf{ID},\mathsf{t}})$: On input the public parameter $\mathsf{mpk} = (\mathsf{r.mpk}, \mathsf{h.mpk})$, a partial decrypted ciphertext $\mathsf{ct}'_{\mathsf{ID},\mathsf{t}} = \mathsf{h.ct}'_{\mathsf{ID},\mathsf{t}}$ and a decryption key $\mathsf{dk}_{\mathsf{ID},\mathsf{t}} = \mathsf{h.sk}_{\mathsf{ID},\mathsf{t}}$ for identity ID in time period t, run $\mathsf{h}.M' \leftarrow \mathsf{h.Dec}(\mathsf{h.mpk}, \mathsf{h.sk}_{\mathsf{ID},\mathsf{t}}, \mathsf{h.ct}'_{\mathsf{ID},\mathsf{t}})$. If $\mathsf{h}.M' = \perp$, return $\perp$. Otherwise, output a message $M := \mathsf{h}.M'$.

Correctness. The correctness of the constructed SR-HIBE scheme Π follows from that of the underlying RHIBE scheme $\mathsf{r}.\Pi$ and the HIBE scheme $\mathsf{h}.\Pi$.

Theorem 1. *If the underlying RHIBE scheme* $\mathsf{r}.\Pi$ *satisfies selective-identity (resp. adaptive-identity) security and the underlying* $(L+1)$*-level HIBE scheme* $\mathsf{h}.\Pi$ *satisfies selective-identity (resp. adaptive-identity) security, then the constructed constructed SR-HIBE scheme* Π *satisfies SSR-sID-CPA (resp. SSR-aID-CPA) security.*

Proof sketch (of Theorem 1). The strategies that an adversary used can be divided into the following cases:

- Type-I: $\mathcal{A}$ issues valid private key reveal queries on at least one $\mathsf{ID} \in \mathsf{prefix}(\mathsf{ID}^*)$.
  - Type-I-i^*: $\mathcal{A}$ issues a valid private key reveal queries on $\mathsf{ID}^*_{[i^*]}$ but not on any $\mathsf{ID} \in \mathsf{prefix}(\mathsf{ID}^*_{[i^*-1]})$.
    - Type-I-i^*-1: $\mathcal{A}$ issues a valid public key reveal query on ID^*. In this case, ID^* must be revoked before t^*.
    - Type-I-i^*-2: $\mathcal{A}$ issues valid secret key reveal queries on at least one $\mathsf{ID}' \in \mathsf{prefix}(\mathsf{ID}^*)$.
    - Type-I-i^*-3: $\mathcal{A}$ issues a valid public key reveal query on ID^* and valid secret key reveal queries on at least one $\mathsf{ID}' \in \mathsf{prefix}(\mathsf{ID}^*)$.
    - Type-I-i^*-4: $\mathcal{A}$ does not issue a valid public key reveal query on ID^* and valid secret key reveal queries on any $\mathsf{ID}' \in \mathsf{prefix}(\mathsf{ID}^*)$.
- Type-II: The adversary does not issue valid private key reveal queries on any $\mathsf{ID} \in \mathsf{prefix}(\mathsf{ID}^*)$.

By the strategy-dividing lemma in [8], in order to prove the theorem, it is sufficient to show that for each type of adversary, its advantage is negligible.

3.1 Generic Construction of SR-IBE

When the maximal hierarchical depth $L = 1$, we obtain a generic construction of SR-IBE from RIBE with DKER and two-level HIBE. Compared with the SR-IBE in [10], our construction has shorter ciphertext size when instantiated with pairing since we use the "double encryption" technique. While Ma and Lin [9] gave a generic construction of RIBE with DKER from any IBE scheme and two-level HIBE scheme. Combining their work with our construction, we can get a generic construction of SR-IBE scheme from any IBE scheme and two-level HIBE scheme.

Observe that [9] and [10] also gave the generic construction of SR-IBE scheme. In their work, the sender chooses a random message M_1 and set the message

$M_2 = M \oplus M_1$, and the server can get one of M_1 and M_2 while the recipient can recover the other one. Since the server may be untrusted, if he sends something that is different from what he obtained, then the recipient cannot gain the real message M. While in our construction, the server only can get a HIBE ciphertext on M, if he has dishonest behavior, then the recipient cannot decrypt to recover the message M and thus can detect this case. Thus, our construction can guarantee both the integrity and privacy of messages.

Acknowledgement. We thank the anonymous reviewers and editors for helpful comments. All authors are supported by the National Natural Science Foundation of China (Grant No. 61932019, No. 61772521, No. 61772522) and Key Research Program of Frontier Sciences, CAS (Grant No. QYZDB-SSW-SYS035).

References

1. Agrawal, S., Boneh, D., Boyen, X.: Efficient lattice (H)IBE in the standard model. In: Gilbert, H. (ed.) EUROCRYPT 2010. LNCS, vol. 6110, pp. 553–572. Springer, Heidelberg (2010). https://doi.org/10.1007/978-3-642-13190-5_28
2. Boldyreva, A., Goyal, V., Kumar, V.: Identity-based encryption with efficient revocation. In: Proceedings of the 2008 ACM Conference on Computer and Communications Security - CCS 2008, pp. 417–426 (2008)
3. Boneh, D., Boyen, X.: Efficient selective-ID secure identity-based encryption without random oracles. In: Cachin, C., Camenisch, J.L. (eds.) EUROCRYPT 2004. LNCS, vol. 3027, pp. 223–238. Springer, Heidelberg (2004). https://doi.org/10.1007/978-3-540-24676-3_14
4. Boneh, D., Franklin, M.: Identity-based encryption from the weil pairing. In: Kilian, J. (ed.) CRYPTO 2001. LNCS, vol. 2139, pp. 213–229. Springer, Heidelberg (2001). https://doi.org/10.1007/3-540-44647-8_13
5. Boyen, X., Li, Q.: Towards tightly secure lattice short signature and id-based encryption. In: Cheon, J.H., Takagi, T. (eds.) ASIACRYPT 2016. LNCS, vol. 10032, pp. 404–434. Springer, Heidelberg (2016). https://doi.org/10.1007/978-3-662-53890-6_14
6. Döttling, N., Garg, S.: Identity-based encryption from the Diffie-Hellman assumption. In: Katz, J., Shacham, H. (eds.) CRYPTO 2017. LNCS, vol. 10401, pp. 537–569. Springer, Cham (2017). https://doi.org/10.1007/978-3-319-63688-7_18
7. Gentry, C., Peikert, C., Vaikuntanathan, V.: Trapdoors for hard lattices and new cryptographic constructions. In: Proceedings of the 40th Annual ACM Symposium on Theory of Computing - STOC 2008, pp. 197–206 (2008)
8. Katsumata, S., Matsuda, T., Takayasu, A.: Lattice-based revocable (hierarchical) IBE with decryption key exposure resistance. In: Public-Key Cryptography - PKC 2019, pp. 441–471 (2019)
9. Ma, X., Lin, D.: A generic construction of revocable identity-based encryption. IACR Cryptology ePrint Archive, 2019:299 (2019)
10. Meng, F.: Server-aided revocable identity-based encryption revisited. IACR Cryptology ePrint Archive, 2019:1442 (2019)
11. Qin, B., Deng, R.H., Li, Y., Liu, S.: Server-aided revocable identity-based encryption. In: Pernul, G., Ryan, P.Y.A., Weippl, E. (eds.) ESORICS 2015. LNCS, vol. 9326, pp. 286–304. Springer, Cham (2015). https://doi.org/10.1007/978-3-319-24174-6_15

12. Shamir, A.: Identity-based cryptosystems and signature schemes. In: Blakley, G.R., Chaum, D. (eds.) CRYPTO 1984. LNCS, vol. 196, pp. 47–53. Springer, Heidelberg (1985). https://doi.org/10.1007/3-540-39568-7_5
13. Waters, B.: Efficient identity-based encryption without random oracles. In: Cramer, R. (ed.) EUROCRYPT 2005. LNCS, vol. 3494, pp. 114–127. Springer, Heidelberg (2005). https://doi.org/10.1007/11426639_7
14. Waters, B.: Dual system encryption: realizing fully secure IBE and HIBE under simple assumptions. In: Halevi, S. (ed.) CRYPTO 2009. LNCS, vol. 5677, pp. 619–636. Springer, Heidelberg (2009). https://doi.org/10.1007/978-3-642-03356-8_36
15. Yamada, S.: Asymptotically compact adaptively secure lattice IBEs and verifiable random functions via generalized partitioning techniques. In: Katz, J., Shacham, H. (eds.) CRYPTO 2017. LNCS, vol. 10403, pp. 161–193. Springer, Cham (2017). https://doi.org/10.1007/978-3-319-63697-9_6

Fully Secure ABE with Outsourced Decryption against Chosen Ciphertext Attack

Ti Wang[1,2], Yongbin Zhou[1,2(✉)], Hui Ma[1,2], Yuejun Liu[1,2], and Rui Zhang[1,2]

[1] State Key Laboratory of Information Security, Institute of Information Engineering, Chinese Academy of Sciences, Beijing 100093, China
zhouyongbin@iie.ac.cn

[2] School of Cyber Security, University of Chinese Academy of Sciences, Beijing 100049, China

Abstract. Attribute-based encryption (ABE) provides fine-grained access control on encrypted data, but it is not suitable for limited-resource devices due to the inefficiency of decryption. To solve this problem, Green et al. proposed a new paradigm named attribute-based encryption with outsourced decryption (OD-ABE). It allows a proxy with a transformation key delegated from the user to transform any ABE ciphertext into a constant size ciphertext. While full security against chosen ciphertext attack (CCA) is generally considered as the strongest security notion for an ABE system, none of existing OD-ABE schemes achieves full security and CCA security simultaneously. In this paper, we propose the full CCA security model for OD-ABE and construct concrete (ciphertext-policy and key-policy) OD-ABE schemes that are fully CCA-secure in the random oracle model. Specifically, most complex operations of decryption as well as the verification of ciphertexts can be offloaded to the proxy in our schemes. We make detailed performance evaluations in the Charm framework. The experimental results indicate that the user saves significantly on both bandwidth and time during decryption.

Keywords: Attribute-based encryption · Outsourced decryption · Full security · Chosen ciphertext security

1 Introduction

Cloud computing is a quite fascinating service paradigm for data sharing. To ensure confidentiality, users may outsource encrypted data to the public cloud. Attribute-Based Encryption (ABE), introduced by Sahai and Waters [33] and refined by Goyal et al. [18], is a suited solution for this concern. It provides fine-grained access control and encryption functionalities simultaneously. Specifically, there are two main flavors of ABE. In Ciphertext-Policy ABE (CP-ABE) [6, 12, 37], ciphertexts are associated with access policies and keys are associated

Y. Wu and M. Yung (Eds.): Inscrypt 2020, LNCS 12612, pp. 83–103, 2021.
https://doi.org/10.1007/978-3-030-71852-7_6

with sets of attributes. A key will decrypt a ciphertext if and only if the set of attributes satisfies the access policy. Alternatively, in Key-Policy ABE (KP-ABE) [4,18,32] the roles are flipped.

Although ABE achieves powerful and flexible access control, the communication and computation overhead of decryption is quite high. The ciphertext size, as well as the pairing and exponentiation operations during decryption usually grow linearly with the complexity of the access policy. It severely limits the usage for limited-resource devices and essentially impedes ABE from wide-range deployment. To solve this problem, Green et al. [19] proposed the concept of attribute-based encryption with outsourced decryption (OD-ABE). It allows a proxy (such as the cloud server) to transform any ABE ciphertext into a constant-size El Gamal-style ciphertext, while the proxy learns nothing about the underlying plaintext. The user needs only compute one exponentiation and no pairings to recover the message. Subsequently, a series of work [29–31,35] has been dedicated to design OD-ABE schemes for various applications.

When constructing a concrete ABE scheme, there are two aspects of security should be considered: (1) *Full security* or *selective security*. Take CP-ABE for example, a fully (or adaptively) secure scheme [2,10,11,17,22,23,26,27] provides confidentiality for data encrypted under policies chosen anytime during a system's life-cycle, even after the system parameters have been published and several keys have been distributed. On the contrary, selectively secure schemes [4,6,12,18,32,37] can only guarantee security for policies that are declared upfront, before the system is deployed. (2) *CCA security* or *CPA security*. It is well-known that the security against chosen ciphertext attack (CCA) is generally considered as the strongest notion that does not allow any bit of the ciphertext to be altered. While the security against chosen plaintext attack (CPA) only provides the basic confidentiality for a cryptosystem.

As far as we know, none of existing OD-ABE schemes achieves full security and CCA security simultaneously. There exist the following serious technical problems. (1) It seems infeasible to make a security proof of OD-ABE that could be a black box reduction to fully secure ABE schemes. When the adversary makes a query for some transformation key before the challenge phase, the reduction algorithm could not adopt the strategy in selective security model. Otherwise, it would have to abort the simulation or the simulation would be distinguishable from the real game. (2) Submitting ciphertexts to validity testing is crucial to achieve CCA security. However, if we apply techniques like the FO transformation [16] and require the user to verify original ABE ciphertexts, the communication and computation overhead will become so heavy, and hence the outsourced decryption mechanism is meaningless.

Our Contribution. In this paper, we propose fully secure ABE schemes with outsourced decryption against chosen ciphertext attack. Firstly, we construct a basic OD-CP-ABE scheme based on the CP-ABE proposed by Agrawal and Chase [2], and make a dual system encryption type proof to show the scheme is fully CPA-secure. The simulator could generate all (semi-functional) transformation keys for the adversary in the proof. Next, we transform the basic scheme into a CCA-secure one without compromising the efficiency of decryption. The main idea is to apply the "Encryption + Proof of Knowledge" construction [1,34] to make the ciphertext *publicly checkable*, which allows the proxy to execute some parts of the verification of original ciphertexts. Therefore, the user needs only verify transformed ciphertexts according to the FO transformation [16]. The same techniques are applied to construct a fully CCA-secure OD-ABE scheme in KP setting.

Moreover, we implement our OD-CP-ABE scheme in the Charm framework [3] to evaluate the practical performance. The experimental results indicate that the user saves significantly on both bandwidth and time during decryption.

1.1 Related Work

Lewko et al. [23] proposed the first fully secure ABE scheme by adapting the dual system encryption technique of [24,36]. The construction is secure under three assumptions used by Lewko and Waters [24] in composite order bilinear groups. Lewko and Waters [26] presented a fully secure CP-ABE scheme in prime order groups while matching the efficiency of the state of the art selectively secure systems. Subsequently, a series of simpler and improved constructions of ABE schemes with full security have been presented [2,10,11,17,22,27].

The OD-ABE schemes proposed by Green et al. [19] could achieve a relaxed variant of CCA security, called replayable CCA security [8]. Zuo et al. [39] proposed a concrete selectively CCA-securc CP-ABE with outsourced decryption, by applying the CHK [7] and FO [16] techniques. In terms of generic conversions, Goyal et al. [18] presented a method for transforming a CPA-secure KP-ABE to a CCA-secure one. Yamada et al. [38] proposed generic conversions for both CP and KP flavors. Due to the reasons talked above, these methods are not suitable to construct an OD-ABE scheme with full CCA security, which is our main concern in this paper.

1.2 Paper Organization

The remaining paper is organized as follows. In Sect. 2, we give notations and definitions used in the paper. In Sect. 3, we formally define OD-ABE systems and their security model. In Sect. 4, we present a basic OD-CP-ABE scheme that is fully CPA-secure. In Sect. 5, we present our proposal for fully CCA-secure OD-CP-ABE scheme and give the details of security proof in the proposed security model. In Sect. 6, we give the construction of an OD-KP-ABE scheme with full CCA security. In Sect. 7, we make performance evaluations of our OD-CP-ABE scheme. At last, we conclude the paper in Sect. 8.

2 Preliminary

2.1 Notations

For $n \in \mathbb{N}$, $[n] = \{1, 2, \ldots, n\}$. If S is a set, $s \xleftarrow{\$} S$ denotes the operation of selecting an element s uniformly at random from S. $\mathbf{M}_i$ and $\mathbf{M}_{i,j}$ denote the ith row and the (i,j)th element of a matrix $\mathbf{M}$, respectively. $\mathbf{M}^\top$ denotes the transpose of $\mathbf{M}$. λ denotes the security parameter, and $negl(\lambda)$ denotes a negligible function, i.e., $\forall n > 0$, $\exists \lambda_0 \in \mathbb{N}$, s.t., $\lambda > \lambda_0$, $negl(\lambda) < 1/\lambda^n$.

2.2 Definitions

Definition 1 (Access Structure [5]**).** Let $\mathcal{U}$ be the attribute universe. An access structure on $\mathcal{U}$ is a collection $\mathbb{A}$ of non-empty sets of attributes, i.e. $\mathbb{A} \subseteq 2^{\mathcal{U}} \setminus \{\emptyset\}$. The sets in $\mathbb{A}$ are called the authorized sets, and the sets not in $\mathbb{A}$ are called unauthorized sets. Additionally, an access structure is called monotone for $\forall B, C$, if $B \in \mathbb{A}$ and $B \subseteq C$, then $C \in \mathbb{A}$.

Definition 2 (Monotone Span Program (MSP) [2,21]**).** A monotone span program is given by a matrix $\mathbf{M}$ of size $n_1 \times n_2$ over $\mathbb{Z}_p$ and a mapping $\pi : \{1, \ldots, n_1\} \to \mathcal{U}$. Let $\mathcal{S}$ be a set of attributes and $I = \{i | i \in \{1, \ldots, n_1\}, \pi(i) \in \mathcal{S}\}$ be the set of rows in $\mathbf{M}$ that belong to $\mathcal{S}$. We say that an MSP $(\mathbf{M}, \pi)$ accepts $\mathcal{S}$ if there exists a linear combination of rows in I that gives $(1, 0, \ldots, 0)$. More formally, there should exist coefficients $\{\gamma_i\}_{i \in I}$ such that

$$\sum_{i \in I} \gamma_i \mathbf{M}_i = (1, 0, \ldots, 0).$$

Denote $\mathcal{F}$ as a monotone boolean formula with AND and OR gates, where each input is associated with an attribute in $\mathcal{U}$. Lewko and Waters [25] proposed a simple and efficient method to convert any $\mathcal{F}$ into an MSP $(\mathbf{M}, \pi)$, where each entry in $\mathbf{M}$ is either a 0, 1 or -1. Note that it is always possible to pick coefficients that are either 0 or 1 for the resulting MSP, irrespective of the attribute set $\mathcal{S}$.

Definition 3 (Σ-Protocol [13]**).** Let $\mathcal{R}$ be a binary relation. That is, $\mathcal{R}$ is a subset of $\{0,1\}^* \times \{0,1\}^*$, where the only restriction is that if $(x, w) \in \mathcal{R}$, then the length of w is at most $p(|x|)$, for some polynomial $p()$. For some $(x, w) \in \mathcal{R}$, we may think of x as an instance of some computational problem, and w as a witness for x. A two-party protocol π between the prover $\mathcal{P}$ and verifier $\mathcal{V}$ is a Σ-protocol for relation $\mathcal{R}$ if:

- Three-move form: π is of the following form.
  1. $\mathcal{P}$ sends $\mathcal{V}$ a commitment U.
  2. $\mathcal{V}$ chooses a random challenge c and sends it to $\mathcal{P}$.
  3. $\mathcal{P}$ returns a response z to $\mathcal{V}$, and $\mathcal{V}$ decides to accept or reject based on the values (x, U, c, z).
- Completeness: If $\mathcal{P}$ and $\mathcal{V}$ follow the protocol on common input x and private input w to $\mathcal{P}$ where $(x, w) \in \mathcal{R}$, then $\mathcal{V}$ always accepts.
- Special soundness: There exists a polynomial-time algorithm extractor that given any x and any pair of accepting transcripts (U, c, z) and (U, c', z') for x, where $c \neq c'$, outputs w such that $(x, w) \in \mathcal{R}$.
- Special honest verifier zero knowledge: There exists a probabilistic polynomial-time (PPT) simulator, which on input x and a random c outputs an accepting transcript of the form (U, c, z), with the same probability distribution as transcripts generated by the real protocol.

Definition 4 (Bilinear Maps). Let GroupGen be an asymmetric pairing group generator that takes as input a security parameter λ and outputs a tuple $\mathsf{par} = (p, \mathbb{G}_1, \mathbb{G}_2, \mathbb{G}_T, e, g, h)$, where $\mathbb{G}_1$, $\mathbb{G}_2$ and $\mathbb{G}_T$ are three multiplicative cyclic groups of prime order $p \in \Theta(2^\lambda)$, g, h are the generator of $\mathbb{G}_1, \mathbb{G}_2$ respectively, and $e : \mathbb{G}_1 \times \mathbb{G}_2 \to \mathbb{G}_T$ is an efficiently computable bilinear map satisfying that:

1. Bilinearity: $\forall g \in \mathbb{G}_1, h \in \mathbb{G}_2$ and $\forall a, b \in \mathbb{Z}_p^*$, we have $e(g^a, h^b) = e(g, h)^{ab}$.
2. Non-degeneracy: $e(g, h) \neq 1$, whenever g, h are not the identity of $\mathbb{G}_1, \mathbb{G}_2$.

Definition 5 (Decisional Linear (DLIN) Assumption [14]**).** An asymmetric pairing group generator GroupGen satisfies the decisional linear assumption if for all PPT adversaries $\mathcal{A}$, there exists a negligible function *negl* such that:

$$|\Pr[\mathcal{A}(\lambda, \mathsf{par}, D, T_0) = 1] - \Pr[\mathcal{A}(\lambda, \mathsf{par}, D, T_1) = 1]| \leq negl(\lambda),$$

where $\mathsf{par} = (p, \mathbb{G}_1, \mathbb{G}_2, \mathbb{G}_T, e, g, h) \leftarrow \mathsf{GroupGen}(\lambda)$, $a_1, a_2, s_1, s_2, s \xleftarrow{\$} \mathbb{Z}_p^*$, $D = (g^{a_1}, g^{a_2}, h^{a_1}, h^{a_2}, g^{a_1 s_1}, g^{a_2 s_2}, h^{a_1 s_1}, h^{a_2 s_2})$, $T_0 = (g^{s_1+s_2}, h^{s_1+s_2})$, $T_1 = (g^s, h^s)$.

3 ABE with Outsourced Decryption

3.1 Syntax of OD-ABE

Let $\mathcal{S}$ represent an attribute set and $\mathbb{A}$ an access structure. For generality, we will define $(\mathcal{I}_k, \mathcal{I}_e)$ as the inputs to the key generation and encryption functions respectively. In a CP-ABE scheme $(\mathcal{I}_k, \mathcal{I}_e) = (\mathcal{S}, \mathbb{A})$, while in a KP-ABE scheme, we have $(\mathcal{I}_k, \mathcal{I}_e) = (\mathbb{A}, \mathcal{S})$. We define the function f as follows:

$$f(\mathcal{I}_k, \mathcal{I}_e) = \begin{cases} 1 & if\ \ \mathcal{I}_k \in \mathcal{I}_e\ in\ CP-ABE\ setting \\ 1 & if\ \ \mathcal{I}_e \in \mathcal{I}_k\ in\ KP-ABE\ setting \\ 0 & otherwise. \end{cases}$$

A CP-ABE (resp., KP-ABE) with outsourced decryption, OD-CP-ABE (resp., OD-KP-ABE), for access structure space $\mathcal{G}$ is a tuple of PPT algorithms:

- **Setup**$(\lambda, \mathcal{U}) \to (\mathrm{PK}, \mathrm{MSK})$. The probabilistic setup algorithm takes as input a security parameter λ and a universe description $\mathcal{U}$, and outputs the public parameters PK and the master secret key MSK. We implicitly assume that all the following algorithms take PK as input.
- **KeyGen**$(\mathrm{MSK}, \mathcal{I}_k) \to (\mathrm{TK}, \mathrm{RK})$. The probabilistic key generation algorithm takes as input the master secret key MSK and an attribute set (resp., access structure) $\mathcal{I}_k$, and outputs a transformation key TK and a retrieving key RK corresponding to $\mathcal{I}_k$.
- **Encrypt**$(\mathsf{msg}, \mathcal{I}_e) \to \mathrm{CT}$. The probabilistic encryption algorithm takes as input a message msg from the message space $\mathcal{M}$ and an access structure (resp., attribute set) $\mathcal{I}_e$, and outputs a ciphertext CT corresponding to $\mathcal{I}_e$.

- **Transform**(TK, CT) $\rightarrow$ TCT or $\perp$. The deterministic transformation algorithm takes as input a transformation key TK corresponding to $\mathcal{I}_k$ and a ciphertext CT encrypted under $\mathcal{I}_e$, and outputs a transformed ciphertext TCT if $f(\mathcal{I}_k, \mathcal{I}_e) = 1$. Otherwise, it outputs $\perp$.
- **Decrypt**(RK, TCT) $\rightarrow$ msg or $\perp$. The deterministic decryption algorithm takes as input a retrieving key RK corresponding to $\mathcal{I}_k$ and a transformed ciphertext TCT that was originally encrypted under $\mathcal{I}_e$, and outputs msg if $f(\mathcal{I}_k, \mathcal{I}_e) = 1$. Otherwise, it outputs $\perp$.

Correctness. For the fixed security parameter $\lambda \in \mathbb{N}$ and the universe description $\mathcal{U}$, the OD-CP-ABE correctness property requires that for all $\mathcal{S} \subseteq \mathcal{U}$, all $\mathbb{A} \in \mathcal{G}$, all $\mathsf{msg} \in \mathcal{M}$, all (PK, MSK) $\in$ **Setup**(λ, $\mathcal{U}$) and all (TK, RK) $\in$ **KeyGen**(MSK, $\mathcal{S}$):

$$\textbf{Decrypt}(\text{RK}, \textbf{Transform}(\text{TK}, \textbf{Encrypt}(\mathsf{msg}, \mathbb{A}))) = \mathsf{msg}, \text{ if } f(\mathcal{S}, \mathbb{A}) = 1.$$

OD-KP-ABE correctness is defined analogously, with the last inputs to **KeyGen** and **Encrypt** reversed.

3.2 Security Model for OD-ABE

We recall the security definition introduced in [19]. Let $\Pi_{\text{OD-ABE}}$ = (**Setup**, **KeyGen**, **Encrypt**, **Transform**, **Decrypt**) be an OD-ABE scheme for access structure space $\mathcal{G}$, and consider the following experiment for an adversary $\mathcal{A}$, parameter λ and attribute universe $\mathcal{U}$.

The OD-ABE Experiment $\mathsf{Exp}^{\text{CCA}}_{\mathcal{A},\Pi_{\text{OD-ABE}}}(\lambda, \mathcal{U})$:
Setup. The challenger $\mathcal{C}$ runs **Setup**(λ, $\mathcal{U}$) to obtain (PK, MSK) and returns PK to $\mathcal{A}$.

Phase 1. $\mathcal{C}$ initializes an empty table T, an empty set D and an integer $j = 0$. Proceeding adaptively, $\mathcal{A}$ can repeatedly make any of the following queries:

- **Create**($\mathcal{I}_k$): $\mathcal{C}$ sets $j = j + 1$. It runs **KeyGen**(MSK, $\mathcal{I}_k$) to obtain (TK, RK) and stores the entry $(j, \mathcal{I}_k, \text{TK}, \text{RK})$ in table $\mathcal{T}$. It returns TK to $\mathcal{A}$. Note that **Create** can be repeatedly queried with the same input.
- **Corrupt**(i): $\mathcal{C}$ retrieves the ith entry $(i, \mathcal{I}_k, \text{TK}, \text{RK})$ in table $\mathcal{T}$ and sets $\mathcal{D} := \mathcal{D} \cup \{\mathcal{I}_k\}$. It returns RK to $\mathcal{A}$.
- **Decrypt.CT**(i, CT): $\mathcal{C}$ retrieves the ith entry $(i, \mathcal{I}_k, \text{TK}, \text{RK})$ in table $\mathcal{T}$ and returns the output of **Decrypt**(RK, **Transform**(TK, CT)) to $\mathcal{A}$.
- **Decrypt.TCT**(i, TCT): $\mathcal{C}$ retrieves the ith entry $(i, \mathcal{I}_k, \text{TK}, \text{RK})$ in table $\mathcal{T}$ and returns the output of **Decrypt**(RK, TCT) to $\mathcal{A}$. Note that it simply returns $\perp$ if TCT is not generated from **Transform**(TK, $\cdot$).

Challenge. $\mathcal{A}$ submits two equal length messages $\mathsf{msg}_0^*, \mathsf{msg}_1^*$ and a value $\mathcal{I}_e^*$ as the challenge tuple, where for all $\mathcal{I}_k \in \mathcal{D}$, $f(\mathcal{I}_k, \mathcal{I}_e^*) \neq 1$. $\mathcal{C}$ picks $b \xleftarrow{\$} \{0, 1\}$ and returns the challenge ciphertext $\text{CT}^* = \textbf{Encrypt}(\mathsf{msg}_b^*, \mathcal{I}_e^*)$ to $\mathcal{A}$.

Phase 2. Phase 1 is repeated with the restriction that $\mathcal{A}$ cannot query:

- **Corrupt**(i) that would result in a value $\mathcal{I}_k$ which satisfies $f(\mathcal{I}_k, \mathcal{I}_e^*) = 1$ being added to $\mathcal{D}$.
- **Decrypt.CT**(i, CT^*) that $f(\mathcal{I}_k, \mathcal{I}_e^*) = 1$.
- **Decrypt.TCT**(i, TCT^*) that $f(\mathcal{I}_k, \mathcal{I}_e^*) = 1$ and $\mathrm{TCT}^* =$ **Transform**$(\mathrm{TK}, \mathrm{CT}^*)$, where TK is of the ith entry in table $\mathcal{T}$.

Guess. $\mathcal{A}$ outputs a guess b' of b. The output of the experiment is 1 iff $b' = b$.

Definition 6 (Full CCA Security). An OD-ABE is fully CCA-secure (or secure against adaptive chosen ciphertext attack) if for all PPT adversaries $\mathcal{A}$, there exists a negligible function *negl* such that:

$$\left|\Pr[\mathsf{Exp}^{\mathrm{CCA}}_{\mathcal{A},\Pi_{\mathrm{OD\text{-}ABE}}}(\lambda, \mathcal{U}) = 1] - 1/2\right| \leq negl(\lambda).$$

CPA Security. We say that an OD-ABE scheme is CPA-secure (or secure against chosen plaintext attack) if we remove decryption oracles **Decrypt.CT** and **Decrypt.TCT** in the CCA security experiment.

Selective Security. We say that an OD-ABE scheme is selectively secure if we add an **Init** stage before **Setup** where the adversary outputs the challenge $\mathcal{I}_e^*$, instead of waiting until **Challenge**.

4 An OD-CP-ABE Scheme with Full CPA Security

4.1 Construction

First, we construct a basic ciphertext-policy attribute-based encryption with outsourced decryption (OD-CP-ABE) based on the CP-ABE scheme called FAME in [2]. The basic scheme is described as follows:

- **Setup**$(\lambda, \mathcal{U})$. Call $\mathsf{GroupGen}(\lambda)$ to obtain $\mathsf{par} = (p, \mathbb{G}_1, \mathbb{G}_2, \mathbb{G}_T, e, g, h)$. Let $\mathcal{U} = \{0,1\}^*$. Choose a one-way collision-resistant cryptographic hash function $\mathcal{H}_1 : \{0,1\}^* \rightarrow \mathbb{G}_1$, and choose $a_1, a_2, b_1, b_2, d_1, d_2, d_3 \xleftarrow{\$} \mathbb{Z}_p^*$. Output $\mathrm{PK} = (\mathsf{par}, \mathcal{H}_1, H_1 = h^{a_1}, H_2 = h^{a_2}, T_1 = e(g,h)^{d_1 a_1 + d_3}, T_2 = e(g,h)^{d_2 a_2 + d_3})$, $\mathrm{MSK} = (a_1, a_2, b_1, b_2, g^{d_1}, g^{d_2}, g^{d_3})$.
- **KeyGen**$(\mathrm{MSK}, \mathcal{S})$. Choose $r_1, r_2, \beta \xleftarrow{\$} \mathbb{Z}_p^*$ and compute $K_0 = (h^{\beta b_1 r_1}, h^{\beta b_2 r_2}, h^{\beta(r_1+r_2)})$. Choose $\sigma \xleftarrow{\$} \mathbb{Z}_p^*$ and for $t \in [2]$, compute

$$K_{1,t} = g^{\beta d_t} \cdot \mathcal{H}_1(011t)^{\frac{\beta b_1 r_1}{a_t}} \cdot \mathcal{H}_1(012t)^{\frac{\beta b_2 r_2}{a_t}} \cdot \mathcal{H}_1(013t)^{\frac{\beta(r_1+r_2)}{a_t}} \cdot g^{\frac{\beta\sigma}{a_t}}.$$

  Set $K_1 = (K_{1,1}, K_{1,2}, g^{\beta(d_3-\sigma)})$. For all $y \in \mathcal{S}$, $t \in [2]$, choose $\sigma_y \xleftarrow{\$} \mathbb{Z}_p^*$ and compute

$$K_{y,t} = \mathcal{H}_1(y1t)^{\frac{\beta b_1 r_1}{a_t}} \cdot \mathcal{H}_1(y2t)^{\frac{\beta b_2 r_2}{a_t}} \cdot \mathcal{H}_1(y3t)^{\frac{\beta(r_1+r_2)}{a_t}} \cdot g^{\frac{\beta\sigma_y}{a_t}}.$$

  Set $K_y = (K_{y,1}, K_{y,2}, g^{-\beta\sigma_y})$. Output $\mathrm{TK} = (\mathcal{S}, K_0, K_1, \{K_y\}_{y\in\mathcal{S}})$, $\mathrm{RK} = \beta$.

- **Encrypt**($\mathsf{msg} \in \mathbb{G}_T, \mathbb{A} = (\mathbf{M}, \pi)$). Choose $s_1, s_2 \xleftarrow{\$} \mathbb{Z}_p^*$ and compute

$$C_m = T_1^{s_1} \cdot T_2^{s_2} \cdot \mathsf{msg}, \quad C_0 = (H_1^{s_1}, H_2^{s_2}, h^{s_1+s_2}).$$

Suppose $\mathbf{M}$ has n_1 rows and n_2 columns. For $i \in [n_1]$ and $l \in [3]$, compute

$$C_{i,l} = [\mathcal{H}_1(\pi(i)l1) \cdot \prod_{j=1}^{n_2} \mathcal{H}_1(0jl1)^{\mathbf{M}_{i,j}}]^{s_1} \cdot [\mathcal{H}_1(\pi(i)l2) \cdot \prod_{j=1}^{n_2} \mathcal{H}_1(0jl2)^{\mathbf{M}_{i,j}}]^{s_2}.$$

Set $C_i = (C_{i,1}, C_{i,2}, C_{i,3})$ and output $\mathrm{CT} = (\mathbb{A}, C_m, C_0, \{C_i\}_{i \in [n_1]})$.
- **Transform**(TK, CT). If $f(\mathcal{S}, \mathbb{A}) = 0$, output $\perp$. Otherwise, compute constants $\{\gamma_i\}_{i \in I}$ that satisfy $\sum_{i \in I} \gamma_i \mathbf{M}_i = (1, 0, \dots, 0)$ and

$$\mathsf{num} = \prod_{l \in [3]} e(\prod_{i \in I} C_{i,l}^{\gamma_i}, K_{0,l}), \quad \mathsf{den} = \prod_{l \in [3]} e(K_{1,l} \cdot \prod_{i \in I} K_{\pi(i),l}^{\gamma_i}, C_{0,l}),$$

where $K_{0,1}, K_{0,2}, K_{0,3}$ denote the first, second and third elements of K_0; the same for C_0. Output $\mathrm{TCT} = (C_m, \mathsf{kem} = \mathsf{num}/\mathsf{den})$.
- **Decrypt**(RK, TCT). Compute and output $\mathsf{msg} = C_m \cdot \mathsf{kem}^{1/\beta}$.

Theorem 1. *The basic scheme is fully CPA-secure under the DLIN assumption on asymmetric pairing groups in the random oracle model.*

4.2 Security Analysis

As discussed in [19], to prove the full security of an OD-ABE scheme, it seems infeasible to make a black box reduction to fully secure schemes. Accordingly, we make a dual system encryption type proof that would go along the lines of FAME [2], with the exception that in the hybrid stage of the proof all transformation keys will be set (one by one) to be semi-functional including those that could transform the eventual challenge ciphertext.

Proof. First, we give names to various compact forms of keys and challenge ciphertexts that will be used. P and SF stand for pseudo and semi-functional, respectively. Following [10,14], we represent group elements in a succinct way. The descriptions of random oracle $\mathcal{H}_1$ and the sampling algorithm are the same as those in [2], thus we omit them.

A transformation key TK can be in one of the following forms:

- Normal: $K_0 = [\beta \mathbf{Br}]_2$, $K_1 = [\beta \mathbf{d} + \beta \mathbf{U}_1 \mathbf{Br} + \beta \sigma \mathbf{a}^\perp]_1$, $K_y = [\beta \mathbf{W}_y \mathbf{Br} + \beta \sigma_y \mathbf{a}^\perp]_1$.
- P-normal: $K_0 = [\beta(\mathbf{Br} + \hat{r}\mathbf{a}^\perp)]_2$, $K_1 = [\beta \mathbf{d} + \beta \mathbf{U}_1(\mathbf{Br} + \hat{r}\mathbf{a}^\perp) + \beta \sigma \mathbf{a}^\perp]_1$, $K_y = [\beta \mathbf{W}_y(\mathbf{Br} + \hat{r}\mathbf{a}^\perp) + \beta \sigma_y \mathbf{a}^\perp]_1$, where $\hat{r} \xleftarrow{\$} \mathbb{Z}_p^*$.
- P-normal$^\bigstar$: $K_0 = [\beta(\mathbf{Br} + \hat{r}\mathbf{a}^\perp)]_2$, $K_1 = [\beta \mathbf{d} + \beta \mathbf{U}_1(\mathbf{Br} + \hat{r}\mathbf{a}^\perp)]_1$, $K_y = [\beta \mathbf{W}_y(\mathbf{Br} + \hat{r}\mathbf{a}^\perp)]_1$.
- Normal$^\bigstar$: $K_0 = [\beta \mathbf{Br}]_2$, $K_1 = [\beta \mathbf{d} + \beta \mathbf{U}_1 \mathbf{Br}]_1$, $K_y = [\beta \mathbf{W}_y \mathbf{Br}]_1$.

- P-SF*: $K_0 = [\beta(\mathbf{Br} + \hat{r}\mathbf{a}^\perp)]_2$, $K_1 = [\beta\mathbf{d} + \beta\mathbf{U}_1(\mathbf{Br} + \hat{r}\mathbf{a}^\perp) + \beta\alpha\mathbf{a}^\perp]_1$, $K_y = [\beta\mathbf{W}_y(\mathbf{Br} + \hat{r}\mathbf{a}^\perp)]_1$, where $\alpha \xleftarrow{\$} \mathbb{Z}_p^*$.
- SF*: $K_0 = [\beta\mathbf{Br}]_2$, $K_1 = [\beta\mathbf{d} + \beta\mathbf{U}_1\mathbf{Br} + \beta\alpha\mathbf{a}^\perp]_1$, $K_y = [\beta\mathbf{W}_y\mathbf{Br}]_1$.

where a separate $\beta \xleftarrow{\$} \mathbb{Z}_p^*$ is used for each TK. By setting the retrieving key RK $= \beta$, it is clear that all forms of TK with the corresponding RK are essentially identical to the secret key SK in the proof of FAME.

A ciphertext CT can be in one of the following forms:

- Normal*: $C_0 = [\mathbf{As}]_2$, $C_m = [\mathbf{d}^\mathsf{T}\mathbf{As}]_T \cdot \mathsf{msg}_b$, $C_i = [\mathbf{W}_{\pi(i)}^\mathsf{T}\mathbf{As} + \sum_{j=1}^{n_2} \mathbf{M}_{i,j}\mathbf{U}_j^\mathsf{T}\mathbf{As}]_1$.
- SF*: $C_0 = [\mathbf{As} + \hat{s}\mathbf{b}^\perp]_2$, $C_m = [\mathbf{d}^\mathsf{T}(\mathbf{As} + \hat{s}\mathbf{b}^\perp)]_T \cdot \mathsf{msg}_b$, $C_i = [\mathbf{W}_{\pi(i)}^\mathsf{T}(\mathbf{As} + \hat{s}\mathbf{b}^\perp) + \sum_{j=1}^{n_2} \mathbf{M}_{i,j}\mathbf{U}_j^\mathsf{T}(\mathbf{As} + \hat{s}\mathbf{b}^\perp)]_1$, where $\hat{s} \xleftarrow{\$} \mathbb{Z}_p^*$.
- Rnd*: $C_0 = [\mathbf{As} + \hat{s}\mathbf{b}^\perp]_2$, $C_m = [\mathbf{d}^\mathsf{T}(\mathbf{As} + \hat{s}\mathbf{b}^\perp)]_T \cdot \mathsf{msg}^\star$, $C_i = [\mathbf{W}_{\pi(i)}^\mathsf{T}(\mathbf{As} + \hat{s}\mathbf{b}^\perp) + \sum_{j=1}^{n_2} \mathbf{M}_{i,j}\mathbf{U}_j^\mathsf{T}(\mathbf{As} + \hat{s}\mathbf{b}^\perp)]_1$, where $\mathsf{msg}^\star \xleftarrow{\$} \mathbb{G}_T$.

Then, we provide the description of hybrids. Denote Q as the total number of **Create** queries. For notational purposes, we think of $\mathsf{Hyb}_{2,3,0}$ and $\mathsf{Hyb}_{4,3,0}$ as another way of denoting Hyb_1 and Hyb_3, respectively.

- Hyb_0: The one where $\mathcal{C}$ and $\mathcal{A}$ interact according to the security definition of the basic scheme, in which $\mathcal{H}_1$ is assumed to behave like a random oracle.
- Hyb_1: All transformation keys are Normal, the challenge ciphertext CT* is Normal*.
- Group-I hybrids for $q = 1, \ldots, Q$:
  - $\mathsf{Hyb}_{2,1,q}$: Same as Hyb_1, except that first $q-1$ keys are Normal*, qth key is P-Normal, and rest are Normal.
  - $\mathsf{Hyb}_{2,2,q}$: Same as $\mathsf{Hyb}_{2,1,q}$, except that qth key is P-Normal*.
  - $\mathsf{Hyb}_{2,3,q}$: Same as $\mathsf{Hyb}_{2,2,q}$, except that qth key is Normal*.
- Hyb_3: Same as $\mathsf{Hyb}_{2,3,Q}$, except that CT* is SF*.
- Group-II hybrids for $q = 1, \ldots, Q$:
  - $\mathsf{Hyb}_{4,1,q}$: Same as Hyb_3, except that first $q-1$ keys are SF*, qth key is P-Normal*, and rest are Normal*.
  - $\mathsf{Hyb}_{4,2,q}$: Same as $\mathsf{Hyb}_{4,1,q}$, except that qth key is P-SF*.
  - $\mathsf{Hyb}_{4,3,q}$: Same as $\mathsf{Hyb}_{4,2,q}$, except that qth key is SF*.
- Hyb_5: Same as $\mathsf{Hyb}_{4,3,Q}$, except that CT* is Rnd*.

At last, we show the indistinguishability of hybrids. In both FAME and the basic scheme, the adversary can not query for any secret keys SK* or RK* that could decrypt the challenge ciphertext CT*. However, the adversary gets all TK* in the basic scheme. We argue that when changing the forms of transformation keys and the challenge ciphertext, the indistinguishability of every pair of hybrids holds under the DLIN assumption just like in the dual system proof of FAME.

Note that all kinds of transformation keys could correctly transform normal ciphertexts. We need only demonstrate that the transformed ciphertexts $\mathrm{TCT}^* = \mathbf{Transform}(\mathrm{TK}^*, \mathrm{CT}^*)$ of every pair of hybrids are indistinguishable from the view of the adversary. In Group-I and Group-II hybrids, we consider TK^* is generated in the qth **Creat** query.

- Hyb_0: $\mathrm{TCT}^* = ([\mathbf{d}^\top \mathbf{A}\mathbf{s}]_T \cdot \mathsf{msg}_b, [-\beta \mathbf{d}^\top \mathbf{A}\mathbf{s}]_T)$.
- Hyb_1: TCT^* is identical to that in Hyb_0, so $\mathsf{Hyb}_0 \approx \mathsf{Hyb}_1$.
- Group-I hybrids for $q = 1, \ldots, Q$:
  - $\mathsf{Hyb}_{2,1,q}$: TCT^* is identical to that in Hyb_1, so $\mathsf{Hyb}_{2,1,q} \approx \mathsf{Hyb}_1$. With the following two indistinguishable hybrids, finally we have $\mathsf{Hyb}_{2,1,q} \approx \mathsf{Hyb}_{2,3,q-1}$.
  - $\mathsf{Hyb}_{2,2,q}$: TCT^* is identical to that in $\mathsf{Hyb}_{2,1,q}$, so $\mathsf{Hyb}_{2,1,q} \approx \mathsf{Hyb}_{2,2,q}$.
  - $\mathsf{Hyb}_{2,3,q}$: TCT^* is identical to that in $\mathsf{Hyb}_{2,2,q}$, so $\mathsf{Hyb}_{2,2,q} \approx \mathsf{Hyb}_{2,3,q}$.
- Hyb_3: $\mathrm{TCT}^* = ([\mathbf{d}^\top(\mathbf{A}\mathbf{s} + \hat{s}\mathbf{b}^\perp)]_T \cdot \mathsf{msg}_b, [-\beta \mathbf{d}^\top(\mathbf{A}\mathbf{s} + \hat{s}\mathbf{b}^\perp)]_T)$. Note that if $\hat{s}$ is uniformly random, then so is to $\mathbf{A}\mathbf{s} + \hat{s}\mathbf{b}^\perp$. Hence, TCT^* is identically distributed to that in $\mathsf{Hyb}_{2,3,Q}$, and $\mathsf{Hyb}_{2,3,Q} \approx \mathsf{Hyb}_3$.
- Group-II hybrids for $q = 1, \ldots, Q$:
  - $\mathsf{Hyb}_{4,1,q}$: TCT^* is identical to that in Hyb_3, so $\mathsf{Hyb}_{4,1,q} \approx \mathsf{Hyb}_3$. With the following two indistinguishable hybrids, finally we have $\mathsf{Hyb}_{4,1,q} \approx \mathsf{Hyb}_{4,3,q-1}$.
  - $\mathsf{Hyb}_{4,2,q}$: $\mathrm{TCT}^* = ([\mathbf{d}^\top(\mathbf{A}\mathbf{s} + \hat{s}\mathbf{b}^\perp)]_T \cdot \mathsf{msg}_b, [-\beta \mathbf{d}^\top(\mathbf{A}\mathbf{s} + \hat{s}\mathbf{b}^\perp)) - \beta\alpha\mathbf{a}^\perp\hat{s}\mathbf{b}^\perp]_T)$. Note that the extra component $\beta\alpha\mathbf{a}^\perp\hat{s}\mathbf{b}^\perp$ results in the simulator producing an incorrect correlation between TK^* and CT^*. Nevertheless, the last component of TCT^* is blinded by a random factor $\beta \xleftarrow{\$} \mathbb{Z}_p^*$. Since the adversary cannot query the corresponding $\mathrm{RK}^* = \beta$, this correlation remains hidden from the point of view of the adversary. Hence, $\mathsf{Hyb}_{4,1,q} \approx \mathsf{Hyb}_{4,2,q}$.
  - $\mathsf{Hyb}_{4,3,q}$: TCT^* is the same as $\mathsf{Hyb}_{4,2,q}$. Hence, $\mathsf{Hyb}_{4,2,q} \approx \mathsf{Hyb}_{4,3,q}$.
- Hyb_5: $\mathrm{TCT}^* = ([\mathbf{d}^\top(\mathbf{A}\mathbf{s} + \hat{s}\mathbf{b}^\perp)]_T \cdot \mathsf{msg}^\star, [-\beta \mathbf{d}^\top(\mathbf{A}\mathbf{s} + \hat{s}\mathbf{b}^\perp)) - \beta\alpha\mathbf{a}^\perp\hat{s}\mathbf{b}^\perp]_T)$. $\mathsf{Hyb}_{4,3,Q} \approx \mathsf{Hyb}_5$ can be proved in a manner similar to $\mathsf{Hyb}_{4,1,q} \approx \mathsf{Hyb}_{4,2,q}$.

Finally, Hyb_0 is indistinguishable from Hyb_5 that contains no information about the messages submitted by the adversary, proving the argument. This completes the proof.

5 An OD-CP-ABE Scheme with Full CCA Security

Before giving our fully CCA-secure OD-CP-ABE scheme, we would like to present some intuitions. The main idea to realize CCA security for public key encryption is to allow the decryptor to have the ability to check the validity of the ciphertext. In our scheme, we apply the FO transformation [16] on the basic scheme to make the transformed ciphertext checkable. The user can recover the randomness used in the encryption and then execute re-encryption to check the validity. However, it is noteworthy that the scheme is *privately checkable* and hence not efficient. In the decryption phase, the user should download the original ciphertext and compare it with the re-encryption result. Thus the communication and computation overhead is proportional to the complexity of the access policy. Though it achieves CCA security, the outsourced decryption mechanism is meaningless. To solve this problem, we outsource some parts of the verification to the proxy in our scheme. Specifically, we use the "Encryption + Proof of Knowledge" construction [1,34] to make the original ciphertext *publicly checkable*. A (non-interactive) zero knowledge proof of knowledge is attached behind the ciphertext, to prove the ciphertext is well-formed. Hence, we can achieve CCA security without efficiency compromise during decryption.

5.1 Σ-protocol Used in the Schemes

We describe a Σ-protocol for proving that a tuple (A, B, C, D) is of the following relation. The relation is similar to the discrete logarithm equality [9].

$$\mathcal{R} = \{(x, w) \mid x = (p, \mathbb{G}_1, \mathbb{G}_2, H_1, H_2, h, P, Q, A, B, C, D), w = (s_1, s_2), \\ A = H_1^{s_1}, B = H_2^{s_2}, C = h^{s_1+s_2}, D = P^{s_1}Q^{s_2}\},$$

where it is to be understood that p is the prime order of groups $\mathbb{G}_1$ and $\mathbb{G}_2$, that $H_1, H_2, h, A, B, C \in \mathbb{G}_2$, that $P, Q, D \in \mathbb{G}_1$ and that $s_1, s_2 \in \mathbb{Z}_p^*$. Note that the relation $\mathcal{R}$ involving two groups $\mathbb{G}_1$ and $\mathbb{G}_2$ is non-trivial to verify, even with the help of the bilinear map bilinearity $e(g^a, h^b) = e(g, h)^{ab}$.

The Σ-protocol $\pi_{\mathcal{R}}$ works as follows:

1. $\mathcal{P}$ chooses $u_1, u_2 \xleftarrow{\$} \mathbb{Z}_p^*$, computes and sends the following values to $\mathcal{V}$.
$$U_1 = H_1^{u_1}, \quad U_2 = H_2^{u_2}, \quad U_3 = h^{u_1+u_2}, \quad U_4 = P^{u_1}Q^{u_2}.$$
2. $\mathcal{V}$ chooses $c \xleftarrow{\$} \mathbb{Z}_p^*$ and sends it to $\mathcal{P}$.
3. $\mathcal{P}$ computes $z_1 = cs_1 + u_1, z_2 = cs_2 + u_2$ and sends them to $\mathcal{V}$. $\mathcal{V}$ accepts if the following hold, else it rejects:
$$H_1^{z_1} = A^c U_1, \quad H_2^{z_2} = B^c U_2, \quad h^{z_1+z_2} = C^c U_3, \quad P^{z_1}Q^{z_2} = D^c U_4.$$

Theorem 2. *$\pi_{\mathcal{R}}$ is an honest verifier zero knowledge proof of knowledge of $w = (s_1, s_2)$ for $(x, w) \in \mathcal{R}$, under the discrete log assumption in $\mathbb{G}_1$ and $\mathbb{G}_2$.*

Proof. We prove the properties of the three-move protocol $\pi_{\mathcal{R}}$.

1. Correctness: This protocol is obviously complete. If the prover truly does know the witness $w = (s_1, s_2)$, then
$$\begin{aligned} H_1^{z_1} &= H_1^{cs_1+u_1} = (H_1^{s_1})^c H_1^{u_1} = A^c U_1, \\ H_2^{z_2} &= H_2^{cs_2+u_2} = (H_2^{s_2})^c H_2^{u_2} = B^c U_2, \\ h^{z_1+z_2} &= h^{cs_1+u_1} h^{cs_2+u_2} = (h^{s_1+s_2})^c h^{u_1+u_2} = C^c U_3, \\ P^{z_1}Q^{z_2} &= P^{cs_1+u_1}Q^{cs_2+u_2} = (P^{s_1}Q^{s_2})^c (P^{u_1}Q^{u_2}) = D^c U_4. \end{aligned}$$
So the verifier's test of acceptance is valid.

2. Special soundness: The extractor interacts with the prover, which is on the same random tape, to obtain two convincing transcripts $(U_1, U_2, U_3, U_4, c, z_1, z_2)$ and $(U_1, U_2, U_3, U_4, c', z'_1, z'_2)$, where $z_1 = cs_1 + u_1, z_2 = cs_2 + u_2, z'_1 = c's_1 + u_1, z'_2 = c's_2 + u_2$. Then it can extract the witness
$$s_1 = (z_1 - z'_1)/(c - c'), \quad s_2 = (z_2 - z'_2)/(c - c').$$
3. Special honest verifier zero knowledge: The simulator takes $(p, \mathbb{G}_1, \mathbb{G}_2, H_1, H_2, h, P, Q, A, B, C, D)$ and a random c as input. It outputs a transcript by sampling $z_1, z_2 \xleftarrow{\$} \mathbb{Z}_p^*$, and computing
$$U_1 = H_1^{z_1} A^{-c}, \quad U_2 = H_2^{z_2} B^{-c}, \quad U_3 = h^{z_1+z_2} C^{-c}, \quad U_4 = P^{z_1} Q^{z_2} D^{-c}.$$
The simulated transcript is accepting by inspection, and its proof elements are uniformly random, matching the distribution in a real proof.

AND Composition. In our OD-ABE schemes, all attribute components of the ciphertext should be proved well-formed. It is easy to construct a Σ-protocol for an "AND" compound relation of some $n \in \mathbb{N}$: $\mathcal{R} = \{(x, w) \mid x = (p, \mathbb{G}_1, \mathbb{G}_2, H_1, H_2, h, P_i, Q_i, A, B, C, D_i), w = (s_1, s_2), A = H_1^{s_1}, B = H_2^{s_2}, C = h^{s_1+s_2}, D_i = P_i^{s_1} Q_i^{s_2}, i \in [n]\}$. Simply have $\mathcal{P}$ prove all in parallel with a single challenge c.

Applying Fiat-Shamir Heuristic [15]. The protocol can be transformed into a non-interactive one. $\mathcal{P}$ hashes $(H_1, H_2, h, P, Q, A, B, C, D, U_1, U_2, U_3, U_4)$ to obtain the challenge c, then computes z_1, z_2. The proof is (c, z_1, z_2). To verify, $\mathcal{V}$ reconstructs $(\widetilde{U}_1, \widetilde{U}_2, \widetilde{U}_3, \widetilde{U}_4)$ and checks that hashing $(H_1, H_2, h, P, Q, A, B, C, D, \widetilde{U}_1, \widetilde{U}_2, \widetilde{U}_3, \widetilde{U}_4)$ yields c.

5.2 Construction

Next, we propose the OD-CP-ABE construction. The **Setup** and **KeyGen** algorithms operate exactly as in the basic scheme, except that the public parameters also include the description of a key derivation function $\mathcal{KDF} : \mathbb{G}_T \to \{0,1\}^k$ and two one-way collision-resistant cryptographic hash functions $\mathcal{H}_2 : \mathbb{G}_T \times \{0,1\}^k \times \{1,2\} \to \mathbb{Z}_p^*$, $\mathcal{H}_3 : \{0,1\}^* \to \mathbb{Z}_p^*$. The remaining algorithms are as follows:

- **Encrypt**($\mathsf{msg} \in \{0,1\}^k, \mathbb{A} = (\mathbf{M}, \pi)$). Choose $\mathsf{ran} \xleftarrow{\$} \mathbb{G}_T, u_1, u_2 \xleftarrow{\$} \mathbb{Z}_p^*$ and compute
$$s_1 = \mathcal{H}_2(\mathsf{ran}, \mathsf{msg}, 1), \qquad s_2 = \mathcal{H}_2(\mathsf{ran}, \mathsf{msg}, 2),$$
$$C_r = T_1^{s_1} \cdot T_2^{s_2} \cdot \mathsf{ran}, \qquad C_m = \mathcal{KDF}(\mathsf{ran}) \oplus \mathsf{msg},$$
$$C_0 = (H_1^{s_1}, H_2^{s_2}, h^{s_1+s_2}), \qquad U_0 = (H_1^{u_1}, H_2^{u_2}, h^{u_1+u_2}).$$

Suppose $\mathbf{M}$ has n_1 rows and n_2 columns. For $i \in [n_1]$ and $l \in [3]$, compute

$$P_{i,l} = \mathcal{H}_1(\pi(i)l1) \cdot \prod_{j=1}^{n_2} \mathcal{H}_1(0jl1)^{\mathbf{M}_{i,j}}, \quad Q_{i,l} = \mathcal{H}_1(\pi(i)l2) \cdot \prod_{j=1}^{n_2} \mathcal{H}_1(0jl2)^{\mathbf{M}_{i,j}},$$

$$C_{i,l} = P_{i,l}^{s_1} \cdot Q_{i,l}^{s_2}, \qquad U_{i,l} = P_{i,l}^{u_1} \cdot Q_{i,l}^{u_2}.$$

Compute $c = \mathcal{H}_3(H_1, H_2, h, C_0, U_0, \{P_i, Q_i, C_i, U_i\}_{i\in[n_1]})$ and $z_1 = cs_1 + u_1$, $z_2 = cs_2 + u_2$. Output $\mathrm{CT} = (\mathbb{A}, C_r, C_m, C_0, \{C_i\}_{i\in[n_1]}, c, z_1, z_2)$.

- **Transform**(TK, CT). If $f(\mathcal{S}, \mathbb{A}) = 0$, output $\perp$. Otherwise, check the validity of CT as follows:
  1. According to $\mathbb{A}$, for $i \in [n_1]$ and $l \in [3]$, compute $P_{i,l}$, $Q_{i,l}$ and
  $$\widetilde{U}_0 = (H_1^{z_1} \cdot C_{0,1}^{-c}, H_2^{z_2} \cdot C_{0,2}^{-c}, h^{z_1+z_2} \cdot C_{0,3}^{-c}), \quad \widetilde{U}_{i,l} = P_{i,l}^{z_1} \cdot Q_{i,l}^{z_2} \cdot C_{i,l}^{-c}.$$
  2. If $c \neq \mathcal{H}_3(H_1, H_2, h, C_0, \widetilde{U}_0, \{P_i, Q_i, C_i, \widetilde{U}_i\}_{i\in[n_1]})$, output $\perp$.

  Compute constants $\{\gamma_i\}_{i\in I}$ that satisfy $\sum_{i\in I} \gamma_i \mathbf{M}_i = (1, 0, \ldots, 0)$ and
  $$\mathsf{num} = \prod_{l\in[3]} e(\prod_{i\in I} C_{i,l}^{\gamma_i}, K_{0,l}), \quad \mathsf{den} = \prod_{l\in[3]} e(K_{1,l} \cdot \prod_{i\in I} K_{\pi(i),l}^{\gamma_i}, C_{0,l}).$$
  Output $\mathrm{TCT} = (C_r, C_m, C_{0,1}, C_{0,2}, \mathsf{kem} = \mathsf{num}/\mathsf{den})$.
- **Decrypt**(RK, TCT). Compute $\mathsf{ran} = C_r \cdot \mathsf{kem}^{1/\beta}$, $\mathsf{msg} = C_m \oplus \mathcal{KDF}(\mathsf{ran})$, $s_1 = \mathcal{H}_2(\mathsf{ran}, \mathsf{msg}, 1)$, $s_2 = \mathcal{H}_2(\mathsf{ran}, \mathsf{msg}, 2)$. If $C_r = T_1^{s_1} \cdot T_2^{s_2} \cdot \mathsf{ran}$, $\mathsf{kem} = (T_1^{s_1} \cdot T_2^{s_2})^{-\beta}$, $C_{0,1} = H_1^{s_1}$ and $C_{0,2} = H_2^{s_2}$, output msg. Otherwise, $\perp$.

Correctness. By the correctness of $\pi_{\mathcal{R}}$, FAME [2] and the scheme in [19], we have if $f(\mathcal{S}, \mathbb{A}) = 1$, decryption recovers the correct message with probability 1.

Theorem 3. *The proposed OD-CP-ABE scheme is fully CCA-secure under the DLIN assumption on asymmetric pairing groups in the random oracle model.*

5.3 Security Analysis

Proof. Assume there is a PPT adversary $\mathcal{A}$ that can attack the OD-CP-ABE scheme in the full CCA security model with non-negligible probability. We can construct a PPT algorithm $\mathcal{B}$ to attack the basic scheme in the full CPA security model with non-negligible probability.

Setup. $\mathcal{B}$ receives the public parameters $\mathrm{PK} = (\mathsf{par}, \mathcal{H}_1, H_1, H_2, T_1, T_2)$ from the challenger $\mathcal{C}$ of the basic scheme, and returns them to $\mathcal{A}$.

Phase 1. $\mathcal{B}$ initializes an empty table $\mathcal{T}$, three empty lists $\mathcal{L}_1, \mathcal{L}_2, \mathcal{L}_3$, an empty set $\mathcal{D}$ and an integer $j = 0$. It answers the queries from $\mathcal{A}$ as follows:

- **Random Oracle** $\mathcal{KDF}(\mathsf{ran})$: If there is an entry (ran, r) in $\mathcal{L}_1$, $\mathcal{B}$ returns r. Otherwise, it choose $r \xleftarrow{\$} \{0,1\}^k$, records (ran, r) in $\mathcal{L}_1$ and returns r.

- **Random Oracle** $\mathcal{H}_2(\mathsf{ran}, \mathsf{msg}, t)$ for $t \in [2]$: If there is an entry $(\mathsf{ran}, \mathsf{msg}, t, s_t)$ in $\mathcal{L}_2$, $\mathcal{B}$ returns s_t. Otherwise, it chooses $s_t \xleftarrow{\$} \mathbb{Z}_p^*$, records $(\mathsf{ran}, \mathsf{msg}, t, s_t)$ in $\mathcal{L}_2$ and returns s_t.
- **Random Oracle** $\mathcal{H}_3(\mathsf{string})$: If there is an entry (string, c) in $\mathcal{L}_3$, $\mathcal{B}$ returns c. Otherwise, it chooses $c \xleftarrow{\$} \mathbb{Z}_p^*$, records (string, c) in $\mathcal{L}_3$ and returns c.
- **Create**$(\mathcal{S})$: $\mathcal{B}$ sets $j = j + 1$. It retransmits **Create**$(\mathcal{S})$ to $\mathcal{C}$ to obtain TK as the return, and stores the entry $(j, \mathcal{S}, \mathrm{TK})$ in table $\mathcal{T}$.
- **Corrupt**(i): $\mathcal{B}$ retrieves the ith entry $(i, \mathcal{S}, \mathrm{TK})$ in table $\mathcal{T}$. It retransmits **Corrupt**(i) to $\mathcal{C}$ to obtain RK as the return, and sets $\mathcal{D} := \mathcal{D} \cup \{\mathcal{S}\}$.
- **Decrypt.CT**(i, CT): $\mathcal{B}$ parses $\mathrm{CT} = (\mathbb{A}, C_r, C_m, C_0, \{C_i\}_{i\in[n_1]}, c, z_1, z_2)$ and acts as follows:
  1. $\mathcal{B}$ retrieves the ith entry $(i, \mathcal{S}, \mathrm{TK})$ in $\mathcal{T}$. If $f(\mathcal{S}, \mathbb{A}) = 0$, it returns $\perp$.
  2. $\mathcal{B}$ checks the validity of CT as in the **Transform** algorithm. If it does not pass, $\mathcal{B}$ returns $\perp$.
  3. $\mathcal{B}$ searches the pairs (ran, r) in $\mathcal{L}_1$ and $(\mathsf{ran}, \mathsf{msg}, 1, s_1), (\mathsf{ran}, \mathsf{msg}, 2, s_2)$ in $\mathcal{L}_2$. These pairs should satisfy $C_r = T_1^{s_1} \cdot T_2^{s_2} \cdot \mathsf{ran}$, $C_m = r \oplus \mathsf{msg}$, $C_{0,1} = H_1^{s_1}$ and $C_{0,2} = H_2^{s_2}$. If zero matches are found, it returns $\perp$. If more than one matches are found, it aborts the simulation. Otherwise, it returns msg.
- **Decrypt.TCT**(i, TCT): $\mathcal{B}$ parses $\mathrm{TCT} = (C_r, C_m, C_{0,1}, C_{0,2}, \mathsf{kem})$ and acts as follows:
  1. $\mathcal{B}$ retrieves the ith entry $(i, \mathcal{S}, \mathrm{TK})$ in $\mathcal{T}$. If $f(\mathcal{S}, \mathbb{A}) = 0$, it returns $\perp$.
  2. $\mathcal{B}$ searches the pairs (ran, r) in $\mathcal{L}_1$ and $(\mathsf{ran}, \mathsf{msg}, 1, s_1), (\mathsf{ran}, \mathsf{msg}, 2, s_2)$ in $\mathcal{L}_2$. These pairs should satisfy $C_r = T_1^{s_1} \cdot T_2^{s_2} \cdot \mathsf{ran}$, $C_m = r \oplus \mathsf{msg}$, $C_{0,1} = H_1^{s_1}$ and $C_{0,2} = H_2^{s_2}$. If zero matches are found, it returns $\perp$. If more than one matches are found, it aborts the simulation.
  3. $\mathcal{B}$ checks the validity of TCT as follows. It randomly chooses a message $\mathsf{msg}' \xleftarrow{\$} \mathbb{G}_T$ and an access structure $\mathbb{A}'$ such that $f(\mathcal{S}, \mathbb{A}') = 1$. It runs **Encrypt**$(\mathsf{msg}', \mathbb{A}')$ with the randomness (s_1, s_2) in the previous step to obtain CT' and runs **Transform**$(\mathrm{TK}, \mathrm{CT}')$ to obtain $\mathrm{TCT}' = (\cdot, \cdot, \cdot, \cdot, \mathsf{kem}')$. If $\mathsf{kem} \neq \mathsf{kem}'$, it returns $\perp$. Otherwise, it returns msg.

Challenge. $\mathcal{A}$ submits two equal length messages $\mathsf{msg}_0^*, \mathsf{msg}_1^*$ from the message space $\{0,1\}^k$ and an access structure $\mathbb{A}^*$. $\mathcal{B}$ acts as follows:

1. $\mathcal{B}$ chooses random "messages" $\mathsf{ran}_0, \mathsf{ran}_1 \xleftarrow{\$} \mathbb{G}_T$ and passes $(\mathsf{ran}_0, \mathsf{ran}_1, \mathbb{A}^*)$ on to $\mathcal{C}$ to obtain $\mathrm{CT} = (\mathbb{A}^*, C_r^*, C_0^*, \{C_i^*\}_{i\in[n_1]})$.
2. $\mathcal{B}$ chooses $c^*, z_1^*, z_2^* \xleftarrow{\$} \mathbb{Z}_p^*$ and computes $U_0 = (H_1^{z_1^*} C_{0,1}^{*-c^*}, H_2^{z_2^*} C_{0,2}^{*-c^*}, h^{z_1^*+z_2^*} C_{0,3}^{*-c^*})$. According to $\mathbb{A}^*$, for $i \in [n_1]$ and $l \in [3]$, it computes $P_{i,l}$, $Q_{i,l}$ and $U_{i,l} = P_{i,l}^{z_1^*} Q_{i,l}^{z_2^*} C_{i,l}^{*-c^*}$. It records $((H_1, H_2, h, C_0, U_0, \{P_i, Q_i, C_i, U_i\}_{i\in[n_1]}), c^*)$ in $\mathcal{L}_3$.
3. $\mathcal{B}$ chooses a random value $C_m^* \xleftarrow{\$} \{0,1\}^k$ and returns $\mathrm{CT}^* = (\mathbb{A}^*, C_r^*, C_m^*, C_0^*, \{C_i^*\}_{i\in[n_1]}, c^*, z_1^*, z_2^*)$.

Phase 2. Almost the same as Phase 1, but with the specified restrictions. Besides, for a query **Decrypt.CT**(i, CT) from $\mathcal{A}$, $\mathcal{B}$ parses $\mathrm{CT} = (\mathbb{A}, C_r, C_m, C_0, \{C_i\}_{i\in[n_1]}, c, z_1, z_2)$ and acts as follows:

1. $\mathcal{B}$ retrieves the ith entry $(i, \mathcal{S}, \mathrm{TK})$ in $\mathcal{T}$. If $f(\mathcal{S}, \mathbb{A}) = 0$, it returns $\perp$.
2. $\mathcal{B}$ checks the validity of CT as in the **Transform** algorithm. If it does not pass, $\mathcal{B}$ returns $\perp$.
3. If $(C_r, C_m, C_{0,1}, C_{0,2}) \neq (C_r^*, C_m^*, C_{0,1}^*, C_{0,2}^*)$, $\mathcal{B}$ searches the pairs (ran, r) in $\mathcal{L}_1$ and $(\mathsf{ran}, \mathsf{msg}, 1, s_1), (\mathsf{ran}, \mathsf{msg}, 2, s_2)$ in $\mathcal{L}_2$. These pairs should satisfy $C_r = T_1^{s_1} \cdot T_2^{s_2} \cdot \mathsf{ran}$, $C_m = r \oplus \mathsf{msg}$, $C_{0,1} = H_1^{s_1}$ and $C_{0,2} = H_2^{s_2}$. If zero matches are found, it returns $\perp$. If more than one matches are found, it aborts the simulation. Otherwise, it returns msg.
4. Else, $(C_r, C_m, C_{0,1}, C_{0,2}) = (C_r^*, C_m^*, C_{0,1}^*, C_{0,2}^*)$. Then we must have $(C_{0,3}, \{C_i\}_{i\in[n_1]}, c, z_1, z_2) \neq (C_{0,3}^*, \{C_i^*\}_{i\in[n_1]}, c^*, z_1^*, z_2^*)$. $\mathcal{B}$ rewinds $\mathcal{A}$ to obtain the witnesses (s_1^*, s_2^*). If $\mathsf{ran}_0 = T_1^{s_1^*} \cdot T_2^{s_2^*}$, $\mathcal{B}$ halts the simulation and outputs 0 as the final guess. Otherwise, it halts and outputs 1.

Guess. Eventually, $\mathcal{A}$ must either output a bit or abort, either way $\mathcal{B}$ ignores it. Next, $\mathcal{B}$ searches through lists $\mathcal{L}_1$ and $\mathcal{L}_2$ to see if the values ran_0 or ran_1 appear as the first element of any entry, i.e., that $\mathcal{A}$ issued a query of the form $\mathcal{KDF}(\mathsf{ran}_b)$ or $\mathcal{H}_2(\mathsf{ran}_b, \cdot, \cdot)$. If neither or both values appear, $\mathcal{B}$ outputs a random bit as its guess. If only value ran_b appears, $\mathcal{B}$ outputs b as its guess.

It is clear that from the view of $\mathcal{A}$, the above simulation is indistinguishable from the real experiment. According to the analysis in [16], the simulation will abort with a negligible probability. Therefore, we obtain the theorem.

6 An OD-KP-ABE Scheme with Full CCA Security

At last, we propose a key-policy attribute-based encryption with outsourced decryption (OD-KP-ABE) based on the KP-ABE scheme in [2] as follows:

- **Setup**$(\lambda, \mathcal{U})$. Same as that of OD-CP-ABE.
- **KeyGen**$(\mathrm{MSK}, \mathbb{A} = (\mathbf{M}, \pi))$. Choose $r_1, r_2, \beta \xleftarrow{\$} \mathbb{Z}_p^*$ and compute $K_0 = (h^{\beta b_1 r_1}, h^{\beta b_2 r_2}, h^{\beta(r_1+r_2)})$. Suppose $\mathbf{M}$ has n_1 rows and n_2 columns. Choose $\sigma'_2, \ldots, \sigma'_{n_2} \xleftarrow{\$} \mathbb{Z}_p^*$. For $i \in [n_1]$ and $t \in [2]$, choose $\sigma_i \xleftarrow{\$} \mathbb{Z}_p^*$ and compute

$$K_{i,t} = [\mathcal{H}_1(\pi(i)1t) \cdot \prod_{j=2}^{n_2} \mathcal{H}_1(0j1t)^{\mathbf{M}_{i,j}}]^{\frac{\beta b_1 r_1}{a_t}} \cdot [\mathcal{H}_1(\pi(i)2t) \cdot \prod_{j=2}^{n_2} \mathcal{H}_1(0j2t)^{\mathbf{M}_{i,j}}]^{\frac{\beta b_2 r_2}{a_t}} \cdot$$
$$[\mathcal{H}_1(\pi(i)3t) \cdot \prod_{j=2}^{n_2} \mathcal{H}_1(0j3t)^{\mathbf{M}_{i,j}}]^{\frac{\beta(r_1+r_2)}{a_t}} \cdot g^{\frac{\beta\sigma_i}{a_t}} \cdot g^{\beta d_t \mathbf{M}_{i,1}} \cdot \prod_{j=2}^{n_2} g^{\frac{\beta\sigma'_j}{a_t}\mathbf{M}_{i,j}}$$

$$K_{i,3} = g^{-\beta\sigma_i} \cdot g^{\beta d_3 \mathbf{M}_{i,1}} \cdot \prod_{j=2}^{n_2} g^{-\beta\sigma'_j \mathbf{M}_{i,j}}$$

Output $\mathrm{TK} = (\mathbb{A}, K_0, \{K_i\}_{i\in[n_1]})$, $\mathrm{RK} = \beta$.

- **Encrypt**(msg $\in \{0,1\}^k, \mathcal{S}$). Choose ran $\xleftarrow{\$} \mathbb{G}_T, u_1, u_2 \xleftarrow{\$} \mathbb{Z}_p^*$ and compute

$$s_1 = \mathcal{H}_2(\mathsf{ran}, \mathsf{msg}, 1), \qquad s_2 = \mathcal{H}_2(\mathsf{ran}, \mathsf{msg}, 2),$$
$$C_r = T_1^{s_1} \cdot T_2^{s_2} \cdot \mathsf{ran}, \qquad C_m = \mathcal{KDF}(\mathsf{ran}) \oplus \mathsf{msg},$$
$$C_0 = (H_1^{s_1}, H_2^{s_2}, h^{s_1+s_2}), \qquad U_0 = (H_1^{u_1}, H_2^{u_2}, h^{u_1+u_2}).$$

For all $y \in \mathcal{S}$ and $l \in [3]$, compute

$$P_{y,l} = \mathcal{H}_1(yl1), \quad Q_{y,l} = \mathcal{H}_1(yl2), \quad C_{y,l} = P_{y,l}^{s_1} \cdot Q_{y,l}^{s_2}, \quad U_{y,l} = P_{y,l}^{u_1} \cdot Q_{y,l}^{u_2}.$$

Compute $c = \mathcal{H}_3(H_1, H_2, h, C_0, U_0, \{P_y, Q_y, C_y, U_y\}_{y \in \mathcal{S}})$ and $z_1 = cs_1 + u_1$, $z_2 = cs_2 + u_2$. Output $\mathrm{CT} = (\mathcal{S}, C_r, C_m, C_0, \{C_y\}_{y\in\mathcal{S}}, c, z_1, z_2)$.
- **Transform**(TK, CT). Same as that of OD-CP-ABE except that for any $i \in I$, $C_{\pi(i)}$ is used to compute num and K_i to compute den. Also, note that there is no K_1 component in TK.
- **Decrypt**(RK, TCT). Same as that of OD-CP-ABE.

Correctness and security of this scheme can be proved in a manner very similar to that of the proposed OD-CP-ABE scheme.

7 Performance Evaluations

We give both theoretical and experimental analyses of the proposed OD-CP-ABE scheme, and compare it with the underlying ABE scheme FAME [2]. For consistency in the comparison, we use FAME as a key encapsulation mechanism (KEM), and the message to be encrypted is an element in $\mathbb{G}_T$.

7.1 Theoretical Analysis

Computation Cost Comparison. Table 1 shows the computation cost comparison of OD-CP-ABE with FAME. We only consider the modular exponentiation and pairing computation since they are significantly more expensive than other operations [20]. Compared with FAME, the encryption algorithm of OD-CP-ABE additionally generates a proof of knowledge, whose computation cost is almost the same as that of generating an ABE ciphertext. In the decryption of FAME, there are 6 pairing computations and the number of modular exponentiation grows linearly with the complexity of the access policy. While in OD-CP-ABE, most operations are offloaded to the proxy in the transformation algorithm, leaving only 6 exponentiations in the decryption.

Communication Cost Comparison. Table 2 compares the communication cost of OD-CP-ABE with FAME. Compared with FAME, the original ciphertext of OD-CP-ABE contains 3 more elements in $\mathbb{Z}_p$ for the proof of knowledge, which is quite shorter than the size of an ABE ciphertext. In the decryption phase, FAME needs to transmit all ciphertext parts used in decryption, the number of which is proportional to the complexity of the access policy. While in OD-CP-ABE, the transformed ciphertext is transmitted with constant size of 2 elements in $\mathbb{G}_2$ and 3 elements in $\mathbb{G}_T$.

Table 1. Computation cost comparison[a]

Schemes	Encryption	Transformation	Decryption
FAME [2]	$6n_1E_1 + 3E_2 + 2E_T$	$\times$	$6\|I\|E_1 + 6P$
OD-CP-ABE	$12n_1E_1 + 6E_2 + 2E_T$	$(6\|I\| + 9n_1)E_1 + 6E_2 + 6P$	$2E_2 + 4E_T$

[a] E_1, E_2, E_T and P denote a modular exponentiation in $\mathbb{G}_1$, $\mathbb{G}_2$, $\mathbb{G}_T$ and a pairing computation, respectively. n_1 and $|I|$ indicate the number of rows of $\mathbf{M}$ and the number of attributes used in decryption, respectively.

Table 2. Communication cost comparison[b]

Schemes	Transfer size during encryption	Transfer size during decryption
FAME [2]	$3n_1\|\mathbb{G}_1\| + 3\|\mathbb{G}_2\| + 2\|\mathbb{G}_T\|$	$3\|I\|\|\mathbb{G}_1\| + 3\|\mathbb{G}_2\| + 2\|\mathbb{G}_T\|$
OD-CP-ABE	$3\|\mathbb{Z}_p\| + 3n_1\|\mathbb{G}_1\| + 3\|\mathbb{G}_2\| + 2\|\mathbb{G}_T\|$	$2\|\mathbb{G}_2\| + 3\|\mathbb{G}_T\|$

[b] $|\mathbb{Z}_p|$, $|\mathbb{G}_1|$, $|\mathbb{G}_2|$ and $|\mathbb{G}_T|$ denote the size of an element in $\mathbb{Z}_p$, $\mathbb{G}_1$, $\mathbb{G}_2$ and $\mathbb{G}_T$, respectively. n_1 and $|I|$ indicate the number of rows of $\mathbf{M}$ and the number of attributes used in decryption, respectively. We omit the additive overhead in order to transmit the access structure.

7.2 Experimental Analysis

We utilize the Charm framework [3] to evaluate the practical performance of the proposed OD-CP-ABE scheme, and make a comparison with FAME. The schemes use the BN254 curve from Pairing-Based Cryptography library [28] and the HKDF implementation from OpenSSL. All running times are measured on a MacBook Pro laptop with an Intel Quad-Core i5 CPU @2.3 GHz and 8 GB RAM running macOS Catalina 10.15.6 and Python 3.7.4.

Experiment Setting. We use access policies of type (A_1 *and* A_2 *and* ... *and* A_l) as in Green et al. [19] because all the l attributes are required for decryption. We set 20 distinct policies with l increasing from 5 to 100, repeat each instance 20 times and eventually take the average. Policies are converted into MSPs according to the method in [25], and all instances are completely independent to each other. The test data to be encrypted is a random element in $\mathbb{G}_T$.

Execution Time. As depicted in Fig. 1(a) and (b), we show the time cost of algorithms. In Fig. 1(a), FAME.Encrypt Time is about 88 ms–967 ms and OD-CP-ABE.Encrypt takes almost the double time, about 158ms–1823 ms. In Fig. 1(b), FAME.Decrypt Time is always about 428 ms while OD-CP-ABE.Decrypt Time is always about 77 ms, which saves up to 82% on time. OD-CP-ABE.Transform Time is about 590 ms–1872 ms.

Transfer Size. Figure 1(c) and (d) illustrate the transfer overhead of algorithms. In Fig. 1(c), the CT size of FAME is 678–6663 bytes and that of OD-CP-ABE is a bit longer with 60 bytes in each instance. In Fig. 1(d), the transfer size of FAME during decryption is exactly the same as that during encryption, while OD-CP-ABE always takes only 802 bytes during decryption.

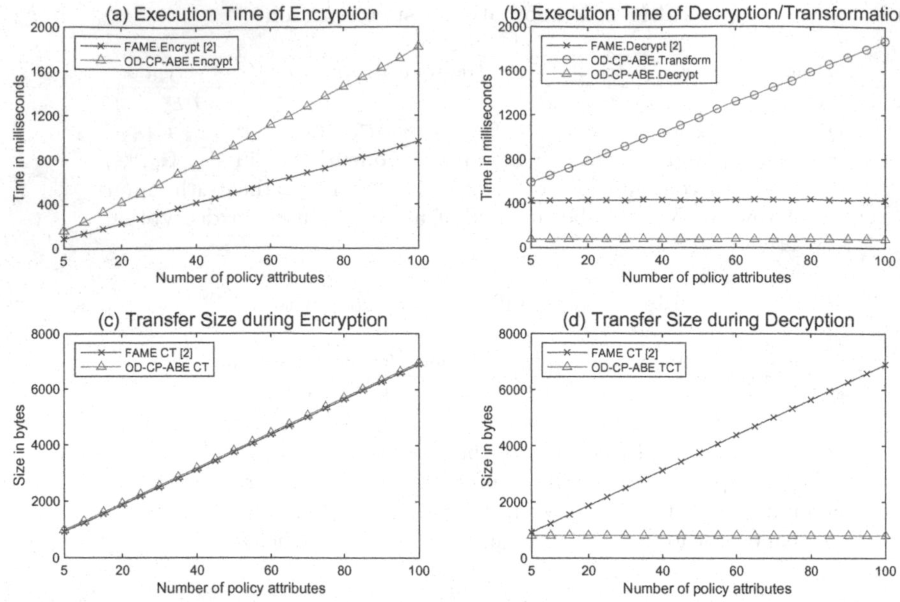

Fig. 1. Experimental results.

8 Conclusions

In this paper, we investigate the full CCA security of attribute-based encryption with outsourced decryption (OD-ABE). Particularly, we propose the full CCA security model for OD-ABE and construct fully CCA-secure OD-ABE schemes in both CP and KP setting. We make detailed performance evaluations, and the experiment results indicate that the user saves significantly on both bandwidth and time during decryption. However, the computation cost during encryption in our schemes is almost double that of the underlying ABE schemes. In the future, we will focus on designing OD-ABE with more efficient encryption.

Acknowledgements. The authors would like to thank the anonymous reviewers for their valuable comments. This work was supported in part by the National Natural Science Foundation of China (Nos. 61632020, U1936209, 62002353, 61772520, 61802392, and 61972094), in part by the Beijing Natural Science Foundation (No. 4192067), in part by the Key Research and Development Project of Zhejiang Province (Nos. 2017C01062 and 2020C01078), and in part by the Beijing Municipal Science & Technology Commission (Nos. Z191100007119007 and Z191100007119002).

References

1. Abe, M.: Securing "encryption + proof of knowledge" in the random oracle model. In: Preneel, B. (ed.) CT-RSA 2002. LNCS, vol. 2271, pp. 277–289. Springer, Heidelberg (2002). https://doi.org/10.1007/3-540-45760-7_19

2. Agrawal, S., Chase, M.: FAME: fast attribute-based message encryption. In: Proceedings of the 2017 ACM SIGSAC Conference on Computer and Communications Security, CCS 2017, pp. 665–682. ACM (2017)
3. Akinyele, J.A., et al.: Charm: a framework for rapidly prototyping cryptosystems. J. Cryptogr. Eng. **3**(2), 111–128 (2013)
4. Attrapadung, N., Libert, B., de Panafieu, E.: Expressive key-policy attribute-based encryption with constant-size ciphertexts. In: Catalano, D., Fazio, N., Gennaro, R., Nicolosi, A. (eds.) PKC 2011. LNCS, vol. 6571, pp. 90–108. Springer, Heidelberg (2011). https://doi.org/10.1007/978-3-642-19379-8_6
5. Beimel, A.: Secure schemes for secret sharing and key distribution. Ph.D. thesis, Israel Institute of Technology, Technion, Haifa, Israel (1996)
6. Bethencourt, J., Sahai, A., Waters, B.: Ciphertext-policy attribute-based encryption. In: 2007 IEEE Symposium on Security and Privacy, S&P 2007, pp. 321–334. IEEE Computer Society (2007)
7. Canetti, R., Halevi, S., Katz, J.: Chosen-ciphertext security from identity-based encryption. In: Cachin, C., Camenisch, J.L. (eds.) EUROCRYPT 2004. LNCS, vol. 3027, pp. 207–222. Springer, Heidelberg (2004). https://doi.org/10.1007/978-3-540-24676-3_13
8. Canetti, R., Krawczyk, H., Nielsen, J.B.: Relaxing chosen-ciphertext security. In: Boneh, D. (ed.) CRYPTO 2003. LNCS, vol. 2729, pp. 565–582. Springer, Heidelberg (2003). https://doi.org/10.1007/978-3-540-45146-4_33
9. Chaum, D., Pedersen, T.P.: Wallet databases with observers. In: Brickell, E.F. (ed.) CRYPTO 1992. LNCS, vol. 740, pp. 89–105. Springer, Heidelberg (1993). https://doi.org/10.1007/3-540-48071-4_7
10. Chen, J., Gay, R., Wee, H.: Improved dual system ABE in prime-order groups via predicate encodings. In: Oswald, E., Fischlin, M. (eds.) EUROCRYPT 2015, Part II. LNCS, vol. 9057, pp. 595–624. Springer, Heidelberg (2015). https://doi.org/10.1007/978-3-662-46803-6_20
11. Chen, J., Gong, J., Kowalczyk, L., Wee, H.: Unbounded ABE via bilinear entropy expansion, revisited. In: Nielsen, J.B., Rijmen, V. (eds.) EUROCRYPT 2018, Part I. LNCS, vol. 10820, pp. 503–534. Springer, Cham (2018). https://doi.org/10.1007/978-3-319-78381-9_19
12. Cheung, L., Newport, C.C.: Provably secure ciphertext policy ABE. In: Proceedings of the 2007 ACM Conference on Computer and Communications Security, CCS 2007, pp. 456–465. ACM (2007)
13. Damgård, I.: On sigma-protocols. Lectures on cryptologic protocol theory. Faculty of Science, University of Aarhus (2010)
14. Escala, A., Herold, G., Kiltz, E., Ràfols, C., Villar, J.L.: An algebraic framework for Diffie-Hellman assumptions. J. Cryptology **30**(1), 242–288 (2017)
15. Fiat, A., Shamir, A.: How to prove yourself: practical solutions to identification and signature problems. In: Odlyzko, A.M. (ed.) CRYPTO 1986. LNCS, vol. 263, pp. 186–194. Springer, Heidelberg (1987). https://doi.org/10.1007/3-540-47721-7_12
16. Fujisaki, E., Okamoto, T.: Secure integration of asymmetric and symmetric encryption schemes. J. Cryptology **26**(1), 80–101 (2013)
17. Gong, J., Wee, H.: Adaptively secure ABE for DFA from k-lin and more. In: Canteaut, A., Ishai, Y. (eds.) EUROCRYPT 2020, Part III. LNCS, vol. 12107, pp. 278–308. Springer, Cham (2020). https://doi.org/10.1007/978-3-030-45727-3_10
18. Goyal, V., Pandey, O., Sahai, A., Waters, B.: Attribute-based encryption for fine-grained access control of encrypted data. In: Proceedings of the 13th ACM Conference on Computer and Communications Security, CCS 2006, pp. 89–98. ACM (2006)

19. Green, M., Hohenberger, S., Waters, B.: Outsourcing the decryption of ABE ciphertexts. In: 20th USENIX Security Symposium. USENIX Association (2011)
20. Guillevic, A.: Comparing the pairing efficiency over composite-order and prime-order elliptic curves. In: Jacobson, M., Locasto, M., Mohassel, P., Safavi-Naini, R. (eds.) ACNS 2013. LNCS, vol. 7954, pp. 357–372. Springer, Heidelberg (2013). https://doi.org/10.1007/978-3-642-38980-1_22
21. Karchmer, M., Wigderson, A.: On span programs. In: Proceedings of the Eigth Annual Structure in Complexity Theory Conference, pp. 102–111. IEEE Computer Society (1993)
22. Kowalczyk, L., Wee, H.: Compact adaptively secure ABE for NC^1 from k-Lin. In: Ishai, Y., Rijmen, V. (eds.) EUROCRYPT 2019, Part I. LNCS, vol. 11476, pp. 3–33. Springer, Cham (2019). https://doi.org/10.1007/978-3-030-17653-2_1
23. Lewko, A., Okamoto, T., Sahai, A., Takashima, K., Waters, B.: Fully secure functional encryption: attribute-based encryption and (hierarchical) inner product encryption. In: Gilbert, H. (ed.) EUROCRYPT 2010. LNCS, vol. 6110, pp. 62–91. Springer, Heidelberg (2010). https://doi.org/10.1007/978-3-642-13190-5_4
24. Lewko, A., Waters, B.: New techniques for dual system encryption and fully secure HIBE with short ciphertexts. In: Micciancio, D. (ed.) TCC 2010. LNCS, vol. 5978, pp. 455–479. Springer, Heidelberg (2010). https://doi.org/10.1007/978-3-642-11799-2_27
25. Lewko, A., Waters, B.: Unbounded HIBE and attribute-based encryption. In: Paterson, K.G. (ed.) EUROCRYPT 2011. LNCS, vol. 6632, pp. 547–567. Springer, Heidelberg (2011). https://doi.org/10.1007/978-3-642-20465-4_30
26. Lewko, A., Waters, B.: New proof methods for attribute-based encryption: achieving full security through selective techniques. In: Safavi-Naini, R., Canetti, R. (eds.) CRYPTO 2012. LNCS, vol. 7417, pp. 180–198. Springer, Heidelberg (2012). https://doi.org/10.1007/978-3-642-32009-5_12
27. Lin, H., Luo, J.: Compact adaptively secure ABE from k-lin: beyond NC^1 and towards NL. In: Canteaut, A., Ishai, Y. (eds.) EUROCRYPT 2020, Part III. LNCS, vol. 12107, pp. 247–277. Springer, Cham (2020). https://doi.org/10.1007/978-3-030-45727-3_9
28. Lynn, B.: The pairing-based cryptography library. http://crypto.stanford.edu/pbc
29. Ma, H., Zhang, R., Wan, Z., Lu, Y., Lin, S.: Verifiable and exculpable outsourced attribute-based encryption for access control in cloud computing. IEEE Trans. Dependable Secur. Comput. **14**(6), 679–692 (2017)
30. Ma, H., Zhang, R., Yang, G., Song, Z., He, K., Xiao, Y.: Efficient fine-grained data sharing mechanism for electronic medical record systems with mobile devices. IEEE Trans. Dependable Secur. Comput. **17**(5), 1026–1038 (2020)
31. Ning, J., Cao, Z., Dong, X., Liang, K., Ma, H., Wei, L.: Auditable σ-time outsourced attribute-based encryption for access control in cloud computing. IEEE Trans. Inf. Forensics Secur. **13**(1), 94–105 (2018)
32. Ostrovsky, R., Sahai, A., Waters, B.: Attribute-based encryption with non-monotonic access structures. In: Proceedings of the 2007 ACM Conference on Computer and Communications Security, CCS 2007, pp. 195–203. ACM (2007)
33. Sahai, A., Waters, B.: Fuzzy identity-based encryption. In: Cramer, R. (ed.) EUROCRYPT 2005. LNCS, vol. 3494, pp. 457–473. Springer, Heidelberg (2005). https://doi.org/10.1007/11426639_27
34. Shoup, V., Gennaro, R.: Securing threshold cryptosystems against chosen ciphertext attack. J. Cryptology **15**(2), 75–96 (2002)

35. Wang, T., Ma, H., Zhou, Y., Zhang, R., Song, Z.: Fully accountable data sharing for pay-as-you-go cloud scenes. IEEE Trans. Dependable Secur. Comput. https://doi.org/10.1109/TDSC.2019.2947579
36. Waters, B.: Dual system encryption: realizing fully secure IBE and HIBE under simple assumptions. In: Halevi, S. (ed.) CRYPTO 2009. LNCS, vol. 5677, pp. 619–636. Springer, Heidelberg (2009). https://doi.org/10.1007/978-3-642-03356-8_36
37. Waters, B.: Ciphertext-policy attribute-based encryption: an expressive, efficient, and provably secure realization. In: Catalano, D., Fazio, N., Gennaro, R., Nicolosi, A. (eds.) PKC 2011. LNCS, vol. 6571, pp. 53–70. Springer, Heidelberg (2011). https://doi.org/10.1007/978-3-642-19379-8_4
38. Yamada, S., Attrapadung, N., Hanaoka, G., Kunihiro, N.: Generic constructions for chosen-ciphertext secure attribute based encryption. In: Catalano, D., Fazio, N., Gennaro, R., Nicolosi, A. (eds.) PKC 2011. LNCS, vol. 6571, pp. 71–89. Springer, Heidelberg (2011). https://doi.org/10.1007/978-3-642-19379-8_5
39. Zuo, C., Shao, J., Wei, G., Xie, M., Ji, M.: Chosen ciphertext secure attribute-based encryption with outsourced decryption. In: Liu, J.K., Steinfeld, R. (eds.) ACISP 2016 Part I. LNCS, vol. 9722, pp. 495–508. Springer, Cham (2016). https://doi.org/10.1007/978-3-319-40253-6_30

An Efficient CCA-Secure Access Control Encryption for Any Policy

Gaosheng Tan[1,2], Rui Zhang[1,2(✉)], Hui Ma[1], and Yang Tao[1]

[1] State Key Laboratory of Information Security (SKLOIS), Institute of Information Engineering (IIE), Chinese Academy of Sciences (CAS), Beijing 100093, China
{tangaosheng,r-zhang,mahui,taoyang}@iie.ac.cn
[2] School of Cyber Security, University of Chinese Academy of Sciences (UCAS), Beijing 100049, China

Abstract. Access control encryption (ACE) is a useful concept introduced by Damgård, Haagh and Orlandi in TCC 2016, which not only protects the data privacy but also controls the information flow. However, their DDH-based scheme suffered from the ciphertext revealing attack (CRA) introduced by Badertscher, Matt and Maurer in Asiacrypt 2017 and just satisfied chosen plaintext attack (CPA) security. Badertscher, Matt and Maurer strengthened the security model to chosen ciphertext attack (CCA) security and constructed a CCA secure scheme under Naor-Yung paradigm. However, they did not indicate how to fix the DDH-based scheme proposed by Damgård, Haagh and Orlandi. Their CCA secure scheme is inefficient and complicated due to the non-interactive zero knowledge proofs (NIZKs) of a very complicated relation. And their scheme is constructed just for limited communication policies.

In this paper, we generalize the DDH-based scheme proposed by Damgård, Haagh and Orlandi and fix its flaw in a very efficient way. Then, we construct a CCA secure ACE scheme, which is efficient, simple, constructed for any communication policy and can be instantiated from many kinds of standard assumptions including the lattice assumptions. Finally, we propose two instantiations respectively based on the lattice assumptions and the decisional bilinear Diffie-Hellman (DBDH) assumption.

Keywords: Access Control Encryption · CCA security · Efficient

1 Introduction

Access control encryption (ACE), first proposed by Damgård, Haagh and Orlandi in TCC 2016 [5], is a novel and useful concept which not only determines who can read the message (read rights) but also determines who can send the message (write rights). The former function can be realized by the traditional public key encryption, such as the identity-based encryption, and only

Y. Wu and M. Yung (Eds.): Inscrypt 2020, LNCS 12612, pp. 104–112, 2021.
https://doi.org/10.1007/978-3-030-71852-7_7

the receiver who has the decryption key can read the message. But the latter function is not considered in nearly all kinds of the traditional public key encryption concepts. This function is also very useful in some systems, especially in those with multiple security levels. For example, in a local area network, a user with the top-secret role, who usually possesses large sensitive information, should not send messages in his computer to the users with the public role, even he is corrupted. ACE provides these two kinds of functions, then can prevent the leakage of the information with the top-secret level even the host is corrupted.

In [5], an ACE scheme based on DDH assumption is constructed. However, it suffers from the CRA attack (the sender, without *ek*, generates the legal *c* by attaining the legal ciphertexts under *ek*) found by Badertscher, Matt and Maurer due to the flaw of its security model. In [2], it introduced the role respecting security model to resist CRA and constructed a CCA secure scheme based on the NIZKs [6] and the homomorphic public key encryption (PKE) [3] under Naor-Yung design paradigm [12]. However, they did not fix the DDH-based ACE scheme in [5] and essentially their method is difficult to extent to the CPA secure scheme. Their scheme is very complicated and inefficient due to NIZKs. Furthermore, their CCA secure scheme is just constructed for limited polices. Constructing an efficient CCA secure scheme for more useful policies is left as one open problem in [2].

Our Contributions. We first generalize the DDH-based ACE scheme in [5] and fix its flaw to resist the CRA attack with a very efficient way. Then, we propose a general but efficient construction of the CCA secure scheme for any policy. Our construction can be instantiated from many kinds of standard assumptions, including the lattice assumptions. Therefore, our CCA secure scheme can also be post quantum secure. Finally, we give two concrete constructions of the CCA secure schemes based on the learning with error (LWE) [14] and short integer solution (SIS) [7] assumptions and the DBDH assumption [17].

Efficient CPA Secure Scheme Resisting CRA. We generalize the DDH-based scheme in [5] and propose a CPA secure scheme based on the homomorphic PKE and a pseudorandom function (PRF). Our scheme resists the CRA attack introduced in [2] and is nearly as efficient as the original DDH-based scheme if our scheme is instantiated from the DDH assumption. It has the same ciphertext size as the original and the cost is only some calculation of the PRF.

General and Efficient CCA Secure Construction for Any Policy. We propose a general CCA secure construction of the ACE scheme based on the identity based encryption (IBE), the strong one-time signature (sOTS) and the PRF. Inspired by Canetti-Halevi-Katz transform (CHK transform) [4], we construct a more efficient CCA secure ACE scheme. In our scheme, the form of the ciphertext c is (vk, c_1, c_2, σ), where vk is the verifying key of sOTS, c_1 and c_2 are the ciphertexts of IBE and σ is the signature of (c_1, c_2). The sanitizer will check the signature and if the signature is valid, it will just dispose (vk, c_1, c_2) and the signature is not sent to the receiver(the ciphertext of c is required to satisfy CCA security, but c' is not).

Table 1. Comparison of existed constructions and ours

Construction	CPA/CCA	No-CRA	PQC	Any policy	Complexity of ciphertext
DDH-based in [5]	CPA	×	×	√	$O(N)$
iO-based in [5]	CPA	√	–	√	$O(\text{polylog}(N))$
[6]	CPA	√	×	×	$O(\text{polylog}(N))$
[11]	CPA	√	×	√	$O(\text{polylog}(N))$
[15]	CPA	×	√	√	$O(N)$
[2]	CCA2	√	×	×	$O(\text{polylog}(N))$
Our CPA framework	CPA	√	√	√	$O(N)$
Our CCA framework	CCA2	√	√	√	$O(N)$

Instantiations Based on Lattice or DBDH Assumptions. We give two instantiations of the general CCA secure constructions. One is based on the LWE and SIS assumptions, which is post quantum secure. The other one is based on the DBDH assumptions, which is more efficient. The main challenge is to construct the IBE scheme with IND-ID-CON property. We prove that Gentry-Peikert-Vaikuntanathan IBE (GPV-IBE) scheme [7] and Waters IBE scheme satisfy the IND-ID-CON property.

Related Work and Comparison. Damgård, Haagh and Orlandi also proposed an ACE scheme with the polylogarithmic complexity of the ciphertext size for any policy [5], and their scheme is based on the indistinguishability obfuscation. Fuchsbauer, Gay, Kowalczyk and Orlandi proposed a scheme with the polylogarithmic complexity based on the standard pairing assumption [6]. But their communication policy is restricted. Kim and Wu proposed an ACE scheme with polylogarithmic complexity for any policy and their scheme is based on standard assumptions [11]. They utilized a digital signature scheme, a predicate encryption scheme [10] and a single-key functional encryption scheme [10,13]. In order to control the information flow, their functional encryption needs to support randomized functionality [1,9]. Tan et al. constructed a LWE-based ACE scheme [15]. However, all these schemes are just CPA secure. We show a concrete comparison with these schemes in Table 1.

Note that N is the number of the security levels or the users in the system. For a local network, N maybe is small. Then our schemes maybe are more suite for these systems due to the simple and efficient structure of our basic scheme (for single user system, i.e. one sender, one sanitizer and one receiver).

2 Preliminary

In this section, we review some useful notations and definitions.

Notations. Let $\mathbb{Z}$ be the integer set. For a positive integer of p, $\mathbb{Z}_p$ represents the set of $\{0, 1, \ldots, p-1\}$. For a positive integer n, let $[n]$ denote the set $\{1, 2, \ldots, n\}$.

Denote the vector by the bold lower case letters (e.g. $\mathbf{u}$, $\mathbf{v}$) and the matrix by the bold upper case letters (e.g. $\mathbf{A}$). If x is a string, let $|x|$ denote its length. If S is a set then $s \leftarrow S$ denotes the operation of picking an elements s of S uniformly at random. Let χ be a distribution, $x \leftarrow \chi$ represents choosing x according χ. Denote the algorithm by the calligraphy letters $\mathcal{A}, \mathcal{B}$. We write $z \leftarrow \mathcal{A}^{\mathcal{O}(\cdot)}(x, y, \ldots)$ to indicate that $\mathcal{A}$ is an algorithm with inputs $(x, y, \ldots)$, queries to $\mathcal{O}(\cdot)$ and an output z. If $k \in \mathbb{N}$, a function $f(k)$ is negligible if $\exists$ $k_0 \in \mathbb{N}$, $\forall$ $k > k_0$, $f(k) \leq 1/k^c$, where $c > 0$ is a constant. We denote a negligible function as $\mathrm{negl}(\cdot)$.

Identity Based Encryption. An IBE scheme consists of four algorithms, denoted as $\mathbf{IBE} = (\mathbf{KG}_{\mathsf{ibe}}, \mathbf{Ext}_{\mathsf{ibe}}, \mathbf{Enc}_{\mathsf{ibe}}, \mathbf{Dec}_{\mathsf{ibe}})$. The following property are useful in our work.

Let $\mathbf{IBE.CONVERT}(\cdot, \cdot)$, called the identity converting algorithm, be a probability algorithm, which takes the identity id and the ciphertext c under id as the inputs and outputs a 'new' identity id' and a ciphertext c' under id', denoted as $(id', c') \leftarrow \mathbf{IBE.CONVERT}(id, c)$. The following definition shows the property we need about **IBE.CONVERT**.

Definition 1 (Indistinguishable Identity Converting Property). *Let λ be the security parameter and **IBE** be the identity based encryption scheme. Denote $\mathcal{ID}$ as the identity space of **IBE**. Let $U(\mathcal{ID})$ be the uniform distribution over $\mathcal{ID}$. Then **IBE** is called satisfying the indistinguishable identity converting property, if there is an efficient **IBE.CONVERT** algorithm, for any $(id, c) \in \mathcal{ID} \times \mathcal{C}_{ibe}$, where $m = \mathbf{Dec}_{ibe}(sk_{id}, id, c)$, $(id', c') \leftarrow \mathbf{IBE.CONVERT}(vk, c)$, it holds that*

1. *The distribution of id' is computationally indistinguishable from $U(\mathcal{ID})$.*
2. *The ciphertext c' has the same security as c and $\mathbf{Dec}_{ibe}(sk_{id'}, id', c') = m$.*

Access Control Encryption. The ACE scheme consists of five PPT algorithms $\mathbf{ACE} = (\mathbf{Setup}, \mathbf{KG}, \mathbf{Enc}, \mathbf{San}, \mathbf{Dec})$. Concretely, $(pp, msk) \leftarrow \mathbf{Setup}(1^\lambda, P)$, where λ is the security parameter and $P : [n] \times [n] \rightarrow \{0, 1\}$ is the security policy. $k \leftarrow \mathbf{KG}(msk, i, t)$, where $i \in \{0, 1, \ldots, n+1\}$ is the identity of the user, $t \in \{sen, rec, san\}$ is the role, and $k \in \{ek_i, dk_i, rk\}$ is the encryption key, the decryption key or the re-randomized key. $c \leftarrow \mathbf{Enc}(ek_i, m)$, $c' \leftarrow \mathbf{San}(rk, c)$ and $m' \leftarrow \mathbf{Dec}(dk_j, c')$.

The correctness of ACE requires that $\Pr[m' \neq m]$ is negligible about λ for any legally generated keys and ciphertexts. There exist the CPA-security model including No-Read Rule, No-Write Rule and Role-Respecting against chosen plaintext attack (NR-CPA, RW-CPA and RR-CPA) and the CCA-security model including No-Read Rule, No-Write Rule and Role-Respecting against chosen ciphertext attack (NR-CCA, NW-CCA and RR-CCA). We give tow constructions of ACE satisfying these two security models respectively.

3 General Constructions

In this section, we give two general constructions of the ACE schemes respectively satisfy the CPA security model and the CCA security model.

The General Construction of the CPA-Secure Scheme. Here, we present the general construction of the ACE scheme satisfying the CPA-security model. We mainly propose the construction of a system with a single identity, namely, with one sender, one sanitizer and one receiver, denoted as **1-ACE** and the scheme for the multiple users can be easily attained from the single-identity scheme. Let $\mathbf{PKE} = (\mathbf{KG}_{\text{pke}}, \mathbf{Enc}_{\text{pke}}, \mathbf{Dec}_{\text{pke}})$ be a homomorphic public key encryption scheme with IND-CPA security. We use "+" to denote the homomorphic operation of the ciphertext of **PKE**. Let $\mathbf{F}_k(\cdot)$ be a pseudorandom function (PRF) with secret key k. Assume that PRF maps the ciphertext space $\mathcal{C}_{\text{pke}}$ of **PKE** into its plaintext space $\mathcal{M}_{\text{pke}}$. Our construction of **1-ACE** with CPA-security is as follows.

- $(pp, msk) \leftarrow \mathbf{Setup}(1^\lambda, P)$: Taking a security parameter λ and a communication policy P as inputs, the setup algorithm invokes $(sk_{\text{pke}}, pk_{\text{pke}}) \leftarrow \mathbf{KG}_{\text{pke}}(1^\lambda)$ and $k \leftarrow \mathbf{KG}_{\text{prf}}(1^\lambda)$ and outputs the master secret key $msk = (sk_{\text{pke}}, k)$ and the public parameter $pp = (pk_{\text{pke}}, P, \lambda)$.
- $k' \leftarrow \mathbf{KG}(msk, i, t)$: Taking a master secret key msk, an identity $i \in \{1, 2\}$ and a role $t \in \{sen, rec, san\}$ as inputs,
  - for $(msk, 1, sen)$, it outputs sender's encryption key $ek_1 = k$.
  - for $(msk, 1, rec)$, it outputs receiver's decryption key $dk_1 = sk_{\text{pke}}$.
  - for $(msk, 2, san)$, it outputs sanitizer's re-randomized key $rk = k$.
- $c \leftarrow \mathbf{Enc}(ek_1, m)$: Taking an encryption key ek_1 and a message m as inputs, it computes $c_1 = \mathbf{Enc}_{\text{pke}}(pk_{\text{pke}}, m)$ and $c_2 = \mathbf{Enc}_{\text{pke}}(pk_{\text{pke}}, \mathbf{F}_k(c_1))$, and outputs the ciphertext $c = (c_1, c_2)$.
- $c' \leftarrow \mathbf{San}(rk, c)$: Taking a re-randomized key rk and a ciphertext c as inputs, it chooses a random integer r, then creates $c_3 \leftarrow \mathbf{Enc}_{\text{pke}}(pk_{\text{pke}}, \mathbf{F}_k(c_1))$ and computes $c' = r(c_2 - c_3) + c_1$ and outputs c'.
- $m' \leftarrow \mathbf{Dec}(dk_1, c')$: Taking a decryption key dk_1 and a ciphertext c' as inputs, it invokes $m' \leftarrow \mathbf{Dec}_{\text{pke}}(sk_{\text{pke}}, c')$ and outputs m'.

Note that when $P(i, j) = 0$, the part of the ciphertext at slot j for the receiver j is chosen randomly from the ciphertext space.

Correctness. Let λ be the security parameter and P be the policy. For pp, msk, ek_1, dk_1, rk legally generated as **1-ACE**, if **PKE** can be decrypted correctly for any 'fresh' ciphertext and homomorphically genenrated ciphertext, then it holds that $m = \mathbf{Dec}(dk_1, \mathbf{San}(rk, \mathbf{Enc}(ek_1, m)))$ for any $m \in \mathcal{M}_{\text{PKE}}$ and the proof is straightforward.

Theorem 1 (Security). *Let λ be the security parameter and P be the policy. For the **1-ACE** scheme constructed as above, if **PKE** is IND-CPA secure and $\mathbf{F}_k$ is pseudorandom. Then the* **1-ACE** *scheme satisfies NR-CPA, NW-CPA and*

RR-CPA security. In particular, for any adversary $\mathcal{A}$ of **1-ACE** *scheme with running time T, there is an adversary $\mathcal{A}'$ to break* **PKE** *such that*

$$Adv^{pp\text{-}cpa}_{\textbf{1-ACE},\mathcal{A}}(\lambda) \leq Adv^{ind\text{-}cpa}_{\textbf{PKE},\mathcal{A}'}(\lambda)$$
$$Adv^{sa\text{-}cpa}_{\textbf{1-ACE},\mathcal{A}}(\lambda) \leq 2Adv^{ind\text{-}cpa}_{\textbf{PKE},\mathcal{A}'}(\lambda)$$
$$Adv^{nw\text{-}cpa}_{\textbf{1-ACE},\mathcal{A}}(\lambda) \leq \frac{1}{2}Adv^{ind\text{-}cpa}_{\textbf{PKE},\mathcal{A}'}(\lambda) + 2Adv_{\textbf{PRF}}(\lambda) + negl(\lambda)$$
$$Adv^{rr\text{-}cpa}_{\textbf{1-ACE},\mathcal{A}}(\lambda) \leq \frac{1}{2}Adv^{ind\text{-}cpa}_{\textbf{PKE},\mathcal{A}'}(\lambda) + 2Adv_{\textbf{PRF}}(\lambda) + negl(\lambda)$$

The running time of $\mathcal{A}'$ is almost equal to T.

The General Construction of the CCA-Secure Scheme. In this section, we give a general construction of ACE with CCA-security. We also mainly construct an ACE scheme (**1-ACE**) for the single identity. Let **IBE** = ($\mathbf{KG}_{\text{ibe}}$, $\mathbf{Ext}_{\text{ibe}}$, $\mathbf{Enc}_{\text{ibe}}$, $\mathbf{Dec}_{\text{ibe}}$) be a homomorphic IBE-scheme. Denote its identity converting algorithm as **IBE.CONVERT**$(\cdot,\cdot)$ and the homomorphic operation as "+". Let **SIG** = ($\mathbf{KG}_{\text{sig}}$, **S**, **V**) be a strong one-time signature scheme. Let $\mathbf{F}_k$ be a pseudorandom function with the secret key k. The **1-ACE** scheme for a single identity with CCA security is as follows.

- $(pp, msk) \leftarrow \mathbf{Setup}(1^\lambda, P)$:Taking a security parameter λ and a policy P as inputs, it invokes $(msk_{\text{ibe}}, mpk_{\text{ibe}}) \leftarrow \mathbf{KG}_{\text{ibe}}(1^\lambda)$ and $k \leftarrow \mathbf{KG}_{\text{prf}}(1^\lambda)$, then outputs $msk = (msk_{\text{ibe}}, k)$ and a public parameter $pp = (mpk_{\text{ibe}}, P, \lambda)$.
- $k' \leftarrow \mathbf{KG}(msk, i, t)$: Taking a master secret key msk, an identity $i \in \{1, 2\}$ and a role $t \in \{sen, rec, san\}$ as inputs,
  - for $(msk, 1, sen)$, it outputs sender's encryption key $ek_1 = k$.
  - for $(msk, 1, rec)$, it outputs receiver's decryption key $dk_1 = msk_{\text{ibe}}$.
  - for $(msk, 2, san)$, it outputs sanitizer's re-randomized key $rk = k$.
- $c \leftarrow \mathbf{Enc}(ek_1, m)$: Taking an encryption key ek_1 and a message m as inputs, it invokes $(sk_s, vk_s) \leftarrow \mathbf{KG}_{\text{sig}}(1^\lambda)$, then computes $c_1 = \mathbf{Enc}_{\text{ibe}}(mpk_{\text{ibe}}, vk_s, m)$, $c_2 = \mathbf{Enc}_{\text{ibe}}(mpk_{\text{ibe}}, vk_s, \mathbf{F}_k(c_1))$ and creates a signature $\sigma = \mathbf{S}(sk_s, (c_1, c_2))$. It outputs a ciphertext $c = (vk_s, c_1, c_2, \sigma)$.
- $c' \leftarrow \mathbf{San}(rk, c)$: Taking the re-randomized key rk and ciphertext c as inputs, it verifies whether σ is a valid signature for (c_1, c_2) by $\mathbf{V}(vk_s, (c_1, c_2), \sigma)$. If the result is 0, it ignores this ciphertext and stops. Otherwise, it chooses a random integer r and creates $c_3 \leftarrow \mathbf{Enc}_{\text{ibe}}(mpk_{\text{ibe}}, vk_s, \mathbf{F}_k(c_1))$. It attains $c_4 = r(c_2 - c_3) + c_1$ and $c' = (vk', c'_4) \leftarrow$ **IBE.CONVERT**(vk_s, c_4). Broadcast c' to every receiver.
- $m' \leftarrow \mathbf{Dec}(dk_1, c')$: Taking a decryption key dk_1 and a ciphertext c' as inputs, it extracts a decryption key $sk_{vk'} \leftarrow \mathbf{Ext}_{\text{ibe}}(msk_{\text{ibe}}, vk')$, then computes a message $m' \leftarrow \mathbf{Dec}_{\text{ibe}}(sk_{vk'}, c'_4)$ and outputs m'.

Theorem 2 (Security). *Let λ be the security parameter and P be the policy. Assume that the* ***IBE*** *scheme is IND-aID-CPA secure with homomorphic and IND-ID-CON property, the one-time signature* ***SIG*** *satisfies sEUF-CMA, and*

F_k is pseudorandom, then the **1-ACE** *scheme constructed as above satisfies NR-CCA (Payload Privacy against Chosen Ciphertext Attack, PP-CCA and Sander Anonymity against Chosen Ciphertext Attack, SA-CCA), NW-CCA and RR-CCA security. In particular, for any PPT adversary $\mathcal{A}$ of* **1-ACE**, *assume that it makes q_D decryption queries and its running time is T. There is a PPT adversary $\mathcal{A}'$ to break the* **IBE** *scheme such that,*

$$Adv^{pp\text{-}cca}_{\mathbf{1-ACE},\mathcal{A}}(\lambda) \le Adv^{ind\text{-}aid\text{-}cpa}_{\mathbf{IBE},\mathcal{A}'}(\lambda) + Adv^{seuf\text{-}cma}_{\mathbf{SIG}}(\lambda) + negl(\lambda)$$
$$Adv^{sa\text{-}cca}_{\mathbf{1-ACE},\mathcal{A}}(\lambda) \le 2Adv^{ind\text{-}aid\text{-}cpa}_{\mathbf{IBE},\mathcal{A}'}(\lambda) + 2Adv^{seuf\text{-}cma}_{\mathbf{SIG}}(\lambda) + negl(\lambda)$$
$$Adv^{nw\text{-}cca}_{\mathbf{1-ACE},\mathcal{A}}(\lambda) \le 2Adv^{ind\text{-}aid\text{-}cpa}_{\mathbf{IBE},\mathcal{A}'}(\lambda) + 2Adv_{\mathbf{PRF}}(\lambda) + negl(\lambda)$$
$$Adv^{rr\text{-}cca}_{\mathbf{1-ACE},\mathcal{A}}(\lambda) \le 2Adv^{ind\text{-}aid\text{-}cpa}_{\mathbf{IBE},\mathcal{A}'}(\lambda) + 2Adv_{\mathbf{PRF}}(\lambda) + negl(\lambda)$$

and the running time of $\mathcal{A}'$ is $T + q_D(T_E + T_D)$, where T_E is the running time of the secret key extraction algorithm and T_D is the running time of the decryption algorithm of ***IBE***.

The proof of Theorem 2 is very similar to the proof of CHK-transform in [4]. The decryption query can be answered by the key extraction query of IBE. Then the proof is similar to the proof of Theorem 1.

4 Instantiation

It is easy to instantiate the CPA secure ACE scheme based on ElGamal encryption, Paillier encryption or many lattice-based encryption schemes, such as the schemes in [3,8], with a pseudorandom function. In this section, we focus on instantiating the CCA secure ACE scheme. One is based on the learning with error (LWE) and short integer solution (SIS) assumptions. The other one is based on the decisional bilinear Diffie-Hellman (DBDH) assumption. By the limits of the space, we only show the construction of its identity converting algorithm in detail.

The Instantiation Based on LWE and SIS. This instantiation of the CCA secure ACE scheme is based on the IBE scheme proposed by Gentry, Peikert and Vaikuntanathan (GPV-IBE) [7], the strong one-time signature also in [7], called probabilistic full domain hash (PFDH) scheme in [7]. The identity converting algorithm of **GPV-IBE.CONVERT** is constructed as follows.

$(id', c') \leftarrow$ **GPV-IBE.CONVERT**(id, c): Let $\{\mathbf{u}_i\}_{i\in[l]} = H(id)$. Parse $c = \{(\mathbf{p}_i, c_i)\}_{i\in[l]}$. For $i \in [l]$, choose $\mathbf{z}_i \leftarrow \chi^m$, then compute $\mathbf{u}'_i = \mathbf{u}_i + \mathbf{A}\mathbf{z}_i$ and $c'_i = c_i + \mathbf{z}_i^T\mathbf{p}_i$. Output $id' = \{\mathbf{u}'_i\}_{i\in[l]}$ and $c' = \{(\mathbf{p}_i, c'_i)\}_{i\in[l]}$.

The Instantiation Based on DBDH. This instantiation of the CCA secure ACE scheme is based on Waters IBE scheme [17] and the strong one-time signature scheme in [16]. The identity converting algorithm of Waters IBE is as follows.

$(id', c') \leftarrow$ **WATERS-IBE.CONVERT**(id, c): Let $v = H(id)$, $u = u' \prod_{v_i=1} u_i$. Choose $x \leftarrow \mathbb{Z}_q$. Output $id' = ug^x$ and $c' = (c_1, c_2, c_3(c_2)^x)$.

5 Conclusion

We proposed an efficient CCA-secure Access Control Encryption scheme for any policy. Our scheme can be instantiated from the standard assumptions, especially from the lattice assumption. Thus, our scheme can be post quantum security. Finally, we give two instantiations from the LWE and SIS assumptions and the DBDH assumption.

Acknowledgements. The authors would like to thank the anonymous reviewers for their valuable comments. This work was supported in part by National Natural Science Foundation of China (Nos. 61772520, 61802392, 61972094, 61472416, 61632020), in part by Key Research and Development Project of Zhejiang Province (Nos. 2017C01062, 2020C01078), in part by Beijing Municipal Science and Technology Commission (Project Number Z191100007119007 and Z191100007119002).

References

1. Agrawal, S., Wu, D.J.: Functional encryption: deterministic to randomized functions from simple assumptions. In: Coron, J.-S., Nielsen, J.B. (eds.) EUROCRYPT 2017. LNCS, vol. 10211, pp. 30–61. Springer, Cham (2017). https://doi.org/10.1007/978-3-319-56614-6_2
2. Badertscher, C., Matt, C., Maurer, U.: Strengthening access control encryption. In: Takagi, T., Peyrin, T. (eds.) ASIACRYPT 2017. LNCS, vol. 10624, pp. 502–532. Springer, Cham (2017). https://doi.org/10.1007/978-3-319-70694-8_18
3. Brakerski, Z., Gentry, C., Vaikuntanathan, V.: (leveled) fully homomorphic encryption without bootstrapping. In: Innovations in Theoretical Computer Science 2012, Cambridge, MA, USA, 8–10 January 2012, pp. 309–325. ACM (2012)
4. Canetti, R., Halevi, S., Katz, J.: Chosen-ciphertext security from identity-based encryption. In: Cachin, C., Camenisch, J.L. (eds.) EUROCRYPT 2004. LNCS, vol. 3027, pp. 207–222. Springer, Heidelberg (2004). https://doi.org/10.1007/978-3-540-24676-3_13
5. Damgård, I., Haagh, H., Orlandi, C.: Access control encryption: enforcing information flow with cryptography. In: Hirt, M., Smith, A. (eds.) TCC 2016. LNCS, vol. 9986, pp. 547–576. Springer, Heidelberg (2016). https://doi.org/10.1007/978-3-662-53644-5_21
6. Fuchsbauer, G., Gay, R., Kowalczyk, L., Orlandi, C.: Access control encryption for equality, comparison, and more. In: Fehr, S. (ed.) PKC 2017. LNCS, vol. 10175, pp. 88–118. Springer, Heidelberg (2017). https://doi.org/10.1007/978-3-662-54388-7_4
7. Gentry, C., Peikert, C., Vaikuntanathan, V.: Trapdoors for hard lattices and new cryptographic constructions. In: STOC 2008, pp. 197–206. ACM, New York (2008)
8. Gentry, C., Sahai, A., Waters, B.: Homomorphic encryption from learning with errors: conceptually-simpler, asymptotically-faster, attribute-based. In: Canetti, R., Garay, J.A. (eds.) CRYPTO 2013, Part I. LNCS, vol. 8042, pp. 75–92. Springer, Heidelberg (2013). https://doi.org/10.1007/978-3-642-40041-4_5
9. Goyal, V., Jain, A., Koppula, V., Sahai, A.: Functional encryption for randomized functionalities. In: Dodis, Y., Nielsen, J.B. (eds.) TCC 2015. LNCS, vol. 9015, pp. 325–351. Springer, Heidelberg (2015). https://doi.org/10.1007/978-3-662-46497-7_13

10. Katz, J., Sahai, A., Waters, B.: Predicate encryption supporting disjunctions, polynomial equations, and inner products. In: Smart, N. (ed.) EUROCRYPT 2008. LNCS, vol. 4965, pp. 146–162. Springer, Heidelberg (2008). https://doi.org/10.1007/978-3-540-78967-3_9
11. Kim, S., Wu, D.J.: Access control encryption for general policies from standard assumptions. In: Takagi, T., Peyrin, T. (eds.) ASIACRYPT 2017. LNCS, vol. 10624, pp. 471–501. Springer, Cham (2017). https://doi.org/10.1007/978-3-319-70694-8_17
12. Naor, M., Yung, M.: Public-key cryptosystems provably secure against chosen ciphertext attacks. In: STOC 1990, pp. 427–437. ACM, New York (1990)
13. O'Neill, A.: Definitional issues in functional encryption. IACR Cryptology ePrint Archive (2010)
14. Regev, O.: On lattices, learning with errors, random linear codes, and cryptography. In: STOC 2005, pp. 84–93. ACM, New York (2005)
15. Tan, G., Zhang, R., Ma, H., Tao, Y.: Access control encryption based on LWE. In: APKC@AsiaCCS 2017, pp. 43–50. ACM, New York (2017)
16. Teranishi, I., Oyama, T., Ogata, W.: General conversion for obtaining strongly existentially unforgeable signatures. In: Barua, R., Lange, T. (eds.) INDOCRYPT 2006. LNCS, vol. 4329, pp. 191–205. Springer, Heidelberg (2006). https://doi.org/10.1007/11941378_14
17. Waters, B.: Efficient identity-based encryption without random oracles. In: Cramer, R. (ed.) EUROCRYPT 2005. LNCS, vol. 3494, pp. 114–127. Springer, Heidelberg (2005). https://doi.org/10.1007/11426639_7

Distributed Key Generation for SM9-Based Systems

Rui Zhang[1,2](✉), Huan Zou[1,2](✉), Cong Zhang[1,2](✉), Yuting Xiao[1,2](✉), and Yang Tao[1](✉)

[1] State Key Laboratory of Information Security, Institute of Information Engineering, Chinese Academy of Sciences, Beijing 100195, China
{r-zhang,zouhuan,zhangcong,xiaoyuting,taoyang}@iie.ac.cn
[2] School of Cyber Security, University of Chinese Academy of Sciences, Beijing 100049, China

Abstract. Identity-Based Cryptography (IBC) is a useful tool for the security of IoT devices, but securely deploying this cryptographic technique to the IoT systems is quite challenging. For instance, a leakage of the master secret key will result in the leakage of all IoT devices' private keys. SM9 is the only approved IBC algorithm standard in China. It is critical to have mechanisms to protect the SM9 master secret keys. In this work, to reduce the risk of the master secret key leakage, we propose a (t, n)-threshold distributed private key generation scheme for SM9 with some techniques from multiparty computation. Our scheme is compatible with all the three SM9 sub-algorithms (i.e., the encryption, signature and key agreement). It is also provably secure and completely eliminates the single point of failures in SM9 that is concerned by the industry. The experimental analysis indicates that the proposed scheme is efficient, e.g., up to 1 million private key generation requests can be handled per day.

Keywords: Identity-Based Cryptography · SM9 · Distributed Key Generation · Threshold cryptography

1 Introduction

Identity-Based Cryptography (IBC) where user's public key is an arbitrary string, is a promising tool for securing the Internet of Things (IoT). In IBCs, all users' private keys are generated from a master secret key *msk* being privately held by a trusted third party—the Private Key Generator (PKG). Such centralized key generation nature, however, inevitably makes the PKG a single point of failures that is harmful to both system robustness and security: once the single PKG crashes, the user private key generation service halts immediately; once the single PKG is corrupted, the master secret key *msk* is leaked as a consequence. In fact, the *msk* leakage problem is of big concern when integrating IBCs to a

Y. Wu and M. Yung (Eds.): Inscrypt 2020, LNCS 12612, pp. 113–129, 2021.
https://doi.org/10.1007/978-3-030-71852-7_8

deployed IoT system. Usually, a user device private key S_{ID} is generated from msk, burned into the device and never changed. It is always more profitable to attack msk than each single device private key. But keeping msk safe seems to be a difficult task. For instance, the master secret key leakage of PlayStation 3[1] has caused tremendous losses.

In general, there are two approaches known in the literature to deal with the msk leakage problem of IBCs. The first approach, such as the certificate-based cryptography [13,15] and certificate-less public key cryptography [3,5,17], lets users contribute to their own private keys with the help of a PKG. Even if the PKG's msk is compromised, the user's private key remains safe as long as the user's secret kept confidential. But this type of solution generally loses in transmission efficiency, since the receiver's certificate or self-generated public key has to be pre-published. Considering IoT networks are often multi-hop routing based, poor transmission efficiency makes this approach less attractive and for most low-cost IoT devices this approach is actually impractical.

The second approach to deal with the msk leakage problem is to adopt the Distributed Key Generation (DKG), by distributing the power of user private key generation among multiple parties rather than a single PKG. The n Key Privacy Authorities (KPAs) based scheme [18] and the n Trusted Authorities (TAs) based scheme [9] allow the n trusted parties to pick their secret keys freely. Both schemes are general methods applicable to all IBC schemes, but they are not compatible with the IBC algorithms after user private key generation (e.g., the encryption, signature and key agreement). In contrast, within schemes following a t-out-of-n DKG fashion, the n PKGs must ensure that their secret keys are sharing one msk. These schemes [7,14,19,20,23] are often based on the Shamir secret sharing or homomorphic Paillier encryption primitive: the former which we refer to as (t, n)-threshold distributed key generation [7,14,23] focuses on the general t-out-of-n case; the latter which we refer to as two-party distributed key generation [19,20] generally focuses on the 2-out-of-2 case specifically. Since the distributedly generated user public/private key keep their original forms, the resulting schemes have good compatibility but heavily rely on concrete mathematical structures. For some IBC schemes with poor homomorphic properties, these schemes could be particularly complicated and inefficient.

SM9 is a Chinese standard for IBC [1,2] that consists of three sub-algorithms: a digital signature scheme, a key agreement scheme and an encryption scheme. Table 1 compares four DKG solutions feasible for SM9. The (t, n)-threshold DKG seems to be the most desirable one, since only it completely eliminates the single point of failures in SM9 where both the security and robustness are achieved.

Difficulties of (t, n)-Threshold DKG for SM9. As stated before, the construction of (t, n)-threshold DKG heavily relies on concrete IBC schemes' mathematical structures. Earlier techniques based on the IBC scheme proposed by Boneh and Franklin [7] (BF-IBC), and proposed by Sakai and Kasahara [14] (SK-IBC) cannot be directly adopted to SM9. For schemes enjoying fully homomor-

[1] The Sony PS3 and Bitcoin crypto hacks. https://tinyurl.com/udg5tyg.

Table 1. Distributed user private key generation schemes for SM9

	Construction	Round	*need a* Secure channel	*eliminate* Key escrow	Compatible	Robust
n KPAs based	Generic	N/A	×	√	×	×
n TAs based	Generic	N/A	√	√	×	×
Two party based	Specific	2	×	√	√	×
(t, n)-threshold based (this work)	Specific	1	√	√	√	√

† Since no negotiation happens among key generation authorities, the "Round" item for the KPA and TA based schemes are listed as not applicable (N/A). A scheme is *compatible* if it doesn't modify the IBC algorithms after private key generation, and is *robust* if key generation authorities can go offline without interrupting the private key generation. *Key escrow* refers to the situation that a single PKG can generate all users' private keys.

phic property like BF-IBC [7], where the user private key $S_{\text{ID}} = [msk]h_{\text{ID}}$ with $[\cdot]$ denoting the elliptic curve scalar multiplication operation and h_{ID} denoting an elliptic curve point hashing from a user's identity string, it is quite straightforward to generate a t-privately Shamir share of $S_{\text{ID}} = [msk]h_{\text{ID}}$ from a t-privately msk share. Whereas in SM9 [10], the user private key $S_{\text{ID}} = [\frac{msk}{msk+F(\text{ID})}]P_2$ with $F(\text{ID})$ denoting the hash value of a user's identity string and P_2 denoting the generator of an additive elliptic curve point group. It is hard for a PKG holding a t-privately Shamir share of msk to generate a t-privately Shamir share of the user private key $S_{\text{ID}} = [\frac{msk}{msk+F(\text{ID})}]P_2$, since msk appears both in the numerator and denominator. This further positions challenges for constructing an efficient (t, n)-threshold DKG for SM9.

Our Contributions. In this paper, we investigate the problem of distributed key generation for SM9 and propose a scheme where both the master secret key msk and user private key S_{ID} are generated in a (t, n)-threshold way. To the best of our knowledge, the proposed (t, n)-threshold Distributed Private Key Generation ((t, n)-DPKG)[2] is the first work that completely eliminates the single point of failures in SM9. Besides security and robustness, our scheme also presents an efficient distributed extraction protocol for the *exponent inversion* IBE family, an open challenge in [14]. By removing one semi-honest BGW distributed multiplication protocol [4,16], the round complexity of our protocol is only 1-round, while the best known solution [14] was with 3-rounds.

Related Work. To reduce the risk of msk leakage, (t, n)-DPKG divides msk into n shares. Each PKG privately holds a share and generates a private key fragment for the user. t PKGs or less cannot derive any information about the

[2] DKG vs. DPKG: DPKG is a branch of DKG. Within IBCs, DPKG captures the property of distributedly generating user private keys more precisely. Besides user private keys, our scheme also generates the master secret key distributedly.

msk, and the complete user private key S_{ID} can only be extracted from at least $t+1$ S_{ID} fragments. Thus (t,n)-DPKG relies heavily on concrete mathematical structures of IBE schemes. Boneh and Franklin [7] came up with the first (t,n)-DPKG scheme based on BF-IBE. As BF-IBE user private key enjoys fully homomorphic property, their scheme allows non-interactive partial private key generation. In comparison, designing such schemes for the *exponent inversion* IBE family [8] (e.g., SK-IBE [21] and SM9-IBE [10]) is not that straightforward. Facilitated by the *sharing the inverse of a shared secret* multiparty computation protocol [6], Smart and Geisler developed a (t,n)-DPKG scheme for SK-IBE [14]. Their scheme requires 3-rounds interaction between PKGs during the partial private key generation phase and a more efficient protocol remains open. Kate and Goldberg then revisited above schemes in [14], and extended them to malicious PKG case with non-interactive proofs of knowledge.

In particular, we notice Xu et al. [23] have presented a similar (t,n)-threshold distributed private key generation solution for SM9. But some insufficiencies exist in Xu et al.'s solution: (1) *correctness.* By distributing $\frac{1}{msk}$ among n PKGs, Xu et al.'s scheme successfully extracts the user private key, but it seems very hard to extract the master public key $P_{pub}=[msk]P_1$ from the shares of $\frac{1}{msk}$ to further extract the user public key. Our scheme shares msk instead, and facilitated by multiparty computation techniques, our scheme can efficiently extract both the user public/private keys from the shares of msk; (2) *completeness.* Xu et al.'s solution didn't describe how to share $\frac{1}{msk}$ among n PKGs in the setup phase. Whereas, we present a completely distributed master key generation protocol which removes the need of pre-distributing msk; (3) *efficiency.* In Xu et al.'s scheme, the distributed extraction phase requires 3-rounds interaction of PKGs. Whereas, only 1-round is needed in our scheme.

2 Preliminaries

Notations. For an integer n, $[n]$ denotes the set $\{1,2,\ldots,n\}$. For a real number n, $\lfloor n \rfloor$ denotes the greatest integer less than or equal to n. Given a set I, $|I|$ denotes the cardinality of I. Vector $\boldsymbol{v}$ having n components is denoted as $\boldsymbol{v}^n$ with n being a non-negative integer. The set of all finite binary strings as $\{0,1\}^*$. If A is an algorithm, then $\mathsf{A}(x) \to y$ means that running the algorithm A with x as its input gets the output y. Furthermore, we let $y \leftarrow \mathsf{A}(x)$ denote the output y of running the algorithm A with x as its input. The term PPT is abbreviated for probabilistic polynomial-time. A function $negl(\cdot)$ is called negligible, if for any polynomial $p(\cdot)$, there exists some λ_0 such that $negl(\lambda) \leq 1/p(\lambda)$ for every $\lambda > \lambda_0$. Throughout the paper, λ will denote the security parameter.

2.1 (t,n)-Secret Sharing

Definition 1 ((t,n)-Secret Sharing). *A (t,n)-secret sharing in the finite field $\mathbb{F}_p$ is a pair of algorithms* (Share, Reconstruct)*:*

- $\mathsf{Share}(s, 1^\lambda)$: *A probabilistic algorithm takes as input the security parameter* 1^λ *and a secret* $s \in \mathbb{F}_p$. *It returns* n *shares* $\{s_1, \ldots, s_n\}$ *of* s.
- $\mathsf{Reconstruct}(s_{i_1}, \ldots, s_{i_{t+1}})$: *A deterministic algorithm takes as input at least* $t+1$ *shares* $\{s_{i_1}, \ldots, s_{i_{t+1}}\}$ *of some secret. It returns the secret* s, *that is,* $\mathsf{Reconstruct}(s_{i_1}, \ldots, s_{i_{t+1}}) \rightarrow s$.

Definition 2 (Perfect Security of (t, n)-Secret Sharing). *A* (t, n)*-secret sharing scheme (*Share, Reconstruct*) in finite field* $\mathbb{F}_p$ *is of perfect security if the following properties hold:*

- *Correctness:* $\forall s \in \mathbb{F}_p, \forall I \subset [n]$ *s.t.* $|I| > t, \Pr[\mathsf{Reconstruct}(s_i : i \in I, s_1, \ldots, s_n \leftarrow \mathsf{Share}(s)) = s] = 1$
- *Security:* $\forall s, s' \in \mathbb{F}_p, \forall I \subset [n]$ *s.t.* $|I| \leq t$, *the two distributions are the same:* $\{\{s_i\}_{i \in I} : \{s_1, \ldots, s_n\} \leftarrow \mathsf{Share}(s)\}$ $\{\{s'_i\}_{i \in I} : \{s'_1, \ldots, s'_n\} \leftarrow \mathsf{Share}(s')\}$.

2.2 Identity-Based Encryption with a Single PKG

Boneh and Franklin [7] formalized an Identity-Based Encryption (IBE) scheme as four algorithms:

- $\mathsf{Setup}(1^\lambda) \rightarrow (msk, mpk)$: The setup algorithm takes 1^λ as its input. It returns a master public key mpk and a master secret key msk.
- $\mathsf{Extract}(mpk, msk, \mathrm{ID}) \rightarrow S_{\mathrm{ID}}$: The private key extraction algorithm takes as input a key pair (mpk, msk) and an identity $\mathrm{ID} \in \{0,1\}^*$. It returns a user private key S_{ID} for identity ID.
- $\mathsf{Enc}(mpk, \mathrm{ID}, m) \rightarrow c$: The encryption algorithm takes as input the master public key mpk, an identity ID, and a message m. It returns a ciphertext c.
- $\mathsf{Dec}(mpk, S_{\mathrm{ID}}, c) \rightarrow m$ or $\perp$: The decryption algorithm takes as input the master public key mpk, a user private key S_{ID}, and a ciphertext c. It returns a message m or $\perp$ denoting a failure.

Boneh and Franklin [7] also formalized the security notion of an IBE scheme as IND-ID-CCA secure, by defining the following two-stage game between an adversary $\mathcal{A}$ and a challenger $\mathcal{C}$:

- **Setup**. $\mathcal{C}$ runs the setup algorithm and obtains (mpk, msk). Then $\mathcal{C}$ sends mpk to $\mathcal{A}$ and keeps msk to respond $\mathcal{A}$'s queries.
- **Phase 1**. $\mathcal{A}$ adaptively makes private key extraction queries and decryption queries. For a private key extraction query $\langle \mathrm{ID} \rangle$, $\mathcal{C}$ returns S_{ID} to $\mathcal{A}$ by running $\mathsf{Extract}(mpk, msk, \mathrm{ID})$; For a decryption query $\langle \mathrm{ID}, c \rangle$, $\mathcal{C}$ sends decrypted c to $\mathcal{A}$ by running $\mathsf{Dec}(mpk, \mathsf{Extract}(mpk, msk, \mathrm{ID}), c)$.
- **Challenge**. $\mathcal{A}$ outputs a tuple $\{m_0, m_1, \mathrm{ID}^*\}$ where m_0 and m_1 are two distinct messages with the same length, ID^* is an identity for which $\mathcal{A}$ never issues a private key extraction query in Phase 1. Then $\mathcal{C}$ picks a random bit $b \in \{0,1\}$, and sends c_b^* to $\mathcal{A}$ by computing $c_b^* = \mathsf{Enc}(mpk, \mathrm{ID}^*, m_b)$.

- **Phase 2.** $\mathcal{A}$ continues to make private key extraction queries and decryption queries. $\mathcal{C}$ responds just as Phase 1 except for the private key extraction query $\langle \text{ID}^* \rangle$ and the decryption query $\langle \text{ID}^*, c_b^* \rangle$.
- **Guess.** $\mathcal{A}$ outputs a guess $b' \in \{0, 1\}$ of b and wins the game if $b' = b$.

Definition 3 (IND-ID-CCA Security of IBE Scheme). *An IBE scheme is secure in the IND-ID-CCA model if for any* PPT *adversary $\mathcal{A}$, there exists a negligible function $ngel(\cdot)$ satisfying:*

$$Adv_{\mathcal{A}}^{IND\text{-}ID\text{-}CCA_{IBE}} = 2|Pr[b' = b] - \frac{1}{2}| \leq negl(\lambda).$$

2.3 The SM9 Private Key Generation

There are 3 sub-algorithms, namely encryption, signature, key agreement in SM9; their key generation is essentially the same. Besides, our proposal will only affect the key generation phase. Due to space limitation, here we only introduce some necessary notions used in the SM9 private key generation. For complete SM9 schemes, one can redirect to [10] for more details.

Let a bilinear pairing mapping define as $\hat{e} : \mathbb{G}_1 \times \mathbb{G}_2 \rightarrow \mathbb{G}_T$, where $\mathbb{G}_1$, $\mathbb{G}_2$ are additive groups and $\mathbb{G}_T$ is a multiplicative group. All three groups have prime order p. $\mathbb{G}_1$ and $\mathbb{G}_2$ are generated by $P_1 \in \mathbb{G}_1$, $P_2 \in \mathbb{G}_2$, respectively. Assume a random $s \in \mathbb{Z}_p^*$ is chosen as a global master secret key and the master public key for SM9 encryption scheme can be defined as $P_{pub} = [s]P_1$. Then the private key extraction algorithm computes the user's public key as $Q_{\text{ID}} = [F(\text{ID})]\, P_1 + P_{pub}$ and the user's private key as $S_{\text{ID}} = \left[\frac{s}{s+F(\text{ID})}\right] P_2$,

2.4 Dealerless Replicated Secret Sharing Protocol $\mathcal{P}_{\text{rep}}^{\sigma}$

$\mathcal{P}_{\text{rep}}^{\sigma}$ is a protocol that allows n players to jointly determine a random secret σ of a t-privately replicated secret sharing scheme, without a trusted dealer:

$$\mathcal{P}_{\text{rep}}^{\sigma}(\mathcal{G}, \ldots, \mathcal{G}) = (\sigma_1, \ldots, \sigma_n)$$

The input for each player is the public system parameters $\mathcal{G} = \{t, n, p\}$, where t is the threshold, n is the number of players and p is a prime number. The output for each player P_i is a t-privately replicated share σ_i of secret σ. The protocol proceeds as follows: each player $P_{i,i\in[n]}$ chooses a random secret $\mu_i \in \mathbb{Z}_p$ and shares μ_i to player $P_{j,j\in[n]}$ according to the replicated secret sharing scheme [22]. The share that P_i sends to P_j is denoted as $\mathcal{R}_{(t,n)}^{\mu_i}(j)$. Then $P_{i,i\in[n]}$ outputs $\sigma_i = \sum_{j=1}^{n} \mathcal{R}_{(t,n)}^{\mu_j}(i)$. Finally, the shares $\{\sigma_1, \ldots, \sigma_n\}$ determine a random replicated secret scheme $\mathcal{R}_{(t,n)}^{\sigma}$ where $\sigma = \mu_1 + \ldots + \mu_n$ and $\sigma_i = \mathcal{R}_{(t,n)}^{\sigma}(i)$.

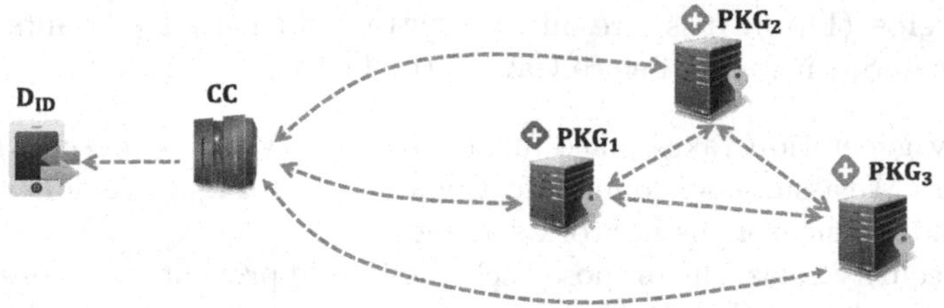

Fig. 1. Architecture of the distributed private key generation scheme

2.5 Share Conversion Algorithm

$\mathsf{Conv}^{*}_{(t,n)}$ is a share conversion algorithm used in the Pseudo-Random Secret Sharing (PRSS) protocol [12,22] that locally converts player $P_{i,i\in[n]}$'s t-privately replicated share $\mathcal{R}^{\sigma}_{(t,n)}(i)$ to a t-privately pseudo-random Shamir share $\mathcal{S}^{z}_{(t,n)}(i)$ sharing a pseudo-random secret z. st is a common input for all n players.

$$\mathsf{Conv}^{*}_{(t,n)}(\mathcal{R}^{\sigma}_{(t,n)}(i), st) \rightarrow \mathcal{S}^{z}_{(t,n)}(i)$$

$\mathsf{Conv}^{0}_{(2t,n)}$ is a share conversion algorithm used in the Pseudo-Random Zero Sharing (PRZS) protocol [12,22] that locally converts player $P_{i,i\in[n]}$'s t-privately replicated share $\mathcal{R}^{\sigma}_{(t,n)}(i)$ to a $2t$-privately pseudo-random Shamir share $\mathcal{S}^{0}_{(2t,n)}(i)$ sharing secret 0. st is a common input for all n players.

$$\mathsf{Conv}^{0}_{(2t,n)}(\mathcal{R}^{\sigma}_{(t,n)}(i), st) \rightarrow \mathcal{S}^{0}_{(2t,n)}(i)$$

3 Threshold Distributed Private Key Generation for IBE

In this section, we introduce the system model, formal definition and properties of (t,n)-threshold Distributed Private Key Generation ((t,n)-DPKG) for IBE.

3.1 System Model and Security

The proposed distributed private key generation scheme involves 3 entities shown in Figure 1. Their characteristics and functionalities are introduced as follows:

- **Private Key Generator (PKG):** It is a powerful entity holding a master secret key share, who generates private key fragments for IoT devices.
- **Combine Center (CC):** It is a stateless entity, whose major task is to perform some complex cryptographic computation. CC collects private key fragments $S^{(i)}_{\mathrm{ID}}$ from PKGs, extracts the complete private key S_{ID} by combing the $S^{(i)}_{\mathrm{ID}}$ fragments then installs S_{ID} into the IoT device. Once the S_{ID} has been successfully installed, CC immediately erases the memory related to S_{ID}.

- **IoT Device ($\mathrm{D_{ID}}$):** It is a resource-constrained entity. $\mathrm{D_{ID}}$ wants to get its private key S_{ID} installed before leaving the factory.

Since key generation takes place inside the factory, not exposed in an open environment. We assume all communications shown in Fig. 1 are done via secure channels under synchronous network setting.

For the security goals, the proposed scheme should prevent two types of adversaries – one residing in the private key generation centers, and the other residing in the private key combine center.

- **Corrupted PKG Coalition.** We assume the adversary can control up to t PKGs, learning at most t master secret key shares. Specifically, we assume the adversary is *static* – the corrupted PKG set is fixed before the game. Since behaviors deviating the predefined rules will be quickly detected, the corrupted PKG coalition is assumed to be *semi-honest* – they will fulfill faithfully promised tasks. The security goal is that this corrupted PKG coalition learns no more information than its members' master secret key shares.
- **Corrupted CC.** The adversary residing at the combine center is assumed to be *active*. It is able to generate arbitrary legal identities representing IoT devices and normally interact with PKGs. The security goal is to ensure that this adversary learns no more information than S_{ID} for which it has queried.

3.2 Security Definition

In this part, we revisit the security definition of (t, n)-DPKG for IBE proposed by Kate and Goldberg [14]. For comprehension, these schemes are described within the background of the proposed system model. An IBE scheme with (t, n)-threshold distributed private key generation consists of four components:

- The distributed setup: $\mathsf{DSetup}(t, n, \mathcal{G}) \rightarrow (msk_i, \boldsymbol{mpk}^{n+1})$. Each $\mathrm{PKG}_{i, i\in[n]}$ takes in a threshold t, the number of PKGs n and public system parameters $\mathcal{G}$. It returns a t-privately share msk_i of msk and a vector $\boldsymbol{mpk}^{n+1} = \{mpk_1, \ldots, mpk_n, mpk\}$, where mpk_i denotes the i_{th} share of mpk.
- The distributed extraction: it involves a *distributed extraction* protocol $\mathsf{DExtract}$ ran by PKGs and a $\mathsf{Combine}$ algorithm locally ran by the CC.

$$\mathsf{DExtract}(\mathrm{ID}, msk_i, mpk) \rightarrow S_{\mathrm{ID}}^{(i)}$$
$$\mathsf{Combine}(S_{\mathrm{ID}}^{(1)}, S_{\mathrm{ID}}^{(2)}, \ldots, S_{\mathrm{ID}}^{(m)}) \rightarrow S_{\mathrm{ID}}$$

  In $\mathsf{DExtract}$, each $\mathrm{PKG}_{i, i\in[n]}$ takes in an identity ID, a t-privately share msk_i of msk and mpk. It will output a t-privately share $S_{\mathrm{ID}}^{(i)}$ of the device private key S_{ID}. Having received $m \geq t+1$ shares of S_{ID}, CC will run the $\mathsf{Combine}$ algorithm to compute S_{ID}.
- The encryption: $\mathsf{Enc}(mpk, \mathrm{ID}, m) \rightarrow c$. It is the same as the single PKG.
- The decryption: $\mathsf{Dec}(mpk, S_{\mathrm{ID}}, c) \rightarrow m$ or $\perp$. It is the same as the single PKG.

Kate and Goldberg [14] formalized the security notion of (t, n)-DPKG for IBE as IND-ID-CCA secure, by defining an IND-ID game that a challenger $\mathcal{C}$ plays against a Byzantine adversary who can control up to t PKGs and make them behave arbitrarily. In this work, we assume the corrupted PKGs are semi-honest instead of malicious, so we have made two modifications to Kate and Goldberg's IND-ID game definition [14]: (1) proofs for private key shares are not required, since the semi-honest assumption implies that all PKGs will fulfill their tasks faithfully and will always generate correct shares as required; (2) only $n \geq t$ is required, instead of $n \geq 2t+1$ required by the malicious PKG assumption. The IND-ID game under the semi-honest PKG assumption is defined as:

Before the game, the adversary $\mathcal{A}_{(t,n)}$ fixes a set of corrupted PKGs denoted as A with $|A| \leq t$ (for general purpose, we assume $|A| = t$), and the challenger $\mathcal{C}$ will simulate the rest $n-t$ honest PKGs denoted as B with $|B| = n-t$.

- **Setup**. $\mathcal{C}$ simulates $\text{PKG}_{i,i\in B}$ and runs the distributed setup protocol with $\mathcal{A}_{(t,n)}$. In the end, $\mathcal{A}_{(t,n)}$ will receive $\boldsymbol{msk}^t = \{msk_i\}_{i\in A}$ contains t shares of msk for $\text{PKG}_{i,i\in A}$, and $\boldsymbol{mpk}^{n+1} = \{mpk_1, \ldots, mpk_n, mpk\}$ contains n shares of mpk generated by $\text{PKG}_{i,i\in A\cup B}$ and mpk.
- **Phase 1**. $\mathcal{A}_{(t,n)}$ adaptively makes private key extraction $\langle \text{ID} \rangle$ queries and decryption $\langle \text{ID}, c \rangle$ queries. For a $\langle \text{ID}, c \rangle$ query, $\mathcal{C}$ decrypts c using its msk then sends decrypted c to $\mathcal{A}_{(t,n)}$. For a $\langle \text{ID} \rangle$ query, $\mathcal{C}$ simulates $\text{PKG}_{i,i\in B}$ running the distributed private key extraction protocol with $\mathcal{A}_{(t,n)}$, and sends $\boldsymbol{S}_{\text{ID}}^{n-t}$ to $\mathcal{A}_{(t,n)}$ where $\boldsymbol{S}_{\text{ID}}^{n-t} = \{S_{\text{ID}}^{(i)}\}_{i\in B}$ are shares of S_{ID} generated by $\text{PKG}_{i,i\in B}$.
- **Challenge**. $\mathcal{A}_{(t,n)}$ outputs a tuple $\{m_0, m_1, \text{ID}^*\}$ where m_0 and m_1 are two distinct messages with the same length, an identity ID^* for which $\mathcal{A}_{(t,n)}$ never issues a private key extraction query in Phase 1. Then $\mathcal{C}$ picks a random bit $b \in \{0,1\}$, and sends c_b^* to $\mathcal{A}_{(t,n)}$ by computing $c_b^* = \mathsf{Enc}(mpk, \text{ID}^*, m_b)$.
- **Phase 2**. $\mathcal{A}_{(t,n)}$ continues to make private key extraction queries and decryption queries. $\mathcal{C}$ responds just as Phase 1 except for the private key extraction query $\langle \text{ID}^* \rangle$ and the decryption query $\langle \text{ID}^*, c_b^* \rangle$.
- **Guess**. $\mathcal{A}_{(t,n)}$ outputs a guess $b' \in \{0,1\}$ of b and wins the game if $b' = b$.

Definition 4 (IND-ID-CCA Security of IBE Scheme With (t, n)-DPKG). *With (t,n)-threshold distributed private key generation, an IBE scheme is secure in the IND-ID-CCA model if for any* PPT *adversary $\mathcal{A}_{(t,n)}$, there exists a negligible function $ngel(\cdot)$ satisfying:*

$$Adv_{\mathcal{A}_{(t,n)}}^{IND\text{-}ID\text{-}CCA_{(t,n)\text{-}IBE}} = 2|Pr[b' = b] - \frac{1}{2}| \leq negl(\lambda).$$

In fact, $\mathcal{A}_{(t,n)}$ depicted in the above IND-ID-CCA game models an attacker $\mathcal{A}'$ who corrupts t PKGs as well as the CC. $\mathcal{A}_{(t,n)}$'s failure in the IND-ID-CCA game also indicates that attacker $\mathcal{A}'$ learns no more information than t corrupted PKGs' msk shares and the device private keys S_{ID} for IDs it has queried for.

4 Construction of (t,n)-DPKG for SM9

As the (t,n)-threshold Distributed Private Key Generation ((t,n)-DPKG) won't change the original forms of user public/private key, it is compatible with the original SM9 algorithms after user private key extraction. Hence we only focus on the first two phases – distributed setup and extraction. Construction of (t,n)-DPKG for SM9 relies on (t,n)-Shamir secret sharing, and the challenging task is to let $\mathrm{PKG}_{i,i\in[n]}$ holding a t-privately Shamir share msk_i to generate a t-privately Shamir share of $S_{\mathrm{ID}} = [\frac{msk}{msk+F(\mathrm{ID})}]P_2$. To do this, we first rewrite S_{ID} as $[1 - \frac{F(\mathrm{ID})}{msk+F(\mathrm{ID})}]P_2$, and employ a *sharing the inverse of a shared secret* protocol [6] enabling PKG_i holding a msk share msk_i to obtain a t-privately Shamir share θ_i of $\frac{1}{msk+F(\mathrm{ID})}$. Then PKG_i can locally convert θ_i to a t-privately Shamir share of $S_{\mathrm{ID}} = [\frac{msk}{msk+F(\mathrm{ID})}]P_2$ by computing $[1-F(\mathrm{ID})\cdot\theta_i]P_2$. Besides, to reduce interactions between PKGs, an auxiliary variable σ and share conversion algorithms $\mathsf{Conv}^*_{(t,n)}$ and $\mathsf{Conv}^0_{(2t,n)}$ are introduced to provide Shamir shares.

A. System Bootstrapping
In this phase, n PKGs are supposed to collaboratively determine the following public system parameters:

(1) Determine PKG group size n and threshold t such that $n \geq 2t + 1$.[3] If unsatisfied, decline to proceed.
(2) Agree on parameters $\mathcal{G} = \{1^\lambda, \mathbb{G}_1, \mathbb{G}_2, \mathbb{G}_T, p, \hat{e}, P_1, P_2, H_v, hid\}$ required by the SM9-IBE scheme [10].

B. Distributed Setup
In this phase, n PKGs jointly determine a secret msk where $\mathrm{PKG}_{i,i\in[n]}$ obtains a t-privately msk share msk_i.

- $\mathsf{DSetup}(t,n,\mathcal{G}) \rightarrow (msk_i, \boldsymbol{mpk}^{n+1})$: is a protocol jointly ran by n PKGs.

(1) $\mathrm{PKG}_{i,i\in[n]}$ jointly runs the $\mathcal{P}^\sigma_{\mathrm{rep}}$ protocol defined in Sect. 2.4, that is, $\mathcal{P}^\sigma_{\mathrm{rep}}(\{t,n,p\}) \rightarrow \sigma_i$. At the end of $\mathcal{P}^\sigma_{\mathrm{rep}}$ execution, n PKGs will collaboratively determine a global secret σ and $\mathrm{PKG}_{i,i\in[n]}$ will privately output σ_i, which represents a t-privately replicated share $\mathcal{R}^\sigma_{(t,n)}(i)$ sharing the secret σ.
(2) $\mathrm{PKG}_{i,i\in[n]}$ locally runs the PRSS share conversion algorithm $\mathsf{Conv}^*_{(t,n)}(\sigma_i, st_0) \rightarrow s_i$, where st_0 is a string representing an agreed-upon initial global state (e.g. Lamport timestamp). The private output s_i is a t-privately pseudo-random Shamir share, sharing the master secret key s.
(3) $\mathrm{PKG}_{i,i\in[n]}$ *publicly* outputs a t-privately Shamir share mpk_i of mpk by computing $mpk_i = [s_i]P_1$.

[3] $n \geq 2t+1$ is required because the distributed extraction phase of SM9 involves secret reconstruction from $2t$-privately Shamir shares.

(4) $\text{PKG}_{i,i\in[n]}$ reconstructs the master public key mpk by performing Lagrange polynomial interpolation on received $m \geq t+1$ mpk shares. That is, $mpk = \sum_{i=1}^{m}[c_i]mpk_i$ where $c_i = \prod_{j=1,j\neq i}^{m} \frac{-j}{i-j}$.

(5) $\text{PKG}_{i,i\in[n]}$ *privately* outputs $msk_i = \{\sigma_i, s_i\}$ and *publicly* outputs $\boldsymbol{mpk}^{n+1} = \{mpk_1, \ldots, mpk_n, mpk\}$. Here, s_i is a t-privately Shamir share of the master secret key of SM9 and σ_i is an auxiliary variable to generate Shamir shares (all Shamir shares can be re-computed from σ_i including s_i). To avoid confusion, the master secret key of SM9 is denoted as s instead of msk in the following discussions.

C. Distributed Private Key Extraction

This phase includes a DExtract protocol jointly ran by n PKGs where $\text{PKG}_{i,i\in[n]}$ will generate a private key fragment $S_{\text{ID}}^{(i)}$ for the IoT device D_{ID}, and a Combine algorithm locally ran by the CC where the CC will extract the complete private key S_{ID} from the received private key fragments.

- $\mathsf{DExtract}(\text{ID}, msk_i, mpk) \rightarrow S_{\text{ID}}^{(i)}$: is a protocol collaboratively ran by n PKGs.

(1) $\text{PKG}_{i,i\in[n]}$ locally computes $x_i = s_i + F(\text{ID})$, which is a t-privately Shamir share sharing secret $x = s + F(\text{ID})$.

(2) $\text{PKG}_{i,i\in[n]}$ locally invokes $\mathsf{Conv}^{*}_{(t,n)}(\sigma_i, st) \rightarrow r_i$, where r_i is a pseudo-random t-privately Shamir share sharing some pseudo-random secret r. Here, st denotes the current agreed-upon global state.

(3) $\text{PKG}_{i,i\in[n]}$ locally invokes $\mathsf{Conv}^{0}_{(2t,n)}(\sigma_i, st) \rightarrow y_i$, where y_i is a $2t$-privately pseudo-random Shamir share sharing secret 0.

(4) $\text{PKG}_{i,i\in[n]}$ locally computes $z_i = x_i \cdot r_i + y_i$, which is a $2t$-privately *pseudo-random* Shamir share sharing secret $z = x \cdot r$, with $x = s + F(\text{ID})$.

(5) $\text{PKG}_{i,i\in[n]}$ first reveals z_i to the rest $n-1$ PKGs, then reconstructs the $2t$-privately secret z. This step requires at least $2t+1$ PKGs to be online, that is, $n \geq 2t+1$.

(6) $\text{PKG}_{i,i\in[n]}$ locally computes $\omega_i = 1 - F(\text{ID}) \cdot \theta_i$, where $\theta_i = \frac{r_i}{z}$ is a t-privately pseudo-random Shamir share of $\frac{1}{s+F(\text{ID})}$. Therefore, ω_i is a t-privately pseudo-random Shamir share of $\frac{s}{s+F(\text{ID})}$.

(7) $\text{PKG}_{i,i\in[n]}$ sends $S_{\text{ID}}^{(i)} = [\omega_i]P_2$ to CC.

In [14], Geisler and Smart reconstructed the product of x and r based on t-privately Shamir shares of $x \cdot r$. However, to obtain this t-privately share, $\text{PKG}_{i,i\in[n]}$ has to run a semi-honest BGW distributed multiplication protocol [4] with the remaining $n-1$ PKGs. We reconstruct $x \cdot r$ from $2t$-privately Shamir shares instead, where $\text{PKG}_{i,i\in[n]}$ can locally obtain its $2t$-privately Shamir share of $x \cdot r$. In this way, we avoid invoking one distributed multiplication protocol and only 1 round interaction between PKGs are needed to recover the secret $x \cdot r$ from its $2t$-privately Shamir shares.

Having received $m \geq t+1$ private key fragments from PKGs, CC invokes the Lagrange polynomial interpolation algorithm to obtain the complete private key.

- $\mathsf{Combine}(S_{\text{ID}}^{(1)}, \ldots, S_{\text{ID}}^{(m)}) \rightarrow S_{\text{ID}}$: is an algorithm locally ran by the CC. CC derives the complete key via:

$$S_{\text{ID}} = \sum_{i=1}^{m} [c'_i] S_{\text{ID}}^{(i)}, \quad \text{where } c'_i = \prod_{j=1, j \neq i}^{m} \frac{-j}{i-j}.$$

Correctness Analysis. To show above construction is correct, we only need to show that the device public/private key generated in a (t, n)-threshold way is the same as the one generated in a centralized way. For the device public key, we only need to show that the master public key $mpk = [s]P_1$ is correctly extracted from $mpk_i = [s_i]P_1$ fragments. Namely, the equation $mpk = [s]P_1 = \sum_{i=1}^{m} [c_i] mpk_i$ should hold where c_i denotes the Lagrange coefficient. Guaranteed by the correctness of (t, n)-threshold Shamir secret sharing, $mpk = [s]P_1 = [\sum_{i=1}^{m} c_i s_i]P_1 = \sum_{i=1}^{m} [c_i s_i]P_1 = \sum_{i=1}^{m} [c_i] mpk_i$ where $mpk_i = [s_i]P_1$. Therefore, the device public key can be correctly extracted. Similarly, we can verify that the device private key can be correctly extracted too.

5 Security Analysis

In this section, we prove that the distributed form of PKGs won't downgrade the security level of SM9 schemes by reducing the multiple PKG scenario to a single PKG scenario. Specifically, we choose SM9-IBE as an illustration. In [11], Cheng gave a rigorous proof of SM9-IBE as IND-ID-CCA secure, so we have:

Theorem 1. *If SM9-IBE scheme is secure in the IND-ID-CCA model, then SM9-IBE scheme with* (t, n)-DPKG *is secure in the IND-ID-CCA model.*

Proof. The central idea of the proof is that, if there exists an adversary $\mathcal{A}_{(t,n)}$ that wins the IND-ID-CCA game under the (t, n)-DPKG setting with advantage ϵ, then we are able to construct a simulator $\mathcal{S}$ to win the IND-ID-CCA game under the single PKG setting with the same advantage ϵ. The key step in this reduction is to create a simulator $\mathcal{S}$ which can perfectly simulate a view for $\mathcal{A}_{(t,n)}$ in a real attack. Specifically, we denote the pre-fixed corrupted PKG set chosen by $\mathcal{A}_{(t,n)}$ as A with $|A| = t$, and the remaining honest PKG set simulated by $\mathcal{S}$ as B with $|B| = n - t$.

■ **Setup.** $\mathcal{S}$ simulates $\text{PKG}_{i, i \in B}$ and runs the distributed setup protocol with $\mathcal{A}_{(t,n)}$. In the end, $\mathcal{A}_{(t,n)}$ receives $(\boldsymbol{msk}^t, \boldsymbol{mpk}^{n+1})$ where $\boldsymbol{msk}^t = \{msk_i\}_{i \in A}$ contains t shares of msk for $\text{PKG}_{i, i \in A}$, and $\boldsymbol{mpk}^{n+1} = \{mpk_1, \ldots, mpk_n, mpk\}$ contains n shares of mpk generated by $\text{PKG}_{i, i \in A \cup B}$ and the mpk.

As $\mathcal{S}$ wants to leverage $\mathcal{A}_{(t,n)}$ to help it answer the challenge proposed by the challenger $\mathcal{C}$ under the single PKG setting, $\mathcal{S}$ should convince $\mathcal{A}_{(t,n)}$ that: 1) $\mathcal{A}_{(t,n)}$'s output $\boldsymbol{msk}^t$ are t shares of the msk chosen by the challenger $\mathcal{C}$ even if $\mathcal{S}$ has no idea about the msk chosen by $\mathcal{C}$; 2) $\mathcal{A}_{(t,n)}$'s output $\boldsymbol{mpk}^n$ generated by $\text{PKG}_{i, i \in A \cup B}$ are n shares of the mpk chosen by $\mathcal{C}$. Concretely, $\mathcal{S}$ works as:

(1) $\mathcal{S}$ gets mpk from $\mathcal{C}$, by running a setup algorithm with $\mathcal{C}$.

(2) $\mathcal{S}$ runs the $\mathcal{P}^{\sigma}_{\text{rep}}$ protocol (defined in Sect. 2.4) with $\mathcal{A}_{(t,n)}$ by simulating $\text{PKG}_{i,i\in B}$, where $\mathcal{S}$ randomly chooses secret μ_i for $\text{PKG}_{i,i\in B}$. At the end of the $\mathcal{P}^{\sigma}_{\text{rep}}$ protocol execution, $\mathcal{A}_{(t,n)}$ will obtain t shares $\boldsymbol{\sigma}^t$ of σ for $\text{PKG}_{i,i\in A}$. Then $\mathcal{A}_{(t,n)}$ can compute the t master secret key shares $\boldsymbol{s}^t \leftarrow \mathsf{Conv}^*_{(t,n)}(\boldsymbol{\sigma}^t, st_0)$, and the t master public key shares $\boldsymbol{mpk}^t \leftarrow [\boldsymbol{s}^t]P_1$. Since the simulator $\mathcal{S}$ chooses secrets for $n-t$ honest PKG nodes randomly, $\mathcal{S}$ can perfectly simulate the view for $\mathcal{A}_{(t,n)}$ in a $\mathcal{P}^{\sigma}_{\text{rep}}$ protocol. After running the $\mathcal{P}^{\sigma}_{\text{rep}}$ protocol with $\mathcal{S}$, $\mathcal{A}_{(t,n)}$ obtains $(\{\boldsymbol{\sigma}^t, \boldsymbol{s}^t\}, \boldsymbol{mpk}^t)$ for $\text{PKG}_{i,i\in A}$. Since (t,n)-DPKG for SM9 requires $n-t \geq t+1$, $\mathcal{S}$ holding $n-t$ shares of σ is able to derive all the outputs of $\mathcal{A}_{(t,n)}$.

(3) $\mathcal{S}$ computes the $\boldsymbol{mpk}^{n-t}$ generated by $\text{PKG}_{i,i\in B}$, by performing Lagrange polynomial interpolation with $\boldsymbol{mpk}^t$ generated by $\text{PKG}_{i,i\in A}$ and mpk. This ensures the n shares $\boldsymbol{mpk}^n$ generated by $\text{PKG}_{i,i\in A\cup B}$ are sharing the secret mpk. Then $\mathcal{S}$ sends $\boldsymbol{mpk}^{n-t}$ and mpk to $\mathcal{A}_{(t,n)}$.

(4) $\mathcal{A}_{(t,n)}$ outputs $(\{\boldsymbol{\sigma}^t, \boldsymbol{s}^t\}, \boldsymbol{mpk}^{n+1})$, where $\boldsymbol{msk}^t$ is denoted as $\{\boldsymbol{\sigma}^t, \boldsymbol{s}^t\}$.

Guaranteed by the perfect security of (t,n)-Shamir secret sharing, $\mathcal{A}_{(t,n)}$ holding only t shares $\boldsymbol{s}^t$ of some master secret key s' (s' is the master secret key determined by $\mathcal{S}$ and $\mathcal{A}_{(t,n)}$ running the $\mathcal{P}^{\sigma}_{\text{rep}}$ protocol), cannot tell if $\boldsymbol{s}^t$ is sharing the secret s' or the secret msk chosen by $\mathcal{C}$. Hence the simulation is correct.

■ **Phase 1.** $\mathcal{A}_{(t,n)}$ adaptively makes private key extraction $\langle\text{ID}\rangle$ queries and decryption $\langle\text{ID}, c\rangle$ queries. For a $\langle\text{ID}, c\rangle$ query, $\mathcal{S}$ passes the query and decrypted c back and forth between $\mathcal{A}_{(t,n)}$ and $\mathcal{C}$. For a $\langle\text{ID}\rangle$ query, $\mathcal{S}$ simulates $\text{PKG}_{i,i\in B}$ running the distributed private key extraction protocol with $\mathcal{A}_{(t,n)}$, and sends $\boldsymbol{S}^{n-t}_{\text{ID}} = \{S^{(i)}_{\text{ID}}\}_{i\in B}$ generated by $\text{PKG}_{i,i\in B}$ to $\mathcal{A}_{(t,n)}$. Concretely, $\mathcal{S}$ works as:

(1) $\mathcal{S}$ gets S_{ID} from $\mathcal{C}$, by forwarding $\mathcal{A}_{(t,n)}$'s $\langle$ ID $\rangle$ query to $\mathcal{C}$.

(2) $\mathcal{S}$ runs the $\mathsf{DExtract}$ protocol with $\mathcal{A}_{(t,n)}$ by simulating $\text{PKG}_{i,i\in B}$, where $\mathcal{S}$ needs to simulate $z_{i,i\in B}$ for $\mathcal{A}_{(t,n)}$. To simulate $z_{i,i\in B}$, $\mathcal{S}$ first computes $z_{i,i\in A}$. Then $\mathcal{S}$ chooses a random z. Next, $\mathcal{S}$ computes $z_{i,i\in B}$ with $z_{i,i\in A}$ and z, ensuring that the $2t$-privately Shamir shares $\{z_i\}_{i\in A\cup B}$ are sharing the secret z. Finally, $\mathcal{S}$ sends $z_{i,i\in B}$ to $\mathcal{A}_{(t,n)}$.

(3) $\mathcal{S}$ computes $\boldsymbol{S}^{n-t}_{\text{ID}}$ generated by $\text{PKG}_{i,i\in B}$. First, $\mathcal{S}$ computes $\boldsymbol{S}^{t}_{\text{ID}} = \{S^{(i)}_{\text{ID}}\}_{i\in A}$. Then $\mathcal{S}$ computes $\boldsymbol{S}^{n-t}_{\text{ID}} = \{S^{(i)}_{\text{ID}}\}_{i\in B}$, by performing Lagrange polynomial interpolation with $\boldsymbol{S}^{t}_{\text{ID}}$ and the S_{ID}. This ensures the t-privately Shamir shares $\{S^{(i)}_{\text{ID}}\}_{i\in A\cup B}$ are sharing the secret S_{ID} returned by the challenger $\mathcal{C}$.

(4) $\mathcal{S}$ sends $\boldsymbol{S_{\text{ID}}}^{n-t}$ to $\mathcal{A}_{(t,n)}$.

In the simulation, $\boldsymbol{S}^{n}_{\text{ID}} = \{S^{(i)}_{\text{ID}}\}_{i\in A\cup B}$ are random shares to $\mathcal{A}_{(t,n)}$, since z are randomly chosen by $\mathcal{S}$. The view is consistent with what $\mathcal{A}_{(t,n)}$ has seen in a real distributed private key extraction protocol. $\mathcal{A}_{(t,n)}$ holding only t shares of z and without any prior-knowledge of z, views z as completely random distribution (guaranteed by perfect security of (t,n)-Shamir secret sharing), which means the i_{th} key fragment $S_{\mathrm{ID}}^{(i)} = [1 - F(\mathrm{ID}) \cdot \frac{r_i}{z}]P_2$ is actually a random share to $\mathcal{A}_{(t,n)}$. Thus the simulation is correct.

■ **Challenge.** $\mathcal{A}_{(t,n)}$ sends a tuple $\{m_0, m_1, \mathrm{ID}^*\}$ to $\mathcal{S}$, where m_0 and m_1 are two distinct messages with the same length, an identity ID^* which has never been queried in Phase 1. $\mathcal{S}$ forwards the tuple to $\mathcal{C}$. $\mathcal{C}$ picks a random bit $b \in \{0, 1\}$, and sends c_b^* to $\mathcal{S}$ by computing $c_b^* = \mathsf{Enc}(mpk, \mathrm{ID}^*, m_b)$. $\mathcal{S}$ passes c_b^* to $\mathcal{A}_{(t,n)}$.

■ **Phase 2.** $\mathcal{A}_{(t,n)}$ continues to make private key extraction queries and decryption queries. $\mathcal{S}$ responds just as Phase 1 except for the private key extraction query $\langle \mathrm{ID}^* \rangle$ and the decryption query $\langle \mathrm{ID}^*, c_b^* \rangle$.

■ **Guess.** $\mathcal{A}_{(t,n)}$ outputs a guess $b' \in \{0, 1\}$ of b. Then $\mathcal{S}$ outputs b' as its guess.

Obviously, the advantage of $\mathcal{S}$ is the same as $\mathcal{A}_{(t,n)}$'s, because $\mathcal{A}_{(t,n)}$'s guess is exactly what $\mathcal{S}$ needs to attack the IBE scheme under the single PKG setting:

$$\begin{aligned} Adv_{\mathcal{S}}^{\text{IND-ID-CCA}_{\text{IBE}}} &= 2|Pr[b' = b : \mathcal{S} \to b'] - \frac{1}{2}| = 2|Pr[b' = b : \mathcal{A}_{(t,n)} \to b'] - \frac{1}{2}| \\ &= Adv_{\mathcal{A}_{(t,n)}}^{\text{IND-ID-CCA}_{(t,n)\text{-IBE}}} = \epsilon \end{aligned} \tag{1}$$

Since the SM9-IBE scheme under the single PKG setting is IND-ID-CCA secure, we have $\epsilon \leq negl(\lambda)$ for some negligible function $negl(\cdot)$. Combing with (1), we come to the conclusion that the SM9-IBE scheme under the (t, n)-DPKG setting is IND-ID-CCA secure, too.

6 Performance Evaluation

In this section, we first present implementation details of the proposed (t, n)-DPKG. Then we focus on the tradeoff between the system security, robustness and efficiency that inherently existed in the threshold key generation. Finally, we justify the feasibility of integrating (t, n)-DPKG to a deployed system, by comparing a $(2, 6)$-DPKG instance with the centralized private key generation.

A. Implementation Details

We construct our code in C and C++, based on the MIRACL library for elliptic curve cryptography. Benchmark tests are done with google benchmark. We have six PKGs deployed on three Alibaba Cloud simple application servers having 1 CPU core with 2 GB RAM, each running two PKG instances. The round-trip latencies among them are 3 ms∼17 ms. We implement CC as a relatively resource-constrained virtual machine on Virturalbox, which is assigned to only 400 MB RAM, 1 CPU core and the CPU frequency is set to 360 MHz. The operating system for PKG/CC is Ubuntu Server 18.04/14.04 LTS.

B. The Tradeoff Between the Security, Robustness and Efficiency

Although (t, n)-DPKG tackles the inherent *single point of failures* problem of IBC schemes, the system security and robustness come at a price. There is an inherent tradeoff between the system security, robustness and efficiency in (t, n)-DPKG , which can be adjusted via the (t, n)-threshold. Table 2 presents

Table 2. (t, n)-threshold's impact on various overheads

	Communication (sent bytes)	Computation Time	Storage (bytes)
PKG at setup	$32(n-1)\binom{n-1}{t}$	$\binom{n-1}{t}\mathcal{T}_{\mathsf{h}} + \mathcal{T}_{\mathsf{pm}}$	$32\binom{n-1}{t} + n\mathcal{L}^{\mathsf{addr}}$
PKG at extract	$32(n-1)$	$(t-1)\binom{n-1}{t}\mathcal{T}_{\mathsf{h}} + \mathcal{T}_{\mathsf{pm}}$	
CC at setup	0	$(t+1)\mathcal{T}_{\mathsf{pm}}$	$n\mathcal{L}^{\mathsf{addr}}$
CC at extract	$n\mathcal{L}^{\mathsf{id}}$	$(t+1)\mathcal{T}_{\mathsf{pm}}$	

† $\mathcal{L}^{\mathsf{id}}$ and $\mathcal{L}^{\mathsf{addr}}$ are the byte-length of the IoT device's identity and the ip address of the PKG respectively. $\mathcal{T}_{\mathsf{h}}$ and $\mathcal{T}_{\mathsf{pm}}$ stand for the time complexity of hashing and elliptic curve scalar multiplication operation respectively.

how the storage overhead, communication overhead and computation overhead change with the (t, n)-threshold. Due to space limitation, Table 2 only lists the most significant item that affects the overhead. In conjunction with Table 2, we can get the following conclusions:

- Small (t, n)-threshold values are preferable in terms of efficiency, as the overheads on PKG/CC will increase exponentially/linearly with increasing (t, n).
- Large (t, n)-threshold values are preferable in terms of security and robustness. Since in the proposed (t, n)-DPKG scheme for SM9, the security connotation is that *at most t PKGs can be corrupted without exposing the master secret key*; the robustness connotation is that *at most* $n - 2t - 1$ *PKGs can go offline half the way without interrupting the user private key generation service.*
- To strike a good tradeoff between the system security, robustness and efficiency, a recommended range for the number of private key generators n is between 3 and 10. On the one hand, (t, n)-DPKG for SM9 requires $n \geq 2t + 1$ and $t > 0$ which implies $n \geq 3$. On the other hand, according to the experiment we find out that after n has climbed to a certain value (roughly around $n = 10$), a slight increase in t will result in the boom of overheads on the PKG side. One can choose the t value on the need, but increasing t will result in increasing system security while decreasing system robustness, and vice versa.

C. Comparison to the Centralized Private Key Generation

A major concern of the proposed (t, n)-DPKG scheme for SM9 is about efficiency, that is, if (t, n)-DPKG is too slow to be integrated into a deployed system. Indeed, efficiency is a practical concern since the key generation centers may need to generate substantial private keys for distinct IDs. To inspect efficiency, we instantiate a $(2, 6)$-DPKG instance and compare it with the centralized key generation setting. We can tell from the outcome presented in Table 3 that when the (t, n)-threshold is small ($t = 2$ and $n = 6$ in our case), the proposed (t, n)-DPKG for SM9 can easily handle up to 1 million private key generation requests per day (only 21ms is required handling per request in $(2, 6)$-DPKG). For IoT device manufactories equipped with much more productive settings, they can trade efficiency for security and robustness by working with larger (t, n) values.

Table 3. Comparison between the centralized key generation and (2, 6)-DPKG

	Communication Traffic	Computation Time on PKG	Computation Time on CC	Key Generation Time	Secure	Robust
Centralized	43 Bytes	1.54 ms	N/A	1.54 ms	×	×
(2, 6)-DPKG	1218 Bytes	2.11 ms	33.49 ms	21.32 ms	√	√

† We assume the IoT device identity's byte-length $\mathcal{L}^{\mathsf{id}} = 10$. The key generation time refers to the time that the PKGs deal with a private key generation request, which excludes the time of combining private key fragments.

7 Conclusion

In this paper, to deal with the master secret key leakage problem in SM9, we propose a (t, n)-threshold Distributed Private Key Generation ((t, n)-DPKG) solution with some techniques from multiparty computation. The proposed scheme achieves better master secret key protection, and doesn't require any modification of original SM9 algorithms after the user private key generation. Besides enhanced security and robustness, we conduct experiments and the results show that with a small (t, n)-threshold value, the proposed scheme can achieve a good balance between the system security, robustness and efficiency.

Acknowledgements. The authors would like to thank the anonymous reviewers for their valuable comments. This work was supported in part by National Natural Science Foundation of China (Nos. 61772520, 61802392, 61972094, 61472416, 61632020), in part by Key Research and Development Project of Zhejiang Province (Nos. 2017C01062, 2020C01078), in part by Beijing Municipal Science and Technology Commission (Project Number Z191100007119007 and Z191100007119002).

References

1. GM/T 0044.1-2016: identity-based cryptographic algorithms SM9-part 1: General. Technical report (2016)
2. GM/T 0044.5-2016: identity-based cryptographic algorithms SM9-part 5: Parameter definition. Technical report (2016)
3. Al-Riyami, S.S., Paterson, K.G.: Certificateless public key cryptography. In: Laih, C.-S. (ed.) ASIACRYPT 2003. LNCS, vol. 2894, pp. 452–473. Springer, Heidelberg (2003). https://doi.org/10.1007/978-3-540-40061-5_29
4. Asharov, G., Lindell, Y.: A full proof of the BGW protocol for perfectly secure multiparty computation. J. Cryptology **30**(1), 58–151 (2017)
5. Baek, J., Safavi-Naini, R., Susilo, W.: Certificateless public key encryption without pairing. In: Zhou, J., Lopez, J., Deng, R.H., Bao, F. (eds.) ISC 2005. LNCS, vol. 3650, pp. 134–148. Springer, Heidelberg (2005). https://doi.org/10.1007/11556992_10
6. Bar-Ilan, J., Beaver, D.: Non-cryptographic fault-tolerant computing in constant number of rounds of interaction. In: Rudnicki, P. (ed.) PODC 1989, pp. 201–209. ACM (1989)

7. Boneh, D., Franklin, M.: Identity-based encryption from the Weil pairing. In: Kilian, J. (ed.) CRYPTO 2001. LNCS, vol. 2139, pp. 213–229. Springer, Heidelberg (2001). https://doi.org/10.1007/3-540-44647-8_13
8. Boyen, X.: General *Ad Hoc* encryption from exponent inversion IBE. In: Naor, M. (ed.) EUROCRYPT 2007. LNCS, vol. 4515, pp. 394–411. Springer, Heidelberg (2007). https://doi.org/10.1007/978-3-540-72540-4_23
9. Chen, L., Harrison, K., Soldera, D., Smart, N.P.: Applications of multiple trust authorities in pairing based cryptosystems. In: Davida, G., Frankel, Y., Rees, O. (eds.) InfraSec 2002. LNCS, vol. 2437, pp. 260–275. Springer, Heidelberg (2002). https://doi.org/10.1007/3-540-45831-X_18
10. Cheng, Z.: The SM9 cryptographic schemes. IACR Cryptology ePrint Archive 2017, 117 (2017). https://eprint.iacr.org/2017/117.pdf
11. Cheng, Z.: Security analysis of SM9 key agreement and encryption. In: Guo, F., Huang, X., Yung, M. (eds.) Inscrypt 2018. LNCS, vol. 11449, pp. 3–25. Springer, Cham (2019). https://doi.org/10.1007/978-3-030-14234-6_1
12. Cramer, R., Damgård, I., Ishai, Y.: Share conversion, pseudorandom secret-sharing and applications to secure computation. In: Kilian, J. (ed.) TCC 2005. LNCS, vol. 3378, pp. 342–362. Springer, Heidelberg (2005). https://doi.org/10.1007/978-3-540-30576-7_19
13. Gao, W., Wang, G., Wang, X., Chen, K.: Generic construction of certificate-based encryption from certificateless encryption revisited. Comput. J. **58**(10), 2747–2757 (2015)
14. Geisler, M., Smart, N.P.: Distributing the key distribution centre in Sakai–Kasahara based systems. In: Parker, M.G. (ed.) IMACC 2009. LNCS, vol. 5921, pp. 252–262. Springer, Heidelberg (2009). https://doi.org/10.1007/978-3-642-10868-6_15
15. Gentry, C.: Certificate-based encryption and the certificate revocation problem. In: Biham, E. (ed.) EUROCRYPT 2003. LNCS, vol. 2656, pp. 272–293. Springer, Heidelberg (2003). https://doi.org/10.1007/3-540-39200-9_17
16. Goldwasser, S., Ben-Or, M., Wigderson, A.: Completeness theorems for non-cryptographic fault-tolerant distributed computing. In: STOC, pp. 1–10 (1988)
17. Lai, J., Kou, W.: Self-generated-certificate public key encryption without pairing. In: Okamoto, T., Wang, X. (eds.) PKC 2007. LNCS, vol. 4450, pp. 476–489. Springer, Heidelberg (2007). https://doi.org/10.1007/978-3-540-71677-8_31
18. Lee, B., Boyd, C., Dawson, E., Kim, K., Yang, J., Yoo, S.: Secure key issuing in id-based cryptography. In: Hogan, J.M., Montague, P., Purvis, M.K., Steketee, C. (eds.) ACSW Frontiers 2004, CRPIT, vol. 32, pp. 69–74 (2004)
19. Lindell, Y.: Fast secure two-party ECDSA signing. In: Katz, J., Shacham, H. (eds.) CRYPTO 2017. LNCS, vol. 10402, pp. 613–644. Springer, Cham (2017). https://doi.org/10.1007/978-3-319-63715-0_21
20. Long, Y., Xiong, F.: Collaborative generations of SM9 private key and digital signature using homomorphic encryption. In: ICCCS 2020, pp. 76–81. IEEE (2020)
21. Sakai, R., Kasahara, M.: Id based cryptosystems with pairing on elliptic curve. IACR Cryptology ePrint 2003, 54 (2003). https://eprint.iacr.org/2003/054.pdf
22. Smart, N.P.: Cryptography Made Simple. Information Security and Cryptography. Springer, Cham (2016). https://doi.org/10.1007/978-3-319-21936-3
23. Xu, S., Ren, X., Yuan, F., Guo, C., Yang, S.: A secure key issuing scheme of SM9. Comput. Appl. Softw. **37**(01) (2020)

Post-quantum Crypto

Chosen Ciphertext Attacks Secure Inner-Product Functional Encryption from Learning with Errors Assumption

Kelly Yun[1,2(✉)] and Rui Xue[1,2(✉)]

[1] State Key Laboratory of Information Security, Institute of Information Engineering, Chinese Academy of Sciences, Beijing 100093, China
{yuankaili,xuerui}@iie.ac.cn

[2] School of Cyber Security, University of Chinese Academy of Sciences, Beijing 100049, China
yunkaili15@mails.ucas.ac.cn

Abstract. Functional Encryption (FE) is an ambitious generalization of public key encryption (PKE), which overcomes the all-or-nothing feature and is an emerging technique for cloud computing. Security against chosen ciphertext attacks (CCA) is the *de facto* level of security required for PKE used in practice. We first show a generic construction from (selective id) chosen plaintext attacks secure identity-based functional encryption (sIBFE-CPA) to CCA secure FE, which is efficient and interesting, resulting in constructing CPA, even CCA FE is to construct CPA IBFE. Then we give an instantiation of sIBFE scheme for inner product (IP) functions from standard learning with errors (LWE) assumption, which applying our transformation gives the first CCA secure IPFE under the same assumption.

Keywords: Functional encryption · Identity-based functional encryption · Chosen ciphertext attacks security · Inner product · Learning with errors.

1 Introduction

FE is an ambitious generalization of PKE which overcomes the all-or-nothing, user-based access to encrypted data and enables fine grained, role-based access to the data. Namely, FE comes equipped with a key generation algorithm that utilizes a master secret key to generate decryption keys sk_F corresponding to functions F where the key holders only learn $F(x)$ from a ciphertext $\mathrm{Enc}(x)$ and no more information about x is revealed. This is well suited for cloud computing

Supported by Beijing Municipal Science & Technology Commission (Project Number: Z191100007119006), National Natural Science Foundation of China grants No. 61772514, and National Key R&D Program of China (2017YFB1400700).

Y. Wu and M. Yung (Eds.): Inscrypt 2020, LNCS 12612, pp. 133–147, 2021.
https://doi.org/10.1007/978-3-030-71852-7_9

platforms and remote untrustworthy servers to store sensitive private data and allow users to request the result of the function F computing on the underlying data.

The definition of FE was first formalized by [18,40] which gave indistinguishability (IND-based) and simulation (SIM-based) security model, and identity-based encryption (IBE) [3,14,16,21,22,29,44], attribute-based encryption (ABE) [11,17,30,32,43], predicate encryption (PE) [4,31,35,36,39] and other concrete functionalities [19,46] in a general framework could all be regarded as specific function classes of FE. And IBFE formalized by Yun et al. [48] which adds identity *id* to the input to KeyGen and Encrypt algorithms and in the game, adversary cannot query secret keys under challenge identity id*, is also a special class and could be easily realized from fully fledged FE schemes.

However, the only existing FE schemes for general function [9,25,27,47] were constructed from some strong assumptions, e.g. indistinguishability obfuscation (iO) or multi-linear maps machinery, and existing constructions [24,28] were found to be insecure [23,33]. Conversely, there is also some fascinating work that constructs iO from FE schemes [8,12,13,26]. So constructing unbounded FE schemes from standard assumptions is a fascinating problem and the final aim in this area.

Recently Abdalla et al. [1] built FE for IP surprisingly and efficiently from standard assumptions like the Decision Diffie-Hellman (DDH) and LWE assumptions. Later, Agrawal et al. [5] promoted their schemes from selective security to adaptive security and gave an additional construction from Decision Composite Residuosity (DCR) assumption. Then Wang et al. [45] promoted their proof, especially under the standard LWE assumption avoiding the multi-hint extended learning with errors assumption (meLWE). The above schemes are CPA secure, which ensures that the plaintext is protected from any eavesdropping that adversary is infeasible to determine which message was actually encrypted. CCA security guarantees security against active adversary who may obtain decryptions of ciphertexts or may modify messages. As we have already mentioned, CCA is the *de facto* level of security required used in practice. Benhamouda et al. [10] presented the first CCA secure IPFE from projective hash functions (PHF) with homomorphic properties, which gave up on the lattice-based concrete constructions, because existing constructions from lattices are not satisfied with the required properties. This motivates the following question:

Can we build CCA secure IPFE scheme under the standard LWE assumption?

1.1 Our Results

We answer the above question affirmatively. We first show a generic construction from sIBFE-CPA to CCA secure FE. Then we give an instantiation of sIBFE for IP from standard LWE assumption, which applying our transformation gives the first CCA secure IPFE under the same assumption.

Our result is powerful and interesting, resulting in constructing CPA, even CCA FE is to construct CPA IBFE. For instance, beyond IP functions, Yun et al.

[48] presented an IBFE for quadratic functions construction from standard LWE assumption in the random oracle model. Thus, applying our transformation, there is also a CCA FE for quadratic functions scheme in the random oracle model from LWE assumption.

Overview of Techniques. IBFE, on the one hand, can be regarded as FE under identity-based control, and on the other hand, we can think it as an extension of IBE what only allows certain identity owners to decrypt partial information or function values. There are so many IBE schemes from different kinds of assumptions, so we think maybe we can gain some interesting results.

CCA security is the go-to security nowadays. To achieve CCA security, there is not only PHF method, competitively in efficiency but also BCHK [15] transformation which transforms CPA IBE to CCA PKE. So using their methods, we obtain a generic transformation from CPA IBFE to CCA FE which has almost the same high efficiency. Besides IBFE, we only need a strong one time signature which prevents malleability of the ciphertexts.

We then combine IBE [3] and IPFE [5] to obtain a sIBIPFE. Recently Wang et al. [45] promoted the proof of IPFE scheme under standard LWE assumption, which avoids meLWE by using noise re-randomized technique from [34], so we obtain a sIBIPFE from the same assumption and our security proof can be reduced to their proof besides some IBE techniques.

1.2 Related Work

Nandi and Pandit [38] gave a conversion from CPA to CCA FE which have delegation or verifiability property, which does not adapt to hidden index predicate encryption and hence for a general FE.

Benhamouda et al. [10] presented the first CCA secure IPFE from projective hash functions (PHF) with homomorphic properties, which gave up on the lattice-based concrete constructions, because existing constructions from lattices are not satisfied with the required properties, and as a byproduct, they introduce a tag-based functional encryption (TBFE). Note that TBFE is weaker than IBFE, especially in its verifiability. Namely, the KeyGen algorithm does not refer to an identity verification.

Yun et al. [48] formalized the identity-based functional encryption definition and indistinguishability security (IND-IBFE-CPA), and presented an IBFE for quadratic functions construction from standard LWE assumption in the random oracle model. Thus, applying our transformation, there is also a CCA FE for quadratic functions scheme in the random oracle model from LWE assumption.

Abdalla et al. [2] recently revisit FE with fine-grained access control owing to its efficiency and interest, and they give an IBFE scheme for IP almost as ours, and applying our transformation, there is also a CCA IPFE, which is more interesting.

1.3 Organization

In Sect. 2, we introduce some definitions of some primitives and its security. We present our construction from sIBFE to FE and its proof in Sect. 3. Section 4 first introduces some necessary notations and some lemmas, algorithms and assumptions from lattice-based cryptography and then presents an instantiation of sIBIPFE scheme. In Sect. 5, we briefly analyze its security. We conclude and propose some open problems in Sect. 6.

2 Preliminary

2.1 Functional Encryption

We recall the syntax of FE, as defined by [18], and indistinguishability based CCA definition [10].

Definition 1 (Functionality). *A functionality F defined over ($\mathcal{K}$, $\mathcal{M}$) is a function F: $\mathcal{K} \times \mathcal{M} \to \Sigma \cup \{\perp\}$ where $\mathcal{K}$ is a key space, $\mathcal{M}$ is a message space and Σ is an output space which does not contain the special symbol $\perp$. For IP, F($\mathcal{K}$, $\mathcal{M}$) $= <\mathcal{K}, \mathcal{M}>$.*

Definition 2 (Functional Encryption). *A functional encryption scheme FE for a functionality F is a tuple of four algorithms FE = (Setup, KeyGen, Encrypt, Decrypt) that work as follows:*

Setup(1^λ) *takes as input a security parameter 1^λ and outputs a master key pair (mpk, msk).*

KeyGen(msk, K) *takes as input the master secret key and a key (i.e. a function) $K \in \mathcal{K}$, and outputs a secret key sk_K.*

Encrypt(mpk, M) *takes as input the master public key mpk and a message M $\in \mathcal{M}$, and outputs a ciphertext C.*

Decrypt(mpk, sk_K, C) *takes as input a secret key sk_K and a ciphertext C, and returns an output $v \in \Sigma \cup \{\perp\}$.*

For correctness, it is required that for all (mpk, msk) $\leftarrow$ Setup(1^λ), all keys $K \in \mathcal{K}$ and all messages $M \in \mathcal{M}$, if $sk_K \leftarrow$ KeyGen(msk, K) and $C \leftarrow$ Encrypt(mpk, M), then it holds with overwhelming probability that Decrypt(sk_K, C) = F(K, M) whenever F(K, M) $\neq \perp$.

Definition 3 (IND-FE-CCA Security). *For a functional encryption scheme FE for a functionality F over ($\mathcal{K}$, $\mathcal{M}$), security against chosen ciphertext attacks (IND-FE-CCA, for short) if no PPT adversary has non-negligible advantage in the following game:*

1. *The challenger runs (mpk, msk) $\leftarrow$ Setup(1^λ) and gives mpk to $\mathcal{A}$.*

2. *The adversary $\mathcal{A}$ adaptively makes secret key and decryption queries. At each secret key query, $\mathcal{A}$ chooses a key $K \in \mathcal{K}$ and obtains $sk_K \leftarrow KeyGen(msk, K)$. At each decryption query, $\mathcal{A}$ chooses a ciphertext C' and $K \in \mathcal{K}$, then the challenger computes $sk_K \leftarrow KeyGen(msk, K)$ and sends back $Decrypt(sk_K, C')$.*
3. *Adversary $\mathcal{A}$ chooses a pair of distinct messages M_0, $M_1 \in \mathcal{M}$ such that $F(K, M_0) = F(K, M_1)$ holds for all Keys K queried in the previous phase. The challenger computes $C^* \leftarrow Encrypt(mpk, M_\beta)$ and return C^* to $\mathcal{A}$.*
4. *Adversary $\mathcal{A}$ makes further secret key queries for arbitrary keys $K \in \mathcal{K}$ under the requirement that $F(K, M_0) = F(K, M_1)$, and further decryption queries (C', K) under the requirement that $C' \neq C^*$.*
5. *Adversary $\mathcal{A}$ eventually outputs a bit $\beta' \in \{0,1\}$ and wins if $\beta' = \beta$. The adversary's advantage is defined to be $Adv_{\mathcal{A}}(\lambda) := |Pr[\beta' = \beta] - 1/2|$.*

We then recall the definitions of IBFE and its security by [48].

Definition 4 (Identity-Based Functional Encryption). *An identity-based functional encryption (IBFE) scheme for a functionality F is a tuple of four algorithms IBFE = (Setup, KeyGen, Encrypt, Decrypt) that work as follows:*

Setup(1^λ) *takes as input a security parameter 1^λ and outputs a master key pair (mpk, msk).*

KeyGen(msk, id, K) *takes as input the master secret key, an $id \in \mathcal{ID}$ and a key (a.k.a. a function) $K \in \mathcal{K}$, and outputs a secret key sk_K.*

Encrypt(mpk, id, M) *takes as input the master public key mpk, an $id \in \mathcal{ID}$ and a message $M \in \mathcal{M}$, and outputs a ciphertext C.*

Decrypt(mpk, sk_K, C) *takes as input a secret key sk_K and a ciphertext C, and returns an output $v \in \Sigma \cup \{\perp\}$.*

For correctness, it is required that for all (mpk, msk) $\leftarrow Setup(1^\lambda)$, all $id \in \mathcal{ID}$, all keys $K \in \mathcal{K}$ and all messages $M \in \mathcal{M}$, if $sk_K \leftarrow KeyGen(msk, id, K)$ and $C \leftarrow Encrypt(mpk, id, M)$, then it holds with overwhelming probability that $Decrypt(sk_K, C) = F(K, M)$ whenever $F(K, M) \neq \perp$.

Definition 5 (IND-IBFE-CPA Security). *For an identity-based functional encryption scheme for a functionality F over $(\mathcal{K}, \mathcal{M})$, security against chosen-plaintext attacks (IND-IBFE-CPA, for short) if no PPT adversary has non-negligible advantage in the following game:*

1. *The challenger runs (mpk, msk) $\leftarrow Setup(1^\lambda)$ and gives mpk to $\mathcal{A}$.*
2. *The adversary $\mathcal{A}$ adaptively makes secret key queries. At each query, $\mathcal{A}$ chooses an identity $id \in \mathcal{ID}$ and a key $K \in \mathcal{K}$ and obtains $sk_K \leftarrow KeyGen(msk, id, K)$.*
3. *Adversary $\mathcal{A}$ chooses an identity $id^* \in \mathcal{ID}$ and a pair of distinct messages M_0, $M_1 \in \mathcal{M}$ such that $F(K, M_0) = F(K, M_1)$ holds for all Keys K queried in the previous phase. The chanllenger computes $C^* \leftarrow Encrypt(mpk, id^*, M_\beta)$ and return C^* to $\mathcal{A}$.*
4. *Adversary $\mathcal{A}$ makes further secret key queries for arbitrary identities $id \in \mathcal{ID}$ and keys $K \in \mathcal{K}$, but under the restriction that $id \neq id^*$ and $F(K, M_0) = F(K, M_1)$.*

5. *Adversary $\mathcal{A}$ eventually outputs a bit $\beta' \in \{0,1\}$ and wins if $\beta' = \beta$.* *The adversary's advantage is defined to be $Adv_{\mathcal{A}}(\lambda) := |Pr[\beta' = \beta] - 1/2|$.*

The selective id security (IND-sIBFE-CPA) has the further requirement that the challenge identity is selected by the adversary before the public key is generated.

Finally, we recall definitions of signature and its strong one-time security.

Definition 6 (Signature). *A signature is a tripple of PPT algorithms (Gen, Sign, Vrfy) such that:*

***Gen**(1^λ) takes as input the security parameter 1^λ and outputs a verification key vk and a signing key sk.*

***Sign**(sk, m) takes as input a signing key sk and a messages m, and outputs a signature σ.*

***Vrfy**(vk, m, σ) takes as input a verification key vk, a message m, and a signature σ, outouts 1 if accept, otherwise 0.*

Definition 7 (Strong Unforgeable One Time Signature (OTS-sUF-CMA)). *If the success probability of any PPT adversary $\mathcal{A}$ in the following game is negligible in the security parameter λ:*

1. *Gen(1^λ) outputs (vk, sk) and the adversary is given 1^λ and vk.*
2. *Query: $\mathcal{A}(1^\lambda$, vk) is given access to the oracle Sign(sk, .) at most once. Let (m, σ) be the query message and signature.*
3. *Forge: The adversary $\mathcal{A}$ outputs a signature (m^*, σ^*).* *We say the adversary succeeds if $Vrfy_{vk}(m^*, \sigma^*) = 1$ but $(m^*, \sigma^*) \neq (m, \sigma)$.*

3 A Genneric Construction from CPA-sIBFE to CCA FE

Given an IBFE scheme = ($Setup', KeyGen', Encrypt', Decrypt'$), which is selective id secure against chosen plaintext attacks (IND-sIBFE-CPA), we construct a FE scheme = ($Setup, KeyGen, Encrypt, Decrypt$) secure against chosen ciphertext attacks (IND-FE-CCA). In the construction, we use a strong one-time signature scheme Sig = ($Gen, Sign, Vrfy$). The construction proceeds as follows:

Setup(1^λ) runs $Setup'(1^\lambda)$ to obtain (mpk', msk'), then mpk $= mpk'$ and msk $= msk'$.

KeyGen(msk, K) runs $KeyGen'(msk, id, K)$ to obtain (sk'_K, id), and outputs a secret key $sk_K = (sk'_K$, id).

Encrypt(mpk, M) runs (vk, sk) $\leftarrow Gen(1^\lambda)$ and $C' \leftarrow Encrypt'$(mpk, vk, M), and computes $\sigma \leftarrow Sign_{sk}(C')$ outputs a ciphertext C $= (vk, C', \sigma)$.

Decrypt(mpk, sk_K, C) first checks whether id = vk and $Vrfy_{vk}(C', \sigma)$ =1 or not. If not, output $\perp$, otherwise output $Decrypt'(mpk, sk'_K, C')$.

Correctness is obvious. We give some intuition why FE scheme is CCA secure. Let (vk*, C*, σ*) be the challenge. It should be clear that C* hides plaintext. Then we claim that decryption oracle queries cannot help adversary determining the plaintext.

Theorem 1. *If IBFE is IND-sIBFE-CPA secure and Sig is a strong one-time signature scheme, then FE is IND-FE-CCA secure.*

Proof. Let $\mathcal{A}$ be an adversary attacking the CCA security of FE, $\mathcal{B}$ be an adversary attacking the CPA security of IBFE. Say a ciphertext (vk, C, σ) is valid if $Vrfy_{vk}(id||C', \sigma) = 1$. Let (vk*, C*, σ*) be the challenge.

If vk = vk*, the decryption oracle reply $\perp$, so the advantage of $\mathcal{A}$ is the probability of the strong one time signature forge successfully.

If vk $\neq$ vk*, the decryption oracle will not help the adversary, so the advantage of $\mathcal{A}$ is the advantage of $\mathcal{B}$.

Then, we have

$$Adv_{\mathcal{A}}^{FE-CCA} \leq Adv_{\mathcal{B}}^{IBFE-CPA} + Adv^{OTS-sUF-CMA}.$$

4 Instantiations of Identity-Based Inner Product Functional Encryption

4.1 Lattices Preliminary

Notations. We denote vectors by lower-case bold letters (e.g. $\mathbf{x}$) and are always in column form (respectively, $\mathbf{x}^\top$ is a row vector). Matrices are denoted by upper-case bold letters (e.g. $\mathbf{A}$) and treat them with their ordered column vector sets $[\mathbf{a}_1, \mathbf{a}_2, ...]$. We let $\mathbf{M_1}|\mathbf{M_2}$ denote the (ordered) concatenation of the column vector sets of $\mathbf{M_1}$ and $\mathbf{M_2}$, $\mathbf{M_1}||\mathbf{M_2}$ denote the (ordered) concatenation of the row vector sets of $\mathbf{M_1}$ and $\mathbf{M_2}$, and vectors are similar. For a vector $\mathbf{x}$, we let $\|\mathbf{x}\|$ denote its l_2 norm and $\|\mathbf{x}\|_\infty$ denote its infinity norm. Similarly, for matrices $\|\cdot\|$ and $\|\cdot\|_\infty$ denote their l_2 and infinity norms respectively.

An m-dimensional lattice $\mathcal{L}$ is a discrete additive subgroup of $\mathbb{R}^m$. Given positive integers n, m, q and a matrix $\mathbf{A} \in \mathbb{Z}_q^{n\times m}$, we let $\Lambda_q^\perp(\mathbf{A})$ denote the lattice $\{\mathbf{x} \in \mathbb{Z}^m : \mathbf{A}\cdot\mathbf{x} = \mathbf{0} \bmod q\}$ and $\Lambda_q(\mathbf{A})$ denote the lattice $\{\mathbf{y} \in \mathbb{Z}^m : \mathbf{y} = \mathbf{A}^\top \cdot \mathbf{s} \bmod q$ for some $\mathbf{s} \in \mathbb{Z}^n\}$. For $\mathbf{u} \in \mathbb{Z}_q^n$, we let $\Lambda_q^{\mathbf{u}}(\mathbf{A})$ denote the coset $\{\mathbf{x} \in \mathbb{Z}^m : \mathbf{A}\cdot\mathbf{x} = \mathbf{u} \bmod q\}$. Note that if $\mathbf{t} \in \Lambda_q^{\mathbf{u}}(\mathbf{A})$ then $\Lambda_q^{\mathbf{u}}(\mathbf{A}) = \Lambda_q^\perp(\mathbf{A}) + \mathbf{t}$ and hence $\Lambda_q^{\mathbf{u}}(\mathbf{A})$ is a shift of $\Lambda_q^\perp(\mathbf{A})$.

Discrete Gaussians. Let σ be any positive real number, $\mathbf{c} \in \mathbb{R}^m$. The Gaussian distribution $\mathcal{D}_{\sigma,\mathbf{c}}$ centered at $\mathbf{c}$ with parameter σ is defined by the probability distribution function $\rho_{\sigma,\mathbf{c}}(\mathbf{x}) = exp(-\pi\|\mathbf{x}-\mathbf{c}\|^2/\sigma^2)$. For any set $\mathcal{L} \subset \mathbb{R}^m$, define $\rho_{\sigma,\mathbf{c}}(\mathcal{L}) = \sum_{\mathbf{x}\in\mathcal{L}} \rho_{\sigma,\mathbf{c}}(\mathbf{x})$. The discrete Gaussian distribution $\mathcal{D}_{\mathcal{L},\sigma,\mathbf{c}}$ over $\mathcal{L}$ centered at $\mathbf{c}$ with parameter σ is defined by the probability distribution function $\mathcal{D}_{\mathcal{L},\sigma,\mathbf{c}}(\mathbf{x}) = \rho_{\sigma,\mathbf{c}}(\mathbf{x})/\rho_{\sigma,\mathbf{c}}(\mathcal{L})$ for all $\mathbf{x} \in \mathcal{L}$.

The following lemma states that the total Gaussian measure on any translate of the lattice is essentially the same.

Lemma 1 ([29,37]). *For any m-dimensional lattice Λ, $\sigma \geq \omega(\sqrt{\log m})$, $\mathbf{c} \in \mathbb{R}^m$, $\epsilon \in (0,1)$, we have*

$$\rho_{\sigma,\mathbf{c}}(\Lambda) \in [\frac{1-\epsilon}{1+\epsilon}, 1]\cdot\rho_\sigma(\Lambda)$$

A sample from a discrete Gaussian with parameter σ is at most $\sqrt{m}\sigma$ away from its center $\mathbf{c}$ with overwhelming probability.

Lemma 2 ([29,37]). *For any m-dimensional lattice Λ, $m > n$, center $\mathbf{c}$, $\sigma \geq \omega(\sqrt{\log m})$, we have*

$$Pr[\|\mathbf{x} - \mathbf{c}\| > \sqrt{m}\sigma | \mathbf{x} \leftarrow \mathcal{D}_{\Lambda,\sigma,\mathbf{c}}] \leq negl(n).$$

There is an upper bound on the probability of a discrete Gaussian, equivalently, it is a lower bound on the min-entropy of the distribution.

Lemma 3 ([29]). *For any m-dimensional lattice Λ, $\sigma \geq \omega(\sqrt{\log m})$, center $\mathbf{c}$, positive $\epsilon > 0$, and $\mathbf{x} \in \Lambda$, we have*

$$\mathcal{D}_{\Lambda,\sigma,\mathbf{c}} \leq \frac{1+\epsilon}{1-\epsilon} \cdot 2^{-m}.$$

In particular, for $\epsilon < \frac{1}{3}$, the min-entropy of $\mathcal{D}_{\Lambda,\sigma,\mathbf{c}}$ is at least $m - 1$.

Ajtai et al. [6,7] showed how to sample an essentially uniform $\mathbf{A}$, along with a relatively short basis $T_{\mathbf{A}}$.

Lemma 4 ([6,7]). *Let n, q, m be positive integers with $q > 2$ and $m \geq 5n \log q$. There is a probabilistic polynomial-time(PPT) algorithm **TrapGen** that outputs a pair ($\mathbf{A} \in \mathbb{Z}_q^{n\times m}$, $T_{\mathbf{A}} \in \mathbb{Z}^{m\times m}$) where the distribution of $\mathbf{A}$ is statistically close to uniform over $\mathbb{Z}_q^{n\times m}$ and $\|T_{\mathbf{A}}\| \leq m \cdot \omega(\sqrt{\log m})$.*

Gentry et al. [29] showed that if $\mathrm{ISIS}_{q,m,2\sigma\sqrt{m}}$ is hard, $f_{\mathbf{A}} : \mathbb{Z}_q^m \to \mathbb{Z}_q^n$ with $f_{\mathbf{A}}(\mathbf{e}) = \mathbf{Ae} \bmod q$ is one-way function, even collision resistant function where $\|\mathbf{e}\| \leq \sqrt{m}\sigma$. Note that for $m > 2n\log q, \sigma > \omega(\sqrt{\log m}), f_{\mathbf{A}}$ is subjective for almost all $\mathbf{A}$, and the distribution of $\mathbf{u} = \mathbf{Ae} \bmod q$ is statistically close to uniform over $\mathbb{Z}_q^n$. Furthermore, fix $\mathbf{u} \in \mathbb{Z}_q^n$, a short basis for $\Lambda^{\perp}(\mathbf{A})$ can be used to efficiently sample short vectors from $f_{\mathbf{A}}^{-1}(\mathbf{u})$ without revealing any information about the short basis $T_{\mathbf{A}}$.

Lemma 5 ([29]). *Let n, q, m be positive integers with $q \geq 2$ and $m \geq 2n \log q$. There is a PPT algorithm **SamplePre** that on input of $\mathbf{A} \in \mathbb{Z}_q^{n\times m}$, a basis $T_{\mathbf{A}}$ for $\Lambda_q^{\perp}(\mathbf{A})$, a vector $\mathbf{u} \in \mathbb{Z}_q^n$ and an integer $\sigma \geq \|\widetilde{T_{\mathbf{A}}}\| \cdot \omega(\sqrt{\log m})$, the distribution of the output of $\mathbf{e} \leftarrow$ **SamplePre**$(\mathbf{A}, T_{\mathbf{A}}, \mathbf{u}, \sigma)$ is with negligible statistical distance of $\mathcal{D}_{\Lambda_q^{\mathbf{u}}(\mathbf{A}),\sigma}$.*

Lemma 6 ([3]). *Let $q > 2$, full rank $\mathbf{A}, \mathbf{B} \in \mathbb{Z}_q^{n\times m}$, a basis $\mathbf{T_A}$ of $\Lambda_q^{\perp}(\mathbf{A})$, a matrix $\mathbf{U} \in \mathbb{Z}_q^{n\times l}$ and $\sigma \geq \|\widetilde{T_{\mathbf{A}}}\| \cdot \omega(\sqrt{\log m})$. Then there exists PPT algorithm **SampleLeft**$(\mathbf{A}, \mathbf{T_A}, \mathbf{B}, \mathbf{U}, \sigma)$ output a matrix $\mathbf{Z} \in \mathbb{Z}_q^{2m\times l}$, distributed statistically close to $\mathcal{D}_{\Lambda_q^{\mathbf{U}}(\mathbf{A}|\mathbf{B}),\sigma}$.*

Lemma 7 ([3,21]). *Let $q > 2$, full rank $\mathbf{A} \in \mathbb{Z}_q^{n\times m}$, a matrix $\mathbf{R}$, $\mathbf{U} \in \mathbb{Z}_q^{n\times l}$ and $y \neq 0 \in \mathbb{Z}_q$, and $\sigma = \sqrt{5} \cdot (1 + \|\mathbf{R}\|_2) \cdot \omega(\sqrt{\log m})$. Then there exists PPT algorithm **SampleRight**$(\mathbf{A}, \mathbf{R}, y, \mathbf{U}, \sigma)$ output a matrix $\mathbf{Z} \in \mathbb{Z}_q^{2m\times l}$, distributed statistically close to $\mathcal{D}_{\Lambda_q^{\mathbf{U}}(\mathbf{A}|\mathbf{AR}+y\mathbf{G}),\sigma}$.*

Lemma 8 ([3]). *Let* $\mathbf{R}$ *be a matrix chosen uniformly at random from* $\{\pm 1\}^{k\times m}$. *There exists a universal constant* C, *then*

$$Pr[\|\mathbf{R}\| > C\sqrt{k+m}] \leq \frac{1}{e^{k+m}}.$$

Lemma 9 ([3]). *Let* q *prime and* $m > (n+1)\log q + \omega(\log n)$. *Let* $\mathbf{R}$ *be chosen uniformly from* $\{\pm 1\}^{m\times k}$ *mod q, with k polynomial in n. Let* $\mathbf{A}$, $\mathbf{B}$ *be chosen uniformly from* $\mathbb{Z}_q^{n\times m}$ *and* $\mathbb{Z}_q^{n\times k}$. *Then, for every* $\mathbf{r} \in \mathbb{Z}_q^m$, *we have the distributions* ($\mathbf{A}$, $\mathbf{AR}$, $\mathbf{R}^\top\mathbf{r}$) *and* ($\mathbf{A}$, $\mathbf{B}$, $\mathbf{R}^\top\mathbf{r}$) *are statistically close.*

Lemma 10 ([3]). *Let* q *be a prime and* n *a positive integer. We say that a function* $H : \mathbb{Z}_q^n \to \mathbb{Z}_q^{n\times n}$ *is an encoding with full rank differences when:*
1. for all distinct u, $v \in \mathbb{Z}_q^n$, *the matrix* $H(u)$-$H(v) \in \mathbb{Z}_q^{n\times n}$ *has full rank.*
2. H *must be computable in polynomial time in* $n\log q$.

Lemma 11 ([34]). **NoiseReRand**$(\mathbf{Z}, \mathbf{b}+\mathbf{r}, \sigma, \tau)$: *Let* $\mathbf{b} \in \mathbb{Z}_q^m$ *and* $\mathbf{r} \leftarrow \mathcal{D}_\sigma^m$. *Given a matrix* $\mathbf{Z} \in \mathbb{Z}^{m\times l}$, $\tau \in \mathbb{R}^+$ *such that* $\tau^2 > s_1(\mathbf{Z}^\top\mathbf{Z})$, *it first samples* $\mathbf{c} \leftarrow \mathcal{D}_\sigma^m$, $\mathbf{r}_1 = (\tau^2\mathbf{I}_l - \mathbf{Z}\mathbf{Z}^\top)^{\frac{1}{2}}\mathbf{r}_2$, *where* $\mathbf{r}_2 \leftarrow \mathcal{D}^l_{\sqrt{2}\sigma}$. *Then it samples* $\mathbf{r}_3 \leftarrow \mathcal{D}_{\mathbb{Z}^l - \mathbf{r}_1, \sqrt{2}\sigma\tau}$. *Outputs* $\mathbf{Z}^\top\mathbf{b} + \mathbf{Z}^\top(\mathbf{r}+\mathbf{c}) + \mathbf{r}_1 + \mathbf{r}_3$, *where* $\mathbf{r}_1 + \mathbf{r}_3$ *is distributed close to* $\mathcal{D}_{\mathbb{Z}_m, 2\sigma\tau}$.

4.2 Learning with Errors

We review the learning with errors (LWE) problem for the most part from [42].

We first introduce the error distribution χ, that is, the normal (Gaussian) distribution on $\mathbb{T}$ with mean 0 and standard deviation $\alpha/\sqrt{2\pi}$ having density function $\frac{1}{\alpha}exp(-\pi x^2/\alpha^2)$. Its discretized normal distribution χ_α on $\mathbb{Z}_q$ denoted to be the distribution of $\lfloor q \cdot X \rceil$ mod q, where X is a random variable with distribution χ and $\lfloor x \rceil$ is the closest integer to x $\in \mathbb{R}$.

The following lemma about the distribution χ_α will be needed to show that decryption works correctly.

Lemma 12 ([3]). *Let* $\mathbf{x} \in \mathbb{Z}^m$ *and* $\mathbf{r} \leftarrow \chi_\alpha^m$, *then the quantity* $|\mathbf{x}^\top\mathbf{r}|$ *treated as an integer in* $[0, q-1]$ *satisfies*

$$|\mathbf{x}^\top\mathbf{r}| \leq \|\mathbf{x}\|q\alpha\omega(\sqrt{\log m}) + \|\mathbf{x}\|\sqrt{m}/2$$

with all but negligible probability in m.

For an integer $q \geq 2$ and some probability distribution χ over q, $\mathbf{s} \in \mathbb{Z}_q^n$, define $A_{\mathbf{s},\chi}$ to be the distribution on $\mathbb{Z}_q^n \times \mathbb{Z}_q$ of the variable $(\mathbf{a}, \mathbf{a}^\top\mathbf{s} + x)$ induced by choosing $\mathbf{a}$ uniformly at random from $\mathbb{Z}_q^n$, $x \leftarrow \chi$.

Learning with Errors (Decision Version). For an integer $q = q(n)$ and a distribution χ on $\mathbb{Z}_q$, $\text{LWE}_{q,\chi}$ is to distinguish between the distribution $A_{\mathbf{s},\chi}$ for some uniform secret $\mathbf{s} \leftarrow \mathbb{Z}_q^n$ and the uniform distribution on $\mathbb{Z}_q^n \times \mathbb{Z}_q$(via oracle access to the distribution).

Regev [42] demonstrated that for certain moduli q and Gaussian error distribution χ_α, $\text{LWE}_{q,\chi_\alpha}$ is as hard as solving several standard worst-case lattice problems using a quantum algorithm.

Theorem 2 ([42]). *Let $\alpha(n) \in (0,1)$ and $q(n)$ be a prime such that $\alpha \cdot q \geq 2\sqrt{n}$. If there exists an efficient (possibly quantum) algorithm that solves LWE_{q,χ_α}, then there exists an efficient quantum algorithm for approximating SIVP and GapSVP to with $O(n/\alpha)$ factors in the worst case.*

Peikert et al. [20,41] showed that there is a classical reduction from GapSVP to the LWE problem.

4.3 Construction

Setup$(1^n,\ 1^l,\ P, V)$: Utilize **TrapGen** to generate $\mathbf{A} \in \mathbb{Z}_q^{n\times m}$ and trapdoor $T_\mathbf{A} \subset \Lambda_q^\perp(\mathbf{A})$ where $\mathbf{A}$, is statistically close to uniform, and $T_\mathbf{A} \in \mathbb{Z}^{m\times m}$. Choose $\mathbf{B} \leftarrow \mathbb{Z}_q^{n\times m}$, $\mathbf{U} \leftarrow \mathbb{Z}_q^{n\times l}$, Set $\|\mathbf{x}\|_\infty = P$ and $\|\mathbf{y}\|_\infty = V$, $K = lPV$. Define mpk $:= \{\mathbf{A}, \mathbf{B}, \mathbf{U}, K, P, V\}$ and msk $:= \{T_\mathbf{A}\}$.

Keygen$(msk, id, \mathbf{y})$: running **SampleLeft**$(\mathbf{A}, T_\mathbf{A}, \mathbf{B}+H(id)\mathbf{G}, \mathbf{U}, \sigma)$ to sample $\mathbf{Z}_{id} \in \mathbb{Z}^{2m\times l}$ such that $(\mathbf{A}|\mathbf{B} + H(id)\mathbf{G})\mathbf{Z}_{id} = \mathbf{U}$. Compute and return the secret key $sk_{id,\mathbf{y}} = (\mathbf{Z}_{id} \cdot \mathbf{y})$.

Encrypt$(mpk, id,\ \mathbf{x})$:] Sample $\mathbf{s} \leftarrow \mathbb{Z}_q^n$, $\mathbf{R} \leftarrow \{\pm 1\}^{m\times m}$ uniformly at random, $\mathbf{r}_1 \leftarrow \chi_{q,\alpha}^{2m}$ and $\mathbf{r}_2 \leftarrow \chi_{q,\alpha}^{l}$, $\mathbf{r}_3 \leftarrow \chi_{q,\tau}^{l}$ and compute

$$\mathbf{f} = (\mathbf{I}_m|\mathbf{R})^\top \mathbf{r}_1$$
$$\mathbf{c}_1 = (\mathbf{A}|\mathbf{B} + H(id)\mathbf{G})^\top \mathbf{s} + \mathbf{f}$$
$$\mathbf{c}_2 = \mathbf{U}^\top \mathbf{s} + \mathbf{r}_2 + \mathbf{r}_3 + \lfloor \frac{q}{K} \rfloor \cdot \mathbf{x}$$

Then, return C $:= (\mathbf{c}_1,\ \mathbf{c}_2)$.

Decrypt$(mpk, sk_{id,\mathbf{y}}, C)$: Compute $\mu' = \mathbf{y}^\top \mathbf{c}_2 - sk_{id,\mathbf{y}}^\top \mathbf{c}_1$ mod q and output the value $\mu \in \{-K+1, ..., K-1\}$ that minimizes $|\ (\lfloor \frac{q}{K} \rfloor) \cdot \mu - \mu'\ |$.

4.4 Parameters and Correctness

$\mu' = \mathbf{y}^\top \mathbf{c}_2 - sk_{id,\mathbf{y}}^\top \mathbf{c}_1 = \mathbf{y}^\top \mathbf{U}^\top \mathbf{s} + \mathbf{y}^\top \mathbf{r}_2 + \mathbf{y}^\top \mathbf{r}_3 + \lfloor \frac{q}{K} \rfloor < \mathbf{x}, \mathbf{y} > - \mathbf{y}^\top \mathbf{Z}_{id}^\top (\mathbf{A}|\mathbf{B} + H(id)\mathbf{G})^\top \mathbf{s} - \mathbf{y}^\top \mathbf{Z}_{id}^\top \mathbf{f}$, and $(\mathbf{A}|\mathbf{B} + H(id)\mathbf{G})\mathbf{Z}_{id} = \mathbf{U}$. Then, we have
error $= \mathbf{y}^\top \mathbf{r}_2 + \mathbf{y}^\top \mathbf{r}_3 - \mathbf{y}^\top \mathbf{Z}_{id}^\top \mathbf{f}$.
Note that $\|\mathbf{Z}_{id}\| \leq \sigma\sqrt{2ml}$, $\|\mathbf{R}\| \leq C\sqrt{2m}$.
Then, **error** $\leq lV(\alpha q + \tau q) + 4C\alpha q \sigma m \sqrt{lnm} V$

In order to ensure the correctness, we let **error** $\leq \lfloor \frac{q}{K} \rfloor / 4$. We set

$$q > 4KlV(\alpha q + \tau q) + 16CK\alpha q \sigma m \sqrt{lnm} V$$

Additionally, ensure that **TrapGen** can work. We set

$$m \geq 6n \log q, \qquad \sigma > m\omega(\log m)$$

And the scheme is secure under standard LWE assumption. We set

$$\alpha q > 2\sqrt{n}, \qquad \tau > C' m\sigma(2\sqrt{n} + \sqrt{m})$$

5 Security Analysis

Theorem 3. *If LWE_{q,χ_α} is hard with the parameters set as above, then the IBIPFE scheme is IND-sIBFE-CPA secure.*

Proof. Let $\mathcal{A}$ be an adversary attacking the CPA security of sIBFE. $\mathcal{A}$ first announce the challenge identity id*. Choose $\mathbf{R}^* \leftarrow \{\pm 1\}^{m \times m}$, Let $\mathbf{B} = \mathbf{AR}^*$-H(id*)$\mathbf{G}$. Then, in secret key queries phase, we use **SampleRight**($\mathbf{A}$, $\mathbf{R}^*$, H(id)-H(id)*, $\mathbf{U}$, σ) to answer the secret keys.
Because ($\mathbf{A}$, $\mathbf{B}$, $\mathbf{R}^*\mathbf{r}_1$) is statistically close to ($\mathbf{A}$, $\mathbf{AR}^*$, $\mathbf{R}^*\mathbf{r}_1$), and we let $(\mathbf{A}|\mathbf{AR}^*)\mathbf{Z}_{id} = \mathbf{U}$, then we have

$$\begin{aligned}
\mathbf{c}_1 &= (\mathbf{A}|\mathbf{AR}^*)^\top \mathbf{s} + (\mathbf{I}_m|\mathbf{R}^*)^\top \mathbf{r}_1 \\
&= (\mathbf{I}_m|\mathbf{R}^*)^\top (\mathbf{A}^\top \mathbf{s} + \mathbf{r}_1) \\
&= (\mathbf{I}_m|\mathbf{R}^*)^\top \mathbf{ct}_1^{\mathbf{ALS}} \\
\mathbf{c}_2 &= \mathbf{U}^\top \mathbf{s} + \mathbf{r}_2 + \mathbf{r}_3 + \lfloor \frac{q}{K} \rfloor \cdot \mathbf{x}_\beta \\
&= \mathbf{Z}_1^\top \mathbf{A}^\top \mathbf{s} + \mathbf{Z}_2^\top \mathbf{R}^{*\top} \mathbf{A}^\top \mathbf{s} + \lfloor \frac{q}{K} \rfloor \cdot \mathbf{x}_\beta + \mathbf{r}_2 + \mathbf{r}_3 \\
&= \mathbf{ct}_2^{\mathbf{ALS}} + \mathbf{NoiseReRand}(\mathbf{R}^*\mathbf{Z}_2, \mathbf{ct}_1^{\mathbf{ALS}}, \alpha q, \tau)
\end{aligned}$$

Then indistinguishability of ciphertexts is reduced to ALS [5] and their promotion [45].

6 Conclusions and Open Problems

We showed a generic construction from (selective id) chosen plaintext attack secure identity-based functional encryption (sIBFE-CPA) to CCA secure FE. Then we give an instantiation of sIBFE for inner product from standard learning with errors (LWE) assumption, which applying our transformation gives the first CCA secure IPFE under the same assumption. But directly constructing a CCA IPFE, especially from competitive PHF is still appealing and meaningful.

We showed the power of IBFE, so we appeal for more constructions for more practical function classes for IBFE.

Lattice-based cryptography have many fascinating properties not found in other types of cryptography, but related techniques are still limited to construct and prove some primitives(e.g. FE), so whether we can construct an FE scheme for polynomial functions from standard assumptions is an appealing open problem.

References

1. Abdalla, M., Bourse, F., De Caro, A., Pointcheval, D.: Simple functional encryption schemes for inner products. In: Katz, J. (ed.) PKC 2015. LNCS, vol. 9020, pp. 733–751. Springer, Heidelberg (2015). https://doi.org/10.1007/978-3-662-46447-2_33
2. Abdalla, M., Catalano, D., Gay, R., Ursu, B.: Inner-product functional encryption with fine-grained access control. Cryptology ePrint Archive, Report 2020/577 (2020). https://eprint.iacr.org/2020/577
3. Agrawal, S., Boneh, D., Boyen, X.: Efficient lattice (H)IBE in the standard model. In: Gilbert, H. (ed.) EUROCRYPT 2010. LNCS, vol. 6110, pp. 553–572. Springer, Heidelberg (2010). https://doi.org/10.1007/978-3-642-13190-5_28
4. Agrawal, S., Freeman, D.M., Vaikuntanathan, V.: Functional encryption for inner product predicates from learning with errors. In: Lee, D.H., Wang, X. (eds.) ASIACRYPT 2011. LNCS, vol. 7073, pp. 21–40. Springer, Heidelberg (2011). https://doi.org/10.1007/978-3-642-25385-0_2
5. Agrawal, S., Libert, B., Stehlé, D.: Fully secure functional encryption for inner products, from standard assumptions. In: Robshaw, M., Katz, J. (eds.) CRYPTO 2016. LNCS, vol. 9816, pp. 333–362. Springer, Heidelberg (2016). https://doi.org/10.1007/978-3-662-53015-3_12
6. Ajtai, M.: Generating hard instances of the short basis problem. In: Wiedermann, J., van Emde Boas, P., Nielsen, M. (eds.) ICALP 1999. LNCS, vol. 1644, pp. 1–9. Springer, Heidelberg (1999). https://doi.org/10.1007/3-540-48523-6_1
7. Alwen, J., Peikert, C.: Generating shorter bases for hard random lattices. In: International Symposium on Theoretical Aspects of Computer Science, STACS 2009, pp. 75–86 (2009)
8. Ananth, P., Jain, A.: Indistinguishability obfuscation from compact functional encryption. In: Gennaro, R., Robshaw, M. (eds.) CRYPTO 2015. LNCS, vol. 9215, pp. 308–326. Springer, Heidelberg (2015). https://doi.org/10.1007/978-3-662-47989-6_15
9. Ananth, P., Sahai, A.: Functional encryption for turing machines. In: Kushilevitz, E., Malkin, T. (eds.) TCC 2016. LNCS, vol. 9562, pp. 125–153. Springer, Heidelberg (2016). https://doi.org/10.1007/978-3-662-49096-9_6
10. Benhamouda, F., Bourse, F., Lipmaa, H.: CCA-secure inner-product functional encryption from projective hash functions. In: Fehr, S. (ed.) PKC 2017, Part II. LNCS, vol. 10175, pp. 36–66. Springer, Heidelberg (2017). https://doi.org/10.1007/978-3-662-54388-7_2
11. Bethencourt, J., Sahai, A., Waters, B.: Ciphertext-policy attribute-based encryption. In: 2007 IEEE Symposium on Security and Privacy, pp. 321–334, May 2007
12. Bitansky, N., Nishimaki, R., Passelègue, A., Wichs, D.: From cryptomania to obfustopia through secret-key functional encryption. In: Hirt, M., Smith, A. (eds.) TCC 2016. LNCS, vol. 9986, pp. 391–418. Springer, Heidelberg (2016). https://doi.org/10.1007/978-3-662-53644-5_15

13. Bitansky, N., Vaikuntanathan, V.: Indistinguishability obfuscation from functional encryption. In: Proceedings of the 2015 IEEE 56th Annual Symposium on Foundations of Computer Science (FOCS), FOCS 2015, Washington, DC, USA, pp. 171–190 (2015)
14. Boneh, D., Boyen, X.: Secure identity based encryption without random oracles. In: Franklin, M. (ed.) CRYPTO 2004. LNCS, vol. 3152, pp. 443–459. Springer, Heidelberg (2004). https://doi.org/10.1007/978-3-540-28628-8_27
15. Boneh, D., Canetti, R., Halevi, S., Katz, J.: Chosen-ciphertext security from identity-based encryption. SIAM J. Comput. **36**(5), 1301–1328 (2007)
16. Boneh, D., Franklin, M.: Identity-based encryption from the Weil pairing. In: Kilian, J. (ed.) CRYPTO 2001. LNCS, vol. 2139, pp. 213–229. Springer, Heidelberg (2001). https://doi.org/10.1007/3-540-44647-8_13
17. Boneh, D., et al.: Fully key-homomorphic encryption, arithmetic circuit ABE and compact garbled circuits. In: Nguyen, P.Q., Oswald, E. (eds.) EUROCRYPT 2014. LNCS, vol. 8441, pp. 533–556. Springer, Heidelberg (2014). https://doi.org/10.1007/978-3-642-55220-5_30
18. Boneh, D., Sahai, A., Waters, B.: Functional encryption: definitions and challenges. In: Ishai, Y. (ed.) TCC 2011. LNCS, vol. 6597, pp. 253–273. Springer, Heidelberg (2011). https://doi.org/10.1007/978-3-642-19571-6_16
19. Boneh, D., Waters, B.: Conjunctive, subset, and range queries on encrypted data. In: Vadhan, S.P. (ed.) TCC 2007. LNCS, vol. 4392, pp. 535–554. Springer, Heidelberg (2007). https://doi.org/10.1007/978-3-540-70936-7_29
20. Brakerski, Z., Langlois, A., Peikert, C., Regev, O., Stehlé, D.: Classical hardness of learning with errors. In: Proceedings of the Forty-fifth Annual ACM Symposium on Theory of Computing, STOC 2013, New York, NY, USA, pp. 575–584 (2013)
21. Cash, D., Hofheinz, D., Kiltz, E., Peikert, C.: Bonsai trees, or how to delegate a lattice basis. In: Gilbert, H. (ed.) EUROCRYPT 2010. LNCS, vol. 6110, pp. 523–552. Springer, Heidelberg (2010). https://doi.org/10.1007/978-3-642-13190-5_27
22. Cocks, C.: An identity based encryption scheme based on quadratic residues. In: Honary, B. (ed.) Cryptography and Coding 2001. LNCS, vol. 2260, pp. 360–363. Springer, Heidelberg (2001). https://doi.org/10.1007/3-540-45325-3_32
23. Coron, J.-S., Lee, M.S., Lepoint, T., Tibouchi, M.: Cryptanalysis of GGH15 multilinear maps. In: Robshaw, M., Katz, J. (eds.) CRYPTO 2016. LNCS, vol. 9815, pp. 607–628. Springer, Heidelberg (2016). https://doi.org/10.1007/978-3-662-53008-5_21
24. Garg, S., Gentry, C., Halevi, S.: Candidate multilinear maps from ideal lattices. In: Johansson, T., Nguyen, P.Q. (eds.) EUROCRYPT 2013. LNCS, vol. 7881, pp. 1–17. Springer, Heidelberg (2013). https://doi.org/10.1007/978-3-642-38348-9_1
25. Garg, S., Gentry, C., Halevi, S., Zhandry, M.: Functional encryption without obfuscation. In: Kushilevitz, E., Malkin, T. (eds.) TCC 2016. LNCS, vol. 9563, pp. 480–511. Springer, Heidelberg (2016). https://doi.org/10.1007/978-3-662-49099-0_18
26. Garg, S., Mahmoody, M., Mohammed, A.: When does functional encryption imply obfuscation? In: Kalai, Y., Reyzin, L. (eds.) TCC 2017. LNCS, vol. 10677, pp. 82–115. Springer, Cham (2017). https://doi.org/10.1007/978-3-319-70500-2_4
27. Garg, S., Gentry, C., Halevi, S., Raykova, M., Sahai, A., Waters, B.: Candidate indistinguishability obfuscation and functional encryption for all circuits. In: 2013 IEEE 54th Annual Symposium on Foundations of Computer Science (FOCS), vol. 0, pp. 40–49, October 2014
28. Gentry, C., Gorbunov, S., Halevi, S.: Graph-induced multilinear maps from lattices. In: Dodis, Y., Nielsen, J.B. (eds.) TCC 2015. LNCS, vol. 9015, pp. 498–527. Springer, Heidelberg (2015). https://doi.org/10.1007/978-3-662-46497-7_20

29. Gentry, C., Peikert, C., Vaikuntanathan, V.: Trapdoors for hard lattices and new cryptographic constructions. In: Proceedings of the Fortieth Annual ACM Symposium on Theory of Computing, STOC 2008, New York, USA, pp. 197–206 (2008)
30. Gorbunov, S., Vaikuntanathan, Vi., Wee, H.: Attribute-based encryption for circuits. In: Proceedings of the Forty-fifth Annual ACM Symposium on Theory of Computing, STOC 2013, New York, USA, pp. 545–554 (2013)
31. Gorbunov, S., Vaikuntanathan, V., Wee, H.: Predicate encryption for circuits from LWE. In: Gennaro, R., Robshaw, M. (eds.) CRYPTO 2015. LNCS, vol. 9216, pp. 503–523. Springer, Heidelberg (2015). https://doi.org/10.1007/978-3-662-48000-7_25
32. Goyal, V., Pandey, O., Sahai, A., Waters, B.: Attribute-based encryption for fine-grained access control of encrypted data. In: Proceedings of the 13th ACM Conference on Computer and Communications Security, CCS 2006, New York, USA, pp. 89–98 (2006)
33. Hu, Y., Jia, H.: Cryptanalysis of GGH map. In: Fischlin, M., Coron, J.-S. (eds.) EUROCRYPT 2016. LNCS, vol. 9665, pp. 537–565. Springer, Heidelberg (2016). https://doi.org/10.1007/978-3-662-49890-3_21
34. Katsumata, S., Yamada, S.: Partitioning via non-linear polynomial functions: more compact IBEs from ideal lattices and bilinear maps. In: Cheon, J.H., Takagi, T. (eds.) ASIACRYPT 2016, Part II. LNCS, vol. 10032, pp. 682–712. Springer, Heidelberg (2016). https://doi.org/10.1007/978-3-662-53890-6_23
35. Katz, J., Sahai, A., Waters, B.: Predicate encryption supporting disjunctions, polynomial equations, and inner products. In: Smart, N. (ed.) EUROCRYPT 2008. LNCS, vol. 4965, pp. 146–162. Springer, Heidelberg (2008). https://doi.org/10.1007/978-3-540-78967-3_9
36. Lewko, A., Okamoto, T., Sahai, A., Takashima, K., Waters, B.: Fully secure functional encryption: attribute-based encryption and (hierarchical) inner product encryption. In: Gilbert, H. (ed.) EUROCRYPT 2010. LNCS, vol. 6110, pp. 62–91. Springer, Heidelberg (2010). https://doi.org/10.1007/978-3-642-13190-5_4
37. Micciancio, D., Regev, O.: Worst-case to average-case reductions based on gaussian measures. In: IEEE Symposium on Foundations of Computer Science, pp. 372–381 (2004)
38. Nandi, M., Pandit, T.: Generic conversions from CPA to CCA secure functional encryption. Cryptology ePrint Archive, Report 2015/457 (2015). https://eprint.iacr.org/2015/457
39. Okamoto, T., Takashima, K.: Hierarchical predicate encryption for inner-products. In: Matsui, M. (ed.) ASIACRYPT 2009. LNCS, vol. 5912, pp. 214–231. Springer, Heidelberg (2009). https://doi.org/10.1007/978-3-642-10366-7_13
40. O'Neill, A.: Definitional issues in functional encryption. Cryptology ePrint Archive, Report 2010/556 (2010). https://eprint.iacr.org/2010/556
41. Peikert, C.: Public-key cryptosystems from the worst-case shortest vector problem: extended abstract. In: Proceedings of the Forty-First Annual ACM Symposium on Theory of Computing, STOC 2009, New York, NY, USA, pp. 333–342 (2009)
42. Regev, O.: On lattices, learning with errors, random linear codes, and cryptography. In: Proceedings of the Thirty-Seventh Annual ACM Symposium on Theory of Computing, STOC 2005, New York, NY, USA, pp. 84–93 (2005)
43. Sahai, A., Waters, B.: Fuzzy identity-based encryption. In: Cramer, R. (ed.) EUROCRYPT 2005. LNCS, vol. 3494, pp. 457–473. Springer, Heidelberg (2005). https://doi.org/10.1007/11426639_27

44. Shamir, A.: Identity-based cryptosystems and signature schemes. In: Blakley, G.R., Chaum, D. (eds.) CRYPTO 1984. LNCS, vol. 196, pp. 47–53. Springer, Heidelberg (1985). https://doi.org/10.1007/3-540-39568-7_5
45. Wang, Z., Fan, X., Liu, F.-H.: FE for inner products and its application to decentralized ABE. In: Lin, D., Sako, K. (eds.) PKC 2019. LNCS, vol. 11443, pp. 97–127. Springer, Cham (2019). https://doi.org/10.1007/978-3-030-17259-6_4
46. Waters, B.: Functional encryption for regular languages. In: Safavi-Naini, R., Canetti, R. (eds.) CRYPTO 2012. LNCS, vol. 7417, pp. 218–235. Springer, Heidelberg (2012). https://doi.org/10.1007/978-3-642-32009-5_14
47. Waters, B.: A punctured programming approach to adaptively secure functional encryption. In: Gennaro, R., Robshaw, M. (eds.) CRYPTO 2015. LNCS, vol. 9216, pp. 678–697. Springer, Heidelberg (2015). https://doi.org/10.1007/978-3-662-48000-7_33
48. Yun, K., Wang, X., Xue, R.: Identity-based functional encryption for quadratic functions from lattices. In: Naccache, D., et al. (eds.) ICICS 2018. LNCS, vol. 11149, pp. 409–425. Springer, Cham (2018). https://doi.org/10.1007/978-3-030-01950-1_24

CSURF-TWO: CSIDH for the Ratio (2 : 1)

Xuejun Fan[1,3], Song Tian[1,3](✉), Xiu Xu[2], and Bao Li[1,3]

[1] State Key Laboratory of Information Security, Institute of Information Engineering, Chinese Academy of Sciences, Beijing, China
tiansong@iie.ac.cn
[2] China Academy of Information and Communications Technology, Beijing, China
[3] School of Cyber Security, University of Chinese Academy of Sciences, Beijing, China

Abstract. The Commutative Supersingular Isogeny Diffie-Hellman key exchange (CSIDH) uses supersingular elliptic curves of Montgomery form over $\mathbb{F}_p$ with $p \equiv 3 \pmod 8$, while CSURF considered those of Montgomery$^-$ form with $p \equiv 7 \pmod 8$. The two protocols both have ratio (1:1) between the coefficients and the $\mathbb{F}_p$-isomorphism classes. Castryck and Decru showed that the ratio became (2:1) when Montgomery supersingular curves with endomorphism ring $\mathbb{Z}[(1+\sqrt{-p})/2]$ and $p \equiv 7 \pmod 8$ were considered. The fact that the coefficients are not unique for each $\mathbb{F}_p$-isomorphism class is the major obstacle to use this case in the scheme.

In this article, we remedy the ratio (2:1) by dividing the coefficients into two orbits and show that there exist the unique representatives of $\mathbb{F}_p$-isomorphism classes in each orbit, which leads to new pools of hard homogeneous space and our resulting protocol CSURF-TWO. Moreover, we give more explicit formulae for 2-isogenies running in each orbit, which offer a noticeable speedup of about 5.69% to CSIDH. We also refresh the sample interval and gain a speed-up of about 0.839%. Changing the form of elliptic curves offers no extra security, while 0 is no longer the startup parameter and thus precomputation for $\pm\frac{3}{\sqrt{2}}$ in $\mathbb{F}_p$ is needed.

Keywords: CSIDH · CSURF · Montogomery curves · Ideal class action

1 Introduction

Isogeny-based cryptography [13] was first proposed by Couveignes in 1997 [15] and then re-proposed by Rostovtsev and Stolbunov independently [16] in 2006, named CRS. Luca De Feo et al. [10] gave a method to accelerate the scheme which required that the orders of the elliptic curves over finite fields must have small primes as factors. The requirement is hard to achieve by ordinary elliptic curves, while easy to be satisfied by supersingular elliptic curves over $\mathbb{F}_p$ as long as $p = kl_1 \cdots l_n - 1$ with l_i small primes. Since CRS scheme has a

Y. Wu and M. Yung (Eds.): Inscrypt 2020, LNCS 12612, pp. 148–156, 2021.
https://doi.org/10.1007/978-3-030-71852-7_10

subexponential-time quantum attack [7], Jao and De Feo introduced supersingular isogeny Diffie-Hellman key exchange (SIDH) [4,8], relying on the isogenies between supersingular elliptic curves, which can thwart the quantum attack proposed by Kuperberg [5]. As a disadvantage, SIDH has an active attack [11] which prevents static private keys.

To perform the acceleration [10] and avoid the active attack [11], Commutative Supersingular Isogeny Diffie-Hellman key exchange (CSIDH) [9] was proposed using Montgomery$^+$ supersingular curves of over a finite field $\mathbb{F}_p$ with $p \equiv 3 \pmod 8$, which have endomorphism ring $\mathcal{O} = \mathbb{Z}[\sqrt{-p}]$ and thus live on the floor of the isogeny graph. It uses hard homogeneous space $\mathrm{cl}(\mathcal{O}) \times \mathcal{ELL}(\mathcal{O}) \rightarrow \mathcal{ELL}(\mathcal{O})$, the set of $\mathbb{F}_p$-isomorphism classes of supersingular elliptic curves with the action of the ideal class group. Applying similar statement to the surface, consisting of $\mathbb{F}_p$-isomorphism class of endomorphism ring $\mathbb{Z}[(1+\sqrt{-p})/2]$, Castryck and Decru proposed CSURF using Montgomery$^-$ supersingular curves over $\mathbb{F}_p$ with $p \equiv 7 (\mathrm{mod}\ 8)$ and gained some improvements [12]. CSIDH and CSURF work over the ratio (1:1), which implies the coefficients can be the unique representation for the $\mathbb{F}_p$-isomorphism class. Now it leaves us with the case with Montgomery$^+$ curves and $p \equiv 7 (\mathrm{mod}\ 8)$.

In this article, as our main contribution, we consider the Montgomery$^+$ supersingular elliptic curves over $\mathbb{F}_p$ with $p \equiv 7 (\mathrm{mod}\ 8)$ whose endomorphism rings are isomorphic to $\mathbb{Z}[(1+\sqrt{-p})/2]$. This case is unsatisfactory since the ratio becomes (2:1) instead of (1:1), which immediately leads to a discussion about how can the coefficients uniquely represent the $\mathbb{F}_p$-isomorphism classes. We divide $M^+_{p,\mathbb{Z}[(1+\sqrt{-p})/2]}$, the set of coefficients of supersingular Montgomery$^+$ curves on the surface, into two independent orbits and prove that every two coefficients corresponding to same $\mathbb{F}_p$-isomorphism class can be separated into the two orbits according to specific criteria. Moreover, the closure of each orbit under the action of $\mathrm{cl}(\mathbb{Z}[(1+\sqrt{-p})/2])$ makes it deserve a new protocol CSURF-TWO. The appearance of 2-isogenies yields 5.69% faster performance than CSIDH, while the compact 2-isogenies formulae removing rescalings only yield a little bit faster performance than CSURF since the rescalings only happen twice, at the beginning and the end of the chain of 2-isogenies. Furthermore CSURF-TWO uses a new sample interval of the secret keys, which brings in a speed-up for about 0.839% than the original one. However, as a disadvantage, 0 can be no longer the starting coefficient and the precomputation of $\frac{3}{\sqrt{2}}$ is needed in our new protocol.

Organization. In Sect. 2, we recall, besides CSIDH and CSURF, some basic results on ideal class groups and isogenies over $\mathbb{F}_p$. In Sect. 3, we give some essential conclusions about the two orbits of the Montgomery coefficients. In Sect. 4, we implement our new protocol CSURF-TWO and compare the performance with CSIDH and CSURF. In Sect. 5, we give a conclusion.

2 Preliminaries

2.1 The Endomorphism Ring and Ideal Class Group

For a supersingular elliptic curve E defined over $\mathbb{F}_p$, its Frobenius endomorphism π satisfies the characteristic equation $\pi^2+p=0$. The $\mathbb{F}_p$-rational endomorphism ring $\mathrm{End}_{\mathbb{F}_p}(E)$ is an order $\mathcal{O}$ of the imaginary quadratic field $K=\mathbb{Q}(\sqrt{-p})$ [2,6]. The group $P(\mathcal{O})$ consisting of all principal fractional ideals of $\mathcal{O}$ is a subgroup of the abelian group $I(\mathcal{O})$ consisting of the invertible fractional ideals. So we can define the ideal-class group of $\mathcal{O}$ as $\mathrm{cl}(\mathcal{O})=I(\mathcal{O})/P(\mathcal{O})$, of which the elements should be denoted as $[\mathfrak{a}]$. Let $\mathcal{ELL}(\mathcal{O})$ be the set of elliptic curves whose endomorphism rings are isomorphic to $\mathcal{O}$. The action of $\mathfrak{a}$ on a given elliptic curve E can be determined by the kernel $E[\mathfrak{a}]=\{P\in E \mid \forall\phi\in\mathfrak{a},\phi(P)=O\}$, and thus can be represented by an isogeny $\mathfrak{a}: E\rightarrow E/E[\mathfrak{a}]$. Since the principal ideal corresponds to the endomorphism, different ideals in the same ideal class lead to the same codomain. So we write $[\mathfrak{a}]E$ for $E/E[\mathfrak{a}]$ to highlight the group action and stress that the composition of the isogenies corresponds to the multiplication of the ideal classes. We now give a formal theorem about the group action.

Theorem 1. *Let $\mathcal{O}$ be an order of an imaginary quadratic field and let $\mathcal{ELL}(\mathcal{O})$ be the set of isomorphism classes of elliptic curves whose endomorphism rings are isomorphic to $\mathcal{O}$. Then the ideal class* $\mathrm{cl}(\mathcal{O})$ *acts freely and transitively on $\mathcal{ELL}(\mathcal{O})$. The map is*

$$\begin{aligned}\mathrm{cl}(\mathcal{O})\times\mathcal{ELL}(\mathcal{O})&\rightarrow\mathcal{ELL}(\mathcal{O})\\ [\mathfrak{a}]\quad\times\quad E\quad&\mapsto\quad E/E[\mathfrak{a}].\end{aligned}$$

2.2 CSIDH and CSURF

Using the properties of supersingular elliptic curves over $\mathbb{F}_p$ and the isogenies between them, Castryck et al. [9] CSIDH. They choose Montgomery models over $\mathbb{F}_p$ with $p=4\cdot l_1\cdots l_n-1$, so that and $E(\mathbb{F}_p)$ has $\mathbb{F}_p$-rational subgroups of order l_i. The properties ensure $l\mathcal{O}=\mathfrak{l}_i\cdot\bar{\mathfrak{l}}_i=(l_i,\pi-1)\cdot(l_i,\pi+1)$. The action of the ideal class of $\mathfrak{l}$ (resp. $\bar{\mathfrak{l}}$) can be computed entirely over $\mathbb{F}_p$ by applying Vélu formulae [3] to E (resp. its quadratic twist E^t), the reason being that only $\mathbb{F}_p$-rational points are involved. Finding a generator of the kernel used in the Vélu formulae requires full-size multiplication which dominates the cost of it. Different from previous protocols, CSIDH uses the coefficient A defining the curve $E_A: y^2=x^3+Ax^2+x$ as the shared key and a vector $(e_1,\cdots,e_n)$ as the private key. The protocol using the $E_0/\mathbb{F}_p: y^2=x^3+x$ as the starting curve is in the style of Diffie-Hellman, see Fig. 1.

CSURF changes the form of the curves into Montgomery$^-$ over $\mathbb{F}_p$ with $p=4\cdot 2\cdot l_1\cdots l_n-1$, which implies the endomorphism ring becomes $\mathcal{O}_K=\mathbb{Z}[(1+\sqrt{-p})/2]$. And the whole protocol is similar with CSIDH, with the exception of different beginning elliptic curve, $E_0: y^2=x^3-x$, and range of the

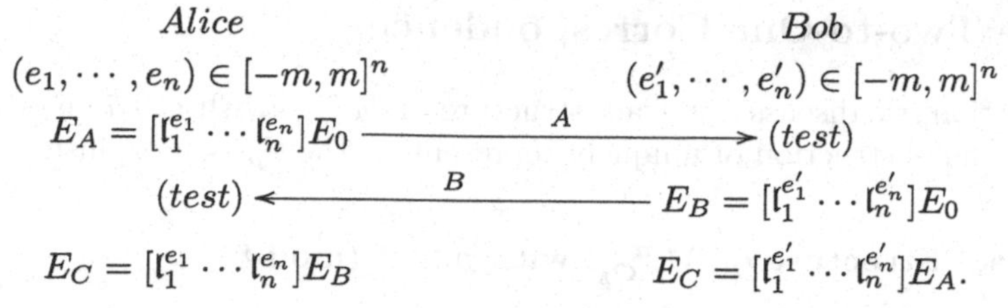

$$\begin{array}{ccc} \textit{Alice} & & \textit{Bob} \\ (e_1,\cdots,e_n)\in[-m,m]^n & & (e'_1,\cdots,e'_n)\in[-m,m]^n \\ E_A=[\mathfrak{l}_1^{e_1}\cdots\mathfrak{l}_n^{e_n}]E_0 & \xrightarrow{\quad A \quad} & (test) \\ (test) & \xleftarrow{\quad B \quad} & E_B=[\mathfrak{l}_1^{e'_1}\cdots\mathfrak{l}_n^{e'_n}]E_0 \\ E_C=[\mathfrak{l}_1^{e_1}\cdots\mathfrak{l}_n^{e_n}]E_B & & E_C=[\mathfrak{l}_1^{e'_1}\cdots\mathfrak{l}_n^{e'_n}]E_A. \end{array}$$

Fig. 1. CSIDH. The "(test)" represents the test of the supersingularity.

exponent vectors. Castryck and Decru [12, Table 1] gave the ratio of the number of Montgomery$^{\pm}$ coefficients to that of $\mathbb{F}_p$-isomorphism classes of supersingular elliptic curves, which is shown in Table 1, where $|M^{+}_{p,\mathcal{O}}|$ and $|M^{-}_{p,\mathcal{O}}|$ denote the number of coefficients of supersingular Montgomery curves and supersingular Montgomery^{-} curves over $\mathbb{F}_p$ with endomorphism ring $\mathcal{O}$, respectively. To highlight the differences between two forms of elliptic curves, we sometimes denote Montgomery curves as Montgomery^{+} curves in later sections.

Table 1. The ratio between number of the coefficients and of $\mathbb{F}_p$-isomorphism classes

		$(\lvert M^{+}_{p,\mathcal{O}}\rvert : \lvert\mathcal{ELL}(\mathcal{O})\rvert)$	$(\lvert M^{-}_{p,\mathcal{O}}\rvert : \lvert\mathcal{ELL}(\mathcal{O})\rvert)$
$p \equiv 3 \pmod 8$	$\mathcal{O}=\mathbb{Z}[\frac{1+\sqrt{-p}}{2}]$	0	(3:1)
	$\mathcal{O}=\mathbb{Z}[\sqrt{-p}]$	(1:1)	0
$p \equiv 7 \pmod 8$	$\mathcal{O}=\mathbb{Z}[\frac{1+\sqrt{-p}}{2}]$	(2:1)	(1:1)
	$\mathcal{O}=\mathbb{Z}[\sqrt{-p}]$	(1:1)	0
$p \equiv 1 \pmod 4$		0	0

CSIDH and CSURF are respectively based on the ratio of the color blue and red. We mainly consider the ratio $(2:1)$ in later sections. To give further notation and explain the existence of the ratio $(2:1)$, we review the following lemma whose proof can be found in [12]. Note that for a square a in $\mathbb{F}_p$ we denote by $\sqrt{a}$ the unique square root which is again a square.

Lemma 1. *Every elliptic curve $E/\mathbb{F}_p \in \mathcal{ELL}(\mathbb{Z}[\frac{1+\sqrt{-p}}{2}])$ with $p \equiv 7 \pmod 8$ comes with three distinguished points of order 2:*

- *P^{-}: The x-coordinate of its halves are not defined over $\mathbb{F}_p$.*
- *P_1^{+}: Its halves are defined over $\mathbb{F}_p$.*
- *P_2^{+}: Its halves are not defined over $\mathbb{F}_p$, but their x-coordinates are.*

According to [12, Lemma 4], the Montgomery^{-} curves $E_B : y^2 = x^3+Bx^2-x$ in the identical case as Lemma 1 has $P^{-} = (0,0)$, $P_1^{+} = (\frac{-B+\sqrt{B^2+4}}{2}, 0)$ and $P_2^{+} = (\frac{-B-\sqrt{B^2+4}}{2}, 0)$. The two Montgomery^{+} models are obtained by translating P_1^{+} or P_2^{+} to $(0,0)$ and then scaling down to the exact form.

3 The Two-to-One Correspondence

In this section, we discuss the exact structure of $M^+_{p,\mathcal{O}_K}$ with $p \equiv 7 \pmod 8$ and overcome the obstruction of uniquely representing the $\mathbb{F}_p$-isomorphism class.

3.1 Exact Structure of $M^+_{p,\mathcal{O}_K}$ with $p \equiv 7 \pmod 8$

From Sect. 2.2, we get $|M^+_{p,\mathcal{O}_K}| : |\mathcal{ELL}(\mathcal{O}_K)| = 2:1$ when $p \equiv 7 \pmod 8$ and the Montgomery$^+$ models can be obtained from Montgomery$^-$ model by ϕ^+ and ϕ^-, translating P_2^+ or P_1^+ to $(0,0)$. So we can handle the exact structure of $M^+_{p,\mathcal{O}_K}$ by the following lemma.

Lemma 2. *Let $p \equiv 7 \pmod 8$ and $M^+_{p,\mathcal{O}_K} = \{A \in \mathbb{F}_p \mid$ supersingular elliptic curve$E_A : y^2 = x^3 + Ax^2 + x \in \mathcal{ELL}(\mathbb{Z}[\frac{1+\sqrt{-p}}{2}])\}$, then $M^+_{p,\mathcal{O}_K} = I \cup J$ where the sets I and J respectively come from translating P_2^+ or P_1^+ to $(0,0)$. More concretely, $J = \{-A : A \in I\}$ and $J \cap I = \emptyset$.*

Proof. Every element in $M^+_{p,\mathcal{O}_K}$ comes from ϕ^+ and ϕ^-, translating P_2^+ or P_1^+ to $(0,0)$, and I and J are denoted as the resulting sets of them. It is easily to get that $J \cap I = \emptyset$.

Focusing on $J = \{-A | A \in I\}$, we first show if $A \in M^+_{p,\mathcal{O}_K}$, then $-A \in M^+_{p,\mathcal{O}_K}$. Since E_{-A} is the quadratic twist of E_A, they have same supersingularity and thus the only need is to prove E_{-A} has full $\mathbb{F}_p$-rational 2-torsion to confirm its endomorphism ring $\mathbb{Z}[(1+\sqrt{-p})/2]$, which can be easily checked since $A^2 - 4$ is a square in $\mathbb{F}_p$. So each element in $M^+_{p,\mathcal{O}_K}$ has opposite again in $M^+_{p,\mathcal{O}_K}$.

Assume the curve E_A is obtained by the isomorphism $\phi^+ : E_B^- \to E_A : (x,y) \mapsto (\alpha^+ x + \gamma^+, \beta^+ y)$ which positions P_2^+ at $(0,0)$, i.e. $A \in I$. By considering the quadratic twist, $E_{-A} : y^2 = x^3 - Ax^2 + x$ is isomorphic to $E_{-B}^- : y^2 = x^3 - Bx^2 - x$ through the isomorphism $\phi'^+ : E_{-B}^- \to E_{-A} : (x,y) \mapsto (\alpha^+ x - \gamma^+, \beta^+ y)$. We then analyze the above two isomorphisms to get more exact structure. According to the correspondence between the points of order 2, we see that ϕ^+ satisfies

$$\begin{cases} \gamma^+ = \dfrac{-A - \sqrt{A^2-4}}{2}, \\ \alpha^+ \dfrac{-B + \sqrt{B^2-4}}{2} + \gamma^+ = \dfrac{-A + \sqrt{A^2-4}}{2}, \\ \alpha^+ \dfrac{-B - \sqrt{B^2-4}}{2} + \gamma^+ = 0. \end{cases} \tag{1}$$

Using the Eq. (1), we note that ϕ'^+ positions the $P_1^+ = (\frac{B+\sqrt{B^2+4}}{2}, 0)$ in E_{-B}^- at $(0,0)$ in E_{-A}, which means it is exact ϕ^- over E_{-B}^- and $-A \in J$. So we can construct I (resp. J) by acting ϕ^+ (resp. ϕ^-) on all Montgomer$^-$ supersingular curves and then gathering the coefficients of the resulting Montgomery$^+$ curves. In this way, the elements in J are actually the opposites of those in I, which ends the proof.

By the foregoing proof, the exact distribution of the two Montgomery$^+$ coefficients A and A', corresponding to the same $\mathbb{F}_p$-isomorphism class, satisfies that $A \in I$ if and only if $A' \in J$. The following proposition tackles the unique representative problem for our family of CSIDH instantiations.

Proposition 1. *Assume $p \equiv 7 \pmod 8$ and consider a supersingular elliptic curve E over $\mathbb{F}_p$. Then $\mathrm{End}_{\mathbb{F}_p}(E) \cong \mathcal{ELL}(\mathbb{Z}[\frac{1+\sqrt{-p}}{2}])$ if and only if there exists a unique element A in I and another unique element A' in J such that E is $\mathbb{F}_p$-isomorphic to the curves $E_A : y^2 = x^3 + Ax^2 + x$ and $E_{A'} : y^2 = x^3 + A'x^2 + x$ simultaneously.*

Proof. First assume E is $\mathbb{F}_p$-isomorphic to E_A and $E_{A'}$ for some $A \in I$ and $A' \in J$. By the definition of $M^+_{p,\mathcal{O}_K}$ in Lemma 2, we can conclude $\mathrm{End}_{\mathbb{F}_p}(E) = \mathrm{End}_{\mathbb{F}_p}(E_A) = \mathrm{End}_{\mathbb{F}_p}(E_{A'}) \cong \mathcal{ELL}(\mathbb{Z}[\frac{1+\sqrt{-p}}{2}])$.

Now suppose $\mathrm{End}_{\mathbb{F}_p}(E) \cong \mathcal{ELL}(\mathbb{Z}[\frac{1+\sqrt{-p}}{2}])$, there exists a unique Montgomery$^-$ curve $E^-_B : y^2 = x^3 + Bx^2 - x$ isomorphic to E. It immediately follows from the Lemma 2 that E is isomorphic to Montgomery$^+$ curves with a coefficients in I and another in J. The uniqueness of Montgomery$^-$ curve [12] directly yields the uniqueness in our case, so we omit the details and end the proof.

3.2 The Isogenies of Odd Degree

We now construct a variant of Theorem 1 as the backboneon of our protocol in Sect. 4 by using the Velu's isogeny formulae (in version of [1, Proposition 1]).

Theorem 2. *If $p \equiv 7 \pmod 8$ then the map:*

$$\rho : \begin{cases} \mathrm{cl}(\mathbb{Z}[(1+\sqrt{-p})/2]) \times I \to I, \\ \mathrm{cl}(\mathbb{Z}[(1+\sqrt{-p})/2]) \times J \to J \end{cases}$$

sending $([\mathfrak{a}], A)$ to $[\mathfrak{a}] \times A = (A - 3\sum_{P \neq \infty \in E_A[\mathfrak{a}]}(x(P) - \frac{1}{x(P)})) \cdot \prod_{P \neq \infty \in E_A[\mathfrak{a}]} x(P)$ is well-defined free and transitive group action. Here, we assume that the ideal $\mathfrak{a}$ representing $[\mathfrak{a}]$ has odd norm.

Proof. In [12, Theorem 3], Castryck and Decru proposed a well-defined free and transitive group action $\rho^- : \mathrm{cl}(\mathbb{Z}[(1+\sqrt{-p})/2]) \times M^-_{p,\mathcal{O}_K} \to M^-_{p,\mathcal{O}_K}$. So we consider the isomorphism ϕ^+ and define

$$\mathrm{cl}(\mathbb{Z}[(1+\sqrt{-p})/2]) \times I \to I : ([\mathfrak{a}], A) \mapsto \phi^+(\rho^-([\mathfrak{a}], (\phi^+)^{-1}(A))),$$

which is a well-defined free and transitive group action because ϕ^+ is a bijection. It is suffices to show this matches with ρ. We construct a diagram in the following two ways:

- We quotient out by $E_A[\mathfrak{a}]$ for $A \in I$ using the formulae in [1, Proposition 1], yielding a curve E_a. Note that the isogeny corresponds to the group action ρ and maps $(0, 0)$ to $(0, 0)$. We continue by applying the isomorphism $(\phi^+)^{-1}$ proposed in Sect. 3.1 to arrive at the set $M^-_{p,\mathcal{O}_K}$.

- Conversely, we apply $(\phi^+)^{-1}$ on E_A, arriving at the coefficient of E_B^- in set $M^-_{p,\mathcal{O}_K}$. It also maps $E_A[\mathfrak{a}]$ to $E_B^-[\mathfrak{a}]$, which we quotient out in turn. The isogeny by means of the formulae from [12, Proposition 2] corresponds to the group action ρ^-, taking us to $M^-_{p,\mathcal{O}_K}$.

Thus we obtain the $\rho \circ \phi^+ = \phi^+ \circ \rho^-$ which implies that $\rho = \phi^+ \circ \rho^- \circ (\phi^+)^{-1}$.

Similarly, the proof for the action on J employs the isomorphism ϕ^- to obtain a commutative diagram. So I and J are two independent orbits under the action of ideal class group $\mathrm{cl}(\mathbb{Z}[(1+\sqrt{-p})/2])$.

The exact formula of $[\mathfrak{a}] \times A$ directly comes from [1, Proposition 1]. Since the $\mathbb{F}_p$-isogenies map point $(0,0)$ to $(0,0)$ with same properties, they keep the (non-)squareness of $A+2$ and hence the closure of each orbit.

4 Implementation and Comparison

In this section, we utilize Theorem 2 to design a variant of CSURF-512, CSURF-TWO, acting on I or J rather than $M^-_{p,\mathcal{O}_K}$. For that sake of comparison, we propose CSURF-TWO with same finite field as CSURF-512, while we use a new near-optimal sample range $[-141,141]\times[-4,4]^3\times[-6,6]^{13}\times[-5,5]^{33}\times[-4,4]^{24}$.

To put everything back to Montgomery$^+$ curves, we change the starting curve of CSURF-512 $E^- : y^2 = x^3 - x$ into $E : y^2 = x^3 \pm \frac{3}{\sqrt{2}}x^2 + x$, which are in the same $\mathbb{F}_p$-isomorphism class with E^-. Note that $-\frac{3}{\sqrt{2}}$ and $\frac{3}{\sqrt{2}}$ are in orbits I and J respectively. Our protocols based on I and J have high degree of similarity, except for the starting curve and the formulae of 2-isogenies. So we only implement CSURF-TWO based on the orbit I.

Our protocol can be viewed as a near-copies of CSIDH and CSURF. It is built from CSURF-like action of $\mathrm{cl}(\mathbb{Z}[(1+\sqrt{-p})/2])$ on I or J, the sets consisting of some Montgomery$^+$ curves like in CSIDH. The scheme has same formulae to compute actions of ideals as CSIDH, with the exception of 2-isogenies, which bring in a noticeable speed-up of about 5.69%. When compared with CSURF, our formulae of 2-isogenies are more explicit on account of omitting the rescalings between Montgomery$^-$ models and Montgomery$^+$ models. Although it only leads to an unobtrusive speed-up since the rescalings are only needed twice in the whole program, the more compact formulae can help with understanding and implementation. We implement our new intervals and the original one on CSURF-TWO and compare the performance of them. The new one omits the computation of the 389-isogenies and increase that of 2-isogenies, which speeds up the resulting protocol by about 0.839%.

5 Conclusion

In the article, we consider Montgomery supersingular curves with endomorphism ring $\mathbb{Z}[(\sqrt{-p}+1)/2]$ and $p \equiv 7 \pmod 8$. Castryck and Decru showed that there exists two-to-one correspondence between the coefficients and $\mathbb{F}_p$-isomorphism classes, which prevents the unique representative of the $\mathbb{F}_p$-isomorphism class. So we divide the two coefficients in same $\mathbb{F}_p$-isomorphism class into two orbits I and J to imply the one-to-one correspondence and then offer a new protocol CSURF-TWO based on each orbit. In our protocol, the 2-isogenies offer a noticeable speedup of about 5.69% to CSIDH. We also propose a new interval to sample secret keys offering 0.839% speed-up without lost of security.

Acknowledgments. We thank the anonymous Inscrypt2020 reviewers for their helpful comments. This work was supported by MMJJ20180207, the National Natural Science Foundation of China (Grant Nos. 61772515) and Beijing Municipal Science & Technology Commission (Project Number: Z191100007119006).

References

1. Renes, J.: Computing isogenies between Montgomery curves using the action of (0, 0)[C]. In: International Conference on Post-Quantum Cryptography, vol. 10786, pp. 229–247 (2018)
2. Delfs, C., Galbraith, S.D.: Computing isogenies between supersingular elliptic curves over $\mathbb{F}_p$ [J]. Des. Codes Crypt. **78**(2), 425–440 (2016)
3. Moody, D., Shumow, D.: Analogues of Vélu's formulas for isogenies on alternate models of elliptic curves. Math. Comput. **300**, 1929–1951 (2016)
4. Jao, D., De Feo, L.: Towards quantum-resistant cryptosystems from supersingular elliptic curve isogenies. In: International Workshop on Post-Quantum Cryptography, vol. 7071, pp. 19–34 (2011)
5. Kuperberg, G.: A subexponential-time quantum algorithm for the dihedral hidden subgroup problem. SIAM J. Comput. **35**(1), 170–188 (2005)
6. W C. Waterhouse. Abelian varieties over finite fields. Annales Scientifiques de l École Normale Supérieure **2**(4), 56–62(7) (1971)
7. Childs, A., Jao, D., Soukharev, V.: Constructing elliptic curve isogenies in quantum subexponential time. J. Math. Cryptol. **8**(1), 1–29 (2014)
8. Costello, C., Hisil, H.: A simple and compact algorithm for SIDH with arbitrary degree isogenies. In: Takagi, T., Peyrin, T. (eds.) ASIACRYPT 2017. LNCS, vol. 10625, pp. 303–329. Springer, Cham (2017). https://doi.org/10.1007/978-3-319-70697-9_11
9. Castryck, W., Lange, T., Martindale, C., Panny, L., Renes, J.: CSIDH: an efficient post-quantum commutative group action. In: Peyrin, T., Galbraith, S. (eds.) ASIACRYPT 2018. LNCS, vol. 11274, pp. 395–427. Springer, Cham (2018). https://doi.org/10.1007/978-3-030-03332-3_15
10. De Feo, L., Kieffer, J., Smith, B.: Towards practical key exchange from ordinary isogeny graphs. In: Peyrin, T., Galbraith, S. (eds.) ASIACRYPT 2018. LNCS, vol. 11274, pp. 365–394. Springer, Cham (2018). https://doi.org/10.1007/978-3-030-03332-3_14
11. Galbraith, S.D., Petit, C., Shani, B., Ti, Y.B.: On the security of supersingular isogeny cryptosystems. In: Cheon, J.H., Takagi, T. (eds.) ASIACRYPT 2016. LNCS, vol. 10031, pp. 63–91. Springer, Heidelberg (2016). https://doi.org/10.1007/978-3-662-53887-6_3
12. Castryck, W., Decru, T.: CSIDH on the surface. Post-Quantum Cryptography. In: 11th International Conference, PQCrypto 2020, vol. 12100, pp. 111–129 (2020)

13. De Feo, L.: Mathematics of Isogeny Based Cryptography. CoRR, abs/1711.04062 (2017). http://arxiv.org/abs/1711.04062
14. Costello, C., Smith, B.: Montgomery curves and their arithmetic. J. Cryptogr. Eng. **8**(3), 227–240 (2017). https://doi.org/10.1007/s13389-017-0157-6
15. Couveignes, J.M.: Hard homogeneous spaces. IACR Cryptology ePrint Archive. http://eprint.iacr.org/2006/291
16. Rostovtsev, A., Stolbunov, A.: Public-key cryptosystem based on isogenies. IACR Cryptology ePrint Archive. http://eprint.iacr.org/2006/145

Group Key Exchange Protocols from Supersingular Isogenies

Xuejun Fan[1,2], Xiu Xu[3(✉)], and Bao Li[1,2]

[1] State Key Laboratory of Information Security, Institute of Information Engineering, Chinese Academy of Sciences, Beijing, China
[2] School of Cyber Security, University of Chinese Academy of Sciences, Beijing, China
[3] China Academy of Information and Communications Technology, Beijing, China
xuxiu@caict.ac.cn

Abstract. Group key exchange (GKE) protocols get much attention in current research with increasing applicability in numerous group-oriented and collaborative applications. In this paper, we propose three schemes on supersingular isogenies. They all have two rounds. Two of them are optimizations of Burmester and Desmedt's protocols without authentication. Our methods are more efficient in the view of communication and computation time. Another one is a provably secure constant round post-quantum authenticated group key exchange (AGKE) protocol, which is built from the first GKE protocol. This proposed scheme achieves security following the security notion namely the eGBG model which considers forward secrecy, KCI resilience and the leakage of ephemeral keys. We give formal proofs for its AKE security, mutual authentication and contributiveness. We also give a comparison of these existing GKE and AGKE protocols.

Keywords: Supersingular isogeny · Post Quantum · Group key exchange · Authenticated group key exchange

1 Introduction

Group Key Exchange. A group key exchange (GKE) protocol allows a group of parties to agree upon a common secret session key over a public network. GKE protocols are applicable in various real world communication networks such as ad-hoc networks, wireless sensor networks and so on. So far, several GKE protocols have been proposed, most of which are extended from two-party key exchange protocols [4–6, 13]. However, this GKE protocol can only be secure against passive adversaries.

Authenticated group key exchange (AGKE) protocols are essential for multiple parties to establish a session key in the presence of active adversaries. There have been plenty of literatures about constant-round AGKE protocols [2, 10, 22, 28]. Particularly, Katz and Yung [22] brought forward a scalable complier that converts any unauthenticated GKE protocol into an authenticated

Y. Wu and M. Yung (Eds.): Inscrypt 2020, LNCS 12612, pp. 157–173, 2021.
https://doi.org/10.1007/978-3-030-71852-7_11

one by adding one round and performing signing and verification operations. In terms of security models, BCPQ model [3] was the first security model for GKE protocols, along with KS model [21], BGS model [7], BM model [8] and CCGJJ model [23]. These models consider the indistinguishability of computed group keys and forward secrecy. GBG model [11] also takes key compromise impersonation (KCI) resilience into account. In eGBG model [29], they extend the GBG security by additionally considering the leakage of ephemeral keys. So any non-trivial combination of the long-term key and ephemeral key can be revealed under this model. It is called the resistance to MEX attacks in CK^+ model [20] which is the strongest model for the two-party AKE.

Supersingular Isogeny Diffie-Hellman Key Exchange (SIDH). Apart from lattice, code, hash and multivariate cryptography, supersingular elliptic curve isogeny is one of the most attractive candidates for post-quantum cryptography. The best-known protocols are supersingular isogeny Diffie-Hellman key exchange (SIDH) [14] and supersingular isogeny key encapsulation (SIKE) [24] submitted to NIST. They are based on the hard problem of computing isogenies between supersingular elliptic curves. Recently the very important problem of designing AKE schemes from the basic SIDH primitive has been studied in [17,18,25,27]. They note that there are several challenges in adapting the security proof of existing well-designed AKE schemes to the SIDH case. We also find it is difficult to construct AGKE protocols from the existing schemes such as SIKE.

1.1 Our Contributions

1. We propose two two-round post-quantum group key exchange protocols based on supersingular isogenies. The first one is an optimization of supersingular isogenies Burmester and Desmedt (SIBD) protocol [16]. Since the BD protocol has been pointed out that the shorting coming is high communication overhead and the tree based GKE protocols are considered superior [19], the second one is a combination of SIDH and BDII [6]. In the two schemes, we change the way to compute the session key by performing addition instead of multiplications in the finite field. So they have a much higher efficiency and are more acceptable for the tiny processors. We also give a formal security proof against the passive adversaries for the first one.
2. We propose a two-round post-quantum authenticated group key exchange protocol based on our first group key exchange protocol. It is proved to be eGBG secure which considers forward secrecy, KCI resilience and the leakage of ephemeral keys. We give formal proofs for its AKE security, mutual authentication and contributiveness.
3. Finally, we have an analysis about the complexity including the round number, the communication size and computation cost. Compared with the existing AGKE protocol on supersingular isogenies [2], our scheme has much less isogeny computation cost and higher communication efficiency.

1.2 Related Works

There has been relatively little work looking at candidate post quantum group key exchange protocols. Apon et al. [1] proposed an unauthenticated GKE by generalizing the Burmester-Desmedt protocol to the Ring-LWE setting. As for group key exchange on isogenies, Furukawa et al. [16] proposed two multi-party key exchange protocols based on supersingular isogeny. The first one is a generalized SIDH variant with $p = f \cdot \prod_{i=1}^{n} \ell_i^{e_i} \pm 1$, which is of $n-1$ rounds. The second one is a variant of the classic Burmester-Desmedt (SIBD) key exchange protocol [4] with many multiplication operations. Azarderakhsh et al. [2] constructed a n-party key agreement which is sequential from party to party and ensures each party applies their own private information before sending the next messages. This scheme provides authentication without extra cost such as signatures. However, this scheme also works in the case that $p = f \cdot \prod_{i=1}^{n} \ell_i^{e_i} \pm 1$, so if the number of users n changes, the public prime p will have to be changed. Furthermore, this scheme involves too much isogeny computation and point computation. Each user has to compute $n-1$ isogenies and $(n-1)n$ image points. And the number of bits communicated by any single user reaches up to $O(\lambda n^2)$, where n is the number of users and λ is the security parameter. They also did not provide a formal security proof. Fujioka et al. [15] also proposed one-round AGKE protocols on isogenies from cryptographic invariant maps, but their schemes are based on commutative SIDH (CSIDH) which is about group actions on the set of supersingular curves defined over a prime field. We can see that it is urgent and meaningful of further research on GKE and AGKE on supersingular isogenies.

Outline. The rest of this paper is organized as follows. Section 2 gives basic notations for SIDH key exchange protocol, related assumptions, and the description of the secure model. Section 3 describes the two improved group key exchange protocols on supersingular isogeny, and gives a formal security proof for the first one. Section 4 describes an authenticated group key exchange protocol with a detailed security proof. Section 5 compares the complexity of the proposed schemes with the previous. Section 6 gives a conclusion.

2 Preliminaries

2.1 SIDH

We recall briefly the SIDH protocol using the same notation as [14,24]. Let p be a large prime of the form $p = \ell_0^{e_0} \ell_1^{e_1} \cdot f \pm 1$, where ℓ_0 and ℓ_1 are two small primes, and f is an integer cofactor. Then we can construct a supersingular elliptic curve E_0 defined over $\mathbb{F}_{p^2}$ of order $|E_0(\mathbb{F}_{p^2})| = (\ell_0^{e_0} \ell_1^{e_1} \cdot f)^2$. Let $\mathbb{Z}_m$ be the ring of residue class modulo m. The subgroup $E_0[m]$ is isomorphic to $\mathbb{Z}_{\ell_0^{e_0}} \times \mathbb{Z}_{\ell_1^{e_1}}$. Let P_0, Q_0 be two points that generate $E_0[\ell_0^{e_0}]$ and P_1, Q_1 be two points that generate $E_0[\ell_1^{e_1}]$. The public parameters are $(E_0; P_0, Q_0; P_1, Q_1; \ell_0, \ell_1, e_0, e_1)$.

The SIDH works as follows. Alice chooses her secret key k_a from $\mathbb{Z}_{\ell_0^{e_0}}$ and computes the isogeny $\phi_A : E_0 \rightarrow E_A$ whose kernel is the subgroup $\langle R_A \rangle =$

$\langle P_0+[k_a]Q_0\rangle$. She then sends to Bob her public key which is E_A together with the two points $\phi_A(P_1), \phi_A(Q_1)$. Similarly, Bob chooses his secret key k_b from $\mathbb{Z}_{\ell_1^{e_1}}$ and computes the isogeny $\phi_B : E_0 \to E_B$ with kernel subgroup $\langle R_B\rangle = \langle P_1+[k_b]Q_1\rangle$. He sends E_B together with the two points $\phi_B(P_0), \phi_B(Q_0)$ to Alice. To get the shared secret, Alice computes the isogeny $\phi_{BA} : E_B \to E_{BA}$ with kernel subgroup $\langle\phi_B(P_0) + [k_a]\phi_B(Q_0)\rangle$. Similarly, Bob computes the isogeny ϕ_{AB} : $E_A \to E_{AB}$ with kernel subgroup $\langle\phi_A(P_1) + [k_b]\phi_A(Q_1)\rangle$. Since the composed isogeny $\phi_{AB} \circ \phi_A$ has the same kernel $\langle R_A, R_B\rangle$ as $\phi_{BA} \circ \phi_B$, Alice and Bob can share the same j-invariant $j(E_{AB}) = j(E_{BA})$.

It will be helpful to have a crypto-friendly description of SIDH for the presentation of our AKEs. We follow the treatment of Fujioka et al. [17]. In what follows, we assume $\{t, s\} = \{0, 1\}$, and denote the public parameters by $\mathfrak{g} = (E_0; P_0, Q_0, P_1, Q_1)$ and $\mathfrak{e} = (\ell_0, \ell_1, e_0, e_1)$. We define the sets of supersingular curves and those with an auxiliary basis as

$$\begin{aligned}
\mathrm{SSEC}_p &= \{\text{supersingular elliptic curves } E \text{ over } \mathbb{F}_{p^2} \text{ with } E(\mathbb{F}_{p^2}) \simeq (\mathbb{Z}_{\ell_0^{e_0}\ell_1^{e_1}f})^2\};\\
\mathrm{SSEC}_A &= \{(E; P'_t, Q'_t)|E \in \mathrm{SSEC}_p, (P'_t, Q'_t) \text{ is basis of } E[\ell_t^{e_t}]\};\\
\mathrm{SSEC}_B &= \{(E; P'_s, Q'_s)|E \in \mathrm{SSEC}_p, (P'_s, Q'_s) \text{ is basis of } E[\ell_s^{e_s}]\}.
\end{aligned}$$

Let $\mathfrak{a} = k_a$ and $\mathfrak{b} = k_b$, then we define,

$$\begin{aligned}
\mathfrak{g}^{\mathfrak{a}} &= (E_A; \phi_A(P_t), \phi_A(Q_t)) \in \mathrm{SSEC}_A, \text{where } R_A = P_s + [k_a]Q_s, \phi_A : E_0 \to E_A = E_0/\langle R_A\rangle;\\
\mathfrak{g}^{\mathfrak{b}} &= (E_B; \phi_B(P_s), \phi_B(Q_s)) \in \mathrm{SSEC}_B, \text{where } R_B = P_t + [k_b]Q_t, \phi_B : E_0 \to E_B = E_0/\langle R_B\rangle;\\
(\mathfrak{g}^{\mathfrak{b}})^{\mathfrak{a}} &= j(E_{BA}), \text{ where } R_{BA} = \phi_B(P_s) + [k_a]\phi_B(Q_s), \phi_{BA} : E_B \to E_{BA} = E_B/\langle R_{BA}\rangle;\\
(\mathfrak{g}^{\mathfrak{a}})^{\mathfrak{b}} &= j(E_{AB}), \text{ where } R_{AB} = \phi_A(P_t) + [k_b]\phi_A(Q_t), \phi_{AB} : E_A \to E_{AB} = E_A/\langle R_{AB}\rangle.
\end{aligned}$$

We emphasize that we define $\mathfrak{g}^{\mathfrak{a}}$ and $\mathfrak{g}^{\mathfrak{b}}$ as groups while $(\mathfrak{g}^{\mathfrak{b}})^{\mathfrak{a}}$ and $(\mathfrak{g}^{\mathfrak{a}})^{\mathfrak{b}}$ are defined to be j-invariants. That is not a mathematical mistake and aims to combine the classical Diffie-Hellman with SIDH. By this notation, the SIDH looks almost exactly like the classical Diffie-Hellman. The public parameters are $\mathfrak{g}$ and $\mathfrak{e}$. Alice chooses a secret key $\mathfrak{a}$ and sends $\mathfrak{g}^{\mathfrak{a}}$ to Bob, while Bob chooses a secret key $\mathfrak{b}$ and sends $\mathfrak{g}^{\mathfrak{b}}$ to Alice. The shared key is $j = (\mathfrak{g}^{\mathfrak{b}})^{\mathfrak{a}} = (\mathfrak{g}^{\mathfrak{a}})^{\mathfrak{b}}$.

2.2 Standard SIDH Assumptions

We describe two standard assumptions about supersingular isogeny based on the crypto-friendly notation. Let $s \neq t$ and $s, t \in \{0, 1\}$.

Definition 1 (SI-CDH Assumption [14,17]**).** *The SI-CDH problem is that, given public parameters $\mathfrak{g}$ and $\mathfrak{e}$, and $\mathfrak{g}^{\mathfrak{a}}$, $\mathfrak{g}^{\mathfrak{b}}$ where $\mathfrak{a} \leftarrow \mathbb{Z}_{\ell_s^{e_s}}$, $\mathfrak{b} \leftarrow \mathbb{Z}_{\ell_t^{e_t}}$, compute the j-invariant $(\mathfrak{g}^{\mathfrak{a}})^{\mathfrak{b}} = (\mathfrak{g}^{\mathfrak{b}})^{\mathfrak{a}}$. For any PPT algorithm $\mathcal{A}$, we define the advantage of solving SI-CDH problem as $Adv_{\mathcal{A}}^{sicdh} = Pr[j' = (\mathfrak{g}^{\mathfrak{a}})^{\mathfrak{b}} | j' \leftarrow \mathcal{A}(\mathfrak{g}, \mathfrak{e}, \mathfrak{g}^{\mathfrak{a}}, \mathfrak{g}^{\mathfrak{b}})]$. The SI-CDH assumption states: for any PPT algorithm $\mathcal{A}$, the advantage of solving SI-CDH problem is negligible.*

Definition 2 (SI-DDH Assumption [14,17]**).** *Let* $\mathfrak{g}$ *and* $\mathfrak{e}$ *be that defined in SI-CDH assumption. Let* D_0 *and* D_1 *be two distributions defined as:*

$$D_1 := \{\mathfrak{e}, \mathfrak{g}, \mathfrak{g}^{\mathfrak{a}}, \mathfrak{g}^{\mathfrak{b}}, (\mathfrak{g}^{\mathfrak{a}})^{\mathfrak{b}} | \mathfrak{a} \leftarrow \mathbb{Z}_{\ell_s^{e_s}}, \mathfrak{b} \leftarrow \mathbb{Z}_{\ell_t^{e_t}}\},$$
$$D_0 := \{\mathfrak{e}, \mathfrak{g}, \mathfrak{g}^{\mathfrak{a}}, \mathfrak{g}^{\mathfrak{b}}, (\mathfrak{g}^{\mathfrak{s}})^{\mathfrak{t}} | \mathfrak{a}, \mathfrak{s} \leftarrow \mathbb{Z}_{\ell_s^{e_s}}, \mathfrak{b}, \mathfrak{t} \leftarrow \mathbb{Z}_{\ell_t^{e_t}}\}.$$

The SI-DDH problem is that given a random sample from D_b *depending on* $b \leftarrow \{0,1\}$*, guess* b*. The advantage of solving SI-DDH problem for any PPT algorithm* $\mathcal{A}$ *is* $\mathsf{Adv}_{\mathcal{A}}^{siddh} = 2|Pr[b' = b | b' \leftarrow \mathcal{A}(\mathfrak{d}_b \leftarrow D_b), b \leftarrow \{0,1\}] - 1/2|$*. The SI-DDH assumption states: for any PPT algorithm* $\mathcal{A}$*, the advantage of solving SI-DDH problem is negligible.*

2.3 Extended GBG Model

We describe the extended GBG (eGBG) model [29] for GAKE protocols below. This model considers the key compromise impersonation (KCI) attack, the maximal exposure (MEX) attack and the breaking of weak perfect forward secrecy (wPFS). This eGBG model captures almost the same properties as G-CK$^+$ model which extends the CK$^+$ model for two parties to the group setting [26].

Participants. Suppose there are total n participants $\mathcal{U} = \{U_1, U_2, ..., U_n\}$ and the protocol may run among any subset U of these parties. Each participant is allowed to run multiple instances concurrently. The i-th instance of participant U can be represented by $\prod_U^i$. We set the session identifier as sid and the partner identifier pid.

Adversary Model. The security of GAKE protocol is defined by a series of games between the challengers and adversaries $\mathcal{A}$. In the games, $\mathcal{A}$ must solve a challenge on the test session by issuing the following queries in any sequence:

- $\mathsf{Execute}(\prod_U^i)$: It returns the messages exchanged during the honest execution $\prod_U^i$. This is what the passive attacks do.
- $\mathsf{Send}(\prod_U^i, m)$: This query returns the reply generated by instance $\prod_U^i$ during the normal execution of the protocol.
- $\mathsf{RevealKey}(\prod_U^i)$: This query outputs the group session key if the instance $\prod_U^i$ is accepted.
- $\mathsf{Corrupt}(U_i)$: This query models the reveal of the long-term secret key. The participant is honest if the adversary has not made any Corrupt query.
- $\mathsf{EphemeralKeyReveal}(\prod_U^i)$: The adversary makes this query to obtain the ephemeral key of U for instance $\prod_U^i$.
- $\mathsf{Test}(\prod_U^i)$: This query can be made only once during the execution of the accepted instance $\prod_U^i$.

Now we discuss the the notations of AKE security, mutual authentication and contributiveness defined in eGBG model.

AKE Security. The adversary $\mathcal{A}$ could make a sequence of the queries described above. During the Test query, the challenger randomly picks a bit b. If $b = 1$, the oracle generates a random value in the key space; if $b = 0$, it reveals the session key. The adversary wins the game if the session is fresh and the guess of the adversary is correct, i.e. $b' = b$. The advantage of the adversary $\mathcal{A}$ is defined as $\mathsf{Adv}_{\mathcal{A}} = |2\Pr[\mathcal{A} \text{ wins}] - 1|$. The protocol is said to be a secure unauthenticated group key exchange (GKE) protocol if there is no polynomial time passive adversary $\mathcal{A}$ with non-negligible advantage $\mathsf{Adv}_{\mathcal{A}}^{\mathsf{GKE}}$. We say that protocol is a secure authenticated group key exchange (AGKE) protocol if there is no polynomial time active adversary $\mathcal{A}$ with non-negligible advantage $\mathsf{Adv}_{\mathcal{A}}^{\mathsf{AGKE}}$.

Mutual Authentication (MA Security) [29]**.** Mutual authentication requires that parties who complete the protocol execution should output identical session keys and that each party should be ensured of the identity of the other participating parties. An adversary $\mathcal{A}_{ma}$ against the mutual authentication is allowed to make Execute, Send, RevealKey, Corrupt, EphemeralKeyReveal queries. The adversary $\mathcal{A}_{ma}$ violates the mutual authentication property of the AGKE protocol if at some points during the protocol run, there exists an uncorrupted instance $\prod_U^i$ that has been accepted with a session key sk_U^i and another party $U' \in \mathsf{pid}_U^i$ that is uncorrupted at the time $\prod_U^i$ accepts such that

1. there is no instance $\prod_{U'}^j$ with $(\mathsf{pid}_{U'}^j, \mathsf{sid}_{U'}^j) = (\mathsf{pid}_U^i, \mathsf{sid}_U^i)$ or
2. there is no instance $\prod_{U'}^j$ with $(\mathsf{pid}_{U'}^j, \mathsf{sid}_{U'}^j) = (\mathsf{pid}_U^i, \mathsf{sid}_U^i)$ that has accepted with $sk_{U'}^j \neq sk_U^i$.

Let $\mathsf{Adv}_{\mathcal{A}_{ma}}$ be the success probability of $\mathcal{A}_{ma}$ winning the mutual authentication game. If $\mathsf{Adv}_{\mathcal{A}_{ma}}$ is negligible in the security parameter λ, then we say the protocol provides mutual authentication in the presence of insiders.

Contributiveness [29]**.** A GKE protocol under this notion resists the key control attacks where a proper subset of insiders tries to predetermine the resulting session key. An adversary $\mathcal{A}_{con}$ against the contributiveness is allowed to make Execute, Send, RevealKey, Corrupt, EphemeralKeyReveal queries. It operates in two stages prepare and attack as follows:

- prepare. $\mathcal{A}_{con}$ queries the instances of π and outputs some state information ζ along with a key $\tilde{k}$.
  At the end of the prepare stage, a set $\prod$ is built such that $\prod$ consists of all the uncorrupted instances which have been asked either Execute or Send queries.
- attack. On input $(\zeta, \prod)$, $\mathcal{A}_{con}$ interacts with the instances of π as in the prepare stage.
  At the end of this stage, $\mathcal{A}_{con}$ outputs (U_i, j) and wins the game if an instance π_i^j at an uncorruptes party U_i has terminated accepting $\tilde{k}$ with $\pi_i^j \notin \prod$.

Let $\mathsf{Adv}_{\mathcal{A}_{con}}$ be the success probability of $\mathcal{A}_{con}$ winning the contributiveness game. If $\mathsf{Adv}_{\mathcal{A}_{con}}$ is negligible in the security parameter λ, then we say the protocol provides contributiveness in the presence of insiders.

3 Improved Group Key Exchange on Supersingular Isogeny

Inspired by [4–6,16], we combine SIDH with BD and BDII protocol respectively and propose a more efficient group key exchange on supersingular isogeny by performing addition instead of multiplications. We also compare the efficiency, the communication size and the security of the GEK schemes in Table 1.

3.1 Improved SIBD Protocol

Furukawa et al. [16] proposed a generalization of BDI, called SIBD, using SIDH as the underlying key exchange. We optimize it by changing multiplication into addition and give security proof against the passive adversaries.

The public parameters are the same as those in SIDH, except that there are n users indexed by $1, 2, ..., n$. Users are organized logically in a cycle, such as $U_{n+1} = U_1$. When n is odd, then one party needs to behave as two independent machines virtually. So we just consider the case where n is even.

Round 1. Each U_i randomly chooses $k_i \in \mathbb{Z}_{\ell_s^{e_s}}$ and computes $R_i = P_s + k_i Q_s$, where $s = i \pmod 2$. U_i computes the isogeny $\phi_i : E \to E_i = E/\langle R_i \rangle$. Then it sets $sk_i^1 = k_i$ and broadcasts $pk_i^1 = (E_i, \phi_i(P_{1-s}), \phi_i(Q_{1-s}))$ to U_{i-1} and U_{i+1}.

Round 2. User U_i takes the keys pk_{i-1}^1, pk_{i+1}^1 and sk_i^1 to execute SIDH key exchange and obtain $K_i^L = j_{i-1,i}$ and $K_i^R = j_{i,i+1}$, where $j_{i-1,i}$ and $j_{i,i+1}$ represent the j-invariants of $E_{i-1}/\langle \phi_{i-1}(P_s)+k_i\phi_{i-1}(Q_s)\rangle$ and $E_{i+1}/\langle \phi_{i+1}(P_s)+k_i\phi_{i+1}(Q_s)\rangle$, respectively. Then user U_i broadcasts $pk_i^2 = u_i = j_{i,i+1} - j_{i-1,i}$.

Key Computation. Each user U_i uses hash function $H : \{0,1\}^* \to \{0,1\}^\lambda$, where λ is the security parameter and computes its session key

$$K_i = H(nj_{i-1,i} + (n-1)u_i + (n-2)u_{i+1} + ... + 2u_{i-3} + u_{i-2}).$$

It can be easily verified that $K_i = H(j_{1,2} + ... + j_{n,1}) = K$ for all i.

We stress that the costs of addition in finite fields can be ignored when compared with the multiplication costs, which is the main reason of the efficiency improvement. The requirement of KE-security, i.e. indistinguishability of computed group keys with respect to passive adversaries, states the basic security requirement for any GKE protocol. We now give a formal security proof.

Theorem 1. *Under the SI-DDH assumption, the improved SIBD GKE protocol is secure against passive adversary in random oracle and achieves forward secrecy. Precisely, if there are n users and the adversary $\mathcal{A}$ makes q_E calls to the* Execute *oracle, this protocol satisfies* $\mathsf{Adv}_{\mathcal{A}}^{\mathsf{GKE}}(q_E) \leq 2n\mathsf{Adv}_{\mathcal{A}}^{\mathsf{SIDDH}} + \frac{2nq_E}{p}$.

Proof. Suppose that there is an adversary $\mathcal{A}$ for the improved SIBD GKE protocol. Then we construct an algorithm $\mathcal{D}$ to solve the SI-DDH problem with non-negligible advantage. Since there is no long-term secret key, Corrupt query can be ignored by $\mathcal{A}$. So this protocol obviously achieves forward secrecy. $\mathcal{A}$ can query Execute, RevealKey and Test oracles. Suppose $T = (pk_i^1, pk_i^2)$ is a transcript of an execution of the GKE protocol and K is the resulting session key. We define two distributions Real and Fake, where Real is just the original protocol while Fake represents that all the pk_i^2 are uniformly chosen in $\mathbb{F}_{p^2}$ subject to the constraint $\sum_i pk_i^2 = 0$. We write $\mathfrak{g}^{\mathfrak{k}_i} \triangleq (E_i, \phi_i(P_{1-s}), \phi_i(Q_{1-s}))$, where $\phi_i : E \rightarrow E_i = E/\langle P_s + \mathfrak{k}_i Q_s \rangle$.

$$\mathsf{Real} = \left\{ \begin{array}{l} \mathfrak{k}_1, ..., \mathfrak{k}_n \in \mathbb{Z}_{\ell_s^{e_s}}; pk_1^1 = \mathfrak{g}^{\mathfrak{k}_1}, ..., pk_n^1 = \mathfrak{g}^{\mathfrak{k}_n}, \\ K_1^R = K_2^L = j(\mathfrak{g}^{\mathfrak{k}_1\mathfrak{k}_2}), ..., K_n^R = K_1^L = j(\mathfrak{g}^{\mathfrak{k}_n\mathfrak{k}_1}); \\ pk_1^2 = K_1^R - K_1^L, ..., pk_n^2 = K_n^R - K_n^L; \\ T = (pk_1^1, ..., pk_n^1; pk_1^2, ..., pk_n^2); \\ K = H(nj(\mathfrak{g}^{\mathfrak{k}_{i-1}\mathfrak{k}_i}) + (n-1)pk_i^2 + (n-2)pk_{i+1}^2 + ... + pk_{i-2}^2). \end{array} : (T, K) \right\},$$

$$\mathsf{Fake} = \left\{ \begin{array}{l} \mathfrak{k}_1, ..., \mathfrak{k}_n \in \mathbb{Z}_{\ell_s^{e_s}}; pk_1^1 = \mathfrak{g}^{\mathfrak{k}_1}, ..., pk_n^1 = \mathfrak{g}^{\mathfrak{k}_n}, \\ K_1^R = K_2^L = j(\mathfrak{g}^{\mathfrak{s}_1\mathfrak{s}_2}), ..., K_n^R = K_1^L = j(\mathfrak{g}^{\mathfrak{s}_n\mathfrak{s}_1}); \mathfrak{s}_1, ..., \mathfrak{s}_n \in \mathbb{Z}_{\ell_s^{e_s}}; \\ pk_1^2 = K_1^R - K_1^L, ..., pk_n^2 = K_n^R - K_n^L; \\ T = (pk_1^1, ..., pk_n^1; pk_1^2, ..., pk_n^2); \\ K = H(nj(\mathfrak{g}^{\mathfrak{k}_{i-1}\mathfrak{k}_i}) + (n-1)pk_i^2 + (n-2)pk_{i+1}^2 + ... + pk_{i-2}^2). \end{array} : (T, K) \right\}.$$

Claim 1. For any algorithm $\mathcal{A}$, we have $|\Pr[(T, K) \leftarrow \mathsf{Real} : \mathcal{A}(T, K) = 1] - \Pr[(T, K) \leftarrow \mathsf{Fake'} : \mathcal{A}(T, K) = 1]| \leq \mathsf{Adv}_{\mathcal{A}}^{\mathsf{SIDDH}} + \frac{1}{p}$, where

$$\mathsf{Fake'} = \left\{ \begin{array}{l} \mathfrak{k}_1, ..., \mathfrak{k}_n \in \mathbb{Z}_{\ell_s^{e_s}}; pk_1^1 = \mathfrak{g}^{\mathfrak{k}_1}, ..., pk_n^1 = \mathfrak{g}^{\mathfrak{k}_n}, \\ K_1^R = K_2^L = j(\mathfrak{g}^{\mathfrak{k}_1\mathfrak{k}_2}), ..., K_{n-1}^R = K_n^L = j(\mathfrak{g}^{\mathfrak{k}_{n-1}\mathfrak{k}_n}), \\ K_n^R = K_1^L = j(\mathfrak{g}^{\mathfrak{s}_n\mathfrak{s}_1}); \mathfrak{s}_1, \mathfrak{s}_n \in \mathbb{Z}_{\ell_s^{e_s}}; \\ pk_1^2 = K_1^R - K_1^L, ..., pk_n^2 = K_n^R - K_n^L; \\ T = (pk_1^1, ..., pk_n^1; pk_1^2, ..., pk_n^2); \\ K = H(nj(\mathfrak{g}^{\mathfrak{k}_{i-1}\mathfrak{k}_i}) + (n-1)pk_i^2 + (n-2)pk_{i+1}^2 + ... + pk_{i-2}^2). \end{array} : (T, K) \right\}.$$

Proof. Suppose there is a distinguisher $\mathcal{D}$ for SI-DDH problem using algorihtm $\mathcal{A}$. On the input $(\mathfrak{g}^{\mathfrak{a}}, \mathfrak{g}^{\mathfrak{b}}, \mathfrak{g}^{\mathfrak{c}})$ as defined in SIDH, it generates a pair (T, K) according to the below distribution Dist' and then outputs what $\mathcal{A}$ outputs.

$$\mathsf{Dist'} = \left\{ \begin{array}{l} \mathfrak{k}_1, ..., \mathfrak{k}_n \in \mathbb{Z}_{\ell_s^{e_s}}; \\ pk_1^1 = \mathfrak{g}^{\mathfrak{a}}, pk_2^1 = \mathfrak{g}^{\mathfrak{k}_2}, ..., pk_{n-1}^1 = \mathfrak{g}^{\mathfrak{k}_{n-1}}, pk_n^1 = \mathfrak{g}^{\mathfrak{b}}, \\ K_1^R = K_2^L = j(\mathfrak{g}^{\mathfrak{a}\mathfrak{k}_2}), K_2^R = K_3^L = j(\mathfrak{g}^{\mathfrak{k}_2\mathfrak{k}_3}), ..., \\ K_{n-2}^R = K_{n-1}^L = j(\mathfrak{g}^{\mathfrak{k}_{n-2}\mathfrak{k}_{n-1}}), \\ K_{n-1}^R = K_n^L = j(\mathfrak{g}^{\mathfrak{k}_{n-1}\mathfrak{b}}), K_n^R = K_1^L = j(\mathfrak{g}^{\mathfrak{c}}); \\ pk_1^2 = K_1^R - K_1^L, ..., pk_n^2 = K_n^R - K_n^L; \\ T = (pk_1^1, ..., pk_n^1; pk_1^2, ..., pk_n^2); \\ K = H(nj(\mathfrak{g}^{\mathfrak{k}_{i-1}\mathfrak{k}_i}) + (n-1)pk_i^2 + (n-2)pk_{i+1}^2 + ... + pk_{i-2}^2). \end{array} : (T, K) \right\}.$$

The distribution Real and the distribution $\{\mathfrak{a}, \mathfrak{b} \in \mathbb{Z}_{\ell_s^{e_s}}; (T, K) \leftarrow \mathsf{Dist'} : (T, K)\}$ are statistically equivalent if any $\mathfrak{k}_i$ is random. Furthermore, the distribution Fake' and the distribution $\{\mathfrak{a}, \mathfrak{b} \in \mathbb{Z}_{\ell_s^{e_s}}, \mathfrak{c} \neq \mathfrak{a}\mathfrak{b}; (T, K) \leftarrow \mathsf{Dist'} : (T, K)\}$ are statistically equivalent except for a factor of $\frac{1}{p}$. Hence, the two distributions Real and Fake' are statistically equivalent by the reduction of SI-DDH problem.

Claim 2. For any algorithm $\mathcal{A}$, we have $|\Pr[(T,K) \leftarrow \mathsf{Fake}' : \mathcal{A}(T,K) = 1] - \Pr[(T,K) \leftarrow \mathsf{Fake} : \mathcal{A}(T,K) = 1]| \leq (n-1)\mathsf{Adv}_{\mathcal{A}}^{\mathsf{SIDDH}} + \frac{n-1}{p}$.

Proof. The proof can imitate that of Claim 1, so we omit it here.

Claim 3. For any algorithm $\mathcal{A}$, we have $|\Pr[(T,K_0) \leftarrow \mathsf{Fake}; K_1 \leftarrow \mathbb{F}_{p^2}; b \leftarrow \{0,1\} : \mathcal{A}(T,K_b) = b]| = \frac{1}{2}$.

Proof. We can get nothing from the transcript T about the session key $K = H(j_{1,2} + ... + j_{n,1})$, since $pk_1^2 + pk_2^2 + ... + pk_n^2 = 0$. Hence the probability $|Pr[(T,K_0) \leftarrow \mathsf{Fake}; K_1 \leftarrow \mathbb{F}_{p^2}; b \leftarrow \{0,1\} : \mathcal{A}(T,K_b) = b]| = \frac{1}{2}$.

Now $\mathsf{Adv}_{\mathcal{A}}^{\mathsf{GKE}} = |2\Pr[\mathcal{A} \text{ wins}] - 1| = 2|Pr[(T,K_0) \leftarrow \mathsf{Real}, K_1 \leftarrow \mathbb{F}_{p^2}, b \leftarrow \{0,1\} : \mathcal{A}(T,K_b) = b] - \frac{1}{2}| = 2|\Pr[(T,K_0) \leftarrow \mathsf{Real}, K_1 \leftarrow \mathbb{F}_{p^2}, b \leftarrow \{0,1\} : \mathcal{A}(T,K_b) = b] - \Pr[(T,K_0) \leftarrow \mathsf{Fake}, K_1 \leftarrow \mathbb{F}_{p^2}, b \leftarrow \{0,1\} : \mathcal{A}(T,K_b) = b]|$. Sum up the above claims, we can obtain $\mathsf{Adv}_{\mathcal{A}}^{\mathsf{GKE}} \leq 2n\mathsf{Adv}_{\mathcal{A}}^{\mathsf{SIDDH}} + \frac{2n}{p}$.

For q_E times of query, the proceeding is in the similar way. Hence, $\mathsf{Adv}_{\mathcal{A}}^{\mathsf{GKE}}(q_E) = 2|\Pr[(T,K_0) \leftarrow \mathsf{Real}, K \leftarrow \mathbb{F}_{p^2}, b \leftarrow \{0,1\} : \mathcal{A}(T,K_b) = b] - \Pr[(T,K_0) \leftarrow \mathsf{Fake}, K \leftarrow \mathbb{F}_{p^2}, b \leftarrow \{0,1\} : \mathcal{A}(T,K_b) = b]| \leq 2n\mathsf{Adv}_{\mathcal{A}}^{\mathsf{SIDDH}} + \frac{2nq_E}{p}$.

3.2 Improved SIBDII Protocol

Since the BD protocol has high communication overhead, so we consider BDII protocol, which is rather akin to a tree structure and needs $O(\log n)$ communication and computation complexity per user in the multicast version. So we give an optimized SIDH version of the BDII scheme. The n users are indexed by $1, 2, ..., n$ with n even and their places in the binary tree automatically determined by their indexes are illustrated in Fig. 1.

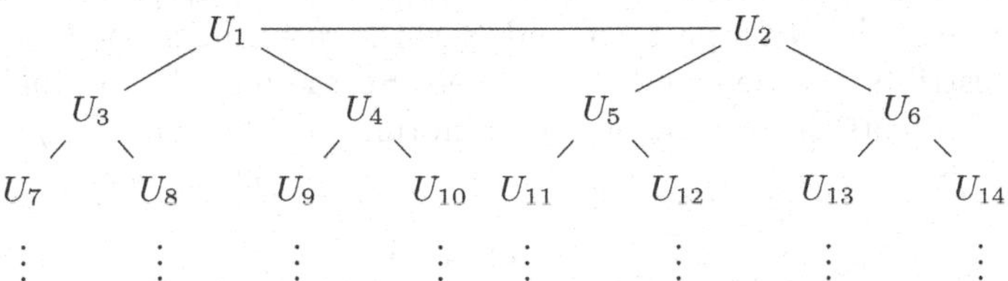

Fig. 1. The Binary tree in BDII scheme

We can find the user U_i is at level $\lfloor \log_2(i+1) \rfloor$ in the ordered tree. Let $parent(i), l_{child}(i)$ and $r_{child}(i)$ be the indexes of the parent, the left child and the right child of U_i, respectively. U_1 and U_2 consider their respective opposite as parent, which insures all but the leaves of the binary tree each have one parent and two children. Let $ancestors(i)$ be the set of indexes of all ancestors of U_i, including i but excluding 1 and 2. To make the computations of U_i and

$U_{parent(i)}$ are in different subgroups of the public elliptic curve, we set $s(1) = 0$ and $s \triangleq s(i) = s(parent(i)) + 1 \pmod 2$, which denote the indexes of the two subgroups. And the public parameters are also the same as those in SIDH.

Round 1. Each user U_i randomly chooses $k_i \in \mathbb{Z}_{\ell_s^{e_s}}$ and computes $R_i = P_s + k_i Q_s$. User U_i computes the isogeny $\phi_i : E \to E_i = E/\langle R_i \rangle$. Then it sets $sk_i^1 = k_i$ and broadcasts $pk_i^1 = (E_i, \phi_i(P_{1-s}), \phi_i(Q_{1-s}))$ to its parent and children.

Round 2. User U_i takes the keys $pk^1_{parent(i)}$, $pk^1_{l_{child}(i)}$, $pk^1_{r_{child}(i)}$ and sk_i^1 to execute
SIDH key exchange and obtain $K_i^P = j_{parent(i),i} = E_{parent(i)}/\langle \phi_{parent(i)}(P_s) + k_i \phi_{parent(i)}(Q_s) \rangle$, $K_i^L = j_{i,l_{child}(i)} = E_{l_{child}(i)}/\langle \phi_{l_{child}(i)}(P_s) + k_i \phi_{l_{child}(i)}(Q_s) \rangle$, and $K_i^R = j_{i,r_{child}(i)} = E_{r_{child}(i)}/\langle \phi_{r_{child}(i)}(P_s) + k_i \phi_{r_{child}(i)}(Q_s) \rangle$. Then it computes and multicasts pk_i^2 to its descendants, where $pk_i^2 = (u_{l_{child}(i)}, u_{r_{child}(i)}) = (j_{parent(i),i} - j_{i,l_{child}(i)}, j_{parent(i),i} - j_{i,r_{child}(i)})$.

Key Computation. Each user U_i uses the hash function $H : \{0,1\}^* \to \{0,1\}^\lambda$, where λ is the security parameter, and computes its session key $K_i = H(j_{parent(i),i} + \sum_{m \in ancestors(i)} X_m)$, where $X_m = j_{parent(parent(m)),parent(m)} - j_{parent(m),m}$.

It can be easily verified that $K_i = H(j_{1,2}) = K$ for all i.

Theorem 2. *Under the SI-DDH assumption, the improved SIBDII GKE protocol is secure against passive adversary in the random oracle model and achieves forward secrecy. Precisely, if there are n users and the adversary $\mathcal{A}$ activates at most k sessions, the GKE protocol satisfies* $\mathsf{Adv}_{\mathcal{A}}^{\mathsf{GKE}}(q_E) \le k(n-1)\mathsf{Adv}_{\mathcal{A}}^{\mathsf{SIDDH}}$.

Proof. Suppose that there is an adversary $\mathcal{A}$ for the improved SIBDII GKE protocol. Then we construct an algorithm $\mathcal{D}$ to solve the SI-DDH problem with non-negligible advantage. Since there is no long-term secret key, Corrupt query can be ignored by $\mathcal{A}$. So this protocol obviously achieves forward secrecy. $\mathcal{A}$ can query Execute, RevealKey and Test oracles. Suppose $T = (pk_i^1, pk_i^2)$ is a transcript of an execution of the GKE protocol and K is the resulting session key. We still define two distributions Real and Fake, where Real is just the original protocol while Fake represents that all the pk_i^2 are uniformly chosen from $(\mathbb{F}_{p^2})^2$. We write $\mathfrak{g}^{\mathfrak{k}_i} \triangleq (E_i, \phi_i(P_{1-s}), \phi_i(Q_{1-s}))$, where $\phi_i : E \to E_i = E/\langle P_s + \mathfrak{k}_i Q_s \rangle$.

$$\mathsf{Real} = \left\{ \begin{array}{l} \mathfrak{k}_1, ..., \mathfrak{k}_n \in \mathbb{Z}_{\ell_s^{e_s}}; \quad pk_1^1 = \mathfrak{g}^{\mathfrak{k}_1}, ..., pk_n^1 = \mathfrak{g}^{\mathfrak{k}_n}; \\ K_1^P = K_2^P = j(\mathfrak{g}^{\mathfrak{k}_1 \mathfrak{k}_2}), \text{ and for } 3 \le i \le \frac{n}{2} - 1 \\ K_i^L = K_{2i+1}^P = j(\mathfrak{g}^{\mathfrak{k}_i \mathfrak{k}_{2i+1}}), K_i^R = K_{2i+2}^P = j(\mathfrak{g}^{\mathfrak{k}_i \mathfrak{k}_{2i+2}}), \\ pk_1^2 = (K_1^P - K_1^L, K_1^P - K_1^R), ..., pk_n^2 = (K_n^P - K_n^L, K_n^P - K_n^R); \\ T = (pk_1^1, ..., pk_n^1; pk_1^2, ..., pk_n^2); \\ K = H(K_i^P + \sum_{m \in ancestors(i)} (K^P_{parent(m)} - K^P_m)). \end{array} : (T, K) \right\},$$

$$\mathsf{Fake} = \left\{ \begin{array}{l} \mathfrak{k}_1, ..., \mathfrak{k}_n \in \mathbb{Z}_{\ell_s^{e_s}}; \quad pk_1^1 = \mathfrak{g}^{\mathfrak{k}_1}, ..., pk_n^1 = \mathfrak{g}^{\mathfrak{k}_n}; \\ K_1^P = K_2^P = j(\mathfrak{g}^{\mathfrak{s}_1 \mathfrak{s}_2}), \text{ and for } 3 \le i \le \frac{n}{2} - 1: \\ K_i^L = K_{2i+1}^P = j(\mathfrak{g}^{\mathfrak{s}_i \mathfrak{s}_{2i+1}}), K_i^R = K_{2i+2}^P = j(\mathfrak{g}^{\mathfrak{s}_i \mathfrak{s}_{2i+2}}), \mathfrak{s}_1, \cdots, \mathfrak{s}_n \in \mathbb{Z}_{\ell_s^{e_s}}; \\ pk_1^2 = (K_1^P - K_1^L, K_1^P - K_1^R), ..., pk_n^2 = (K_n^P - K_n^L, K_n^P - K_n^R); \\ T = (pk_1^1, ..., pk_n^1; pk_1^2, ..., pk_n^2); \\ K = H(K_i^P + \sum_{m \in ancestors(i)} (K^P_{parent(m)} - K^P_m)). \end{array} : (T, K) \right\}.$$

We use hybrid technique to compute $|\Pr[(T, K_0) \leftarrow \mathsf{Real}, K_1 \leftarrow \mathbb{F}_{p^2}, b \leftarrow \{0,1\} : \mathcal{A}(T, K_b) = b] - \Pr[(T, K_0) \leftarrow \mathsf{Fake}, K_1 \leftarrow \mathbb{F}_{p^2}, b \leftarrow \{0,1\} : \mathcal{A}(T, K_b) = b]|$. So we define the distribution Fake^1 as follows.

$$\mathsf{Fake}^1 = \left\{ \begin{array}{l} \mathfrak{k}_1, ..., \mathfrak{k}_n \in \mathbb{Z}_{\ell_s^{e_s}}; \quad pk_1^1 = \mathfrak{g}^{\mathfrak{k}_1}, ..., pk_n^1 = \mathfrak{g}^{\mathfrak{k}_n}; \\ K_1^P = K_2^P = j(\mathfrak{g}^{\mathfrak{s}_1 \mathfrak{s}_2}), \mathfrak{s}_1, \cdots, \mathfrak{s}_n \in \mathbb{Z}_{\ell_s^{e_s}}; \\ \text{for } 3 \leq i \leq \frac{n}{2} - 1 : \\ K_i^L = K_{2i+1}^P = j(\mathfrak{g}^{\mathfrak{k}_i \mathfrak{k}_{2i+1}}), K_i^R = K_{2i+2}^P = j(\mathfrak{g}^{\mathfrak{k}_i \mathfrak{k}_{2i+2}}); \\ pk_1^2 = (K_1^P - K_1^L, K_1^P - K_1^R), ..., pk_n^2 = (K_n^P - K_n^L, K_n^P - K_n^R); \\ T = (pk_1^1, ..., pk_n^1; pk_1^2, ..., pk_n^2); \\ K = H(K_i^P + \sum_{m \in ancestors(i)} (K_{parent(m)}^P - K_m^P)). \end{array} : (T, K) \right\}.$$

Claim 1. For any algorithm $\mathcal{A}$, we have $|\Pr[(T, K_0) \leftarrow \mathsf{Fake}; K_1 \leftarrow \mathbb{F}_{p^2}; b \leftarrow \{0,1\} : \mathcal{A}(T, K_b) = b]| = \frac{1}{2}$.

Claim 2. For any algorithm $\mathcal{A}'$, we have $|\Pr[(T, K) \leftarrow \mathsf{Real} : \mathcal{A}'(T, K) = 1] - \Pr[(T, K) \leftarrow \mathsf{Fake}^1 : \mathcal{A}'(T, K) = 1]| = \frac{k}{2}\mathsf{Adv}_{\mathcal{A}}^{\mathsf{SIDDH}}$, where k is an upper bound on the number of sessions activated by the adversary.

Proof. We have $\frac{1}{k}$ chance that the session actually matches. We now build $\mathcal{D}$ to solve SIDDH in Algorithm 1 and get the final advantage of it is $\mathsf{Adv}_{\mathcal{A}}^{\mathsf{SIDDH}} = \frac{\mathsf{Adv}_{\mathcal{A}'}}{k} = \frac{2|\Pr[(T,K) \leftarrow \mathsf{Real}:\mathcal{A}'(T,K)=1] - \Pr[(T,K) \leftarrow \mathsf{Fake}^1:\mathcal{A}'(T,K)=1]|}{k}$.

Algorithm 1. SIDDH distinguisher $\mathcal{D}$

Input: $E_1, E_2, \phi_1(P_1), \phi_1(Q_1), \phi_2(P_0), \phi_2(Q_0), E'$
Output: d
Invoke $\mathcal{A}'$ and simulate protocol to $\mathcal{A}'$, except for the test session;
Simulate the Round 1; Set $K_1^P = K_2^P = j(E')$ and compute pk_i^2 as in Round 2;
if the selected section is the test session **then**
    $d \leftarrow \mathcal{A}$'s output.
else $d \xleftarrow{R} \{0,1\}$.
end if

Claim 3. For any algorithm $\mathcal{A}$, we have $|\Pr[(T, K) \leftarrow \mathsf{Fake} : \mathcal{A}'(T, K) = 1] - \Pr[(T, K) \leftarrow \mathsf{Fake}^1 : \mathcal{A}'(T, K) = 1]| = k(n - \frac{3}{2})\mathsf{Adv}_{\mathcal{A}}^{\mathsf{SIDDH}}$.

So $\mathsf{Adv}_{\mathcal{A}}^{\mathsf{GKE}} = |2\Pr[\mathcal{A} \text{ wins}] - 1| = 2|Pr[(T, K_0) \leftarrow \mathsf{Real}, K_1 \leftarrow \mathbb{F}_{p^2}, b \leftarrow \{0,1\} : \mathcal{A}(T, K_b) = b] - \frac{1}{2}| = 2|\Pr[(T, K_0) \leftarrow \mathsf{Real}, K_1 \leftarrow \mathbb{F}_{p^2}, b \leftarrow \{0,1\} : \mathcal{A}(T, K_b) = b] - \Pr[(T, K_0) \leftarrow \mathsf{Fake}, K_1 \leftarrow \mathbb{F}_{p^2}, b \leftarrow \{0,1\} : \mathcal{A}(T, K_b) = b]| \leq k(n-1)\mathsf{Adv}_{\mathcal{A}}^{\mathsf{SIDDH}}$.

4 Authenticated Group Key Exchange

According to the improved SIBD protocol (Sect. 3.1), we propose an AGKE protocol that is secure in eGBG model.

These public parameters are the same as the protocol in Sect. 3.1, except that there are two additional hash functions $H_1 : \{0,1\}^* \rightarrow \mathbb{Z}_{\ell_s^{e_s}}$ and $H_2 : \{0,1\}^* \rightarrow \{0,1\}^\lambda$, where λ is the security parameter. We write $\mathfrak{g}^{\mathfrak{a}_i} \triangleq (E_i, \phi_i(P_{1-s}), \phi_i(Q_{1-s}))$, where $\phi_i : E \rightarrow E_i = E/\langle P_s + \mathfrak{a}_i Q_s \rangle$ (Sect. 2.1).

Key Generation: For each user U_i, it chooses $sk_i = \mathfrak{a}_i \in \mathbb{Z}_{\ell_s^{e_s}}$ and computes $pk_i = \mathfrak{g}^{\mathfrak{a}_i}$, where $s = i \pmod 2$. Also, each user needs to generate the verification/signing keys (pk'_i, sk'_i).

Round 1. 1. Each user U_i randomly chooses $k_i \in \mathbb{Z}_{\ell_s^{e_s}}$, computes $\mathfrak{k}'_i = H_1(sk_i, k_i)$ and then computes $Y_i = \mathfrak{g}^{\mathfrak{k}'_i}$. After obtaining Y_i, user U_i destroys $\mathfrak{k}'_i$.
2. Each user U_i sets $M_i^1 = Y_i||\mathsf{pid}$. Then U_i computes a signature $\sigma_i^1 = Sign(sk'_i, M_i^1)$.
3. Each user U_i broadcasts $M_i^1||\sigma_i^1$ to U_{i-1} and U_{i+1}.

Round 2. 1. Each user U_i checks the signatures of U_{i-1} and U_{i+1} by the verification algorithm using the verification keys pk'_{i-1} and pk'_{i+1}. If it fails, then abort. Else, each user U_i computes $t_i^L = H_2(j_{i-1,i})$ and $t_i^R = H_2(j_{i,i+1})$ where $j_{i-1,i}$ and $j_{i,i+1}$ represent the j-invariants of $Y_{i-1}^{\mathfrak{k}'_i}$ and $Y_{i+1}^{\mathfrak{k}'_i}$, respectively. Then set $T_i = t_i^L \oplus t_i^R$.
2. Each user U_i chooses $x_i \in \{0,1\}^\lambda$ and set $M_i^2 = T_i||x_i$ except U_n. U_n computes $mask_n = x_n \oplus t_n^R$ and $H_2(x_n)$ and then sets $M_n^2 = mask_n||T_n||H_2(x_n)$. After that, t_i^L, t_i^R and x_n will be destroyed.
3. U_i computes a signature $\sigma_i^2 = Sign(sk'_i, M_i^2)$ and broadcasts $M_i^2||\sigma_i^2$.

Key Computation
1. U_i verifies all the incoming signatures σ_j^2 and checks whether $T_1 \oplus ... \oplus T_n = 0$.
2. Each U_i recomputes $\mathfrak{k}'_i = H_1(sk_i, k_i)$ and $t_i^L = H_2(j_{i-1,i})$, extracts $x_n = mask_n \oplus T_1 \oplus ... \oplus T_{i-1} \oplus t_i^L$, and then checks $H_2(x_n)$. If all the above checks pass, then set $\mathsf{sid} = H_2(\mathsf{pid}||x_1||...||x_{n-1}||H_2(x_n))$.
3. Each U_i computes the session key $SK = H(\mathsf{sid}||x_1||...||x_n)$.

Remark 1: In Round 1, each U_i doesn't broadcasts its message and signature to to any other user. This can reduce much communication.

Remark 2: The signature scheme used in the above protocol can be any post-quantum signature, not essentially these isogeny-based signatures, since these signatures on supersingular isogeny are impractical at present [12].

Theorem 3. *Suppose that H_1, H_2 and H are random oracles and the signature scheme used in AGKE protocol is UF-CMA secure. Under the SI-CDH assumption, the AGKE protocol is eGBG secure in the random oracle model. Precisely, if there are n users and for any PPT adversary $\mathcal{A}$ against AGKE, there exists $\mathcal{B}$ s.t.* $\mathsf{Adv}_{\mathcal{A}}^{\mathsf{AGKE}} \leq 2n^2 \cdot \mathsf{Adv}^{Sig} + \frac{q_{H_1}^2}{\sqrt{p}} + \frac{q_{H_2}^2}{2^\lambda} + \frac{q_H^2}{2^\lambda} + \frac{q_S^2}{2^{\lambda-1}} + \frac{q_H}{2^{\lambda-1}} + nq_{H_2} \cdot \mathsf{Adv}_{\mathcal{B}}^{\mathsf{SICDH}}$, *where n is the number of users, q_{H_1}, q_{H_2}, q_H are the number of hash oracle queries to H_1, H_2, H, respectively, and q_S is the number of queries to* Send *oracle. And* Adv^{Sig} *denotes the advantage against the UF-CMA security of the signature.*

Proof. We refer the readers to Sect. 2.3 for the definition of eGBG secure. For each game G_i, we define $Succ_i$ as the adversary wins the game.

Game 0: This game corresponds to the real execution, where we do not modify any simulation of the oracles. Hence, $\mathsf{Adv}_{\mathcal{A}}^{\mathsf{AGKE}} \leq |2Pr[Succ_0] - 1|$.

Game 1: In this game, the event Forge happens when the adversary $\mathcal{A}$ succeeds in forging an authenticated message $M_i||\sigma_i$ for user U_i, where M_i was not outputed by any U_i's instance and $\mathsf{Corrupt}$ has not been queried. The probability of $\mathcal{A}$ outputting a valid forgery on behalf of the target party is $\geq \frac{1}{n}$ and probability of not getting the long-term key of the target party is $\geq \frac{1}{n}$, hence using $\mathcal{A}$ we can defeat the existential unforgeability of the underlying signature with probability $\mathsf{Adv}^{Sig} \geq \frac{1}{n^2} Pr[\mathsf{Forge}]$. Then we have $|Pr[Succ_1] - Pr[Succ_0]| \leq Pr[\mathsf{Forge}] \leq n^2 \cdot \mathsf{Adv}^{Sig}$.

Game 2: This game is the same as Game 1 except that $\mathsf{Collision}$ occurs when the random oracles produce a collision. We denote q_{H_1}, q_{H_2} and q_H as the numbers of hash oracle queries to H_1, H_2 and H, respectively. According to the birthday paradox, we can get the probability of collisions of H_1, H_2 and H oracles. Hence,

$$|Pr[Succ_2] - Pr[Succ_1] \leq Pr[\mathsf{Collision}]| \leq \frac{q_{H_1}^2}{2\sqrt{p}} + \frac{q_{H_2}^2}{2^{\lambda+1}} + \frac{q_H^2}{2^{\lambda+1}}.$$

where p is the prime of the finite field $\mathbb{F}_{p^2}$ and λ is the security parameter.

Game 3: This game is the same as Game 2 except that Repeat occurs when different users choose the same random values x_i. We denote q_S as the number of queries to the Send oracle. Hence, $|Pr[Succ_3] - Pr[Succ_2]| \leq Pr[\mathsf{Repeat}] \leq \frac{q_S^2}{2^\lambda}$.

Game 4: This game differs from the previous game by the different answers to the Send queries during the Test session.

The SI-CDH solver $\mathcal{B}$ obtains the tuple $(\mathfrak{g}, \mathfrak{g}^{\mathfrak{a}}, \mathfrak{g}^{\mathfrak{b}})$ and randomly chooses a party U_i. When the Send query is asked, $\mathcal{B}$ sets $A = Y_{i-1}$ and $B = Y_i$ and returns A, B to U_i. Since the eGBG model only allows the adversary to reveal the long-term secret sk_i or the ephemeral key k_i, but not both sk_i and k_i simultaneously. However, we set $\mathfrak{k}_i' = H_1(sk_i, k_i)$ and compute Y_i with $\mathfrak{k}_i'$. So the SI-CDH solver simulates all oracle queries without knowing $a = \mathfrak{k}_i'$ and $b = \mathfrak{k}_{i-1}'$.

If the adversary $\mathcal{A}$ successfully obtained the session key, then $\mathcal{A}$ must know x_n and $t_i^L = H_2(j_{i-1,i})$ where $j_{i-1,i}$ represents $Y_{i-1}^{\mathfrak{k}_i'}$ or $Y_i^{\mathfrak{k}_{i-1}'}$. So the only way for $\mathcal{A}$ to get t_i^L is to ask a hash query with $Y_{i-1}^{\mathfrak{k}_i'}$ or $Y_i^{\mathfrak{k}_{i-1}'}$ to H_2. Then we can solve the SI-CDH problem with the advantage $\mathsf{Adv}_{\mathcal{B}}^{\mathsf{SICDH}}$ in polynomial time.

Hence, according to the above analysis, we have $|Pr[Succ_4] - Pr[Succ_3]| \leq n \cdot q_{H_2} \cdot \mathsf{Adv}_{\mathcal{B}}^{\mathsf{SICDH}}$.

Game 5: The difference between this game and Game 4 is that the test session aborts if the adversary $\mathcal{A}$ issues a query to H with $sid||x_1||...||x_n$. Since the adversary $\mathcal{A}$ does not obtain anything about k_n, then $\mathcal{A}$ guesses it with a probability of $\frac{1}{2^\lambda}$. Hence, $|Pr[Succ_5] - Pr[Succ_4]| \leq \frac{q_H}{2^\lambda}$, where $Pr[Succ_5] = \frac{1}{2}$.

The theorem is proven by summing them up.

Theorem 4. *Suppose that H_1, H_2, H are random oracles and the signature scheme used in AGKE proto3col is UF-CMA secure. $\mathcal{A}_{ma}$ is an adversary that can perform all the queries in Sect. 2.3. Then the AGKE protocol provides mutual authentication security. Precisely,* $\mathsf{Adv}^{AGKE}_{\mathcal{A}_{ma}} \leq n^2 \cdot \mathsf{Adv}^{Sig} + \frac{q_{H_1}^2}{2\sqrt{p}} + \frac{q_{H_2}^2}{2^{\lambda+1}} + \frac{q_H^2}{2^{\lambda+1}} + \frac{q_S^2}{2^\lambda}$, *where* $n, q_{H_1}, q_{H_2}, q_H, q_S, \mathsf{Adv}^{Sig}$ *are the same as those in Theorem 3.*

Proof. We still define $Succ_i$ as the adversary wins the game.

Game 0: This game corresponds to the real execution, where we do not modify any simulation of the oracles. Hence, $\mathsf{Adv}^{\mathsf{AGKE}}_{\mathcal{A}_{ma}} = Pr[Succ_0]$.

Game 1, 2, 3 are same with those in the proof of Theorem 3.

If Game 3 does not abort, then all the honest users can compute the same key. Hence $Pr[Succ_3] = 0$. Sum up the probabilities from Game 0 to Game 3, we can prove Theorem 4.

Theorem 5. *Suppose that H_1, H_2, H are random oracles and the signature scheme used in AGKE protocol is UF-CMA secure. $\mathcal{A}_{con}$ is an adversary that can perform all the queries in Sect. 2.3. Then the AGKE protocol provides contributiveness security. Precisely,* $\mathsf{Adv}^{AGKE}_{\mathcal{A}_{con}} \leq \frac{q_{H_2}^2}{2^{\lambda+1}} + \frac{q_H^2}{2^{\lambda+1}} + \frac{q_S^2}{2^\lambda}$, *where* $n, q_{H_1}, q_{H_2}, q_H,$ *is the number of users,* $q_{H_1}, q_{H_2}, q_H, q_S$ *are the same as those in Theorem 3.*

Proof. We give a proof following the proofs of Theorem 3 and Theorem 4.

Game 0: This game is the real execution. Hence, $\mathsf{Adv}^{\mathsf{AGKE}}_{\mathcal{A}_{ma}} = Pr[Succ_0]$.

Game 1: This game is the case that Repeat occurs. We simulate all oracles in Game 1 except that we half all executions in which Repeat occurs. Hence, $|Pr[Succ_1] - Pr[Succ_0]| \leq Pr[\mathsf{Repeat}] \leq \frac{q_S^2}{2^\lambda}$.

Game 2: This game is the case that Collision for input x_n happens. Then we have $|Pr[Succ_2] - Pr[Succ_1]| \leq Pr[\mathsf{Collision}] \leq \frac{q_{H_2}^2}{2^{\lambda+1}}$.

Game 3: This game is the case that Collision for input $(\mathsf{sid}||x_1||...||x_n)$ occurs. Consequently, $|Pr[Succ_3] - Pr[Succ_2]| \leq Pr[\mathsf{Collision}] \leq \frac{q_H^2}{2^{\lambda+1}}$.

Then sum them up, we get the result.

5 Complexity Analysis

We first give an analysis about our first GKE scheme. We change the traditional way to compute the session key by using addition (subtraction), which has a more obvious practical benefit than multiplication (inverse) in finite field computation. In [16], their SIBD scheme needs to compute a maximum of $\frac{n^2+n}{2}$ multiplications. However, in our scheme in Sect. 3.1, we only need around $(n-1)$ multiplications and n additions. For easier comparison, we set the square operation as multiplication here. For our second GKE scheme, it is a trivial generalization of BDII protocol, which is tree-based and has computational complexity

Table 1. Comparison of GKE and AGKE protocols on supersingular isogenies.

Scheme	Rd	Com	Cost	Assum	Sec	Auth
SIBD [16]	2	$(48n-48)\lambda$	$3\mathsf{Iso}+\frac{n^2+n}{2}\mathsf{M}$	SI-DDH	BCPQ	No
First GKE	2	$(12n+60)\lambda$	$3\mathsf{Iso}+(n-1)\mathsf{M}+n\mathsf{A}$	SI-DDH	BCPQ	No
Second GKE	2	$(12\lfloor\log_2(n+1)\rfloor+96)\lambda$	$4\mathsf{Iso}+(\lfloor\log_2(i+1)\rfloor+1)A$	SI-DDH	BCPQ	No
AJJ19 [2]	2	$O(n^2\lambda)$	$(n-1)\mathsf{Iso}+n(n-1)\mathsf{Point}$	SI-DDH	CK	Yes
Sect. 4	2	$O(n\lambda)$	$4\mathsf{Iso}+2\mathsf{Sign}+(n+1)\mathsf{Ver}$	SI-CDH	eGBG	Yes

$O(\log n)$. The communication efficiency of a GKE protocol can be measured by the number of rounds it takes to complete the total protocol and the size of the messages exchanged by any user. If we require λ bits of quantum security and adopt the parameters chosen in [9] which are considered the most efficient, then the prime is of bit-length 6λ. Each field element needs 12λ since the curve is defined over $\mathbb{F}_{p^2}$. Then one curve and one point both require 12λ bits.

For our AGKE scheme, it has two rounds. During the whole process, any single user has to compute four isogenies (1 in Round 1, 2 in Round 2 and 1 in Key Computation), two signatures and $(n+1)$ verifications. The number of isogeny computation is much smaller than that of [2] where each user computes $n-1$ isogenies and $(n-1)n$ image points.

In the following table, **Rd** denotes the number of communication round. **Com** is the total communication size. **Cost** is the computation cost for each user U_i. **Assum** is the assumptions. **Sec** is the security model. **Auth** denotes if the scheme provides authentication. λ is the security parameter. Iso means the cost to compute an isogeny. M and A mean one multiplication and one addition in $\mathbb{F}_{p^2}$, respectively. Point means the computation of the image point by an isogeny. Sign and Ver are the cost of one signature and verification algorithm.

6 Conclusion

In this paper, we present two improved GKE protocols of BD and BDII style by using SIDH as the underline two-party key exchange. We show our schemes have optimal performance and satisfy quantum security through a reduction to SI-DDH assumption. We then propose a AGKE protocol under the SI-CDH assumption with a formal security proof. To show our schemes are more practical and have stronger security, we also give comparison among the existed protocols.

Acknowledgments. We thank the anonymous Inscrypt'2020 reviewers for their helpful comments. This work was supported by MMJJ20180207, the National Natural Science Foundation of China (Grant Nos. 61772515) and Beijing Municipal Science & Technology Commission (Project Number: Z191100007119006).

References

1. Apon, D., Dachman-Soled, D., Gong, H., Katz, J.: Constant-round group key exchange from the ring-LWE assumption. IACR Cryptology ePrint Archive 2019/398
2. Azarderakhsh, R., Jalali, A., Jao, D., Soukharev, V.: Practical supersingular isogeny group key agreement. IACR Cryptology ePrint Archive 2019/330
3. Bresson, E., Chevassut, O., Pointcheval, D., Quisquater, J. J.: Provably authenticated group Diffie-Hellman key exchange. In Proceedings of the 8th ACM conference on Computer and Communications Security, pp. 255–264. ACM (2001)
4. Burmester, M., Desmedt, Y.: A secure and efficient conference key distribution system. In: De Santis, A. (ed.) EUROCRYPT 1994. LNCS, vol. 950, pp. 275–286. Springer, Heidelberg (1995). https://doi.org/10.1007/BFb0053443
5. Burmester, M., Desmedt, Y.: A secure and scalable group key exchange system. Inf. Process. Lett. **94**(3), 137–143 (2005)
6. Burmester M., Desmedt, Y.: Efficient and secure conference-key distribution. Secur. Protocols **1189**, 119–129 (1997)
7. Bohli, J.M., Gonzalez Vasco, M.I., Steinwandt, R.: Secure group key establishment revisited. Int. J. Inf. Sec. **6**(4), 243–254 (2007)
8. Bresson, E., Manulis, M.: Securing group key exchange against strong corruptions. In ASIACCS 2008, pp. 249–260. ACM Press (2008)
9. Costello, C., Longa, P., Naehrig, M.: Efficient algorithms for supersingular isogeny Diffie-Hellman. In: Robshaw, M., Katz, J. (eds.) CRYPTO 2016. LNCS, vol. 9814, pp. 572–601. Springer, Heidelberg (2016). https://doi.org/10.1007/978-3-662-53018-4_21
10. Desmedt, Y., Lange, T., Burmester, M.: Scalable authenticated tree based group key exchange for ad-hoc groups. In: Dietrich, S., Dhamija, R. (eds.) FC 2007. LNCS, vol. 4886, pp. 104–118. Springer, Heidelberg (2007). https://doi.org/10.1007/978-3-540-77366-5_12
11. Gorantla, M.C., Boyd, C., González Nieto, J.M.: Modeling key compromise impersonation attacks on group key exchange protocols. In: Jarecki, S., Tsudik, G. (eds.) PKC 2009. LNCS, vol. 5443, pp. 105–123. Springer, Heidelberg (2009). https://doi.org/10.1007/978-3-642-00468-1_7
12. Galbraith, S.D., Petit, C., Silva, J.: Identification protocols and signature schemes based on supersingular isogeny problems. In: Takagi, T., Peyrin, T. (eds.) ASIACRYPT 2017. LNCS, vol. 10624, pp. 3–33. Springer, Cham (2017). https://doi.org/10.1007/978-3-319-70694-8_1
13. Ingemarsson, I., Tang, D., Wong, C.: A conference key distribution system. IEEE Trans. Inf. Theory **28**(5), 714–720 (1982)
14. De Feo, L., Jao, D., Plût, J.: Towards quantum-resistant cryptosystems from supersingular elliptic curve isogenies. J. Math. Cryptol. **8**(3), 209–247 (2014)
15. Fujioka, A., Takashima, K., Yoneyama, K.: One-round authenticated group key exchange from isogenies. In: Steinfeld, R., Yuen, T.H. (eds.) ProvSec 2019. LNCS, vol. 11821, pp. 330–338. Springer, Cham (2019). https://doi.org/10.1007/978-3-030-31919-9_20
16. Furukawa, S., Kunihiro, N., Takashima, K.: Multi-party key exchange protocols from supersingular isogenies. In: ISITA 2018, pp. 208–212. IEEE (2018)
17. Fujioka, A., Takashima, K., Terada, S., Yoneyama, K.: Supersingular isogeny Diffie–Hellman authenticated key exchange. In: Lee, K. (ed.) ICISC 2018. LNCS, vol. 11396, pp. 177–195. Springer, Cham (2019). https://doi.org/10.1007/978-3-030-12146-4_12

18. Galbraith, S.D.: Authenticated key exchange for SIDH. IACR Cryptology ePrint Archive 2018/266
19. Kim, Y., Perrig, A., Tsudik, G.: Tree-based group key agreement. ACM Trans. Inf. Syst. Secur. **7**(1), 60–96 (2004)
20. Krawczyk, H.: HMQV: a high-performance secure Diffie-Hellman protocol. In: Shoup, V. (ed.) CRYPTO 2005. LNCS, vol. 3621, pp. 546–566. Springer, Heidelberg (2005). https://doi.org/10.1007/11535218_33
21. Katz, J., Shin, J.S.: Modeling insider attacks on group key-exchange protocols. In: Proceedings of the 12th ACM Conference on Computer and Communications Security, pp. 180–189. ACM (2005)
22. Katz, J., Yung, M.: Scalable protocols for authenticated group key exchange. J. Cryptol. **20**(1), 85–113 (2007)
23. Cohn-Gordon, K., Cremers, C., Gjøsteen, K., Jacobsen, H., Jager, T.: Highly efficient key exchange protocols with optimal tightness. In: Boldyreva, A., Micciancio, D. (eds.) CRYPTO 2019. LNCS, vol. 11694, pp. 767–797. Springer, Cham (2019). https://doi.org/10.1007/978-3-030-26954-8_25
24. Jao, D., Azarderakhsh, R., Campagna, M., et al.: Supersingular Isogeny Key Encapsulation. https://csrc.nist.gov/projects/post-quantum-cryptography/round-2-submissions
25. Longa, P.: A Note on Post-Quantum Authenticated Key Exchange from Supersingular Isogenies. IACR Cryptology ePrint Archive 2018/267
26. Suzuki, K., Yoneyama, K.: Exposure-resilient one-round tripartite key exchange without random oracles. IEICE Trans. Fundam. Electron. Commun. Comput. Sci. **97**(6), 1345–1355 (2014)
27. Xu, X., Xue, H., Wang, K., Au, M.H., Tian, S.: Strongly secure authenticated key exchange from supersingular isogenies. In: Galbraith, S.D., Moriai, S. (eds.) ASIACRYPT 2019. LNCS, vol. 11921, pp. 278–308. Springer, Cham (2019). https://doi.org/10.1007/978-3-030-34578-5_11
28. Tseng, Y.M.: A secure authenticated group key agreement protocol for resource-limited mobile devices. Comput. J. **50**(1), 41–52 (2007)
29. Zhao, J., Gu, D., Gorantla, M. C.: Stronger security model of group key agreement. In: Proceedings of the 6th ACM Symposium on Information, Computer and Communications Security, pp. 435–440. ACM (2011)

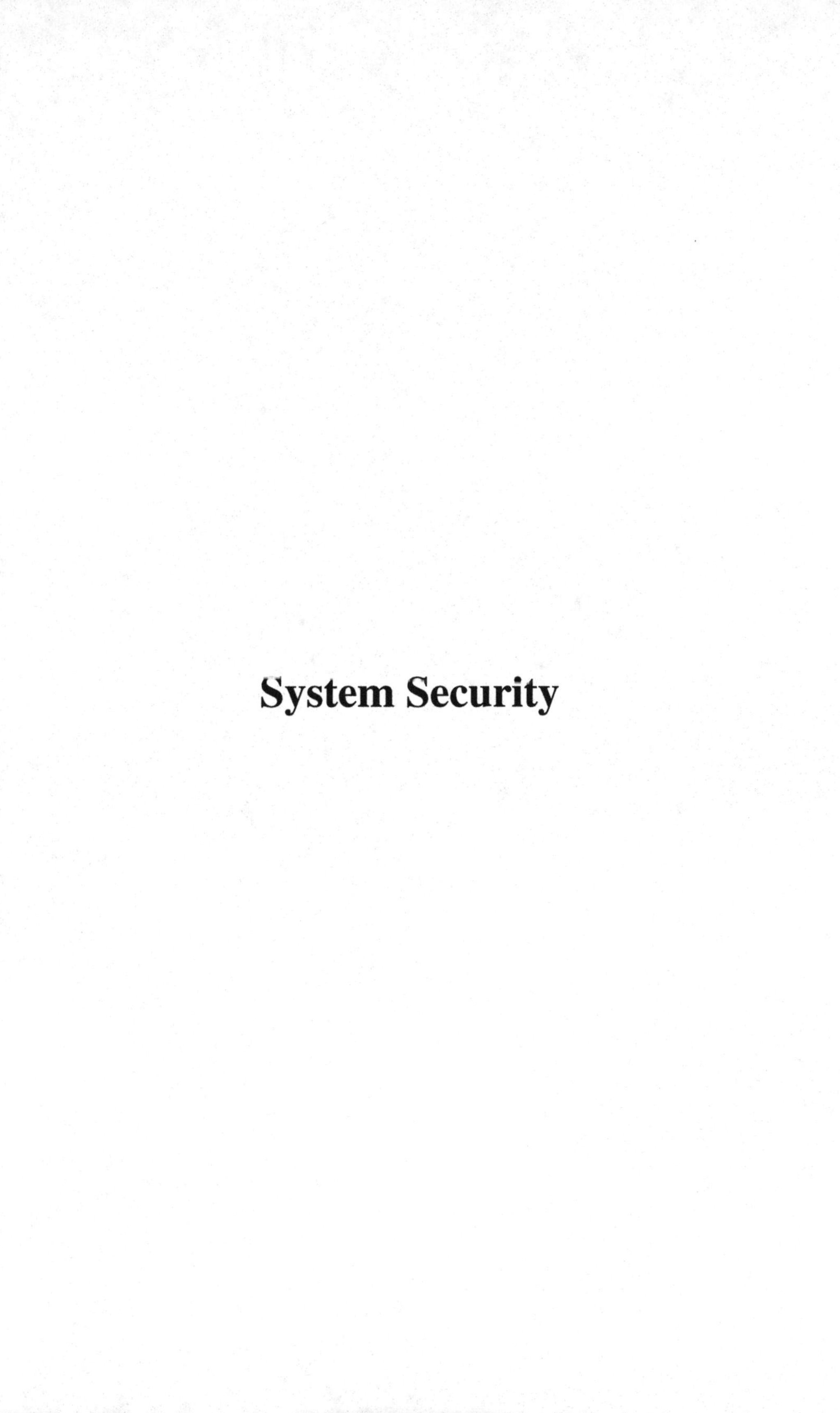

System Security

A Paid Message Forwarding Scheme Based on Social Network

Yifu Geng[1], Bo Qin[1(✉)], Wenchang Shi[1], and Qianhong Wu[2]

[1] School of Information, Renmin University of China, Beijing, China
bo.qin@ruc.edu.cn

[2] School of Cyber Science and Technology, Beihang University, Beijing, China

Abstract. Because of billions of users, the social network is the best choice for person who has an urgent task which needs enough people to participant or that only a few people are able to solve. Inspired by incentive mechanisms for retrieving information from networked agents and motivating the participation of people in crowdsourcing or human tasking systems, we design a paid message forwarding scheme based on social network so that the task will be known to capable persons in a short time. In our scheme, each participant helps solving the task directly or forwards the message he has received. Both kinds of contribution will bring a reward. Additionally, we use Elliptic Curve Digital Signature Algorithm to make the real contribution of participants known to who will pay the reward. Our scheme is shown sybil-proof, incentive compatible, efficient and is proved secure with the assumption that Elliptic Curve Digital Signature Algorithm is safe.

Keywords: Mechanism design · Incentive tree · Sybil attack · Signature algorithm

1 Introduction

The emergence of the Internet has changed the way of information transmission. Billions of social network users make it possible that a message is read by millions of people in a short time. As a result, if person has a task which needs enough people to participant or that only a few people are able to solve, he can ask for help through the social network and of course he is willing to pay for correct responses. The challenge is how to spread the task quickly and accurately with the reward paid according to the real contribution.

One solution is to design an incentive mechanism that encourages each social network user to forward messages about the task to his friends and gives a reward even if he isn't the right person the task is looking for.

A common type of incentive mechanisms for raising user participation in such systems are Incentive Trees. Incentive Trees are referral-based mechanisms in which (1) each participant is rewarded for contributing to the system, and (2) a participant that has already joined the system can make referrals, and

Y. Wu and M. Yung (Eds.): Inscrypt 2020, LNCS 12612, pp. 177–192, 2021.
https://doi.org/10.1007/978-3-030-71852-7_12

thereby solicit new participants to also join the system and contribute to it. The mechanism incentivizes such solicitations by making a solicitor's reward depend on the contributions (and recursively also on their further solicitations, etc.) made by such solicitees. Incentive Trees have been widely used in a variety of domains and under different names, e.g., in referral trees, multi-level marketing schemes, affiliate marketing or even in the form of the infamous illegal Pyramid Schemes. The question of how people can be incentivized using Incentive Trees to participate in crowdsourcing or network-effect systems is starting from the work on Lottery Trees [6], and most prominently through the work by the MIT team on the Red Balloon Challenge [12], which has attracted significant interest from the research community [3,7].

However, few incentive mechanisms have ever discussed the condition that the contribution of a participant p is falsely claimed by another one between p and the root. The root may be cheated by participants. On the other hand, the root may refuse to pay the reward after his task is solved.

In this paper, we construct a paid message forwarding scheme. First, we use elliptic curve digital signature algorithm [8] to build a message forward scheme to make the participants obey the roles. Second, we design a reward distribution mechanism which is an incentive tree and where a node will get fix-split rewards of its children as commission. Third, we prove the paid message forwarding scheme is secure assuming ECDSA is safe.

In our model, the following principles are taken into account:

- **Rational**: All participants should be rational and they will involve in our message forward process for more rewards rather than breaking roles to deprive the source of help.
- **Sybil-Proofness**: Nodes involved in message forward process will be known to the source and rewarded. Intuitively, a greedy node may make multiple false-names (Sybil attack [5]) before sending to his friends. It should make a clever design to prevent nodes from deviating from honest operations.
- **Fairness**: A node will get a reward that matches his contributions. To make our scheme fair, the contributions of each node should be truly delivered to the source and the source distributes rewards according to commitments.
- **Entirety**: The rewards are originally from the source node, thus we hope that it is the source node who sets the method of reward allocation. For each node, he does not have a lot of knowledge of the underlying network. It is better to avoid using many parameters of network property in the design of reward allocation function.
- **Efficiency**: The source should quickly know all the nodes that help transferring the message on finding one of the target nodes. Besides, if there exist lots of target nodes, the source should complete the reward allocation process within acceptable time.

Related Work. The related works about incentive mechanism can be divided into three parts according to the description about social network.

Tree Model. The work by Douceur and Moscibroda on Lottery Trees [6] aims at motivating people to participate in networked systems and bootstrapping such systems by network effect. The paper addresses the following question: Assuming that some system organizer is willing to spend a fixed amount of money incentivizing people to do a specific type of work, how should the system be organized to maximize the resulting work? The authors propose Lottery Trees, formalize a set of desirable properties, prove impossibility results, and devise two nontrivial mechanisms, one of which achieves near-optimality in terms of achieved desirable properties. In the work by Yuezhou Lv and Thomas Moscibroda [10,11], they study Incentive Trees for motivating the participation of people in crowdsourcing or human tasking and define a set of basic, desirable properties which ideally an Incentive Tree Mechanism should satisfy.

Branching Process Model. The model of branching process in P2P network was introduced to analyze query incentive network [9], where they considered a simple branching process in a tree. Cebrian et al. [3] studied the Red Balloon Challenge [12] with split contracts and showed that in contrast to fixed-payment contracts, split contracts are robust to nodes' selfishness. In the above-mentioned works, Sybil-proofness was not explicitly explored. Chen et al. [4] proposed a family of mechanisms for query incentive network, called the direct referral (DR) mechanisms, which allocate most reward to the information holder as well as its direct parent (or direct referral). It was shown that, when designed properly, the direct referral mechanism is Sybil-proof and efficient.

Other Models. In addition to above two models, there has recently been many other works on incentive systems. For example, the Bitcoin system by Babaioff et al. [1] studies a problem similar to multi-level marketing. It uses a game-theoretic solution concept to study a problem in which agents are incentivized to forward sensitive information in such a way that the overall system performance is maximized.

Organization. The rest of the paper is organized as follows: We have shown necessary knowledge about Elliptic Curves digital signature algorithm in Sect. 2. Section 3 gives the definition of Message Path Tree. We have given the message forward model in Sect. 4 and the reward distribution mechanism in Sect. 5. The analysis of our construction is given in Sect. 6.

2 Background

Definition 1 ***(Elliptic Curves EC).*** *Let F_p be a finite field, where p is any prime. The elliptic curve over F_p is described as*

$$E : y^2 = x^3 + Ax + B,$$

where A and B are constants, belonging to F_p, such that $4A^3 + 27B^2 \neq 0$. For all $x, y \in F_p$ there are finitely many pair of points on E, which have coordinates *in* F_p. *We use* $E(F_p)$ *to represent the elliptic curve* E *over* F_p. *In the set* $E(F_p)$ *we always include the point at infinity,which is donated as* $\mathcal{O}$. *The set* $E(F_p)$ *is written as*

$$E(F_p) = \{(x, y) \in F_p \times F_p | y^2 = x^3 + Ax + B\} \cup \{\mathcal{O}\}.$$

Addition Formula of Elliptic Curves. Let P and Q be two distinct points on an elliptic curve E. The sum of P and Q denoted $R = P + Q$ is defined as follows. First draw the line through P and Q; this line intersects the elliptic curve in a third point. Then R is the reflection of this point in the x-axis.

Usually, we use a set of EC domain parameters $D = (E_p(a, b), G, n)$ with the following conditions:

- $E_p(a, b)$ refers to the EC $E(F_p) = \{(x, y) \in F_p \times F_p | y^2 = x^3 + ax + b\} \cup \{\mathcal{O}\}$.
- $G \in E_p(a, b)$ and $G \neq \mathcal{O}$.
- p is an odd prime.
- n is prime and $nG = \mathcal{O}$.

Definition 2 ***(Elliptic Curve Digital Signature Algorithm ECDSA).*** *Given a particular set of EC domain parameters* $D = (E_p(a, b), G, n)$ *and a hash function* H, *an Elliptic Curve Digital Signature Algorithm ECDSA consists of three algorithm:* $KeyGen$, $Sign$ *and* $Verify$.

- $KeyGen(\lambda) \rightarrow (PP, VK, SK)$. *This algorithm takes security parameter* λ *as input. An entity* $\mathcal{A}$ *runs KeyGen and generates a public parameter* $PP = (D, H)$, *public key* VK *and private key* SK. *The key pair is published as following:*
  1. *Select a random integer* d *in the interval* $[1, n - 1]$.
  2. *Compute* $Q = dG$.
  3. $(VK, SK) = (Q, d)$.
- $Sign(M, PP, SK) \rightarrow (\sigma)$. *This algorithm takes as input a message* M, *public parameter* PP *and private key* SK. $\mathcal{A}$ *runs Sign and generates a signature* σ *as:*
  1. *Select a random integer* k, $1 \leq k \leq n - 1$.
  2. *Compute* $kG = (x_1, y_1)$ *and* $r = x_1 \bmod n$. *If* $r = 0$ *then go to step 1.*
  3. *Compute* $k^{-1} \bmod n$.
  4. *Compute* $e = H(M)$.
  5. *Compute* $s = k^{-1}(e + dr) \bmod n$. *If* $s = 0$ *then go to step 1.*
  6. $\sigma = (r, s)$.
- $Verify(\sigma, M, PP, VK) \rightarrow \{0, 1\}$. *This algorithm takes as input a signature* $\sigma = (r, s)$, *a message* M, *the public parameter* PP *and the public key* VK. *Any verifier runs* $Verify$ *to check whether* σ *is a valid signature on* M.
  1. *Verify that* r *and* s *are integers in the interval* $[1, n - 1]$.
  2. *Compute* $e = H(M)$.
  3. *Compute* $w = s^{-1} \bmod n$.
  4. *Compute* $u_1 = ew \bmod n$ *and* $u_2 = rw \bmod n$.

5. *Compute* $X = u_1G + u_2Q$. *If* $X = \mathcal{O}$, *then reject the signature. Otherwise,compute* $v = x_1 \bmod n$ *where* $X = (x_1, y_1)$.
6. *Accept* σ *if and only if* $v = r$.

Definition 3 ***(Elliptic Curve Discrete Logarithm Problem ECDLP).*** *The elliptic curve discrete logarithm problem (ECDLP) is the following: given an elliptic curve* E *defined over a finite field* F_q, *a point* $P \in E(F_q)$ *of order* n, *and a point* $Q = lp$ *where* $0 \leq l \leq n-1$, *determine* l.

Slight variants of ECDSA have been proven existentially unforgeable against chosen-message attack) by Pointcheval and Stern [13] under the assumptions that the ECDLP is hard and that the hash function employed is a random function.

Theorem 1. *ECDSA is safe under the assumptions that the ECDLP is hard and that the hash function employed is a random function.*

3 Model

3.1 Task

As briefly introduced in Sect. 1, the goal of a paid message forwarding scheme is to finish a task. In our scheme, two types of tasks can be finished. One is a difficult question only a few people know the answer, such as missing persons column. Another one is a work that needs a large number of people involved, such as crowd sensing. In both types, the task owner needs to spread a message to a significant number of people.

3.2 Social Network User

The participation of a great quantity of social network users is the key point of our scheme. In our scheme, we use different symbols to represent users: Source (S) is the owner of task who will start the process of paid message forwarding. U is the set of all social network users except S. B is the set of users who are able to finish part of task by themselves. Then we define that $C = \{u | u \in U \text{ and } u \notin B\}$. C is the set of uses who just help forward message.

3.3 Message Path Tree

Definition 4 ***(Message Path Tree).*** *Messages are forwarded from one user to another in the social network for many times. For convenience, we assume that a user can not receive message from different ones. Then, the paths of messages eventually form a tree rooted at Source. We defined the result of our scheme in the social network as a Message Path Tree (MPT).*

Each participant who joins a MPT is represented as a tree node, and a directed edge from a node u to node v indicates that u has forwarded the message to v. Let T_r denote a tree rooted at node r. Formally, we represent a tree T as a set containing nodes n and ordered nodepairs (p, c) that indicate parent-child edges. This representation allows trees to be partially ordered using subset and superset relations. Standard tree properties are assumed to hold.

The following operators on trees are used in the paper: $Sub(T, u)$ is the subtree of T rooted at node u; $Child(T, n)$ indicates the set of node n's children in T; $Height(T, n)$ is the number of edges on the path from node n to the root of tree T.

Besides, we need some other parameters in the rewarding scheme: $Type(T, n)$ describe the class of node n,

$$Type(T, n) = \begin{cases} 1 & if\ n \in B \\ 0 & if\ n \in C \end{cases} \tag{1}$$

A crucial ingredient of MPT is that every participant has a certain amount of measurable contribution. Formally, we model this contribution using a contribution function $C(T, n)$ that maps each node n to the non-negative sum of its accumulated contribution; larger values of $C(T, n)$ indicate greater contributions in the process of message forwarding.

In the sections below, we may have two MPTs (T and T') at the same time. For convenience, we will use $Type(n)$ to represent $Type(T, n)$ while $Type'(n)$ to represent $Type(T', n)$.

4 Message Forwarding

In this section, we describe the process of generating a MPT. When designing message forwarding model, we use ECDSA to make our scheme fair to everyone.

4.1 Forward Strategy

Forward strategy describes what to do for each kind of participants. And the whole process of message forwarding is as following:

1. S announces the message forwarding mechanism, which stipulates rules for period of validity and rewarding the involved agents.
2. S sends the message along with the verification information to his friend.
3. Each node (agent), when receiving the message and tempted by rewards, will continue to forward the message.
4. If a B class node receive the message, he can also send extra special information while helping solving the task of S for more rewards besides Step (3).
5. After a period of time announced in Step (1), S refuses to accept information and thus ends the process of forwarding.

6. S generates a MPT according to all the information he has received from B nodes.
7. S pays the involved nodes according to the MPT.

One significant difference between our model and the previous works is that a B class node will directly submit an answer to S instead of reporting along the opposite direction of message propagation. And S can learn about the real message path from B.

4.2 Message Forwarding Scheme

In this subsection, we will give a detailed description about our Message Forwarding Scheme. Three parts are included in the whole scheme: $SETUP$, $F(orward)$ and $VERIFY$. The Source run $SETUP$ and starts the whole scheme. Both B and C class nodes can run F and transmit messages to their friends. While, $VERIFY$ needs the participation of Source and a B class node. The scheme may come to an end after a period t set by Source or when the task is solved.

- $SETUP(M, \lambda) \rightarrow (PP, PK, SK, IDC_0, SigC_0)$. The algorithm takes as input the security parameter λ and message M which S wants to be forwarded. S runs $SETUP$ and outputs $PP = (D, H, M)$, $PK = d$ and $SK = v_0$, where d and v_0 are random integers in the interval $[1, n-1]$ and a validation information v_0. IDC is a chain of identity while $SigC$ is a chain of signatures. In $SETUP$, S set $IDC_0 = NULL$ and $SigC_0 = NULL$.
- $F(v_{h-1}, IDC_{h-1}, SigC_{h-1}, PK, ID_h) \rightarrow (V_h, IDC_h, SigC_h)$. An agent N_h with identity ID_h and height h receives message $(v_{h-1}, IDC_{h-1}, SigC_{h-1})$ from his friend with $(ID_{h-1}, h-1)$ or Source S. The process seems that N_h is running $ECDSP.Sign$ on message ID_h with private key dv_{h-1}. Agent N_h does the following:
  1. Compute $v_h = H(v_{h-1})$.
  2. Select a random integer k_h,$1 \leq k_h \leq n-1$.
  3. Compute $k_h G = (x_h, y_h)$ and $r_h = x_h$ mod n. If $r_h = 0$ then go to step (1).
  4. Compute $(k_h)^{-1}$ mod n.
  5. Compute $e_h = H(ID_h)$.
  6. Compute $s_h = k_h^{-1}(e_h + dv_{h-1} r_h)$ mod n. If $s_h = 0$ then go to step (1).
  7. N_h's signature is (r_h, s_h).
  8. Compute $IDC_h = IDC_{h-1} \cup \{ID_h\}$.
  9. Compute $SigC_h = SigC_{h-1} \cup \{(r_h, s_h)\}$.
  10. N_h with identity ID_h sends message $(v_h, IDC_h, SigC_h)$ to one of the friends with identity ID_{h+1} or transmits to S.
- $VERIFY(IDC_x, SigC_x, PK, SK) \rightarrow accept/reject$. The B Class node ID_x with height x submits message $(IDC_x, SigC_x)$ and S will verify the message (Algorithm 1). The message $(ID_h, Sig_h = (r_h, s_h))$ will be split from $(IDC_x, SigC_x)$ and verified by S as $ECDSA.Verify$ with key $dv_{h-1}G$:
  1. Verify that r_h and s_h are integers in the interval $[1, n-1]$.

2. Compute $e_h = H(ID_h)$.
3. Compute $w_h = s_h^{-1}$ mod n.
4. Compute $u_{h,1} = e_h w_h$ mod n and $u_{h,2} = r_h w_h$ mod n.
5. Compute $Q_h = dv_{h-1}G$.
6. Compute $P_h = u_{h,1}G + u_{h,2}Q$. If $P_h = \mathcal{O}$, then reject the signature. Otherwise,compute $v_h = x_h$ mod n where $P_h = (x_h, y_h)$.
7. Accept the signature if and only if $v_h = r_h$.

If all the messages (ID_h, Sig_h) for $1 \leq h \leq x$ are accepted, the message submitted by ID_x is valid and S will update the MPT according to IDC.

Algorithm 1. VERIFY Function

Input: Public parameter $PP = (D, H, M)$ PK=(d); Secret parameter SK=(v_0); Submitted message $(IDC_x, SigC_x)$

Output: accept or reject

```
function verify(i, v_{i-1}, ID_i, Sig_i, SK)
    Get (r_i, s_i) from Sig_i
    if r_i, s_i ∈ Z_n^* then
        e_i = H(ID_i)
        w_i = s_i^{-1} mod n
        u_{i,1} = e_i w_i mod n
        u_{i,2} = r_i w_i mod n
        Q_i = (d v_{i-1})G
        (x_i, y_i) = P_i = u_{i,1}G + u_{i,2}Q
        if P_i ≠ O then
            v_i = x_i mod n
            if v_i == r_i then
                return 1
            end if
        end if
    end if
    return 0
end function

function VERIFY(IDC_x, SigC_x, PK, SK)
    Get x from IDC_x
    for i = 1 → x do
        Get ID_i from IDC_x
        Get Sig_i = (r_i, s_i) from SigC_x
        if verify(i, v_{i-1}, ID_i, Sig_i, SK) == 0 then
            return reject
        else
            v_i = H(v_{i-1})
        end if
    end for
    return accept
end function
```

Proof. The correctness of function $VERIFY$ can be proved by the following equation:

$$\begin{aligned} k_h &\equiv s_h^{-1}(e_h + dv_{h-1}r_h) \equiv s_h^{-1}e_h + s^{-1}r_h(dv_{h-1}) \\ &\equiv w_h e_h + w_h r_h(dv_{h-1}) \equiv u_{h,1} + u_{h,2}(dv_{h-1}) \ (mod\ n) \end{aligned} \tag{2}$$

Thus $u_{h,1}G + u_{h,2}Q_h = (u_{h,1} + u_{h,2}dv_{h-1})G = k_h G$, and so $v_h = r_h$ as required.

5 Reward Distribution Mechanism

In our model, participants can contribute to the system by forwarding the message to friends. A reward mechanism is a function that takes as input the MPT, and computes for each $n \in T$ a non-negative real reward, denoted by $R(T, n)$. Similar to conditions in Sect. 2, we use $R(n)$ and $R'(n)$ to represent $R(T, n)$ and $R(T', n)$.

5.1 Desirable Properties

In this section, we define the set of desirable properties that our reward mechanism should ideally satisfy. All these properties are inspired by related properties defined for Lottery Trees [6]; or for multi-level marketing [7]; and they are adjusted appropriately to our MPT model with arbitrary contributions.

Task Solver Incentive (TSI). What S actually need is enough B class users who are able to solve the task together. A reward mechanism satisfies TSI if it provides more reward for a B class participant than a C class one (other conditions remain the same). This encourages participants with ability to continue contributing to the task. Formally, given a message path tree T and a C class node $n \in T$. If n is replaced by a B class node n' (T turns to T') and the type of all other nodes $v \in T \backslash \{u\}$ remains the same, then $R'(n') > R(n)$.

Continuing Forwarding Incentive (CFI). A reward mechanism satisfies CFI if every participant always has an incentive to forward the message and bring new participants. Formally, given a message path tree T and a node $n \in T$. Then a new node u is added to T (T becomes T') and node n is the parent node of u in the new message path tree T'. Then, the reward of n will increase because $R'(n) \geq R(n)$.

Unbounded Reward Opportunity (URO). This property demands that there should be no limit to the reward a participant can potentially receive, even when his own contribution is fixed by constant. Formally, a reward mechanism satisfies URO if for every positive real R, contribution $C(n)$ and positive integer k, there exist k trees $T_1, \cdots, T_k$ attached to node n in message path tree such that $R(n) \geq R$.

Unprofitable Sybil Attack (USA). This property is taken directly from [11], and it captures the classic notion of Sybil resilience. The USA property imposes that no participant can increase his profit purely by pretending to have multiple identities: A reward mechanism satisfies USA if a participant cannot increase his reward by creating a set of C class nodes as Sybil nodes and joining the system. In other words, a participant who makes a certain contribution to the system should never have a benefit of "splitting" himself and its contribution up and making this contributions as two or more identities, even if these "Sybil identities" join the tree as if referring themselves.

5.2 Reward Distribution Mechanism

In this subsection, we will construct a reward distribution mechanism (RDM) which satisfies all properties defined above.

In our reward distribution mechanism, the reward of participant p will be calculated according to p's contribution to the system, which can be divided into two parts: direct contribution and indirect contribution. Direct contribution is whether p is in B class, while indirect contribution is how many B class nodes there are in p's subtree.

For node n, We define the reward from n's direct contribution as $DR(n)$ and the reward from indirect contribution as $IR(n)$. As a result, the total reward $R(n) = DR(n) + IR(n)$.

The idea about how to calculate indirect reward is inspired by the work of MIT team on the Red Balloon Challenge [12]. One participant n forwards the message, one friend u who has received this message will join the message path tree as the child nodes of n. Then n will get β-split of u's reward $(0 < \beta < 1)$. So in our construction, the indirect reward of n can be written as

$$IR(n) = \beta \cdot \sum_{u \in Child(n)} R(u) = \beta \cdot \sum_{u \in Child(n)} [DR(u) + IR(u)].$$

For example, Fig. 1 (left) is part of the whole message path tree, where node n_5 is in B class. In this situation, all ancestors of n_5 will get more reward because of n_5. We use symbol r to indicate $DR(n_5)$, then the extra reward of other nodes is shown in Fig. 1 (right).

To make our RDM satisfy the properties defined above, we define the height of node n in message path tree as $h(n)$ and set

$$DR(n) = \frac{Type(n)}{(1+\beta)^{h(n)}}.$$

Finally, we have

$$R(n) = \frac{Type(n)}{(1+\beta)^{h(n)}} + \beta \cdot \sum_{u \in Child(n)} R(u).$$

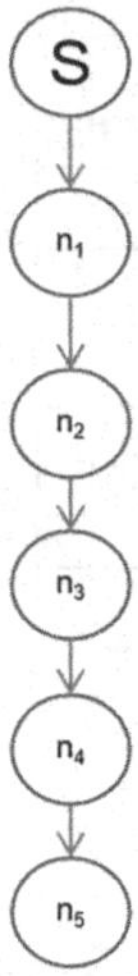

Node	Height	Reward from n_5
n_5	5	r
n_4	4	βr
n_3	3	$\beta^2 r$
n_2	2	$\beta^3 r$
n_1	1	$\beta^4 r$
S	0	0

Fig. 1. A simple situation to show the construction of reward

Lemma 1. *RDM satisfies TSI.*

Proof. Assume a node n interacts with Source and becomes a B class node instead of being a C class node, while all other nodes in the message path tree remain the same. Naturally, we know that indirect reward doesn't change while direct reward increases:

$$IR(n') = IR(n)$$

and

$$DR(n') - DR(n) = \frac{1}{(1+\beta)^{h(n)}}.$$

So, the total reward increases, too.

Lemma 2. *RDM satisfies CFI.*

Proof. Assume a node n forwards message to node u_0 and becomes u_0's parent, while all other nodes in the message path tree remain the same. Then the total reward of n will increase (or remains the same) because

$$R(n') - R(n) = \beta \cdot R(u_0) \geq 0.$$

Lemma 3. *RDM satisfies URO.*

Proof. Given a positive real R, the reward of node n will be greater than R if there exist k B class nodes in n's child nodes and $k > \frac{R}{\beta}$.

Lemma 4. *RDM satisfies USA*

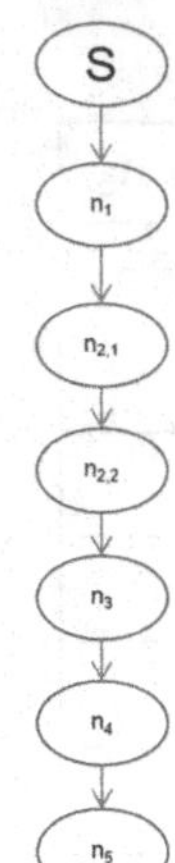

Participant	Node	Height	Reward from n_5
p_5	n_5	6	r'
p_4	n_4	5	βr'
p_3	n_3	4	β^2r'
p_2	$n_{2,2}$	3	β^3r'
	$n_{2,1}$	2	β^4r'
p_1	n_1	1	β^5r'
Source	S	0	0

Fig. 2. Participant p_2 who has C class node n_2 in Fig. 1 launches a Sybil Attack by splitting n_2 into $n_{2,1}$ and $n_{2,2}$

Proof. First, let's consider a simple situation. In Fig. 1, a participant p_2 owns the node n_2, and his extra reward from B class node n_5 is $R = \beta^3 \cdot r$. Now, p_2 has tried to launch a Sybil Attack by splitting n_2 into $n_{2,1}$ and $n_{2,2}$, which is shown in Fig. 2. The total reward of node $n_{2,1}$ and $n_{2,2}$ is $R' = \beta^3 \cdot r' + \beta^4 \cdot r'$. The relation between R and R' is

$$\frac{R'}{R} = \frac{(1+\beta) \cdot r'}{r}.$$

According to the definition of direct reward,

$$\frac{r'}{r} = \frac{(1+\beta)^5}{(1+\beta)^6} = \frac{1}{1+\beta}.$$

Finally, we have $R = R'$. From this situation, we can know that by creating a Sybil nodes, a participant cannot increase the indirect reward from other nodes (not including the Sybil node).

Next, we consider another situation. In Fig. 1, a participant p_5 owns the B class node n_5, and his reward from node n_5 is $R = r$. Now, p_5 has tried to launch a Sybil Attack by splitting n_5 into $n_{5,1}$ and $n_{5,2}$ so that p_5 can create an extra indirect reward from his own direct contribution, which is shown in Fig. 3. The total reward of node $n_{5,1}$ and $n_{5,2}$ is $R' = r' + \beta \cdot r'$. The relation between R and R' is

$$\frac{R'}{R} = \frac{(1+\beta) \cdot r'}{r}.$$

According to the definition of direct reward,

$$\frac{r'}{r} = \frac{(1+\beta)^5}{(1+\beta)^6} = \frac{1}{1+\beta}.$$

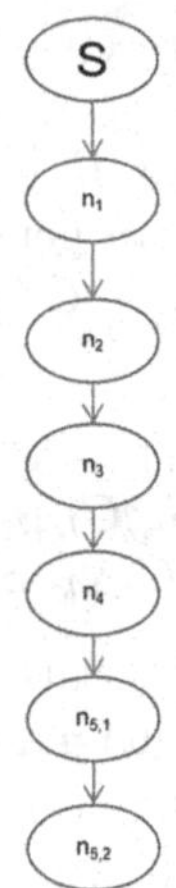

Participant	Node	Height	Reward from $n_{5,2}$
p_5	$n_{5,2}$	6	r'
	$n_{5,1}$	5	$\beta r'$
p_4	n_4	4	$\beta^2 r'$
p_3	n_3	3	$\beta^3 r'$
p_2	n_2	2	$\beta^4 r'$
p_1	n_1	1	$\beta^5 r'$
Source	S	0	0

Fig. 3. Participant p_5 who has B class node n_5 in Fig. 1 launches a Sybil Attack by splitting n_5 into $n_{5,1}$ and $n_{5,2}$

Finally, we have $R = R'$. From this situation, we can know that by creating a Sybil node, a participant cannot increase the reward from Sybil nodes.

In the above two situations, we have selected a chain from the whole message path tree, and only the last node is in B class. In the message path tree, the reward of a node comes from all the B class nodes in subtree. Though the real case seems more complex, we can regard it as superimposition of chains. Besides, if participant p launches a Sybil attack by creating x extra nodes($x > 0$), it is the same as that p creates one new node for x times. We can know p can't increase his total reward in each step. As a result, property USA is obeyed in our RDM.

6 Analysis

6.1 Security

Theorem 2. *Let $\mathcal{A}$ be any adversary against our Paid Message Forwarding Scheme. The following two situations cannot be held at the same time:*

1. *There exists an algorithm P, such that $\mathcal{A}$ can forge a valid message M' and send it to his friends or S.*
2. *$\mathcal{A}$ will get more reward by send M'.*

Proof. To prove Theorem 2, we will discuss two situations separately in Theorem 3 and 4.

Theorem 3. *$\mathcal{A}$ can forge a valid message M' as if there are more participants than reality and the reward of $\mathcal{A}$ won't increase.*

Proof. Assume the height of $\mathcal{A}$ in MPT is L, $\mathcal{A}$ receives message $(v_{L-1}, IDC_{L-1}, SigC_{L-1})$ and ought to send $(v_L, IDC_L, SigC_L)$. As mentioned in Sect. 4, the process of F (forward) seems a node with height L and identity ID_L signs the message ID_L with private key dv_{L-1} and $\mathcal{A}$ can get any v_{L+k} from v_{L-1}. As a result, $\mathcal{A}$ is able to construct $(v_{L+k}, IDC_{L+k}, SigC_{L+k})$ with a positive integer $k \geq 0$ by the following steps:

1) $F(v_L, IDC_L, SigC_L, PK, ID^1_{\mathcal{A}}) \rightarrow (v_{L+1}, IDC_{L+1}, SigC_{L+1})$
2) $F(v_{L+1}, IDC_{L+1}, SigC_{L+1}, PK, ID^2_{\mathcal{A}}) \rightarrow (v_{L+2}, IDC_{L+2}, SigC_{L+2})$
k) $F(v_{L+k-1}, IDC_{L+k-1}, SigC_{L+k-1}, PK, ID^k_{\mathcal{A}}) \rightarrow (v_{L+k}, IDC_{L+k}, SigC_{L+k})$

In this situation, it is as if $\mathcal{A}$ launches a Sybil attack by creating k Sybil nodes with identities $(ID^1_{\mathcal{A}}, ID^2_{\mathcal{A}}, \cdots, ID^k_{\mathcal{A}})$. According to Lemma 4, $\mathcal{A}'s$ reward doesn't increase.

Theorem 4. *It's hard for $\mathcal{A}$ to forge a valid message as if the height of $\mathcal{A}$ in MPT is smaller than reality under the assumptions that ECDSA is safe.*

Proof. Assume that $\mathcal{A}$ can forge a valid message as if the height of $\mathcal{A}$ in MPT is smaller than reality. $\mathcal{A}$ can't know the value of v_{L-2} from v_{L-1} and the hash function H, because of the assumption that H is a random function (Theorem 1). So $\mathcal{A}$ isn't able to reduce his height by legally running FORWARD function.

Then, $\mathcal{A}$ must forge a valid signature on ID_L from the signature (r_{L-1}, s_{L-1}) on ID_{L-1} with private key dv_{L-2} and public key G ($\mathcal{A}$ actually doesn't know $Q_{L-1} = dv_{L-2}G$). This process is harder than $\mathcal{A}$ breaks a ECDSA under a chosen-message attack.

Different from ECDSA, the private parameter v_0 is known to not only the source but also the nodes at height 1. If the node of participant p is at height 1, he tends to keep v_0 in secrete because there exists no extra reward for him. As a result, if all the participants are rational, $\mathcal{A}$ can't get v_{L-2} from nodes at lower height.

6.2 Other Assumptions

Besides security assumption, some other assumptions are significant in the paper. As introduced in Sect. 1, we assume that all nodes are rational. It is also an assumption that S will obey the roles all the time in our scheme. Considering the following two conditions:

1. S refuses to pay the reward.
2. S distorts the message path tree.

The solution of the former is to execute the process of paying on the blockchain using a smart contract [2]. And in the latter condition, S will open all the submitted message and parameters to the public. In our construction, these information will generates the only MPT. Besides, introducing a third party for supervision is also practicable.

Collusion is not considered in our scheme, which is one target of our future work.

6.3 Efficiency

The efficiency of our scheme is based on that of ECDSA. We set the computation cost of $ECDSA.Sign$, $ECDSA.Verify$, hash function as C_S, C_V and C_H. Then the computation cost of F is $C_S + C_H$ and $VERIFY$ is $h \cdot (C_V + C_H)$ where h is the number of ID in IDC. For S, $VERIFY$ will be executed many times according to the number of B class node in MPT. Some results can be stored for less time.

7 Conclusion

In this paper, we designed a paid message forwarding scheme based on social network. Compared with other related works, we first propose a cryptography scheme in incentive network so that the path of messages is proved to be true and rewards will be distributed correctly.

In our model, each node is inspired to receive and send messages and the process eventually forms a Message Path Tree. The source finishes his task with the help of participants and allocates rewards according to the MPT. We use incentive tree model for motivation and cryptography for fairness. Our scheme is shown sybil-proof, incentive compatible, efficient and easy to forward.

Acknowledgement. This paper is supported by the National Key R&D Program of China through project 2017YFB0802500, by the National Cryptography Development Fund through project MMJJ20170106, by the foundation of Science and Technology on Information Assurance Laboratory through project 61421120305162112006, the Natural Science Foundation of China through projects 61972019, 61932011, 61772538, 61672083, 61532021, 61472429, 91646203 and 61402029.

References

1. Babaioff, M., Dobzinski, S., Oren, S., Zohar, A.: On bitcoin and red balloons. ACM SIGECOM Exchanges **10**(3), 56–73 (2011)
2. Buterin, V., et al.: A next-generation smart contract and decentralized application platform
3. Cebrian, M., Coviello, L., Vattani, A., Voulgaris, P.: Finding red balloons with split contracts: robustness to individuals' selfishness. In: Forty-fourth Acm Symposium on Theory of Computing (2012)
4. Chen, W., Wang, Y., Yu, D., Zhang, L.: Sybil-proof mechanisms in query incentive networks. In: Proceedings of the Fourteenth ACM Conference on Electronic Commerce, pp. 197–214 (2013)
5. Douceur, J.R.: The sybil attack. In: Peer-to-peer Systems. In: First International Workshop, Iptps, Cambridge, MA, USA, March, Revised Papers (2002)
6. Douceur, J.R., Moscibroda, T.: Lottery trees: motivational deployment of networked systems. ACM SIGCOMM Comput. Commun. Rev. **37**(4), 121–132 (2007)
7. Emek, Y., Karidi, R., Tennenholtz, M., Zohar, A.: Mechanisms for multi level marketing. In: EC 2011: Proceedings of the 12th ACM Conference on Electronic Commerce. ACM (January 2011). https://www.microsoft.com/en-us/research/publication/mechanisms-for-multi-level-marketing/

8. Johnson, D., Menezes, A., Vanstone, S.: The elliptic curve digital signature algorithm (ECDSA). Int. J. Inf. Secur. **1**(1), 36–63 (2001)
9. Kleinberg, J., Raghavan, P.: Query incentive networks. In: 2005 46th Annual IEEE Symposium on Foundations of Computer Science, FOCS 2005 (2005)
10. Lv, Y., Moscibroda, T.: Incentive networks. ACM SIGARCH Comput. Architect. News **38**(3), 106–116 (2015)
11. Lv, Y., Moscibroda, T.: Fair and resilient incentive tree mechanisms. Distrib. Comput. **29**(1), 1–16 (2016)
12. Pickard, G., et al.: Time-critical social mobilization. Science **334**(6055), 509–512 (2011)
13. Pointcheval, D., Stern, J.: Security proofs for signature schemes. In: Maurer, U. (ed.) EUROCRYPT 1996. LNCS, vol. 1070, pp. 387–398. Springer, Heidelberg (1996). https://doi.org/10.1007/3-540-68339-9_33

WebSmell: An Efficient Malicious HTTP Traffic Detection Framework Using Data Augmentation

Tieming Chen[1], Zhengqiu Weng[1,2(✉)], YunPeng Chen[1], Chenqiang Jin[1], Mingqi Lv[1], Tiantian Zhu[1], and Jianhong Lin[3]

[1] College of Computer Science and Technology, Zhejiang University of Technology, Hangzhou 310023, China
derisweng@163.com

[2] Department of Information Technology, Wenzhou Polytechnic, Wenzhou 325035, China

[3] Zhejiang Ponshine Technology Joint Stock Company, Hangzhou 310010, China

Abstract. With the increasing complexity of cyberspace infrastructure and its applications, cyberattack is becoming ubiquitous and evolving rapidly. As one of the basic techniques to cyberattack awareness, network traffic anomaly detection has been facing diverse challenges such as low detection ability, huge cost of training data collection, weak generalization of classification model. In this paper, we present ***WebSmell***, a framework that conducts malicious HTTP traffic detection using deep learning with data augmentation based on keywords library avoidance. The proposed method can improve the cross-dataset detection ability, reduce the input cost of training dataset, and make deep learning model have strong generalization even with a small training dataset.

Keywords: Data augmentation · Malicious web traffic · Anomaly detection · Deep learning

1 Introduction

As an effective means of protection, malicious HTTP traffic detection can not only detect known attacks, but also identify unknown attacks, which has become one of the key techniques in network situation awareness [1]. Current malicious HTTP traffic detection methods can be roughly divided into two categories, signature detection and anomaly detection. The signature detection mainly constructs the detection model for known attacks. Although this method has high accuracy, it cannot detect unknown attacks. The strategy of anomaly detection is to create rules based on the traffic of normal behaviors. Any traffic that violates the rules will be identified as an attack behavior, which has certain detection ability for unknown attacks. However, this detection strategy is similar to the white list mechanism, and all rules are set in a certain range in advance [2]. Once the user produces unexpected but still normal operational traffic will be misjudged as malicious traffic. In addition, most of current anomaly detection often require a large number of traffic samples for training. It is not so easy to obtain traffic samples, especially

Y. Wu and M. Yung (Eds.): Inscrypt 2020, LNCS 12612, pp. 193–201, 2021.
https://doi.org/10.1007/978-3-030-71852-7_13

malicious traffic payloads. Due to the lack of training samples, it is difficult to extract features effectively, resulting in weak over fitting and generalization ability.

In summary, there exists the challenges such as low cross-dataset detection ability, huge cost of training data collection, weak generalization ability of classification model. Therefore, it is necessary to design a method that can achieve a better malicious traffic detection performance by training the model with only a small number of training samples.

In this paper, we focus on HTTP traffic detection, treat the training traffic data as text, and propose the ***WebSmell*** framework with a special data augmentation method for HTTP traffic detection. The main contributions of our works include 1) A data augmentation method based on Keywords Library Avoidance (KLA) is proposed. 2) An effective method on malicious HTTP traffic detection is proposed based on semi-supervised text classification model. 3) Various experimental performance tests on the whole proposed approaches for model optimization are individually evaluated.

The rest of this paper is listed as follows. Section 2 introduces the related works. Section 3 describes our proposed ***WebSmell*** framework. Section 4 shows the performance results. Finally, we conclude the paper in Sect. 5.

2 Related Work

Most of the current data augmentation methods [3–5] are suitable for image or time-series data, for example, by shifting the image, transforming the angle of view, transforming the size, using co-training [6] and applying Gaussian noise [7], which make the added noise data have lower level of information distortion. However, these methods are not suitable for the augmentation task of text data. For text data, existing researches have proposed the method of synonym substitution [8] and the method of constructing weighted undirected graph [9]. However, this method is suitable for texts such as articles and Q&A, which mainly studies the semantic association characteristics. It is difficult to extract features through simple regular matching using the word-order structure of web traffic.

In the aspect of text data augmentation, it is unreasonable to use image or speech recognition signal conversion to increase data because the sequence of characters will affect the syntax and semantics. Data augmentation aims at creating novel and realistic-looking training data without changing its label [10]. Moreover, most of the characters in web traffic data are independent or meaningless encoding and non-semantic. Therefore, we need to enhance the web traffic data on the basis of retaining most keywords in the malicious traffic.

In terms of malicious traffic detection, many studies have used different models and data pre-processing methods to extract web traffic characteristics. Park et al. [11] proposed a method for anomaly detection of HTTP based on a character-level binary image transformation, which is superior to the traditional heuristic machine learning method for selecting input features. Zolotukhin et al. [12] proposed an anomaly detection method for web attacks by analyzing HTTP logs. Yang et al. [13] designed a CGRU (convolutional gated-recurrent-unit) neural network for malicious URLs detection based on characters as text classification features. Yu et al. [14] proposed a Bi-LSTM (bidirectional long short-term memory), which using a method based on special character segmentation. Cretu-Ciocarlie [15] proposed a content anomaly detector, which was used to detect malicious traffic and "suspicious" network packets by modeling a high-order N-grams hybrid model. Lee [16] presented an anomalous traffic detection method based on network traffic entropy.

The above work is to use a variety of models and extract different features to model and classify the traffic, but most of the work in the data pre-processing part uses simple N-grams word segmentation or data statistics. Using simple data statistics to pre-process the traffic will lead to the problem that the traffic data characteristics can not be well preserved. And in most of the web traffic, there are no semantic association characters and encoding characters, then using N-grams to extract keywords of different lengths will generate a large number of coded characters and invalid strings, while traditional malicious keywords are often not reserved.

3 Methodology

3.1 WebSmell Framework

The overall architecture of ***WebSmell*** proposed in this paper is shown in Fig. 1, where the process represented by the solid line is the model training process, and the dotted line is the detection process of sample to be predicated.

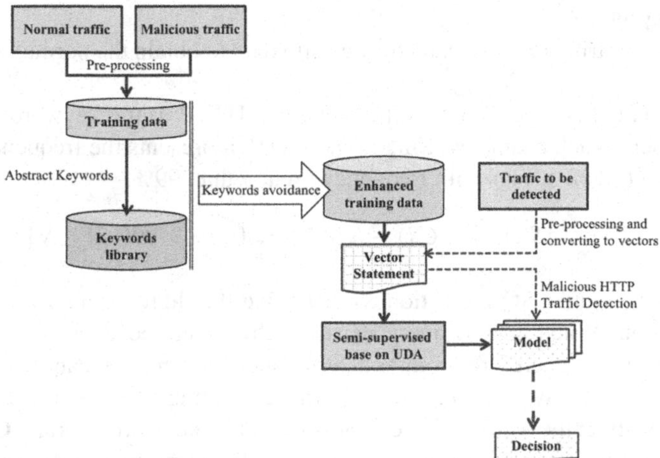

Fig. 1. System architecture of ***WebSmell.*** Including mixing normal traffic data and malicious traffic data after preprocessing, obtaining keywords library to generate augmentation samples and get the enhanced training dataset using KLA, converting the specified.

The training data is a dataset obtained by mixing normal traffic data and malicious traffic data after pre-processing. The keywords library is a set which divides the training dataset according to the special symbols and retains the high-frequency strings. The enhanced training dataset is based on the keyword avoidance after sample enhancement. The vector statement is a vector obtained by converting the specified data through Word2vec.

3.2 Data Augmentation

3.2.1 Traffic Parsing and Keyword Extraction

In this paper, the malicious HTTP traffic is divided into three categories: XSS, SQL injection, and directory traversal. Since the attack payload of most web attacks exist in the request path and request data of HTTP traffic, they need first be parsed to form samples. The following pre-processing is required: 1) Data extraction. Extract the request path in the Get request and the request data in the Post request. 2) Data cleaning. Perform URL decoding, lower case characters, remove spaces and other invalid characters on the extracted data to obtain the final samples.

3.2.2 Keyword Library Generation

In order to process the text data effectively, we first divide the text into a large number of independent units. The keyword library generation steps are as follows:

Step1. Divide malicious HTTP traffic into three categories and extract valid data to obtain XSS samples, SQL injection samples and directory traversal samples, and extract normal HTTP traffic samples.
Step2. The XSS, SQL injection and directory traversal samples were divided into strings respectively to obtain XSS strings set *AS*, SQL injection strings set *BS* and directory traversal string set *CS*.
Step3. Divide the string of the normal traffic valid data to obtain the normal traffic string set *N*.
Step4. Equation (1) is used to obtain the malicious HTTP traffic keywords library *W*, where j represents each character string in the set, P_j represents the frequency of string *j*, and *NS* is a set of all strings with frequency greater than 99%.

$$W = (AS \cup BS \cup CS) - NS, NS = \{\mathrm{j}, P_j > 99\%, j \in N\} \tag{1}$$

In order to recognize SQL injection correctly, we should focus on the characteristic in SQL injection. When a SQL query exists in the requested data, it is most likely a malicious request. Therefore, common SQL query statements can be recorded as keywords. The ideal way is to analyze web traffic wording patterns based on training samples, and abstract the web traffic keywords to build a keywords library. Considering the existence of various special symbols in web traffic, extracting the substring of two special symbols as one word simplifies the segmentation process. At the same time, the 28 special characters in web traffic (including., “”’ < > + −_* = { }()[] ~ /\#:;?!-&@) are used as the basis for segmentation.

3.2.3 KLA-Based Data Augmentation

As the keywords library is the key to transform the training samples into the word vector representation, and it comes from the training samples, so we should reserve the keywords to the greatest extent. At the same time, non-keyword strings should be randomly replaced. The rules of random noise replacement are listed in Table 1.

Table 1. Rules of random noise replacement.

	Rules of random noise replacement
Rule 1	Keep all keywords in the keyword library
Rule 2	Remain the symbols % $# @ unchanged
Rule 3	Numbers are randomized to other numbers in the range of 0–9
Rule 4	English characters are randomized to other English characters in the range of a–z

It is obvious that the SQL syntax no longer conforms to the specification (error syntax), and there is only one where statement that is suspected to be SQL injection syntax, which makes the weight of word matrix decline, and it is difficult to be effectively identified in model training phase. According to the above rules, the generated noise data and the keywords of malicious traffic have been reserved, while other characters have been changed.

4 Experimental Evaluations

This article collects a set of open source WAF request dataset from Fsecrurify based on HTTP protocol as training set and test set. Randomly select 45,000 malicious traffic with malicious behavior characteristics and 45,000 normal traffic, we randomly divided them into training set and test set according to a ratio of 3.5:1. At the same time, we collect 6465 wild malicious traffic (hereinafter referred to as wild malicious traffic) recorded by honeypot server (deployed in March 2019) as a generalization performance test dataset.

The ratio of malicious traffic samples to normal traffic samples in the training set is 1:1, both of which are 35000. And the ratio in the test set is also 1:1, both of which are 10000. There are 6465 wild malicious traffic dataset, including 614 SQL injection samples, 4093 XSS samples, and 1758 directory traversal samples.

4.1 Data Augmentation Effectiveness

This experiment explores the influence of using different data nosing ratios on the model detection effect, and finally find the best noise ratio. The experimental results are shown in Fig. 2.

The results show that adding a small amount of noise data in the training set can improve the accuracy and generalization rate of the model and improve the performance of model detection. However, after exceeding the ratio threshold, the model will be over-fitted, the accuracy or generalization rate of the model will decline, and the overall recognition and detection performance will show a downward trend.

4.2 Pre-processing Influence

This experiment explores the performance of various data pre-processing methods on the detection effect of learning model. In the pre-processing step, our method (10%

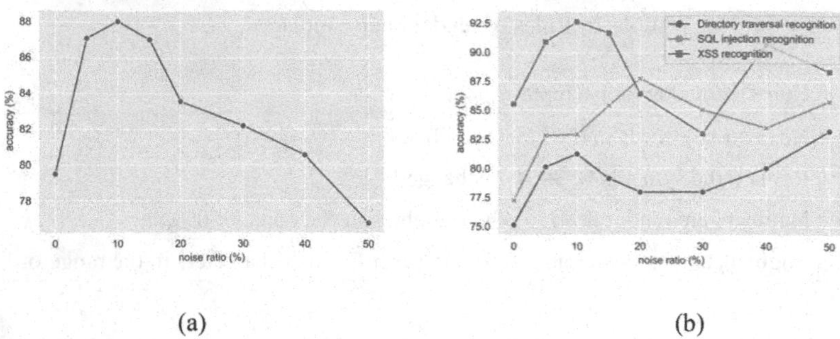

(a) (b)

Fig. 2. (a) Effect of different noise ratio on model performance. (b) The influence of different noise ratio on the model generalization with different types of malicious HTTP traffic.

noise in the training set) and the methods of [11, 13] and [14] are used to obtain the corresponding training models. The performance of models trained by different data pre-processing methods was compared in four aspects: sample size, detection rate, false alarm rate and accuracy. The method proposed in this paper has higher accuracy and lower false alarm rate, and the overall performance is optimal compared with other existing methods when using small training traffic samples.

Table 2. Comparison of generalization ability between noisy training model and non noisy training model.

Noise ratio	Accuracy of training dataset	Accuracy of wild malicious traffic
WebSmell (10%)	88.08%	85.66%
WebSmell (non noisy)	86.49%	80.34%

Using the method in this paper, the models obtained from the non noisy training set and the 10% noisy training set were used to perform detection classification on the same test set respectively. The comparison results are shown in Table 2. It can be seen that the noise-adding model can adapt to the new samples well, ensure the relatively stable performance of the model in training samples and test samples, and have a strong generalization ability, indicating that the noise-adding can effectively improve the generalization ability of the model.

4.3 Detection Performance with Different Models

One of the main purposes of ***WebSmell*** is to verify the effectiveness of the data augmentation method in the DL-based detection algorithms. For the sake of demonstration we choose two classic DL algorithm here for comparison, one is TextCNN [17], the other is based on UDA [18] (see Fig. 3). That is to say, one is classically using supervised learning while the other is recently introduced semi-supervised. The experimental results are shown in Table 3 and Table 4.

We compared the performance of the detection between the supervised learning model and the semi-supervised learning model under the data pre-processing method (optimal parameters) in the actual malicious traffic. Dataset is composed of honeypot web target deployed in real network environment. Honeypot container is CentOS7.0 system. Finally, 120000 traffic records are collected, and 30000 records of each kind of traffic obtained according to IDS and WAF classification. Since IDS and WAF are relatively mature and have high reliability, the detection results of them are regarded as accurate results, while the test model results are used as reference results. By comparing the actual results obtained by the test model with the IDS and WAF test results, the real-world performance results of the model in Table 4 (Accuracy of wild dataset) can be obtained.

In the real-world detection, the overall detection effect of the model is slightly lower than that of the training phase due to the more complex coding obfuscation strategy and the multiple detection bypass methods of the attacker. At the same time, the performance of the semi-supervised learning model is always better than that of the supervised learning model.

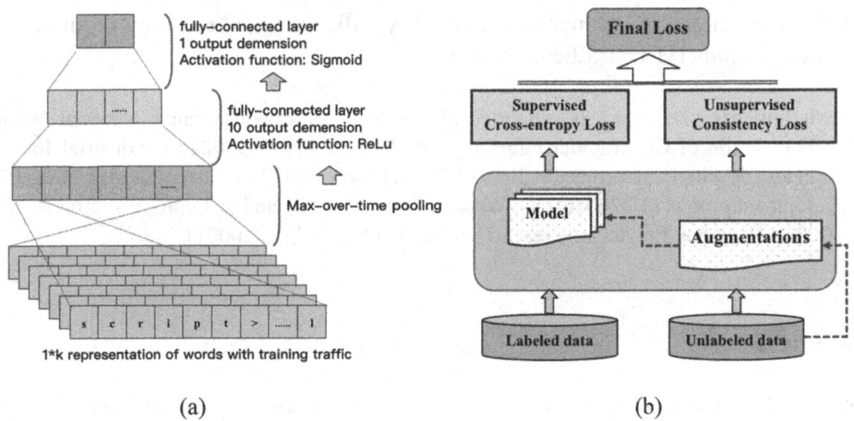

Fig. 3. (a) TextCNN-based architecture. (b) UDA-based semi-supervised training procedure.

Table 3. The performance comparison between supervised learning and semi-supervised learning.

Learning model	TPR	Precision	Recall	F-measure	Accuracy
Supervised learning	96.03%	82.86%	96.03%	88.96%	88.08%
Semi-supervised learning	98.43%	98.08%	38.30%	55.09%	96.43%

Table 4. The generalization ability comparison between supervised learning and semi-supervised learning.

Learning model	Accuracy of training dataset	Accuracy of wild dataset
Supervised learning	88.18%	85.17%
Semi-supervised learning	96.43%	89.13%

5 Conclusions

In this paper, we present the system ***WebSmell*** to detect the malicious HTTP traffic through UDA-based neural network with data augmentation. Our contribution to the research community is the design, implementation, and evaluation of ***WebSmell*** that autonomously abstracts the web traffic keywords to build a keywords library, extends data according to augmentation facilities, detect the malicious HTTP traffic by enhanced learning model.The experiment of malicious HTTP traffic detection using deep learning with data augmentation proves that our ***WebSmell*** has good performance even in real network environment. It can meet the generality, efficiency and usability requirements jointly in malicious HTTP traffic detection.

Acknowledgments. This work is supported in part by the following grants: National Natural Science Foundation of China under Grant (No. 61772026 and U1936215); Industrial Internet innovation and development project in 2019 (TC190H3WN); 2020 industrial Internet innovation and development project (TC200H01V); Wenzhou key scientific and technological projects (No. ZG2020031); Wenzhou Polytechnic research projects (No. WZY2020001).

References

1. Ahmed, M., Mahmood, A., Hu, J., et al.: A survey of network anomaly detection techniques. J. Netw. Comput. Appl. 19–31(2016)
2. Zhong, Z., Zheng, L., et al.: Random erasing data augmentation. In: AAAI, vol. 34, no. 7 (2017)
3. Taylor, L., Nitschke, G.: Improving deep learning using generic data augmentation (2017)
4. Zhao, A., Balakrishnan, G., et al.: Data augmentation using learned transformations for one-shot medical image segmentation. In: IEEE CVPR, pp. 8543–8553 (2019)
5. Sprengel, E., Jaggi, M., et al.: Audio based bird species identification using deep learning techniques (2016)
6. Zhu, T., Weng, Z., et al.: A hybrid deep learning system for real-world mobile user authentication using motion sensors. Sensors **20**(14), 3876 (2020)
7. Zhu, T., Weng, Z., et al.: ESPIALCOG: General, Efficient and Robust Mobile User Implicit Authentication in Noisy Environment. IEEE TMC(2020).
8. Zolotukhin, M., Hämäläinen, T., et al.: Analysis of HTTP requests for anomaly detection of web attacks. In: 2014 IEEE 12th DASC, pp. 406–411. IEEE (2014)
9. Arzhakov, A., Troitskiy, S., et al.: Development and implementation a method of detecting an attacker with use of HTTP network protocol. In: 2017 IEEE Conference of Russian Young Researchers in Electrical and Electronic Engineering, pp. 100–104. IEEE (2017)

10. Cavnar, W., Trenkle, J.: N-gram-based text categorization. In: Proceedings of SDAIR-94, 3rd Annual Symposium on Document Analysis and Information Retrieval, vol. 161175 (1994)
11. Park, S., Kim, M., Lee, S.: Anomaly detection for http using convolutional autoencoders. IEEE Access **6**, 70884–70901 (2018)
12. Zolotukhin, M., Hämäläinen, T., et al.: Analysis of HTTP requests for anomaly detection of web attacks. In: 2014 IEEE 12th International Conference on Dependable, Autonomic and Secure Computing, pp. 406–411. IEEE (2014)
13. Yang, W., Zuo, W., Cui, B.: Detecting malicious URLs via a keyword-based convolutional gated-recurrent-unit neural network. IEEE Access **7**, 29891–29900 (2019)
14. Yu, Y., Liu, G., Yan, H., et al.: Attention-based Bi-LSTM model for anomalous HTTP traffic detection. In: 2018 ICSSSM, pp. 1–6. IEEE (2018)
15. Cretu-Ciocarlie, G.F., Stavrou, A., Locasto, M.E., Stolfo, S.J.: Adaptive anomaly detection via self-calibration and dynamic updating. In: Kirda, E., Jha, S., Balzarotti, D. (eds.) RAID 2009. LNCS, vol. 5758, pp. 41–60. Springer, Heidelberg (2009). https://doi.org/10.1007/978-3-642-04342-0_3
16. Lee, E., Paek, S., et al.: Apparatus and method for detecting anomalous traffic: U.S. Patent (2010)
17. McQueen, M., McQueen, T., et al.: Empirical estimates and observations of 0day vulnerabilities. In: 42nd Hawaii International Conference on System Sciences, pp. 1–12. IEEE (2009)
18. Xie, Q., Dai, Z., et al.: Unsupervised data augmentation for consistency training. arXiv preprint arXiv:1904.12848 (2019)

Blockchain-Based Efficient Public Integrity Auditing for Cloud Storage Against Malicious Auditors

Shanshan Li[1], Chunxiang Xu[1], Yuan Zhang[1,4](✉), Anjia Yang[2], Xinsheng Wen[1], and Kefei Chen[3]

[1] School of Computer Science and Engineering, University of Electronic Science and Technology of China, Chengdu, China
zhangyuan@uestc.edu.cn, zy_loye@126.com
[2] College of Cyber Security, Jinan University, Guangzhou, China
[3] Department of Mathematics, Hangzhou Normal University, Hangzhou, China
[4] Key Laboratory of Dynamic Cognitive System of Electromagnetic Spectrum Space, Ministry of Industry and Information Technology, Nanjing University of Aeronautics and Astronautics, Nanjing, China

Abstract. Public integrity auditing enables a user to delegate a third-party auditor (TPA) to periodically audit the integrity of the outsourced data. Whereas, the security of public auditing schemes relies on the trustworthiness of TPA: once TPA misbehaves, the data integrity auditing would be invalidated. In this paper, we propose a blockchain-based efficient public integrity auditing scheme to resist misbehaved TPA, where the user is required to check the behaviors of TPA in a much longer period compared with that of the data integrity auditing performed by TPA. To free users from heavy computation costs during the checking, our scheme uses two key techniques. We first design a smart contract to (1) enable TPA to record each auditing entry (which records the information about each auditing task) into the blockchain and (2) ensure the validity of each recorded entry. Then, we propose an auditing record chain built on the Ethereum blockchain to link all auditing entries corresponding to the same data in the chronological order. By doing so, the user only needs to check the last auditing entry generated by TPA to verify the trustworthiness of TPA (i.e., whether TPA has correctly performed the prescribed auditing tasks). Compared with existing schemes, where the user has to check multiple entries one by one, our scheme achieves the same security guarantee with constant and low costs in terms of communication and computation.

Keywords: Public auditing · Data integrity · Ethereum blockchain · Cloud storage · Smart contract

1 Introduction

Cloud storage is an important application in our daily life, which has brought lots of benefits, such as saving the local storage space, providing convenience

Y. Wu and M. Yung (Eds.): Inscrypt 2020, LNCS 12612, pp. 202–220, 2021.
https://doi.org/10.1007/978-3-030-71852-7_14

for users, improving resource utilization and so on [1–4]. Although users have gained great benefits from these services, data outsourcing raises many security concerns. One of the most severe problems is data integrity. Since users would not physically control their outsourced data, they are anxious about the integrity of the outsourced data. The integrity of outsourced data is being put at risk due to both internal and external threats in reality [5,6]. For example, the cloud server may hide an incident of data corruption to keep a good reputation and a hacker, who has compromised the cloud server, may tamper with a target user's data for profits. Worse still, a misbehaved cloud server may intentionally delete part of outsourced data to reduce the storage costs [6,7]. Therefore, the integrity of outsourced data should be verified periodically to ensure that the cloud server well maintains the data intact.

Public integrity auditing is a paradigm that enables users to delegate data integrity auditing tasks to a third-party auditor (TPA). Existing public integrity auditing schemes [5,7–9] are constructed on homomorphic signatures and utilize a sampling auditing paradigm: the outsourced data is split into multiple blocks; each data block is associated with an authentication tag that is constructed on a homomorphic signature (e.g., [10]); TPA chooses a random subset of all blocks and checks their integrity by verifying the corresponding tags. If the subset of blocks is well maintained, the integrity of the entire data set is ensured. In addition, due to the development of the homomorphic signature, TPA is able to verify the tags without needing to download the corresponding blocks from the cloud server.

On the other hand, existing public integrity auditing schemes [5,7–9] also bear a strong assumption that TPA is honest and reliable. In these schemes, if TPA is compromised, the integrity auditing would be invalidated [11,12]. Specifically, a malicious TPA may always claim that the outsourced data is well maintained even without auditing the data integrity. Worse still, the malicious TPA may collude with the cloud server to generate a bias auditing result by biasing the randomness of the subset blocks (i.e., always choosing the well-maintained blocks to audit) to keep a good reputation of the cloud server [11]. Much more trickily, the malicious TPA would procrastinate on the scheduled auditing, which makes the timely detection of data corruption impossible [6].

To resist malicious TPA, existing schemes (e.g., [6,12]) require the user to audit the behavior of TPA in a much longer period compared with that of the data integrity auditing performed by TPA. The user needs to audit whether TPA correctly performs the integrity auditing tasks on time, which guarantees that once TPA misbehaves, it could be detected by the user. However, in such a scheme [6], to ensure that TPA has honestly performed the prescript auditing tasks in a long period of time, the user needs to check the auditing records generated by TPA one by one. Consequently, the computation costs on the user side are linear to the number of auditing tasks that TPA has performed. Furthermore, a user may delegate TPA to audit multiple outsourced files, during such a period, the user has to bear a huge computation delay which is not only proportional to the number of auditing records for each file, but also proportional to the number of files she/he outsourced. As such, reducing the computation costs on the user side is of critical importance such that the user can check the reliability of TPA with an affordable delay, even if the user equips a low-power device.

In this paper, we propose a blockchain-based efficient public integrity auditing against malicious TPA that significantly reduces the checking delay on the user side. The computation costs on the user side are reduced by utilizing two key techniques. The first one is that the validity of each auditing record (i.e., an entry recording the information about the corresponding auditing task) is verified by a smart contract; The second one is that all auditing entries corresponding to the same data performed by TPA form an auditing record chain [13] with the aid of the Ethereum blockchain, such that the user only needs to verify the validity of the last record on the chain to check the validity of all the auditing records on the chain. Specifically, the contributions of this paper are described as follows:

- We design a smart contract on the Ethereum blockchain for data integrity auditing, which is triggered by TPA for recording information about each integrity auditing entry into the blockchain and guarantees the validity of entries.
- We propose an efficient public auditing scheme against malicious TPA. The scheme employs an auditing record chain built on the Ethereum blockchain, which ensures the linkability of each auditing entry. A user only needs to check the validity of the last entry on the chain (rather than all of the entries) to verify the TPA's behavior, which significantly improves the efficiency on the user side, compared with the existing schemes.
- We analyze the security of our scheme to prove that our scheme can resist various attacks. We conduct a performance evaluation to demonstrate that our scheme is efficient in terms of communication and computation overhead.

2 Preliminaries

2.1 Terminology

Bilinear Maps. Let G be an additive group, and G_T is a multiplicative cycle group. G and G_T have the same prime order p. P is the generator of G. A bilinear map is that $e : G \times G \rightarrow G_T$ with three properties. Bilinearity: for $P, Q \in G$ and $a, b \in {Z_p}^*$: $e(aP, bQ) = e(P, Q)^{ab}$; Nondegeneracy: $e(P, Q) \neq 1$ for all $P, Q \in G$ and $P \neq Q$; Computability: there exists an efficiently computable algorithm for computing e.

Pseudorandom Function. Let $F : \{0,1\}^* \times \{0,1\}^* \rightarrow \{0,1\}^*$ be an efficient, length-preserving, keyed function. F is a pseudorandom function if for all probabilistic polynomial-time distinguishers D, there is a negligible function $negl$ such that: $|\Pr[D^{F_k(\cdot)}(1^n) = 1] - \Pr[D^{f(\cdot)}(1^n) = 1]| \leq negl(n)$, where the first probability is taken over uniform choice of $k \in \{0,1\}^n$ and the randomness of D, and the second probability is taken over uniform choice of $f \in Func_n$ and the randomness of D, where $Func_n$ denotes the set of all functions mapping n-bit strings to n-bit strings [14].

Pseudorandom Generator. Let l be a polynomial and let T be a deterministic polynomial-time algorithm such that for any n and any input $s \in \{0,1\}^n$, the result $T(s)$ is a string of length $l(n)$ [14]. T is a pseudorandom generator if the following conditions hold: for any n it holds that $l(n) > n$; for any polynomial-time algorithm D, there is a negligible function $negl$ such that $|\Pr[D(T(s)) = 1] - \Pr[D(r) = 1]| \leq negl(n)$, where the first probability is taken over uniform choice of $s \in \{0,1\}^n$ and the randomness of D, the second probability is taken over uniform choice of $r \in \{0,1\}^{l(n)}$ and the randomness of D. We call l the expansion factor of T.

Blockchain. The blockchain servers as an underlying technology in current digital currency and online payment system—Bitcoin [15]. Existing schemes [16,17] have shown that blockchain technology could prove to be much more significant than Bitcoin. The blockchain consists of multiple blocks and each block contains a timestamp, the hash value of the previous block, a nonce (a random number for verifying the hash), and multiple transactions. The first block of the chain is called "genesis block", while generating a new block, the miners collect all validate transactions and the miners compute a valid nonce such that the hash value of the newly generated block is less than or equal to a value provided by the blockchain system. This process is defined as the Proof of Work (PoW) consensus, which is the core of the Bitcoin blockchain [15].

Another prominent application of PoW consensus is Ethereum blockchain [18], which focuses on providing a platform to facilitate building decentralized applications on its blockchain and is more expressive than Bitcoin blockchain [19]. In Ethereum blockchain, the ledger is a state transition system, where the state consists of the ownership status of all existing Ethers and the state transition function which takes a state and a transaction as input, and outputs a new state as the result [6]. In general, Ethereum blockchain has two types of accounts: externally owned accounts and contract accounts, controlled by private keys and their contract code, respectively. The externally owned account can create and sign a transaction. However, the contract account would receive a message once the smart contract code is activated, which allows it to read and write to internal storage [20]. The smart contract has an expressive programming language and the code is stored directly on the blockchain, which is the key difference between the Ethereum blockchain and the Bitcoin blockchain. There are three properties in blockchain systems: chain consistency, chain quality, chain growth [21–23]. With the fundamental properties, the blockchain acts as a bulletin board and a secure source of randomness in some studies [2,6].

2.2 System and Adversary Models

As shown in Fig. 1, there are three entities in a public integrity auditing scheme: users (data owner), the cloud server, and a third-party auditor (TPA).

• Users: users are data owners, they outsource their data to the cloud server and would access the outsourced data as needed. To guarantee the integrity of the outsourced data, users employ TPA to periodically verify the outsourced data. Furthermore, users check the auditing results generated by TPA in a longer period of time (compared with the data integrity auditing performed by TPA).

• Cloud server: the cloud server is subject to the cloud service provider and provides users with cloud storage services. The cloud server generates the public auditing proofs for TPA's auditing.

• Third-party auditor: TPA periodically verifies the integrity of the outsourced data, records the verification result entry to the Ethereum blockchain, and informs users once their data is corrupted.

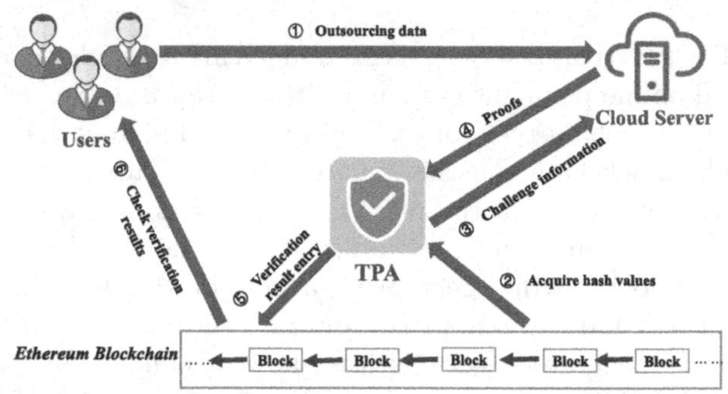

Fig. 1. System model

In the adversary model, we consider three types of threats as follows.

• Semi-trusted cloud server. The cloud server is a semi-trusted entity, it may deceive TPA and/or users and make them believe that the outsourced data is well maintained for keeping a good reputation. Here, by "semi-trusted", we mean that the cloud server would deceive TPA and/or users (i.e., it would deviate from the prescribed scheme) if and only if its profits can be increased by utilizing such a strategy.

• Misbehaved TPA. We follow the existing thread model of malicious TPA [6,11]. TPA may collude with the cloud server to hide the fact of data corruption, and may not perform data integrity auditing on schedule.

• Malicious users. Malicious users may intentionally accuse the cloud server or TPA's correct behaviors.

2.3 Design Goals

To achieve the secure and efficient public auditing under the aforementioned model, our scheme should achieve three goals as follow.

• Functionality. The scheme is able to allow TPA to periodically audit the outsourced data and allows the users to check the trustworthiness of TPA.

• Security. If and only if the cloud server well maintains the outsourced data, can it pass the TPA's auditing; Collusion between any two entities cannot deceive the other entity.

• Efficiency. TPA is able to audit the integrity of outsourced data without needing to download the data set; A user is able to check the TPA's behaviors during a long period of time with a constant and slight cost.

3 The Proposed Scheme

3.1 Overview of the Proposed Scheme

In this section, we give an overview of our scheme, focusing on the challenge addressed by our scheme.

Time in our scheme is divided into fixed and pre-determined time-intervals called *period*. A period describes the frequency at which the user checks the TPA's behaviors. In addition, each period is further divided into multiple time-intervals called *epoch*. An epoch is determined by the user and prescribes the frequency at which TPA audits the integrity of outsourced data.

As described before, in a public auditing scheme, to ensure the trustworthiness of TPA, the user is required to check the TPA's behaviors in a much longer period of time (compared with the epoch). The TPA's behaviors are described by multiple entries, where each entry records the interaction messages between TPA and the cloud server during one auditing task. In existing schemes [6,12], the user has to check all entries one by one, which incurs heavy costs in terms of communication and computation and takes a long delay. This problem would be further exacerbated by the fact that the user always wants to perform the above operations using a low-powerful device (e.g., smartphone). Therefore, the main challenge in this work is how to significantly reduce the checking costs on the user.

The above challenge is addressed by using two key techniques.

We design a smart contract on the Ethereum blockchain for data integrity auditing. Such a smart contract is triggered by TPA. At the end of each epoch, TPA extracts the hash values of the latest ϵ confirmed blocks in Ethereum blockchain. These hash values are utilized to compute the challenged blocks to ensure the randomness of the challenge, due to (ϵ, ι)-chain quality [6]. Upon receiving the challenged blocks, the cloud server generates the corresponding proofs and sends back to TPA. Then TPA verifies the validity and triggers the smart contract to record the auditing entries into the blockchain. Here, the functionality of the smart contract is not only to record these entries, but also to guarantee the validity of each entry generated by TPA. There are three functions in the smart contract. The first one is to verify whether the ϵ blocks are consecutive and newly generated based on the height of the current Ethereum blockchain (for the sake of brevity, in this work, we set $\epsilon = 12$). The second one is to verify the validity of the auditing proofs generated by the cloud server. The third one is to record the valid auditing entries into the blockchain. Additionally, TPA stores a log file for all auditing information in its local storage.

To enable the user to check the TPA's behaviors with a constant and slight cost in terms of communication and computation, we construct an auditing record chain [13] based on the Ethereum blockchain for the same data. As a result, all entries corresponding to the same data form a chain in the chronological order, which ensures that the validity of the last entry can reflect the validity of all entries on the chain. Specifically, each block on the chain contains the current epoch's auditing proofs, the height of the block recording current and

Table 1. The log file

Recorded content	Height of current block	Hash value of chosen blocks	Proofs information
$h_1(t^{(1)}\Vert\sigma^{(1)}\Vert\mu^{(1)}\Vert\tau^{(1)})\Vert Bl_{\omega}^{(1)}\Vert Bl_{\eta}^{(1)}$	$t^{(1)}$	$B_t^{(1)}, B_{t-1}^{(1)}, B_{t-2}^{(1)}, \cdots, B_{t-11}^{(1)}$	$\sigma^{(1)}, \mu^{(1)}, \tau^{(1)}$
$h_1(t^{(2)}\Vert\sigma^{(2)}\Vert\mu^{(2)}\Vert\tau^{(2)})\Vert Bl_{\omega}^{(2)}\Vert Bl_{\eta}^{(2)}$	$t^{(2)}$	$B_t^{(2)}, B_{t-1}^{(2)}, B_{t-2}^{(2)}, \cdots, B_{t-11}^{(2)}$	$\sigma^{(2)}, \mu^{(2)}, \tau^{(2)}$
...	...	...	...
$h_1(t^{(\varphi)}\Vert\sigma^{(\varphi)}\Vert\mu^{(\varphi)}\Vert\tau^{(\varphi)})\Vert Bl_{\omega}^{(\varphi)}\Vert Bl_{\eta}^{(\varphi)}$	$t^{(\varphi)}$	$B_t^{(\varphi)}, B_{t-1}^{(\varphi)}, B_{t-2}^{(\varphi)}, \cdots, B_{t-11}^{(\varphi)}$	$\sigma^{(\varphi)}, \mu^{(\varphi)}, \tau^{(\varphi)}$

previous epoch's auditing proofs. With such a binding mechanism, all auditing entries corresponding to the same data performed by TPA would form an auditing record chain such that any one of them is corrupted, the chain is broken. During the **Check Verification** phase, a user firstly checks the consistency between the auditing results and the content required from the log file. Then, the user checks the validity of the latest entry recorded in the blockchain. If both checking results are successful, the correctness, integrity, and timeliness of auditing entries can be ensured.

3.2 Construction of the Proposed Scheme

Our scheme consists of three entities: the user ($\mathcal{U}$), the cloud server ($\mathcal{CS}$), a third-party auditor (TPA).

Setup. With the security parameter l, the system initializes public parameters as follows:

- G is the an additive group with the prime order p and the generator P, G_T is a multiplicative group. G and G_T determine a bilinear map $e : G \times G \rightarrow G_T$.
- $\mathcal{U}$ randomly chooses γ as his/her secret key sk, the public key pk can be computed as $y = \gamma P$. $\mathcal{U}$ also generates a random signing keypair (spk, ssk).
- $h_1(\cdot) : \{0,1\}^* \rightarrow Z_p^*$, $h_2 : \{0,1\}^* \rightarrow G$ are two hash functions.
- Choose a pseudorandom permutation $\pi_{key}(\cdot)$ and a pseudorandom function $f_{key}(\cdot)$ [14].

The system parameters are $\{l, G, G_T, e, \pi_{key}(\cdot), f_{key}(\cdot), h_1(\cdot), h_2(\cdot)\}$.

Outsource. $\mathcal{U}$ interacts with $\mathcal{CS}$, and outsources the data M to $\mathcal{CS}$.

- Using the erasure code algorithm [24], $\mathcal{U}$ divides M into n blocks and splits each block into s sectors. Each sector is denoted by $M = \{m_{ij}\}, 1 \leq i \leq n, 1 \leq j \leq s$.
- $\mathcal{U}$ chooses a random data name $name \in Z_p^*$ for the outsourced data M, randomly chooses an element set $\{U_1, U_2, \cdots, U_s\} \leftarrow G$.
- $\mathcal{U}$ computes the data tag $\tau \leftarrow \tau_0 \| Sig_{ssk}(\tau_0)$, where $\tau_0 = name\|U_1\| U_2\| \cdots \|U_s$.
- For each sector m_{ij}, $1 \leq j \leq s$, $\mathcal{U}$ computes the verification tag $\sigma_i = \gamma \cdot (h_2(i\|name) + \sum\limits_{j=1}^{s} m_{ij}U_j)$.
- $\mathcal{U}$ outsources $\{M, \{\sigma_i\}, \tau\}$ to $\mathcal{CS}$ for storage.

Audit. During each predetermined epoch, TPA interacts with $\mathcal{CS}$ to audit the integrity of the outsourced data.

- TPA extracts the lasted confirmed 12 hash values $\{B_{t-11}, B_{t-10}, B_{t-9}, \cdots, B_t\}$ from the Ethereum blockchain, where t is the hight of the newly confirmed block under the current time.
- TPA sends the set $(\{B_{t-11}, B_{t-10}, B_{t-9}, \cdots, B_t\}, t)$ to $\mathcal{CS}$.
- Upon receiving the set, $\mathcal{CS}$ computes two seeds:
$\theta_1 = h_1(B_t||B_{t-1}||B_{t-2}||\cdots||B_{t-11}||1)$,
$\theta_2 = h_1(B_t||B_{t-1}||B_{t-2}||\cdots||B_{t-11}||2)$.
- $\mathcal{CS}$ computes challenged index-coefficient pairs as $k_i = \pi_{\theta_1}(i), v_{k_i} = f_{\theta_2}(i), i = 1, 2, 3, \cdots, c$, where c is the number of challenged blocks and is determined the security parameter l.
- For each $j \in [1, s]$, $\mathcal{CS}$ computes the set $\mu = \{\mu_1, \mu_2, \cdots, \mu_s\}$ by $\mu_j = \sum_{i=k_1}^{k_c} v_i m_{ij}$, and generates aggregated verification tag $\sigma = \sum_{i=k_1}^{k_c} v_i \sigma_i$.
- $\mathcal{CS}$ sends the proof information $\{\sigma, \mu, \tau\}$ to TPA.
- Upon receiving the proof information, TPA verifies the data integrity as follows:
  - TPA uses the verification key *psk* of $\mathcal{U}$ to verify the signature on τ. If the signature is invalid, TPA takes the verification result as *Reject*.
  - TPA computes two seeds:
  $\theta_1 = h_1(B_t||B_{t-1}||B_{t-2}||\cdots||B_{t-11}||1)$,
  $\theta_2 = h_1(B_t||B_{t-1}||B_{t-2}||\cdots||B_{t-11}||2)$.
  - TPA computes the index-coefficient pairs as $k_i = \pi_{\theta_1}(i), v_{k_i} = f_{\theta_2}(i), i = 1, 2, 3, \cdots, c$.
  - TPA verifies the data integrity by checking the equation $e(\sigma, P) \stackrel{?}{=} e(\sum_{i=k_1}^{k_c} v_i \cdot h_2(i||name) + \sum_{j=1}^{s} \mu_j \cdot U_j, y)$.
- After the verification, TPA runs the smart contract *contract* (described in Algorithm 1), which verifies whether the 12 blocks $\{B_t, B_{t-1}, B_{t-2}, \cdots, B_{t-11}\}$ used are consecutive under the current height of block, verifies the validity of the proofs $\{\sigma, \mu, \tau\}$, and records the valid information $\{h_1(t||\sigma||\mu||\tau)||Bl_\omega||Bl_\eta\}$ into the contract storage. Bl_ω is the height of the block recording the current epoch's valid information, $Bl_\eta(\eta \leq \omega)$ is the height of the block recording the previous epoch's valid information. The process is depicted in Fig. 2.
- TPA also generates a log file in its local storage as follows:
  - At the end of each epoch, TPA generates an entry as $\{h_1(t||\sigma||\mu||\tau)||Bl_\omega|| Bl_\eta, t, B_t||B_{t-1}||B_{t-2}||\cdots||B_{t-11}, \sigma, \mu, \tau\}$.
  - TPA stores the entries to a log file as described in Table 1.

Check Verification. At the end of each period, $\mathcal{U}$ interacts with TPA to check the auditing entries generated in this period.

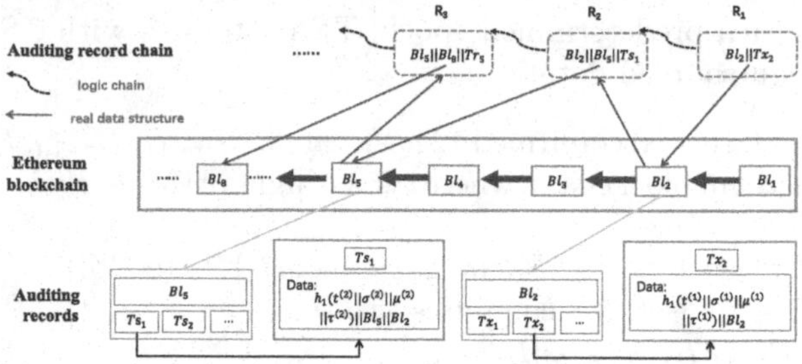

Fig. 2. Auditing record chain structure

Algorithm 1: Smart contract algorithm

Require:
$B_t, B_{t-1}, B_{t-2}, ..., B_{t-11}, \sigma, \mu, \tau$
Ensure:
$true$ or $false$ or $error$
if $(B_t, B_{t-1}, B_{t-2}, ..., B_{t-11})$ are consecutive and well-timed **then**
  if $(e(\sigma, P) = e(\sum_{i=k_1}^{k_c} v_i \cdot h_2(i||name) + \sum_{j=1}^{s} \mu_j \cdot U_j, y)$ **then**
    record $true||h_1(t||\sigma||\mu||\tau)||Bl_w||Bl_\eta$;
  else
    record $false||Bl_w||Bl_\eta$;
  end if
else
  record $error$;
end if

- $\mathcal{U}$ requires the all recorded contents $(h_1(t^{(1)}||\sigma^{(1)}||\mu^{(1)}||\tau^{(1)})||Bl_\omega^{(1)}||Bl_\eta^{(1)}, h_1(t^{(2)}||\sigma^{(2)}||\mu^{(2)}||\tau^{(2)})||Bl_\omega^{(2)}||Bl_\eta^{(2)}, \cdots, h_1(t^{(\varphi)}||\sigma^{(\varphi)}||\mu^{(\varphi)}||\tau^{(\varphi)})||Bl_\omega^{(\varphi)}||Bl_\eta^{(\varphi)})$ and the last entry $(h_1(t^{(\varphi)}||\sigma^{(\varphi)}||\mu^{(\varphi)}||\tau^{(\varphi)})||Bl_\omega^{(\varphi)}||Bl_\eta^{(\varphi)}, t^{(\varphi)}, B_t^{(\varphi)}, B_{t-1}^{(\varphi)}, B_{t-2}^{(\varphi)}, \cdots, B_{t-11}^{(\varphi)}, \sigma^{(\varphi)}, \mu^{(\varphi)}, \tau^{(\varphi)}, \mathit{Accept/Reject})$ stored in the log file from TPA.
- $\mathcal{U}$ acquires the auditing record chain recording the same data's auditing entries from the Ethereum blockchain.
- $\mathcal{U}$ checks the consistence of the verification results recorded into the Ethereum blockchain and the content required from the log file. If any of them is inconsistent, $\mathcal{U}$ would argue the credibility of TPA; Otherwise, $\mathcal{U}$ checks the validity of the last entry as follows:
  - $\mathcal{U}$ first acquires $t^{(\varphi)}$ and $t^{(\varphi)} + 13$, derives physical time, and verifies the time whether matches the agreed one. If the time does not match the agreed one, the checking result is false.

- $\mathcal{U}$ extracts the hash values of 12 latest confirmed blocks before the block $Bl_t^{(\varphi)}$, generates the two seeds as

$$\theta_1^{(\varphi)} = h_1(B_t^{(\varphi)}||B_{t-1}^{(\varphi)}||B_{t-2}^{(\varphi)}||\cdots||B_{t-11}^{(\varphi)}||1),$$
$$\theta_2^{(\varphi)} = h_1(B_t^{(\varphi)}||B_{t-1}^{(\varphi)}||B_{t-2}^{(\varphi)}||\cdots||B_{t-11}^{(\varphi)}||2),$$

  and checks the consistence between the generated seeds and the last entry in the second row.
- $\mathcal{U}$ uses his/her verification key psk to verify the signature on $\tau^{(\varphi)}$. If the signature is invalid, the checking result is false.
- $\mathcal{U}$ computes the index-coefficient pairs as $k_i^{(\varphi)} = \pi_{\theta_1}(i), v_{k_i}^{(\varphi)} = f_{\theta_2}(i), i = 1, 2, 3, \cdots, c$.
- $\mathcal{U}$ checks the verification result by justify the equation $e(\sigma^{(\varphi)}, P) \stackrel{?}{=} e(\sum_{i=k_1^{(\varphi)}}^{k_c^{(\varphi)}} v_i^{(\varphi)} \cdot h_2(i||name) + \sum_{j=1}^{s} \mu_j^{(\varphi)} \cdot U_j^{(\varphi)}, y)$. If the equation does not hold, the checking result is false, otherwise, the checking result is true.

3.3 On the Necessity of TPA

Intuitively, we can remove TPA and only require the smart contract mechanism to perform the auditing tasks. Such smart contract-based public auditing of the data integrity mechanism has been proposed in [25,26]. Specifically, to regulate the behaviors of the cloud server, the smart contract-based public auditing schemes introduce a fair arbitration mechanism, i.e., automatic penalization. At the beginning of smart contract deployment, each user and the cloud server take a certain amount of deposit as input, respectively. After each auditing, if the outsourced data is well maintained, the smart contract would send the user's deposit to the cloud server's account as the charge of the storage service. Otherwise, the smart contract would send the cloud server's deposit to the user's account as the compensations.

However, as part of our contribution, we point out that such a fair arbitration is unsatisfactory in reality, due to the following reasons.

• Once the outsourced data is corrupted, the smart contract would automatically transfer the cloud server's deposit to the user as the compensations. In reality, neither holding accountable nor demanding compensation is the main objective for a public auditing scheme. We stress that the main objective of public auditing schemes is to detect data corruption and inform the user as soon as possible (within one time-interval that TPA audits the data integrity). However, in the above fair arbitration mechanism, only if the user checks her/his blockchain account, can she/he detect the data corruption. Actually, requiring the users to periodically check her/his blockchain account is very inefficient in reality. If a user is able to meet this requirement, she/he may directly utilize the private auditing scheme [7] to verify the integrity of outsourced data. Therefore, to enable the user to obtain the data corruption timely, TPA plays an important role in the public auditing schemes.

• In reality, the cloud server needs to serve multiple users simultaneously. For each user, the cloud server is required to take a certain amount of deposit as input for the smart contract. As a consequence, the total amount of deposit of the cloud server is proportional to the number of users, which brings huge costs for the cloud server. Furthermore, the price of Ether (as well as other value tokens of blockchains) fluctuates frequently and volatility. Such an instability would bring economic losses both for users and the cloud server. We take the following scene as an example, at the beginning of a period, the price of 1 Ether is $10. Here, both a user and the cloud server deposit 1 Ether as input. At the end of this period, the price of 1 Ether is $20. At this time, the smart contract has been triggered to perform the auditing tasks. If some auditing result shows that the data is corrupted, the cloud server should compensate for its misbehavior. The smart contract would send 1 Ether to the user's account. Consequently, due to price fluctuation, the cloud server paid an extra $10 for the user. If the auditing result shows that the outsourced data is well maintained, the user should pay the storage service charge to the cloud server. The smart contract would send 1 Ether to the cloud server's account. Here, the user paid an extra $10 for the cloud server. In addition, regarding to the case of multiple users, the cloud server has to hold a large number of Ethers for deposit. Therefore, the cloud server bears a more serious risk of loss than the user due to price fluctuations.

4 Security Analysis

In this section, we analyze the security of our scheme with respect to the adversary model described in Sect. 2.

4.1 Resistance Against the Semi-trusted Cloud Server

A semi-trusted cloud server may hide the incident of data corruption by forging a proof information to deceive TPA.

Theorem 1. *An aggregate signature σ for a set of blocks $\{k_i\}, i = 1, 2, \cdots, c$ in our scheme is existentially unforgeable under adaptively chosen-message attacks.*

Proof. To prove the above Theorem, we define a game as follows.

- A challenger $\mathcal{S}$ runs the **Setup** to initiate the system and generate the public parameters PP. $\mathcal{S}$ sends PP to an adversary $\mathcal{A}$.
- Upon receiving PP, $\mathcal{A}$ randomly chooses the i-th block messages $\{m_{ij}\}, j = 1, 2, \cdots, s$, requests $\mathcal{U}$'s signature on the i-th block messages, and sends it to $\mathcal{S}$.
- On receiving the query, $\mathcal{S}$ generates the corresponding signature σ_i, and sends σ_i to $\mathcal{A}$.
- $\mathcal{A}$ repeats the above query on different blocks.
- Finally, $\mathcal{A}$ outputs an aggregate signature σ.

$\mathcal{A}$ wins the game if and only if satisfying the following two conditions:

- σ is a valid aggregate signature.
- $\sigma_k, k \in [k_1, k_c]$ is not submitted during the queries.

Here, we prove the advantage that $\mathcal{A}$ wins Game is negligible.

Supposing $\mathcal{A}$ wants to generate an aggregate signature about the set of blocks $\{k_i\}, i = 1, 2, \cdots, c$. A dishonest prover would response $\mathcal{A}$ with $\mu'_1, \mu'_2, \cdots, \mu'_s$ together with σ'. If the responses from an honest prover, the response is $\mu_1, \mu_2, \cdots, \mu_s$ with a valid signature σ. By the correctness of the scheme, we know that the valid response satisfies the verification equation as follows:

$$e(\sigma, P) = e(\sum_{i=k_1}^{k_c} v_i h_2(i||name) + \sum_{j=1}^{s} \mu_j U_j, y).$$

and for the adversary's outputs, we have that

$$e(\sigma', P) = e(\sum_{i=k_1}^{k_c} v_i h_2(i||name) + \sum_{j=1}^{s} \mu'_j U_j, y).$$

where $y = \gamma \cdot P$ is the challenger's public key. We know that, for all $j = 1, 2, \cdots, s$, if $\mu'_j = \mu_j$, then $\sigma' = \sigma$, which contradicts our assumption above. Thus, for $1 \leq j \leq s$, if we define $\Delta\mu_j = \mu_j{}' - \mu_j$, then, there is at least one $\{\Delta\mu_j\}$ is nonzero.

Let $\mathcal{A}$ be an elliptic curve discrete algorithm problem (ECDLP) attacker who is given $P, \gamma \cdot P, h \in G$ and needs to compute $\gamma \cdot h$. Here, we show that if $\mathcal{A}$ is able to forge a signature with a probability, then $\mathcal{S}$ would break the ECDLP by the same probability.

- During the **Setup** phase, the public key y is set to $\gamma \cdot P$. That means, $\mathcal{S}$ does not know the secret key γ.
- $\mathcal{S}$ simulates the random oracle h_2. It has a list of queries and responses to keep consistently. When it answers a query from $\mathcal{A}$, $\mathcal{S}$ randomly chooses r from $Z_p{}^*$ and responds $rP \in G$ to $\mathcal{A}$.
- $\mathcal{A}$ selects a random i-th block, where $i \in [k_1, k_c]$, and sends the messages $\{m_{ij}\}, j = 1, 2, \cdots, s$ to $\mathcal{S}$.
- Upon receiving the query, $\mathcal{S}$ randomly chooses $name \in Z_p{}^*$. For each $j, 1 \leq j \leq s$, $\mathcal{S}$ randomly chooses $\alpha_j, \beta_j \in Z_p{}^*$ and sets $U_j = \alpha_j \cdot P + \beta_j \cdot h$. For each different i, $\mathcal{S}$ randomly chooses $r_i \in Z_p{}^*$, and generates the random oracle at i as follows:

$$h_2(i||name) = r_i \cdot P - (\sum_{j=1}^{s} \alpha_j m_{ij} P + \sum_{j=1}^{s} \beta_j m_{ij} h).$$

Then, $\mathcal{S}$ can compute σ_i, since $\mathcal{S}$ has

$$h_2(i||name) + \sum_{j=1}^{s} m_{ij}U_j = r_i \cdot P - (\sum_{j=1}^{s} \alpha_j m_{ij} P + \sum_{j=1}^{s} \beta_j m_{ij} h) + \sum_{j=1}^{s} m_{ij}U_j$$
$$= r_i \cdot P - (\sum_{j=1}^{s} \alpha_j m_{ij} P + \sum_{j=1}^{s} \beta_j m_{ij} h) + \sum_{j=1}^{s} m_{ij}(\alpha_j \cdot P + \beta_j \cdot h)$$
$$= r_i \cdot P.$$

Consequently, $\mathcal{S}$ generates the signature $\sigma_i = r_i \cdot (h_2(i||name) + \sum_{j=1}^{s} m_{ij}U_j)$.

- $\mathcal{A}$ repeats the query on different $i, i \in [k_1, k_c]$, and $\mathcal{S}$ answers it as above.
- Finally, $\mathcal{A}$ generates an aggregate signature σ'.
- $\mathcal{S}$ computes the equation as follows:

$$e(\sigma' - \sigma, P) = e(\sum_{j=1}^{s} \Delta\mu_j U_j, y) = e(\sum_{j=1}^{s} \Delta\mu_j(\alpha_j \cdot P + \beta_j \cdot h), y)$$
$$= e(\sum_{j=1}^{s} \Delta\mu_j \alpha_j \cdot P, y) + e(\sum_{j=1}^{s} \Delta\mu_j \beta_j \cdot h, y),$$

and rearranges terms yields as follows:

$$e(\sigma' - \sigma - \sum_{j=1}^{s} \Delta\mu_j \alpha_j \cdot y, P) = e(\sum_{j=1}^{s} \Delta\mu_j \beta_j \cdot h, y) = e(h, y)^{\sum_{j=1}^{s} \Delta\mu_j \beta_j}.$$

- $\mathcal{S}$ can solve ECDLP by the equation as follows:

$$\gamma \cdot h = (\sigma' - \sigma - \sum_{j=1}^{s} \Delta\mu_j \alpha_j \cdot y) \cdot (\sum_{j=1}^{s} \Delta\mu_j \beta_j)^{-1}.$$

By doing so, $\mathcal{S}$ can solve ECDLP using the $\mathcal{A}$'s outputs. However, in reality, ECDLP is a difficult problem, $\mathcal{A}$ cannot forge a valid signature under adaptively chosen-message attack.

4.2 Resistance Against the Misbehaved TPA and Malicious Users

The misbehaved TPA may collude with the semi-trusted cloud server to hide the fact of data corruption, and may not perform data integrity auditing on schedule.

Theorem 2. *In our scheme, the misbehaved TPA can the cloud server cannot predetermine the hash values of the block generated at a future time.*

Proof. In our scheme, the challenged blocks are computed by the random seeds. These seeds are generated the hash values of the latest 12 confirmed blocks in the Ethereum blockchain according to the corresponding time. Thus, the randomness of these seeds can be ensured by the chain quality of blockchain. In addition, the miners cannot be incentivized by the malicious TPA to generate a target block due to the preimage resistance property of hash functions. Specifically, if the malicious TPA wants to audit the well-maintained data blocks, he has to incentivize the miners to generate 12 continuous target blocks in the blockchain. In reality, since the hash value of future blocks cannot be predicted and the miners cannot break the preimage resistance of the hash functions, the malicious TPA cannot collude with the cloud server to generate a bias auditing result using the well-preserved blocks.

In our scheme, TPA is required to audit the data integrity at the prescribed time, the auditing result entries are recorded in the Ethereum blockchain, where these entries are tamper-resistant and unforgeable. Thus, if TPA does not audit data integrity on schedule, users would detect the misbehavior.

The malicious users may intentionally accuse the cloud server or TPA's honest behaviors. In our scheme, during the **Check Verification** phase, all users can check the auditing results, if there is a malicious user deliberately accuse the honest cloud server or TPA, other honest users would break the lie if they execute the valid verification result.

5 Performance Evaluation

We implement experiment in JAVA with JPBC using a computer with a single Intel Core i7-3720QM, 2.6 GHz CPU, 8 GB of RAM. SHA-2 is implemented in the hash functions. We select 80 bits security level for analysis, the size of RSA modulus is selected $|N|=1024$, and the curve of field size is 159 bits.

5.1 Communication Overhead

In this section, we compare the communication costs between our scheme with CPVPA [6] and SWP [7]. The comparison result is depicted in Fig. 3, which shows that the communication overhead is proportional to the number of challenged blocks in SWP scheme, while it is constant in CPVPA and our scheme.

5.2 Computation Overhead

We first estimate the basic cryptographic operations as Table 2.

Table 2. Notation of operations

Notation	Description
$Hash_{Z_p^*}$	Hash a value to $Z_p{}^*$
$Hash_G$	Hash a value to G
Mul_G	Multiplication in group G
$Mul_{Z_p^*}$	Multiplication in $Z_p{}^*$
Prf	A pseudorandom function
$Add_{Z_p^*}$	Addition in $Z_p{}^*$
Add_G	Addition in G
$Pair_{G_T}$	Computing pairing e

Table 3. Computation costs on the cloud server side

Schemes	Computation costs
SWP [7]	$c \cdot Mul_G + c \cdot Add_G + c \cdot Mul_{Z_p^*} + c \cdot Add_{Z_p^*}$
CPVPA [6]	$c \cdot Mul_G + c \cdot Add_G + c \cdot Mul_{Z_p^*} + c \cdot Add_{Z_p^*} + 2c \cdot Prf + 2 \cdot Hash_{Z_p^*}$
Our scheme	$c \cdot Add_G + c \cdot Mul_{Z_p^*} + c \cdot Add_{Z_p^*} + 2c \cdot Prf$

We show the computation costs on the cloud server side of our scheme, CPVPA [6], and SWP [7] in Table 3. Here, c denotes the number of challenged blocks during each auditing. Since our scheme is based on an addition group, thus, our scheme requires less computation cost on the cloud server side.

We show the computation costs on the TPA side of our scheme, CPVPA [6], and SWP [7] in Table 4. Here, c is the number of challenged blocks during each auditing and s is the number of sectors in our scheme.

In Fig. 4, we give a comparison of computation overhead between our scheme, SWP [7] and CPVPA [6] in cloud server side and TPA side. According to the experiment results, we can see that the costs of our scheme in server side and TPA side are much less than existing schemes [6,7], namely, our scheme is much more efficient.

We show the computation costs on the user side during the **Check Verification** phase in Table 5, where c is the number of challenged blocks and N is the number of all entries in a long period of users. The table shows that, during the **Check Verification** phase, the computation costs of user side in CPVPA is proportional to the number of auditing entries in this period. To show in more detail, we depict a linear graph as shown in Fig. 5. Compared with existing public auditing schemes, only our scheme and CPVPA [6] require the user to audit the behavior of TPA. According to Fig. 5, we can learn that compared with CPVPA, our scheme extremely reduces the checking costs for users.

In our scheme, we allow TPA to run a smart contract to record the valid auditing records into the Ethereum blockchain. Here, the smart contract contains three functions. The first one is to verify the continuity of 12 blocks corresponding to the height of the block at that time. The second one is to verify the proofs generated by the cloud server, namely performing the auditing by the smart

Table 4. Computation costs on TPA side

Schemes	Computation costs
SWP [7]	$2 \cdot Pair_{G_T} + (c+1) \cdot Mul_G + c \cdot Add_G + c \cdot Hash_G$
CPVPA [6]	$4 \cdot Pair_{G_T} + (3c+2) \cdot Mul_G + 3c \cdot Add_G + (c+4) \cdot Hash_G + (2c+3) \cdot Hash_{Z_p^*} + 2c \cdot Mul_{Z_p^*} + 2c \cdot Prf$
Our scheme	$2 \cdot Hash_{Z_p^*} + 2c \cdot Prf + 2Pair_{G_T} + c \cdot Hash_G + (c+s) \cdot Mul_G + (c+s-1) \cdot Add_G$

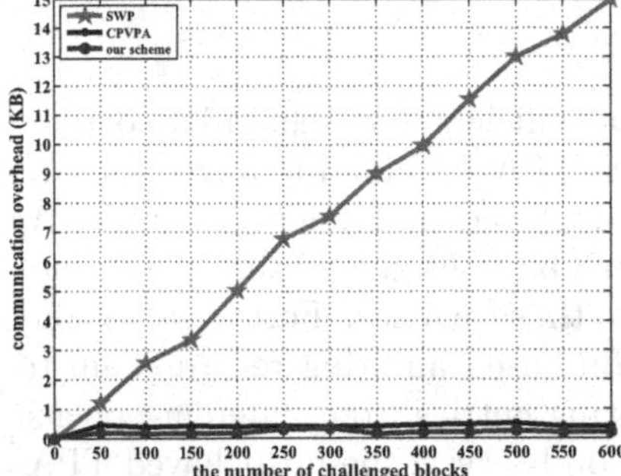

Fig. 3. The communication overhead

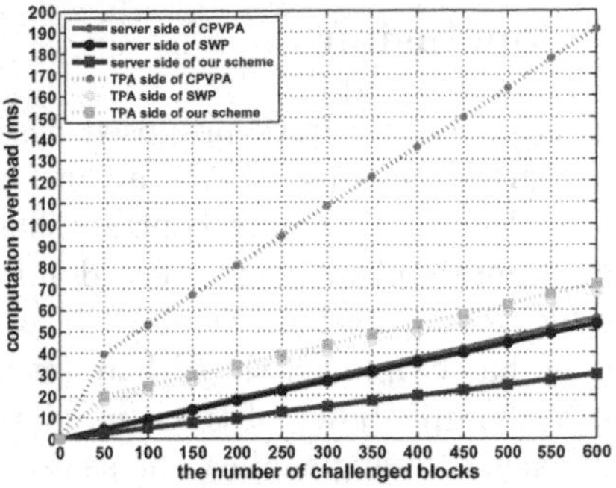

Fig. 4. Computation overhead

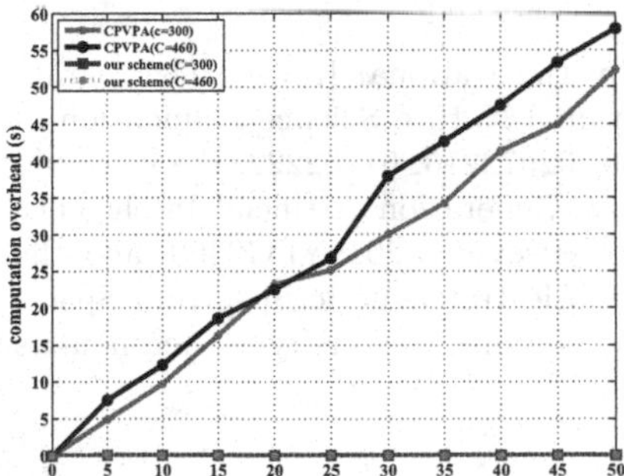

Fig. 5. Computation overhead of users

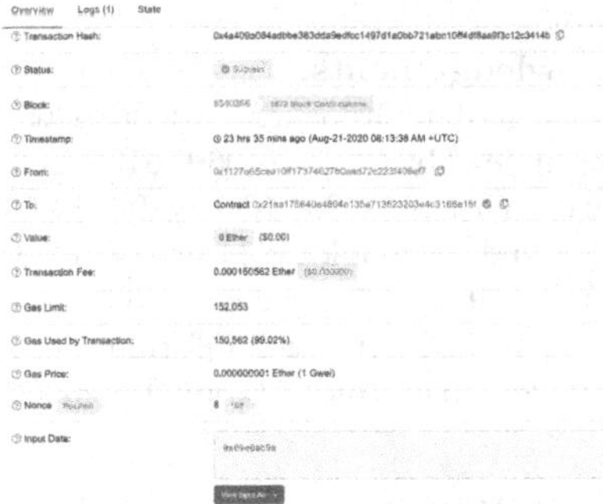

Fig. 6. Result of smart contract

contract. The last one is to record the auditing entries into the blockchain. To achieve the second functionality, the smart contract has to compute a bilinear pairing operation and make a judgment. We have found that there have been some works on Ethereum blockchain to support pairing operations [27] and the code is uploaded in Github [28]. To verify the correctness of this algorithm, we test it in the Ethereum blockchain and show the experiment in Fig. 6. As shown in Fig. 6, gas consumption is acceptable for Ethereum blockchain. Thus, the bilinear operation performed by the smart contract is feasible in practice.

Table 5. Computation costs on user side

Schemes	Computation costs during the **Check Verification** phase
CPVPA [6]	$N \cdot (4 \cdot Pair_{G_T} + (3c+2) \cdot Mul_G + 3c \cdot Add_G + (c+4) \cdot Hash_G + (2c+3) \cdot Hash_{Z_p^*} + 2c \cdot Mul_{Z_p^*} + 2c \cdot Prf)$
Our scheme	$2 \cdot Hash_{Z_p^*} + 2c \cdot Prf + 2Pair_{G_T} + c \cdot Hash_G + (c+s) \cdot Mul_G + (c+s-1) \cdot Add_G$

6 Conclusion

In this paper, we have proposed a secure and efficient blockchain-based public integrity auditing scheme against malicious TPA for cloud storage systems. In our scheme, a smart contract has been deployed and triggered by TPA. Such a mechanism would record information about each auditing entry into the blockchain and guarantee the validity of those entries. Furthermore, our scheme has employed the Ethereum blockchain-based auditing record chain to ensure the linkability of the same data's auditing entries from different epochs. Our scheme resists against the semi-trusted cloud server, the misbehaved TPA, and the malicious users. Compared with existing schemes, our scheme reduces the computation costs on the user side while keeping constant communication overhead.

Acknowledgements. This work is supported by the National Key R&D Program of China under Grant 2017YFB0802000, the National Nature Science Foundation of China under Grant 61872060, 61370203, 62002050, 62072215, 61702222, the Chengdu Innovation Project 2019-YF05-02029-GX, the New Generation Artificial Intelligence Science and Technology Major Project of Sichuan Province 2019YFG0400, and the Key Laboratory of Dynamic Cognitive System of Electromagnetic Spectrum Space, Ministry of Industry and Information Technology, Nanjing University of Aeronautics and Astronautics under Grant KF20202110.

References

1. Li, S., Xu, C., Zhang, Y.: CSED: client-side encrypted deduplication scheme based on proofs of ownership for cloud storage. J. Inf. Security Appl. **46**, 250–258 (2019)
2. Zhang, X., Zhao, J., Xu, C., Li, H., Wang, H., Zhang, Y.: CIPPPA: conditional identity privacy-preserving public auditing for cloud-based wbans against malicious auditors, IEEE Trans. Cloud Comput. 1–14, (2019), to appear. https://doi.org/10.1109/TCC.2019.2927219
3. Yang, A., Xu, J., Weng, J., Zhou, J., Wong, D.S.: Lightweight and privacy-preserving delegatable proofs of storage with data dynamics in cloud storage. IEEE Trans. Cloud Comput. 1–14 (2018). https://doi.org/10.1109/TCC.2018.2851256
4. Zhang, X., Xu, C., Wang, H., Zhang, Y., Wang, S.: FS-PEKS: lattice-based forward secure public-key encryption with keyword search for cloud-assisted industrial internet of things, IEEE Trans. Dependable and Secure Comput. 1–15 (2019). https://doi.org/10.1109/TDSC.2019.2914117

5. Wang, C., Chow, S.S., Wang, Q., Ren, K., Lou, W.: Privacy-preserving public auditing for secure cloud storage. IEEE Trans. Comput. **62**(2), 362–375 (2011)
6. Zhang, Y., Xu, C., Lin, X., Shen, X.S.: Blockchain-based public integrity verification for cloud storage against procrastinating auditors, IEEE Trans. Cloud Comput. 1–15 (2019). https://doi.org/10.1109/TCC.2019.2908400
7. Shacham, H., Waters, B.: Compact proofs of retrievability. In: Pieprzyk, J. (ed.) ASIACRYPT 2008. LNCS, vol. 5350, pp. 90–107. Springer, Heidelberg (2008). https://doi.org/10.1007/978-3-540-89255-7_7
8. Ateniese, G., et al.: Provable data possession at untrusted stores. In: Proceedings of CCS, pp. 598–609 (2007)
9. Wang, C., Wang, Q., Ren, K., Lou, W.: Privacy-preserving public auditing for data storage security in cloud computing. In: Proceedings of INFOCOM. IEEE, pp. 1–9 (2010)
10. Boneh, D., Lynn, B., Shacham, H.: Short signatures from the weil pairing, In: Proceedings of ASIACRYPT, pp. 514–532 (2001)
11. Zhang, Y., Xu, C., Yu, S., Li, H., Zhang, X.: SCLPV: secure certificateless public verification for cloud-based cyber-physical-social systems against malicious auditors. IEEE Trans. Comput. Social Syst. **2**(4), 159–170 (2015)
12. Armknecht, F., Bohli, J.-M., Karame, G.O., Liu, Z., Reuter, C.A.: Outsourced proofs of retrievability. In: Proceedings of CCS. ACM, pp. 831–843 (2014)
13. Zhang, Y., Lin, X., Xu, C.: Blockchain-based secure data provenance for cloud storage. In: Proceedings of ICICS, pp. 3–19 (2018)
14. Katz, J., Lindell, Y.: Introduction to modern cryptography. Chapman and Hall/CRC (2014)
15. Nakamoto, S.: Bitcoin: A peer-to-peer electronic cash system. Technical Report, Manubot (2019)
16. Swan, M.: Blockchain: Blueprint for a new economy. OReilly Media Inc. (2015)
17. Underwood, S.: Blockchain beyond bitcoin (2016)
18. Wood, G.: Ethereum: a secure decentralised generalised transaction ledger. Ethereum Project Yellow Paper **151**(2014), 1–32 (2014)
19. Gencer, A.E., Basu, S., Eyal, I., van Renesse, R., Sirer, E.G.: Decentralization in bitcoin and ethereum networks. In: Meiklejohn, S., Sako, K. (eds.) FC 2018. LNCS, vol. 10957, pp. 439–457. Springer, Heidelberg (2018). https://doi.org/10.1007/978-3-662-58387-6_24
20. Buterin, V.: A next-generation smart contract and decentralized application platform, White Paper, vol. 3, no. 37 (2014)
21. Li, M., Zhu, L., Lin, X.: Efficient and privacy-preserving carpooling using blockchain-assisted vehicular fog computing. IEEE Internet of Things J. **6**(3), 4573–4584 (2018)
22. Li, M., Weng, J., Yang, A., Liu, J.-N., Lin, X.: Towards blockchain-based fair and anonymous ad dissemination in vehicular networks. IEEE Trans. Vehicular Technol. 1–12 (2019) to appear. https://doi.org/10.1109/TVT.2019.2940148
23. Li, M., Weng, J., Yang, A., Lu, W., Zhang, Y., Hou, L., Liu, J.-N., Xiang, Y., Deng, R.H.: Crowdbc: a blockchain-based decentralized framework for crowdsourcing. IEEE Trans. Parallel Distrib. Syst. **30**(6), 1251–1266 (2018)
24. Rizzo, L.: Effective erasure codes for reliable computer communication protocols. ACM SIGCOMM Comput. Commun. Rev. **27**(2), 24–36 (1997)
25. Yuan, H., Chen, X., Wang, J., Yuan, J., Yan, H., Susilo, W.: Blockchain-based public auditing and secure deduplication with fair arbitration. Inf. Sci. 1–36 (2020), to appear. https://doi.org/10.1016/j.ins.2020.07.005

26. Xu, Y., Ren, J., Zhang, Y., Zhang, C., Shen, B., Zhang, Y.: Blockchain empowered arbitrable data auditing scheme for network storage as a service. IEEE Trans. Services Comput. **13**(2), 289–300 (2019)
27. Staffie: How can we verify bgls aggregate signatures in solidity (2018). https://ethereum.stackexchange.com/questions/51421/how-can-we-verify-bgls-aggregate-signatures-in-solidity
28. https://gist.github.com/BjornvdLaan/ca6dd4e3993e1ef392f363ec27fe74c4

E-SGX: Effective Cache Side-Channel Protection for Intel SGX on Untrusted OS

Fan Lang[1,3], Huorong Li[4], Wei Wang[1,3(✉)], Jingqiang Lin[2,3], Fengwei Zhang[5], Wuqiong Pan[6], and Qiongxiao Wang[1,3]

[1] State Key Laboratory of Information Security, Institute of Information Engineering, Chinese Academy of Sciences, Beijing 100089, China
wangwei@iie.ac.cn

[2] School of Cyber Security, University of Science and Technology of China, Hefei 230027, Anhui, China

[3] School of Cyber Security, University of Chinese Academy of Sciences, Beijing 100089, China

[4] Alibaba Group, Hangzhou, China

[5] SUSTech, Shenzhen, China

[6] Ant Financial Services Group, Hangzhou, China

Abstract. Cache side-channels are among the major weaknesses of Intel SGX. We mitigate this weakness with E-SGX, an effective defensive approach against all known access-driven/trace-driven cache side-channel attacks from privileged code. The core idea of E-SGX is to monopolize the whole CPU during security-critical executions, breaking the concurrent execution condition of access-driven/trace-driven cache side-channel attacks. To achieve this, E-SGX employs several SGX threads within the same enclave: one application thread and a few dummy threads together hold all CPU cores. A key challenge is to ensure all those enclave threads are scheduled exclusively to occupy all CPU cores with an untrusted OS scheduler. E-SGX addresses this challenge by providing effective mechanisms to detect violations of exclusive scheduling: challenge-response check of dummy threads aliveness and detection of asynchronous enclave exits, both performed with a carefully selected period. Comparing to existing approaches, E-SGX is capable of defending against access-driven/trace-driven cache side-channel attacks not only from the sibling logical core but from across all physical cores.

Keywords: Software Guard Extension · Side-channel attack · Cryptographic keys

This work was supported by National Cryptography Development Fund (Award No. MMJJ20180221) and National Natural Science Foundation of China (Grant No. 61772518).

Y. Wu and M. Yung (Eds.): Inscrypt 2020, LNCS 12612, pp. 221–243, 2021.
https://doi.org/10.1007/978-3-030-71852-7_15

1 Introduction

Intel Software Guard Extensions (SGX) [6,14,21,29] protect user-level sensitive code and data against modification or disclosure from other processes, the untrusted OS, and even physical attackers. SGX provides applications with trusted execution environments (TEE), called enclaves, whose memory areas are isolated from the OS by hardware. The memory areas used by the enclaves are encrypted using processor-specific keys. SGX distinguishes different enclaves in hardware-level by the code measurement of the enclaves.

While Intel SGX provides isolation at a logical level, physical resources such as caches are still shared by all programs including SGX-protected programs, to support efficient multiplexing of workloads. This enables different forms of side-channel attacks across isolation boundaries. Wenhao Wang *et al.* identify 8 potential attack vectors about side channel including cache, TLB, DRAM modules, etc. [42]. Cache side-channel attacks are worrisome in particular, which has been shown to be a serious threat to the confidentiality of SGX-protected programs in realistic scenarios. Brasser *et al.* extracted 70% of a 2048-bit RSA key with 300 repeated executions by Prime+Probe cache monitoring [8]. Schwarz *et al.* extracted 96% of an RSA private key from a single trace and recovered the full RSA private key in an automated attack from 11 traces within 5 mins [38]. Johannes *et al.* [20] extracted an AES secret key in less than 10 s by Neve and Seifert's elimination method, as well as a cache probing mechanism on Intel PMC. The-state-of-art attacks, Meltdown [26] and Spectre [24], exploit Out-of-Order Execution and Speculative Execution, which are originally designed for performance optimization in modern processors, to extract secrets from vulnerable applications and OS kernel by cache side channels. SGX enclaves are also vulnerable to Meltdown [9] and Spectre [12]. After Meltdown and Spectre, a series of Microarchitectural Data Sampling (MDS) attacks appeared [10,36,37]. They can leak information through microarchitectural buffers and also extract secrets by cache side-channels. The latest research shows that MDS attacks are also effective against SGX [2,35].

Two necessary requirements to perform access-driven/trace-driven cache side-channel attacks are: (1) the adversarial code executes concurrently with the victim code; and (2) the adversarial code shares caches with the victim code. Most of prior countermeasures [13,15,18,25,39–41] to mitigate cache side-channel attacks are targeted at breaking the cache sharing condition. Some try to prevent adversarial observation of shared caches using Hardware Transaction Memory (e.g., Intel TSX [33]), which ensures no cache within a transaction can be observed by other threads without being detected [13,18,40]. Some try to make it more difficult or even impossible for an attacker to locate shared caches by randomizing the address space layout or control flow of victim programs [7,15,17,25,34,39]. Some try to totally eliminate cache sharing by disabling caching of critical memory [41] and disabling Hyper-Threading [28]. There are also some solutions trying to prevent the adversarial code from executing concurrently with the victim code [11,31]. A major approach is occupying the sibling logical core of the main thread with a dummy thread, and ensuring that no adversarial code could take its place.

However, they can only defeat attacks launched from the sibling logical core, since they rely on cache access time measurement to detect dummy thread anomalies. In fact, there have been attacks from different physical cores against SGC. At present, neither the *VERW* instruction issued by Intel nor the above-mentioned defense schemes can effectively mitigate these attacks.

In this paper, we propose E-SGX (enhanced SGX), a defensive approach against various known access-driven/trace-driven cache side-channel attacks from privileged code, including OS kernel and hypervisor. At its core, our approach monopolizes the whole CPU during the execution of security-critical operations. Unlike the above mentioned schemes which can only prevent attacks from the sibling logical core, E-SGX prevents concurrent execution of adversarial code from any physical cores, which breaks the concurrent execution condition of access-driven/trace-driven cache side-channel attacks thoroughly. To achieve this, E-SGX employs two types of SGX threads within the same enclave: a main thread and a few dummy threads. The main thread runs on a logical CPU core to realize the application functionality, so we also call it the *computing thread* in the remainder. On each of the other logical CPU cores, whether within the same physical core or not, runs a dummy thread. The computing thread and the dummy threads together hold all the CPU cores. E-SGX requests exclusive scheduling for all these enclave threads during the execution. Only if all dummy threads are scheduled on different logical CPU cores exclusively and running properly, which implies the prerequisites for attacks are never met, the computing thread will continue the execution.

A significant challenge is to ensure these enclave threads occupy all the logical CPU cores reliably, especially with an untrusted or even malicious OS scheduler. As E-SGX relies on the OS scheduler for exclusive scheduling, a malicious OS scheduler might fool the computing thread into believing that all dummy threads are running properly, and tempt it to continue the execution. E-SGX addresses this challenge by providing a mechanism to detect all violations of exclusive scheduling. We develop a different approach from that of cache access time measurement [11,31], to empower E-SGX with the ability to detect attacks from all CPU cores. The mechanism works as follows. First, the computing thread periodically challenges the dummy threads to check if they are running properly, at a frequency higher than the time it takes for an unexpected enclave exit, i.e., an Asynchronous Enclave Exit (AEX). Then, upon receiving positive responses from the dummy threads, the computing thread detects whether an AEX has occurred due to interruptions. All challenge and response messages are protected by SGX. Note that adversarial cache side-channel attack code has to interrupt at least one enclave thread to have a chance to execute. An attack may have occurred if the computing thread hasn't received timely responses from the dummy threads or has detected an AEX. The computing thread addresses such an alarm according to application-specific policies, for example, self-terminating the execution.

We implement E-SGX based on the Intel Linux SGX SDK [5]. At present, all known cache side-channel attacks [19,27,32,43] need to execute concurrently with the victim program. The experimental results show that those cache side-channel attacks are detected by E-SGX at a very early stage when they try to interrupt any of the dummy threads or the computing thread, which is a necessary condition for the attacks to continue. This is achieved by selecting an appropriate detection period so that the adversary cannot afford to launch an attack without being detected by two consecutive detection acts.

Additionally, we have evaluated the performance of E-SGX in mbed TLS (formerly known as PolarSSL) [3] and Nginx web server [4] on Intel NUC6 with a 4-core i3-6100U processor. The experimental results show that, (1) it takes twice the original time for cryptographic routines of mbed TLS to proceed with E-SGX, and (2) E-SGX brings moderate overheads to the Nginx web server while such overheads decrease as the number of concurrent requests increases. As such, we can conclude that E-SGX can defend against all access-driven cache side-channel attacks at the cost of performance. It is favorable for programs that are not computation-intensive while requiring strong security, like authentication modules at client side, typically.

Contributions. In summary, our main contributions are:

- We propose E-SGX, an approach that can mitigate all known access-driven/trace-driven cache side-channel attacks against Intel SGX without trusting system software (i.e., OS or hypervisor).
- We propose an idea of using AEX time as the response threshold to determine whether an SGX thread located in any core is online, which can defend against side-channel attacks in the shared LLC .
- We have implemented a prototype of E-SGX on an SGX-enabled physical machine and evaluated its effectiveness and performance against mainstream benchmarks including mbed TLS and Nginx.

2 Preliminaries and Related Work

2.1 Intel Software Guard Extensions

Intel SGX protects user-level sensitive code and data against modification or disclosure from other processes, the untrusted OS, and even physical attackers. To achieve this, SGX provides applications with trusted execution environments, called enclaves, which are isolated from the OS by CPU hardware, and encrypts the memory areas used by the enclaves using processor-specific keys. Intel SGX identifies enclaves and distinguishes different enclaves in hardware-level by their measurements, which is the hash of an enclave's contents. Enclaves with different measurements are considered as totally different and are isolated from each other.

The execution of an enclave may be interrupted by certain events, such as interruptions. Such events cause control to transition to an address outside the enclave. SGX will exit the enclave before invoking the event handler. The process of leaving an enclave is called an Asynchronous Enclave Exit (AEX). To protect the secrecy of the enclave, an AEX automatically saves the state of certain general-purpose registers as well as the exit reason of the AEX to *GPRSGX* region of the State Save Area (SSA) of a Thread Control Structure (TCS) [22], which is a thread local storage within enclave memory.

2.2 Cache Side-Channel Attacks

Cache Side-Channel Attacks on SGX Enclaves. Cache side-channel attacks are the main threats to SGX-protected applications. Although cache side-channel attackers, privileged or unprivileged, cannot access the memory inside an enclave, they may generate frequent interruptions to interrupt the execution of the enclave and leverage such frequent interruptions to set up fine-grained cache side-channel attacks, for example, Prime+Probe attacks, on L1 cache to extract secret keys. For an unprivileged attacker, he can exploit the vulnerabilities of the underlying OS or hypervisor to generate interruptions. For a privileged attacker who can control the scheduling of processor resources, he can generate even more frequent interruptions simply by programming hardware interrupt controllers (e.g., the Advanced Programmable Interrupt Controller (APIC)). As such, he can preempt and intercept the control flows of the enclave's execution in manipulable ways at a high frequency. Additionally, a privileged attacker can reduce the background noise which are key obstacles in unprivileged cache side-channel attacks. The privileged attacker can achieve this by, e.g., pinning the attack process to a dedicated CPU core and disabling the preemption on that core to make sure no other processes are scheduled on it.

Brasser *et al.* and Schwarz *et al.* Leaked key information from enclave. Both achieved it through prime + probe cache side-channel attack. Some recent researches such as Foreshadow [9] and SGAxe [35], they steal the secret information inside the enclave by transient instructions, and finally leak the secret through the cache side-channels.

Cache Side-Channel Attacks Across Physical Cores. In recent years, in addition to cache side-channel attacks from the sibling logical core, attacks from the non-sibling logical cores have also appeared. It is mainly aimed at some internal buffers shared by multiple physical cores, such as LLC, staging buffers, etc. Because of the more complex structure and more noise, side-channel attacks from the non-sibling logical cores are very difficult to implement in the Intel SGX environment.

Recently, there have been much research on side-channel attacks against LLC. Liu *et al.* [27], Disselkoen *et al.* [16] and Craig Disselkoen *et al.* [16] each designed an LLC based cache side-channel attacks to extract key information. Unfortunately, SGX can not protect against this type of attack. Moghimi *et al.* [30] proposed an attack named CacheZoom which is able to virtually track all memory accesses of SGX enclaves. The CacheZoom was implemented in L1 cache,however it can be as well implemented in LLC.

In addition to attacks against LLC, the latest attack named CrossTalk [2] uses staging buffers readable by all CPU cores to perform transient execution attacks in all cores and extract the ECDSA key of the entire secure enclave running on the independent CPU core via cache side-channel. Crosstalk is an kind of MDS attack, which exploit staging buffers shared by all cores to launch attacks from the non-sibling logical cores.

2.3 Defense Against Cache Side-Channel

Shih *et al.* proposed a solution, called T-SGX [40], works by compiling the enclave application into a collection of TSX transactions. By handling page faults within the transaction abort handler first before trapping into the kernel, T-SGX can suppress the notification of errors to the underlying OS, which means that the OS cannot know whether a page fault has occurred during the transaction, and thus thereby completely eradicates the known controlled-channel attack. A similar solution is Cloak [18]. Cloak deterministically preloads all sensitive code and data into the caches at the beginning of a transaction and instruments HTM to prevent any cache misses on the code and data. This way, Cloak prevents adversarial observation of cache misses on sensitive code and data, and provides strong protection against all known cache-based side-channel attacks. However, both Cloak and T-SGX may require keeping all sensitive code and data in cache during the transaction, incurring large write and read sets. Such large write and read sets will tend to incur frequent transaction aborts.

Tromer *et al.* suggested disable caching of critical memory, which can totally eliminate cache sharing [41]. This is an attractive approach to prevent cache side-channel attacks since modern processors support selectively disabling page caching. However, it is inapplicable for SGX-protected programs, in that: (1) SGX logic relies on caching and (2) disabling caching on other cores relies on the OS, which is untrusted under SGX threat model, and SGX-protected programs cannot verify whether caching has been disabled.

Closely related to our solution is the research by Chen *et al.*. Their solution, called Déjà Vu [13], works by building into enclave execution the ability to check application program execution time at the granularity of paths in its control-flow graph. It implements a software reference clock that is protected by Intel TSX to provide the enclave execution a trustworthy source of time measurement. By requesting the reference clock thread, a computing thread within the enclave can detect privileged side-channel attacks by observing the timing difference of the execution with or without AEXs. Chen *et al.* presented HYPERRACE, an LLVM-based tool for instrumenting SGX enclave programs to eradicate all side-channel threats due to Hyper-Threading [11]. They created a shadow thread for each enclave thread, asked the underlying untrusted OS to schedule both threads on the same physical core, and verified that the communication between the threads using a shared variable inside the enclave did take place in the shared L1 data cache, which indicated that the OS had scheduled the threads as expected. Oleksii Oleksenko et al. also take advantage of the cache access time to defend against cache side-channel attacks by occupying sibling threads [31]. However, they are weak in defending against side-channel attacks from different physical cores. In this paper we address this problem in the design of E-SGX.

3 Threat Model

We consider access-driven/trace-driven cache side-channel attacks against the execution of security-critical operations in SGX enclaves. By security-critical operations, we refer to the operations performing on cryptographic keys, for example, RSA private key operations (i.e., signing and decrypting operations), which are typically short-lived.

The goal of an attacker is to capture cryptographic keys from SGX enclaves. The attacker can reveal secrets in turn. To serve this purpose, the attacker is assumed to have full control over the OS, capable of generating interruptions to preempt the execution of SGX enclaves, and tracing their control flow or data flow at a cache line granularity. The attacker can block, delay, replay, read, and modify all messages outside enclaves while the direct inspection of enclave memory is prohibited by SGX. The attacker cannot break through CPU and compromise SGX enclaves from inside. Especially, the attacker has no access to processor-specific keys.

We assume that the untrusted OS is willing to provide an execution environment as well as enough continuous time to the SGX enclave that is exclusively scheduled. Violation of this requirement will result in self-termination of SGX enclave execution (assuming the program is configured with policies to do so), which leads to denial-of-service (DoS). The detection of such violations uses the methods we propose in this paper. Especially, the untrusted OS restarting the enclave abnormally, e.g., frequently restarting the execution, is also considered as a violation of the requirement. This can be mitigated by introducing a remote party to monitor the start of the enclave, in a way that the enclave requests a token from the remote party to get run, so that the execution can be forbidden by refusing to send the token if the enclave is detected being restarted abnormally. In this paper, we do not focus on mitigating such restarting attacks. DoS attacks are also out of the scope of this paper, as a malicious OS can easily do so by not scheduling SGX enclave execution.

4 E-SGX Design

4.1 Architecture

The architecture of E-SGX is illustrated in Fig. 1. The security-critical operations that run inside the SGX enclave are contained in a computing thread, which is accompanied by several dummy threads within the same enclave. The total number of the computing thread and the dummy threads equals that of the logical CPU cores. Both the computing thread and dummy threads are scheduled on different logical CPU cores exclusively by the untrusted OS. The untrusted OS failing to do so will cause these threads to go offline or suffer interruptions.

The computing thread preloads all the code and data required by security-critical operations into memory at the very beginning in case of page-faults during the execution. Before starting a security-critical operation, the computing thread resets memory and cache that will be used. After that, the computing

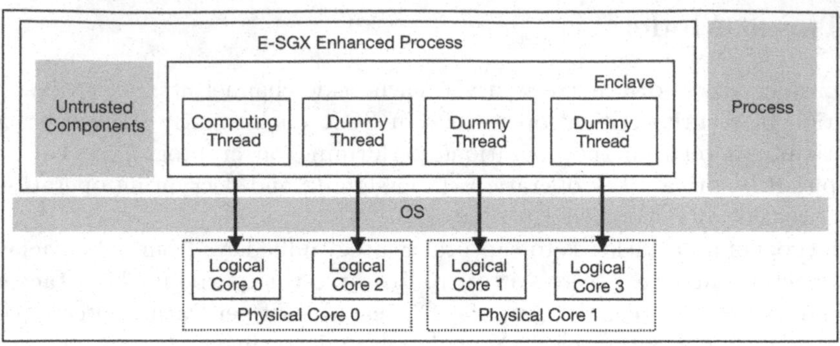

Fig. 1. The architecture of E-SGX. Blocks in gray are untrusted, which include the untrusted components of the processes and the entire OS kernel.

thread challenges the dummy threads to check if they are running properly and waits for the responses, at a frequency higher than the time it takes for an AEX (see detailed explanation in Sect. 4.4). Upon receiving the challenge from the computing thread, each dummy thread syncs its latest running state immediately in response if it holds a core and is running properly. If a dummy thread is offline due to being not scheduled on core or being interrupted, it cannot respond in time. The computing thread checks the timeliness of the responses from the dummy threads and detects whether an AEX has occurred. Only if all the responses are in time and no AEX is detected, the computing thread will continue executing the security-critical operation. Otherwise, it will self-terminate the execution. At the end of the execution, the computing thread again resets the memory and cache used during the execution.

Both challenge and response messages are transferred through a trusted communication channel protected by SGX, which cannot be manipulated by the OS without being noticed.

4.2 Enable Trusted Communication Among Enclave Threads

To protect the challenge-response messages transferred among enclave threads from being modified or forged, it is necessary to construct a trusted communication channel. A straightforward and efficient solution is to use enclave global variables shared by all enclave threads to securely deliver the messages. The enclave global variables act as a billboard to store the challenges and responses, whose values are compared by the computing thread to verify the timeliness of the responses. The above approach can benefit from the features provided by SGX, in that all memory within the enclave is protected and cannot be manipulated by even privileged attackers without being noticed. But a key problem of such a solution is that, writing operations on the shared global variables are simultaneous because in E-SGX all enclave threads are running in parallel. Such simultaneous writing may cause frequent cache access conflicts, making the global variables inconsistent in different enclave threads.

We improve this solution by skillfully configuring the shared global variables with additional access policies. E-SGX defines different shared global variables for the computing thread and the dummy threads, which are denoted by *Challenge* and *State[i]* respectively. *Challenge* is for the computing thread to keep the latest challenge message, while *State[i]* is for the i-th dummy thread to keep its response message. We make both *Challenge* and *State[i]* meet the following requirements:

- Both *Challenge* and *State[i]* are located at different cache lines and are readable for all enclave threads.
- *Challenge* can only be written by the computing thread while *State[i]* can only be written by the i-th dummy thread.

These requirements eliminate cache conflicts when writing global variables, making sure that (1) there is no simultaneous writing to the same global variables; and (2) each enclave thread can only write its own global variable. We have verified that message transfer among enclave threads using this improved solution is very efficient, more than one order of magnitude faster than that using thread locks.

4.3 Attack Detection

In E-SGX, all logical CPU cores are held by enclave threads and thus adversarial code has to interrupt at least one enclave thread to get a chance to run. Such context switches will induce AEXs and make the enclave thread go offline. Specifically, if the interrupted thread is a dummy thread, it will go offline and fail to respond to the challenge in time; if the interrupted thread is the computing thread, it will detect an AEX after being resumed from the interruption. Both of those circumstances can be detected by the computing thread, i.e., the computing thread can detect such an interruption. The computing thread performs attack detection periodically by checking running states of the dummy threads and detecting AEXs in sequence during security-critical operations. Figure 2 shows the state transition diagram of attack detection. The details of the two detection mechanisms are as follow.

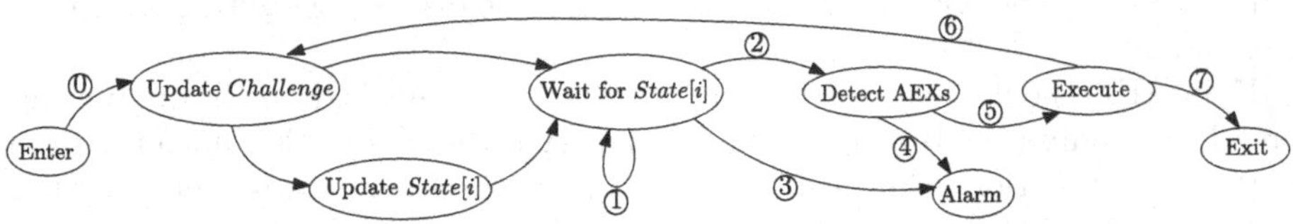

Fig. 2. Attack detection state transition diagram. ⓪ Initiate environment – reset internal memory; ① Not all $State[i]$ are updated; ② All $State[i]$ are updated in time; ③ Time out; ④ AEXs are detected; ⑤ No AEX is detected; ⑥ Time is up and execution is not finished – perform the periodic detection again; ⑦ Execution is finished – reset internal memory.

Checking Dummy Threads Aliveness. The purpose of checking the running states of the dummy threads is to ensure that all dummy threads are scheduled on different logical CPU cores exclusively by the untrusted or even malicious OS and are running properly, or in another word, *alive*. To achieve this, E-SGX enables the computing thread to challenge all dummy threads using one-time messages and check the responses. If a dummy thread cannot respond to the challenge in time due to, for example, being not scheduled or being interrupted, it is considered being offline.

As shown in Fig. 2, at the beginning of a new detection period, the computing thread generates a one-time message randomly as a new challenge, writes it to *Challenge* as an update, and uses the updated *Challenge* to check the dummy threads. After that, the computing thread waits for the update of all *State[i]* of the dummy threads until all of them have been updated to the new *Challenge* or time out. In the meanwhile, the i-th dummy thread continually reads *Challenge* and uses the fetched value to update its *State[i]* immediately. *State[i]* will be updated to the latest *Challenge* immediately if the i-th dummy thread is running properly on a logical CPU core. If all *State[i]* have been updated to the new *Challenge* in time, which indicates all the dummy threads still hold those logical CPU cores exclusively and are running properly, the computing thread performs an AEX detection; otherwise, namely a timeout occurs, the computing thread will know that the i-th dummy thread is offline possibly due to, for example, being interrupted by adversarial code, and will abort the execution and raise an alarm.

Detecting AEXs. After checking all dummy threads, the computing thread performs an AEX detection to make sure that it itself has not been interrupted. E-SGX enables the computing thread to do so by providing it an interface inside the enclave to check the exit reasons of AEXs. As described by Intel in [22], the processor automatically saves the exit reasons of AEXs to *SSA.GPRSGX.EXITINFO*, located within enclave thread local area. *VECTOR* and *EXIT_TYPE* fields of *EXITINFO* keep the number and type of exception reported inside an enclave. The interface determines whether an AEX has occurred by checking the two fields and returns a boolean result to the computing thread. Note that E-SGX only concerns about the occurrence of an AEX rather than what the exact exit reasons are, so it makes no difference whether a malicious OS overwrites the exit reasons by means like triggering arbitrary interrupts.

If no AEX is detected, which means no attack is launched on the computing thread, the computing thread continues security-critical execution until the time is up or the execution is finished, as shown in Fig. 2. Otherwise, namely an AEX is detected, the computing thread will abort the execution and raise an alarm.

4.4 Detection Period Selection

The computing thread performs attack detection periodically during the execution of security-critical operations. We denote the detection period as T. T has an influence on the security of E-SGX. For example, if T is longer than the time it takes for an entire security-critical operation, the computing thread will perform attack detection only once during the entire security-critical operation, which is only nominal. To guarantee the effectiveness of attack detection, T should be no longer than the time it takes for an AEX (briefly called an AEX duration). In fact, the time it takes for the adversary to successfully launch an attack won't be less than an AEX duration, as he must interrupt an enclave thread to kick-start an attack, which will always incur an AEX.

If T is longer than an AEX duration, the adversary will be able to launch a cache side-channel attack without being detected. For example, the adversarial code interrupts a dummy thread and resumes it before the computing thread times out waiting for the response. In this example, the computing thread has no awareness that a dummy thread had been interrupted. It is considered more secure to adopt a smaller T since it brings more intensive attack detection.

On the other hand, T also has an influence on the performance of E-SGX. To demonstrate more clearly how T affects the performance of E-SGX, we divide a complete detection period into different time parts. The time spent on security-critical operations is denoted by t, and the time spent on attack detection is denoted by t_0. Both t and t_0 are measured in clock cycles. We use the time utilization ratio (denoted as r), i.e., the ratio of t in a complete detection period, as an indicator of the performance. r can be approximated by:

$$r = \frac{t}{T} = \frac{T - t_0}{T} = 1 - \frac{t_0}{T}$$

where t_0 is almost constant. This is reasonable since for a given slice of code, e.g., the implementation of attack detection including checking dummy threads aliveness and detecting AEXs, its execution time in clock cycles is independent of processor speeds. It can be proved that r is monotonically increasing at T, i.e., and a larger r indicates higher performance. For a very small T, the execution may spend most of the time on attack detection, leading to a significant decline in the performance of security-critical operations. Thus, it is not recommended to make T too small.

E-SGX allows applications to specify their own detection period. Setting T to a relatively small value can allow for early-state attack detection and more adequate reaction time. However, it is preferable to set the detection period to an AEX duration.

4.5 Attack Reaction

When an alarm is raised, which indicates that an attack has possibly occurred, the computing thread addresses such an alarm according to application-specific policies. E-SGX allows users to specify application-specific policies. This is preferable since it is unlikely that there is a single best policy for all detected attacks across a wide variety of applications. For applications that require strong security, such as online banking, they can specify strict policies, for example, self-terminating the execution and refresh cryptographic keys. For applications that are not sensitive to security, they can adopt moderate policies, for example, ignoring a few suspect alarms. Such moderate policies make E-SGX tolerant to some AEXs triggered by Non-Maskable Interrupts. Also, moderate policies enable the applications to process huge sensitive data without incurring page faults. Our focus is on providing reliable detection of AEXs during the execution of security-critical operations rather than the specific policies for different applications.

5 Security Analysis

By performing access-driven/trace-driven cache side-channel attacks, attackers aim to extract cryptographic keys from enclaves by measuring the timing differences between cache hits and misses to collect cache access-patterns. Recall that the attackers are prohibited by SGX from directly inspecting enclave memory nor can the attackers break processor package. The attackers can be either privileged or unprivileged. They can set up fine-grained attacks by frequently interrupting one or more enclave threads and preempting the execution of security-critical operations. If the attackers are privileged, they can trigger even more frequent interrupts, for example, one interrupt per instruction, by programming hardware interrupt controllers (e.g., APIC) to do so. Nevertheless, all these interrupts will incur AEXs.

We analyze the security of E-SGX from two aspects: (1) attacks on the computing thread; and (2) attacks on the dummy threads.

5.1 Attacks on Computing Thread

In E-SGX it is the computing thread rather than the dummy threads that performs the security-critical operations, which operates on cryptographic keys. Thus, the attackers have to interrupt the computing thread and then resume it to collect a cache access-pattern by side-channel (recall that to carry out a cache side-channel attack, an attacker has to manipulate cache to be a known state, wait for victim activity, and examine what has changed). When the computing thread is interrupted, an AEX is incurred and the exit reason of the AEX is automatically saved in *SSA.GPRSGX.EXITINFO* by the processor. After being resumed, the computing thread can finally detect the AEX by checking the exit reason. Thus, attacks on the computing thread can be detected.

However, there does exist a vulnerable window before the computing thread detects the AEX. During such a vulnerable window, the attackers can trace the execution of security-critical operations. By programming hardware interrupt controllers, the attackers can even interrupt the computing thread per instruction, maximizing the traces they can get in the vulnerable window. Note that the size of the vulnerable window is not larger than one detection period since the AEX will finally be detected within one detection period.

Cache side-channel attackers extract cryptographic keys by observing the access-patterns of the keys. In E-SGX, by launching an attack, the number of

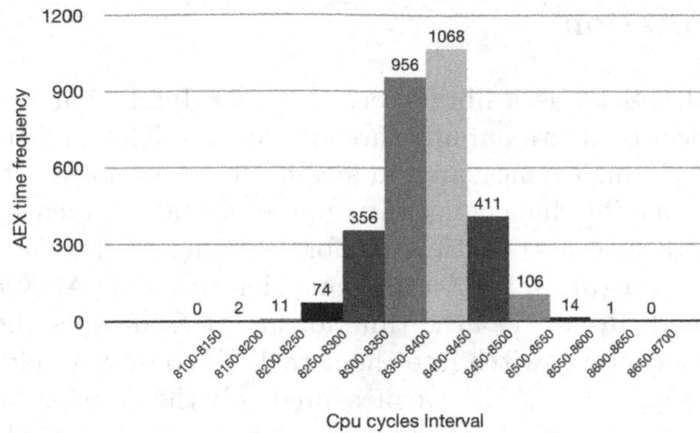

Fig. 3. The distribution of AEX duration occurs once.

bits of a key that the attackers can observe within the vulnerable window is very limited. For example, less than 4 bits of an RSA private key can be observed in the vulnerable window, since RSA employs one Montgomery multiplication operation [23] to process every bit of the private key and there are less than 4 Montgomery multiplication operations can be proceeded in an AEX duration (an AEX costs at least 8150 cycles while one Montgomery multiplication operation costs 2314 cycles in our platform, as shown below). Note that the attackers successfully observing access-patterns of the key does not mean that they can extract the keys correctly.

An application can set the detection period to a small value and thus allow for more frequent attack detection, to shrink the vulnerable window and restrain the attack effect of the adversary. More importantly, the risk of key leakage can be eliminated by adopting strict application-specific attack reaction policies, for example, altering the cryptographic key and restarting the security-critical operation when necessary.

5.2 Attacks on Dummy Threads

By interrupting one of the dummy threads, attackers would have a chance to execute in parallel with the computing thread and carry out a cache side-channel attack from a co-located logical CPU core. The interrupted dummy thread will be offline and unable to update its *State[i]* in time, resulting in the computing thread time out waiting for the response when challenging the interrupted dummy thread. Thus, by challenging the dummy threads, the computing thread can detect attacks on the dummy threads. Interrupting a dummy thread takes an AEX duration, during which the computing thread will time out waiting for the response. Thus, there is no vulnerable window for this scenario.

6 Implementation

We implemented E-SGX as a library based on the Intel Linux SGX SDK [5], providing interfaces to create dummy threads, detect AEXs, and specify policies in respond to an alarm. We measured in advance three important time values of E-SGX: (1) the time for challenging the dummy threads, which was 456 cycles on average (no attack occurs) (2) the time for detecting AEXs, which was several dozens of cycles; and (3) an AEX duration. Measuring an AEX duration was a little complicated. Recall that the time for an AEX includes the time for an enclave exit and a context switch into the kernel. To conservatively estimate the minimum time needed by an AEX, we measured only the time for an enclave exit, which could be approximated to the time spent in an empty OCall. Because the AEX duration directly determines the value of the E-SGX detection period, so we repeatedly measured the AEX duration 3000 times and recorded its distribution. As shown in Fig. 3, the AEX duration is 8404 cycles on average and the minimum is 8150 cycles. To ensure that the E-SGX detection mechanism can be triggered at any time, the detection cycle length should be shorter than the AEX duration. So we set the detection period to 8100 cycles. As we all know that the time in clock cycles it takes for a given slice of code is independent of processor speeds. As such, we pre-measured all the three-time values of E-SGX in non-enclave mode, leveraging the *rdtscp* instruction.

The E-SGX detection phase is mainly divided into two steps. The first step is the detection of the dummy threads. As shown in Listing 1.1 in appendix A, each dummy thread has a *State[i]* to store the *Challenge*, which is assigned by the computing thread. Especially, the size of the *State[i]* is aligned to the cache line size, which can effectively avoid cache line read and write conflicts. In addition, we closed the compiler optimization fo each dummy thread' *State[i]*, which prevents reading errors during periodic detection due to cache content not being updated in time. The second step is to detect whether an AEX has occurred in the computing thread. As shown in Listing 1.2 in Appendix A, we modified the SGXSDK to make the judgment according to the state of SSA.GPRSGX.EXITINFO. And then the SGXAPI and detection of the dummy thread will be called by the computing thread, as shown in Listing 1.3 in Appendix A.

We employed the OS to schedule all E-SGX enclave threads in a **SCHED_FIFO** way (First-in-first-out scheduling) with the highest priority. A **SCHED_FIFO** thread runs until either it is blocked by an I/O request, it is preempted by a higher priority thread, or it calls *sched_yield* to relinquish the processor. Scheduling in **SCHED_FIFO** with the highest priority ensures that E-SGX threads are first scheduled and probably not preempted by other processes, making E-SGX more practical. If **SCHED_FIFO** E-SGX threads are preempted, E-SGX resets the environment and tries again.

7 Evaluation

7.1 Experiment Setup

Our experiments were conducted on an Intel NUC6 with an SGX-enabled i3-6100U processor and 8GB DRAM. The processor was designed for low power (15W) usage and had 4 logical cores (denoted by core 0, core 1, core 2, core 3, respectively), whose maximum frequency is 2.3 GHz. The size of EPC was 128 MB. The operating system was Ubuntu 16.04 with Linux kernel version 4.13.0. Connections to the Intel NUC6 were via the local area network (`ping` about 0.55 ms). We used GCC 5.4.0 to compile the source code including the Linux SGX SDK.

7.2 Security Evaluation

We considered all known access-driven/trace-driven cache side-channel attacks, both of which incurred interruptions, and evaluated the security of E-SGX from three aspects: (1) we validated that E-SGX could detect such interruptions on any one of the enclave threads; (2) we measured the size of the vulnerable window before the computing thread detected such interrupts and showed that it was very limited, less than a detection period; and (3) we validated that manipulated CPU speeds did not break (1) and (2).

To make such evaluations intuitive, we applied E-SGX to protect a carefully designed program. This program did nothing but count from a predefined valuc N to zero in the computing thread. N was large enough, e.g., 10^5, so that it took multiple detection periods to count from N to zero. We pre-measured the time in clock cycles for the computing thread to count from N to zero. The computing thread would exit the execution if counting was finished or an interruption was detected. To make it simple and intuitive, the counter was located outside enclave in purpose, so that we could directly observe it even if the computing thread terminated itself. We instrumented the OS kernel to trigger interrupts to preempt one of the dummy threads and the computing thread respectively, executed adversarial code and observed the final counter value as well as the execution time for the computing thread.

Validating Interrupt Detection. Under E-SGX protection, to launch a cache side-channel attack, whether using flush+reload or other cache side-channel attack means, the attacker needs to interrupt at least one thread. In such a carefully designed program, we could verify whether E-SGX had detected interrupts by checking the counter value: if the value of the counter is greater than zero, it indicates that E-SGX has detected the interrupts and terminated itself. Note that the interrupts can be caused by either event: (1) the dummy threads being hung up; (2) an AEX happens to the computing thread. To test the first case, we hung up a dummy thread 10^6 times, and the interrupts are detected correctly every time. To test the second case, we deliberately induce an AEX 10^6 times and the interrupts are also detected every time.

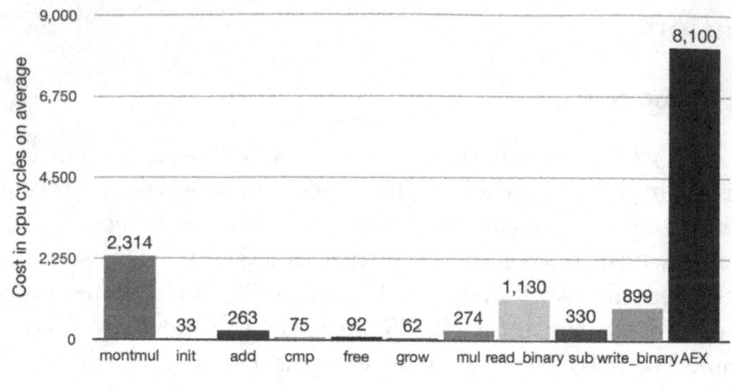

Fig. 4. lower-level functions CPU costs (in cycles).

Measuring Vulnerable Window Size. To measure the vulnerable window size, we enabled adversarial code to record the counter value immediately when it interrupted an enclave thread and executed itself. We measured the difference between the recorded counter value and the final counter value as an indicator of the vulnerable window size. The results showed that for all the tests, the difference between the two counter values was less than 1540. Note that it took about 4 cycles for each decrement. As such, the vulnerable window size was less than 6160 cycles, less than a detection period, 8100 cycles (less than an AEX duration). So any attack launched during the vulnerable window will surely be detected afterwards.

Manipulated CPU Speeds. To verify whether manipulated CPU speeds have an impact on E-SGX, we scaled down the operating frequency of the logical CPU core [1], where the computing thread ran on, from the maximum 2.3 GHz to the minimum 800 MHz on our platform, and then repeated above tests. The results were the same. This is as expected, since all times are measured in CPU clock cycles, and for the same code, the time in clock cycles it takes to execute is independent of processor speeds though the time in seconds does depend. As such, an advanced attacker cannot benefit from manipulating processor speeds in E-SGX.

7.3 Performance Evaluation

To verify the practicability of E-SGX, we mainly carried out two sets of experiments. First, we use E-SGX to protect the digital signature algorithm in mbed TLS [3]. And then we use ngnix [4] to transfer openssl as a third-party library, which runs in an E-SGX scene. So we measured the running cycles of some frequently called lower-level functions in mbed TLS RSA signature implementation and openssl RSA encryption implementation. As shown in Fig. 4, the most time-consuming operation is the Montgomery operation that costs 2314 cycles, which is one third of an AEX duration. And other operations are much shorter than an AEX duration.

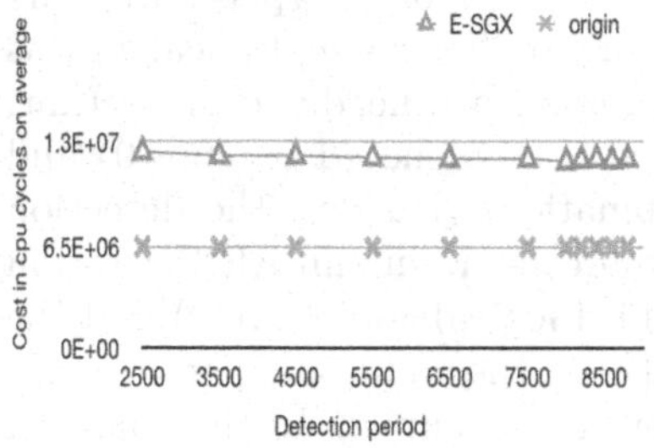

(a) The number of CPU clock cycles spent on the RSA private key operation in the original model and the E-SGX modely.

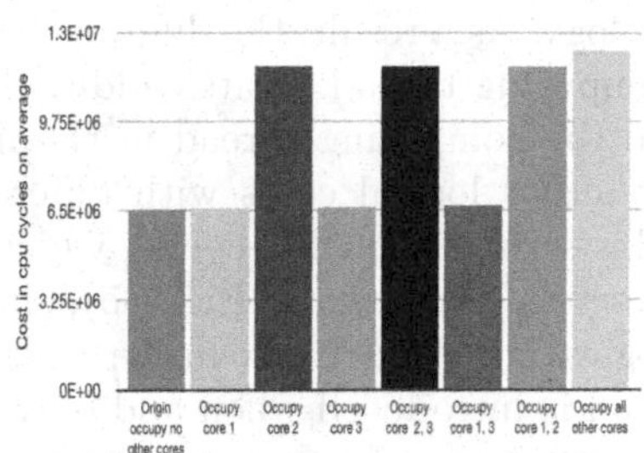

(b) Performance overhead when occupying different logical cores with dummy threads.

Fig. 5. mbed TLS library

Performance in mbed TLS. We applied E-SGX to protect RSA private key operations in mbed TLS. We consider that to capture long-term cryptographic keys, typically private keys (e.g., RSA private key) is the primary goal of an attacker, since capturing temporary symmetric keys (e.g., AES key) or actual secrets are useful for only one session while acquiring long-term private keys grants full access.

Private key operations, i.e., signing and decrypting, were done by calling *rsa_private* in mbed TLS. *rsa_private* consisted of a series of lower-level functions, such as *mpi_add_mpi*, *mpi_mul_mpi*, *mpi_montmul* (Montgomery multiplication [23]), etc. We indexed those lower-level functions and pre-measured the time in clock cycles for each of them (noted as t_i for lower-level function i, e.g., t_3 for *mpi_montmul* was 2314 cycles). We dynamically maintained the remaining available time (noted as t_r) to execute. In each detection period, t_r was initiated to $T - t_0$. If t_r was larger than t_i, which indicated the remaining time was enough to execute lower-level function i, updated $t_r = t_r - t_i$ and executed lower-level function i; otherwise turned to next period. We measured the average clock cycles for a private key operation with and without E-SGX. The detection period for E-SGX varied from 2500 cycles to 8800 cycles.

E-SGX protected operations cost more time than the original ones. We can learn from Fig. 5(a) that when the detection period is less than 8000 cycles, the time penalty in E-SGX protected operations goes down when the detection period increases. This result is in line with the conclusion in Sect. 4.4 that the performance of E-SGX is monotonically increasing as the detection period grows. While the detection period is larger than 8000 cycles, the change in performance overhead is not obvious, because at this moment the additional performance overhead is mainly caused by the dummy threads. Specifically, the logical cores in a same physical core share the L1/L2 cache, the execution engine and the system bus interface, which means the two logical cores almost evenly share the computing capability of the physical core which supports Hyper-Threading Technology. As a result, the dummy thread running on the same physical core as the computing thread creates additional performance overhead. To prove that, we run the computing thread in the first logical core (denoted by core 0) and occupy other logical cores with different combinations. Besides, the detection period is set to 8100 CPU cycles, which is less than the minimum AEX duration we detected. As shown in Fig. 5(b), since the third logical core (core 2) and the first logical core (core 0) are in the same physical core, the additional performance overhead is introduced when and only when core 2 is occupied. In this manner, turning off Hyper-Threading can be an option for E-SGX users to maintain the original performance of the protected single-threaded operations (i.e., the computing thread), since there will be no dummy thread acting as a resource competitor on the same physical core.

In summary, when we set the detection period to 8100 CPU cycles and turn on Hyper-Threading, compared to the original mbed TLS which takes 6.5084×10^6 CPU cycles to produce an RSA signature, mbed TLS with E-SGX spends 1.2336×10^7 CPU cycles. The performance overhead is 47.24%. And when we turn off Hyper-Threading, mbed TLS with E-SGX only spends 6.6706×10^6 CPU cycles. The performance overhead drops to 2.43%.

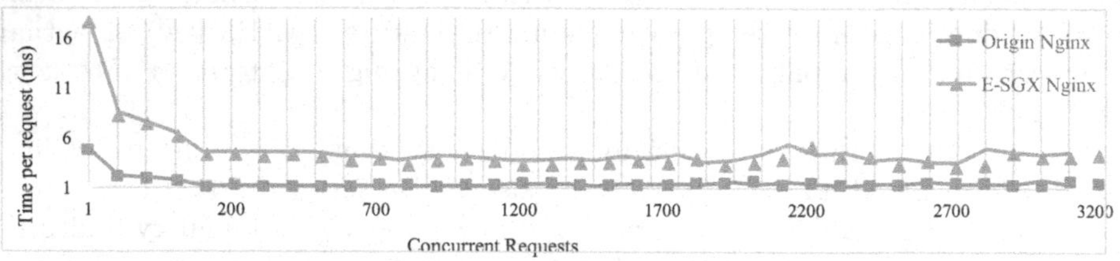

Fig. 6. Nginx calls the original openssl and E-SGX's openssl environment for each https access request time. The number of concurrent requests varies from 1 to 3, 200.

Performance in Nginx. We ported Nginx to support openssl. We created two Nginx web servers with same configurations, hosting default welcome pages—one was running with origin openssl (Origin Nginx) while the other one was running in an E-SGX scene (E-SGX Nginx). We benchmarked the web servers, with the number of concurrent requests varied from 1 to 3200. Before each test, the web servers were restarted to clear out any potential caching or other issues that may interfere with results. All requests to the web servers were through local area network.

First of all, unexpectedly, we can learn from Fig. 6 that E-SGX protected web server can also benefit from concurrency just like the origin one. This is because E-SGX is just one part of the web server and the protected web server can still use all concurrent resources outside E-SGX, though E-SGX monopolizes the whole CPU and wastes resources during security-critical operations. Figure 6 also shows that time per request in E-SGX protected web server is greater than that in the origin one at any concurrent level, especially when the concurrent level is lower than 150. This shows that our E-SGX does induce performance overhead to web server. However, as the concurrency level goes higher, the performance in E-SGX protected web server increases fast and closes to the original one. This is possibly because (1) E-SGX can also benefit from concurrency; and (2) the number of requests that queue up to await increases when the concurrency level goes high, and requests have to spend more time in waiting. As such, the overhead introduced by E-SGX becomes less significant at higher levels of concurrency. As also shown in Fig. 6, both web servers cannot benefit more from concurrency when the level of concurrency is higher than 200, and even gain performance overhead instead.

8 Discussion

Human Effort. The functionalities of E-SGX rely on its attack detection mechanism that is performed periodically, so enhancing an application with E-SGX scheme requires the developer to manually divide the source code into code snippets separated by lines that implement periodic detection. The reform involves CPU cycle measurements of low-level functions of the target application, which is application specific and somewhat time consuming. Though, such reform could be once and for all. Nevertheless, the automatic E-SGX reform of applications can be expected as well.

Security with Overhead. When Hyper-Threading is on, E-SGX introduces an overhead of 47% to the execution of its protection target according to Sect. 7.3, since it affects the shared computation resource by occupying the sibling logical core. However, by carefully selecting and tailoring the code area that is protected by E-SGX, we can minimize the impact on system performance, which also conforms to the design philosophy of Intel SGX. Nevertheless, as stated in Sect. 1, E-SGX is most favorable for programs that are not computation-intensive while requiring strong security, like authentication modules at client side, typically.

Single-threaded vs. Multiple-threaded. E-SGX requires that the dummy threads occupy all the other cores when the computing thread of the application executes security-critical operations and be scheduled exclusively by the computing thread. It will be difficult to confirm all of the cores has been occupied if more than one computing threads are being executed simultaneously, due to the complexity in scheduling. So currently for E-SGX, we require that the application should be single-threaded (only one computing thread present), which is also the normal case for many client-side applications. We are also working on the multi-threaded version of E-SGX which are more preferable for server-side programs that demands concurrency.

9 Conclusion

In this paper, we present an approach to mitigate one of the main weaknesses of Intel SGX: cache side-channel attacks. Our approach employs several SGX threads from the same enclave to hold all logical CPU cores exclusively to break the concurrent execution condition of access-driven/trace-driven cache side-channel attacks, and use a mechanism which take advantage of AEX time to detect any interrupts to enclave threads. Our approach can mitigate all known access-driven/trace-driven cache side-channels and even page-fault side-channels, as well as other interruption-based and exception-based attacks, at a cost of some overhead. It is favorable for programs that are not computation-intensive while requiring strong security.

A Implementation Code

Listing 1.1. Dummy thread algorithm

```
void ecall_seize_core(size_t) {
        do {state[CPU] = challenge;}while(!exit);
}
bool is_all_se_online() {
        for(int i =0;i<CORE_PER_CPU;i++)
        if(challenge != state[i])
        return false;
        return true;
}
```

Listing 1.2. AEX algorithm

```
void SGXAPI sgx_get_thread_exit_info
(int *vector,int *exit_type,int *valid){
        thread_data = get_thread_data();
        ssa_gpr = thread_data->first_ssa_gpr;
        exit_info = &ssa_gpr->exit;
        *vector = exit_info->vector;*exit_type =
            exit_info->exit_type;*valid =
            exit_info->valid;
}
bool SGXAPI sgx_is_exception_happen(){
        sgx_get_thread_exit_info(&vector,&
            exit_type,&valid);
        if(vector||exit_type_type||valid) return
            1;
        return 0;
}
```

Listing 1.3. Computing thread algorithm

```
...
sgx_read_rand(challange,
sizeof(challange));
do {
        if(is_all_se_online()&&sgx_is_exception()
            ){
                ... //detection pass, continue
                break;}
}while(!is_timeout);
```

References

1. cpufreqd. http://manpages.ubuntu.com/manpages/precise/man8/cpufreqd.8.html
2. CrossTalk. http://cve.mitre.org/cgi-bin/cvename.cgi?name=CVE-2020-0543
3. mbed TLS. https://tls.mbed.org
4. Nginx. http://nginx.org
5. SGX SDK. https://software.intel.com/en-us/sgx-sdk
6. Anati, I., Gueron, S., Johnson, S., Scarlata, V.: Innovative technology for CPU based attestation and sealing. In: Proceedings of the 2nd International Workshop on Hardware and Architectural Support for Security and Privacy, vol. 13 (2013)
7. Brasser, F., et al.: DR.SGX: hardening SGX enclaves against cache attacks with data location randomization. CoRR abs/1709.09917 (2017), http://arxiv.org/abs/1709.09917
8. Brasser, F., Müller, U., Dmitrienko, A., Kostiainen, K., Capkun, S., Sadeghi, A.R.: Software grand exposure: SGX cache attacks are practical. arXiv preprint arXiv:1702.07521, p. 33 (2017)
9. Bulck, J.V., et al.: Foreshadow: extracting the keys to the intel SGX kingdom with transient out-of-order execution. In: 27th USENIX Security Symposium, USENIX Security 2018, Baltimore, MD, USA, August 15–17, 2018, pp. 991–1008 (2018). https://www.usenix.org/conference/usenixsecurity18/presentation/bulck
10. Canella, C., et al.: Fallout: leaking data on meltdown-resistant cpus. In: Cavallaro, L., Kinder, J., Wang, X., Katz, J. (eds.) Proceedings of the 2019 ACM SIGSAC Conference on Computer and Communications Security, CCS 2019, London, UK, November 11–15, 2019. pp. 769–784. ACM (2019). https://doi.org/10.1145/3319535.3363219
11. Chen, G., et al.: Racing in hyperspace: closing hyper-threading side channels on SGX with contrived data races. In: 2018 IEEE Symposium on Security and Privacy (SP). IEEE Computer Society, Los Alamitos, CA, USA (2018). https://doi.org/10.1109/SP.2018.00024
12. Chen, G., Chen, S., Xiao, Y., Zhang, Y., Lin, Z., Lai, T.H.: SGXPECTRE Attacks: Leaking Enclave Secrets via Speculative Execution. arXiv preprint arXiv:1802.09085 (2018)
13. Chen, S., Zhang, X., Reiter, M.K., Zhang, Y.: Detecting privileged side-channel attacks in shielded execution with Déjá Vu. In: Proceedings of the 2017 ACM on Asia Conference on Computer and Communications Security, pp. 7–18. ACM (2017)

14. Costan, V., Devadas, S.: Intel SGX Explained. IACR Cryptology ePrint Archive **2016**, 86 (2016)
15. Crane, S., Homescu, A., Brunthaler, S., Larsen, P., Franz, M.: Thwarting cache side-channel attacks through dynamic software diversity. In: NDSS, pp. 8–11 (2015)
16. Disselkoen, C., Kohlbrenner, D., Porter, L., Tullsen, D.M.: Prime+abort: A timer-free high-precision L3 cache attack using intel TSX. In: 26th USENIX Security Symposium, USENIX Security 2017, Vancouver, BC, Canada, August 16–18, 2017. pp. 51–67 (2017). https://www.usenix.org/conference/usenixsecurity17/technical-sessions/presentation/disselkoen
17. Goldreich, O., Ostrovsky, R.: Software protection and simulation on oblivious rams. J. ACM **43**(3), 431–473 (1996). https://doi.org/10.1145/233551.233553
18. Gruss, D., Lettner, J., Schuster, F., Ohrimenko, O., Haller, I., Costa, M.: Strong and efficient cache side-channel protection using hardware transactional memory. In: USENIX Security Symposium (2017)
19. Gruss, D., Maurice, C., Wagner, K., Mangard, S.: Flush+flush: a fast and stealthy cache attack. In: Detection of Intrusions and Malware, and Vulnerability Assessment - 13th International Conference, DIMVA 2016, San Sebastián, Spain, July 7–8, 2016, Proceedings, pp. 279–299 (2016). https://doi.org/10.1007/978-3-319-40667-1_14
20. Götzfried, J., Eckert, M., Schinzel, S., Müller, T.: Cache attacks on intel SGX (2017)
21. Hoekstra, M., Lal, R., Pappachan, P., Phegade, V., Del Cuvillo, J.: Using innovative instructions to create trustworthy software solutions, p. 11 (2013)
22. Intel: Intel Software Guard Extensions Programming Reference, October 2014, reference no. 329298–002US
23. Koc, C.K., Acar, T.: Montgomery multiplication in GF (2k). Designs, Codes and Cryptography **14**(1), 57–69 (1998)
24. Kocher, P., et al.: Spectre Attacks: Exploiting Speculative Execution. ArXiv e-prints (2018)
25. Kuvaiskii, D., et al.: SGXBOUNDS: Memory safety for shielded execution. In: Proceedings of the Twelfth European Conference on Computer Systems, pp. 205–221. ACM (2017)
26. Lipp, M., et al.: Meltdown. ArXiv e-prints (2018)
27. Liu, F., Yarom, Y., Ge, Q., Heiser, G., Lee, R.B.: Last-level cache side-channel attacks are practical. In: 2015 IEEE Symposium on Security and Privacy (SP), pp. 605–622. IEEE Computer Society, Los Alamitos, CA, USA (may 2015). https://doi.org/10.1109/SP.2015.43, https://doi.ieeecomputersociety.org/10.1109/SP.2015.43
28. Marshall, A., Howard, M.: Security best practices for developing windows azure applications (2010)
29. McKeen, F., et al.: Innovative instructions and software model for isolated execution. HASP@ ISCA 10 (2013)
30. Moghimi, A., Irazoqui, G., Eisenbarth, T.: Cachezoom: how SGX amplifies the power of cache attacks (2017)
31. Oleksenko, O., Trach, B., Krahn, R., Silberstein, M., Fetzer, C.: Varys: protecting SGX enclaves from practical side-channel attacks. In: 2018 USENIX Annual Technical Conference, USENIX ATC 2018, Boston, MA, USA, July 11–13, 2018, pp. 227–240 (2018). https://www.usenix.org/conference/atc18/presentation/oleksenko

32. Osvik, D.A., Shamir, A., Tromer, E.: Cache attacks and countermeasures: the case of AES. In: Topics in Cryptology - CT-RSA 2006, The Cryptographers' Track at the RSA Conference 2006, San Jose, CA, USA, February 13–17, 2006, Proceedings. pp. 1–20 (2006). https://doi.org/10.1007/11605805_1
33. Rajwar, R., Dixon, M.: Intel transactional synchronization extensions. In: Intel Developer Forum San Francisco, vol. 2012 (2012)
34. Rane, A., Lin, C., Tiwari, M.: Raccoon: closing digital side-channels through obfuscated execution. In: 24th USENIX Security Symposium, USENIX Security 15, Washington, D.C., USA, August 12–14, 2015, pp. 431–446 (2015). https://www.usenix.org/conference/usenixsecurity15/technical-sessions/presentation/rane
35. van Schaik, S., Kwong, A., Genkin, D., Yarom, Y.: Sgaxe: How sgx fails in practice (2020). http://cacheoutattack.com/files/SGAxe.pdf
36. van Schaik, S., et al.: RIDL: rogue in-flight data load. In: 2019 IEEE Symposium on Security and Privacy, SP 2019, San Francisco, CA, USA, May 19–23, 2019, pp. 88–105. IEEE (2019). https://doi.org/10.1109/SP.2019.00087
37. Schwarz, M., et al.: Zombieload: cross-privilege-boundary data sampling. In: Cavallaro, L., Kinder, J., Wang, X., Katz, J. (eds.) Proceedings of the 2019 ACM SIGSAC Conference on Computer and Communications Security, CCS 2019, London, UK, November 11–15, 2019, pp. 753–768. ACM (2019). https://doi.org/10.1145/3319535.3354252
38. Schwarz, M., Weiser, S., Gruss, D., Maurice, C., Mangard, S.: Malware guard extension: using SGX to conceal cache attacks. In: Polychronakis, M., Meier, M. (eds.) DIMVA 2017. LNCS, vol. 10327, pp. 3–24. Springer, Cham (2017). https://doi.org/10.1007/978-3-319-60876-1_1
39. Seo, J., et al.: SGX-shield: enabling address space layout randomization for SGX programs. In: Proceedings of the 2017 Annual Network and Distributed System Security Symposium (NDSS), San Diego, CA (2017)
40. Shih, M.W., Lee, S., Kim, T., Peinado, M.: T-SGX: eradicating controlled-channel attacks against enclave programs. In: Proceedings of the 2017 Annual Network and Distributed System Security Symposium (NDSS), San Diego, CA (2017)
41. Tromer, E., Osvik, D.A., Shamir, A.: Efficient cache attacks on AES, and countermeasures. J. Cryptol. **23**(1), 37–71 (2010)
42. Wang, W., Chen, G., Pan, X., Zhang, Y., Wang, X.: Leaky cauldron on the dark land: understanding memory side-channel hazards in SGX. In: the 2017 ACM SIGSAC Conference (2017)
43. Yarom, Y., Falkner, K.: Flush+reload: a high resolution, low noise, l3 cache side-channel attack. In: Usenix Conference on Security Symposium (2014)

Privacy Protection

Public Verifiable Private Decision Tree Prediction

Hailong Wang[1,2,3](✉), Yi Deng[1,2,3], and Xiang Xie[4]

[1] The State Key Laboratory of Information Security, Institute of Information Engineering, Chinese Academy of Sciences, Beijing, China
wanghailong9065@iie.ac.cn

[2] The School of Cyber Security, University of Chinese Academy of Sciences, Beijing, China

[3] The State Key Laboratory of Cryptology, P. O. Box 5159, Beijing, China

[4] PlatOn, Shenzhen, China

Abstract. Decision tree is a favored prediction model in machine learning and data mining. With the fast development and wide application of machine learning, the privacy of decision tree prediction is a rising concern.

In this paper, We construct a specific purpose NIZK for privacy-preserving decision tree prediction. The protocol allows the server who holds a decision tree model to convince others the result of the decision tree on an encrypted data sample, without leaking private information about the decision tree. Our protocol has high efficiency in both prover time and verifier time, and the proof size is only several KBs. With such NIZK, we can build a public verifiable private decision tree prediction system. In this system, a client can query the result of the server's decision tree on its encrypted feature vector, and anyone who has only the access to public information can verify the validity of the result.

Keywords: NIZK · Decision tree prediction · Privacy-preserving

1 Introduction

With the development of machine learning, there are many companies who hold some machine learning models providing consulting or assessment services by evaluating user's information. For example, many people use the Zhima Credit Score what is provided by Alipay as a person's credit rating. In most cases, we require privacy for the model, because training this model may take a lot of cost or use a lot of sensitive information. On the flip side, the service provider also needs to provide something to make sure that users can verify the validity of the results. Consider another specific scenario, the government wants to build a building and invite public bidding. The government holds a decision-making model which will evaluate the bids of bidding companies. On the one hand, this decision-making model should be kept confidential; On the other hand, to prevent cheating and corruption, the correctness of the evaluation results should be public verifiable. It means that anyone who has access to public information can verify the correctness of the results.

Y. Wu and M. Yung (Eds.): Inscrypt 2020, LNCS 12612, pp. 247–256, 2021.
https://doi.org/10.1007/978-3-030-71852-7_16

Decision Trees [FHT01] is among the most popular machine learning techniques. As the name suggests, decision tree consists of a collection of nodes arranged in a tree structure and each decision node is associated with a threshold value which makes a test on the query. Prediction process simply corresponds to tree traversal and the leaf node at the end of this traversal path is associated with a classification label, which is the result of this prediction process. Since its structure is simple and easy to explain, decision tree models are favored by many users and have been widely used in many fields and scenarios such as credit-risk assessment [KTG06].

Zero-knowledge (ZK) proofs (of knowledge) [GMR89] are fundamental cryptographic tools. They allow a prover to convince a verifier, who has access to a circuit C, that there exists a witness w for which $C(w) = 1$ without leaking any extra information. To make ZK proofs practical, in recent years, several efficient ZK proof systems have been developed such as zero-knowledge succinct non-interactive arguments of knowledge [Gro10, Gro16, BSCTV14, GGPR13, PHGR13]. These ZK proofs can also be used in decision tree prediction, while we noticed that all of them are general purpose ZK proofs. We must transfer the statement that we want to prove into a suitable format that will bring lots of computation overhead.

In this work, we develop a specific purpose non-interactive zero-knowledge proof (NIZK) for decision tree prediction, And we also give a public verifiable decision tree prediction system. In our settings, the client holds a feature vector x, the server holds a decision tree $\mathcal{M}$, and the client wants to query the result $c = \mathcal{M}(x)$. We require that the server returns the result c to the client along with a NIZK proof so that the client can verify the validity of the result.

1.1 Our Contributions

In this paper, we give a specific purpose NIZK proof for decision tree prediction, which can be used to prove the correctness of the decision tree prediction results without leaking extra information. Our construction is very efficient on both proving and verifying, the proof consists of only $5d + 2(\log_2 l + \log_2 d) + 4$ group elements and $4d + 5$ $\mathbb{Z}_p$ elements, where d is the depth of the decision tree. With such NIZK proof, we give a public verifiable private decision tree prediction system.

2 Preliminaries

In this section, we define some notations and review some basic definitions of cryptographic primitives used in this paper. We also introduce some background knowledge about decision trees used in our work.

Notations. Let $[n]$ be the set of integers $\{1, 2, ..., n\}$, $\mathbb{Z}_p$ be the ring of integers modulo p. With $[a, b]$, we denote the set of all integers from a to b, means $\{a, a + 1, ..., b\}$. For a set S, we write $x \leftarrow S$ to denote a uniform draw x from

S. Let λ be the security parameter, Λ be a interactive protocol, Π be a non-interactive protocol, and π be the proof in a non-interactive protocol. A function $\mathsf{negl}(\lambda)$ is said to be negligible if for all polynomial $p(\lambda)$, it holds that $\mathsf{negl}(\lambda) \leq 1/p(\lambda)$ for sufficiently large $\lambda \in \mathbb{N}$. Let PPT stands for probabilistic polynomial-time. Let $\mathcal{MS}$ be the plaintext space and $\mathcal{R}$ be the randomness space.

2.1 Cryptographic Primitives

Elgamal Encryption. Elgamal [ElG85] is a widely used PKE scheme. It works in a cyclic groups which the discrete logarithm problem is hard. We will give the details of Elgamal below

- Assuming Elgamal works on a cyclic group $\mathbb{G}$, and g is a base element in $\mathbb{G}$.
- $(h; s) \leftarrow \mathsf{KGen}(1^\lambda)$, where h is public-key and s is secret key. It holds that $h = g^s$.
- $c = (c_1, c_2) \leftarrow \mathsf{Enc}(h, m; r) = (g^r, g^m h^r)$, c is the ciphertext of m under public-key h and randomness r.
- $\mathsf{Dec}(s, c) = \mathsf{Dec}(s, (c_1, c_2))$, firstly compute $c_1^{-s} c_2 = g^{-sr} h^r g^m = g^m$, then compute the logarithm m of g^m to g. Outputs m as the decryption of c.

2.2 Decision Trees

Decision trees are frequently encountered in machine learning and can be used for classification and regression. We will introduce some necessary background knowledge about decision tree model.

Decision Tree. A *decision tree* (DT) is a map $\Phi : \mathbb{Z}^n \rightarrow \mathbb{Z}$, implements the function on an n dimensional *feature space*. In practical scenarios, the feature space is usually $\mathbb{R}^n$, so we use a fixed-point encoding of the values. We refer to element $x \in \mathbb{Z}^n$ as a *feature vector* and denote a finite set $\{c_1, c_2, ...c_k\} \in \mathbb{Z}^k$ as the *classification label set*. The decision tree maps a feature vector to an element in classification label set and the decision at each decision node is a comparison between the assigned threshold and associated feature values.

Node Indices. Given a complete binary decision tree (all the decision trees can be transformed into a complete binary tree by increasing the depth of the tree and introducing "dummy" nodes), we set 1 to be the index of the root node. And we label the remaining nodes inductively: given an internal node with index v, let $2v$ be its left child and $2v + 1$ be its right child. We also refer to the node with index v as the node v.

Paths in Complete Binary Trees. We use bit strings to represent paths in a complete binary trees. Specifically, given a complete binary tree $\mathcal{M}$ with depth d, we specify a path by a bit string $b = b_1, b_2, ..., b_d \in \{0, 1\}^d$, where b_i denotes whether we visit the left child or the right child when we are at a node at level i (in this work, we visit the left child when $b_i = 0$ and the right child when $b_i = 1$). Starting at the root node (level 1), and traversing according to the bit string b, then we define a unique path in $\mathcal{M}$.

Decision Tree Prediction. Given a feature vector $x = (x_1, x_2, ..., x_n)$ and a decision tree $\mathcal{M}$, starting at the root node 1, the *decision tree prediction* evaluates at each reached node v_i the decision bit $b_i \leftarrow [x_{\text{att}(v_i)} \geq \text{thr}(v_i)]$ and moves to the left (if $b_i = 0$) or right (if $b_i = 1$) subsequent node. At the end, this prediction process returns the label of the reached leaf node as the result of the computation. We denote it $\mathcal{M}(x)$.

3 Our Construction

3.1 Overview

Here we will describe our construction briefly to give readers a general intuition. In the setup phase, the server should encrypt his decision tree $\mathcal{M}$ and make the encrypted decision tree $\hat{\mathcal{M}}$ public. $\hat{\mathcal{M}}$ can be used as public information to verify the correctness of the output results. In the query phase, the client encrypts his feature vector under the server's public key and send the ciphertexts to the server. The security of the encryption will protect the privacy of the client from others except the server. In the response phase, after receiving the query, the server decrypts the ciphertexts and obtain a plain feature vector, then computes the result of $\mathcal{M}$ on the vector by the standard decision tree prediction.

The server also need to provide a NIZK proof to prove that result is correct. By in-depth observation, the validity of the result is indeed the correctness of all the comparison on the decision path. In our construction, we show the correctness of each comparison by proving the difference between threshold value and correspond attribute value is in correct range. Formally, we define such a statement $\mathsf{st}_{\text{correct}}$ as

$$\{(g, h, X, Y) | \exists m, r \text{ s.t. } X = g^r \wedge Y = h^r g^m \wedge c \in \mathsf{Range}\}$$

where Range is the correct range we need. And for ease of analysis, we can write such statement as

$$\mathsf{st}_{\text{correct}} = \mathsf{st}_{\text{enc}} \wedge \mathsf{st}_{\text{range}}$$

where

$$\mathsf{st}_{\text{enc}} = \{(g, h, X, Y) | \exists m, r \text{ s.t. } X = g^r \wedge Y = g^m h^r\}$$

$$\mathsf{st}_{\text{range}} = \{(g, h, Y) | \exists m, r \text{ s.t. } Y = g^m h^r \wedge m \in \mathsf{Range}\}$$

We apply *bulletproof* [BBB+18] as our range proof for $\mathsf{st}_{\text{range}}$. Here we point out that the security of bulletproof is based on the discrete logarithm assumption, but in our settings, the secret key of the server is indeed the discrete logarithm of public keys. With the knowledge of such secrete key, the server can convince the verifier a false statement which breaks the soundness of bulletproof. And the server can only learn the plain message, it generally does not know the correspond randomness. It means the server does not know all the witness for $\mathsf{st}_{\text{correct}}$.

Our solution is encrypting the same plaintext under new public keys whose discrete logarithm keeps secret to the server. And hence, we also need to provide a proof to ensure that the two ciphertexts encrypt the same value under different public keys. We define such a statement

$$\mathsf{st}_{\mathsf{equi}} = \{(g, h_1, h_2, C_1, C_2) : \exists m, s_1, r_2 \ s.t. \ m = \mathsf{Dec}(s_1, C_1) \wedge C_2 = \mathsf{Enc}(h_2, m; r_2)\}$$

3.2 Data Structure

To present our constructions, we give some necessary description of data structures here. For convenience, we only consider complete binary trees and set the right child of v to be the next node of the decision path when $b = 1$ and the left child to be the next node when $b = 0$.

Definition 1. *Data Structure For a decision tree model $\mathcal{M}$, We let* Node *be a data structure that for each node v defines the following notations:*

- v.thre *stores the threshold value* thr(v) *of the node v.*
- v.ain *stores the associated index* att(v) *of the node v.*

We denote $\mathcal{D}$ by the set of decision nodes which have the described data structure and $\mathcal{L}$ by the set of such leaf nodes. It is clear that $\mathcal{M}$ can be rewritten as $\mathcal{M} = (\mathcal{D}, \mathcal{L})$. We can encrypt the threshold values of $\mathcal{M}$ and obtain a corresponding decision tree $\hat{\mathcal{M}} = (\hat{\mathcal{D}}, \mathcal{L})$, where $\hat{v} \in \hat{\mathcal{D}}$ is same as $v \in \mathcal{D}$ except the threshold values they stored. It means that $\hat{v}$.thre stores the ciphertexts of v.thre.

3.3 Building Blocks

Setup. In this step, the system generates the necessary parameters and establish the initial state. Specifically, on inputs security parameter λ, it outputs public parameters *pp*, which includes group $\mathbb{G}$ and associated parameters (p, g) where p is the order and g is the base element. And *pp* also includes a global public key h_{pub} of $\mathsf{ElGamal}$ encryption scheme and l which is the bit length of the threshold value in plain decision tree $\mathcal{M}$. Then on inputs λ and *pp*, outputs the server's key-pair.

Setup

- On inputs λ, outputs $pp = (\mathbb{G}, p, g, h_{\text{pub}}, l)$
- For the server, run $(pk_S, sk_S) \leftarrow \text{keygen}(pp, \lambda)$.
- The server holds a decision tree $\mathcal{M} = (\mathcal{D}, \mathcal{L})$ with data structures described above, encrypts all the threshold values of v in $\mathcal{D}$ and obtain an encrypted decision tree $\hat{\mathcal{M}}$. That is to say, in $\hat{\mathcal{M}}$, $\hat{v}$.thre stores the ciphertexts of thr(v) under ther server's public key pk_S. The server exposes $\hat{\mathcal{M}}$ to all.

Bulletproof. Bulletproof is a very efficient range proof in practice and supports batching. We employ bulletproof $\Lambda_{\text{bullet}} = (\mathsf{Setup}, P, V)$ for $\mathsf{st}_{\text{range}}$. To avoid repetition, we refer the readers to [BBB+18] for more details.

Lemma 1. *Assuming the hardness of discrete logarithm problem, Λ_{bullet} is a public coin SHVZK arguments.*

Sigma protocol for st_{enc}. Here we give a sigma protocol for the knowledge proof of ElGamal ciphertexts.

Protocol Λ_{enc}

- **Common inputs:** $\mathsf{st}_{\text{enc}} = (g, h, X, Y)$.
- **private inputs:** the plaintext m, the randomness r.

1. P: Randomly chooses $b_1, b_2 \leftarrow \mathbb{Z}_p$, computes $a_1 = g^{b_1}$, $a_2 = h^{b_1} g^{b_2}$. Then sends a_1, a_2 to the V.
2. V: Randomly chooses $e \leftarrow \mathbb{Z}_p$, and sends e to the P.
3. P: Upon receiving challenge e, computes $z_1 = re + b_1$, $z_2 = me + b_2$.
4. V: Upon receiving z_1, z_2, checks that:
   - if $g^{z_1} = a_1 X^e$;
   - if $g^{z_2} h^{z_1} = a_2 Y^e$;

   If all the check pass, accepts; Otherwise, rejects.

Lemma 2. *Protocol Λ_{enc} is a Σ−protocol for statement st_{enc}.*

Proof. This proof is trivial, we omit the details here due to the space limitations.

NIZK for $\mathsf{st}_{\text{correct}}$. Let Λ_{correct} be the sequential composition of Λ_{enc} and Λ_{bullet} as described in [CMTA19].

Lemma 3. *Protocol Λ_{correct} is a public-coin SHVZK arguments of knowledge for $\mathsf{st}_{\text{correct}}$.*

The proof for Lemma 3 has appeared in [CMTA19], to avoid repetition, we refer readers to [CMTA19] for more details. And in this paper, we apply Fiat-Shamir heuristic to achieve corresponding non-interactive protocol and we denote the non-interactive form by Π_{equi}.

NIZK for $\mathsf{st}_{\text{equi}}$. As described above, we need a NIZK proof for the plaintext equivalence between two ciphertexts. Below, we will give the concrete description of our construction.

Protocol Λ_{equi}

- **Common inputs:** $\mathsf{st}_{\text{equi}} = (g, h_1, h_2, C_1, C_2)$, where $C_1 = (c_1, d_1)$, $C_2 = (c_2, d_2)$.
- **private inputs:** the plaintext m, the secret key s_1 where $h_1 = g^{s_1}$ and randomness r_2 used in C_2.
- Note that $c_1 = g^{r_1}$, $d_1 = g^m h_1^{r_1}$, $c_2 = g^{r_2}$, $d_2 = g^m h_2^{r_2}$, and it is easy to verify that $d_2 = d_1 c_1^{-s_1} h_2^{r_2}$. The P has no idea about r_1.

1. P: Randomly chooses $b_1, b_2 \leftarrow \mathbb{Z}_p$, computes $a_1 = g^{b_1}$, $a_2 = g^{b_2}$, $a_3 = c_1^{b_1} h_2^{-b_2}$. Then sends a_1, a_2, a_3 to the V.
2. V: Randomly chooses $e \leftarrow \mathbb{Z}_p$, and sends e to the P.
3. P: Upon receiving challenge e, computes $z_1 = s_1 e + b_1$, $z_2 = r_2 e + b_2$.
4. V: Upon receiving z_1, z_2, checks that:
   - if $g^{z_1} = h_1^e a_1$ and $g^{z_2} = c_2^e a_2$;
   - if $d_2^e d_1^{-e} c_1^{z_1} h_2^{-z_2} = a_3$.

   If all the check pass, accepts; Otherwise, rejects.

Lemma 4. *Protocol Λ_{equi} is a $\Sigma-$protocol for statement* $\mathsf{st}_{\text{equi}}$.

Proof. (Perfect) Completeness and special HVZK are trivial.

We only give the proof sketch for the special soundness. By standard rewinding technology, we can extract s_1, b_1, r_2, b_2. Substitute z_1, z_2 with $s_1 e+b_1, r_2 e+b_2$ into the third verification, we have $(d_2 d_1^{-1} c_1^{d_1} h_2^{-r_2})^e c_1^{b_1} h_2^{-b_2} = a_3$ which is satisfied for two different e, e'. $d_2 d_1^{-1} c_1^{d_1} h_2^{-r_2}$ must be the identity of the group $\mathbb{G}$, we have that $d_2 = d_1 c_1^{-s_1} h_2^{r_2}$, and this equation holds iff C_1, C_2 correspond to a same plaintext m. That is to say, the plaintext m we obtained from C_1 is also the plaintext of C_2.

We can also apply Fiat-Shamir heuristic to achieve a corresponding non-interactive protocol and we denote the non-interactive form by Π_{equi}.

3.4 NIZK for Decision Tree Prediction

Here we put all building blocks together to achieve a NIZK proof for decision tree prediction. In our settings, the prover holds a decision tree $\mathcal{M}$ and a key-pair. The verifier only knows the prover's public key and the encrypted decision tree $\hat{\mathcal{M}}$. Given an ecnrypted feature vector $(c_1, c_2, ..., c_n)$, a classification label y and an associated decision path $(b_1, b_2, ..., b_d)$, the prover will prove that y is indeed the correct output of $\mathcal{M}$ on the plaintexts of $(c_1, c_2, ..., c_n)$.

Π_{DTP}: NIZK for Decision Tree Prediction

1. **Common inputs:** $\hat{\mathcal{M}}$, classification label y, decision path $(b_1, b_2, ..., b_d)$, encrypted feature vector $(c_1, c_2, ..., c_n)$, the bit length l of threshold values, pp.
2. **Private inputs:** the plain feature vector $(x_1, x_2, ..., x_n)$, plain decision tree $\mathcal{M}$.
3. **Prove:** The prover
   - sets $v_0 = 1$, that is to say, let v_0 to be the root node.
   - for each $i \in \{1, 2, ..., d\}$, if $b_i = 1$, sets $v_i = 2v_{i-1} + 1$, else let $v_i = 2v_{i-1}$.
   - for each $j \in \{0, ..., d-1\}$, randomly chooses a $r_j \leftarrow \mathbb{Z}_p$, computes ct_j homomophicly according to b_{j+1}, then computes the corresponding ciphertext CT_j under the global public key.
   - for each $j \in \{0, ..., d-1\}$, invokes Π_{equi} and computes $\pi_j.\text{equi} \leftarrow \Pi_{\text{equi}}.\mathsf{Prove}(h_{\text{pub}}, pk_{\text{S}}, g, \mathrm{ct}_j, \mathrm{CT}_j; r_j, sk_{\text{S}}, (-1)^{b_j+1}(v_j.\text{thre} - x_{v_j.\text{ain}}))$.
   - for each $j \in \{0, ..., d-1\}$, invokes Π_{correct} and computes $\pi_j.\text{correct} \leftarrow \Pi_{\text{correct}}.\mathsf{Prove}(g, h_{\text{pub}}, X_j, Y_j; r_j, y_j)$ to prove that y_j is in the range $[0, 2^l - 1]$, where y_j is the corresponding plaintext and $\mathrm{CT}_j = (X_j, Y_j)$.
   - sends $\pi_{\text{DTP}} = \{\pi_j.\text{equi}, \pi_j.\text{correct}, \mathrm{CT}_j\}_{j \in \{0, \dots, d-1\}}$ to the verifier.
4. **Verify:** The verifier receives proof π_{DTP}, then
   - for each $j \in \{0, ..., d-1\}$, computes ct'_j homomophicly according to b_{j+1} and checks $\Pi_{\text{equi}}.\mathsf{Verify}(\mathrm{ct}'_j, \mathrm{CT}_j, pk_{\text{S}}, h_{\text{pub}}, g)$. If all checks pass, continues. Else, rejects.
   - for each $j \in \{0, ..., d-1\}$, writes CT_j in the Elgmal ciphertext form (X_j, Y_j), then checks $\Pi_{\text{correct}}.\mathsf{Verify}(g, h_{\text{pub}}, X_j, Y_j)$. If all checks pass, accepts; Otherwise, rejects.

Theorem 1. *Π_{DTP} is a NIZK protocol.*

Proof. It is easy to see that $\Pi_{\text{DTP}} = \Pi_{\text{correct}} \wedge \Pi_{\text{equi}}$. And Π_{correct} and Π_{equi} are both NIZK, then the proof of this theorem follows from the property of AND−proofs.

Optimizations. After executing Π_{enc} and Π_{equi}, we prove the knowledge of the plaintext and the randomness twice. We can put them in one protocol to reduce the repetition. For a (n, d, m)−tree, one π_{DTP} proof consists $5d + 2(\log_2 l + \log_2 d) + 4$ $\mathbb{G}$ elements and $4d + 5$ $\mathbb{Z}_p$ elements.

Application. With such NIZK for decision tree prediction, we will give a brief description of a public verifiable private decision tree prediction system which is a straightforward application of Π_{DTP}.

- Builds the initial state of the system by the **Setup** step.
- The client encrypts his feature vector under the server's public key, and sends the ciphertexts to the server.

- After receiving the query, the server decrypts the ciphertexts and obtains a plain feature vector, then computes the output of his decision tree on such feature vector, and invorks Π_{DTP} to compute a corresponding NIZK proof. Sends the results and the proof to the client.

Note that the output results and the corresponding proof can be verified by anyone who has the access to these public informations. It means that the client can use such proof as his "certificate" of this results (maybe his credit evaluation score). And anyone else can learn nothing about both the server's and the client's private information.

4 Implementation and Evaluation

We implement the NIZK protocol Π_{DTP} and we will evaluate its performance on prover time, verifier time, proof size. Our implementation is written in rust and use the library libsecp256k1 which is used in many cryptocurrency systems. libsecp256k1 uses the elliptic curv secp256k1 which has 128 bit security, and one secp256k1 point is stored as 33 bytes (32 bytes plus 1 bit). When implement Π_{DTP}, we use batching bulletproof to prove d instances, it will saves a lot communication overhead. To make $\Lambda_{\mathrm{correct}}$ and Λ_{equi} non-interactive in the random oracle model, we instantiate the random oracle with SHA-256. All our codes runs on a personal computer with a Intel Core i7-9700k CPU. And all the codes is using a single thread. We run the experiments many times on different decision trees which has different depth d. Besides, we fix the bit length $l = 32$. The results about Π_{DTP} are summarized in Table 1.

Table 1. The performance of Π_{DTP}.

Depth	$d = 4$	$d = 8$	$d = 16$
Prover time	59.3 ms	122.2 ms	244.7 ms
Verifier time	15.9 ms	28.4 ms	54.7 ms
Proof size	2.58 KB	3.82 KB	6.23 KB

[a] n is set to be 20 and l is set to be 32.
[b] KB is short for KiloBytes.

From the table, we can see that the efficiency of Π_{DTP} is reasonable in practice. The proof size is several KBs, the prover time and the verifier time scale linearly with the depth d and they are all only on the order of milliseconds.

Acknowledgments. This work was supported by PlatON, the National Natural Science Foundation of China (Grant No. 61932019, No. 61772521 and No. 61772522), Key Research Program of Frontier Sciences, CAS (Grant No. QYZDB-SSW-SYS035), and the Open Project Program of the State Key Laboratory of Cryptology.

References

[BBB+18] Bünz, B., Bootle, J., Boneh, D., Poelstra, A., Wuille, P., Maxwell, G.: Bulletproofs: short proofs for confidential transactions and more. In: 2018 IEEE Symposium on Security and Privacy (SP), pp. 315–334. IEEE (2018)

[BSCTV14] Ben-Sasson, E., Chiesa, A., Tromer, E., Virza, M:. Succinct non-interactive zero knowledge for a von Neumann architecture. In: 23rd {USENIX} Security Symposium ({USENIX} Security 2014), pp. 781–796 (2014)

[CMTA19] Chen, Y., Ma, X., Tang, C., Au, M.H.: PGC: pretty good decentralized confidential payment system with auditability. Cryptology ePrint Archive, Report 2019/319 (2019). https://eprint.iacr.org/2019/319

[ElG85] ElGamal, T.: A public key cryptosystem and a signature scheme based on discrete logarithms. IEEE Trans. Inf. Theory **31**(4), 469–472 (1985)

[FHT01] Hastie, T., Tibshirani, R., Friedman, J.: The Elements of Statistical Learning. SSS. Springer, New York (2009). https://doi.org/10.1007/978-0-387-84858-7

[GGPR13] Gennaro, R., Gentry, C., Parno, B., Raykova, M.: Quadratic span programs and succinct NIZKs without PCPs. In: Johansson, T., Nguyen, P.Q. (eds.) EUROCRYPT 2013. LNCS, vol. 7881, pp. 626–645. Springer, Heidelberg (2013). https://doi.org/10.1007/978-3-642-38348-9_37

[GMR89] Goldwasser, S., Micali, S., Rackoff, C.: The knowledge complexity of interactive proof systems. SIAM J. Comput. **18**(1), 186–208 (1989)

[Gro10] Groth, J.: Short pairing-based non-interactive zero-knowledge arguments. In: Abe, M. (ed.) ASIACRYPT 2010. LNCS, vol. 6477, pp. 321–340. Springer, Heidelberg (2010). https://doi.org/10.1007/978-3-642-17373-8_19

[Gro16] Groth, J.: On the size of pairing-based non-interactive arguments. In: Fischlin, M., Coron, J.-S. (eds.) EUROCRYPT 2016. LNCS, vol. 9666, pp. 305–326. Springer, Heidelberg (2016). https://doi.org/10.1007/978-3-662-49896-5_11

[KTG06] Koh, H.C., Tan, W.C., Goh, C.P.: A two-step method to construct credit scoring models with data mining techniques. Int. J. Bus. Inf. **1**(1) (2006)

[PHGR13] Parno, B., Howell, J., Gentry, C., Raykova, M.: Pinocchio: nearly practical verifiable computation. In: 2013 IEEE Symposium on Security and Privacy, pp. 238–252. IEEE (2013)

P2A: Privacy Preserving Anonymous Authentication Based on Blockchain and SGX

Tianlin Song[1,3], Wei Wang[1,3(✉)], Fan Lang[1,3], Wenyi Ouyang[1,3], Qiongxiao Wang[1,3], and Jingqiang Lin[2,3]

[1] State Key Laboratory of Information Security, Institute of Information Engineering, Chinese Academy of Sciences, Beijing 100089, China
wangwei@iie.ac.cn

[2] School of Cyber Security, University of Science and Technology of China, Hefei 230027, Anhui, China

[3] School of Cyber Security, University of Chinese Academy of Sciences, Beijing 100089, China

Abstract. Modern Identify-as-a-Service solutions solve the problems of burdensome user credential management and non-uniform security strength, by introducing an Identity Provider (IdP) that holds the users' identities and grants a user one-time access tokens when he/she tries to login to different online applications (known as the Relying Parties, RPs). However, the non-negligible problem of privacy leakage during authentication largely remains unattended. In this paper, we propose a ***P**rivacy **P**reserving **A**nonymous Authentication Scheme* (P2A) with Blockchain and Intel Software Guard Extensions (SGX). The IdP in *P2A* manages the users' identities by issuing different kinds of transactions in the Blockchain, covering the registration, update, freeze/thaw, and deletion of identities. When the user wants to login to an RP, instead of asking for an one-time token from the IdP, he can generate an identity proof locally with SGX and login to the RP with an RP-specific pseudonym (PN). By resorting to the Blockchain, the RP will be convinced that the PN is associated with some registered identity on IdP and specific attributes of the user are satisfactory, without obtaining the real identity and raw attributes of the user. In this way, privacy leakages to the IdP and RPs are eliminated. *P2A* has a few exciting new features and security analysis shows it can resist various attacks even under strict assumptions.

Keywords: Privacy Preserving · Anonymous Authentication · Intel Software Guard Extensions · Blockchain

1 Introduction

Authentication is the process of determining whether the identity a user declares is authentic. A simple authentication method is to compare the username and pass-

This work was supported by National Cryptography Development Fund (Award No. MMJJ20180221).

Y. Wu and M. Yung (Eds.): Inscrypt 2020, LNCS 12612, pp. 257–276, 2021.
https://doi.org/10.1007/978-3-030-71852-7_17

word entered by the user with the original copies stored on the application server. However, the increasing number of online applications results in heavy burden for the users in managing large numbers of accounts and credentials. What's worse, the security strength of the online applications vary and the security of the user accounts can not be guaranteed. To address the above problems, a few unified authentication protocols have been proposed and adopted in the past years, such as SAML [1], OAuth [2], and OpenID Connect [3]. In systems that apply these protocols, when a user who has registered on the identity provider (IdP) wants to access an application (known as the Relying Party, RP), he can get an authentication assertion from the IdP, which will be forwarded to the RP along with his access request. After that, the RP can confirm the user's identity by verifying the assertion and allow (or disallow) the access. However, such protocols suffer from privacy leakage, e.g., unnecessary identity attributes may be obtained by the RP from the assertion, and the specific login action is leaked to the IdP.

In this paper, we propose an *privacy preserving anonymous authentication scheme* (P2A) based on Blockchain and Intel SGX [4–7]. With SGX, a user can create an SGX enclave containing a verification program *prog*, and get an SGX CPU signed quote *quote*. *quote* will be sent to the remote verifier to prove that *prog* has been correctly initialized and executed, and the outputs of *prog* are believable. The roles in *P2A* include the users, an identity provider (IdP), some relying parties (RPs), and a Blockchain. The IdP holds all the identities with the help of the Blockchain. It can change the state of an identity by issuing different types of transactions onto the Blockchain. To register a new identity, a *registration* transaction will be issued. To update the attributes of the identities, an *update* transaction will be issued. To freeze a valid identity or thaw a frozen identity, a *freeze/thaw* transaction will be issued. To remove an identity from the identity set on the Blockchain, a *deletion* transaction will be issued. An identity Merkle tree will be kept on the Blockchain network with all the registered identity commitments as leaves, and the Merkle tree will be modified once a new transaction is published and verified. The changes will take effect immediately after the Merkle tree has been modified. A new user should register an identity on the IdP, and the identity will be valid after the IdP has issued a registration transaction onto the Blockchain. A valid user can generate an identity proof with a pseudonym using SGX. The proof will be sent to the RP and convince the RP that the pseudonym is associated with some valid identity on the Blockchain, and that the attributes of the user fulfill the individual requirements of the RP, without disclosing the real identity and raw attributes of the user.

Owing to its new design philosophy, *P2A* has a few good features.

User Authentication Independent of the IdP. In the traditional unified authentication schemes, the user relies on the IdP in every authentication trial, as a result, the IdP knows clearly when and for which application the user is authenticated. In *P2A*, a user can generate an identity proof with Intel SGX and be authenticated by an RP with the proof, without the participation of the IdP. Zero participation of the IdP in the authentications means that the use of the user's identity is kept secret against the IdP.

Non-leakage Proof of User Attributes Fulfillment. Conventionally, an RP may obtain some sensitive user attributes to ensure the user fulfills its login requirements, e.g. collect the user's age to ensure that he/she is adult, which is more than necessary. In *P2A*, an identity proof generated by the user can be used to prove that the verification program *prog* compiled by the RP has been initialized and executed correctly, and the outputs of *prog* are believable. Using the proof, the user can convince the RP that the identity attributes can meet the requirements of the RP, without revealing any attribute value. Thus the user attributes will be preserved against the RP.

Isolated Pseudonyms Across RPs. A valid user can anonymously login to different RPs with RP-specific pseudonyms. In the system initialization procedure, every RP needs to upload their RPIds onto the Blockchain. A user can generate one and only one pseudonym with an RP's RPId. Different RPs can not analyze whether any two pseudonyms are associated with the same user. Meanwhile, the IdP can not know the pseudonyms of an identity, even by launching a conspiracy attack with all the RPs.

Accountable Identity Management. When the IdP issue a transaction onto the Blockchain, the identity Merkle tree will be modified and a new root rt_{new} will be generated and the old root rt_{old} will be replaced. Note that all identity management operations are realized based on the operations to the Blockchain. So the operations of the IdP on the user identities are accountable for the users, since all the transactions on the Blockchain are verifiable and irreversible. This accountability feature outperforms the existing unified authentication protocols.

We analyze the security of our proposed scheme, and find that *P2A* is secure against different types of attacks. The assumption on the adversaries covers curious IdP, curious RPs, malicious users, and conspiracy attackers. These attackers may launch proof forgery attack, proof replay attack, attributes theft attack, identity tracking attack, and conspiracy attack. We can conclude that *P2A* is not only privacy preserving but also provides reliable authentication functionalities.

The rest of this paper is organized as follows. The background is described in Sect. 2. In Sect. 3, we introduce the design goals and models of this paper. Section 4 provides the details of *P2A*. The security analysis will be provided in Sect. 5.1, followed by the discussion in Sect. 6. The conclusion will be given in Sect. 8.

2 Background

2.1 Blockchain

Blockchain was first proposed by Satoshi Nakamoto in 2008 [8]. In a narrow sense, the Blockchain is a type of chain data structure that combines data blocks in a sequential manner in a chronological order, and it is an unmodifiable distributed ledger guaranteed by cryptography. Blockchain can be regard as a distributed database that records all the transactions and states, maintained by every node in a decentralized network. In a centralized system, the center often has too much power, resulting in information asymmetry. The security of many centralized systems can only be built on the strong security assumption that the center is trusted. However, in practice, this assumption is often not true for various reasons. The decentralization feature can free the system design from the premise that the center is trusted, thereby improving the security of the system and preventing systemic risks caused by a single point of failure of the center. Before Blockchain, methods such as timestamp were often used to ensure the order of the data generation time. These methods not only put higher requirements on developers in the design of the system scheme, but also often assumed the existence of a trusted third party. The emergence of Blockchain is a convenient and efficient solution to ensure the order of the data generation time, which is guaranteed by cryptography. Considering the efficiency, the previous consensus protocols of distributed systems only allow a small number of nodes to participate. However, all the nodes in a Blockchain network ensure data consistency through several consensus protocols, such as *Proof of Work* (PoW) [8] and *Proof of Stake* (PoS) [9]. The consensus protocols have greatly increased the number of nodes that can participate in a distributed system. The large number of nodes participating in the consensus enhances the robustness of the system, and it is difficult for malicious nodes to tamper with the information on the Blockchain. Blockchain has been widely used for privacy protection, such as some anonymous cryptocurrencies [10–12] and Privacy-Preserving Smart Contracts [13]. In this article, we will use a Blockchain as a trusted bulletin board (BB) for the above advantages, which keeps the data chronological, verifiable, and traceable.

2.2 Merkle Tree

A Merkle tree is a tree where every non-leaf node is the hash of a data block, which is composed of its child nodes, as shown in Fig. 1-a. Given a path from a leaf to the root rt of the tree, the leaf can be verified that it belongs to a tree and the root of the tree is rt. For example, for the $leaf_2$ in the Fig. 1-b, the path can be expressed as $path_2 := (right, h_{01}; left, leaf_3)$.

Merkle tree is widely used in various information system to help verify some data in data storage, processing, and transmission. In decentralized anonymous payment (DAP) schemes of Zerocash [10], which lets users pay each other directly and privately, Merkle tree is applied for proving that the commitment of a coin is one of all the historical commitments.

2.3 SGX and Attestation

Intel Software Guard Extensions (SGX) is a set of instructions and mechanisms for memory accesses added to recent-model Intel®Architecture processors [4]. With SGX, a process can run in a Trusted Execution Environment (TEE), which is known as an enclave in SGX. The code and data in an enclave are stored in Processor Reserved Memory (PRM), which can not be accessed by other software.

SGX can generate a proof *quote*, with which a remote system can verify that a program runs in a SGX-protected enclave. When an enclave is created, the CPU

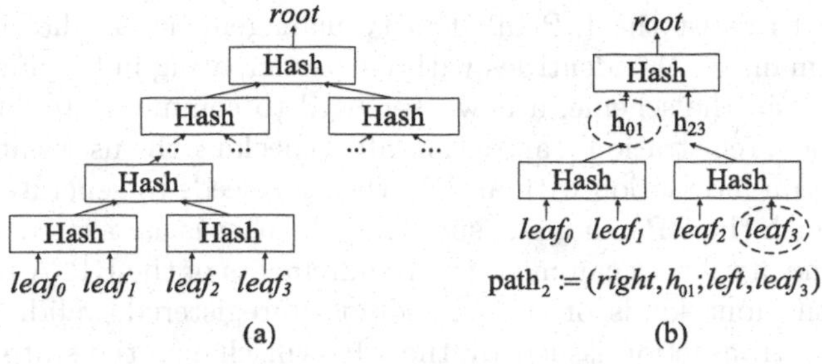

Fig. 1. Merkle Tree

will generate a measurement of the initial state. The software in the enclave can request for a report including the measurement and some supplementary data. The report will be signed by a group signature scheme to produce a *quote*, with which a remote system can verify the report by accessing Intel's Attestation Service (IAS). Each report struct includes a 256-bit field for User Data. This field can be occupied by the hash value for some auxiliary data a, which will be shared to the remote verifier. And in our proposed scheme, some input parameters, which we defined as secret data x, need to be kept from the verifier. SGX can help increase privacy and security for consensus [14,15], smart contracts [16], and data storage [17] for the Blockchain.

In this paper, a *quote* of the Intel SGX remote attestation will be informally generated as follows:

$$quote = \Sigma_{Intel}[auxiliary\ data\ hash].$$

3 Design Goals and Models

3.1 Design Goals

To effectively mitigate the risk of privacy leakage, as far as we are concerned, an ideal authentication scheme should achieve the following goals:

- The login actions of the user to RPs are unknown to the IdP.
- The user can anonymously login to any RP with an RP-specific pseudonym, and convince the RP that the pseudonym is associated with some valid identity held by the IdP.
- The user can convince an RP that his attributes meet the requirements of the RP, without revealing any raw values of the attributes.
- The identity operation logs are unmodifiable and accountable for the users.

3.2 System Model

Four kinds of roles will participate in our proposed scheme, including the users, an *identity provider* (IdP), some *relying parties* (RP), and a Blockchain. Different from the traditional Unified Authentication Schemes, we introduce a Blockchain as a platform to assist the IdP in identity management, as shown in Fig. 2. The IdP only manages the identities without participating in the authentication procedure. To join the scheme, a new user need to communicate with the IdP, which will issue a registration transaction after checking the user's attributes. In an authentication interaction with an RP, the user needs to generate an identity proof, with which the RP can make sure that the user is associated with a valid identity and the attributes can meet the requirements of the RP. A user identity is in one of the four kinds of states, include unregistered, valid, frozen, and deleted. A new transaction issued by the IdP will change the state into a new state, as shown in Fig. 3.

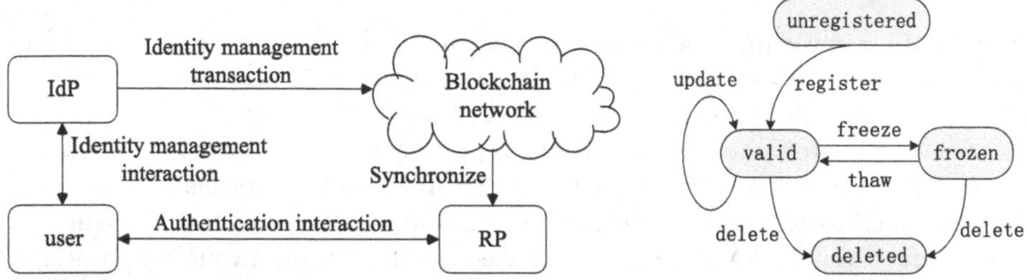

Fig. 2. System Model.

Fig. 3. State transition

3.3 Attack Model

An attacker is one of the following four kinds of attackers, malicious user, curious IdP, curious RP, and conspiracy attacker. A malicious user is a user who want to generate a fake authentication. A curious IdP is assumed to be curious about the associated pseudonyms of the registered users. A curious RP is assumed to be curious about the associated identity attributes of the authenticated identity. And the conspiracy attackers are assumed to be more than two curious RPs or the curious IdP and more than one curious RP.

The following types of attacks are considered in our anonymous authentication scheme.

- *Proof Forgery Attack*: By an proof forgery attack, we mean that an attacker attempts to forge an identity proof, with which a victim RP will misunderstand that the attacker's identity is valid and the identity attributes is verified. However, in fact, the identity attributes verification function may output 0 (unqualified), or even the user identity is not in the set of all the registered identities.
- *Proof Replay Attack*: By an proof replay attack, we mean that one or several identity proofs from a user has been obtained by the attacker, who attempts to reused the proofs for a new authentication interaction with the RP.
- *Attributes Theft Attack* A curious RP is assumed to attempt to get the identity attributes of the authenticated pseudonyms from the received proofs and the publicly accessible attributes on the Blockchain.

- *Identity Tracking Attack* A curious IdP is assumed to attempt to compute the pseudonym which should be used in an identity proof with an RP by a registered user.
- *Conspiracy Attack* Two or more RPs may share all their knowledge of the authenticated pseudonyms to analyze whether two pseudonyms authenticated on two different are associated with the same user. Similarly, the IdP and more than one RP may share the knowledge of the registered identities and the authenticated pseudonyms to analyze the associations between the pseudonyms and the Ids.

4 Privacy Preserving Anonymous Authentication

We describe the roles and key procedures of the proposed privacy preserving anonymous authentication scheme in this section.

4.1 Roles

Figure 2 summarizes the entities and interactions in our proposed *P2A*, where the participants include users, an identity provider, relying parties, and the Blockchain.

Identity Provider. An identity provider (IdP) is responsible for the management of the user identity, including operations such as user registration, update, freeze/thaw, and deletion. The operations are specifically publishing corresponding transactions (TX) on the Blockchain, including registration TX, update TX, freeze/thaw TX, and deletion TX.

A new user needs to send a registration request to the IdP firstly. when receiving a registration request from a user, the IdP should verify user identity attributes and issue a registration TX onto the Blockchain if the request is valid. The registration TX contains the salted hash value of the identity attributes, and the salt value only kept by the user and the IdP, so the identity attributes will be only known by the user and the IdP. For user registration, the IdP needs to compile a function TEE_r which will run in a user's SGX-protected enclave. An identity commitment cm will be computed in TEE_r with the identity attributes $Attr$ and user secret key s as inputs. SGX CPU of the user will sign a quote $quote_r$ to prove to the IdP that cm is well-formed with $Attr$.

When a user identity attributes needs to be updated for some reason, the IdP will issue a update TX onto the Blockchain. After the update TX is published on the Blockchain, the user can generate identity proofs with new identity attributes, and the old identity attributes will be unavailable immediately. For user update, the IdP needs to compile a function TEE_m which will run in a user's SGX-protected enclave. A new identity commitment cm_{new} will be computed in TEE_r with s and new identity attributes $Attr_{new}$. And SGX CPU of the user will sign a quote $quote_m$ to prove to the IdP that (i) cm is well-formed with $Attr_{new}$ and (ii) s has not been modified. When a user identity has to be frozen/unfrozen, the IdP needs to issue a freeze/thaw TX onto the Blockchain.

Then the identity is frozen or thawed. If the identity is frozen, the identity can not be used for authentication before being thawed. When a user identity needs to be deleted, the IdP needs to issue a deletion TX onto the Blockchain. Then the associated identity will be removed from the Blockchain, and can not be used to generate valid identity proofs. We assume the IdP is honest but curious, which means that the transactions issued by the IdP are credible, but the IdP may be curious about the user's authentication behavior, such as the user Login behavior on an RP. So, in our proposed system, a user can generate an identity proof by itself, without communication with the IdP. A user only needs to access the IdP when the identity needs to be registered, updated, or frozen/thawed. So the IdP can get nothing about user's authentication behavior. And we have further strengthened the level of privacy protection with cryptography so that even the IdP and an RP share information and launch a conspiracy attack, they can still know nothing about the association between the user identity attributes on the IdP and the pseudonym on the RP.

The IdP can only modify identity status by issuing transactions on the Blockchain, which is publicly accessible for the user. So all identity operation logs in *P2A* are accountable for the users.

Relying Party. A relying party (RP) is generally an information system where users need to use identity proofs for identity authentication. In our scheme, an RP is assumed to be associated with a unique identity number which we called RPId. An RP needs to compile a function TEE_a which will run in a user's SGX-protected enclave. TEE_a will check if the user owns one of the valid identities on the Blockchain and if the user's identity attributes meets the requirements of the RP. The requirements of the RP are defined by the RP, and can be formalized as an identity attributes verification function (IVF): $b \leftarrow IVF(A, v)$, where A is the set of identity attributes, and v is the requirement parameter. For example, if an RP requires users to be older than 18, the v can be the date 18 years old, and the $VF(A, v)$ will output 1 (qualified) if and only if v is larger than the date of birth parsed from A. When receiving an identity proof from a user, an RP will check the proof and accept the authentication if the proof is valid. A pseudonym PN can be parsed from the proof, with which the RP can determine if the authentication behaviors are coming from the same user.

User. A user is assumed to register and update identity on the IdP, and to be authenticated by the RPs. When registering on the IdP, the user should get TEE_r compiled by the IdP firstly and generate a signed $quote_r$ to prove to the IdP that a identity commitment cm is well-formed with the correct identity attributes. $quote_r$ will be packaged into a registration request to the IdP. Then a new identity will be registered onto the Blockchain with a registration TX being issued by the IdP after the registration request has been verified. Similarly, before requesting for identity update, a user needs to get TEE_u compiled by the IdP, and generate a signed $quote_m$. $quote_m$ will be packaged into a update request to the IdP. Then the associated identity will be modified with a update TX being issued by the IdP after the update request has been verified.

Different from traditional unified authentication schemes such as SAML2.0 and OpenId-Connect, in P2A, a user who has successfully registered on the IdP, can generate an identity proof locally when needed, without communicating with the IdP. When authenticated by an RP, a user will get TEE_a from the RP firstly. The user will generate a quote $quote_a$, a pseudonym PN and the authentication result b after calling the TEE_a with some parameters downloaded from the Blockchain and the valid identity attributes as inputs. An identity proof, including $quote_a$, PN, b, and some other auxiliary parameters, will be sent to the RP. Then the identity authentication will be successful if the proof is verified. An valid identity can be used to generate only one PN for an RP.

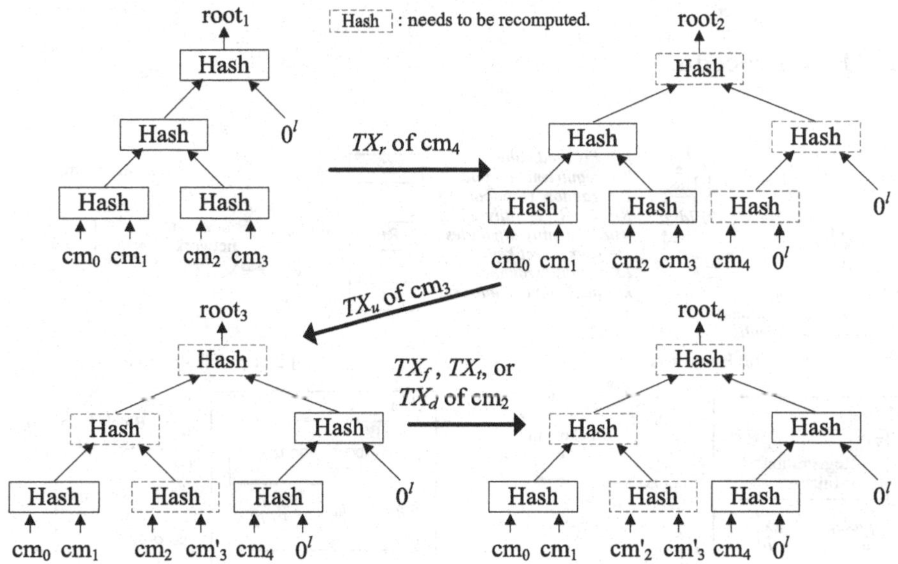

Fig. 4. In this picture, we take a three-tier Merkle tree as an example, to illustrate how the Merkle tree changes when a registration TX, a modification TX, a freeze/thaw TX, or a deletion TX has been published on the Blockchain. The l is the size of the hash function output. For a TX_f or TX_t, $cm_2' =\sim cm_2$, and for a TX_d, $cm_2' = 1 \parallel 0^{l-1}$.

Blockchain. In our proposed scheme, only the IdP can issue and publish transactions, which means that a transaction without a valid signature signed by the IdP will be rejected by every nodes in the Blockchain network. Five kinds of transactions (TX) will be issued on the Blockchain, including registration TX, update TX, freeze/thaw TX, and deletion TX. All the TXs can be accessed by every RP and user. When the IdP has issued and uploaded a TX onto the Blockchain network, the nodes which have received the TX should check it. If the TX is valid, it may be included into a new block for the Blockchain. The consensus on a new block of all the nodes means that the TXs in the new block should be verified by all the nodes.

Every node should manage a Merkle tree locally for user identity. A leaf of the tree is an valid identity commitment. When a new block is created, every node should parse all the TXs from the new block, and modify the Merkel tree accordingly. A node can parse an commitment cm from a new registration TX, and added cm into the Merkle tree as a leaf. A node can parse a new commitment cm_{new} and an old commitment cm_{old} from a update TX, and replace cm_{old} with cm_{new} in the Merkle tree. A node can parse a commitment cm from a freeze/thaw TX, and change it to the bitwise negation. A node can parse a commitment cm from a deletion TX, and remove it from the Merkle tree. The RPs and the IdP need to read the data on the Blockchain frequently, so for them, an efficient way is to maintain a Blockchain node and interact with the node.

4.2 Key Procedures

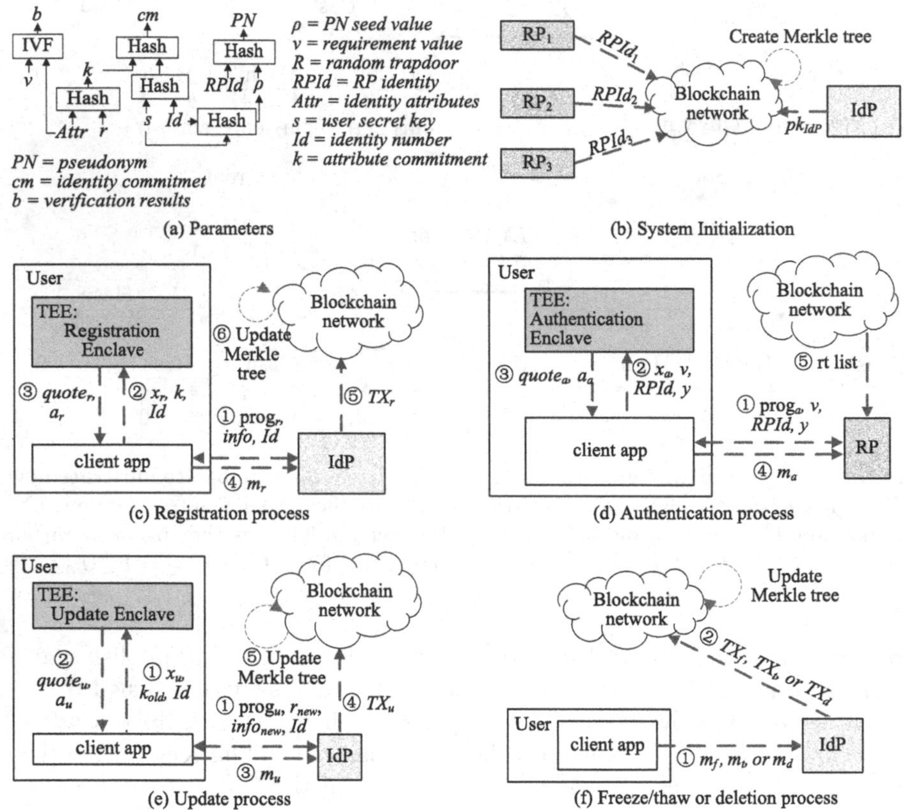

Fig. 5. Paremeters and key procedures.

In this section, we will present the details of the *P2A* . The data structure used in *P2A* is described in Fig. 5 (a). We will give the explanations on the key procedures in the scheme, including system initialization, identity registration, anonymous authentication, identity update, identity freeze/thaw, and identity deletion.

System Initialization. In the system initialization procedure, the IdP generate a public-private key pair (pk_{IdP}, sk_{IdP}). The public key pk_{IdP} will be synchronized to every Blockchain nodes, and the private key sk_{IdP} will be used to issue transactions onto the Blockchain. Every RP identity number (RPId) is synchronized to the Blockchain and accessible for every one. The RPIds of any two RPs should be different, and an RPId synchronization from a new RP will be refused by the Blockchain network if the RPId has been used by another RP. The Blockchain generates an empty Merkle tree without any identity, which means that every node of the Blockchain network create an empty Merkle tree locally.

Registration on the IdP. The identity registration procedure is shown as Fig. 5 (c). A new user who want to use *P2A* should register an identity with the IdP. The user communicates with the IdP to get the identity attributes *Attr* and an unique identity number Id. Id and *Attr* are recognized by the user and the IdP. The user then gets the SGX-compliant registration verification program $prog_r$ compiled by the IdP, and create an registration enclave TEE_r with $prog_r$. The user samples a random secret key s and set s as the secret data x_r of $prog_r$. The user samples a random trapdoor r and compute the attribute commitment k. The inputs of $prog_r$ are (x_r, k, Id), and the outputs are $(quote_r, a_r)$. A registration message $m_r := (quote_r, a_r, r)$ will be sent to the IdP in a secure manner. The $quote_r$ can be used to prove to the IdP that $prog_r$ has been running in an SGX-enclave and the a_r is believable, and the a_r can be parsed as (k, Id, cm). After having verified the $quote_r$, the IdP issues a registration TX TX_r, which includes $quote_r$, a_r, and a signature σ, onto the Blockchain. The Blockchain will accept the TX if the signature and the $quote_r$ are both valid and the identity number Id parsed from a_r is unique. Once a new registration TX has been published, every node will update the identity Merkle tree locally as described in Sect. 4.1.

In the Algorithm 1, we describe how the user constructs a registration message, how the IdP issues a registration TX, and how the Blockchain Verify a registration TX. The details of the pseudocode of $quote_r$ are described in Algorithm 2.

Authentication on the Relying Party. The participants in an authentication procedure include a registered user, an RP, and the Blockchain. The interactions between them are shown in Fig. 5 (d). The identity proof will be generated by the user locally and sent to the RP. The identity attributes *Attr*, the trapdoor r, the secret key s, and the identity number Id are kept locally by the user. The user gets the path *path* from the Blockchain, with which the current root rt can be computed from its registered identity commitment cm. The user also gets the RP identity number $RPId$ from the Blockchain and generated the extensibility

Algorithm 1. Registration. Secret data x_r is kept by the user and auxiliary data a_r is sent to the IdP.

Generate a registration message
- INPUTS:
- identity number Id
- identity attributes $Attr$
- user secret key s
- a trapdoor r
- OUTPUTS:
- registration message m_r

1. Compute $k = Hash(Attr \parallel r)$.
2. Create an enclave $\mathbf{TEE_r}$.
3. Set $x_r := (s)$.
4. Call $prog_r()$ in $\mathbf{TEE_r}$.
5. $quote_r, a_r \leftarrow prog_r(x_r, k, Id)$.
6. Set $m_r := (quote_r, a_r, r)$.
7. **Return** m_r.

Issue a registration transaction
- INPUTS:
- identity number Id
- identity attributes $Attr$
- registration message m_r
- IdP private key sk_{IdP}
- OUTPUTS:
- registration transaction TX_r if m_r is valid

1. Set $b' = 1$.
2. Set $b' = 0$ if A or RN is invalid.
3. Parse m_r as $(quote_r, a_r, r)$
4. Parse a_r as (k, Id, cm)
5. Set $b' = 0$ if $k \neq Hash(Attr \parallel r)$.
6. Parse $quote_r$ and get the auxiliary hash h_r.
7. Set $b' = 0$ if $h_r \neq Hash(a_r)$.
8. Check $quote_r$ by accessing IAS.
9. Set $b' = 0$ if $quote_r$ is invalid.
10. Compute $\sigma := Sig_{sk_{IdP}}(quote_r, a_r)$ if $b' = 1$.
11. **Return** $TX_r := (quote_r, a_r, \sigma)$ **if** $b' = 1$.

Verify a registration transaction
- INPUTS:
- a registration transaction TX_r
- the IdP's public key pk_{IdP}
- current Merkle tree mt
- OUTPUTS:
- a Merkle tree

1. Set $b' = 1$.
2. Parse TX_r as $(quote_r, a_r, \sigma)$.
3. Check σ with pk_{IdP}.
4. Set $b' = 0$ if σ is invalid.
5. Parse a_r as (k, RN, cm).
6. Parse $quote_r$ and get the auxiliary hash h_r.
7. Set $b' = 0$ if $h_r \neq Hash(a_r)$.
8. Check $quote_r$ by accessing IAS.
9. Set $b' = 0$ if $quote_r$ is invalid.
10. Add cm into mt if $b' = 1$.
11. **Return** mt.

Algorithm 2. Registration verification program ($prog_r$): A new user can prove that cm is the commitment of its identity attributes $Attr$ and identity number Id.

Function $prog_r(x_r, k, Id)$
Parse x_r as s.
  $cm = (k \parallel Hash(s \parallel Id))$
  $a_r = (k, Id, cm)$
$h_r = Hash(a_r)$
$quote_r{:=}\Sigma_{intel}[h_r]$
Return $quote_r, a_r$

parameters y for this authentication process, including a timestamp T, a random challenge number CN sampled by the RP, the public key of the user, etc. The user will communicate with the RP and get the SGX-compliant authentication verification program $prog_a$ compiled by the RP, and the requirement parameters

v. The user then creates an authentication enclave TEE_a with $prog_a$. The inputs of $prog_a$ are $(Attr, r, s, Id, path, RPId, y)$, and the outputs are an authentication message m_a, which should be sent to the RP in a secure manner. When receiving m_a, the RP will parse m_a as $(quote_a, a_a)$, and parse a_a as $(rt, PN, RPId, y, b, v)$. The RP will accept the authentication request if the following holds: (i) $b = 1$; (ii) rt is one of the several newest historical roots of the Merkle tree; (iii) $quote_a$ is valid and the h_a parsed from $quote_a$ is the hash value of a_a; (iv) T and CN parsed from y is correct.

The details of the authentication procedure and the pseudocode of $quote_a$ is described in Algorithm 3 and Algorithm 4.

Algorithm 3. Authentication. Secret data x_a is kept by the user and auxiliary data a_a is sent to the IdP.

Generate an authentication request

- INPUTS:
  - identity number Id
  - identity attributes $Attr$
  - user secret key s
  - a trapdoor r
  - path $path$ from commitment cm to root rt.
  - relying party ID $RPId$
  - RP's requirement parameters v
  - extensibility parameters y
- OUTPUTS:
  - an authentication message m_a

1. Create an enclave $\mathbf{TEE_a}$.
2. Set $x_a := (Attr, r, s, Id, path)$.
3. Call $prog_a()$ in $\mathbf{TEE_a}$.
4. $quote_a, a_a \leftarrow prog_a(x_a, v, RPId, y)$.
5. Set $m_a := (quote_a, a_a)$.
6. **Return** m_a.

Verify an authentication message

- INPUTS:
  - an authentication message m_a
  - relying party ID $RPId$
  - root list of several newest historical root $list_{rt}$
- OUTPUTS:
  - bit b', equals 1 if m_a is valid.

1. Parse m_a as $(quote_a, a_a)$.
2. Parse a_a as $(rt, PN, RPId, y, b, v)$.
3. Set $b' = b$.
4. Set $b' = 0$ if $rt \notin list_{rt}$.
5. Parse $quote_a$ and get the auxiliary hash h_a.
6. Set $b' = 0$ if $h_r \neq Hash(a_a)$.
7. Check $quote_a$ by accessing IAS.
8. Set $b' = 0$ if $quote_a$ is invalid.
9. Parse y and get timestamp T and random challenge number CN
9. Set $b' = 0$ if T or CN is wrong.
9. **Return bit** b'.

User Identity Update. In our proposed scheme, the attributes of a registered identity can be updated for some reason. For example, the user email address or phone number needs to be modified. So we designed an identity update process, with which a registered user can update its identity attributes while keep the secret key s and the identity number Id unmodified, so that the associated pseudonym numbers (PN) will be kept unchanged. The participants of the update procedure include the IdP, the user, and the Blockchain, and the interactions are shown in Fig. 5 (f). The new identity attributes $Attr_{new}$ and new trapdoor r_{new} should also be recognized by both the user and the IdP. The user

Algorithm 4. Authentication program ($prog_a$):

Function $prog_a(x_a, v, RPId, y)$.
Parse x_a as $(Attr, r, s, Id, path)$
$k = Hash(Attr \parallel r)$.
$cm = Hash(k \parallel Hash(s \parallel Id))$.
$rt = gen\_root\_from\_leaf(cm, path)$.
$\rho = Hash(Id \parallel s)$.
$PN = Hash(RPId \parallel \rho)$.
$b = IVF(A, v)$.
$a_a = (rt, RPId, PN, b, v, y)$.
$h_a = Hash(a_a)$.
$quote_a := \Sigma_{intel}[h_a]$.
Return $quote_a, a_a$.

will compute a new identity attribute commitment k_{new} with $Attr_{new}$ and r_{new}). The user will communicate with the IdP and get the SGX-compliant update program $prog_u$ compiled by the IdP. The inputs of $prog_u$ include (s, k_{old}, k_{new}) and the outputs are a quote $quote_u$ and the auxiliary data a_u. $quote_u$ can be used to prove to the IdP that the secret key s and the identity number Id are kept unchanged for the updated identity. An update message m_u will be sent to the IdP and the IdP will issued an associated update TX TX_u onto the Blockchain. The TX_u includes $quote_u$, A_u, and a signature σ. The old identity commitment cm_{old} and the new identity commitment cm_{new} can be parsed from a_u. Each Blockchain node will update the Merkle tree when receiving TX_u by change the cm_{old} to cm_{new}.

The details of the update procedure and the pseudocode of $quote_u$ is described in Algorithm 5 and Algorithm 6.

User Identity Freeze, Thaw, and Deletion. In our anonymous authentication scheme, a registered identity can be frozen, and a frozen identity can also be thawed. The IdP can freeze/thaw an identity by issuing a freeze/thaw TX with or without the identity freeze request from the user. A freeze/thaw transaction TX_f or TX_t includes the current associated identity commitment cm_{old}, and a signature $\sigma_f/\sigma_t := Sig_{sk_{IdP}}(cm_{old})$. When a new TX_f or TX_t has been published on the Blockchain, each Blockchain node will modify the Merkle tree accordingly after verifying the signature of the transaction. Each node will parse the transaction and get the old identity commitment cm_{old} and the Merkle tree will be modified by changing cm_{old} to its bitwise negation $cm_{new} =\sim cm_{old}$. A frozen identity can not be used for authentication because the user can not find the valid (k', s', Id') so that $\sim cm = Hash(k' \parallel Hash(s' \parallel Id'))$ in polynomial time. And a thawed identity can be revived because $cm =\sim (\sim (cm))$.

When a registered identity needs to be deleted from the set of valid identities, the IdP will issue a deletion transaction TX_d. Each node can parse TX_d and get an identity commitment cm from TX_d. Then each node will replace cm with $1 \parallel 0^{l-1}$ as shown in Fig. 4.

Algorithm 5. Update user attributes.

Generate update request

• INPUTS:
- old identity attributes $Attr_{old}$
- new identity attributes $Attr_{new}$
- old trapdoor r_{old}
- new trapdoor r_{new}
- identity number Id
- secret key s

• OUTPUTS:
- an identity update request message m_u

1. Compute $k_{old} = Hash(Attr_{old} \| r_{old})$.
2. Compute $k_{new} = Hash(Attr_{new} \| r_{new})$.
3. Create an enclave $\mathbf{TEE_u}$.
4. Set $x_u = (s)$.
5. Call the function $prog_u(x_u, k_{old}, k_{new}, Id)$ in $\mathbf{TEE_u}$.
6. $quote_u, a_u \leftarrow prog_u(x_u, k_{old}, k_{new}, Id)$.
7. Set $m_u := (quote_u, a_u)$.
8. **Return** m_u.

Issue an update transaction

• INPUTS:
- old identity attributes $Attr_{old}$
- new identity attributes $Attr_{new}$
- old trapdoor r_{old}
- new trapdoor r_{new}
- an identity update request message m_u

• OUTPUTS:
- an update TX TX_u

1. Parse m_u as $(quote_u, a_u)$.
2. Parse a_u as $(k_{old}, k_{new}, cm_{old}, cm_{new}, Id)$.
3. Set $b' = 1$.
4. Set $b' = 0$ if $k_{old} \neq Hash(Attr_{old} \| r_{old})$.
5. Set $b' = 0$ if $k_{new} \neq Hash(Attr_{new} \| r_{new})$.
6. Parse $quote_u$ and get the auxiliary hash h_u.
7. Set $b' = 0$ if $h_u \neq Hash(a_u)$.
8. Check $quote_u$ by accessing IAS.
9. Set $b' = 0$ if $quote_a$ is invalid.
10. Set $b' = 0$ if Id is valid.
11. Compute $\sigma_u := Sig_{sk_{IdP}}(quote_u, a_u)$ if $b' = 1$.
12. **Return** $TX_u := (quote_u, a_u, \sigma_u)$ **if** $b' = 1$.

Verify an update transaction

• INPUTS:
- current Merkle tree mt
- an update TX TX_u

• OUTPUTS:
- a new Merkle tree mt_new

1. Set $b' = 1$.
2. Parse TX_u as $(quote_u, a_u, \sigma_u)$.
3. Check σ_u with pk_{IdP}.
4. Set $b' = 0$ if σ_u is invalid.
5. Parse $quote_u$ and get the auxiliary hash h_u.
6. Set $b' = 0$ if $h_u \neq Hash(a_u)$.
7. Parse a_u as $(k_{old}, k_{new}, cm_{old}, cm_{new}, Id)$.
8. Set $b' = 0$ if $cm_{old} \notin mt$.
9. Update mt to mt_{new} by replacing cm_{old} with cm_{new} if $b' = 1$.
10. Return mt_{new}.

Algorithm 6 Update program $(prog_u)$.

Function $prog_u(x_u, k_{old}, k_{new}, Id)$
Parse x_u as (s).
$cm_{old} = Hash(k_{old} \| Hash(s \| Id))$
$cm_{new} = Hash(k_{new} \| Hash(s \| Id))$
$a_u = (k_{old}, k_{new}, cm_{old}, cm_{new}, Id)$
$h_u = Hash(a_u)$
$quote_u := \Sigma_{intel}[h_u]$
Return $quote_u, a_u$

5 Analysis

5.1 Security Analysis

In this section, we will demonstrate that *P2A* can resist the attacks mentioned in Sect. 3.3.

Proof Forgery Attack. An proof forgery attacker will attempt to generate a forge $quote_a^*$ to deceive an RP that the user has been authenticated successfully in the local created SGX enclave. However, in fact, the user is not associated with any registered identity or the identity attributes is non-compliant for the RP's requirement. The proof forgery attack will failed in *P2A*. Firstly, the SGX CPU signed quote $quote_a^*$ ensures that the authentication verification function has been initialized and executed correctly, and auxiliary data $a_a^* = (rt^*, RPId^*, PN^*, b^*, v^*, y^*)$ can not be modified out of SGX enclave. If a user want to use an unregistered, frozen, or deleted identity for authentication, the rt^* can not be the current Merkle tree root because the rt^* is not computed from any leaf of the Merkle tree. Another attack manner for the attacker is to use a registered identity with the non-compliant identity attributes, which, however, will be found by the RP because $b = 0$ or v^* is wrong.

Proof Replay Attack. An Proof replay attacker is assumed to have stolen the authentication request m_a of a victim user, and attempts to reuse m_a for impersonate the victim to login the RP. However, in m_a, the random challenge number CN and the time stamp T are embedded in the extensibility parameters y, which is part of the auxiliary data a_a and cannot be modified by the attacker. And the RP will reject the authentication because T is expired and CN is not correct.

Attributes Theft Attack. A attributes theft attacker, such as a curious RP, is assumed to be curious about the identity attributes $info$ and the number Id of the authenticated users. They attempts to get knowledge about $info$ and Id from the authentication request m_a. However, $info$ and Id are embedded in the secret data x_a which will kept secretly against the RP. The RP can parse a_a from m_a, and parse a_a as $(rt, PN, RPId, y, b, v)$, with which the RP can know nothing about $info$ and Id because of the one-way property of the hash function.

Identity Tracking Attack. A identity tracking attacker is assumed as a curious IdP. The IdP attempts to compute the pseudonyms associated with the registration request m_r. The IdP can parse a_r from m_r, and parse a_r as (k, Id, m). However, the secret key s will be kept privately against the IdP, so the IdP cannot compute the PN seed value ρ with the equation $\rho = Hash(Id \parallel s)$, and of course cannot compute the PN with the equation $PN = Hash(RPId \parallel \rho)$.

Conspiracy Attack. Without loss of generality, we assume that a conspiracy attacker know two the authenticated requests m_{a1}, m_{a2} and a registration request m_r. The attacker attempts to analyze whether m_{a1} and m_{a2} belong to the same user, or whether m_r is associated with m_{a1}. The first problems is equivalent to analyzing whether PN_1 and PN_2 are computed with the same PN seed value ρ, and the second problem is equivalent to analyzing whether Id can be used to compute a PN seed value $\rho' = Hash(Id \parallel s)$ so that PN_1 can be computed with ρ. These two problems are difficult because the properties of the hash function, so the conspiracy attacks will be failed.

5.2 Performance Analysis

We built a prototype system and analyzed the communication overhead, calculation overhead, and Blockchain space overhead of the transactions. Without loss of generality, we Set the size of each parameter in Fig. 5(a) as shown in Table 1. We deployed the client in an Ubuntu1804 system with a CPU model of Intel(R)Core(TM) i5-6300U CPU @2.40 GHz 2.5 GHz and a system memory of 16 GB. In each procedure of the system, the most of the computational overhead is generated during calculating quotes. We have measured that during the registration, authentication, and update process, the client takes about 522 ms to generate the quote.

Both IdP and RP can download the certificate chain and deploy the server locally, so the interaction with the IAS server provided by Intel can be omitted, and thus the communication overhead caused by the interaction with the IAS server when verifying the quote can be omitted. And $prog_a$,$prog_r$, and $prog_u$ can be embedded into the client in advance, without the need for temporary download. In the registration procedure, the communication overhead is mainly composed of the interaction between the client and the IdP, and uploading of m_r, the size of which is 1244 bytes. In the authentication procedure, the user needs to download the v, RPId, and y, 96 bytes in total, and upload m_a, the size of which is 1277 bytes. The user also needs to download the *path* from his commitment cm to the current root rt, the size of which is 2056 bytes. In the update procedure, the user needs to upload a m_u, 1276 bytes in total.

In our proposed scheme, the transations onto the Blockchain only generated during the low-frequency operations such as registration, update, freeze, thaw, and deletion. Therefore, the space requirement for the blockchain is not high, and public chains such as Ethereum can be used for deployment. The size of the transactions required for registration and update is 1180 and 1244 bytes, and the size of the transactions for freeze, thaw, and deletion operations is only 103 bytes.

Table 1. Parameter size

Paremeter	Size (byte)	Paremeter	Size (byte)
b	1	k,cm,PN,ρ	32
Attr	1024	path	32*64+64/8
σ_*	71	s,r,RPId,Id,v,y,rt	32
a_r	96	$quote_r$, $quote_a$, $quote_u$	1116
a_u	160	a_a	161
m_r	1244	m_a	1277
m_u	1276	TX_u	1244
TX_r	1180	TX_f, TX_t, TX_d	103

6 Discussions

The Security of SGX. Our proposed P2A scheme is based on the security assumption that the quote generated by SGX cannot be forged. At present, most attacks against the SGX system are to obtain confidential information in the Enclave through side channels. In this solution, the Enclave is created on the user's local device, so there is no need to worry about the privacy leakage caused by the Enclave being attacked by the side channel. Nilsson et al. [18] has proposed that the attestation key might be extracted. However, some solutions [19,20] can also be used in our scheme to prevent clients from forging quotes.

The Storage of Identity Attributes. In this article, we assume that the user's identity attributes is stored on the user's local computer. If having to use the identity on a new computer, the user can easily recover all parameters with the help of the IdP, as long as the user keeps the secret key s. The user can login the IdP and download $info$, r, and Id kept by the IdP.

The Tolerance of Latency in Merkle Tree Modification. In the authentication procedure, the user will prove to the RP that the commitment of his identity is one leaf of the current Merkle tree with the newest root rt_n, where n is the number of all the versions of the Merkle tree. However, due to the network delay and processing delay, the Merkle tree will be changed during the authentication interaction. So, the RP will accept the authentication request if the root parsed from the request is in the list of the several newest historical roots. The number of roots in the list can be individually set by every RPs.

The Number of Pseudonyms for a User on a Single RP. According to the equation $PN = Hash(RPId \parallel \rho)$, a user can only generate one PN with an RPId. If an RP want to allow a registered user is associated with n PNs on it, it can keep n RPIds. And if an RP do not need to know whether two authentications are requested from the same identity, it can remove the RPId and the PN from the auxiliary data. And thus the user do not need to generate a PN for the RP.

Tracking Malicious Identities. The purpose of *P2A* is to protect the identity attributes in the authentication, and the PNs can not be tracked by the RPs and the IdP as designed in Sect. 4. However, for some relying parties to track illegal pseudonyms, a trusted *tracking authority* (TA) can be added into *P2A*. The public-private key pair (pk_{TA}, sk_{TA}) will be generated by the TA, and pk_{TA} will be publicly accessible. Every user needs to encrypted the PN seed value ρ with pk_{TA} and get the cipher-text $c := Enc_{pk_{TA}}(\rho)$. c will be computed in the registration enclave TEE_r and added into the auxiliary data a_r, together with pk_{TA}. So with a_r and $quote_r$ the user can prove to others that c is the cipher-text of his PN seed value encrypted with pk_{TA}. c can be decrypted by the TA to get ρ, and thus all the PNs associated with rho can be computed by the TA. c and the identity commitment cm os the same user will be packaged into the same registration transaction, so that the TA will know all the PNs of a commitment. When having been proved that a PN needed to be tracked, the TA will return the associated commitment, with which the IdP can figure out the identity attributes of the malicious user. The TA does not need to participate in the registration procedure, so it can be offline and only need to synchronize all the registration transactions in a secure manner.

7 Related Work

In Security Assertion Markup Language 2.0 (SAML 2.0) [1], the identity provider and a service provider can exchange data through redirected access of the user's browser. With SAML 2.0, once a user's identity has been authenticated by the identity provider, he can login to other applications directly without having to enter his username and password. OAuth 2.0 (Open Authorization) [2] is an open standard that allows users to allow third-party applications to access private resources (such as photos, videos, contact lists) that the user has stored on a website without providing a username and password to the third party application. And OpenID Connect 1.0 [3] is a simple identity layer on top of the OAuth 2.0 protocol. With the OpenID Connect 1.0 the user can realize unified authentication.

Zhang et al. [14] and Milutinovic et al. [15] allow miners to generate proof-of-useful-work (PoUW) for the Blockchain consensus protocols. Instead of calculating useless hash values, PoUW can be generated by providing trustworthy remote attestation with SGX on CPU cycles they devote to inherently useful workloads, and thus avoiding wasting computational resources. Matetic et al. [21] propose a rollback protection system called ROTE with SGX that realizes integrity protection as a distributed system.

8 Conclusions

In this paper, we propose an privacy preserving anonymous authentication scheme for protecting user identity related privacy in the authentication interactions with online applications. *P2A* is designed based on Blockchain and Intel SGX. Owing to its design philosophy, *P2A* supports user authentication independent of the IdP, non-leakage proof of user attributes fulfillment, isolated pseudonyms across RPs, and accountable identity management. The security analysis demonstrates that the proposed scheme is secure under the strict assumption of malicious user, curious relying party, curious identity provider, and the conspiracy attackers. We can conclude that *P2A* is a secure and reliable authentication scheme that provides exciting privacy preserving features.

References

1. Scott, C., Jahan, M., Rob, P., Eve, M.: Metadata for the oasis security assertion markup language (saml) v2. 0 (2005)
2. Dick, H.: The oauth 2.0 authorization framework (2012)
3. Nat, S., John, B., Mike, J., de Medeiros, B., Mortimore, C.: Openid connect core 1.0 incorporating errata set 1. The OpenID Foundation, specification (2014)
4. Costan, V., Devadas, S.: Intel sgx explained. IACR Cryptology ePrint Archive **2016**(086), 1–118 (2016)
5. Ittai, A., Shay, G., Simon, J., Vincent, S.: Innovative technology for cpu based attestation and sealing. In: Proceedings of the 2nd International Workshop on Hardware and Architectural Support for Security and Privacy, vol. 13. ACM New York, NY, USA (2013)
6. Matthew, H., Reshma, L., Pradeep, P., Vinay, P., Juan Del, C.: Using innovative instructions to create trustworthy software solutions. HASP@ ISCA, 11 (2013)
7. Frank, M., et al.: Innovative instructions and software model for isolated execution. Hasp@ isca, 10(1), 56–63 (2013)
8. Satoshi, N.: Bitcoin: a peer-to-peer electronic cash system. http://bitcoin.org/bitcoin.pdf (2008)
9. Wood, G., et al.: Ethereum: a secure decentralised generalised transaction ledger. Ethereum Project Yellow Paper **151**(2014), 1–32 (2014)
10. Sasson, E.B., et al.: Zerocash: decentralized anonymous payments from bitcoin. In: 2014 IEEE Symposium on Security and Privacy, pp. 459–474. IEEE (2014)
11. Van Saberhagen, N.: Cryptonote v **2** (2013)
12. Evan, D., Daniel, D.: Dash: a privacycentric cryptocurrency. GitHub. https://www.github.com/dashpay/dash/wiki/Whitepaper (2015)
13. Ahmed, K., Andrew, M., Elaine, S., Zikai, W., Charalamposm, P.: Hawk: the blockchain model of cryptography and privacy-preserving smart contracts. In: 2016 IEEE Symposium on Security and Privacy (SP), pp. 839–858. IEEE (2016)
14. Fan, Z., Ittay, E., Robert, E., Ari, J., Robbert, V.R.: {REM}: resource-efficient mining for blockchains. In: 26th {USENIX} Security Symposium ({USENIX} Security 17), pp. 1427–1444 (2017)
15. Mitar, M., Warren, H., Howard, W., Maxinder, K.: Proof of luck: an efficient blockchain consensus protocol. In: Proceedings of the 1st Workshop on System Software for Trusted Execution, p. 2. ACM (2016)
16. Yuan, R., Xia, Y.-B., Chen, H.-B., Zang, B.-Y., Xie, J.: Shadoweth: private smart contract on public blockchain. J. Comput. Sci. Technol. **33**(3), 542–556 (2018)
17. Gbadebo, A., Vishal, K., Latifur, K., Kevin, H.: Decentralized iot data management using blockchain and trusted execution environment. In: 2018 IEEE International Conference on Information Reuse and Integration (IRI), pp. 15–22. IEEE (2018)
18. Alexander, N., Pegah, N.B., Joakim, B.: A survey of published attacks on intel SGX. Technical report (2020)
19. Guoxing, C., et al.: Racing in hyperspace: closing hyper-threading side channels on SGX with contrived data races. In: 2018 IEEE Symposium on Security and Privacy (SP), pp. 178–194. IEEE (2018)
20. Oleksii, O., Bohdan, T., Robert, K., Mark, S., Christof, F.: Varys: protecting {SGX} enclaves from practical side-channel attacks. In: 2018 {USENIX} Annual Technical Conference ({USENIX}{ATC} 18), pp. 227–240 (2018)
21. Sinisa, M., et al.: Rote: rollback protection for trusted execution. In: Proceedings of the 26th USENIX Conference on Security Symposium (2017)

Spectrum Privacy Preserving for Social Networks: A Personalized Differential Privacy Approach

Yang Liu, Yong Zeng(✉), Zhihong Liu, and Jianfeng Ma

School of Cyber Engineering, Xidian University, Xi'an 710071, China
yzeng@mail.xidian.edu.cn

Abstract. The characteristics of social networks has always been a hot topic of scientific research. In order to protect the privacy of users, the owner of the private data need to provide privacy protection when providing inquiries or publishing data. Local differential privacy (LDP) is difficult to construct a highly available social networks graph due to its independent perturbation process. Centralized differential privacy usually adds excessive noise due to the structural characteristics of social networks graphs. Higher security usually results in lower availability. Simply implementing any differential privacy mechanism will cause a large amount of data to be disturbed by noise. On the other hand, some spectral based privacy protection methods provide accurate spectrum, however ignore the disclosure of privacy data in spectrum query. Therefore, we propose a spectrum query algorithm based on personalized differential privacy. The algorithm effectively improves data availability by taking advantage of different privacy preferences of users in the social network and the characteristics of the spectrum. To verify the availability of these methods, experimental tests have been carried out in both model networks and actual networks, which shows that the algorithm improves the availability of data when it has the same security.

Keywords: Social networks · Difference privacy · Spectrum

1 Introduction

Social networks are complex networks that reflect the connections between people. With the development of technology, especially the promotion of instant messaging tools, social networks are becoming more and more important. The macroscopic characteristics and structural information of social networks are of great help to the study of human society. However, the security of users' social relationship and personal privacy data in social networks still needs to be studied. Especially the relational privacy of social networks, that is, the connection between people.

The method based on graph-anonymity could not resist the attacks based on background knowledge and consistency [1, 2]. Therefore, the research on the privacy protection of social networks has been transformed into the research based on differential

Y. Wu and M. Yung (Eds.): Inscrypt 2020, LNCS 12612, pp. 277–287, 2021.
https://doi.org/10.1007/978-3-030-71852-7_18

privacy [3–5]. However, due to the strict definition of a unified level of privacy protection, the data availability of the network will be greatly reduced after the centralized differential privacy noise processing is performed on the data [6]. It is unrealistic to assume that everyone has the same privacy protection.

A possible solution is to set a personalized privacy threshold for each user in centralized differential privacy [7]. Jorgensen [8] first proposed a personalized differential privacy (PDP) mechanism at the ICDE conference. This mechanism preprocesses the data, and then applies the differential privacy mechanism to the pre-processed data set. Zhang [9] applied the personalized difference privacy mechanism to the protection of social networks privacy, but there was no conclusion on the selection rules of segmentation and sampling coefficient. Chamikara [10] proposes an efficient and scalable privacy protection algorithm (SEAL) for big data and data streams. However, SEAL's current configuration does not allow distributed data perturbation, and it only limits the utility to privacy-protected data classification. Cui [11] proposed a trust-grained personalized differential privacy (TGDP) mechanism, but trust is influenced by several social factors, and sometimes not every kind of required data is available. In addition, weighing values for different factors are always based on subjective experience.

Social networks not only have unique characteristics. It is also found that the spectrum is closely related to the properties of the graph [12]. Therefore, many spectrum-based privacy protection methods have emerged, such as Singular Value Decomposition (SVD) perturbations [13, 14], eigenvalue decomposition perturbations [14, 15]. These methods lack the security analysis and security model and there is a risk of being reconstructed [14–16]. In addition, most of the existing spectral information privacy protection methods [17] usually adopt the consistent privacy threshold. These methods are also limited by the aforementioned disadvantages of differential privacy.

2 Our Contribution

In this paper, we focus on mitigating the decline in data availability due to differential privacy disturbances. In the above-mentioned traditional differential privacy mechanism, as there always exists a tradeoff between availability and security of data, a higher security generally indicates a lower availability. Simply implementing any differential privacy mechanism will cause a large amount of data to be disturbed by noise. In order to solve these problems, we propose a spectrum query algorithm based on personalized differential privacy. Specifically, our main contributions are summarized as follows. (I) We apply the sampling mechanism to social networks. This mechanism effectively improves data availability while ensuring the same level of privacy security. (II) We use the aggregation mechanism to obtain the optimal solution of the sampling threshold and evaluate the error caused by the sampling. In addition, we apply the algorithm to the privacy protection of spectrum information in social networks. As far as we know, our work is the first to apply a non-uniform privacy sampling mechanism to the spectrum information protection field of social networks.

3 Background and Definition

This paper aims to protect the spectrum of personal relationship data in social networks. So, we define the social networks data set as the weighted graph $G(V, E)$.

Definition 1. If graph G and G' have only one edge with different weights and the change is not more than 1, then G' is called G's weighted neighbor graph.

Definition 2. A privacy specification is a mapping from users to personal privacy preferences. The notation $\Phi u \in (0,1]$ is used to denote the privacy preference corresponding to user $u \in U$.

Definition 3. (Personalized Differential Privacy) [8] Let M be a graph analysis algorithm, which takes graph G as input and outputs $M(G)$. For all output subsets S, pair of neighboring datasets G and G', with $G \sim G'$, it is satisfied:

$$\Pr[M(G) \in S] \leq e^{\Phi^{u}} \cdot \Pr[M(G') \in S] \tag{1}$$

then M satisfies edge weighted ε-PDP.

Singular values and the singular vector are related to network structure closely. With the development of machine learning theory, more and more attention has been paid to spectrum. No matter what kind of spectrum of the graph, it refers to the eigenvalue and singular value of the corresponding matrix, and the spectrum vector refers to the eigenvector and singular vector. Corresponding to spectrum, spectrum decomposition can be divided into eigenvalue decomposition and singular value decomposition. The singular value decomposition is a generalization of eigenvalue decomposition on any matrix.

4 Personalized Differential Privacy Algorithms for Spectral

This section will investigate the realization principle of personalized differential privacy. Secondly, the global sensitivity of the query function is analyzed and proved. The main result in this paper is given as follows.

4.1 The Sampling Mechanism Implements the PDP

Sampling mechanism is a method to design personalized differential privacy algorithm. The probability of the random sampling mechanism depends on the user's privacy threshold, and adds the differential privacy noise to the query results. In the graph data of social networks, the sample object is the edge between nodes. In directed graphs, edge weights and privacy thresholds are determined by the starting node. In an undirected graph, the edge weight is determined by the two related nodes, and the edge privacy threshold depends on the stricter of the two nodes. The sampling mechanism are defined as follows:

Definition 4. (Sampling mechanism) [8] Consider a function f, a graph dataset G, and a privacy specification Φ. Let $RS(G, \Phi, t)$ denote the procedure that independently samples each edge $x \in$ D with probability.

$$\pi_x = \begin{cases} \frac{e^{\min\{\Phi^{x_1}, \Phi^{x_2}\}} - 1}{e^t - 1} & \text{if } \min\{\Phi^{x_1}, \Phi^{x_2}\} < t \\ 1 & \text{otherwise} \end{cases} \tag{2}$$

where $\min\Phi^u \leq t \leq \max\Phi^u$ and maximizes q_ε. Φ^{x1}, Φ^{x2} represents the privacy preference of the two edge-related nodes respectively.

The definition indicates that the privacy preference of the edge is close to 0, and the probability of the edge being selected is greater. When the privacy preference is greater than the privacy threshold t, this edge must be selected. Generally, the closer Φ is to 1, the stricter the user's privacy requirements. Therefore, the probability of edge selection is negatively correlated with the privacy preference of the edge node.

The previous algorithm analyzes the security issues of undirected weighted social networks, and the disturbance of singular values may lead to negative weights in networks that originally contained only positive weights. The sampling algorithm in this paper only uses the existence of the selected edge as a basis for judgment and calculation.

4.2 Privacy Threshold of the Sampling Mechanism

According to the definition of the sampling mechanism, we need to determine the value of the privacy threshold t. Sampling when the tuple's privacy preference is less than the privacy threshold. The smaller the threshold, the fewer tuples discarded by sampling, and the lower the sampling error, but it will cause the differential privacy mechanism to add more noise. When $t = \max\ \Phi^u$, each tuple provides the exact privacy required to meet its privacy preferences, but not necessarily the best utility.

The optimal value of the sampling threshold depends not only on the distribution of data, but also on the set of privacy specifications. One possible mechanism is to analyze the given network data set in advance using the idea of aggregation before sampling, which was investigated in the literature [16–18]. This mechanism divides similar nodes into the same group and calculates the influence of threshold value on the data set through the evaluation function. Specifically, $\Omega = \{g_1, \ldots\ldots, g_n\}$ represents different aggregation strategies. First, the nodes in the original data set are grouped by the aggregation strategy, and $g_n = \{k_1, \ldots\ldots, k_n\}$ represents different nodes in the group. Based on this, the sampling threshold is determined based on the pre-sampling results. At the same time, a quality function needs to be designed to evaluate the aggregation sampling mechanism. Our quality function is like that used in [24], and has two components. The first component captures the errors introduced in the process of sampling, computed as follows:

$$l_{samp}(G, \Phi, \Omega) = \sum_{g_k \in \Omega} \sum_{e \in g_k} \left| c_w - \frac{\sum_{e \in g_k} c_w}{|g_k|} \right| \tag{3}$$

where c_w denotes the number of edges with the weight w in a group. The above sums over the error for all group. The second component captures the sampling loss. Intuitively, we want to capture the number of edges that change after sampling.

$$l_{edge}(G) = \left|\{e|e \in G, e_{weight} \neq e'_{weight}\}\right| \tag{4}$$

Combining the two components, our proposed quality function is

$$q_{\varepsilon}(G, \Phi, \Omega) = -l_{samp}(G, \Phi, \Omega) - l_{edge}(G) \tag{5}$$

According to the aggregation mechanism and quality function evaluation sampling process, we can get a better privacy threshold. Based on the selected privacy threshold and privacy specification set, it can be used to personalize differential privacy algorithms. Detailed steps are shown in Algorithm 1.

Algorithm 1: Random sampling threshold algorithm

Input: Graph G, Privacy Specification Φ, candidates T, Aggregation strategy O
Output: Random sampling threshold t

```
Random sampling threshold algorithm (G, Φ)
For each (t, Ω) ∈ T × O, computes q_ε (G, Φ, Ω)
For each Ω ∈ O do
    For each t ∈ T do
        if q'_ε (G, Φ, Ω') < q_ε (G, Φ, Ω)
            t = t'
Output t
```

4.3 Differential Privacy Perturbation of Spectrum

According to graph theory, a weighted undirected graph G is represented by a matrix A. The matrix $A_{n\times n}$ can be decomposed into singular values $\lambda = (\lambda_1, \lambda_2,\ldots, \lambda_n)$ and corresponding singular vectors $U_n = (u_1, u_2,\ldots, u_n)$, under ε-differential privacy with the given graph G and privacy specification Φ. We first derive the sensitivities for the eigenvalues and eigenvectors. Because the perturbed eigenvectors will no longer be orthogonalized to each other, we finally do a postprocess to normalize and orthogonalize the perturbed eigenvectors according to orthogonalization of vectors with minimal adjustment [15].

Theorem 1. (Global sensitivity of singular value) Let function M take graph G as input, and output the singular value after the disturbance. The global sensitivity of all singular values $\boldsymbol{\lambda} = (\lambda_1, \lambda_2,\ldots, \lambda_n)$ as output value is $\Delta f_1 = \sqrt{2n}$.

Proof. Let G be a weighted undirected graph whose weight adjacency matrix is $A_{n\times n}$. According to definition 2, without losing generality, the edge weight between node v and node u in sampled graph G is changed by 1 as neighbor graph G'. If the perturbation matrix $P = A - A'$, then P is a symmetric matrix where only P_{ij} and P_{ji} have value ± 1

and all other entries are 0. We have the Frobenius norm of P respectively as $||P||_F = \sqrt{2}$. Based on the matrix perturbation theory, we have.

$$\Delta f_1 = \sum_{i=1}^{n} |\bar{\lambda}_i - \lambda_i| \leq \sqrt{n}\sqrt{\sum_{i=1}^{n} (\bar{\lambda}_i - \lambda_i)^2} \leq \sqrt{n}\|P\|_F = \sqrt{2n} \tag{6}$$

So, the global sensitivity of singular value is $\sqrt{2n}$.

Theorem 2. (Global sensitivity of singular vector) Let function M take graph G as input, and output the singular vector after the disturbance. The global sensitivity of each singular vector is

$$\Delta f_2 = \frac{\sqrt{n}}{\min\{|\lambda_i - \lambda_{i-1}|, |\lambda_i - \lambda_{i+1}|\}} \tag{7}$$

Proof. We define the perturbation matrix P and other terminologies the same as those in the proof of Theorem 2. We denote singular vectors of matrix A, A + P respectively as column vectors u_i and $\bar{u}_i$. Based on the matrix perturbation theory, for each eigenvector, we have

$$\Delta f_2 \leq \sqrt{n}\|\bar{u}_i - u_i\|_2 \leq \frac{\sqrt{n}\|Pu_i\|_2}{\min\{|\lambda_i - \lambda_{i-1}|, |\lambda_i - \lambda_{i+1}|\}} \tag{8}$$

Because of the particularity of perturbation matrix P, the 2 norms of P can be obtained directly $\| P \|_2 = 1$. The equation can be obtained. Therefore, the global sensitivity of the singular vector is obtained.

Algorithm 2: Personalized differential privacy algorithm for spectral

Input: Graph G, Privacy Specification Φ

Output: The singular values $\boldsymbol{\lambda} = (\lambda_1, \lambda_2, ..., \lambda_n)$ and corresponding singular vector $U_n = (u_1, u_2, ..., u_n)$ satisfies Φ-Personalized differential privacy.

PDP for social networks (G, i, ε)
1: $t \leftarrow q_\varepsilon$ (G, t, Ω) by Algorithm 1.
2: $G' \leftarrow$ Sampling mechanism(t) to G
3: Decomposition $A(G')$ obtain the singular values $\lambda = (\lambda_1, \lambda_2, ..., \lambda_n)$ and corresponding singular vector $U_n = (u_1, u_2, ..., u_n)$
4: add Laplace noise to λ_n with Δf_1
5: add Laplace noise to u_i with Δf_2
6: Normalize and orthogonalize $u_1, u_2, ..., u_n$
7: Output $\lambda_1, \lambda_2, ..., \lambda_n$ and $u_1, u_2, ..., u_n$

The sampling procedure has definite steps, which are evaluated according to the aggregation mechanism and quality function, so the sampling result and time cost can be calculated, so the method of obtaining the solution is also reproducible and quantifiable.

5 Experiments and Results Analysis

The privacy protection algorithm protects the private data from being leaked and ensures the availability of data, which two are mutually restrictive and indispensable. For security, differential privacy mechanism, which has strict proof in theory and practice to ensure its security is adopted in this paper. As for data availability, it will be tested and analyzed detailed in this section. First, we verify the effectiveness of the new mechanism on the BA scale-free network and the ER random network. The availability of the spectrum was tested and analyzed through numerical experiments. Then, we compared it with the current best personalized differential privacy algorithm (TGDP) [11]. The root mean square error (RMSE) is used to measure the deviation between the observed value and the true value. It reflects the accuracy of the results well, and it quantifies the degree to which the measured data deviates from the true value [20].

5.1 Datasets and Settings

In order to verify the effectiveness of the algorithm, we compared the BA Scale-free network and ER random network. Considering that many actual networks have the characteristics of BA and ER networks, so different types of networks for multiple experiments are generated by these two networks.

In order to develop a set of privacy specifications, we randomly divide users on the network into four groups. Different groups represent people with different requirements for privacy protection. The privacy specification Φu_1 of users in Group G_1 was drawn uniformly at random from the ranges (0.01, 0.25). Similarly, $\{\Phi u_2 \in (0.25,0.5) \mid u_2 \in G_2\}$, $\{\Phi u_3 \in (0.5,0.75) \mid u_3 \in G_3\}$, $\{\Phi u_4 \in (0.75,1) \mid u_4 \in G_4\}$. Each group accounts for different proportions in the population. For example, $P_1 = 0.15$ means that the number of users in Group 1 accounts for 15% of the total and $P_1 + P_2 + P_3 + P_4 = 100\%$.

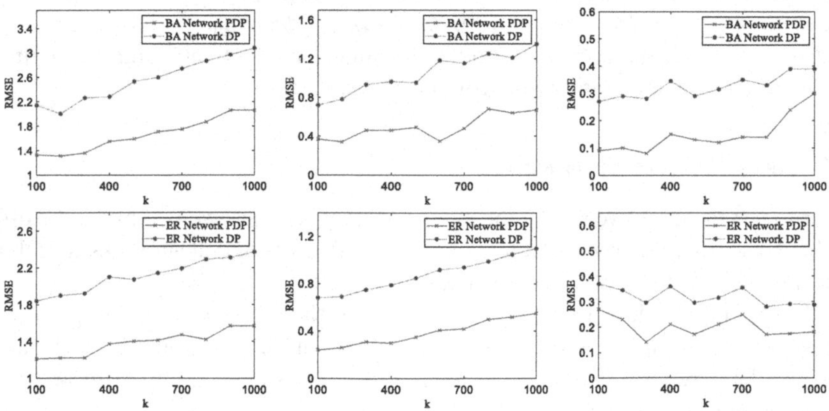

Fig. 1. RMSE of BA Network and ER Network. The minimum privacy preference for the first to third rows is 0.1, 0.5, and 0.9. The density (edges/ nodes) is 20.

5.2 The Impact of Network Data

First, we compared the effectiveness of the algorithm in the two classic networks. Fig 1 shows the result in BA network and ER network, where the thresholds are set that $P_1 = P_2 = P_3 = P_4 = 0.25$. Due to the combination of differential privacy, it does not take the mean of multiple experiments and only shows one of the query results in the figure. The added noise is random, so RMSE is also random. However, it can be seen from Fig. 1 that considering the PDP mechanism has obvious advantages over the traditional DP mechanism. RMSE is lower, meaning that the output is more available. In addition, although the two networks have different characteristics, the noise disturbance of both networks is reduced after considering the PDP mechanism.

Table 1. Comparison of the density of the graph

Graph	$S = 10$		$S = 20$	
	DP	PDP	DP	PDP
BA 1	1.25	0.51	0.72	0.37
ER 1	1.31	0.64	0.68	0.24
BA 2	1.01	0.49	1.10	0.49
ER 2	1.27	0.53	0.85	0.35
BA 3	1.15	0.37	1.35	0.67
ER 3	1.32	0.46	1.10	0.55

Table 1 shows the difference between graphs with different densities. The density S is defined as the ratio of the number of edges to the number of nodes in the graph. The larger S indicates the more complicated the relationship of a graph. In addition, the number of nodes $degree_{\mathrm{BA1}} = degree_{\mathrm{ER1}} = 100$, $degree_{\mathrm{BA2}} = degree_{\mathrm{ER2}} = 500$, $degree_{\mathrm{BA3}} = degree_{\mathrm{ER3}} = 1000$. It can be seen that our algorithm also effectively reduces the impact of the disturbance in the graphs with different densities.

5.3 Impact of Privacy Specification

In order to test the effectiveness of the algorithm in this paper, we compared the differences between different privacy preference distributions of the real networks (Facebook, Twitch and Wiki-Vote Networks downloaded from [21]).

In the experiment shown in Fig. 2, the variable is the proportion of Group G_1 users. Group G_1 represents conservative users. The RMSE of the traditional DP mechanism is always relatively large. So, the traditional DP is not shown in Fig. 2 to accurately compare the impact of different aggregation strategies on the results.

Figure 2 shows that as the number of conservative users increases, the disturbances reduce the availability of data. In addition, the introduction of the aggregation mechanism effectively improves the accuracy of the sampling mechanism. In general, our mechanisms are more effective than traditional DP mechanisms. In addition, Trying

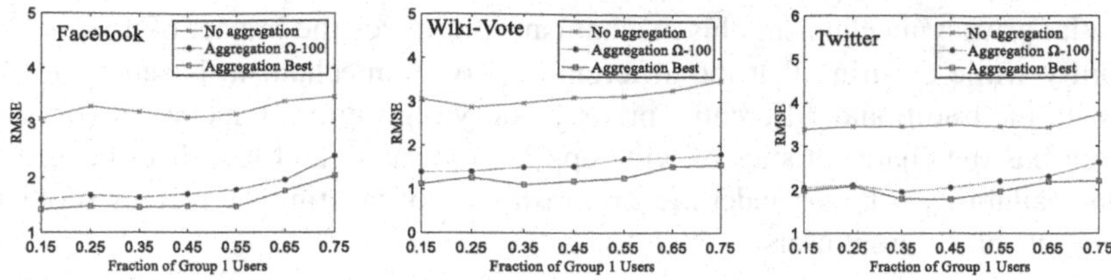

Fig. 2. Impact of Fraction of Group 1 Users

the best aggregation strategy for some time usually produces better results, but usually requires more time to run the algorithm. The sampling threshold selection algorithm affects the sampling process by selecting a better threshold to reduce the impact of conservative users on the overall data availability. This process is affected by user privacy preferences.

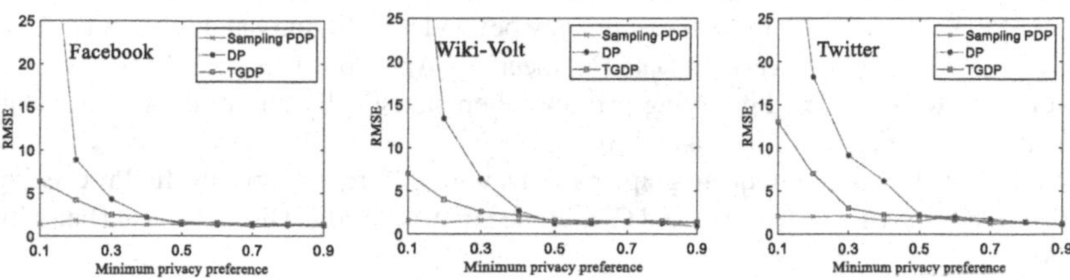

Fig. 3. Impact of Minimum privacy preference

In the experiment shown in Fig. 3, the minimum value of user privacy preference in the data set is artificially restricted to observe the impact of privacy specification on data availability and we compared with the current best personalized differential privacy mechanism (TGDP) [16]. When Minimum privacy preference is 0, the experimental result is equivalent to Fig. 2, $P1 = 0.25$. It can be seen from Fig. 3 that the traditional DP mechanism is greatly affected by the parameters. Because in the DP mechanism, a large amount of noise must be added in order to meet the privacy protection requirements of each user. The personalized differential privacy mechanism has achieved better utility when the privacy preferences of many users are low. Compared with the TGDP mechanism, our algorithm performs better when privacy preferences are low, which means that disturbances cause fewer errors. As shown in Fig. 3, the minimum privacy preference is less than 0.5. When the privacy preference is high, the performance of the two is basically the same, and the performance is better than the traditional differential privacy mechanism.

6 Conclusion

The spectrum is an important attribute of the networks. In order to improve the usability of spectral queries on edge weights in weighted social networks, a spectral query algorithm based on personalized differential privacy is proposed. Compared with the traditional differential privacy mechanism, this mechanism minimizes the impact of noise on data availability while ensuring that the differential privacy mechanism is satisfied. Compared with the traditional differential privacy query algorithm of social networks, this algorithm has the characteristics of wide application range and less disturbance. And the data availability is better under the circumstances of meeting the privacy protection requirements of different users.

Acknowledgements. We would like to thank the anonymous reviewers for their insightful comments. This work was sponsored by the National Natural Science Foundation of China (No. 61941105).

References

1. Cormode, G., Srivastava, D., Yu, T., Zhang, Q.: Anonymizing bipartite graph data using safe groupings. In: Proceedings of the VLDB Endowment, vol. 1, pp. 833–844 (2008)
2. Li, N., Li, T., Venkata, S.: t-closeness: privacy beyond k-anonymity and l-diversity. In: IEEE 23rd International Conference on Data Engineering, April, pp. 106–115 (2007)
3. Dwork, C., Kobliner, Y.: Preserving privacy when statistically analyzing a large database. U.S. Patent Application 11/038,446, (2006).
4. Shen, E., Yu, T.: Mining frequent graph patterns with differential privacy. In: Proceedings of the 19th ACM SIGKDD International Conference on Knowledge Discovery and Data Mining. ACM (2013)
5. Wang, Q.: Real-time and spatio-temporal crowd-sourced social network data publishing with differential privacy. IEEE Trans. Dependable Secure Comput. **15**(4), 591–606 (2016)
6. Baden, R.: Persona: an online social network with user-defined privacy. In: ACM SIGCOMM Computer Communication Review, vol. 39 (2009)
7. Ebadi, H., Sands, D., Schneider, G.: Differential privacy: now it's getting personal. ACM Sigplan Notices **50**, 69–81 (2015)
8. Jorgensen, Z., Yu, T., Cormode, G.: Conservative or liberal? Personalized differential privacy. In: 2015 IEEE 31St International Conference on Data Engineering (2015).
9. Zhang, S., Kang, H., Yan, H.: Privacy preserving for social network relational data based on Skyline computing. J. Comput. Appl. **39**, 1394-1399 (2019)
10. Chamikara, M.A.P., Bertók, P., Liu, D.: An efficient and scalable privacy preserving algorithm for big data and data streams. Comput. Secur. 87, 101570 (2019)
11. Cui, L., Qu, Y., Yu, S., Gao, L.: A Trust-grained personalized privacy-preserving scheme for big social data. In: 2018 IEEE International Conference on Communications (ICC). 20–24 May, pp. 1938–1883 (2018)
12. Van Dam, E.R., Haemers, W.H.: Which graphs are determined by their spectrum. Linear Algebra Appl. **373**, 241–272 (2003)
13. Xu, S., Zhang, J., Han, D.: Singular value decomposition-based data distortion strategy for privacy protection. Knowl. Inf. Syst. **10**, 383–397 (2006)
14. Wu, L., Ying, X., Wu, X.: Reconstruction from randomized graph via low rank approximation. In: Proceedings of the 2010 SIAM International Conference on Data Mining, Society for Industrial and Applied Mathematics, pp. 60–71 (2010)
15. Liu, D., Wang, H., Van Mieghem, P.: Spectral perturbation and reconstructability of complex networks. Phys. Rev. E **81**, 016101 (2010)
16. Yong, Z., Lingjie, Z., Zhongyuan, J.: Security analysis of weighted network anonymity based on singular value decomposition. J. Commun. **39**, 23 (2018)

17. Wang, Y., Wu, X., Wu, L.: Differential privacy preserving spectral graph analysis. In: Pei, J., Tseng, V.S., Cao, L., Motoda, H., Xu, G. (eds.) PAKDD 2013. LNCS (LNAI), vol. 7819, pp. 329–340. Springer, Heidelberg (2013). https://doi.org/10.1007/978-3-642-37456-2_28
18. Dwork, C., Roth, A.: The algorithmic foundations of differential privacy. Found. Trends Theor. Comput. **9**, 211–407 (2014)
19. Li, C., Hay, M., Miklau, G., Wang, Y.: A data-and workload-aware algorithm for range queries under differential privacy. PVLDB **7**(5) (2014)
20. Shekhar S., Xiong H., Zhou X.: Root-Mean-Square Error. Encyclopedia of GIS. Springer, Cham (2017).https://doi.org/10.1007/978-3-319-17885-1_101137
21. Stanford network dataset collection. https://snap.stanford.edu/dat

LPPRS: New Location Privacy Preserving Schemes Based on Ring Signature over Mobile Social Networks

Cailing Cai(✉), Tsz Hon Yuen, Handong Cui, Mingli Wu, and Siu-Ming Yiu

Department of Computer Science, The University of Hong Kong, Pokfulam Road, Pokfulam, Hong Kong
{clcai,thyuen,hdcui,mlwu,smyiu}@cs.hku.hk

Abstract. There are two popular location-based service (LBS) applications: searching k-nearest neighbor Points of Interests (kNN POIs) and finding Nearby Friends (NF) via a social network server (SNS). Nevertheless, both applications are based on users' current locations, and no scheme has been devised yet to merge POIs, NF and SNS together. A series of works were proposed to preserve users' query privacy leaked from service attributes of POIs or location privacy over Mobile Social Networks (MSNs). However, their communication and computation costs are heavy.

In this paper, we design a novel LBS application named **NFPOI**, which allows users to search NF based on a given POI via an SNS. To preserve users' identity privacy, location privacy and query privacy, we firstly propose Location Privacy Preserving schemes based on Ring Signature (**LPPRS**). In our LPPRS, (1) Both user's real identity and real location are kept secret from others effectively. (2) Due to the anonymity of ring signature, the SNS was allowed to return query results while it cannot distinguish the real sender when processing a query message. Thus, the sender's query privacy is preserved even though the SNS knows the actual attributes and locations of POIs. (3) Neither a fully trusted third party (TTP) nor a pre-shared secret key with friends is required. A semi-TTP scheme and a TTP-free scheme were proposed respectively with different trade-offs in efficiency and security level. (4) Communication and computation costs for user side are less than existing works.

Keywords: Location privacy-preserving · Ring signature · Points of interests · Mobile social networks

1 Introduction

Location based services (LBS) are of great importance in our daily life. One LBS application is location-based searching, which allows users to query kNN POIs. For instance, Alice[1] can use the Google map to check how many bars, cinemas, or hospitals are within a radius of 3 km based on her current location.

[1] Alice represents a user or a user's device in this work.

Y. Wu and M. Yung (Eds.): Inscrypt 2020, LNCS 12612, pp. 288–303, 2021.
https://doi.org/10.1007/978-3-030-71852-7_19

Note that searching kNN POIs does not rely on MSNs, i.e., the information in Alice's social network, such as Alice's friend lists.

MSNs construct a sharing medium for individuals' daily communication. Via a SNS, provided by Twitter for instance, users can create profiles and share personal data like videos and pictures with friends in their social networks. Location sharing among social network friends is another popular function of SNS. After uploading a current location to SNS, users can query NF.

The searching goals of the above two functions are individual. One is for kNN POIs but another one is for NF. However, no LBS application achieves the two goals at the same time and thus cannot satisfy some specific cases. For example, Alice is currently in New York and she can search for friends near the hotel in London where she has booked or she can choose a hotel which is more likely near her friends living in London. Motivated by such demands, we design a novel application for searching NF based on a given POI via a SNS. We define it as **NFPOI**, which also allows users to search nearby POIs.

Since both of the LBS applications are based on a user's current and precise location, privacy concerns are raised by sensitive information leakage. The first one is **location privacy** that is revealed from the disclosure of users' exact locations. For instance, some fitness tracking APPs like Strava allows its users to record and share their jogging routes. However, in 2018, it was reported that the location of a secret US army base was leaked by the locations shared in the APP. Another one is **query privacy** leaked from the service attribute of POIs, e.g., amusement services, medical services, catering services, especially when a sender issues POIs query with the same service attribute continuously in a period. For example, if Alice frequently queries bars, an adversary can infer that Alice is an alcoholic and she may face some health issues caused by over drinking. As shown in [1], the adversary also can infer the sender's interests, health condition, eating habits, and so forth by analyzing the sender's POIs. In our LPPRS, a **continuous NFPOI query** refers that a sender continuously searches NF based on POIs with the same service attribute in a period. Otherwise, we denote that the user does a non-continuous NFPOI query.

To protect users' *location privacy*, a number of schemes are proposed, such as k-anonymity [2–5], dummy locations [6–9], obfuscation [10,11], mix zone [12,13], spatial transformation [14,15] and homomorphic encryption (HE) [16–19]. For *query privacy*, private information retrieval (PIR) proposed in [20–23] is a useful algorithm.

The k-anonymity and dummy location are applied to construct a cloak region for a user's location with $k-1$ locations, which can be obtained from the user or a TTP. Different from the dummy location algorithm, the $k-1$ locations of k-anonymity can be exact or dummy. The obfuscation algorithm is to select an appropriate location (not a cloak area) to substitute a user's exact location. For mix zone, a TTP will help a user change her identity when her location is in a specific zone, mixing the user's identity with others, but users cannot change locations. The space transformation is to map a user's location into another space with a one-way transformation. Paillier [16] and BV [17] are two popular HE algorithms applied in privacy-preserving, achieving additive homomorphic and full homomorphic respectively. The PIR allows a user to retrieve POIs from servers with indexes while the user does not reveal any content of POIs. More introductions about locations privacy protection can be found in recent surveys [24–26].

Limitations of Existing Works on Location Privacy and Query Privacy. (1) The k-anonymity algorithm in continuous queries is vulnerable to location-dependent attacks [27] and attackers can recognize users' identities with an anonymized graph [28]. (2) The accuracy is reduced when a query message is processed under a cloak region, e.g., k-anonymity and dummy location. (3) Users need to reveal their exact locations to a TTP, e.g., mix zone. (4) The communications and computations costs for users or servers sides are heavy, e.g., HE, PIR.

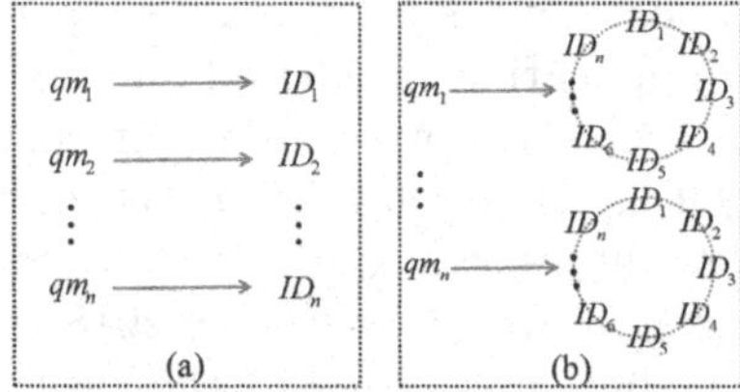

Fig. 1. Linkage between sender's identity and query message.

Furthermore, we find that the linkage between a sender and her query message is revealed to SNS directly in most existing schemes and thus allows SNS to infer more sensitive information, Fig. 1(a). For example, according to the location of POI, e.g., a bar, the sender's location, and her friends' IDs, SNS can infer that the sender's or her friends' future locations may be the specific bar with a high probability. Thus, besides location privacy and query privacy, hiding the linkage between the sender's query message and identity is essential. Since ring signature is a more powerful tool than k-anonymous to achieve anonymity, we apply a RingCT 3.0 algorithm proposed by Yuen et al. [29] to achieve anonymous query, Fig. 1(b). A comparison between k-anonymity and ring signature is presented in Table 1.

Table 1. Comparison between k-anonymity and ring signature

k-anonymity	• Anonymize a sender's exact location for LBS • Cannot resist location-dependent and anonymized graph attack for continuous queries • Cannot satisfy unconditional anonymity and cloak region easily causes vague query results
Ring signature	• Anonymize the linkage between a sender's identity and query message • SNS can only distinguish the real sender with the probability of $1/ring\_size$ even for continuous queries • Allow users to submit an exact location of POI to SNS without compromising the accuracy of query results

In this work, therefore, we design a lightweight and anonymous framework for NFPOI query, which preserves the sender's location privacy, query privacy and identity privacy simultaneously. To the best of our knowledge, no mechanism satisfying all requirements has been proposed yet.

Our Contributions. We propose location privacy-preserving schemes over MSNs based on ring signature (LPPRS) in two different security settings: with Semi-TTP and without TTP. In our scheme 1, there are three entities: User, Social Network Server (SNS) and Cloud Server (CS). CS is a semi-trusted third party. Our scheme 2 is TTP-free. The main contributions of our LPPRS are as follows.

1) **Proposed a novel LBS application over MSNs combining POI and NF together**. Our NFPOI successfully breaks the limitation of either POIs query or NF query. Via a SNS, NFPOI allows users to search NF based on a given POI. Thus, it can be used as a practical LBS searching fashion.
2) **Identity privacy and location privacy are preserved**. Instead of inputting email addresses or telephone numbers to SNS, only ring signature public keys are used to denote users' identities. Thus, users' registration IDs do not reveal any personal information to SNS. Users' location privacy is protected by submitting substitution locations to SNS. Different from algorithms discussed above, it is efficient because no heavy computation or communication cost is involved.
3) **Anonymous query and query privacy are preserved**. Due to the anonymity property of ring signature, although SNS can learn that the query message including exact location and attribute of POI is sent from the ring members, it cannot find out the real sender with an unnegligible probability. Thus, anonymous query is guaranteed in LPPRS. In addition, as it is impossible for SNS to distinguish whether two query messages are sent from the same user, query privacy is preserved after sending continuous queries.
4) **Achieved Semi-TTP and TTP-free**. In LPPRS, only a semi-trusted third party is involved in scheme 1 (Sect. 4.1). Computation cost of CS is trivial, as it only helps users select ring members and forwards messages to SNS. Apart from the sender's identity privacy, user's location privacy and query privacy will not be leaked to CS. Additionally, scheme 2 (Sect. 4.2) removes the need of utilizing a semi-trusted third party by using anonymity networks or anonymous algorithms and requiring the SNS to perform public key encryption.
5) **Achieve session key free**. Different from previous works, users do not share any session key with social network friends in advance, thus avoiding privacy leakage caused by dishonest friends when users share the session key with them.

2 Preliminaries

Ring signature was proposed by Rivest et al. [30] in 2001. A ring is formed by n public keys $\boldsymbol{Y}$ among which one is the signer's public key and the remaining public keys are from $n-1$ other users. The signer generates a ring signature for a message using his own secret key. A verifier can validate the signature for the message with the ring $\boldsymbol{Y}$. The ring signature provides anonymity for the signer in the ring $\boldsymbol{Y}$ without using a trusted third party or a group manager. The unconditional anonymity of ring signature makes the attacker unable to distinguish the actual signer with probability greater than $1/n$, ever though the attacker has infinitely powerful computation and can access to an unbounded number of chosen-message signatures signed with the same ring members.

RingCT 3.0. Many ring signature schemes are proposed since the invention of ring signature. In 2019, Yuen et al. [29] proposed a new ring signature scheme named RingCT3.0 protocol to protect the privacy of a sender in Monero blockchain transaction. To the best of the authors' knowledge, it is the shortest ring signature scheme without trusted setup up to now. Thus, we use the RingCT 3.0 as a building block of our protocol[2].

3 System Descriptions and Threat Model

3.1 System Descriptions

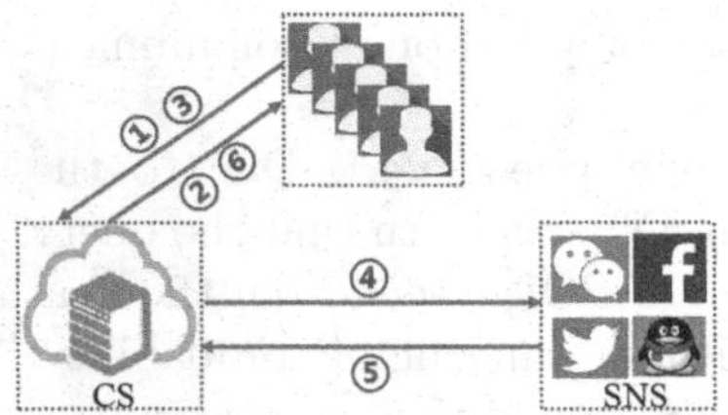

① User asks ring signature members from CS.
② CS selects ring members to the user.
③ User generates a ring signature for query message.
④ CS sends the ring signature to SNS.
⑤ SNS returns query results to CS.
⑥ CS exacts query result with a ring index.

Fig. 2. Framework of Scheme 1.

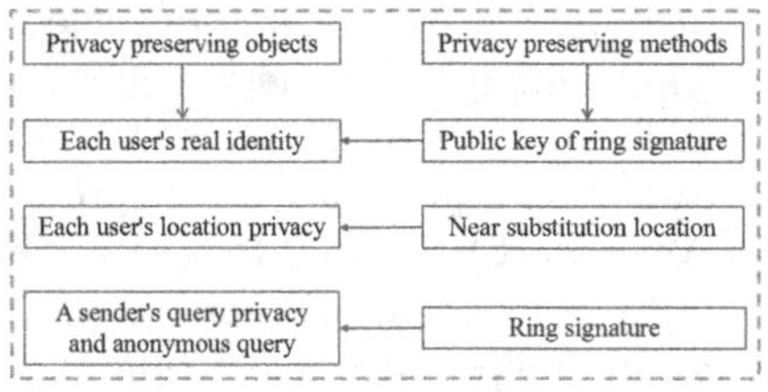

Fig. 3. Privacy preserving objects and methods.

The framework of scheme 1 is shown in Fig. 2. There are three entities: Users, Social Network Server (SNS), Cloud Server (CS). Scheme 2 is TTP-free by moving the setting of CS.

Users. They can access CS and SNS via a smart device such as smartphone, smartwatch, iPad, and so on.

SNS. It carries out users' query messages based on their social network friends lists and locations.

[2] The details of RingCT 3.0 are in the full version.

CS. It assists users in three ways. (1) CS helps users select ring members for each location query. Since Alice's friend list is revealed to SNS, the ring members cannot be selected from Alice's friends simply. Otherwise, SNS can easily recognize that Alice is the sender by checking ring members' common friends. Besides, we require that the ring members must be registered users in SNS. Hence, it is not easy for Alice to construct a ring without the knowledge from users who are not her social friends. (2) CS conveys users' ring signatures to SNS. (3) CS extracts the final encrypted query results sent from SNS with a sender's ring index. It can prevent the sender from decrypting the query results of the $n-1$ decoy ring members. Therefore, this step provides protection against malicious users.

As shown in Fig. 3, the ring signature is applied to sign a sender's query message, and a ring signature public key is used to hide the sender's identity.

Substitution Location (*sl*): It is used to preserve users' exact locations. Similar to the works [10,11], we assume that there are some public buildings such as subway stations, bus stops, supermarkets, etc., around a user's current location. A nearby public location (not a cloak region) will be selected to replace the exact location in LPPRS. The choice is flexible, depending on the user's current location. For example, if Alice's current location is near a subway station exit, then that location is a better substitution.

District of Substitution Location and Ring Members: The district of substitution location represents a larger area, such as a town or a suburb. Since the location of POI is independent on the sender's substitution location, we propose that ring members are selected randomly from users who are in the same district as the sender's.

3.2 System Threat Model

The assumptions of system threat model in LPPRS are as follows.

1) The communications between three entities in LPPRS are via a secure channel. Thus, an eavesdropping attack is not considered in LPPRS.
2) Both CS and SNS are honest-but-curious, which means that they will execute schemes honestly while intend to infer more private information. In general, an entity is defined as a TTP when it knows each user's real identity, location, query message and query result, such as the setting of CT in [31]. Thus, similar to [32], we define that CS in our LPPRS is a semi-trusted entity (semi-TTP) since it does not have users' real query messages, exact locations and real query results.
3) Following to the works [31–33], we assume that CS and SNS cannot be controlled by the same adversary, because they are managed by two individual institutions. In other words, CS and SNS do not collude with each other.
4) CS and SNS can monitor users' information running in the system, respectively, including users' historical substitution locations, query messages, query results, and so on. Meanwhile, both entities receive all public parameters of algorithms applied in the mechanism.

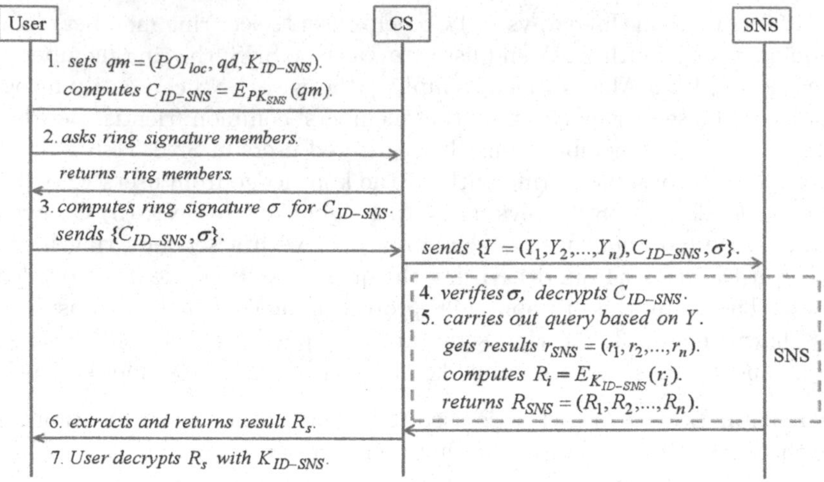

Fig. 4. Steps of NFPOI query in scheme 1.

4 Our LPPRS

4.1 Construction of Scheme 1

Registration in Social Network Server. Alice's registration identity (ID) in SNS is a ring public key Y_A. We suppose that each user's ID is different from others. In LPPRS, based on the location of a POI, uploading personal location to SNS is not the prerequisite for NFPOI query. Thus, if Alice is willing to reveal it to social network friends, she can upload a substitution location sl_A to SNS.

Registration in Cloud Server. Alice's ID in CS is also Y_A. Once Alice updates her ID in SNS, she will send the new ID to CS simultaneously. Different from SNS, CS records Alice's ring and corresponding index of her query message. Besides, instead of sending a sl_A, Alice only sends the district of sl_A to CS once she has updated her location in SNS.

Query Steps. There are seven steps in scheme 1, seeing Fig. 4.

- **Step 1: Alice sets** qm**.** Firstly, to prevent CS from knowing query results sending from SNS, Alice randomly generates a one-time-key K_{ID-SNS} of AES[3]. Instead of sending K_{ID-SNS} to SNS directly, Alice adds the key into a query message denoted by $qm = (POI_{loc}, qd, K_{ID-SNS})$, where POI_{loc} is the exact location of POI, and qd is a radius of query distance. Secondly, Alice encrypts qm to get $C_{ID-SNS} = E_{PK_{SNS}}(qm)$, where PK_{SNS} is a RSA[4] public key of SNS.

[3] AES represents a symmetric encryption algorithm in this work.

[4] RSA represents an asymmetric encryption algorithm in this work. Note that RSA can be replaced by Elliptic Curve Cryptography or other asymmetric encryption algorithms in trade-offs in efficiency and security.

Suppose that Alice desires to search kNN friends within $qd = 2$ km, denoted the query region by $\odot_{qd}$. Due to the distance between a user's real location and substitution location, a border case is that the user's substitution location is outside $\odot_{qd}$, while the user's real location is inside $\odot_{qd}$. Since SNS performs qm based on users' substitution locations, SNS will not add the user to its query result. For this case, we propose that qd sent to SNS is larger than 2 km, e.g., 4 km (double times), flexibly avoiding omitting all kNN friends within $\odot_{qd=2km}$. Besides, we set that results returned by SNS are recorded increasingly based on the distance among POI_{loc} and her friends' locations (seeing Step 5). Thus, Alice can quickly learn about whose location is around and can obtain those friends' exact locations by privately communicating with them.

- **Step 2: Alice asks ring Y from CS.** Based on Alice's district, CS selects $n-1$ ring members from its M_{CS} randomly and keeps the ring index. After that, CS sends ring $Y = (Y_1, Y_2, ..., Y_n)$ to Alice. On the other hand, if Alice does continuous queries, then ring Y and its indexes are the same as the first time during the whole period. Otherwise, ring Y is deleted by CS and Alice after a NFPOI query.
- **Step 3: Alice computes σ for C_{ID-SNS}.** Once Alice obtains the ring Y from CS, Alice keeps her index secretly. Based on RingCT 3.0, Alice computes a ring signature σ for C_{ID-SNS}. After that, Alice sends (C_{ID-SNS}, σ) to CS. For CS, once it receives Alice's query message, it firstly records Alice's ring Y and index. Later, CS sends $(C_{ID-SNS}, \sigma, (Y_1, Y_2, ..., Y_n))$ to SNS.
- **Step 4: SNS verifies σ.** For σ, if it is valid, SNS decrypts C_{ID-SNS} with its RSA private key to get the query message, and keeps the session key K_{ID-SNS} secretly. Otherwise, SNS rejects the query.
- **Step 5: SNS performs qm based on ring Y.** Firstly, due to the anonymity of ring signature, SNS cannot find out that $qm = (POI_{loc}, qd, K_{ID-SNS})$ is sent from Alice. Thus, SNS carries out qm based on $(Y_1, Y_2, ..., Y_n)$ and records results from Y_1 to Y_n sequentially. Denoted query results for ring Y by $r_{SNS} = (r_1, r_2, ..., r_n)$ and r_s is the query result for ring member in Y with index $s, (s = 1, ..., n)$. In general, r_s is a set and its each element is in the form of (d_t, ID_t, sl_t), where t is a number of Y_s' friends whose substitution locations are in $\odot_{qd=4km}$, d_t is a distance satisfying $d_t = dist(POI_{loc}, sl_t) < qd$, and ID_t represents a Y_s' friend. We require that SNS records results according to d_t increasingly. The smaller value of d_t implies the nearer friend. Secondly, SNS encrypts each r_i with the session key K_{ID-SNS} and gets $R_i = E_{K_{ID-SNS}}(r_i)$. Denoted the ciphertext results by $R_{SNS} = (R_1, R_2, ..., R_n)$. Finally, SNS sends R_{SNS} to CS.
- **Step 6: CS extracts result R_s.** After receiving $R_{SNS} = (R_1, R_2, ..., R_n)$ from SNS, CS exacts the result R_s with index s, sends it to Alice, and discards the rest results.
- **Step 7: Alice decrypts R_s.** Finally, Alice can learn about how many friends are nearby the POI by decrypting R_s with K_{ID-SNS}.

4.2 Construction of Scheme 2

Registration in SNS. Firstly, each user generates a RSA public key, denoted as RSA_{ID}. Secondly, since users' IDs are ring public keys, we assume that all IDs in SNS are public. Besides, users' location districts are also published by SNS. Thus, Alice's public information is in the form of (Y_A, RSA_{Y_A}, country/city, district), if she has updated a location to SNS. Otherwise, her public information is (Y_A, $RSA_{Y_A}, \perp, \perp$). Note that all users' social relationships are not published.

Query Steps. Without the setting of CS, there are six steps in scheme 2.

- **Step 1: Alice sets** qm**.** In scheme 2, a symmetric random private key is removed from qm, $qm = (POI_{loc}, qd)$. Next, Alice encrypts qm to get $C_{ID-SNS} = E_{PK_{SNS}}(qm)$.
- **Step 2: Alice selects ring** Y **personally.** Based on the public information offered by SNS, the same as scheme 1, Alice randomly selected ring Y from the same district with her location. If Alice needs continuous queries, then she will keep ring Y and use it to sign new qm during the period of continuous queries. Otherwise, ring Y is deleted after obtaining query results.
- **Step 3: Alice computes** σ **for** C_{ID-SNS}**.** Firstly, Alice computes a ring signature σ for C_{ID-SNS}, and sends message $\{C_{ID-SNS}, \sigma, (Y_1, Y_2, ..., Y_n))\}$ to SNS. Secondly, similar to [18], we assume that the communication between Alice and SNS is via anonymized algorithms [34] or an anonymized network (e.g., Tor[5]).
- **Step 4: SNS verifies** σ**.** (This step is the same as scheme 1.)
- **Step 5: SNS carries out** qm **based on ring** Y**.** Different from scheme 1, SNS encrypts query results $r_{SNS} = (r_1, r_2, ..., r_n)$ with each ring member's RSA_{ID}, getting $R_s = E_{RSA_{Y_s}}(r_s)$, $s = 1, ..., n$. Next, SNS returns $R_{SNS} = (R_1, R_2, ..., R_n)$ to the sender.
- **Step 6: Alice decrypts the query result.** After obtaining R_{SNS}, Alice selects the result with her ring index, and decrypts it with RSA secret key. Note that even though Alice can obtain all ring members' results, she only can obtain her own friends' information by decrypting the result with personal RSA private key.

Note that following to scheme 2, SNS also can apply RSA to encrypt $r_{SNS} = (r_1, r_2, ..., r_n)$ in scheme 1, while considering the setting of CS and the efficiency of AES, we adopt AES to encrypt query results instead of RSA for scheme 1.

5 Schemes Comparison and Security Analysis

5.1 Scheme Comparison

Comparisons among LPPRS and other schemes are shown in Table 2.

[5] https://www.torproject.org/.

Table 2. Comparison between LPPRS and other schemes. The following symbols are used: DS: Digital Signature, FL: friends' list, qt: query type, qd: query distance, qm: query message, σ: ring signature, f: the number of friends, [#x]: runs for x-times.

<table>
<tr><th>Scheme</th><th>User
Comp. cost</th><th>User
Comm. cost</th><th>Server(s)
Comp. cost</th><th>Server(s)
knows</th></tr>
<tr><td>[31]
U-CT-SNS-LS
(TTP: CT)</td><td>DS.Sign
AES[#1+f]</td><td>ID||qt||qd</td><td>CT: pseudonyms & dummy loc
RSA.Enc & RSA.Dec
SNS: DS.Verify
LS: RSA.Enc</td><td>CT & SNS: ID & fake IDs
CT: loc & dummy locs
SNS: FL
LS: fake IDs & dummy locs</td></tr>
<tr><td>[33]
U-SNS-LS</td><td>RSA.Enc
AES[#4]</td><td>ID||qt||qd||loc.cipher</td><td>SNS: pseudonyms & k-anonymity
LS: RSA.Dec & AES[#2]</td><td>SNS: ID & fake IDs & FL
LS: fake ID & real loc</td></tr>
<tr><td>[35]
U-SNS-LS</td><td>Broadcast Enc, DS.Sign
AES[# > 2+f]</td><td>ID||qt||qd</td><td>SNS: pseudonyms & DS.Verify
LS: AES[#2] & DS.Sign</td><td>SNS: ID & fake IDs & FL
LS: fake ID & real loc</td></tr>
<tr><td>[36]
U-SNS</td><td>ORE.Enc[#2]
ORE.QGen
AES[# > f]</td><td>multi-qm.cipher</td><td>SNS: ORE.Cmp
Index construction
Index maintenance</td><td>SNS: ID & loc.cipher</td></tr>
<tr><td>[18]
U-SNS</td><td>CP-ABE
Paillier HE
Functional Enc</td><td>(To a friend)
multi-times comm.</td><td>negligible
(mainly computed by users)</td><td>SNS: ID & FL</td></tr>
<tr><td>[1]
U-LS</td><td>DUMMY-Q
technique</td><td>multi-(loc||POIs)</td><td>LS: multi-query processing</td><td>LS: ID & real loc</td></tr>
<tr><td>[32]
U-SA-LS
(Semi-TTP : SA)</td><td>Hilbert Curve
RSA.Enc</td><td>loc||POI</td><td>SA: anonymity area
compute redundant results
LS: RSA.Dec & loc transform</td><td>SA: ID</td></tr>
<tr><td>[37]
U-LS</td><td>RSA.Enc[#2], RSA.Dec[#2]
Bilinear Pairing[#n]
Deniable Authentication</td><td>multi-times comm.</td><td>LS: RSA.Dec[#2]
RSA.Enc[#2]
Bilinear Pairing</td><td>LS: ID & real qm</td></tr>
<tr><td>Ours. 1
U-CS-SNS
(Semi-TTP : CS)</td><td>RSA.Enc
Ring.Sign
AES</td><td>qm.cipher||σ</td><td>SNS: RSA.Dec
Ring.Verify
AES[#n]</td><td>CS: sender's ring index
SNS: FL & real qm</td></tr>
<tr><td>Ours. 2
U-SNS</td><td>RSA.Enc
Ring.Sign
RSA.Dec</td><td>qm.cipher||σ</td><td>SNS: RSA.Dec
Ring.Verify
RSA.Enc[#n]</td><td>SNS: FL & real qm</td></tr>
</table>

- Column 1 (Scheme): For each scheme, we summarize the involved entities such as User (U), SNS, location server (LS), cloud server (CS). CT represents Cell Tower in [31] and SA represents Semi-Anonymizer in [32]. We also describe the type of TTP used if there is one.
- Column 2 (A user's comp.cost[6]): The cryptographic operations computed by a user are listed. We use [#] to represent the number of times when an algorithm runs by the user multiple times. For example, in [31], the sender runs the AES once in registration period. Besides, a query result includes several locations, encrypted by friends' private keys respectively. Thus, the sender totally needs to perform the AES for (1+f) times, denoted as AES[#1+f], where f is the number of friends of a query result.
- Column 3 (A user's comm.cost[7]): To simplify, we only compare a user's comm.cost of sending query messages, excluding registration and location updating periods. Note that the loc.cipher and qm.cipher represent the ciphertext of location and query message respectively. The multi-times comm. means there are multiple communications between two entities. Unless otherwise specified, the user sends the query to the party connected to U in column 1.
- Column 4 (Comm.cost of server(s)): Its description is similar to column 2.
- Column 5 (Sever knows): We summarize a user's privacy that is revealed to server(s).

Detailed comparisons in different perspectives are given as follows.

TTP. Our scheme 1 and [32] have a semi-TTP, which both cannot obtain users' real IDs and locations, but the semi-TTP in [32] needs to help users perform extra computations for query results. [1,37] are TTP-free schemes, but [1] only focus on preserving user's query privacy, and user's comp.cost and comm.cost are all heavy in [37]. Our scheme 2 is TTP-free, offering privacy-preserving for a user's identity, location and query message simultaneously.

Comp.cost (User and server(s)). In our LPPRS, for each query, the sender only needs to compute the RSA, AES and ring signature one time, respectively. However, in [31,33,35,36], the sender needs to run the RSA or AES several times. Besides, due to the running costs of CP-ABE/Hilbert curve/Bilinear Pairing, user's comp.cost from [18,32,37] are significant. Different from [31,33,35,36], comp.cost for server side in [18] is negligible, since the computation is mainly done by two parties for each query. Comparing to [37], our LPPRS is lightweight as the server does not need to perform the bilinear pairing operations.

Comm.cost (User). In our LPPRS, a query message sent to the server only includes a RSA ciphertext and a ring siganture. However, in [1,36], the sender's query message either contains multiple dummy POIs or multiple locations encrypted with AES. For [18,37], the user has to interact with her friend or the server multi-times. Thus, user's comm.costs in [1,18,36,37] are all heavy.

Server(s) Knows. In our LPPRS, a user's real ID and location are not revealed to any party as they are preserved by a ring public key and a substitution location respectively. However, at least one server knows a user's real identity or location in [1,18,31–33,35–37]. For query privacy, our schemes and [37] allow SNS to obtain an anonymous query message in the form of plaintext. Our LPPRS is based on the ring signature that preserves query privacy perfectly, while [37] enables the sender to deny her behavior when the server tells her data to others, with a deniable ring authentication algorithm.

Searching Method and Session Key. Based on users' current locations, schemes [18,31,33,35,36] and [1,32,37] are designed to offer privacy-preserving for searching kNN NF and POIs respectively. Our NFPOI focuses on NF searching based on a given POI via SNS. In addition, different from [31,33,35,36], we do not require users to share session keys with friends, successfully avoiding privacy leakage from malicious users. Due to the length limitation, we do not show both items in Table 2.

5.2 Security Analysis

In this section, we analyze that the sensitive information that CS and SNS intend to infer is preserved when they perform inference attacks.

For SNS, it knows all users' friends lists, query messages, ring members and some users' substitution locations, while it desires to infer the real sender and users' exact locations. For CS, it stores users' historical and current districts of substitution locations, encrypted query messages, encrypted query results, ring members and ring indexes, while it hopes to acquire the plaintext of users' query message, query results and exact locations.

Inference Attack Resistant: A mechanism is inference attack resistant if an adversary in probabilistic polynomial time cannot infer a user's real value over a possibility ϵ, where ϵ depends on the secure parameter of a specific privacy preserving algorithm.

Property 1. Our LPPRS is inference attack resistant to SNS.

(1) Given a query message signed by Alice Y_A with a ring $Y = (Y_1, Y_2, ..., Y_n)$, the possibility that SNS infers the real sender is $\epsilon = \frac{1}{n}$.

Analysis 1: Firstly, if Alice does not need continuous query, different query message is signed with different ring $Y = (Y_1, Y_2, ..., Y_n)$. Each ring member in Y is selected from whole registration IDs of SNS, as long as they are in the same district as Alice. Besides, the location of POI is independent on Alice's substitution location. Thus, SNS cannot find out Alice by matching each ring member's substitution location with the location of POI. In addition, each ring Y is generated randomly and the ring members are not chosen from Alice's social network friends. Thus, even though SNS has all users' social friends lists, it cannot recognize Alice by checking ring members' common friends, or via performing joint analysis based on a large number of ring signatures.

Secondly, if Alice needs a continuous query, all of her query messages are signed with the same ring and index. Hence, due to the perfect anonymity of ring signature, it is impossible for SNS to find out whether two query messages are sent from the same user. Therefore, without the knowledge of the ring index, even though SNS obtains POI and its exact location, it only has the possibility of $\frac{1}{n}$ to identify Alice as the real sender.

(2) Given a substitution location sending from Alice, the possibility that SNS deduces Alice's exact location is $\epsilon = \frac{1}{w}$.

Analysis 2: Suppose Alice's substitution location is a subway station, and there are 'w' buildings around it. Since the substitution location is selected by Alice secretly, SNS can infer Alice's exact location with the possibility of $\frac{1}{w}$ at most, even though SNS knows that what buildings are near the subway station.

Property 2. Our LPPRS is inference attack resistant to CS.

Analysis 3: As a semi-TTP, CS receives query messages from users and query results from SNS. For Alice's query message $qm = (POI_{loc}, qd, K_{ID-SNS})$, it is encrypted with PK_{SNS}. The corresponding private key of PK_{SNS} is kept by SNS secretly, so CS only owns the ciphertext of Alice's query message.

For query results $R_{SNS} = (R_1, R_2, ..., R_n)$ sending from SNS, they are encrypted by SNS with a systematic key K_{ID-SNS}, generated by Alice secretly and randomly. Hence, given R_{SNS}, without the knowledge of K_{ID-SNS}, CS cannot obtain the plaintexts of them.

For users' locations, CS only obtains districts of users' substitution location, so the possibility that CS can infer Alice's real location is far less than $\frac{1}{w}$.

From analysis 1 and analysis 3, we can conclude that Alice's query privacy and the linkage between her ID and query messages are preserved anonymously. From analysis 2, we can deduce that users' location privacy is also preserved.

6 Evaluation

This section shows that our LPPRS are practical, via evaluating communication and computation costs for the user side and server side, respectively.

- **Comm.cost**: RSA, AES and ring signature (RS) are three main algorithms applied in LPPRS. For RSA and AES, the key length is represented by 2048 bytes and 256 bytes respectively. For 2048-byte RSA with PKCS#1 padding, the ciphertext size is 256 bytes for every 245 bytes message. For a ring size of n, the ring signature size of RingCT 3.0 is $2\lceil\log_2(n)\rceil + 7$ elements in $\mathbb{G}$ and 7 elements in $\mathbb{Z}_p$. Based on Curve 25519, each element in $\mathbb{G}$ and $\mathbb{Z}_p$ has the length of 33 bytes and 32 bytes respectively. Thus, we have $|\sigma| = (2\log n + 7) * 33 + 7 * 32 = 66 \log n + 455$ bytes. For a ring size of 1024, the signature is 1115 bytes.
- **Comp.cost (User):**
    - RSA.Enc. It is used to encrypt query message, $C_{ID-SNS} = E_{PK_{SNS}}(qm)$.
    - RS.Sign. To sign C_{ID-SNS}, a ring signature of RingCT 3.0 is dominated by 3 multi-exponentiations in $\mathbb{G}$ of size $2n+1$, $2n$ and $n+1$ respectively, where n is the size of ring members.
    - AES.Dec. It is performed to get final result r_s. (Scheme 1)
    - RSA.Dec. It is performed to get final result r_s. (Scheme 2)

    Note that the above computations can be done offline by users.
- **Comp.cost (SNS)**
    - RS.Verify. It is dominated by 2 multi-exponentiations in $\mathbb{G}$ of size $2n + 2log_2 n + 1$ and $n + 4$ respectively.
    - RSA.Dec. SNS applies it to decrypt C_{ID-SNS} and obtain qm.
    - Perform qm. SNS calculates results r_{SNS} based on qm and ring Y.
    - AES.Enc. To obtain ciphertexts R_{SNS} of r_{SNS}. (Scheme 1)
    - RSA.Enc. To obtain ciphertexts R_{SNS} of r_{SNS}. (Scheme 2)
- **Comp.cost (CS):** CS does not need to perform any cryptographic algorithm. It just needs to select ring members and forward information between users and SNS.
- **The total running time of LPPRS:** The running time of RS.Sign and RS.Verify of RingCT 3.0 for different ring members n are given in [29]. Referring to the test data of AES and RSA algorithms providing by Crypto++ library[8], the running time in LPPRS for AES or RSA algorithm is negligible. Thus, the total running time of SNS (T_{SNS}) is mainly dominated by the time of RS.Verify ($T_{RS.Verify}$) and the computing time of query message (T_{qm}),

[8] https://www.cryptopp.com/benchmarks.html.

$T_{SNS} \approx T_{RS.Verify} + T_{qm}$. Based on RingCT 3.0, even if the size n of a ring is 1000, its' verification time is less than 3 s. Thus, $T_{RS.Verify}$ does not increase T_{SNS} remarkably. For T_{qm}, it is reasonable to set that SNS calculates results for ring members simultaneously, instead of one by one. Therefore, we can conclude that our LPPRS is practical to protect users' privacy with the ring signature.

7 Conclusion

In this paper, we present a new LBS application named NFPOI, which firstly combines SNS with POI and NF. Additionally, two privacy preserving frameworks (semi-TTP and TTP-free) based on ring signature are proposed in our LPPRS, aiming to offer anonymity for a sender's query message, and preserve the sender's location privacy and query privacy efficiently.

Firstly, ring signature is applied to sign the ciphertext of a query message. Based on the anonymity of ring signature, LPPRS supports SNS to return query results for a query message while it cannot find out who is the real sender. Thus, query privacy is preserved even when the sender does continuous queries. Secondly, a lightweight location privacy preserving algorithm called substitution location is applied to hide users' real locations. Thirdly, no entity in LPPRS is assumed fully trusted and the pre-sharing session key for friends is not required. Furthermore, our LPPRS is secure under inference attacks. Finally, users' communication costs and computation costs are lower than previous works according to comparisons shown in Table 2.

In LPPRS, the anonymity of a query message is related to the size of ring members n, which also influences the computations costs of SNS. Thus, the balance between the anonymity and the ring size n is a trade-off.

References

1. Pingley, A., Zhang, N., Fu, X., Choi, H.-A., Subramaniam, S., Zhao, W.: Protection of query privacy for continuous location based services. In: 2011 Proceedings IEEE INFOCOM, pp. 1710–1718. IEEE (2011)
2. Sweeney, L.: k-anonymity: a model for protecting privacy. Int. J. Uncertain. Fuzziness Knowl.-Based Syst. **10**(05), 557–570 (2002)
3. Gruteser, M., Grunwald, D.: Anonymous usage of location-based services through spatial and temporal cloaking. In: Proceedings of the 1st International Conference on Mobile Systems, Applications and Services, pp. 31–42 (2003)
4. Yang, D., Fang, X., Xue, G.: Truthful incentive mechanisms for k-anonymity location privacy. In: 2013 Proceedings IEEE INFOCOM, pp. 2994–3002. IEEE (2013)
5. Niu, B., Li, Q., Zhu, X., Cao, G., Li, H.: Achieving k-anonymity in privacy-aware location-based services. In: IEEE INFOCOM 2014-IEEE Conference on Computer Communications, pp. 754–762. IEEE (2014)
6. Kido, H., Yanagisawa, Y., Satoh, T.: An anonymous communication technique using dummies for location-based services. In: ICPS 2005. Proceedings. International Conference on Pervasive Services, 2005, pp. 88–97. IEEE (2005)

7. Lu, H., Jensen, C.S., Yiu, M.L.: PAD: privacy-area aware, dummy-based location privacy in mobile services. In: Proceedings of the Seventh ACM International Workshop on Data Engineering for Wireless and Mobile Access, pp. 16–23 (2008)
8. Liu, H., Li, X., Li, H., Ma, J., Ma, X.: Spatiotemporal correlation-aware dummy-based privacy protection scheme for location-based services. In: IEEE INFOCOM 2017-IEEE Conference on Computer Communications, pp. 1–9. IEEE (2017)
9. Sun, G., Song, L., Liao, D., Hongfang, Yu., Chang, V.: Towards privacy preservation for "check-in" services in location-based social networks. Inf. Sci. **481**, 616–634 (2019)
10. Hong, J.I., Landay, J.A.: An architecture for privacy-sensitive ubiquitous computing. In: Proceedings of the 2nd International Conference on Mobile Systems, Applications, and Services, pp. 177–189 (2004)
11. Duckham, M., Kulik, L.: A formal model of obfuscation and negotiation for location privacy. In: Gellersen, H.-W., Want, R., Schmidt, A. (eds.) Pervasive 2005. LNCS, vol. 3468, pp. 152–170. Springer, Heidelberg (2005). https://doi.org/10.1007/11428572_10
12. Beresford, A.R., Stajano, F.: Mix zones: user privacy in location-aware services. In: IEEE Annual Conference on Pervasive Computing and Communications Workshops, 2004. Proceedings of the Second, pp. 127–131. IEEE (2004)
13. Freudiger, J., Shokri, R., Hubaux, J.-P.: On the optimal placement of mix zones. In: Goldberg, I., Atallah, M.J. (eds.) PETS 2009. LNCS, vol. 5672, pp. 216–234. Springer, Heidelberg (2009). https://doi.org/10.1007/978-3-642-03168-7_13
14. Khoshgozaran, A., Shahabi, C.: Blind evaluation of nearest neighbor queries using space transformation to preserve location privacy. In: Papadias, D., Zhang, D., Kollios, G. (eds.) SSTD 2007. LNCS, vol. 4605, pp. 239–257. Springer, Heidelberg (2007). https://doi.org/10.1007/978-3-540-73540-3_14
15. Hu, H., Xu, J., Ren, C., Choi, B.: Processing private queries over untrusted data cloud through privacy homomorphism. In: 2011 IEEE 27th International Conference on Data Engineering, pp. 601–612. IEEE (2011)
16. Paillier, P.: Public-key cryptosystems based on composite degree residuosity classes. In: Stern, J. (ed.) EUROCRYPT 1999. LNCS, vol. 1592, pp. 223–238. Springer, Heidelberg (1999). https://doi.org/10.1007/3-540-48910-X_16
17. Brakerski, Z., Vaikuntanathan, V.: Fully homomorphic encryption from ring-LWE and security for key dependent messages. In: Rogaway, P. (ed.) CRYPTO 2011. LNCS, vol. 6841, pp. 505–524. Springer, Heidelberg (2011). https://doi.org/10.1007/978-3-642-22792-9_29
18. Li, X.-Y., Jung, T.: Search me if you can: privacy-preserving location query service. In: 2013 Proceedings IEEE INFOCOM, pp. 2760–2768. IEEE (2013)
19. Novak, E., Li, Q.: Near-pri: private, proximity based location sharing. In: IEEE INFOCOM 2014-IEEE Conference on Computer Communications, pp. 37–45. IEEE (2014)
20. Ghinita, G., Kalnis, P., Khoshgozaran, A., Shahabi, C., Tan, K.-L.: Private queries in location based services: anonymizers are not necessary. In: Proceedings of the 2008 ACM SIGMOD International Conference on Management of Data, pp. 121–132 (2008)
21. Khoshgozaran, A., Shirani-Mehr, H., Shahabi, C.: SPIRAL: a scalable private information retrieval approach to location privacy. In: 2008 Ninth International Conference on Mobile Data Management Workshops, MDMW, pp. 55–62. IEEE (2008)
22. Papadopoulos, S., Bakiras, S., Papadias, D.: Nearest neighbor search with strong location privacy. Proc. VLDB Endow. **3**(1–2), 619–629 (2010)

23. Paulet, R., Kaosar, M.G., Yi, X., Bertino, E.: Privacy-preserving and content-protecting location based queries. IEEE Trans. Knowl. Data Eng. **26**(5), 1200–1210 (2013)
24. Gupta, R., Rao, U.P.: An exploration to location based service and its privacy preserving techniques: a survey. Wirel. Pers. Commun. **96**(2), 1973–2007 (2017)
25. Liu, B., Zhou, W., Zhu, T., Gao, L., Xiang, Y.: Location privacy and its applications: a systematic study. IEEE Access **6**, 17606–17624 (2018)
26. Almusaylim, Z.A., Jhanjhi, N.Z.: Comprehensive review: privacy protection of user in location-aware services of mobile cloud computing. Wirel. Pers. Commun. **111**(1), 541–564 (2020)
27. Liao, D., Li, H., Sun, G., Anand, V.: Protecting user trajectory in location-based services. In: 2015 IEEE Global Communications Conference (GLOBECOM), pp. 1–6. IEEE (2015)
28. Narayanan, A., Shmatikov, V.: De-anonymizing social networks. In: 2009 30th IEEE Symposium on Security and Privacy, pp. 173–187. IEEE (2009)
29. Yuen, T.H., et al.: RingCT 3.0 for blockchain confidential transaction: shorter size and stronger security. Technical report, Cryptology ePrint Archive, Report 2019/508. To appear in FC 2020 (2019)
30. Rivest, R.L., Shamir, A., Tauman, Y.: How to leak a secret. In: Boyd, C. (ed.) ASIACRYPT 2001. LNCS, vol. 2248, pp. 552–565. Springer, Heidelberg (2001). https://doi.org/10.1007/3-540-45682-1_32
31. Wei, W., Xu, F., Li, Q.: Mobishare: flexible privacy-preserving location sharing in mobile online social networks. In: 2012 Proceedings IEEE INFOCOM, pp. 2616–2620. IEEE (2012)
32. Peng, T., Liu, Q., Wang, G., Xiang, Y., Chen, S.: Multidimensional privacy preservation in location-based services. Futur. Gener. Comput. Syst. **93**, 312–326 (2019)
33. Liu, Z., Li, J., Chen, X., Li, J., Jia, C.: New privacy-preserving location sharing system for mobile online social networks. In: 2013 Eighth International Conference on P2P, Parallel, Grid, Cloud and Internet Computing, pp. 214–218. IEEE (2013)
34. Liu, Y., Han, J., Wang, J.: Rumor riding: anonymizing unstructured peer-to-peer systems. IEEE Trans. Parallel Distrib. Syst. **22**(3), 464–475 (2010)
35. Li, J., Yan, H., Liu, Z., Chen, X., Huang, X., Wong, D.S.: Location-sharing systems with enhanced privacy in mobile online social networks. IEEE Syst. J. **11**(2), 439–448 (2015)
36. Schlegel, R., Chow, C.-Y., Huang, Q., Wong, D.S.: Privacy-preserving location sharing services for social networks. IEEE Trans. Serv. Comput. **10**(5), 811–825 (2016)
37. Zeng, S., Yi, M., He, M., Chen, Y.: New approach for privacy-aware location-based service communications. Wireless Pers. Commun. **101**(2), 1057–1073 (2018)

Secure Sequence

On the Structure Property of PCR's Adjacency Graph with a Prime Order and Its Application of Constructing M-Sequences

Congwei Zhou[1(✉)], Jie Guan[1], Bin Hu[1], and Kuan He[2]

[1] PLA SSF Information Engineering University, Zhengzhou, China
zhoucongwei@qq.com

[2] National Key Laboratory of Science and Technology on Blind Signal Processing, Chengdu, China

Abstract. In this paper we find a deterministic structure respecting the adjacency graph of a pure circulating shift register (PCR) with a prime order, and give a theoretical method for constructing all floor weight class of M-sequences. As a special case of this method, we calculate a lower bound of the number of floor weight class of M-sequences and give their corresponding feedback functions.

Keywords: M-sequences · Adjacency graph · Pure circulating shift register · Spanning tree

1 Introduction

Because of its huge quantity and favorable pseudo-randomness, the M-sequence is widely used in secure communication. In recent decades, the method for constructing M-sequences and their feedback functions is increasingly studied. The common methods are Direct (Cycle joining, Montage [1] and Spanning Tree [2]) and Recursion [3,4]. In [2], it has already been proved that there is an one-to-one correspondence between all spanning trees of PCR's (resp. complementing cycling register's) adjacency graph and all floor (resp. maximum) weight class of M-sequences for the same order. Furthermore, due to the existence of the odd-weight feedback function of M-sequences, in which the odd number is between the floor and maximum weight value, we just find out all floor (resp. maximum) weight feedback functions of M-sequences by Spanning Tree, compare the differences among their minor term parts, and obtain all feedback functions of M-sequences for the same order. Therefore, the study on the structure of PCR's (resp. complementing cycling register's) adjacency graph and the number of its spanning tree is of great significance for constructing M-sequences.

Supported by the National Science Foundation of China under Grant Nos. 61572516.

Y. Wu and M. Yung (Eds.): Inscrypt 2020, LNCS 12612, pp. 307–317, 2021.
https://doi.org/10.1007/978-3-030-71852-7_20

In fact, because the adjacency graph is a multiple oriented graph, it's difficult to express its deterministic structure, and few references describe the structure of PCR's (resp. complementing cycling register's) adjacency graph. In [5], Mykkeltveit first studies on generating and counting the double adjacencies of PCR's adjacency graph, and in [6,7], on the basis of a larger automorphism group on PCR's (resp. complementing cycling register's) adjacency graph, a quantitative result of various characteristics is obtained through a series of its properties of multiple-lines converting to a number theory calculation. But further, the quantitative result limits the imagination of the deterministic structure of PCR's (resp. complementing cycling register's) adjacency graph in a way.

On the other hand, in [8], the method for constructing all floor (resp. maximum) weight class of M-sequences is given by matrix-tree theorem for a generalized multiple oriented graph, and Kang gets the number of all floor (resp. maximum) weight class of M-sequences for order $n \leq 7$ through experimental calculation results. In [9], Mayhew gets the number of all floor (resp. maximum) weight class of M-sequences for order $n \leq 11$ through a similar graph theory approach[8]. That is the best numerical result about the number of all floor (resp. maximum) weight class of M-sequences for order n so far. In [10], for the research on the non-extremal weight class of M-sequences, a theoretical discussion of symmetric groups acting on these sequences is presented. And in [11,12], Mayhew gets the number of all weight class of M-sequences for order $n \leq 6$ and the partial weight class of M-sequences for order $n \leq 7$. These numerical results indicate the difficulty of exhaustive enumeration for order $n > 7$ in a way.

In order to give more numerical results about the number of floor weight class of M-sequences for higher orders ($n > 11$), we present a deterministic structure to describe PCR's adjacency graph with a prime order. And this deterministic structure can directly generate a type of spanning trees and get their number, as well as all spanning trees in theory. For example, we conclude that the number of its spanning trees is at least $2^{498} \cdot 3^{309} \cdot 5^{198} \cdot 7 \cdot 11$ for order $n = 13$ by calculating (see Theorem 4), and this number is more than the total number of all spanning trees for order $n \leq 11$.

The rest of this paper is organized as follows. In Sect. 2 we delimit the adjacency graph and the relationship between its spanning tree and the floor (resp. maximum) weight class of M-sequences based on [2]; In Sect. 3, we present a deterministic structure description on the basis of properties of PCR and its adjacency graph with a prime order, calculate a lower bound of the number of floor weight class of M-sequences and give their corresponding feedback functions; According to the above structure a theoretical construction method for obtaining all floor weight of M-sequences is given in Sect. 4, and we apply it to the order $n = 5$.

2 Preliminaries

The following Definition 1 [2], Lemma 1 and 2 [2] and Theorem 1 [2] are summarized in [2], and we rule the following $\oplus$ to the addition on F_2.

Definition 1. (see [2]): Let $f(X^n) = x_1 \oplus f_0$ be a non-singular shift register feedback function with order n, whose state cycle structure G_f has N_f cycles, and let Γ_f be the adjacency graph of G_f. Then G_f has cycles σ_i as Γ_f has vertices $g_i (i = 1, 2, \cdots, N_f)$. Let $\underline{a} = (a_1, a_2, \cdots, a_n)$ and $\underline{a}^* = (a_1 \oplus 1, a_2, \cdots, a_n)$ be an arbitrary pair of conjugate vertices in G_f. If $\underline{a}$ and $\underline{a}^*$ are in the cycle σ_i and σ_j respectively (i can be j), we use one side to connect the point g_i and g_j, and set this side be $(a_2, \cdots, a_n)$. Consequently, the number of vertices and sides are equal to N_f and 2^{n-1} in Γ_f.

Lemma 1. (see [2]): If Γ_f satisfies the following two conditions:(1) Γ_f has a partial graph of undirected tree; (2) a partial graph of undirected tree of Γ_f consists of $N_f - 1$ sides, then

$$f'(X^n) = f(X^n) \oplus \sum_{i=1}^{N_f-1} x_2^{a_2^{(i)}} x_3^{a_3^{(i)}} \cdots x_n^{a_n^{(i)}}$$

is a feedback function of M-sequences.

Lemma 2. (see [2]) (a necessary condition of the feedback function of M-sequences): Let $wt(f_0)$ be the weight of f_0 in the feedback function. Then correspondingly,

$$Z(n) - 1 \leq wt(f_0) \leq 2^{n-1} - Z^*(n) + 1,$$

and $wt(f_0)$ is odd, where $Z(n)=\frac{1}{n}\sum\limits_{d|n} \phi(d)2^{n/d}$, $Z^*(n) = \frac{1}{2}Z(n) - \frac{1}{2n}\sum\limits_{2d|n} \phi(d)$ $2^{n/2d}$. Meanwhile we say that the weight $Z(n) - 1$ is the floor weight class of feedback function of M-sequences with the order n, and the weight $2^{n-1} - Z^*(n) + 1$ is the maximum weight class of feedback function of M-sequences with the order n.

Theorem 1. (see [2]): There is a one-to-one correspondence between the all spanning trees of PCR's adjacency graph and all floor weight class of M-sequences, so the number of all floor weight class of M-sequences is equal to the number of partial graph of undirected tree of Γ_{x_1}; There is a one-to-one correspondence between all spanning trees of the complementing cycling register's adjacency graph and all maximum weight class of M-sequences, so the number of all maximum weight class of M-sequences is equal to the number of partial graph of undirected tree of $\Gamma_{x_1 \oplus 1}$.

3 The Structure of PCR's Adjacency Graph with a Prime Order

We first give the cycle structure of PCR with a prime order as follows.

Theorem 2. Let $f(X^n)$ be x_1, where n is a prime number greater than 2. Then $N_f = (2^n - 2)/n{+}2$, and the cycle structure satisfies the following properties:

1. the states with different weights are not in the same circle;
2. Let $i(0 < i < n)$ be the weight value of the state. Then the number of cycles is $\binom{n}{i}/n$, which are formed by states with the same weight;
3. There are only 2 circles with the length of 1, which are formed by the state $\mathbf{0}$ and $\mathbf{1}$.

Proof. Take n as a prime number into $Z(n)$. Then we get $N_f = (2^n - 2)/n+2$; By the definition of PCR, the states with different weights are obviously not in the same circle. Because n is a prime number, every circle is in PCR, whose number of states is either 1 or n. And because the number of weight value $i(0 < i < n)$ of states is $\binom{n}{i}$, the number of circles which are formed by states with the same weight, is exactly $\binom{n}{i}/n$. Simultaneously, It is easy to know that there is a circle with a length of 1 if and only if its state is $\mathbf{0}$ or $\mathbf{1}$.

Based on the above cycle structure properties of PCR with a prime order, we can describe the structure of its adjacency graph. In the first place, we define the concept of "level" in the adjacency graph. And let $\binom{n}{i}/n$ be m_i.

Definition 2. In the adjacency graph of PCR with a prime order, the corresponding vertices $g_j^{(i)}(1 \leq j \leq m_i)$ of the state circle which is formed by the weight $i(0 < i < n)$ of states, are on the i-th level. In particular, we say that the corresponding vertex $g^{(0)}$ of the state circle, which is formed by the state $\mathbf{0}$, is on zero level. Correspondingly, the corresponding vertex $g^{(n)}$ of the state circle, which is formed by the state $\mathbf{1}$, is on the n-th level.

Theorem 3. A deterministic structure of PCR's adjacency graph with a prime order satisfies the following conditions:

1. Only vertices on adjoining levels have sides to connect;
2. For each vertex on the $i(1 \leq i \leq \frac{n-1}{2})$-th level, there are i sides connected to vertices on the previous level;
3. For each vertex on the $i(\frac{n+1}{2} \leq i \leq n-1)$-th level, there are $n-i$ sides connected to vertices on the next level;
4. For each vertex on the $\frac{n-1}{2}$-th (resp. $\frac{n+1}{2}$-th) level, there are $\frac{n+1}{2}$ sides connected to vertices on the $\frac{n+1}{2}$-th (resp. $\frac{n-1}{2}$-th) levels.

Proof. Because the weight of a pair of conjugate states must be a difference of 1, only vertices on adjoining levels have sides to connect. Since in the cycles represented by each vertex on the $i(1 \leq i \leq \frac{n-1}{2})$-th level only the most significant bit of i states is 1, according to the definition of the side of adjacency graph, it can be seen that for each vertex on the $i(1 \leq i \leq \frac{n-1}{2})$-th level, there are i sides connected to vertices on the previous level; Since in the cycles represented by the each vertex on the $i(\frac{n+1}{2} \leq i \leq n-1)$-th level only the most significant bit of $n-i$ states are 0, according to the definition of the side of adjacency graph, it can be seen that for each vertex on the $i(\frac{n+1}{2} \leq i \leq n-1)$-th level, there are $n-i$ sides connected to vertices on the next level; Similarly, according to the definition of the side of adjacency graph, it can be seen that for each vertex on the $\frac{n-1}{2}$-th (resp. $\frac{n+1}{2}$-th) level, there are $\frac{n+1}{2}$ sides connected to vertices on the $\frac{n+1}{2}$-th (resp. $\frac{n-1}{2}$-th) levels. At this point, we count the total number of these sides. Since the i-th level has m_i vertices, for $1 \leq i \leq \frac{n-1}{2}$,

$$i \cdot m_i = \binom{n-1}{i-1};$$

for $i(\frac{n+1}{2} \leq i \leq n-1)$,

$$(n-i) \cdot m_i = (n-i) \cdot \binom{n}{n-i} / n = \binom{n-1}{i};$$

And the total number of sides connected to each vertex on the $\frac{n-1}{2}$-th and $\frac{n+1}{2}$-th levels is

$$\frac{n+1}{2} \cdot \binom{n}{\frac{n-1}{2}} / n = \binom{n-1}{\frac{n-1}{2}}.$$

Consequently, the total number of all sides at this point is exactly the expanding combinatorial number of 2^{n-1}.

Theorem 4. The number of the partial graph of undirected tree of PCR's adjacency graph Γ_{x_1} with a prime order, namely the number of all floor weight class of feedback function of M-sequences, is at least

$$\left[\prod_{i=1}^{\frac{n-1}{2}} i^{m_i}\right]^2 \cdot \binom{n-1}{\frac{n-1}{2}}.$$

Proof. According to the concept of partial graph of undirected tree, it can be seen that we need $N_f - 1$ sides to connect N_f vertices. Therefore, for each vertex on the $i(1 \leq i \leq \frac{n-1}{2})$-th level, we can choose one of i sides connected to vertices on the previous level. Then the $\frac{N_f}{2}$ vertices in the upper part of adjacency graph are connected with $\frac{N_f}{2} - 1$ sides, and the upper part of spanning tree is formed; Similarly, for each vertex on the $i(\frac{n+1}{2} \leq i \leq n-1)$-th level, we can choose one of $n-i$ sides connected to vertices on the next level. Then the $\frac{N_f}{2}$ vertices in the lower part of adjacency graph are connected with $\frac{N_f}{2} - 1$ sides, and the lower part of spanning tree is formed; At this point, we only need to choose one of all sides connected to each vertex on the $\frac{n-1}{2}$-th and $\frac{n+1}{2}$-th levels, then the upper and lower part of spanning tree can be connected to form a whole spanning tree. It's easy to see that the upper and lower parts of adjacency graph are symmetrical, and the total number of selectable sides in the corresponding connected upper part of spanning tree is $\prod_{i=1}^{\frac{n-1}{2}} i^{m_i}$. And the total number of all sides in the middle two levels is $\binom{n-1}{\frac{n-1}{2}}$. Consequently, the total number of generated partial graph of undirected tree is at least

$$\left[\prod_{i=1}^{\frac{n-1}{2}} i^{m_i}\right]^2 \cdot \binom{n-1}{\frac{n-1}{2}}.$$

Then, according to Theorem 1, the proof is finished.

Next we discuss the deterministic form of floor weight class of feedback function of M-sequences formed in Theorem 4. Because the weight value has been determined to be $(2^n - 2)/n + 1$, then the floor weight class of feedback function of M-sequences generated in Theorem 4 can be expressed as follows:

$$f(X^n) = x_1 \oplus \sum_{t=1}^{(2^n-2)/n} x_2{}^{a_2^t} x_3{}^{a_3^t} \cdots x_n{}^{a_n^t} \oplus x_2{}^{a_2^l} x_3{}^{a_3^l} \cdots x_n{}^{a_n^l}.$$

Since $f(X^n)$ is a class of feedback functions of M-sequences, Then to determine the corresponding state among minor terms is equal to determine state sets which $(a_1^t, a_2^t, \cdots, a_n^t)$ and $(a_1^l, a_2^l, \cdots, a_n^l)$ belong to. According to the proof process of Theorem 4, there are the following symbol notations:

$$\begin{cases} A_i(1 \le i \le \frac{n-1}{2}) = \{(1, a_2, \cdots, a_n) \,|wt(a_2, \cdots, a_n) = i - 1\} \\ A_i(\frac{n+1}{2} \le i \le n-1) = \{(0, a_2, \cdots, a_n) \,|wt(a_2, \cdots, a_n) = i\} \end{cases}.$$

At the same time, all states in the each set A_i are equivalently classified by the left circular shift R. Let the classified state set be $\{B_j^i\}$, namely

$$B_j^i = \left\{ R^{(k)}\underline{a} \,\middle|\, 0 \le k \le n-1, \underline{a} \in A_i, R^{(k)}\underline{a} \in A_i \right\}.$$

It's easy to see that $\left|B_j^i\right| = i, 1 \le j \le m_i$, namely the state set

$$A_i = \bigcup_{j=1}^{m_i} B_j^i.$$

Consequently, each state $(a_1^t, a_2^t, \cdots, a_n^t)(1 \le t \le (2^n - 2)/n)$ exactly comes from one of state sets B_j^i. At the same time, It's easy to see that

$$(a_1^l, a_2^l, \cdots, a_n^l) \in \{(0, a_2, \cdots, a_n) \,\Big|\, wt(a_2, \cdots, a_n) = \frac{n-1}{2}\}.$$

The above analytic process can be an one-to-one correspondence with the proof of Theorem 4.

4 A Construction Method for Solving All Floor Weight Class of M-Sequences

For the deterministic structure of PCR's adjacency graph with a prime order in Theorem 3, this paper carries out a research on whether it can derive the other floor weight class of M-sequences which are different from them described in Theorem 4, namely generate other types of spanning trees. On account of this deterministic structure, when we select the upper and lower spanning trees, it actually considers that how to merge the two parts into a connected spanning tree. In Theorem 4 we use one side to connect, but in fact we can use multiple sides to connect according to the number of vertices on the middle two levels. Sequentially, when the middle two levels are connected by k sides, the upper and lower spanning trees need to be combined to disconnect $k-1$ sides.

According to the concept of partial graph of undirected tree, it is shown that vertices on the middle two levels have been connected with one side after the formation of upper and lower spanning trees, namely form a branch between the ones and $g^{(0)}(g^{(n)})$. It is assumed that one side on the branch formed by a certain vertex is disconnected in the connected spanning tree (the side can't be connected with $g^{(0)}(g^{(n)})$). Then the number of disconnected sides on the branches formed by vertices on one of the middle two levels will be at most $\binom{n}{\frac{n-1}{2}}/n-1$, otherwise, a connected spanning tree can not be obtained. Consequently in total, at most $2(\binom{n}{\frac{n-1}{2}}/n-1)$ sides are disconnected, namely $k \leq 2\cdot\binom{n}{\frac{n-1}{2}}/n-1$. At the same time, it has been proved that there are at most double sides connected by two vertices in PCR's adjacency graph on the basis of [6]. Therefore, there is a double-side between the corresponding vertices on the middle two levels. At this point if we consider that the role of double-side in the disconnection process, it should be selected before the connection in fact. Consequently it does not affect the maximum value of k.

Figure 1 shows a possible disconnection process when k reaches the maximum value, where the "hyphen" represents one disconnected side on a branch.

In this case, a construction method for solving all floor weight class of M-sequences can be described as follows:

1. Enumerate the weight $\frac{n-1}{2}$ and $\frac{n+1}{2}$ of states, get the correspondence among sides in the middle two levels of PCR's adjacency graph, and calculate the number of double-side groups in the middle two levels. Namely, set the number as $B(n)$. In the meantime, a double-side can be equivalent to one side in the following steps.
2. For $k=1$, the sum of spanning trees is the lower bound described in Theorem 4.
3. For $k=2$, select two sides from $\binom{n-1}{\frac{n-1}{2}} - B(n)$ sides, and there are only two following cases when the two sides are connected in the middle two levels:

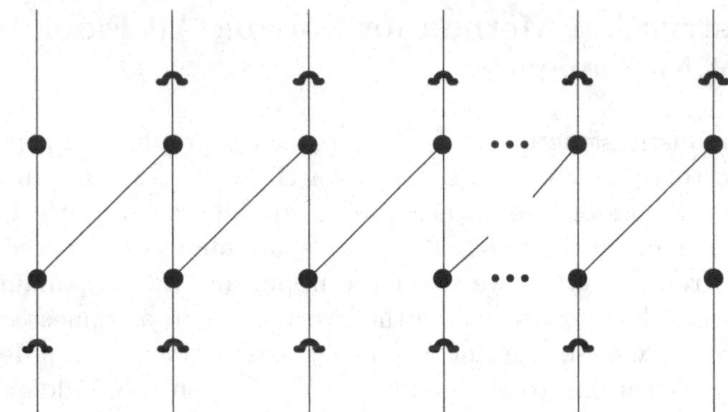

Fig. 1. A schematic diagram of a possible disconnection process when k reaches its the maximum value

(a) One vertex through the two sides is connected to two vertices on the upper (lower) level. Then the disconnected side is on one of two branches corresponding to the two vertices. Accordingly, we count the number of groups in this case as K_2;

(b) Two vertices through the two sides are connected to two vertices on the upper (lower) level. Then the disconnected side is on one of four branches corresponding to the four vertices. Accordingly, the number of groups in this case is $\begin{pmatrix} \binom{n-1}{\frac{n-1}{2}} - B(n) \\ 2 \end{pmatrix} - K_2$.

Note that when we calculate the possibility of disconnected sides, the choices about the original side corresponding to i or $n-i$ possible choices is gone. And the number of possible disconnected sides selected on a branch at this time is $\frac{n-3}{2}$ (excluding the side connected with $g^{(0)}(g^{(n)})$). Consequently, the sum of spanning trees in this case is

$$\sum_{i=2}^{\frac{n-1}{2}} \frac{1}{i} \left\{ 2^{B(n)} \cdot \left[\prod_{i=1}^{\frac{n-1}{2}} i^{m_i} \right]^2 \cdot \frac{n-3}{2} \cdot \left[2 \cdot K_2 + 4 \cdot \left(\begin{pmatrix} \binom{n-1}{\frac{n-1}{2}} - B(n) \\ 2 \end{pmatrix} - K_2 \right) \right] \right\}$$

$$= \sum_{i=2}^{\frac{n-1}{2}} \frac{1}{i} \left\{ 2^{B(n)} \cdot \left[\prod_{i=1}^{\frac{n-1}{2}} i^{m_i} \right]^2 \cdot (n-3) \cdot \left(2 \cdot \begin{pmatrix} \binom{n-1}{\frac{n-1}{2}} - B(n) \\ 2 \end{pmatrix} - K_2\right) \right\}$$

4. For $k = i(2 < i \leq 2 \cdot \binom{n}{\frac{n-1}{2}} / n-1)$, According to the case for $k = 2$, until calculating the total number of spanning trees in the current case on k, finally we count the sum of spanning trees on all values of k, namely the number of all floor weight class of M-sequences.

The rest of this paper takes the order $n = 5$ as an example, giving the steps to solve all floor weight class of M-sequences. Figure 2 shows Γ_{x_1} for the order $n = 5$.

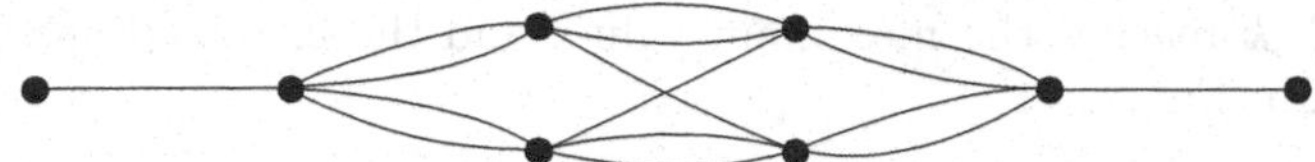

Fig. 2. Γ_{x_1} for the order $n = 5$

1. For $k = 1$, Theorem 4 shows that the sum at this time is $2^5 \cdot 3$. And a spanning tree is shown in Fig. 3.

Fig. 3. A spanning tree of Γ_{x_1} for $k = 1$ (imaginary lines indicate selectable sides)

2. For $k = 2$, at this time a double-side can be regarded as one side marked with short vertical lines. Then according to the above construction we classify spanning trees and the classified spanning trees are shown in Fig. 4.

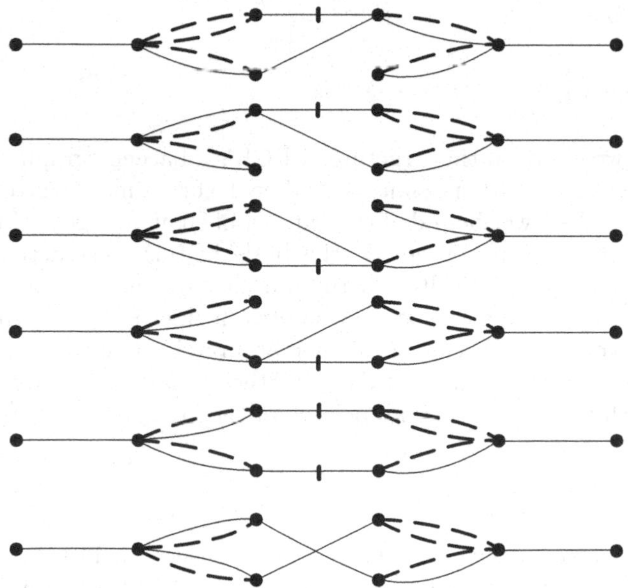

Fig. 4. Spanning trees of Γ_{x_1} for $k = 2$

In turn, the sum of spanning trees is $2^5 + 2^5 + 2^5 + 2^5 + 2^7 + 2^5 = 2^5 \cdot 9$.

3. For $k = 3$, k reaches the maximum value, and the classified spanning trees are shown in Fig. 5.

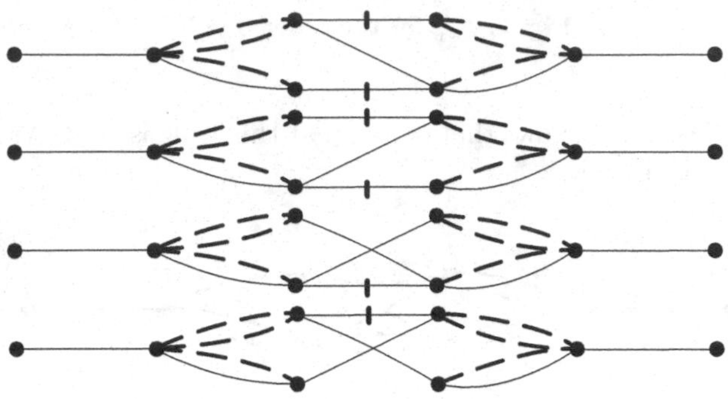

Fig. 5. Spanning trees of Γ_{x_1} for $k = 3$

In turn, the sum of spanning trees is $2^6 + 2^6 + 2^5 + 2^5 = 2^5 \cdot 6$.

In conclusion, for the order $n = 5$, the sum of spanning trees of Γ_{x_1}, namely the number of all floor weight class of M-sequences, is $2^6 \cdot 3^2$, which is consistent with the data in [9].

5 Conclusion

In this paper, we study on the structure of PCR's adjacency graph with a prime order and the number of its spanning trees. For the first time, we give a deterministic structure and a lower bound of the number of spanning trees of PCR's adjacency graph with any prime orders. On this basis, by this construction method on M-sequences, it can theoretically generate all floor weight class of M-sequences. Therefore, as long as the correspondence between sides in the middle two levels of PCR's adjacency graph can be further accurately described, a more accurate lower bound of the number of all floor weight class of M-sequences can be obtained, which is also a research objective of the next step for this paper.

References

1. Gao, H.: A method and proof for finding all M-Sequence and its feedback function for order n. Acta Mathematicae Applicatae Sinica **04**, 316–324 (1979)
2. Wan, Z., Day, Z., Liu, M., et al.: Non-Linear Shift Register. Science Press, Beijing (1978)
3. Lempel, A.: On a homomorphism of the de Bruijn graph and its applications to the design of feedback shift registers. IEEE Trans. Comput. **19**(12), 1204–1207 (1970)
4. Zhao, X., Qi, W.: The construction of de Bruijn sequence based on cascade connection. J. Cryptol. Res. **2**(3), 245–257 (2015)

5. Mykkeltveit, J.: Generating and counting the double adjacencies in a pure circulating shift registers. IEEE Trans. Comput. **24**(3), 299–304 (1975)
6. Feng, K.: On properties of PCR's and CCR's factor-incident graphs. Acta Mathematicae Applicatae Sinica **01**, 1–14 (1982)
7. Kang, Q.: On the multiple-lines in CCR's and PCR's factor-incident graphs. Acta Mathematicae Applicatae Sinica **03**, 352–369 (1986)
8. Kang, Q.: The methods of constructing M-sequence over GF(2). J. Commun. **04**, 2–10 (1983)
9. Mayhew, G.L.: Extreme weight class of de Bruijn sequences. Discrete Math. **256**(1–2), 495–497 (2002)
10. Hauge, E.R., Mykkeltveit, J.: The analysis of De Bruijn sequences of non-extremal weight. Discrete Math. **189**(1–3), 133–147 (1998)
11. Mayhew, G.L.: Weight class distributions of de Bruijn sequences. Discrete Math. **126**(1–3), 425–429 (1994)
12. Mayhew, G.L.: Further results on de Bruijn weight classes. Discrete Math. **232**(1–3), 171–173 (2001)

Symmetric 2-Adic Complexity of Ding-Helleseth Generalized Cyclotomic Sequences of Period pq

Vladimir Edemskiy[1(✉)] and Chenhuang Wu[2,3]

[1] Yaroslav-the-Wise Novgorod State University, Veliky Novgorod, Russia
vladimir.edemsky@novsu.ru

[2] Provincial Key Laboratory of Applied Mathematics, Putian University, Putian 351100, Fujian, China
ptuwch@163.com

[3] School of Computer Science and Engineering, University of Electronic Science and Technology of China, Chengdu 611731, Sichuan, China

Abstract. In this paper, we consider Ding-Helleseth generalized cyclotomic sequences of length pq where p and q are odd distinct primes. We derive symmetric 2-adic complexity of these sequences for any p, q and show that they have high symmetric 2-adic complexity. These results generalize known conclusions of Yan et al. (IEEE Access, 2020, https://doi:10.1109/ACCESS.2020.3012570) about 2-adic complexity of Ding-Helleseth sequences of order 2 and of length pq.

Keywords: 2-adic complexity · Binary sequences · Cyclotomy

1 Introduction

Pseudorandom binary sequences are widely used in many areas of communication and cryptography. These sequences can be efficiently generated by linear feedback shift registers (LFSRs) [3] or feedback with carry shift registers (FCSRs) [8,9]. Linear complexity and 2-adic complexity of a sequence are defined as the length of the shortest LFSR or FCSR respectively, which is capable of generating a given sequence. In a cryptographic application, sequences as a candidate for a keystream encryption system must be of high complexity. The notation of 2-adic complexity of sequence was presented by Klapper and Goresky [8,9]. Later Hu and Feng [6] proposed a new measure which they called symmetric 2-adic complexity. They also showed that symmetric 2-adic complexity is better than 2-adic complexity in measuring the security of a binary periodic sequence.

V. Edemskiy were supported by RFBR-NSFC according to the research project No. 19-51-53003, C. Wu was partially supported by the Projects of International Cooperation and Exchange NSFC-RFBR No. 61911530130, by the National Natural Science Foundation of China No. 61373140, 61772292 and by the Natural Science Foundation of Fujian Province No. 2020J01905.

Y. Wu and M. Yung (Eds.): Inscrypt 2020, LNCS 12612, pp. 318–327, 2021.
https://doi.org/10.1007/978-3-030-71852-7_21

Compared to the linear complexity, the 2-adic complexity of sequences has not been fully researched. The 2-adic complexity of the series of sequences with ideal autocorrelation or good autocorrelation was studied in [5,12,13,16,17] (see also references here). Thus, it is important to study 2-adic complexity of the known sequences and find binary sequences with large linear complexity and high symmetric 2-adic complexity. Its value cannot be less than half of the period, otherwise the sequence will be vulnerable to be attacked by 2-adic of the rational approximation algorithm [8].

In [1], Ding and Helleseth introduced the generalized cyclotomy of order 2 with respect to odd modulo, which includes classical cyclotomy of order 2 as a special case. It is well known that we can obtain binary sequences with high linear complexity using the generalized cyclotomic classes of Ding-Helleseth. There are a lot of papers devoted to study of characteristics of these sequences. In particular, the linear complexity and the autocorrelation of such sequences with period pq is investigated in [2,10,11,18,19](see also references here). In [21], Yan et al. studied 2-adic complexity of family of Ding-Helleseth sequences for $q=p+2$ and in [22] for $\gcd(p-1,q-1)=2$, $p\equiv q\equiv 3 \pmod 4$. They used the method of the determinant of a circulant matrix given in [6] and Gauss periods. Very recently, new method of studying 2-adic complexity was presented in [23]. It uses "Gauss periods" and "Gauss sums" on the finite field $\mathbb{F}_q$ valued in the ring $\mathbb{Z}_{2^{2q}-1}$. In [20], this method was employed to study 2-adic complexity of generalized binary sequences of order 2 and also to generalize the results from [4,14] about the 2-adic comeplxity of the modified Jacobi sequences.

Here in this paper, we will use this interesting approach to study the symmetric 2-adic complexity of Ding-Helleseth binary sequence with period pq in general case. We will obtain the estimate of symmetric 2-adic complexity of these sequences; in particular, we will generalize the results from [21] and [22].

The remainder of this paper is organized as follows. In Sect. 2, some basic concepts are discuss and the main result is presented. In Sect. 3 subsidiary statements are considered. In Sect. 4 the symmetric 2-adic complexity of generalized cyclotomic sequences with period pq is estimated.

2 Preliminaries

We need some preliminary notations and results before we begin. First, we recall the definitions of generalized cyclotomic classes of Ding-Hellesth and sequences for our case. Throughout this paper, we will denote by $\mathbb{Z}_N$ the ring of integers modulo N for a positive integer N, and by $\mathbb{Z}_N^*$ the multiplicative group of $\mathbb{Z}_N$.

Let p and q be two distinct odd primes, $d=\gcd(p-1,q-1)$, and $e=(p-1)(q-1)/d$. Denote by g a common primitive root modulo p and q [7]. Let x be integer satisfying $x\equiv g \pmod p$, $x\equiv 1 \pmod q$ [15]. Then Ding-Helleseth generalized cyclotomic classes of order d modulo pq is defined as

$$D_i=\{g^{i+jd}x^t : j=0,1,\dots,e/d-1,\ t=0,1,\dots,d-1\},\ i=0,1,\dots,d-1.$$

We have the partition

$$\mathbb{Z}_{pq}^* = \bigcup_{i=0}^{d-1} D_i.$$

Denote $P = \{p, 2p, \ldots, (q-1)p\}$, $Q = \{0, q, 2q, \ldots, (p-1)q\}$ and define the following two sets

$$C_0 = \bigcup_{i=0}^{d/2-1} D_{2i}, \quad \text{and } C_1 = \bigcup_{i=0}^{d/2-1} D_{2i+1}.$$

It is clear that $\mathbb{Z}_{pq} = C_0 \cup C_1 \cup P \cup Q$ and $|C_j| = (p-1)(q-1)/2$.

Ding-Helleseth binary sequences $s^\infty = (s_0, s_1, s_2, \ldots)$ of period pq can thus be defined as

$$s_i = \begin{cases} 0, & \text{if } i \pmod{pq} \in C_0 \cup Q, \\ 1, & \text{if } i \pmod{pq} \in C_1 \cup P. \end{cases} \tag{1}$$

The autocorrelation of these sequences was studied in [11] and the linear complexity was considered in [10] for $d = 2$, see also [2,18].

2.1 Main Result

In this paper we will study the symmetric 2-adic complexity of s^∞. First we recall the notation of 2-adic complexity.

Let $s^\infty = \{s_0, s_1, \ldots, s_N\}$ be a binary sequence with period N and $S(x) = s_0 + s_1 x + \cdots + s_{N-1}x^{N-1} \in \mathbb{Z}[x]$. According to [8] the 2-adic complexity of s^∞ can be defined as

$$\Phi(s^\infty) = \left\lfloor \log_2 \left(\frac{2^N - 1}{\gcd(S(2), 2^N - 1)} + 1 \right) \right\rfloor,$$

where $\lfloor x \rfloor$ is the greatest integer that is less than or equal to x.

The symmetric 2-adic complexity of s^∞ is defined by $\bar{\Phi}(s^\infty) = \min(\Phi(s^\infty), \Phi(\tilde{s}^\infty))$, where $\tilde{s}^\infty = (s_{N-1}, s_{N-2}, \ldots, s_0)$ is the reciprocal sequence of s^∞.

For a positive integer $m = 2^a m_0;\ 2 \nmid m_0$, we denote the odd part m_0 of m by $(m)_o$ as in [20]. The main result in this paper is given as follows.

Theorem 1. *Let s^∞ be a binary sequence of period pq defined in* (1). *Then the symmetric 2-adic complexity of s^∞ is given by*

(i) for $q \equiv 3 \pmod 4$

$$\bar{\Phi}(s^\infty) = \left\lfloor \log_2 \left(\frac{2^{pq} - 1}{r_1 r_2} \right) + 1 \right\rfloor,$$

where $r_1 = \gcd((q-1)_o, 2^p - 1)$ and $r_2 = \gcd(p + (p-1)^2(q+1)/4, 2^q - 1)$;

(ii) for $q \equiv 1 \pmod 4$

$$\bar{\Phi}(s^\infty) \geq \left\lfloor \log_2\left(\frac{2^{pq}-1}{r_1 r_3}\right) + 1 \right\rfloor,$$

where $r_3 = \gcd\left(p + (p-1)^2(1-q)/4, 2^q - 1\right)$.

According to Theorem 1 the above mentioned sequences have high symmetric 2-adic complexity. Theorem 1 gives us the exact value of symmetric 2-adic complexity for such sequences for $q \equiv 3 \pmod 4$ and the lower bound for $q \equiv 1 \pmod 4$.

The following conclusions are obvious.

Remark 1. If $(q-1)_o < 1 + 2p$ then $\gcd\left((q-1)_o, 2^p - 1\right) = 1$.

Corollary 1. *Let* s^∞ *be a binary sequence of period* pq *defined in* (1). *Then*

$$\Phi(s^\infty) \geq \left\lfloor \log_2\left(\frac{2^{pq}-1}{\gcd\left((q-1)_o, 2^p - 1\right) \cdot \gcd\left(p + (p-1)^2(1 \pm q)/4, 2^q - 1\right)}\right) + 1 \right\rfloor.$$

These results are consistent with [21,22]. The below statement gives us the lower bound for symmetric 2-adic complexity of these sequences.

Corollary 2. *Let* s^∞ *be a binary sequence of period* pq *defined in* (1). *Then*

$$\bar{\Phi}(s^\infty) \geq pq - p - q.$$

3 Subsidiary Lemmas

First, we will prove some subsidiary statements, and then in the next section derive the 2-adic complexity of s^∞ defined in (1).

The residue classes ring $\mathbb{Z}_{pq} \cong \mathbb{Z}_p \times \mathbb{Z}_q$ relative to isomorphism $\phi(m) = (m \bmod p, m \bmod q)$. Let $G_j = \{g^{j+2u} \bmod q, u = 0, 1, \ldots, (q-3)/2\}, j = 0, 1$. Then G_0 and G_1 are cyclotomic classes of order two modulo q and $|G_j| = (q-1)/2, j = 0, 1$.

Lemma 1. *Let the symbols be the same as before. Then*

$$C_j = \phi^{-1}\left(\mathbb{Z}_p^* \times G_j\right), j = 0, 1.$$

Proof. Let $y \in C_j, j = 0, 1$. Then $y = g^{j+ud}x^v$ for some u, v. By choosing x we see that $y \equiv g^{j+ud} \pmod q$ for even d. Hence $y \bmod q \in G_j$. Since $|C_j| = |\mathbb{Z}_p^* \times G_j|$, $j = 0, 1$, it follows that the statement of this lemma is true. $\square$

3.1 Generalized "Gauss Sums"

In this subsection, we will use the generalization of notation of generalized "Gauss periods" and "Gauss sums" presented in [23].

Let $c \neq 1$ and $\gcd(c, q) = 1$. By definition put $\eta_j(c) = \sum_{i \in G_j} c^i$, $j = 0, 1$. It is clear that $\eta_j(c^u) \equiv \eta_j(c) \pmod{c^q - 1}$ for $u \in G_0$ and

$$\eta_0(c) + \eta_1(c) = (c^q - 1)/(c - 1) - 1. \tag{2}$$

We will use the notation of cyclotomic numbers of order two modulo q in the sequel. By definition cyclotomic number of order two (i, j) is equal to $|(G_i + 1) \cap G_j|$. It is well known that

$$(0,0) = (q-5)/4 \text{ and } (0,1) = (1,0) = (1,1) = (q-1)/4 \text{ for } q \equiv 1 \pmod 4,$$
$$(0,0) = (1,0) = (1,1) = (q-3)/4 \text{ and } (0,1) = (q+1)/4 \text{ for } q \equiv 3 \pmod 4. \tag{3}$$

Lemma 2. *With notation above, we have that $\eta_0(c), \eta_1(c)$ satisfy the congruence:*

(i) $x^2 + x - (q-1)/4 \equiv 0 \pmod{(c^q - 1)/(c - 1)}$ *for* $q \equiv 1 \pmod 4$*;*
(ii) $x^2 + x + (q+1)/4 \equiv 0 \pmod{(c^q - 1)/(c - 1)}$ *for* $q \equiv 3 \pmod 4$.

Proof. By (2) it is sufficient to find $\eta_0(c) \cdot \eta_1(c)$ by modulo $\bmod (c^q - 1)/(c - 1)$. In the proof of this lemma, we will use the integer addition modulo m and the integer multiplication modulo m as the ring operations, where $m = (c^q - 1)/(q - 1)$. According to the definition of $\eta_j(c)$ we have

$$\eta_0(c) \cdot \eta_1(c) = \sum_{i \in G_0,\ j \in G_1} c^{i+j} = \sum_{i \in G_0,\ j \in G_1} c^{i(i^{-1}j+1)} = \sum_{i \in G_0,\ k \in G_1} c^{i(k+1)}.$$

It is well known that $-1 \in G_0$ for $q \equiv 1 \pmod 4$ and $-1 \in G_1$ for $q \equiv 3 \pmod 4$ [7].

Suppose $q \equiv 1 \pmod 4$; then

$$\eta_0(c) \cdot \eta_1(c) = \sum_{k \in (G_1+1) \cap G_0} \eta_0(c) + \sum_{k \in (G_1+1) \cap G_1} \eta_1(c) = (1,0)\eta_0(c) + (1,1)\eta_1(c)$$

since $-1 \in G_0$. Using (2) and (3) we derive the statement of this lemma for $q \equiv 1 \pmod 4$.

Let $q \equiv 3 \pmod 4$. With similar arguments as above we get that here

$$\eta_0(c) \cdot \eta_1(c) = (1,0)\eta_0(c) + (1,1)\eta_1(c) + (q-1)/2.$$

Here $-1 \in G_1$. Again, using of (2) and (3) completes this proof. □

3.2 The Properties of Generating Polynomial

Since $\gcd(p,q)=1$, it follows that there exist integers u,v such that $1=up+vq$. Hence exist $a,b\in\mathbb{N}$ satisfying the congruence $1\equiv ap+bq \pmod{pq}$.

Lemma 3. *Let the symbols be the same as before. Then*

$$\sum_{i\in C_j} 2^i \equiv \eta_j\left(2^{ap}\right)\sum_{f\in\mathbb{Z}_p^*} 2^{fbq} \pmod{2^{pq}-1}, j=0,1.$$

Proof. Suppose $c\in G_j$ for fixed $j=0,1$; then we have

$$\sum_{i\in\phi^{-1}(\mathbb{Z}_p^*\times\{c\})} 2^i \equiv \sum_{i\in\phi^{-1}(\mathbb{Z}_p^*\times\{c\})} 2^{iap+ibq} \equiv 2^{cap}\sum_{f\in\mathbb{Z}_p^*} 2^{fbq} \pmod{2^{pq}-1}.$$

Since $C_j=\bigcup_{c\in G_j}\phi^{-1}\left(\mathbb{Z}_p^*\times\{c\}\right)$ by Lemma 1, this completes the proof of this lemma. □

Proposition 1. *Let s^∞ be defined in* (1)*. Then*

$$S(2)\equiv\eta_1\left(2^{ap}\right)\sum_{f\in\mathbb{Z}_p^*}2^{fbq}+\sum_{i=1}^{q-1}2^{ip} \pmod{2^{pq}-1}. \tag{4}$$

This proposition follows from the definition of sequence in (1) and Lemma 3.

Now we will obtain the congruence for $\tilde{S}(2)$ where $\tilde{S}(x)$ is the generating polynomial of $\tilde{s}^\infty$. First we consider the subsidiary sequence t^∞ defined as

$$t_i=\begin{cases}0, & \text{if } i \pmod{pq}\in C_1\cup Q,\\ 1, & \text{if } i \pmod{pq}\in C_0\cup P.\end{cases} \tag{5}$$

Lemma 4. *Let t^∞ be defined in* (5) *and $T(x)=\sum_{i=0}^{pq-1}x^i$. Then*

$$T(2)\equiv\eta_0\left(2^{ap}\right)\sum_{f\in\mathbb{Z}_p^*}2^{fbq}+\sum_{i=1}^{q-1}2^{ip} \pmod{2^{pq}-1}. \tag{6}$$

This lemma can be proved the same way as Proposition 1.

Proposition 2. *Let s^∞ be defined in* (1) *and $\tilde{s}^\infty=(s_{pq-1},\ldots,s_1,s_0)$. Then*

$$2\tilde{S}(2)\equiv\begin{cases}S(2), & \text{if } q\equiv 1 \pmod 4,\\ T(2), & \text{if } q\equiv 3 \pmod 4,\end{cases} \pmod{2^{pq}-1}.$$

Proof. By definition of $\tilde{s}^\infty$ we see that $\tilde{S}(2)=\sum_{i=1}^{pq}2^{i-1}s_{pq-i}$. Hence

$$2\tilde{S}(2)=\sum_{i=1}^{pq}2^i s_{pq-i}=\sum_{i=0}^{pq-1}2^i s_{pq-i}+2^{pq}s_0-s_{pq}. \tag{7}$$

It is clear that $s_{pq-i} = 1$ for $i \in P$, $s_{pq-i} = 0$ for $i \in Q$ and vice versa.

Let $i \in \mathbb{Z}_{pq}^*$. As noted above we have that $-1 \in G_0$ for $q \equiv 1 \pmod 4$ and $-1 \in G_1$ for $q \equiv 3 \pmod 4$[7]. So, $s_{-i} = 1$ iff $i \in C_1$ for $q \equiv 1 \pmod 4$ and $s_{-i} = 1$ iff $i \in C_0$ for $q \equiv 3 \pmod 4$. In the last case we see that $s_{-i} = t_i$ for for $q \equiv 3 \pmod 4$. Thus this statement follows from (7), (5). □

We finish the section with a few remarks about the greatest common divisor for some numbers. This lemma will be useful in sequel.

Lemma 5. *Let p and q be odd distinct primes and $ap + bq \equiv 1 \pmod{pq}, a, b \in \mathbb{N}$. Then*

(i) $\gcd(2^p - 1, 2^q - 1) = \gcd\left(2^p - 1, 2^{bq} - 1\right) = 1$;
(ii) $\gcd\left(2^{bq} - 1, 2^{pq} - 1\right) = \gcd(2^q - 1, 2^{pq} - 1)$;
(iii) $\gcd(2^q - 1, (2^{pq} - 1)/(2^q - 1)) = \gcd(2^q - 1, p)$.

Proof. We will prove only the second statement. The first statement can be proved the same way and the third is clear.

Since $\gcd(bq, pq) = q$, it follows that there exist m, n such that $q = mbq + npq$. Hence $2^q = 2^{mbq+npq}$. Let r be a divisor of $\gcd\left(2^{bq} - 1, 2^{pq} - 1\right)$. We see that $2^q \equiv 2^{mbq+npq} \equiv 1 \pmod r$. Thus $\gcd\left(2^{bq} - 1, 2^{pq} - 1\right) \mid \gcd(2^q - 1, 2^{pq} - 1)$. The inverse statement is clear and we get the desired conclusion. □

4 The Proof of Main Theorem

Let r be a divisor of $2^{pq} - 1$. We consider three cases.

(i) Let r divides $2^p - 1$. According Lemma 5 we have $2^{bq} - 1 \not\equiv 0 \pmod r$, hence $\sum_{f \in \mathbb{Z}_p^*} 2^{fbq} \equiv -1 \pmod r$. In this case, by (4) we obtain

$$S(2) \equiv -(q-1)/2 + q - 1 \equiv (q-1)/2 \pmod r.$$

As earlier, $(a)_o$ is the odd part of a. Since r is odd, we have

$$\gcd(2^p - 1, S(2)) = \gcd((q-1)_o, 2^p - 1).$$

Similarly, by Proposition 2 and (6) we can prove that $\gcd\left(2^p - 1, \tilde{S}(2)\right) = \gcd\left((q-1)_o, \tilde{S}(2)\right)$.

(ii) Let r divides $2^q - 1$. Here by (4), (6), Proposition 2, Lemma 4 we get

$$S(2) \equiv \eta_1(2^{ap})(p-1) - 1 \pmod r$$

and

$$2\tilde{S}(2) \equiv \begin{cases} \eta_1(2^{ap})(p-1) - 1, & \text{if } q \equiv 1 \pmod 4, \\ \eta_0(2^{ap})(p-1) - 1, & \text{if } q \equiv 3 \pmod 4, \end{cases} \pmod r.$$

Here $ap \equiv 1 \pmod q$.

Suppose $q \equiv 3 \pmod 4$ and r divides $S(2)$ or $\tilde{S}(2)$; then $\gcd(p-1,r)=1$ and $\eta_1(2) \equiv 1/(p-1) \pmod r$ or $\eta_0(2) \equiv 1/(p-1) \pmod r$. According to Lemma 2 in this case we have the congruence

$$1/(p-1)^2 + 1/(p-1) + (q+1)/4 \equiv 0 \pmod r \text{ or } p + (p-1)^2(q+1)/4 \equiv 0 \pmod r.$$

Hence, $\max\left(\gcd\left(2^q-1, S(2)\right), \gcd\left(2^q-1, \tilde{S}(2)\right)\right)$ divides $\gcd\left(p+(p-1)^2(q+1)/4, 2^q-1\right)$.

Vice versa, if r is a divisor of $\gcd\left(p+(p-1)^2(q+1)/4, 2^q-1\right)$. Then r is odd, $\gcd(r,q)=1$ and $\gcd(p-1,r)=1$. Hence by Lemma 2 we get $\eta_1(2) \equiv 1/(p-1) \pmod r$ or $\eta_0(2) \equiv 1/(p-1) \pmod r$. Thus, r is a divisor of $\max\left(\gcd\left(2^q-1, S(2)\right), \gcd\left(2^q-1, \tilde{S}(2)\right)\right)$.

Let $q \equiv 1 \pmod 4$. In this case we can only claim that $\gcd\left(2^q-1, S(2)\right)$ or $\gcd\left(2^q-1, \tilde{S}(2)\right)$ divides $\gcd\left(p+(p-1)^2(1-q)/4, 2^q-1\right)$ by Lemma 2.

(iii) Let r be a prime divisor of $\gcd\left(2^{pq}-1, S(2)\right)$ and r does not divide $(2^p-1)(2^q-1)$. Then the order 2 modulo r equals pq and pq divides $r-1$. Farther, by Lemma 5 we see that r does not divide $2^{bq}-1$ and by (4) we obtain $S(2) \equiv -\eta_1(2^{ap}) - 1 \pmod r$. It follows that $q+1 \equiv 0 \pmod r$ or $q-1 \equiv 0 \pmod r$ by Lemma 2, here $c = 2^{ap}$. We have the contradiction, since $r-1$ is divided by pq in this case. Further, it can be easy to show in the same way that r does not divide $\tilde{S}(2)$.

So, from (i)-(iii) for $q \equiv 3 \pmod 4$ we obtain that

$$\max\left(\gcd\left(2^{pq}-1, S(2)\right), \gcd\left(2^{pq}-1, S(2)\right)\right) = r_1 r_2,$$

where $r_1 = \gcd\left((q-1)_o, 2^p-1,\right)$ and $r_2 = \gcd\left(p+(p-1)^2(q+1)/4, 2^q-1\right)$.

Also for $q \equiv 1 \pmod 4$ we see that

$$\max\left(\gcd\left(2^{pq}-1, S(2)\right), \gcd\left(2^{pq}-1, S(2)\right)\right)$$

divides $\gcd\left((q-1)_o, 2^p-1\right) \cdot \gcd\left(p+(p-1)^2(1-q)/4, 2^q-1\right)$. This completes the proof of Theorem 1.

Remark 2. According to Lemma 4 and Proposition 2, Theorem 1 will be also true for the sequence t^∞ defined in (4).

In conclusion of this section we consider a few examples.

1. Let $q=5$. Here $G_0 = \{1,4\}$ and $G_1 = \{2,3\}$. Thus $\eta_0(2) = 18$ and $\eta_1(2) = 12$.

(i) Suppose $p = 107$; then $\gcd\left(p+(p-1)^2(1-q)/4, 2^q-1\right) = 31$. Further, in this case $1/(p-1) \equiv 1/13 \equiv 12 \pmod{31}$. Hence $\eta_1(2) \equiv 1/(p-1) \pmod{31}$ and $\gcd\left(2^5-1, S(2)\right) = 31$ and $\gcd\left(2^5-1, \tilde{S}(2)\right) = 31$. So, $\bar{\Phi}(s^\infty) = \left\lfloor \log_2\left(\frac{2^{5\cdot 107}-1}{31}+1\right)\right\rfloor = 530$ $(r_3 \neq 0)$.

(ii) Suppose $p = 113$; then again $\gcd\left(p+(p-1)^2(1-q)/4, 2^q-1\right) = 31$. But, in this case $1/(p-1) \equiv 1/19 \equiv 18 \pmod{31}$. Hence $\eta_1(2) \not\equiv 1/(p-1)$

(mod 31) and $\gcd\left(2^5-1, S(2)\right) = \gcd\left(2^5-1, \tilde{S}(2)\right) = 1$. Hence, $\bar{\Phi}(s^\infty) = \left\lfloor \log_2\left((2^{5\cdot 113}-1)+1\right)\right\rfloor = 565$ $(r_3 = 0)$.

2. Let $q = 3$, $p = 5$. Here $\eta_0(2) = 2$ and $\eta_1(2) = 4$. Hence $\eta_0(2) \equiv 1/(p-1) \pmod 7$ and $\eta_1(2) \not\equiv 1/(p-1) \pmod 7$. Thus, $\gcd\left(2^3-1, S(2)\right) = 1$ and $\gcd\left(2^5-1, \tilde{S}(2)\right) = 7$. Hence $\Phi(s^\infty) = 15$, $\Phi(\tilde{s}^\infty) = 12$ and $\bar{\Phi}(s^\infty) = 12$.

5 Conclusion

Sequences generated by FCSRs share many important properties enjoyed by LFSR sequences. Due to the effectiveness of rational approximation algorithm, the 2-adic complexity has been viewed as one of the important security criteria of sequences. We derived symmetric 2-adic complexity of Ding-Helleseth generalized cyclotomic sequences of length pq for any odd distinct primes p, q. We obtained the exact value of symmetric 2-adic complexity of these sequences for $q \equiv 3 \pmod 4$ and the lower bound for $q \equiv 1 \pmod 4$. We generalized known statements about 2-adic complexity Ding-Helleseth sequences of length pq from [21,22]. Our results showed that 2-adic complexity of these sequences is good enough to resist the attack by the rational approximation algorithm.

References

1. Ding, C., Helleseth, T.: New generalized cyclotomy and its applications. Finite Fields Appl. **4**(2), 140–166 (1998)
2. Edemskiy, V., Sokolovskiy, N.: Notes about the linear complexity of Ding-Helleseth generalized cyclotomic sequences of length pq over the finite field of order p or q. In: ITM Web of Conferences, vol. 9, p. 01005 (2017)
3. Golomb, S.W.: Shift Register Sequences. Holden-Day, San Francisco (1967)
4. Hofer, R., Winterhof, A.: On the 2-adic complexity of the two-prime generator. IEEE Trans. Inf. Theory **64**(8), 5957–5960 (2018)
5. Hu, H.: Comments on "a new method to compute the 2-adic complexity of binary sequences". IEEE Trans. Inform. Theory **60**, 5803–5804 (2014)
6. Hu, H., Feng, D.: On the 2-adic complexity and the k-error 2-adic complexity of periodic binary sequences. IEEE Trans. Inf. Theory **54**(2), 874–883 (2008)
7. Ireland, K., Rosen, M.: A Classical Introduction to Modern Number Theory. Graduate Texts in Mathematics. Springer, New York (1990). https://doi.org/10.1007/978-1-4757-2103-4
8. Klapper, A., Goresky, M.: Cryptanalysis based on 2-adic rational approxiamtion. In: CRYPTO 1995, LNCS, vol. 963, pp. 262–273 (1995)
9. Klapper, A., Goresky, M.: Feedback shift registers, 2-adic span, and combiners with memory. J. Cryptol. **10**(2), 111–147 (1997). https://doi.org/10.1007/s001459900024
10. Li, S., Chen, Z., Sun, R., Xiao, G.: On the randomness of generalized cyclotomic sequences of order two and length pq. IEICE Trans. Fundamentals of Electronics, Communications and Computer Sciences E90-A(9), 2037–2041 (2007)

11. Li, S., Chen, Z., Fu, X., Xiao, G.: The autocorrelation values of new generalized cyclotomic sequences of order two and length *pq*. J. Comput. Sci. Technol. **22**(6), 830–834 (2007). https://doi.org/10.1007/s11390-007-9099-2
12. Sun, Y., Wang, Q., Yan, T.: The exact autocorrelation distribution and 2-adic complexity of a class of binary sequences with almost optimal autocorrelation. Cryptography and Communications **10**(3), 467–477 (2017). https://doi.org/10.1007/s12095-017-0233-x
13. Sun, Y., Yan, T., Chen, Z., Wang, L.: The 2-adic complexity of a class of binary sequences with optimal autocorrelation magnitude. Cryptography and Communications **12**(4), 675–683 (2019). https://doi.org/10.1007/s12095-019-00411-4
14. Sun, Y., Wang, Q., Yan, T.: A lower bound on the 2-adic comeplxity of the modified Jacobi sequences. Cryptogr. Commun. **11**(2), 337–349 (2019). https://doi.org/10.1007/s12095-018-0300-y
15. Whiteman, A.L.: A family of difference sets. Illinois J. Math. **6**, 107–121 (1962)
16. Xiao, Z., Zeng X., Sun, Z.: 2-Adic complexity of two classes of generalized cyclotomic binary sequences. Internationl Journal of Foundations of Comput. Sci. 27(7), 879–893 (2016)
17. Xiong, H., Qu, L., Li, C.: A new method to compute the 2-adic complexity of binary sequences. IEEE Trans. Inform. Theory **60**, 2399–2406 (2014)
18. Yan, T., Sun, R., Xiao, G.: Autocorrelation and linear complexity of the new generalized cyclotomic sequences. IEICE Trans. Fundamentals of Electronics, Communications and Computer Sciences E90-A (4), 857–864 (2007)
19. Yan, T., Chen, Z., Xiao, G.: Linear complexity of Ding generalized cyclotomic sequences. Journal of Shanghai University **11**(1), 22–26 (2007). https://doi.org/10.1007/s12095-018-0343-0
20. Yang, M., Feng, K.: Determination of 2-adic complexity of generalized binary sequences of order 2. arXiv:2007.15327
21. Yan, M., Yan, T., Li, Y.: Computing the 2-adic complexity of two classes of Ding-Helleseth generalized cyclotomic sequences of period of twin prime products. arXiv:1912.06134
22. Yan, M., Yan, T., Sun, Y., Sun, S.: The 2-Adic complexity of ding-Helleseth generalized cyclotomic sequences of order 2 and period *pq*. IEEE Access **8**, 140682–140687 (2020). https://doi.org/10.1109/ACCESS.2020.3012570
23. Zhang, L., Zhang, J., Yang, M., Feng, K.: On the 2-Adic complexity of the Ding-Helleseth-Martinsen binary sequences. IEEE Trans. Inform. Theory (2020). https://doi.org/10.1109/TIT.2020.2964171

A Distinguisher for RNGs with LFSR Post-processing

Xinying Wu[1,2,3], Yuan Ma[1,2,3], Tianyu Chen[1,2(✉)], and Na Lv[1,2]

[1] State Key Laboratory of Information Security, Institute of Information Engineering, Chinese Academy of Sciences, Beijing, China
{wuxinying,mayuan,chentianyu,lvna}@iie.ac.cn

[2] Data Assurance and Communications Security Research Center, Chinese Academy of Sciences, Beijing, China

[3] School of Cyber Security, University of Chinese Academy of Sciences, Beijing, China

Abstract. Random number generator (RNG) is a fundamental element in modern cryptography. If the quality of the outputs generated by RNGs is not as well as expected, the cryptographic applications which use the random number service are vulnerable to security threats. In reality, the entropy source of RNGs could be impressible by the changes of environmental factors, resulting in defects in the generated data, such as poor statistical properties. Thus, RNG is generally designed with a preset post-processing module to improve the quality of the output sequences. Linear feedback shift register (LFSR) is one of the frequently used methods for post-processing thanks to the characteristic of simplicity and no reduction in output throughput. However, we point out that even if the statistical properties of the outputs of the entropy source are extremely poor, the sequences processed by LFSR can still pass the statistical test. This undoubtedly increases the security risks in the usage of RNGs. In this work, we propose a distinguisher for the RNGs with LFSR post-processing for the first time. The distinguisher can be used to detect the RNGs with LFSR post processing, and we theoretically prove the sequences before processing can be recovered. On this basis, we design a new statistical test via combining the distinguisher with the Frequency Test in the NIST test suite. The experimental results show that if the sequence is biased before being processed by LFSR, our proposed method can detect it, but the NIST SP 800-22 Test Suite cannot.

Keywords: Random number generator · LFSR · Post-processing · Distinguisher · Randomness test

1 Introduction

Random number generators (RNGs) play a basic and important role in cryptographic systems. The outputs of RNGs are widely used in the generation of cryptographic keys, initial vectors, timestamps, *etc.* The security of many cryptographic algorithms and protocols is based on the randomness of outputs

Y. Wu and M. Yung (Eds.): Inscrypt 2020, LNCS 12612, pp. 328–343, 2021.
https://doi.org/10.1007/978-3-030-71852-7_22

from RNGs. The RNGs can be mainly classified into two types, true RNGs (TRNGs) and pseudo RNGs (PRNGs). TRNGs generally contains three components: entropy source, entropy extraction and post-processing. The entropy source is also called the random source, that is, the randomness in the physical phenomenons used by TRNGs, such as thermal noise and scattering noise in the circuit, Brownian motion, atmospheric noise, radioactive decay, *etc.* The quality of the entropy source directly determines the quality of the random numbers generated by the RNGs. So the entropy source is the core component of a RNG. Entropy extraction is used to collect randomness from the entropy source.

However, the entropy sources are often affected by external factors, such as non-Gaussian noise inside the circuit, changes in external temperature and voltage, *etc.* External factors or inappropriately entropy extraction methods may cause the generated sequences with deviation or correlation. For this reason, designers often add post-processing module to optimize the statistical properties of the sequences and to improve the security of the random number service. The post-processing module in a RNG can eliminate the statistical weakness of the sequence and make it pass the statistical test. Post-processing can reduce the bias, but can never completely eliminate the bias [3]. The common post-processing techniques include XOR corrector [2], Von Neumann corrector [14], H-post-processing and S-post-processing, resilient functions, linear feedback shift register (LFSR), *etc.* The implementation of LFSR is highly efficient and it does not reduce the output throughput. Besides, in hardware, LFSRs are easy to implement and can generate sequences with large periods. Moreover, the sequences they produce have good statistical properties [4]. Therefore, LFSR is often used as a post-processing module in many RNGs [1,5–7], *etc.*

Black-box statistical test is a commonly used method to assess the quality of RNGs, specifically, evaluate whether the output sequence has obvious statistical flaws. It is characterized by versatility (independent of the structure of RNGs) and convenient operation. At present, the commonly used statistical test suites are black-box testing, such as NIST SP 800-22 [13] issued by US National Institute of Standard and Technology (NIST), AIS 20/31 [8] issued by Germany Bundesamt für Sicherheit in der Informationstechnik (BSI), Diehard [11] proposed by Marsaglia, and TestU01 [9] proposed by L'Ecuyer.

The design of RNGs with post-processing is generally able to pass the statistical test, but in fact, the post-processing also masks the defects of the entropy source, especially the LFSR post-processing. The simulation results in Sect. 3 show that a sequence post-processed by the LFSR can pass the NIST SP 800-22 test, even if the statistical properties of the original sequence are extremely poor. The defect of the entropy source essentially affects the quality of the output sequence, which leads to serious security risks in the cryptographic system. However, the traditional/current black-box statistical test cannot detect the defects of the entropy source. Therefore, in this paper, for the RNGs with LFSR post-processing, we propose a distinguisher and a new test item, which can detect the sequence post-processed by LFSR, and recover the original sequence from post-processed one.

In summary, we make the following contributions.

- We simulate the LFSR post-processing structure and expose the sequence post-processed by LFSR can pass NIST SP 800-22 test, even if the statistical properties of the original sequence are extremely poor.
- We propose a distinguisher for the RNGs with LFSR post-processing for the first time. This distinguisher can be used to discriminate whether the LFSR post processor is employed in a RNG or not, and we theoretically prove the sequences before processing can be recovered.
- We design a new statistical test method named LFSR Post-Processing Structure Test which can distinguish the sequences post-processed by LFSR from perfectly random sequences.

The rest of the paper is organized as follows. In Sect. 2, two kinds of LFSR post-processing structures are introduced. In Sect. 3, the simulation results show the LFSR2 post-processing structure can conceal the statistical defects. In Sect. 4, for LFSR2 post-processing structure, we propose a distinguisher and a new test item to detect the sequence post-processed by LFSR. In Sect. 5, the proposed method is verified in simulation.

2 Related Work

LFSR post-processing structure is used in many RNGs. Since in hardware, LFSRs are easy to implement and they can generate sequences with large periods. Moreover, the sequences they produce have good statistical properties [4]. There are two classical types of LFSR processing structures. One structure is the sequence XOR-ed with the output of LFSR, as shown in Fig. 1(a), called LFSR1. This structure is widely used in stream cipher. Zeng *et al.* [15,16] proposed an algorithm to LFSR1 which can recover the seed. For keystream generator based on LFSR1, Merir *et al.* [12] proposed fast correlation attacks to recover the seed of LFSR. For stream cipher based on LFSR1, many scholars have studied this field. Another structure is the random source XOR-ed with the output of LFSR and the result is fed back to the register, as shown in Fig. 1(b), called LFSR2. The LFSR2 structure is widely used in post-processing structure, the RNGs in [1,5–7] used LFSR2-based structure for post-processing.

Structure 1. Figure 1(a) shows one of the LFSR processing structures. At every clock tick, the LFSR1 shifts one bit to the left. The LFSR1 uses the generating polynomial $f(x) = x^{l_0} + x^{l_1} + x^{l_2} + ... + x^{l_{r-1}}$ to generate a feedback bit which is fed into the LFSR1 on the right. Additionally, the feedback bit is XOR-ed with the input bit x_i to get the output bit. Then, we can get the output sequence B that equals sequence A XOR-ed with sequence X (that is $B = A \oplus X$). Zeng *et al.* [15,16] proposed an algorithm to recover sequence X from sequence B based on linear syndrome. The sequence B is the obtained sequence, and the sequence A is generated by LFSR1 whose generating polynomial is known. The sequence

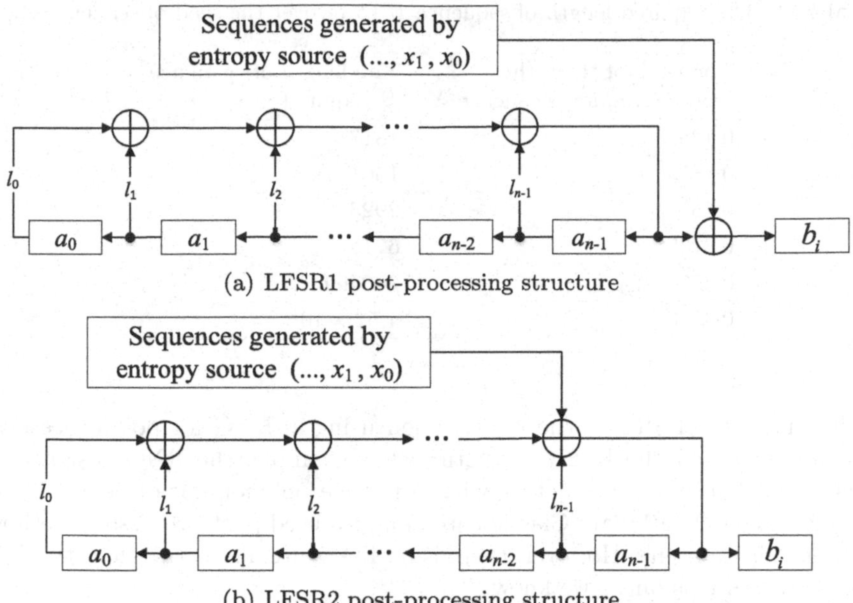

Fig. 1. Two kinds of LFSR post-processing structures

X is an unknown structure sequence, but the probability of '0' in sequence X is greater than that of '1'. The proposed algorithm can recover the sequence A and sequence X.

Zeng *et al.* defined the linear syndrome as $\sigma_{i,k}(f) = \sum_{p=0}^{r-1} b(i-l_k+l_p)$, which is called the signal $b(i)$ the *k-th* linear syndrome with generating polynomial $f(x)$. They calculate $2m+1$ linear syndromes of $b(i)$ and revise the signal $b(i)$ in according with the following rule of majority logic decision. After several rounds of iteration revisions, the resulting sequence $b^{'}(i)$ will be close to sequence A.

$$b^{'}(i) = \begin{cases} b(i)+1 & \text{at least } m+1 \text{ linear syndromes are '1'} \\ b(i) & \text{at least } m+1 \text{ linear syndromes are '0'} \end{cases}$$

When the ratio of '1' in the sequence X is known, the author gives the required length of sequence B to recover the seed of sequence A as shown in Table 1. In Table 1, with the ratio of '1' in the sequence X increasing, the required length of sequence B becomes longer.

Structure 2. Figure 1(b) shows another processing structure based on LFSR with generating polynomial $f(x) = x^{l_0} + x^{l_1} + x^{l_2} + ... + x^{l_{r-1}}$. This structure is the common LFSR post-processing structure in RNGs. At every clock tick, the LFSR shifts one bit to the left, using the generating polynomial to generate a feedback bit. The leftmost bit $a(i)$ is discarded. Besides, the LFSR2 has an input bit x_i that is XOR-ed with the feedback bit and the result is outputted

Table 1. The required length of sequence B to recover the seed of sequence A.

The ratio of '1' in the physical random sequence X	The length of sequence B required
0.125	1817
0.1875	1501
0.25	2923
0.3125	6715
0.375	269469
0.4375	4.52×10^{12}

and fed into the LFSR2 on the right. When using in RNG for post-processing, most designs adopt the LFSR2 structure. For example, the RNG designed by Bucci *et al.* [1] used this structure with primitive polynomials of degree 32 for post-processing. The Mifare Classic cards [5] also used post-processing methods based on this structure. However, there is no literature about the security of the LFSR2 structure as far as we know.

Compared with LFSR2, in LFSR1, the feedback bit is directly fed into the register. While in LFSR2, the feedback bit is firstly XOR-ed with the input bit x_i, and the result is then fed into the register. In LFSR1, the input bits have no influence on the internal of the LFSR1, while in LFSR2, the input bits impact on the internal register.

3 Problem Statement

In this section, LFSR2 post-processing structure is simulated to observe the statistical properties of the output sequences. Sequence X is a biased sequence that simulates the output of entropy source. The bias of sequence X is denoted as s, that is the ratio of '1' in the sequence X is s (namely $P(x_i = 1) = s$). The value of s is from 0.001 to 0.999 in 0.001 step. The sequence X is a random sequence with $P(x_i = 1) = s$, generated by *randsrc* function in Matlab. The simulation uses LFSR2 structure to post-process the sequence X. The degrees of generating polynomials are 32, 48 and 64, alternating the value of s to generate the sequence B with a length of 10^9 bytes. The generating polynomials are shown in Table 2. The generated sequence B is tested by SP 800-22 which includes 15 test items. When using SP 800-22 Test Suite, the tested data are 1000 successive sequences with a length of 1,000,000 bytes. The significance level is 0.01. For the first-level tests, the proportion of sequences that pass the tests is lying in [0.981, 0.999]. The *P-value* in the second-level tests is above 10^{-4}, which indicates the tested sequence can pass the SP 800-22 test.

The simulation results show that when the generating polynomial is $f(x) = x^{32}+x^{30}+x^{24}+x^{21}+x^{20}+x^9+x^8+x^7+x^6+x^2+x^0$ and $s \in [0.001, 0.007]$, except Binary Matrix Rank Test and Linear Complexity Test, the sequence B can pass

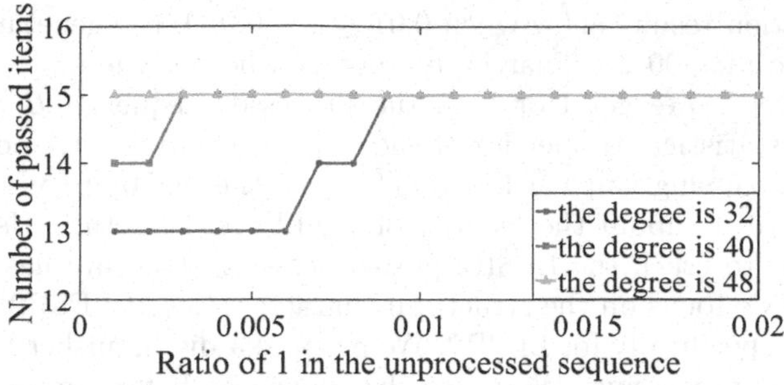

Fig. 2. Number of passing test items in SP 800-22 for different generating polynomials with s increasing

all other tests in SP 800-22. When $s \in [0.008, 0.009]$, except Linear Complexity Test, the sequence B can pass all other tests in SP 800-22. Figure 2 shows the numbers of passed test items in SP 800-22 for different generating polynomials with s increasing. The purpose of Binary Matrix Rank Test is to check for linear dependence among fixed length substrings of the original sequence. The focus of Linear Complexity Test is the length of LFSR. The purpose of this test is to determine whether or not the sequence is complex enough to be considered random. Random sequences are characterized by longer LFSRs. An LFSR that is too short implies non-randomness. This test is based on the Berlekamp-Massey algorithm [13]. However, as shown in Fig. 2, with s increasing, even if the length of LFSR does not change, the generated sequences can pass the Linear Complexity Test. That is a few noises are added to the sequence generated by a short LFSR, then it can pass the Linear Complexity Test and other test items in SP 800-22. For generating polynomial with different degrees, Table 2 shows the values of s, in which the generated sequences can pass SP 800-22. When degree of generating polynomial is 32 and $s = 0.01$, the detailed test report is presented in Table 6 in Appendix.

Table 2. Intervals of s, in which the sequences generated by LFSR2 can pass SP 800-22.

Generating polynomial	Intervals of s
$f(x) = x^{32} + x^{30} + x^{24} + x^{21} + x^{20} + x^9 + x^8 + x^7 + x^6 + x^2 + x^0$	[0.01, 0.989]
$f(x) = x^{40} + x^{32} + x^{30} + x^{27} + x^{25} + x^{18} + x^{16} + x^{15} + x^7 + x^2 + x^0$	[0.003, 0.998]
$f(x) = x^{48} + x^{36} + x^{35} + x^{26} + x^{24} + x^{19} + x^{15} + x^{14} + x^6 + x^4 + x^0$	[0.001, 0.999]

The simulation results show when $0.01 \leq s \leq 0.989$, the generated sequence B can pass the SP 800-22. That is, no matter whether the statistical properties of sequence X are good or bad, the processed sequence B can pass SP 800-22. When statistical properties of the sequence X are extremely poor, the LFSR2 post-processing can mask the defects of the entropy source. However, there is no literature about the security of the LFSR2 structure. Using fast correlation attacks to crack the LFSR2 post-processing structure has a high time complexity. So we focus on the structural characteristics of LFSR2 and propose a distinguisher specifically for LFSR2. We propose a distinguisher for the RNGs with LFSR post-processing. We prove the sequences before processing can be recovered and propose a new test item to detect whether a sequence has been processed by LFSR2.

4 A Distinguisher and a Test Item for LFSR Post-processing Structure

In this section, the structure of LFSR2 is analyzed and the relationship between sequences in LFSR2 is given. Firstly, the linear syndrome of LFSR2 is defined and a distinguisher is proposed based on the linear syndrome. Then, a new test item is designed based on the distinguisher. The test can distinguish sequences post-processed by LFSR from perfectly random sequences.

4.1 A Distinguisher Based on Linear Syndrome

For LFSR2 post-processing structure, on the condition that the structure is known (that is the generating polynomial is known), according to the output sequence, we propose a distinguisher based on linear syndrome (LS-based distinguisher) which can recover the random source sequence. Linear feedback shift register with generating polynomial $f(x) = x^{l_0} + x^{l_1} + x^{l_2} + ... + x^{l_{r-1}}$, the feedback bit equals:

$$a(i + l_0) \oplus a(i + l_1) \oplus ... \oplus a(i + l_{r-2}). \tag{1}$$

For LFSR2, the bit $a(i + l_{r-1})$ fed into the structure is equal to the feedback bit XOR-ed with the input bit $x(i)$. According to Eq. (1), we can get the $a(i+l_{r-1})$:

$$a(i + l_{r-1}) = a(i + l_0) \oplus a(i + l_1) \oplus ... \oplus a(i + l_{r-2}) \oplus x(i). \tag{2}$$

The output bit $b(i)$ is also equal to the feedback bit XOR-ed with the input bit $x(i)$, that is,

$$b(i) = a(i + l_0) \oplus a(i + l_1) + ... \oplus a(i + l_{r-2}) \oplus x(i) = a(i + l_{r-1}). \tag{3}$$

For this structure, we define the linear syndrome as $\sigma_i(f) = \sum_{p=0}^{r-1} b(i + l_p)$ mod 2. According to Eqs. (2) and (3), we can get:

$$\begin{aligned}
\sigma_i(f) &= \sum_{p=0}^{r-1} b(i + l_p) \bmod 2 \\
&= \sum_{p=0}^{r-1} a(i + l_p + l_{r-1}) \bmod 2 \\
&= (\sum_{p=0}^{r-2} a(i + l_{r-1} + l_p) \bmod 2) \oplus a(i + l_{r-1} + l_{r-1}) \\
&= a(i + l_{r-1} + l_{r-1}) \oplus x(i) \oplus a(i + l_{r-1} + l_{r-1}) \\
&= x(i + l_{r-1}).
\end{aligned}$$

The linear syndrome $\sigma_i(f)$ establishes the corresponding relationship between sequence X and sequence B. Hence, the hidden source sequence X can be recovered using the output sequence B.

$$x(i) = \sum_{p=0}^{r-1} b(i - l_{r-1} + l_p) \bmod 2. \tag{4}$$

LS-based distinguisher is based on Eq. (4) to recover the sequence X and analyzes whether X is perfectly random. Let $n = l_{r-1}$, n is the degree of the generating polynomial. When using the LS-based distinguisher, at least n bits of sequence B are needed. While when L (the length of sequence B) $> n$, $L-n$ bits of sequence X can be recovered. The LS-based distinguisher selects bits in sequence B for XOR-ed operation which is very fast. So the efficiency of algorithm is high. The algorithm uses the unique correspondence between sequence B and sequence X. Obviously, the accuracy of the proposed LS-based distinguisher is a hundred percent. The time complexity of the LS-based distinguisher is $O(n)$.

4.2 A New Test Based on the Distinguisher

The sequence post-processed by LFSR2 can pass the SP 800-22, even if the statistical properties of the original sequence are extremely poor. Based on the LS-based distinguisher, a new test item is proposed to detect whether a sequence has been post-processed by LFSR2. The new test item is named LFSR Post-Processing Structure Test, which is called LPP Test for short. For a certain sequence, we need to detect whether it has been post-processed by LFSR2. In Sect. 4.1, a distinguisher is proposed to the structure of LFSR2. When the generating polynomial is known, the input sequence X can be recovered from the output sequence B.

The generating polynomial of LFSR is a primitive polynomial. In $F_2[x]$, the number of N-*th* primitive polynomials is $\varphi(2^N - 1)/N$, where $\varphi(n)$ is the Euler function, representing the number of positive integers that are mutually prime with n in positive integers from 1 to n. On account of the LS-based distinguisher is very fast, we design the LPP Test item that traverses primitive polynomials of degree 32 to 48 to perform the LS-based distinguisher. Then we analyze the properties of the sequences after the LS-based distinguisher to get the result.

Test Purpose. After the LFSR2 post-processing structure, the bad statistical properties of entropy source may be hidden. In Sect. 4.1, a LS-based distinguisher to the structure proposed. Therefore, the sequences post-processed by LFSR2 can be recovered and the deficiency of the physical entropy source can be exposed. The purpose of the test is to detect whether a sequence has been post-processed by LFSR2, and whether the sequence before post-processing is not random.

Test Description. The test item is designed based on the LS-based distinguisher. The test item traverses primitive polynomials to do the LS-based distinguisher of tested sequences. For the recovered sequences, we analyze the properties of them. We can use all the test item in NIST SP 800-22 to analyze the properties. NIST recommends the Frequency Test to be run first. If a sequence fails the Frequency Test, it has a high likelihood of failing other tests, because this provides the most basic evidence for the existence of non-randomness in the sequence, especially non-uniformity [13]. The procedure of this test is simple and the process is fast, so it can optimize the speed. Therefore, we choose the Frequency Test to analyze the properties. In fact, the LS-based distinguisher can be combined with other test items in practice. In this paper, we use the Frequency Test as an example.

Table 3. Parameters using in LPP test

F	The set of primitive polynomials
Num	The number of the primitive polynomials
$F(k, x)$	The k-th primitive polynomial
$n = l_{r-1}$	The degree of the primitive polynomial
L	The length of the sequence B

We design the test algorithm process as follows. Table 3 shows the parameters. In Fig. 3, the process of the LPP Test is presented. Firstly, let $k = 0$, then,

Step 1: If $k \geq Num$, stop and pass the test.
Step 2: Set $k = k+1$; choose the k-th primitive polynomial (that is $f = F(k, x)$); let $i = 0$, $m = L - n$.
Step 3: Calculate $x(i) = \sigma_{i-l_{r-1}}(f)$.
Step 4: If $i < m$, set $i = i + 1$; return step 3.
Step 5: Run Frequency Test, if pass, return step 1; else stop, fail the test.

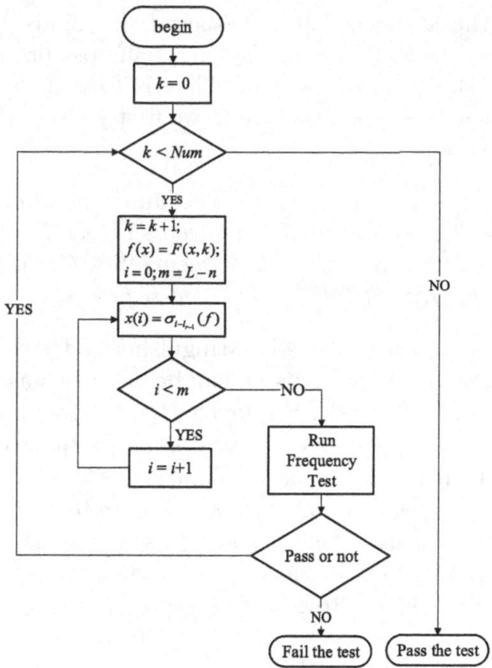

Fig. 3. The process of LPP Test

4.3 Correctness Analysis of the LPP Test

We define the *error test* as a phenomenon of a sequence has not been post-processed by LFSR and pass the SP 800-22. But it fails the LPP Test. *Leakage test* is defined as a phenomenon of an original sequence has large deviation and the sequence after LFSR post-processing can pass the LPP Test. In order to discuss whether there are *error/leakage test*, three situations using the LPP Test is discussed.

- **Situation 1.** Sequence B has been post-processed by LFSR2, and we use the LS-based distinguisher with a matching polynomial (that is, the polynomial for LS-based distinguisher is the same as the polynomial used in post-processing).
- **Situation 2.** Sequence B has been post-processed by LFSR2, and we use the LS-based distinguisher with an dismatching polynomial (that is, the polynomial for LS-based distinguisher is not the polynomial used in post-processing).
- **Situation 3.** Sequence B has not been post-processed by LFSR2, and we use the LS-based distinguisher with any polynomial.

In situation 1, the sequence after LS-based distinguisher is the same as unpost-processed sequence. If the deviation of unpost-processed sequence is large, the sequence cannot pass the test. That is LPP Test will not have the phenomenon of leakage test. For situation 2, we first give a *'shift and add'* property [10] of m-sequences.

Property 1 *For a m-sequence A, 'shift and add' operation means cyclically shifted by i positions (digits) to the left, denoted as* $L^i(A)$. *For polynomial* $f(x) = x^{l_0} + x^{l_1} + x^{l_2} + ... + x^{l_{r-1}}$, $n = l_{r-1}$, *m-sequence* $S \in G(f)$, *when* $t1 > t2 > 0$, *and* $(t1 - t2) \nmid (2^n - 1)$, $L^{t1}(S) \oplus L^{t2}(S)$ *is a m-sequence.*

When the polynomial for LS-based distinguisher is $f(x) = x^{l_0} + x^{l_1} + x^{l_2} + ... + x^{l_{r-1}}$, then the LS-based distinguisher can be described as $X = B \oplus L^{l_0}(B) \oplus L^{l_1}(B) \oplus L^{l_2}(B) \oplus \ldots \oplus L^{l_{r-1}}(B)$. Sequence B is a m-sequence. According to the 'shift and add' property, the sequence X is a m-sequence. So the sequence after LS-based distinguisher is unbiased. That is there is no error test in LPP Test. In situation 3, the sequence B is denoted as $(b(0), b(1)...)$. We only focus on the situation that sequence B is unbiased. If sequence B is biased, it cannot pass the other test item in statistical test. For the test, using any polynomial $f(x) = x^{l_0} + x^{l_1} + x^{l_2} + ... + x^{l_{r-1}}$ to generate sequence x as $x(i) = \sum_{p=0}^{r-1} b(i + l_p)$.

$$\begin{aligned} p(x(i) = 1) &= p(\sum_{p=0}^{r-1} b(i + l_p) = 1) \\ &= p(\sum_{p=0}^{r-2} b(i + l_p) \oplus b(i + l_{r-1}) = 1) \end{aligned}$$

The sequence generated by $\sum_{p=0}^{r-2} b(i + l_p)$ is a m-sequence. So the sequence is balance (that is $(p(\sum_{p=0}^{r-2} b(i + l_p) = 1) = 1/2)$). For sequence B, we have $p((b(i + l_{r-1}) = 1) = 1/2)$. So we have $p(\sum_{p=0}^{r-2} b(i + l_p) \oplus b(i + l_{r-1}) = 1) = 1/2$. So the sequence after LS-based distinguisher is unbiased. That is there is no error test in LPP Test.

In summary, the sequence that has not been post-processed by LFSR and pass the SP 800-22 will not fail the test algorithm. Original sequence has a large deviation and the sequence after LFSR post-processing will not pass the test. The LPP Test we proposed will not have error test or leakage test. It is noted that if a sequence fails the LPP test, it must a have statistical defect. However, the sequences pass the LPP test are not guaranteed to be perfectly random. In this section we give the procedure of LS-based distinguisher and analyze the accuracy of the distinguisher. Additionally, we propose a new test item and analyze the correctness. In next section, LS-based distinguisher and LPP Test are validated in simulation.

5 Validation on the Method in Simulation

In this section, LS-based distinguisher and LPP Test are simulated to validate the method. First of all, the simulated sequences are generated by LFSR2 post-processing structure. Then, LS-based distinguisher experiments are performed with the simulated data and the sequences before post-processing are compared with that after LS-based distinguisher, to illustrate the recovery effect. Moreover, the LPP Test and the SP 800-22 Test Suite are used to test the simulated data and pseudorandom sequences.

5.1 Generation of the Data Sets

The input sequence X is post-processed by LFSR2, then the output sequence is the simulated data set. The degree of the generating polynomial is denoted as n. The sequence X is simulated with deviation s of 0.01, 0.1 and 0.3. Using sequence X, sequences B_0–B_8 are produced with generating polynomials of degree 32, 40, 48. Corresponding relationships between the generating polynomials, bias and sequences are shown in Table 4. In addition, we collect random sequences from pseudorandom number generators, which have perfect statistical properties. The Blum-Blum-Shub (BBS) generator and the Linear Congruential (LC) generator are used to collect sequence B_9 and B_{10}. The pseudorandom sequences are generated by NIST Statistical Test Suite tool, which is called sts-2.1.2.

Table 4. Corresponding relationships between the generating polynomials, bias and sequences

Degree	Generating polynomial	s (the ratio of 1 in X)	Generated sequence
32	$f(x) = x^{32} + x^{30} + x^{24} + x^{21} + x^{20} + x^9 + x^8 + x^7 + x^6 + x^2 + x^0$	0.01	B_0
		0.1	B_1
		0.3	B_2
40	$f(x) = x^{40} + x^{32} + x^{30} + x^{27} + x^{25} + x^{18} + x^{16} + x^{15} + x^7 + x^2 + x^0$	0.01	B_3
		0.1	B_4
		0.3	B_5
48	$f(x) = x^{48} + x^{36} + x^{35} + x^{26} + x^{24} + x^{19} + x^{15} + x^{14} + x^6 + x^4 + x^0$	0.01	B_6
		0.1	B_7
		0.3	B_8

5.2 Validation of LPP Test

Validation of LPP Test is to determine whether there are error or leakage tests. The test experiment is designed with three situations. The common primitive polynomials of degrees from 32 to 48 are chosen. For sequences B_i, there are three situations,

- Situation 1. For $B_0 - B_8$, the results of matching polynomials are observed.
- Situation 2. For $B_0 - B_8$, the results of dismatching polynomials are observed.
- Situation 3. For pseudorandom sequences B_9, B_{10}, the results of all polynomials are observed.

Table 5. Using matching and dismatching polynomials, s' after LS-based distinguisher

Tested sequence	s (the ratio of 1 in X)	Recovery polynomial	s' after LS-based distinguisher
$B_0, B_3, B_6,$	0.01	Dismatching	[0.4999, 0.5]
		Matching	0.01
B_1, B_4, B_7	0.1	Dismatching	[0.4998, 0.5]
		Matching	0.1
B_2, B_5, B_8	0.3	Dismatching	[0.4998, 0.5]
		Matching	0.3
B_9	0.5006	All	[0.4999, 0.5001]
B_{10}	0.4998	All	[0.4999, 0.5]

As shown in Table 5, for the matching polynomials, the recovered sequences X are biased. For the dismatched polynomials, the recovered sequences X are not biased. The pseudorandom sequences are not biased. Therefore, there is no error test or leakage test. The detailed test reports are presented in Appendix. In Appendix, the NIST SP 800-22 and LPP Test reports of sequences B_0 and B_9 is presented. Then, the results of the LPP Test and SP 800-22 Test Suite are compared. The sequences B_0–B_8 post-processed by LFSR2 can pass the SP 800-22 Test Suite, but cannot pass the LPP Test. The sequences B_9 and B_{10} can pass both the SP 800-22 and LPP Test. The LPP Test can be a supplement of the SP 800-22 Test Suite.

6 Conclusion

LFSR post-processing structures are used in many RNGs. The sequences they produce have good statistical properties and can ensure the stability of the outputs quality. However, they mask the defects of the entropy source, when statistical properties of the entropy source sequences are extremely poor. In this paper, we propose a LS-based distinguisher for the RNGs with LFSR post-processing for the first time. We prove the sequences before processing can be recovered from the sequence processed by LFSR. On this basis, we design a new statistical test via combining the distinguisher with the Frequency Test. After the verification experiments, the results demonstrate that if the sequence before LFSR processing has a deviation, our proposed test can detect it, but the NIST Test Suite cannot.

Acknowledgments. This work was partially supported by National Key R&D Program of China (No. 2018YFB0804300), National Natural Science Foundation of China (No. 61872357 and No. 61802396), and Cryptography Development Foundation of China (No. MMJJ20170205, MMJJ20180113).

A Appendix: The Detailed Statistical Test Report

Table 6. NIST SP 800-22 statistical test report of generating sequence, when degree of generating polynomial is 32 and $s = 0.01$.

C1	C2	C3	C4	C5	C6	C7	C8	C9	C10	P-value	Propo	Statistical test
97	104	104	100	98	107	92	101	100	97	0.995578	994/1000	Frequency
129	110	112	113	97	97	85	83	91	83	0.010383	988/1000	BlockFrequency
88	106	112	102	110	87	103	99	90	103	0.620465	990/1000	CumulativeSums
92	112	106	92	104	96	108	85	99	106	0.672470	992/1000	CumulativeSums
109	106	101	111	109	83	103	87	94	97	0.502247	991/1000	Runs
103	100	95	97	105	96	115	94	105	90	0.859637	988/1000	LongestRun
98	96	88	112	101	88	97	111	105	104	0.715679	989/1000	Rank
95	107	100	109	85	85	121	96	94	108	0.235589	990/1000	FFT
102	103	105	86	110	96	99	113	89	97	0.689019	992/1000	NonOverlappingTemplate
99	119	107	94	99	92	87	96	105	102	0.610070	994/1000	OverlappingTemplate
115	93	99	101	98	92	97	98	93	114	0.737915	992/1000	Universal
108	107	107	109	88	103	94	94	89	101	0.749884	991/1000	ApproximateEntropy
59	64	65	66	65	64	58	67	63	62	0.998731	628/633	RandomExcursions
64	62	59	65	48	70	74	71	61	59	0.538952	626/633	RandomExcursionsVariant
114	129	101	98	105	107	89	88	73	96	0.011545	985/1000	Serial
119	112	107	92	97	90	100	99	106	78	0.187581	989/1000	Serial
103	101	83	97	100	103	109	97	100	107	0.870856	986/1000	LinearComplexity

Table 7. NIST SP 800-22 statistical test report of the sequence B_0

C1	C2	C3	C4	C5	C6	C7	C8	C9	C10	P-value	Propo	Statistical test
97	86	94	102	95	111	132	88	104	91	0.056069	991/1000	Frequency
144	102	108	109	100	81	96	102	82	76	0.000102	983/1000	BlockFrequency
93	103	97	91	113	105	85	102	104	107	0.703417	993/1000	CumulativeSums
102	98	105	116	88	97	102	99	87	106	0.686955	993/1000	CumulativeSums
100	93	105	99	89	103	103	92	100	116	0.803720	995/1000	Runs
94	97	103	81	113	111	92	103	111	95	0.415422	990/1000	LongestRun
105	96	106	99	100	95	119	103	84	93	0.556460	987/1000	Rank
113	97	118	93	105	89	104	86	103	92	0.365253	996/1000	FFT
98	112	102	103	105	100	109	87	88	96	0.743915	995/1000	NonOverlappingTemplate
105	89	109	91	93	103	113	109	98	90	0.616305	992/1000	OverlappingTemplate
113	107	100	91	97	111	102	92	96	91	0.745908	995/1000	Universal
103	105	95	100	96	83	103	112	98	105	0.792508	988/1000	ApproximateEntropy
69	65	57	63	64	66	57	58	61	70	0.956968	622/630	RandomExcursions
59	61	65	76	69	66	65	56	60	53	0.704523	626/630	RandomExcursionsVariant
122	110	105	103	86	103	85	101	104	81	0.484646	988/1000	Serial
120	96	89	115	104	94	96	95	103	88	0.344048	981/1000	Serial
99	94	88	92	90	95	122	108	91	121	0.108791	992/1000	LinearComplexity

Table 8. NIST SP 800-22 statistical test report of the sequence B_9

C1	C2	C3	C4	C5	C6	C7	C8	C9	C10	P-value	Propo	Statistical test
92	107	93	103	113	115	102	87	95	93	0.522100	990/1000	Frequency
120	90	111	100	101	95	109	88	97	89	0.348869	988/1000	BlockFrequency
90	117	95	122	97	106	103	87	98	85	0.141256	990/1000	CumulativeSums
91	99	113	98	103	94	113	98	110	81	0.406499	990/1000	CumulativeSums
98	102	101	91	116	94	107	112	91	88	0.534146	993/1000	Runs
97	102	93	104	108	99	101	100	100	96	0.996335	990/1000	LongestRun
87	102	103	115	100	96	100	95	108	94	0.790621	993/1000	Rank
108	125	96	95	109	92	108	79	104	84	0.056785	993/1000	FFT
99	91	120	108	91	111	93	107	82	98	0.228367	991/1000	NonOverlappingTemplate
94	114	115	101	88	111	98	87	100	92	0.383827	995/1000	OverlappingTemplate
98	104	91	108	95	92	95	107	100	110	0.892036	994/1000	Universal
106	93	87	104	112	88	111	98	101	100	0.653773	991/1000	ApproximateEntropy
70	72	76	53	58	62	61	48	64	53	0.203333	610/617	RandomExcursions
54	52	73	75	5 1	64	74	64	50	60	0.108475	610/617	RandomExcursionsVariant
118	92	106	112	107	99	90	108	94	74	0.092597	986/1000	Serial
122	101	111	97	116	86	98	100	88	81	0.072066	989/1000	Serial
93	103	97	96	91	113	104	107	111	85	0.591409	992/1000	LinearComplexity

References

1. Bucci, M., Luzzi, R.: Fully digital random bit generators for cryptographic applications. IEEE Trans. Circuits Syst. I Regul. Pap. **55**(3), 861–875 (2008)
2. Davies, R.B.: Exclusive or (XOR) and hardware random number generators (2002). Accessed 31 May 2013
3. Dichtl, M.: Bad and good ways of post-processing biased physical random numbers. In: Biryukov, A. (ed.) FSE 2007. LNCS, vol. 4593, pp. 137–152. Springer, Heidelberg (2007). https://doi.org/10.1007/978-3-540-74619-5_9
4. Fischer, V., Aubert, A., Bernard, F., Valtchanov, B., Danger, J., Bochard, N.: True random number generators in configurable logic devices. Project ANR-ICTeR, pp. 23–28 (2009)
5. Garcia, F.D., de Koning Gans, G., Muijrers, R., van Rossum, P., Verdult, R., Schreur, R.W., Jacobs, B.: Dismantling MIFARE classic. In: Jajodia, S., Lopez, J. (eds.) ESORICS 2008. LNCS, vol. 5283, pp. 97–114. Springer, Heidelberg (2008). https://doi.org/10.1007/978-3-540-88313-5_7
6. Golic, J.D.: New paradigms for digital generation and post-processing of random data. IACR Cryptology ePrint Archive 2004, 254 (2004)
7. Golic, J.D.: New methods for digital generation and postprocessing of random data. IEEE Trans. Comput. **55**(10), 1217–1229 (2006)
8. Killmann, W., Schindler, W.: A proposal for: Functionality classes for random number generators. ser. BDI, Bonn (2011)
9. L'Ecuyer, P., Simard, R.: Testu01: AC library for empirical testing of random number generators. ACM Trans. Math. Softw. (TOMS) **33**(4), 22 (2007)
10. Lin, Y.: 'Shift and add' property of m-sequences and its application to channel characterisation of digital magnetic recording. IEE Proc. Commun. **142**(3), 135–140 (1995)

11. Marsaglia, G.: Diehard battery of tests of randomness (1995). http://www.stat.fsu.edu/pub/diehard
12. Meier, W., Staffelbach, O.: Fast correlation attacks on certain stream ciphers. J. Cryptol. **1**(3), 159–176 (1988). https://doi.org/10.1007/BF02252874
13. Rukhin, A., Soto, J., Nechvatal, J., Smid, M., Barker, E.: A statistical test suite for random and pseudorandom number generators for cryptographic applications. Technical report, Booz-Allen and Hamilton Inc Mclean Va (2001)
14. Von Neumann, J.: Various techniques used in connection with random digits. Appl. Math. Ser. **12**, 36–38 (1951)
15. Zeng, K., Hung, M.: On the linear syndrome method in cryptanalysis. In: Goldwasser, S. (ed.) CRYPTO 1988. LNCS, vol. 403, pp. 469–478. Springer, New York (1990). https://doi.org/10.1007/0-387-34799-2_32
16. Zeng, K., Yang, C.H., Rao, T.R.N.: An improved linear syndrome algorithm in cryptanalysis with applications. In: Menezes, A.J., Vanstone, S.A. (eds.) CRYPTO 1990. LNCS, vol. 537, pp. 34–47. Springer, Heidelberg (1991). https://doi.org/10.1007/3-540-38424-3_3

On the k-Error Linear Complexities of De Bruijn Sequences

Ming Li(✉), Yupeng Jiang, and Dongdai Lin

State Key Laboratory of Information Security, Institute of Information Engineering, Chinese Academy of Sciences, Beijing 100093, China
{liming,jiangyupeng,ddlin}@iie.ac.cn

Abstract. We study the k-error linear complexities of de Bruijn sequences. Let n be a positive integer and k be an integer less than $\lceil \frac{2^{n-1}}{n} \rceil$. We show that the k-error linear complexity of a de Bruijn sequence of order n is greater than or equal to $2^{n-1}+1$, which implies that de Bruijn sequences have good randomness property with respect to the k-error linear complexity. We also study the compactness of some related bounds, and prove that in the case that $n \geq 4$ and n is a power of 2, there always exists a de Bruijn of order n such that the Hamming weight of $L(\mathbf{s}) \oplus R(\mathbf{s})$ is $\frac{2^{n-1}}{n}$, where $L(\mathbf{s})$ and $R(\mathbf{s})$ denote respectively the left half and right half of one period of this de Bruijn sequence. Besides, some experimental results are provided for the case that n is not a power of 2.

Keywords: k-Error linear complexity · de Bruijn sequence · Nonlinear feedback shift register

1 Introduction

Binary de Bruijn sequences of order n are sequences of period 2^n such that each n-bits tuple appears exactly once in one period. In recent years, de Bruijn sequences have attracted much attentions due to their many good randomness properties such as long period and large complexity, and thus have important applications in communication systems, coding theory and cryptography [1,4,22, 28,31]. In stream cipher designs, de Bruijn sequences are believed to be a class of ideal source sequences which if used instead of linear recurring sequences would make the cipher resistant to many classical attacks and therefore enhance the security greatly [6,29]. However, due to their nonlinearity, de Bruijn sequences seems very difficult to study. Despite years of intensive research some basic problems about them are still open [2,9,15,27,33,34].

One main topic of studying de Bruijn sequences is to investigate their various properties, such as the linear complexity, the correlation property, their distributions and etc. [3,5,10,12,26,32]. Linear complexity is a basic cryptographic criterion of sequences, which measures the linear predictability of sequences. The linear complexities of de Bruijn sequences were first studied by Games et al. [3],

Y. Wu and M. Yung (Eds.): Inscrypt 2020, LNCS 12612, pp. 344–356, 2021.
https://doi.org/10.1007/978-3-030-71852-7_23

where they showed that for the de Bruijn sequences of order n their linear complexities lie in the range of $2^{n-1}+n \leq LC(\mathbf{s}) \leq 2^n-1$. Then Etzion and Lempel showed that the lower bound $2^{n-1}+n$ is attainable [13]. Thereafter the linear complexity distribution of de Bruijn sequences was also studied [11,14].

The concept of k-error linear complexity, proposed by Ding et al., is a generalization of the concept of linear complexity, which measures the stability of sequences in terms of linear complexity [8,24]. If a sequence can be approximated by a sequence with low linear complexity, then this sequence is vulnerable to correlation attacks [25,29], and hence it is not secure to be used in cryptography. The k-error linear complexity of a periodic sequence is defined to be the smallest linear complexity of the sequences obtained by changing no more than k bits of the original sequence per period. The k-error linear complexities of several classes of sequences were studied by Ding et al. [7,8]. An efficient algorithm for calculating the k-error linear complexities of sequences whose periods are powers of 2 was given by Stamp and Martin [30].

In this paper, we study the k-error linear complexities of de Bruijn sequences. Although the linear complexities of de Bruijn sequences have been studied extensively, their k-error linear complexities have not attracted much attention yet. By using the distribution property of de Bruijn sequences and by a known result for the linear complexities of sequences whose periods are powers of 2, we derive a bound for the k-error linear complexities of de Bruijn sequences. Specifically, we show that for a de Bruijn sequence of order n, when $k < \lceil \frac{2^{n-1}}{n} \rceil$ its k-error linear complexity lies in the range of $2^{n-1}+1 \leq LC_k(\mathbf{s}) \leq 2^n-1$. From this bound we know that, de Bruijn sequences have very good randomness property with respect to the k-error linear complexity. Then we analyze the compactness of some ralated bounds. Let $L(\mathbf{s})$ and $R(\mathbf{s})$ be the left half and right half of one period of a de Bruijn sequence, and $L(\mathbf{s}) \oplus R(\mathbf{s})$ be their bit-wise xor. We show that, $w_H(L(\mathbf{s}) \oplus R(\mathbf{s})) \geq \lceil \frac{2^{n-1}}{n} \rceil$, and the lower bound $\lceil \frac{2^{n-1}}{n} \rceil$ is attainable when $k \geq 4$ and k is a power of 2. The proof is constructive and it is based on the frame work of Etzion [13] which constructs a class of de Bruijn sequences whose linear complexity reaches the minimum value $2^{n-1}+n$. For the case that n is not a power of 2 we did some experiments to analyze the compactness of the bound.

The remainder of this paper is organized as follows. Section 2 introduces some preliminaries. In Sect. 3, we show a lower bound for the k-error linear complexities of de Bruijn sequences. In Sect. 4, we analyze the compactness of some related bounds. Section 5 presents some experimental results. Section 6 gives the final conclusions of this paper.

2 Preliminaries

2.1 Feedback Shift Register

An n-stage feedback shift register (FSR) consists of n binary storage cells and a feedback function regulated by a single clock. At every clock pulse, the current state $(s_0, s_1, \ldots, s_{n-1})$ is updated by $(s_1, s_2, \ldots, s_{n-1}, F(s_0, s_1, \ldots, s_{n-1}))$

and the bit s_0 is output. An n-stage FSR can generate 2^n sequences with each sequence corresponding to a different initial state. It is shown by Golomb that all the 2^n output sequences are periodic if and only if the feedback function F is of the form $F = x_0 + f_0(x_1, \ldots, x_{n-1})$. In the following discussions, we always assume the feedback function has this form and we will mostly concentrate on the function $f = x_0 + f_0(x_1, \ldots, x_{n-1}) + x_n$ which we call the characteristic function. The set of 2^n output sequences of the FSR with characteristic function f is denoted by $G(f)$.

Let $\mathbf{s} = (s_i)_{i=0}^{\infty}$ be a periodic sequence. We use per($\mathbf{s}$) to denote the (least positive) period of $\mathbf{s}$. The left shift operator L is defined as: $L^r\mathbf{s} = (s_i)_{i=r}^{\infty}$. Two periodic sequences $\mathbf{s}_1$ and $\mathbf{s}_2$ are called shift equivalent (or simply equivalent) if there exists an integer r such that $\mathbf{s}_1 = L^r\mathbf{s}_2$. According to the shift equivalent relation, the output sequences $G(f)$ are partitioned into equivalent classes $G(f) = [\mathbf{s}_1] \cup [\mathbf{s}_2] \cup \ldots \cup [\mathbf{s}_k]$ such that two sequences are in the same equivalent class if and only if they are equivalent. Each equivalent class is called a cycle, and the partition is called the cycle structure. The cycle $[\mathbf{s}]$ is often written as $[s_0 s_1 \ldots s_{\text{per}(\mathbf{s})-1}]$. It is easy to see that $[\mathbf{s}]$ contains exactly per($\mathbf{s}$) sequences.

An FSR is called a linear feedback shift register (LFSR) if its characteristic function f is linear; otherwise, it is called a nonlinear feedback shift register (NFSR). For an n-stage FSR, the periods of its output sequences are limited by 2^n. If this value is attained, we call the sequences de Bruijn sequences, and the FSR a maximum length FSR.

For a state $\mathbf{S} = (s_0, \ldots, s_{n-2}, s_{n-1})$ its companion is defined as $\mathbf{S}' = (s_0, \ldots, s_{n-2}, \overline{s}_{n-1})$ where $\overline{s}$ denotes the complements of s. Companion states can be used to join two sequences together into a sequence with larger period, which is often called the cycle joining method.

Lemma 1. *[17] Let* $\mathbf{s}$ *and* $\mathbf{s}'$ *be two non-equivalent sequences in* $G(f)$. *If there is a state* $\mathbf{S}$ *on* $\mathbf{s}$ *such that its companion* $\mathbf{S}'$ *is a state on* $\mathbf{s}'$, *then by interchanging the predecessors of* $\mathbf{S}$ *and* $\mathbf{S}'$ *the two sequences* $\mathbf{s}$ *and* $\mathbf{s}'$ *are joined into a single sequence whose period is* per($\mathbf{s}$) + per($\mathbf{s}'$).

2.2 Linear Complexity and k-Error Linear Complexity

For a periodic sequence, its linear complexity is defined to be the length of the shortest LFSR that can generate this sequence. We use $LC(\mathbf{s})$ to denote the linear complexity of the sequence $\mathbf{s}$. Chan et al. studied the sequences whose periods are powers of 2, and gave a bound for their linear complexities [3].

Lemma 2. *[3] Let* $\mathbf{s}$ *be a sequence of period* 2^n. *Then the linear complexity of* $\mathbf{s}$ *lies in the range of*

$$2^{n-1} + 1 \leq LC(\mathbf{s}) \leq 2^n.$$

Since the periods of de Bruijn sequences are powers of 2, their linear complexities satisfy the above range. Moreover, due to the particularity of de Bruijn sequences, their linear complexities have a more compact bound.

Lemma 3. *[3] For de Bruijn sequences of order n with $n \geq 3$, their linear complexities lie in the range of*

$$2^{n-1} + n \leq LC(\mathbf{s}) \leq 2^n - 1.$$

It is conjectured by Chan et al. [3] and then proved by Games and Richard [16] that there are no de Bruijn sequences of order n with linear complexity $2^{n-1} + n + 1$.

The k-error linear complexity of a periodic sequence is defined to be the smallest linear complexity of the sequences obtained by changing no more than k bits of the original sequence per period [8]. Formally, the k-error linear complexity of the periodic sequence $\mathbf{s}$ is

$$LC_k(\mathbf{s}) = \min\{LC(\mathbf{s} \oplus \mathbf{e}) \mid w_H(\mathbf{E}) \leq k, \mathrm{per}(\mathbf{e}) | \mathrm{per}(\mathbf{s})\},$$

where $\mathbf{E}$ is the first per($\mathbf{s}$) bits of $\mathbf{e}$. A systematic study of k-error linear complexity can be found in Ding et al.'s book [8] (see Sect. 5 of [8]).

2.3 $\mathcal{D}$-morphism

The $\mathcal{D}$-morphism, proposed by Lempel [19], is a homomorphism between de Bruijn graphs of order n and order $(n+1)$. Based on the properties of $\mathcal{D}$-morphism, Lempel presented a method to construct de Bruijn sequences of order $(n+1)$ from de Bruijn sequences of order n. The $\mathcal{D}$-morphism can also be treated as a mapping on sequences. Let $\mathbf{s} = (s_i)_{i=0}^{\infty}$ be a sequence. Its imagine under $\mathcal{D}$-morphism is defined to be the sequence $\mathbf{u} = (u_i)_{i=0}^{\infty}$ where $u_i = s_i \oplus s_{i+1}$ for $i \geq 0$. The inverse of $\mathcal{D}$-morphism is defined as $\mathcal{D}^{-1}(\mathbf{s}) = \{\mathbf{v} \mid \mathcal{D}(\mathbf{v}) = \mathbf{s}\}$. It is easy to see that, for any sequence $\mathbf{s}$, $\mathcal{D}^{-1}(\mathbf{s})$ contains exactly two sequences. We denote the two sequences respectively by $\mathcal{D}_0^{-1}(\mathbf{s})$ and $\mathcal{D}_1^{-1}(\mathbf{s})$, that is

$$\mathcal{D}_0^{-1}(\mathbf{s}) = 0, s_0, s_0 \oplus s_1, s_0 \oplus s_1 \oplus s_2, \ldots,$$
$$\mathcal{D}_1^{-1}(\mathbf{s}) = 1, 1 \oplus s_0, 1 \oplus s_0 \oplus s_1, 1 \oplus s_0 \oplus s_1 \oplus s_2, \ldots.$$

Some basic properties of $\mathcal{D}$-morphism are recalled in the following lemma. For a periodic sequence $\mathbf{s} = (s_i)_{i=0}^{\infty}$, its Hamming weight $w_H(\mathbf{s})$ is defined to be the Hamming weight of one period of $\mathbf{s}$, i.e., the number of 1s in the tuple $(s_0, s_1, \ldots, s_{\mathrm{per}(\mathbf{s})-1})$.

Lemma 4. *Let $\mathbf{s}$ be a periodic sequence. Then the two sequences $\mathcal{D}_0^{-1}(\mathbf{s})$ and $\mathcal{D}_1^{-1}(\mathbf{s})$ have the same period. Moreover,*

1. *If the weight of $\mathbf{s}$ is odd, then the two sequences $\mathcal{D}_0^{-1}(\mathbf{s})$ and $\mathcal{D}_1^{-1}(\mathbf{s})$ are shift equivalent, and the period of $\mathcal{D}_0^{-1}(\mathbf{s})$ or $\mathcal{D}_1^{-1}(\mathbf{s})$ is two times the period of $\mathbf{s}$. Furthermore, if the period of $\mathbf{s}$ is even then the weights of $\mathcal{D}_0^{-1}(\mathbf{s})$ and $\mathcal{D}_1^{-1}(\mathbf{s})$ are both even.*
2. *If the weight of $\mathbf{s}$ is even, then the two sequences $\mathcal{D}_0^{-1}(\mathbf{s})$ and $\mathcal{D}_1^{-1}(\mathbf{s})$ are not shift equivalent, and the period of $\mathcal{D}_0^{-1}(\mathbf{s})$ or $\mathcal{D}_1^{-1}(\mathbf{s})$ is equal to the period of $\mathbf{s}$. Furthermore, if the period of $\mathbf{s}$ is even then the weights of $\mathcal{D}_0^{-1}(\mathbf{s})$ and $\mathcal{D}_1^{-1}(\mathbf{s})$ are both odd or both even (depends on the specific sequence $\mathbf{s}$).*

For two characteristic functions $f(x_0, x_1, \ldots, x_n)$ and $g(x_0, x_1, \ldots, x_m)$, their $*$-product is defined to be [18]:

$$f * g = f(g(x_0, x_1, \ldots, x_m), g(x_1, x_2, \ldots, x_{m+1}), \ldots, g(x_n, x_{n+1}, \ldots, x_{n+m})).$$

If we apply $\mathcal{D}^{-1}$ to all the sequences in $G(f)$, we will obtain 2^{n+1} sequences. Actually, these 2^{n+1} sequences are exactly the output sequences of the FSR with characteristic function $f * (x_0 + x_1)$, that is,

$$G(f * (x_0 + x_1)) = \{\mathcal{D}_0^{-1}(\mathbf{s}), \mathcal{D}_1^{-1}(\mathbf{s}) \mid \mathbf{s} \in G(f)\}.$$

More detailed discussions about $\mathcal{D}$-morphism and their application in constructing de Bruijn sequences can be found in [20,21,23].

3 A Lower Bound

In this section, we give a lower bound for the k-error linear complexities of de Bruijn sequences. Firstly, we present a simple property of the sequences whose periods are powers of 2. Let $\mathbf{s} = \{s_i\}_{i=0}^{\infty}$ be a sequence of period 2^n. We use $L(\mathbf{s})$ and $R(\mathbf{s})$ to denote respectively the left half and right half of one period of $\mathbf{s}$, that is,

$$L(\mathbf{s}) = s_0 s_1 \ldots s_{2^{n-1}-1},$$
$$R(\mathbf{s}) = s_{2^{n-1}} s_{2^{n-1}+1} \ldots s_{2^n-1}.$$

By changing some bits in each period of $\mathbf{s}$, we will get a new sequence $\mathbf{s}'$. It is easy to see that, the period of $\mathbf{s}'$ is less than or equal to the period of $\mathbf{s}$. We want to know at least how many bits we need to change in order to make the period of $\mathbf{s}'$ less than 2^n.

Lemma 5. *Let $\mathbf{s} = \{s_i\}_{i=0}^{\infty}$ be a sequence of period 2^n. In order to get a sequence of period less than 2^n we need to change at least m bits in each period of $\mathbf{s}$, where m is the Hamming weight of $L(\mathbf{s}) \oplus R(\mathbf{s})$.*

Proof. Let $\mathbf{s}' = \{s'_i\}_{i=0}^{\infty}$ be the sequence obtained by changing k bits in each period of $\mathbf{s}$. Denote the periods of $\mathbf{s}$ and $\mathbf{s}'$ by $\text{per}(\mathbf{s})$ and $\text{per}(\mathbf{s}')$ respectively. It is easy to see, $\text{per}(\mathbf{s}')$ must be a factor of $\text{per}(\mathbf{s})$. If $\text{per}(\mathbf{s}')$ is less than 2^n, then $\text{per}(\mathbf{s}') \mid 2^{n-1}$. Therefore, we have $s'_i = s'_{i+2^{n-1}}$ for any $0 \le i < 2^{n-1}$. Consider the set

$$U = \{0 \le i \le 2^{n-1} - 1 \mid s_i \ne s_{i+2^{n-1}}\}.$$

In order to make the equation $s'_i = s'_{i+2^{n-1}}$ valid for any $0 \le i < 2^{n-1}$, for each index $i \in U$ one of the two bits s_i and $s_{i+2^{n-1}}$ must be changed. The proof is completed by noting that the number of elements in U is equal to the Hamming weight of $L(\mathbf{s}) \oplus R(\mathbf{s})$. □

In the special case that $\mathbf{s}$ is a de Bruijn sequence, we can derive a bound for the Hamming weight $w_H(L(\mathbf{s}) \oplus R(\mathbf{s}))$.

Theorem 1. *Let* $\mathbf{s}$ *be a de Bruijn sequence of order* n*. Then* $w_H(L(\mathbf{s}) \oplus R(\mathbf{s}))$ *is an even number and it lies in the range of*

$$\left\lceil \frac{2^{n-1}}{n} \right\rceil \leq w_H(L(\mathbf{s}) \oplus R(\mathbf{s})) \leq 2^{n-1}.$$

Proof. Denote by $w_H(\mathbf{s})$ the Hamming weight of one period of $\mathbf{s}$. Then we have $w_H(\mathbf{s}) = w_H(L(\mathbf{s})) + w_H(R(\mathbf{s}))$. Because one period of a de Bruijn sequence contains all the n-bits tuples, we know that $w_H(\mathbf{s}) = 2^{n-1}$ which is an even number. It is easy to see that

$$w_H(L(\mathbf{s}) \oplus R(\mathbf{s})) \equiv w_H(L(\mathbf{s})) + w(R(\mathbf{s})) \pmod{2}.$$

Therefore, $w_H(L(\mathbf{s}) \oplus R(\mathbf{s}))$ is also an even number.

The upper bound in the theorem can be derived by using the inequality

$$w_H(L(\mathbf{s}) \oplus R(\mathbf{s})) \leq w_H(L(\mathbf{s})) + w(R(\mathbf{s})) = w_H(\mathbf{s}) = 2^{n-1}.$$

In the following, we consider the lower bound of $w_H(L(\mathbf{s}) \oplus R(\mathbf{s}))$.

Since the period of $\mathbf{s}$ is 2^n, there exist an index v with $0 \leq v \leq 2^{n-1} - 1$ such that $s_v \neq s_{v+2^{n-1}}$. We shift $\mathbf{s}$ to the left by $v + 1$ bits to obtain a new sequence $\mathbf{t}$ so that the sequence $\mathbf{t}$ has the property $t_{2^{n-1}-1} \neq t_{2^n-1}$. Because $\mathbf{t}$ is shift equivalent with $\mathbf{s}$ we have $w_H(L(\mathbf{t}) \oplus R(\mathbf{t})) = w_H(L(\mathbf{s}) \oplus R(\mathbf{s}))$.

Firstly, we divide $L(\mathbf{t})$ and $R(\mathbf{t})$ into blocks of length n (the length of the last block may less than n). This is illustrated in Fig. 1. Then we compare the i-th blocks of $L(\mathbf{t})$ and $R(\mathbf{t})$ which are denoted by $\mathbf{l}_i$ and $\mathbf{r}_i$ respectively, $0 \leq i \leq \left\lceil \frac{2^{n-1}}{n} \right\rceil - 1$. Because $\mathbf{t}$ is a de Bruijn sequence, the two blocks $\mathbf{l}_i$ and $\mathbf{r}_i$ are different from each other. Remember that $\mathbf{t}$ has the property $t_{2^{n-1}-1} \neq t_{2^n-1}$, so even if the two last blocks of $L(\mathbf{t})$ and $R(\mathbf{t})$ have length less than n they are still different from each other.

From the above discussion, the blocks $\mathbf{l}_i$ and $\mathbf{r}_i$ are different from each other for any $0 \leq i \leq \left\lceil \frac{2^{n-1}}{n} \right\rceil - 1$, which implies that $w_H(\mathbf{l}_i \oplus \mathbf{r}_i) \geq 1$. Then by using the inequality

$$w_H(L(\mathbf{t}) \oplus R(\mathbf{t})) = \sum_i w_H(\mathbf{l}_i \oplus \mathbf{r}_i) \geq \left\lceil \frac{2^{n-1}}{n} \right\rceil,$$

we know that the lower bound in the theorem is also valid. □

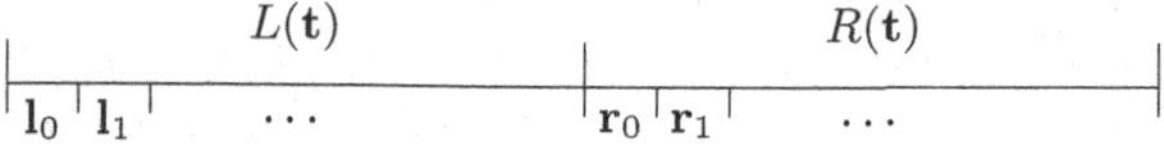

Fig. 1. Divide $L(\mathbf{s})$ and $R(\mathbf{s})$ into blocks

By combining the above theorem with Lemma 2, we can derive a bound for the k-error linear complexities of de Bruijn sequences.

Theorem 2. *Let* $\mathbf{s}$ *be a de Bruijn sequence of order* n*, and* k *be an integer less than* $\lceil \frac{2^{n-1}}{n} \rceil$*. Then the* k*-error linear complexity of* $\mathbf{s}$ *satisfies*

$$LC_k(\mathbf{s}) \geq 2^{n-1} + 1.$$

Proof. From Theorem 1, we know that if $k < \lceil \frac{2^{n-1}}{n} \rceil$ then the sequence obtained by changing k bits in each period of a de Bruijn sequence will still has period 2^n, and hence by Lemma 2 its linear complexity is $\geq 2^{n-1} + 1$. □

4 Compactness of Some Related Bounds

It is shown in Theorem 1 that, for a de Bruijn sequence of order n we have $w_H(L(\mathbf{s}) \oplus R(\mathbf{s})) \geq \left\lceil \frac{2^{n-1}}{n} \right\rceil$. In this section, we study the compactness of this bound. We will show that this lower bound is attainable if $n \geq 4$ and n is a power of 2. The proof is constructive, and it is based on the frame work of Etzion [13] which constructs a class of de Bruijn sequences whose linear complexity reaches the minimum value $2^{n-1} + n$.

For a polynomial $a_0 + a_1 x + \ldots + a_n x^n \in \mathbb{F}_2[x]$, we can associate it with a linear function $a_0 x_0 + a_1 x_1 + \ldots + a_n x_n$. Sometimes it is convenient to use linear functions instead of polynomials. Let $l_n(x)$ be the linear function corresponding to the polynomial $(1+x)^n$. Denote by $G(l_n(x)+1)$ the set of output sequences of the FSR whose characteristic function is $l_n(x)+1$. The reader can verify that:

$$l_{n+1}(x) + 1 = (l_n(x) + 1) * (x_0 + x_1).$$

Hence, the sequences in $G(l_{n+1}(x)+1)$ can be seen as obtained by applying the inverse of the $\mathcal{D}$-morphism to the sequences in $G(l_n(x)+1)$, i.e.,

$$G(l_{n+1}(x) + 1) = \{\mathcal{D}_0^{-1}(\mathbf{s}), \mathcal{D}_1^{-1}(\mathbf{s}) \mid \mathbf{s} \in G(l_n(x) + 1)\}.$$

When $n = 1$, we have $l_1(x)+1 = x_0 + x_1 + 1$ which is the characteristic function of the 1-th order de Bruijn sequence $0101\ldots$. The following lemma recalls some properties of the sequences in $G(l_n(x)+1)$.

Lemma 6. *Let* $G(l_n(x)+1)$ *be the set of output sequences of the FSR whose characteristic function is* $l_n(x)+1$*. Then we have*

1. *The sequences in* $G(l_n(x)+1)$ *all have the same period:* $2^{\lfloor \log n \rfloor + 1}$.
2. *There are* $2^{n - \lfloor \log n \rfloor - 1}$ *cycles in* $G(l_n(x)+1)$.
3. *The sequences in* $G(l_n(x)+1)$ *all have the same linear complexity:* $n+1$.
4. *The weights of the sequences in* $G(l_n(x)+1)$ *are all even, or all odd.*

The formal proofs for the first three properties can be found in [13] (see Fact 2 in [13]). The fourth property is valid because that, according to Lemma 4 if there are two sequences in $G(l_n(x)+1)$, denoted as $\mathbf{s}$ and $\mathbf{t}$, whose weights have different parities, then $\mathcal{D}_0^{-1}(\mathbf{s})$ and $\mathcal{D}_0^{-1}(\mathbf{t})$ would have different periods which contradicts with the property 1 of this lemma.

Now we choose from each cycle in $G(l_n(x)+1)$ a sequence to form a set $F(n)$. By the property 2 of Lemma 6, $F(n)$ consists of $2^{n-\lfloor \log n \rfloor -1}$ sequences. It is shown by Etzon that by properly choosing the sequences it is possible to arrange the sequences in $F(n)$ into pairs $P_i = (\mathbf{a}_i, \mathbf{b}_i)$ with $1 \le i \le 2^{n-\lfloor \log n \rfloor -2}$ so that the following three conditions hold.

1. For each pair P_i, the initial states of $\mathbf{a}_i$ and $\mathbf{b}_i$ form a companion pair.
2. For each i, $\mathbf{a}_i \oplus \mathbf{b}_i = \mathbf{a}_1 \oplus \mathbf{b}_1$.
3. The graph $(V(n), E(n))$, where $V(n) = \{v_i \mid 1 \le i \le 2^{n-\lfloor \log n \rfloor -2}\}$ and $\{v_i, v_j\} \in E(n)$ if and only if $\mathbf{a}_i$ and $\mathbf{a}_j$ have a pair of companion states in the same position (relative to their respective first states), is a connected graph.

Take $n = 4$ for example. By calculation we know that, $G(l_4(x)+1)$ consists of 2 cycles: $C_1 = [10000111]$ and $C_2 = [10010110]$. Let $\mathbf{a}_1 = 10000111\ldots$ and $\mathbf{b}_1 = 10010110\ldots$ be two sequences in C_1 and C_2 respectively. Define $F(4) = \{(\mathbf{a}_1, \mathbf{b}_1)\}$. It is easy to verify that $F(4)$ satisfies the above three conditions (the last two conditions are trivially met).

We remark that in the original paper [13] there is an additional condition: the linear complexity of $\mathbf{a}_1 \oplus \mathbf{b}_1$ is n. However, this condition is actually redundant because for any two sequences $\mathbf{s}$ and $\mathbf{t}$ in $G(l_n(x)+1)$ whose initial states form a companion pair, the linear complexity of $\mathbf{s} \oplus \mathbf{t}$ is always n. A short proof of this fact is given as follows. Write $\mathbf{s} = \{s_i\}_{i=0}^{\infty}$ and $\mathbf{t} = \{t_i\}_{i=0}^{\infty}$. Since $\mathbf{s}$ and $\mathbf{t}$ are sequences in $G(l_n(x)+1)$ they satisfy the recursion of $l_n(x)+1$, i.e., for any $i \ge 0$ we have

$$l_n(s_i, s_{i+1}, \ldots, s_{i+n-1}) \oplus 1 = 0,$$
$$l_n(t_i, t_{i+1}, \ldots, t_{i+n-1}) \oplus 1 = 0.$$

Since $l_n(x)$ is a linear function, by adding the above two equations together we get

$$l_n(s_i \oplus t_i, s_{i+1} \oplus t_{i+1}, \ldots, s_{i+n-1} \oplus t_{i+n-1}) = 0,$$

which implies that $\mathbf{s} \oplus \mathbf{t}$ can be generated by an n-stage LFSR. Therefore, its linear complexity is no more than n. On the other hand, because the first n bits of $\mathbf{s} \oplus \mathbf{t}$ is $(0, \ldots, 0, 1)$, it can not be generated by a LFSR whose length is less than n. So the linear complexity of $\mathbf{s} \oplus \mathbf{t}$ must be n. For this reason, we remove the condition $LC(\mathbf{a}_1 \oplus \mathbf{b}_1) = n$ here. Another thing need to mention is that, in the original paper [13] the existence of such $F(n)$ is proved for any integer $n \ge 8$. But here we consider only the case that n is a power of 2 and the existence of such $F(n)$ for $n = 4$ is already shown, so we can start from $n = 4$.

By using the structure of $F(n)$, Etzion et al. constructed a de Bruijn sequence of order n whose linear complexity attained the minimum value $2^{n-1} + n$. In the following, we show that in the case that $n \ge 4$ and n is a power of 2 the de Bruijn sequence constructed by them also has the property $w_H(L(\mathbf{s}) \oplus R(\mathbf{s})) = \frac{2^{n-1}}{n}$, which by Theorem 1 reaches the lower bound.

Let $(V(n), T)$ be a spanning tree of $(V(n), E(n))$. According to Lemma 1 we can join the sequences $\mathbf{a}_i, 1 \le i \le 2^{n-\lfloor \log n \rfloor -2}$ in $F(n)$ to form a single sequence

a. Notice that if $\mathbf{a}_i$ and $\mathbf{a}_j$ have a pair of companion states in the same position k, then $\mathbf{b}_i$ and $\mathbf{b}_j$ also have a pair of companion states in the same position k. So we can join the sequences $\mathbf{b}_i, 1 \leq i \leq 2^{n-\lfloor \log n \rfloor -2}$ in $F(n)$ to form a single sequence $\mathbf{b}$ in the same manner as we have done for $\mathbf{a}_i$. Then the two sequences $\mathbf{a}$ and $\mathbf{b}$ can be joined together by using their initial states (which are a pair of companion states) to form a de Bruijn sequence $\mathbf{s}$.

Denote the first periods of $\mathbf{a}_1, \mathbf{b}_1, \mathbf{a}, \mathbf{b}$ and $\mathbf{s}$ by $\mathbf{A}_1, \mathbf{B}_1, \mathbf{A}, \mathbf{B}$ and $\mathbf{S}$, respectively. The lengths of the five finite subsequences are $2^{\lfloor \log n \rfloor +1}$, $2^{\lfloor \log n \rfloor +1}$, $2^{n-1}, 2^{n-1}$ and 2^n, respectively. From the construction, we know that $\mathbf{S} = (\mathbf{A}|\mathbf{B})$, the concatenation of $\mathbf{A}$ and $\mathbf{B}$. Furthermore, we have $\mathbf{A} \oplus \mathbf{B} = (\mathbf{A}_1 \oplus \mathbf{B}_1)^k$ where $k = 2^{n-\lfloor \log n \rfloor -2}$ denotes the number of repetitions of $\mathbf{A}_1 \oplus \mathbf{B}_1$.

Theorem 3. *In the case that $n \geq 4$ and n is a power of 2, there exists a de Bruijn sequence $\mathbf{s}$ of order n such that*

$$w_H(L(\mathbf{s}) \oplus R(\mathbf{s})) = \frac{2^{n-1}}{n}.$$

Proof. Because n is a power of 2, we have $(1+x)^n = 1 + x^n$. Hence the characteristic function $l_n(x) + 1$ is actually

$$l_n(x) + 1 = x_0 + x_n + 1,$$

which implies that the two sequences $\mathbf{a}_1$ and $\mathbf{b}_1$ satisfy the recursion $x_n = x_0 + 1$. Then it is easy to see that the sequence $\mathbf{a}_1 \oplus \mathbf{b}_1$ satisfies the recursion $x_n = x_0$. Since the first n bits of $\mathbf{a}_1 \oplus \mathbf{b}_1$ is $0\ldots01$, the sequence $\mathbf{a}_1 \oplus \mathbf{b}_1$ is actually a sequence period of n and its one period is $0\ldots01$. Therefore,

$$\mathbf{A}_1 \oplus \mathbf{B}_1 = (0\ldots01)^2.$$

Then by the discussion before this theorem we have

$$L(\mathbf{s}) \oplus R(\mathbf{s}) = \mathbf{A} \oplus \mathbf{B} = (0\ldots01)^{\frac{2^{n-1}}{n}},$$

which implies that $w_H(L(\mathbf{s}) \oplus R(\mathbf{s})) = \frac{2^{n-1}}{n}$. This completes the proof. □

5 Experimental Results

In the case that n is not a power of 2, the authors don't know whether there exist de Bruijn sequences of order n such that $w_H(L(\mathbf{s}) \oplus R(\mathbf{s})) = \lceil \frac{2^{n-1}}{n} \rceil$. We did some experiments to study the compactness of this bound. The experimental results are given in the following tables.

With the help of C-programming, we generated all the de Bruijn sequences of orders 5 and 6, and calculated the weight $w_H(L(\mathbf{s}) \oplus R(\mathbf{s}))$ for each of them. The distributions of $w_H(L(\mathbf{s}) \oplus R(\mathbf{s}))$ for de Bruijn sequences of orders 5 and 6 are given in Tables 1 and 2, respectively.

Table 1. For de Bruijn sequences of order 5

Weight	4	6	8	10	12	14	16
Num	32	400	992	500	120	4	0

Table 2. For de Bruijn sequences of order 6

Weight	6	8	10	12	14	16	18
Num	696	72828	1098604	5826920	14522584	19616964	15570460
Weight	20	22	24	26	28	30	32
Num	7606696	2300736	433528	54024	4728	96	0

For the de Bruijn sequences of order 7, because their number is 2^{57} which is quite beyond our ability of computation, we randomly chose 10^8 de Bruijn sequences from them and calculated the distribution of $w_H(L(\mathbf{s}) \oplus R(\mathbf{s}))$. The result is given in Table 3.

Table 3. For de Bruijn sequences of order 7 (10^8 times)

Weight	20	22	24	26	28	30	32
Num	85654	471092	2269806	4025700	10578160	16445391	16788011
Weight	34	36	38	40	42	44	
Num	14903633	10321191	6124198	2912212	214137	214131	

From Tables 1 and 2 we know that, when $n = 5$ or 6, the lower bound $\lceil \frac{2^{n-1}}{n} \rceil$ is attainable. For $n = 7$ because the search is not exhaustive, we don't know if the lower bound is attainable.

We can also observe from Tables 1 and 2 that when $n = 5$ or 6, the upper bound 2^{n-1} is not attainable, i.e., there is no de Bruijn sequence satisfying $w_H(L(\mathbf{s}) \oplus R(\mathbf{s})) = 2^{n-1}$. Actually, this result is true for any $n \geq 3$. The reason is that, $w_H(L(\mathbf{s}) \oplus R(\mathbf{s})) = 2^{n-1}$ implies $s_{i+2^{n-1}} = s_i \oplus 1$ for any $0 \leq i \leq 2^{n-1} - 1$, and it has been proved by Chan et al. [3] that there are no such de Bruijn sequences if $n \geq 3$ (see Theorem 2 in [3]).

Table 4 presents all the de Bruijn sequences of order 5 such that $w_H(L(\mathbf{s}) \oplus R(\mathbf{s}))$ reaches the lower bound. There are totally 32 such sequences.

Table 4. All the de Bruijn sequences of order 5 such that $w_H(L(\mathbf{s}) \oplus R(\mathbf{s})) = 4$

0000010001101011 1001010011111011	0000010001101111 1001010011101011
0000010001101111 1010010101100111	0000010010101111 1000110011101101
0000010011100101 1000110111110101	0000010011101111 1000110010101101
0000010011101111 1001010001101011	0000010011111001 0100011010111011
0000010011111001 0100011011101011	0000010011111011 1001010001101011
0000010100011011 0010011101011111	0000010101101111 1010010001100111
0000010101111101 1000110100111001	0000010110101001 1000111110111001
0000010110111001 1000111110101001	0000011010011111 0010001010111011
0000011010110001 0100111011111001	0000011010110001 0100111110111001
0000011010111001 0001010011111011	0000011010111001 0100010011111011
0000011010111001 0100111110110001	0000011010111011 0001010011111001
0000011010111011 0010001010011111	0000011011101010 0010011111001011
0000011011101011 0001010011111001	0000011011111001 0001010011101011
0000011011111001 0100010011101011	0000011011111001 0100111010110001
0000011100110001 0010111110110101	0000011100110101 0010111110110001
0000011111001010 0010011011101011	0000011111010111 0010011011000101

6 Conclusions

We analyzed the k-error linear complexities of de Bruijn sequences. Based on the distribution property of de Bruijn sequences, we showed that for an n-th order de Bruijn sequence, if $k < \lceil \frac{2^{n-1}}{n} \rceil$ then its k-error linear complexity is more than or equal to $2^{n-1} + 1$. We also studied the compactness of some related bounds. Specifically, we showed that if $n \geq 4$ and n is a power of 2 then there exists a de Bruijn sequence of order n such that $w_H(L(\mathbf{s}) \oplus R(\mathbf{s})) = \frac{2^{n-1}}{n}$. Some experimental results are also provided for the case that n is not a power of 2. We hope these experimental results will be helpful for future research.

Acknowledgements. We would like to thank the three anonymous reviewers whose comments helped us a lot in improving the quality of the paper. In particular, the fact that $w_H(L(\mathbf{s}) \oplus R(\mathbf{s})) \neq 2^{n-1}$ is pointed out by the second reviewer. This work was supported by the National Science Foundation of China (Grant Nos. 61902393, 61872359 and 61936008).

References

1. Alhakim, A., Nouiehed, M.: Stretching de Bruijn sequences. Des. Codes Crypt. **85**(2), 381–394 (2017)
2. Amram, G., Ashlagi, Y., Rubin, A., Svoray, Y., Schwartz, M., Weiss, G.: An efficient shift rule for the prefer-max de Bruijn sequence. Discret. Math. **342**(1), 226–232 (2019)

3. Chan, A.H., Games, R.A., Key, E.L.: On the complexities of de Bruijn sequences. J. Comb. Theory Ser. A, **33**(3), 233–246 (1982)
4. Chang, Z., Chrisnata, J., Ezerman, M.F., Kiah, H.M.: Rates of DNA sequence profiles for practical values of read lengths. IEEE Trans. Inf. Theory **63**(11), 7166–7177 (2017)
5. Coppersmith, D., Rhoades, R.C., VanderKam, J.M.: Counting de Bruijn sequences as perturbations of linear recursions. arXiv (2017)
6. Courtois, N.T., Meier, W.: Algebraic attacks on stream ciphers with linear feedback. In: Biham, E. (ed.) EUROCRYPT 2003. LNCS, vol. 2656, pp. 345–359. Springer, Heidelberg (2003). https://doi.org/10.1007/3-540-39200-9_21
7. Ding, C.: Lower bounds on the weight complexities of cascaded binary sequences. In: Seberry, J., Pieprzyk, J. (eds.) AUSCRYPT 1990. LNCS, vol. 453, pp. 39–43. Springer, Heidelberg (1990). https://doi.org/10.1007/BFb0030350
8. Ding, C., Xiao, G., Shan, W. (eds.): The Stability Theory of Stream Ciphers. LNCS, vol. 561. Springer, Heidelberg (1991). https://doi.org/10.1007/3-540-54973-0
9. Dong, J., Pei, D.: Construction for de Bruijn sequences with large stage. Des. Codes Crypt. **85**(2), 343–358 (2017)
10. Dong, Y., Tian, T., Qi, W., Wang, Z.: New results on the minimal polynomials of modified de Bruijn sequences. Finite Fields Appl. **60**, 101583 (2019)
11. Etzion, T.: On the distribution of de Nruijn CR-sequences (corresp.). IEEE Trans. Inf. Theory **32**(3), 422–423 (1986)
12. Etzion, T.: Linear complexity of de Bruijn sequences-old and new results. IEEE Trans. Inf. Theory **45**(2), 693–698 (1999)
13. Etzion, T., Lempel, A.: Construction of de Bruijn sequences of minimal complexity. IEEE Trans. Inf. Theory **30**(5), 705–709 (1984)
14. Etzion, T., Lempel, A.: On the distribution of de Bruijn sequences of given complexity. IEEE Trans. Inf. Theory **30**(4), 611–614 (1984)
15. Gabric, D., Sawada, J., Williams, A., Wong, D.: A successor rule framework for constructing k -ary de Bruijn sequences and universal cycles. IEEE Trans. Inf. Theory **66**(1), 679–687 (2020)
16. Games, R.A.: There are no de Bruijn sequences of span n with complexity $2^{n-1} + n + 1$. J. Comb. Theory Ser. A **34**(2), 248–251 (1983)
17. Golomb, S.W.: Shift Register Sequences (1981)
18. Green, D.H., Dimond, K.R.: Nonlinear product-feedback shift registers. Proc. Inst. Electr. Eng. **117**(4), 681–686 (1970)
19. Lempel, A.: On a homomorphism of the de Bruijn graph and its applications to the design of feedback shift registers. IEEE Trans. Comput. **19**(12), 1204–1209 (1970)
20. Li, C., Zeng, X., Helleseth, T., Li, C., Lei, H.: The properties of a class of linear FSRS and their applications to the construction of nonlinear FSRS. IEEE Trans. Inf. Theory **60**(5), 3052–3061 (2014)
21. Li, M., Jiang, Y., Lin, D.: The adjacency graphs of some feedback shift registers. Des. Codes Crypt. **82**(3), 695–713 (2017)
22. Mandal, K., Gong, G.: Cryptographically strong de Bruijn sequences with large periods. In: Knudsen, L.R., Wu, H. (eds.) SAC 2012. LNCS, vol. 7707, pp. 104–118. Springer, Heidelberg (2013). https://doi.org/10.1007/978-3-642-35999-6_8
23. Mandal, K., Gong, G.: Feedback reconstruction and implementations of pseudorandom number generators from composited de Bruijn sequences. IEEE Trans. Comput. **65**(9), 2725–2738 (2016)
24. Meidl, W., Niederreiter, H.: Linear complexity, k-error linear complexity, and the discrete Fourier transform. J. Complex. **18**(1), 87–103 (2002)

25. Meier, W., Staffelbach, O.: Fast correlation attacks on certain stream ciphers. J. Cryptol. **1**(3), 159–176 (1989)
26. Mykkeltveit, J., Szmidt, J.: On cross joining de Bruijn sequences. IACR Cryptology ePrint Archive 2013, 760 (2013)
27. Rubin, A., Weiss, G.: Mapping prefer-opposite to prefer-one de Bruijn sequences. Des. Codes Crypt. **85**(3), 547–555 (2017)
28. Sawada, J., Williams, A., Wong, D.: A surprisingly simple de Bruijn sequence construction. Discret. Math. **339**(1), 127–131 (2016)
29. Siegenthaler. Decrypting a class of stream ciphers using ciphertext only. IEEE Trans. Comput. **34**(1), 81–85 (1985)
30. Stamp, M., Martin, C.F.: An algorithm for the k-error linear complexity of binary sequences with period 2^n. IEEE Trans. Inf. Theory **39**(4), 1398–1401 (1993)
31. Yang, B., Mandal, K., Aagaard, M.D., Gong, G.: Efficient composited de Bruijn sequence generators. IEEE Trans. Comput. **66**(8), 1354–1368 (2017)
32. Zhang, Z.: Further results on correlation functions of de Bruijn sequences. Acta Mathematicae Applicatae Sinica **2**(3), 257–262 (1985)
33. Zhao, X., Tian, T., Qi, W.: An interleaved method for constructing de Bruijn sequences. Discret. Appl. Math. **254**, 234–245 (2019)
34. Zhou, L., Tian, T., Qi, W., Wang, Z.: Constructions of de Bruijn sequences from a full-length shift register and an irreducible LFSR. Finite Fields Appl. **60**, 101574 (2019)

Digital Signature

A Lattice-Based Fully Dynamic Group Signature Scheme Without NIZK

Yiru Sun[1,2,3](✉) and Yanyan Liu[1,2,3]

[1] SKLOIS, Institute of Information Engineering, UCAS, Beijing 100093, China
{sunyiru,liuyanyan}@iie.ac.cn

[2] School of Cyber Security, University of Chinese Academy of Sciences, Beijing 101408, China

[3] State Key Laboratory of Cryptology, P.O. Box 515, Beijing 100878, China

Abstract. Group signature allows members in a group to sign messages anonymously on behalf of the group. In this paper, we propose the first lattice-based fully dynamic group signature scheme without NIZK based on the work in [Katsumata and Yamada, EUROCRYPT2019]. In order to realize our idea, we present a new indexed ABS scheme by using the Bonsai tree structure [Cash et al., EUROCRYPT2010]. Our fully dynamic group signature scheme satisfies CCA-selfless anonymity, traceability, weak non-frameability, and tracing soundness under the LWE and SIS assumptions. The size of keys and signature grow linearly in the upper bound of the group size in the system.

Keywords: Dynamic group signature · Standard model · LWE · SIS

1 Introduction

Related Work. The group signature was proposed by Chaum and van Heyst [8], which allows members in a group to sign messages anonymously on behalf of the group, while the generated signature does not reveal any information of the signer. When a dispute arises, it allows the group manager to reveal the identity of the original signer according to the signature, which guarantees the binding of the signature and the signer's identity. Because a secure group signature scheme satisfies anonymity and traceability, it becomes one important cryptography primitive to realize anonymous authentication.

Most of the early constructions of group signature scheme are static [2]. In other words, the group is fixed at setup and assume that the group manager is always trustworthy. Subsequently, considering the practical significance, many other properties were considered during the specific construction, for example, the weakened group manager capability [1], the dynamic registration or revocation [4,13]. Considering the post-quantum security of the scheme, lattice-based

Supported by the National Natural Science Foundation of China (Grant No. 61932019, No. 61772521, No. 61772522) and the Key Research Program of Frontier Sciences, CAS (Grant No. QYZDB-SSW-SYS035).

Y. Wu and M. Yung (Eds.): Inscrypt 2020, LNCS 12612, pp. 359–367, 2021.
https://doi.org/10.1007/978-3-030-71852-7_24

cryptography has become a research hot-spot in recent years. Gordon, S. et al. [10] proposed the first lattice-based static group signature scheme, and it was improved to obtain stronger anonymity in [5], the signatures size of the two schemes are all polynomial in N. To reduce the communication cost, it is imperative to reduce the signature size to $O(\log N)$ [16] or make it constant [15]. Subsequently, a lattice-based dynamic group signature scheme [14] was given based on the scheme in [12] by using an accumulator. However, most of the lattice-based group signature schemes are built in RO model, since the constructions of such schemes follow the encryption-then-proof framework, and the proof processes rely heavily on the non-interactive zero-knowledge (NIZK) protocol. It was not until 2018 that some breakthrough emerged on lattice-based NIZK [6,18], so it seems feasible to construct a lattice-based group signature scheme under standard model [11].

Our Work. In this paper, we modify the indexed ABS scheme in [11] by using the Bonsai tree structure [7]. This modification is to facilitate the subsequent construction of our fully dynamic group signature schemes to check whether the user has been revoked by the group manager when signing messages. And fortunately, this modification does not weaken the security properties of the scheme. In other words, our new indexed ABS scheme satisfies correctness, perfect privacy and no-signing-query unforgeability. Then we can improve the unforgeability of the scheme by using the same method as described in [11], i.e. from no-signing-query unforgeability to co-selective unforgeability.

By using our new indexed ABS scheme for a new circuit class $\mathcal{C}_\kappa$, we further give the first lattice-based fully dynamic group signature scheme without NIZK in this paper. During the construction of the scheme, we also use another two schemes as sub-module just like the work in [11]: the SKE scheme with key robustness and IND-CCA anonymity, the OTS scheme with strong unforgeability. And we can prove that our fully dynamic group signature scheme satisfies correctness, CCA-selfless anonymity, traceability, weak non-frameability, and tracing soundness under the standard learning with error (LWE) and small integer solution (SIS) assumptions. Finally, the size of the public parameter, the secret signing key and the signature grow linearly in N that is the upper bound of the group size in the system.

Organization. We recall some definitions, theorems used in the scheme in Sect. 2. And the detailed description of the new indexed ABS scheme is presented in Sect. 3. Finally, our main scheme is constructed and analyzed in Sect. 4.

2 Preliminaries

2.1 Background on Lattice

Let λ be security parameter, n, m, q be integers such that $n = poly(\lambda)$, $m \geq n\lceil \log q \rceil$. $\mathbf{A} \in \mathbb{Z}_q^{n\times m}$, for all $\mathbf{V} \in \mathbb{Z}_q^{n\times m'}$, let $\mathbf{A}_\gamma^{-1}(\mathbf{V})$ be an output distribution of $\mathbf{SampZ}(\gamma)^{m\times m'}$ conditioned on $\mathbf{A}\cdot\mathbf{A}_\gamma^{-1}(\mathbf{V})=\mathbf{V}$. $\mathbf{SampZ}(\gamma)$ is a sampling algorithm for the truncated discrete Gaussian distribution over $\mathbb{Z}$ with parameter $\gamma>0$ whose support is restricted to $z\in\mathbb{Z}$ such that $|z|\le\sqrt{n}\gamma$. A γ-trapdoor for $\mathbf{A}$ is a trapdoor that enable one to sample from the distribution $\mathbf{A}_\gamma^{-1}(\mathbf{V})$ for any $\mathbf{V}$ in time $poly(n,m,m',\log q)$. We slightly overload notation and denote a γ-trapdoor for $\mathbf{A}$ by $\mathbf{A}_\gamma^{-1}$. The gadget matrix $\mathbf{G}\in\mathbb{Z}_q^{n\times m}$ is obtained by padding $\mathbf{I}_n\otimes(1,2,2^2,\cdots,2^{\lceil\log q\rceil})$ with zero columns. Finally, we use the same definition of the function $\mathbf{WldCmp}:\{0,1\}^l\times\{0,1\}^l\times\{0,1\}^l\to\{0,1\}$ as in [11].

For the properties of lattice trapdoor, there exists an efficient procedure $\mathbf{TrapGen}(1^n,1^m,q)$ that outputs $(\mathbf{A},\ \mathbf{A}_{\gamma_0}^{-1})$ where $\mathbf{A}\in\mathbb{Z}_q^{n\times m}$ for some $m=O(n\log q)$ and is 2^{-n} close to uniform, where $\gamma_0=\omega(\sqrt{n\log q\log m})$. Furthermore, the distributions $(\mathbf{A},\mathbf{A}_\gamma^{-1},\mathbf{U},\mathbf{V})$ and $(\mathbf{A},\mathbf{A}_\gamma^{-1},\mathbf{U}',\mathbf{V}')$ are statistically indistinguishable for any $m'=poly(\kappa)$ and $\gamma\ge\gamma_0$, $\mathbf{U}\xleftarrow{\$}\mathbf{SampZ}(\gamma)^{m\times m'}$, $\mathbf{V}=\mathbf{AU}$, $\mathbf{V}\xleftarrow{\$}\mathbb{Z}_q^{n\times m'}$, and $\mathbf{U}'\xleftarrow{\$}\mathbf{A}_\gamma^{-1}(\mathbf{V}')$.

Definition 1 (The small integer solution problem SIS) *[9]. Let n, m, q be integers, the* $\text{SIS}_{n,m,q,\beta}$ problem (in the infinite norm) is as follows: Given a matrix $\mathbf{A}\xleftarrow{\$}\mathbb{Z}_q^{n\times m}$, and a real β, find a nonzero integer vector $\mathbf{z}\in\mathbb{Z}^m$ such that $\mathbf{Az}=\mathbf{0}\mod q$ and $\|\mathbf{z}\|_\infty\le\beta$.

Proposition 1 *[9]. Given a security parameter λ, for any $n=poly(\lambda)$, $m=poly(n)$, $\beta=poly(n)$ and prime $q\ge\beta\sqrt{n}\cdot\omega(\log n)$, the average-case problem* $\text{SIS}_{n,m,q,\beta}$ is as hard as approximating the problem SIVP and GapSVP in the worst case to within certain $\gamma-\beta\cdot\tilde{O}(\sqrt{n})$ factors.

There exists a pair of deterministic algorithm (**PubEval**, **TrapEval**) with the following properties:

1. $\mathbf{PubEval}(\vec{\mathbf{B}},F)\to\mathbf{B}_F$ with $\vec{\mathbf{B}}=[\mathbf{A}\|\mathbf{B}_1\|\cdots\|\mathbf{B}_k]\in\mathbb{Z}_q^{n\times k'm}$, $k'=k+1$, $F:\{0,1\}^{k'}\to\{0,1\}$ is a circuit.
2. $\mathbf{TrapEval}(\vec{\mathbf{R}},F,\mathbf{x})\to\mathbf{R}_{F,\mathbf{x}}$ with $\vec{\mathbf{R}}=[\mathbf{R}_0\|\mathbf{R}_1\|\cdots\|\mathbf{R}_k]\in\mathbb{Z}_q^{m\times mk'}$, $\|\mathbf{R}_i\|_\infty\le\delta$ for $i\in\{0,1,\cdots,k\}$, $\mathbf{x}=(x_0,x_1,\cdots,x_k)\in\{0,1\}^{k'}$, $F:\{0,1\}^{k'}\to\{0,1\}$ is a circuit with depth d. We have $\mathbf{PubEval}(\mathbf{A}\vec{\mathbf{R}}+\mathbf{x}\otimes\mathbf{G})=\mathbf{AR}_{F,\mathbf{x}}+F(\mathbf{x})\mathbf{G}$ where we denote $\mathbf{x}\otimes\mathbf{G}=[x_0\mathbf{G}\|x_1\mathbf{G}\|\cdots\|x_k\mathbf{G}]$. Furthermore, we have $\|\mathbf{R}_{F,\mathbf{x}}\|_\infty\le\delta\cdot m\cdot 2^{O(d)}$.
3. The running time of (**PubEval**, **TrapEval**) is bounded by $poly(k,n,m,2^d,\log q)$.

2.2 The Fully Dynamic Group Signature Scheme

Given a security parameter λ, the syntax of our fully dynamic group signature scheme without NIZK consists the following polynomial time algorithms:

GS.KeyGen$(1^\lambda,1^N)$: Given 1^λ, 1^N, this algorithm is operated by the group manager, outputs public parameter **pp** and key pair $(\mathbf{gpk}=(\mathbf{mpk},\mathbf{pp}),$

msk), and finally initializes the valid member list gul, the tracing secret key list gok, the secret signing key list gsk, the revocation token list grt as $\emptyset$.

GS.UKeyGen$(1^\lambda, \mathbf{pp})$**:** Take 1^λ and **pp** as inputs, the user uses this algorithm to generate its public-secret key pair (**upk**, **usk**).

$\langle$**GS.Join**$(\mathbf{upk}_i, \mathbf{gpk})$, **GS.Issue**$(\mathbf{msk}, \mathbf{gpk}, grt, gok, gsk, gul)\rangle$**:** This is an interactive protocol between a user and the group manager. If the algorithm runs successfully, the user becomes a valid member of the group, the algorithm **GS.Issue** returns the secret signing key to the user, and conserves the user's registration information.

GS.Update$(RL, \mathbf{msk}, gok, gsk, gul)$**:** This algorithm is operated by the group manager to update the users' registration information. Given a revocation list RL, if $RL = \emptyset$, outputs $\perp$. Otherwise, the manager updates the users' public/secret key lists.

GS.Sign$(1^\lambda, \mathbf{gpk}, \mathbf{gsk}_i, \mathbf{M}, C, RL)$**:** On input the group public key **gpk**, a user's secret signing key $\mathbf{gsk}_i$, a message $\mathbf{M} \in \mathcal{M}_\lambda$, a policy $C \in \mathcal{C}_\lambda$, and a revocation list RL, this algorithm outputs a signature $\Sigma = (\mathbf{ovk}, \mathbf{ct}, \sigma_1, \sigma_2)$ on message **M** with $C[\mathbf{ovk}, \mathbf{ct}, RL] = 1$. If the user with $\mathbf{gsk}_i$ is not a valid member of the group, i.e. the user is not registered yet or $\mathbf{grt}^i \in RL$, the algorithm outputs $\perp$.

GS.Vrfy$(\mathbf{gpk}, \mathbf{M}, C, RL, \Sigma)$**:** This is a deterministic algorithm, it outputs $\top$ if Σ is a valid signature on message **M** with policy C, otherwise outputs $\perp$.

GS.Open$(\mathbf{gpk}, \mathbf{gok}, \mathbf{M}, \Sigma)$**:** Given a valid signature Σ on message **M**, this algorithm is operated by the group manager to trace the signer who generated Σ. And returns $\perp$ if the algorithm unable to trace the signature Σ to a particular group member.

The properties required for our fully dynamic group signature scheme are given in the following:

Correctness: This property means that if the signer signs a message honestly, the algorithm **GS.Vrfy** can always output 1, the group manager can trace the identity of the signer who generated the signature by the algorithm **GS.Open** with overwhelming probability.

CCA-Selfless Anonymity: For any PPT adversary $\mathcal{A}$, this property means that it is impossible to distinguish signatures generated by two valid members in the group with a non-negligible probability, even though the adversary $\mathcal{A}$ could corrupt some but not all users, and is given the accesses to the oracle **GS.Sign** and **GS.Open** [11]. In other words, a fully dynamic group signature scheme is CCA-Selfless Anonymity for all PPT adversary $\mathcal{A}$ if $\Pr[\mathbf{Exp}^{anon-b}_{FDGS,\mathcal{A}}(\lambda) = 1] \leq negl(\lambda)$.

Tracing Soundness: For any PPT adversary $\mathcal{A}$, the probability of forging a valid signature that can traced to two different members is negligible, even though the adversary $\mathcal{A}$ could corrupt the group manager and all users [3]. In other words, a fully dynamic group signature scheme satisfies tracing soundness for all PPT adversary $\mathcal{A}$ if $\Pr[\mathbf{Exp}^{trace-sound}_{FDGS,\mathcal{A}}(\lambda) = 1] \leq negl(\lambda)$.

Traceability: For any PPT adversary $\mathcal{A}$, the probability of forging a valid signature that is traced to $\perp$ or a member who did not generate the signature is negligible, even though the adversary $\mathcal{A}$ could corrupt the admitter and some but not all users, and is given the access to the oracle **GS.Sign** [11]. In other words, a fully dynamic group signature scheme is traceable for all PPT adversary $\mathcal{A}$ if $\Pr[\mathbf{Exp}^{trace}_{FDGS,\mathcal{A}}(\lambda) = 1] \leq negl(\lambda)$.

3 A New Indexed Attribute-Based Signature

3.1 The Scheme with No-Signing-Query Unforgeability

The new indexed attribute-based signature scheme is inspired by the indexed ABS in [11]. Let $\{\mathcal{M}_\lambda\}_{\lambda\in\mathbb{N}}$ be a family of message spaces, $\{\mathcal{F}_\lambda\}_{\lambda\in\mathbb{N}}$ be the circuit class that is dealt with in the scheme, where $\mathcal{F}_\lambda$ is a set of circuits $F : \{0,1\}^{k'(\lambda)} \to \{0,1\}$ with depth at most $d_{\mathcal{F}} = O(\log \lambda)$. An indexed ABS scheme for the circuit class $\mathcal{F}_\lambda$ is defined by the following algorithms:

ABS.Setup$(1^\lambda, 1^N) \to (\mathbf{mpk}, \mathbf{msk})$**:** Given a security parameter λ, and input 1^λ and 1^N, it sets the parameters n, m, β, q, γ_0, γ as specified later. And N is the upper bound of the group size, q is a prime number, $k = \lceil \log N \rceil$, $k' = k + 1$. Then, it runs $(\mathbf{A}, \mathbf{A}^{-1}_{\gamma_0}) \xleftarrow{\$} \mathbf{TrapGen}(1^n, 1^m, q)$ with $\mathbf{A} \in \mathbb{Z}_q^{n\times m}$, samples random matrices $\mathbf{B}_j^d \xleftarrow{\$} \mathbb{Z}_q^{n\times m}$ for $d \in \{0,1\}$, $j \in [k]$, random vector $\mathbf{r} \in \{0,1\}^m$, computes $\mathbf{Ar} = \mathbf{u} \in \mathbb{Z}_q^n$, and let $\mathbf{B} = [\mathbf{A}\|\mathbf{B}_1^0\|\mathbf{B}_1^1\| \cdots \|\mathbf{B}_k^0\|\mathbf{B}_k^1]$. We denote i the index of the group member, and $i_1 i_2 \cdots i_k$ is its binary form, then let $\mathbf{B}^i = [\mathbf{A}\|\mathbf{B}_1^{i_1}\| \cdots \|\mathbf{B}_k^{i_k}]$. Finally, it outputs $\mathbf{mpk} = (\mathbf{A}, \{\mathbf{B}^i\}_{i\in[N]}, \mathbf{u})$ and $\mathbf{msk} = (\mathbf{A}^{-1}_{\gamma_0}, \{\mathbf{B}^i\}_{i\in[N]})$.

ABS.KeyGen$(\mathbf{msk}, i, \mathbf{x}) \to \mathbf{sk_x}$**:** On inputs $\mathbf{msk} = (\mathbf{A}^{-1}_{\gamma_0}, \{\mathbf{B}^i\}_{i\in[N]})$, the attribute $\mathbf{x} \in \{0,1\}^{k'}$ that the first bit is 1, and a group member's index $i \in [N]$ with its binary presentation $i_1 i_2 \cdots i_k$, it samples $\mathbf{R}^i \xleftarrow{\$} \mathbf{A}^{-1}_{\gamma_0}(\mathbf{B}^i - \mathbf{x} \otimes \mathbf{G})$ with $\mathbf{R}^i \in \mathbb{Z}_q^{m\times mk'}$ using $\mathbf{A}^{-1}_{\gamma_0}$. Note that $\mathbf{B}^i = \mathbf{AR}^i + \mathbf{x} \otimes \mathbf{G}$ and $\|\mathbf{R}^i\|_\infty \leq \gamma_0\sqrt{n}$ holds by the definition of the distribution $\mathbf{A}^{-1}_{\gamma_0}(\mathbf{B}^i - \mathbf{x}\otimes\mathbf{G})$. Then outputs $\mathbf{sk_x} = (i, \mathbf{R}^i)$.

ABS.Sign$(\mathbf{mpk}, \mathbf{sk_x}, \mathbf{M}, F) \to \sigma$**:** It outputs $\perp$ if $\mathbf{M} \notin \mathcal{M}_\lambda$, $F \notin \mathcal{F}_\lambda$, or $F(\mathbf{x}) = 0$. Otherwise, it first parses $\mathbf{sk_x} = (i, \mathbf{R}^i)$, then computes $\mathbf{B}_F^i = \mathbf{PubEval}(\mathbf{B}^i, F)$ and $\mathbf{R}^i_{F,\mathbf{x}} = \mathbf{TrapEval}(\mathbf{R}^i, F, \mathbf{x})$ such that $\|\mathbf{R}^i_{F,\mathbf{x}}\|_\infty \leq \gamma$. Since $F(\mathbf{x}) = 1$, we have $\mathbf{B}_F^i = \mathbf{AR}^i_{F,\mathbf{x}} + \mathbf{G}$. It then computes $[\mathbf{A}\|\mathbf{B}_F^i]_\beta^{-1}$ from $\mathbf{R}^i_{F,\mathbf{x}}$, and further computes $[\mathbf{A}\|\mathbf{B}_F^1\| \cdots \|\mathbf{B}_F^N]_\beta^{-1}$ from $[\mathbf{A}\|\mathbf{B}_F^i]_\beta^{-1}$. Finally, it samples $\sigma \xleftarrow{\$} [\mathbf{A}\|\mathbf{B}_F^1\| \cdots \|\mathbf{B}_F^N]_\beta^{-1}(\mathbf{u})$ and outputs $\sigma \in \mathbb{Z}^{m(N+1)}$ as a signature of message $\mathbf{M}$.

ABS.Vrfy$(\mathbf{mpk}, \mathbf{M}, F, \sigma) \to \top$ **or** $\perp$**:** It outputs $\perp$ if $F \notin \mathcal{F}_\lambda$ or $\sigma \notin \mathbb{Z}^{m(N+1)}$. Otherwise, it computes $\mathbf{B}_F^i = \mathbf{PubEval}(F, \mathbf{B}^i)$ for $i \in [N]$, then checks whether $\|\sigma\|_\infty \leq \sqrt{n}\beta$, $[\mathbf{A}\|\mathbf{B}_F^1\| \cdots \|\mathbf{B}_F^N] \cdot \sigma = \mathbf{u}$ are valid, if yes outputs $\top$, otherwise outputs $\perp$.

Theorem 1. *Given a security parameter λ, circuit class $\mathcal{F}_\lambda$ with bounded depth $O(\log \lambda)$, $\beta' = 1 + (N+1)m\gamma \cdot \sqrt{n}\beta$. Suppose that the problem* $\mathrm{SIS}^{\infty}_{n,m,q,\beta'}$ *is hard, then the indexed ABS scheme in this paper satisfies correctness, perfect privacy and no-signing-query unforgeability.*

The detailed proof of the theorem is given in the full version. Denote the scheme above as **ABS**, then we can change it into a new indexed ABS scheme **ABS**$'$ that satisfies correctness, perfect privacy and co-selective unforgeability by the same way with [11], where function class $\mathcal{F} = \{\mathcal{F}_\lambda\}_{\lambda \in \mathbb{N}}$ is defined as $\mathcal{F}_\lambda = \{F[\tilde{\mathbf{M}}, C] : \{0,1\}^{k'(\lambda)+2l(\lambda)+1} \to \{0,1\} | \tilde{\mathbf{M}} \in \{0,1\}^{l(\lambda)}, C \in \mathcal{C}_\lambda\}$, $C : \{0,1\}^{k'(\lambda)} \to \{0,1\}$, we won't go into details here.

4 The Fully Dynamic Group Signature Without NIZK

Suppose that the group manager is honest, and the upper bound of the group size is N. We give a construction of fully dynamic group signature scheme from the following building blocks: an indexed ABS scheme **ABS** = (**ABS.Setup**, **ABS.KeyGen**, **ABS.Sign**, **ABS.Vrfy**) with perfect privacy and co-selective unforgeability, an one-time signature scheme **OTS** = (**OTS.KeyGen**, **OTS.Sign**, **OTS.Vrfy**) with strong unforgeability [17], and a secret key encryption scheme **SKE** = (**SKE.Setup**, **SKE.Gen**, **SKE.Enc**, **SKE.Dec**) with key robustness, IND-CCA security, and the decryption circuits depth is $O(\log \lambda)$.

GS.KeyGen$(1^\lambda, 1^N)$**:** This algorithm is operated by the group manager. It runs **SKE.Setup**$(1^\lambda) \to$ **pp** and $(\mathbf{mpk}, \mathbf{msk}) \leftarrow$ **ABS.Setup**$(1^\lambda, 1^{N+1})$. Finally, it outputs $\mathbf{gpk} := (\mathbf{pp}, \mathbf{mpk})$, and initializes $gul, gok, gsk, grt = \emptyset$, where gul is the valid member list, gok is the tracing secret key list, gsk is the secret signing key list, and grt is the revocation token list.

GS.UKeyGen$(1^\lambda, \mathbf{pp})$**:** The users use this algorithm to generate his public key **upk** and secret key **usk**.

$\langle$**GS.Join**$(\mathbf{upk}_i, \mathbf{gpk})$, **GS.Issue**$(\mathbf{msk}, \mathbf{gpk}, grt, gok, gsk, gul)\rangle$**:** It is an interactive protocol between a user and group manager. Suppose that the new user is the ith member in the group with $0 < i \leq N$ and abort otherwise, the algorithm **GS.Join** sends the user's public key $\mathbf{upk}_i$ to the group manager. If the latter agree this application, the algorithm **GS.Issue** firstly receives $\mathbf{K}_i$ that generated by the admitter by running $\mathbf{K}_i \leftarrow$ **SKE.Gen**$(\mathbf{pp} \| \mathbf{upk}_i)$, and $\mathbf{sk}_{i\|\mathbf{K}_i} \leftarrow$ **ABS.KeyGen**$(\mathbf{msk}, i, i\|\mathbf{K}_i)$, sets $\mathbf{gsk}_i = (i, \mathbf{K}_i, \mathbf{sk}_{i\|\mathbf{K}_i})$. Then computes $\mathbf{z} = \sum_{j=1}^{k} \mathbf{B}_j^{i_j} \mathbf{r}_j^{i_j}$ where $\mathbf{r}_1^0, \mathbf{r}_1^1, \cdots, \mathbf{r}_k^0, \mathbf{r}_k^1 \xleftarrow{\$} D_{\mathbb{Z}^m, \sigma'}$. Let $\mathbf{r} = [\mathbf{r}_0 \| \mathbf{r}_1^0 \| \mathbf{r}_1^1 \| \cdots \| \mathbf{r}_k^0 \| \mathbf{r}_k^1]$ where $\mathbf{r}_0 \xleftarrow{\$} \mathbf{A}_{\gamma_0}^{-1}(\mathbf{u} - \mathbf{z})$, $\mathbf{r}^i = [\mathbf{r}_0 \| \mathbf{r}_1^{i_1} \| \cdots \| \mathbf{r}_k^{i_k}]$, so we have $\mathbf{B}^i \mathbf{r}^i = \mathbf{u}$. Then let $\mathbf{grt}^i = \mathbf{A}\mathbf{r}_0$ be a revocation token, includes $\mathbf{grt}^i$ to grt, $\mathbf{gok}_i = \mathbf{K}_i$ to gok, and $\mathbf{gsk}_i$ to gsk, $\mathbf{upk}_i$ to gul. Finally, the algorithm **GS.Issue** sends $\mathbf{gsk}_i$ to the user and outputs grt, gul.

GS.Update$(RL, \mathbf{msk}, gok, gsk, gul)$**:** Suppose that the set of indexes of the revoked members is $RL \subset grt$ with upper bound $N-1$. If $RL = \emptyset$, output $\perp$, otherwise set $gok_{new} = gok \backslash \{\mathbf{K}_j\}_{j \in RL}$, $gsk_{new} = gsk \backslash \{\mathbf{gsk}_j\}_{j \in RL}$, $gul_{new} = guk \backslash \{\mathbf{upk}_j\}_{j \in RL}$.

GS.Sign$(1^\lambda, \mathbf{gpk}, \mathbf{gsk}_i, \mathbf{M}, C, RL)$**:** It runs $(\mathbf{ovk}, \mathbf{osk}) \xleftarrow{\$} \mathbf{OTS.KeyGen}(1^\lambda)$ and $\mathbf{ct} \xleftarrow{\$} \mathbf{SKE.Enc}\ (\mathbf{K}_i, i\|\mathbf{ovk})$, then runs

$$\mathbf{ABS.Sign}(\mathbf{mpk}, \mathbf{sk}_{i,\|\mathbf{K}_i}, C[\mathbf{ovk}, \mathbf{ct}, RL], \mathbf{M}) \rightarrow \sigma_1$$

where $C[\mathbf{ovk}, \mathbf{ct}, RL]$ is defined in the next section. Finally, it runs $\mathbf{OTS.Si}$ $\mathbf{gn}(\mathbf{osk}, \mathbf{M}\|\sigma_1) \rightarrow \sigma_2$, and outputs $\Sigma := (\mathbf{ovk}, \mathbf{ct}, \sigma_1, \sigma_2)$.

GS.Vrfy$(\mathbf{gpk}, \mathbf{M}, C, RL, \Sigma)$**:** It parses $\Sigma = (\mathbf{ovk}, \mathbf{ct}, \sigma_1, \sigma_2)$, then outputs $\top$ if

$$\begin{aligned} &\mathbf{ABS.Vrfy}(\mathbf{mpk}, \mathbf{M}, C[\mathbf{ovk}, \mathbf{ct}, RL], \sigma_1) = \top \\ \wedge \quad &\mathbf{OTS.Vrfy}(\mathbf{ovk}, \mathbf{M}\|\sigma_1, \sigma_2) = \top. \end{aligned}$$

Otherwise, it outputs $\perp$.

GS.Open$(\mathbf{gpk}, \mathbf{gok}, \mathbf{M}, \Sigma)$**:** It runs $\mathbf{GS.Vrfy}(\mathbf{gpk}, \mathbf{M}, C, RL, \Sigma)$ and returns $\perp$ if the verification result is $\perp$. Otherwise, it parses $\Sigma \rightarrow (\mathbf{ovk}, \mathbf{ct}, \sigma_1, \sigma_2)$, computes $d_i \leftarrow \mathbf{SKE.Dec}(\mathbf{K}_i, \mathbf{ct})$ for $i \in [N]$ and outputs the smallest index i such that $d_i \neq \perp$. If there is not such i, it returns $\perp$.

The policy $C[\mathbf{ovk}, \mathbf{ct}, RL](i\|\mathbf{K}_i)$ used in our scheme as follows with hardwired constants **ovk**, **ct** and RL.

1. Parse the input to $i \in [N+1]$ and $\mathbf{K}_i$, if the input does not conform to the format, output 0.
2. If $i = N+1$, output 1.
3. Compute $\mathbf{SKE.Dec}(\mathbf{K}_i, \mathbf{ct}) = i'\|\mathbf{ovk}'$, if $i' = i \wedge \mathbf{grt}^{i'} \notin RL \wedge \mathbf{ovk}' = \mathbf{ovk}$, output 1, otherwise, output 0.

Theorem 2. *If the indexed attribute-based signature scheme* **ABS** *satisfies perfect privacy and co-selective unforgeability, one-time signature scheme* **OTS** *is strongly unforgeable, and the secret key encryption scheme* **SKE** *satisfies correctness, key robustness and IND-CCA security, then the fully dynamic group signature in this paper satisfies correctness, CCA-selfless anonymity, traceability, tracing soundness, and weak non-frameability.*

The detailed proof of the theorem is given in the full version.

References

1. Bellare, M., Shi, H., Zhang, C.: Foundations of group signatures: the case of dynamic groups. In: Menezes, A. (ed.) CT-RSA 2005. LNCS, vol. 3376, pp. 136–153. Springer, Heidelberg (2005). https://doi.org/10.1007/978-3-540-30574-3_11
2. Boneh, D., Boyen, X., Shacham, H.: Short group signatures. In: Franklin, M. (ed.) CRYPTO 2004. LNCS, vol. 3152, pp. 41–55. Springer, Heidelberg (2004). https://doi.org/10.1007/978-3-540-28628-8_3
3. Bootle, J., Cerulli, A., Chaidos, P., Ghadafi, E., Groth, J.: Foundations of fully dynamic group signatures. In: Manulis, M., Sadeghi, A.-R., Schneider, S. (eds.) ACNS 2016. LNCS, vol. 9696, pp. 117–136. Springer, Cham (2016). https://doi.org/10.1007/978-3-319-39555-5_7

4. Boyen, X., Waters, B.: Compact group signatures without random oracles. In: Vaudenay, S. (ed.) EUROCRYPT 2006. LNCS, vol. 4004, pp. 427–444. Springer, Heidelberg (2006). https://doi.org/10.1007/11761679_26
5. Camenisch, J., Neven, G., Rückert, M.: Fully anonymous attribute tokens from lattices. In: Visconti, I., De Prisco, R. (eds.) SCN 2012. LNCS, vol. 7485, pp. 57–75. Springer, Heidelberg (2012). https://doi.org/10.1007/978-3-642-32928-9_4
6. Canetti, R., et al.: Fiat-Shamir: from practice to theory. In: Charikar, M., Cohen, E. (eds.) Proceedings of the 51st Annual ACM SIGACT Symposium on Theory of Computing, STOC 2019, Phoenix, AZ, USA, 23–26 June 2019, pp. 1082–1090. ACM (2019)
7. Cash, D., Hofheinz, D., Kiltz, E., Peikert, C.: Bonsai trees, or how to delegate a lattice basis. In: Gilbert, H. (ed.) EUROCRYPT 2010. LNCS, vol. 6110, pp. 523–552. Springer, Heidelberg (2010). https://doi.org/10.1007/978-3-642-13190-5_27
8. Chaum, D., van Heyst, E.: Group signatures. In: Davies, D.W. (ed.) EUROCRYPT 1991. LNCS, vol. 547, pp. 257–265. Springer, Heidelberg (1991). https://doi.org/10.1007/3-540-46416-6_22
9. Gentry, C., Peikert, C., Vaikuntanathan, V.: Trapdoors for hard lattices and new cryptographic constructions. In: Proceedings of the ACM Conference STOC, Victoria, 17–20 May 2008, pp. 197–206. ACM DL (2008)
10. Gordon, S.D., Katz, J., Vaikuntanathan, V.: A group signature scheme from lattice assumptions. In: Abe, M. (ed.) ASIACRYPT 2010. LNCS, vol. 6477, pp. 395–412. Springer, Heidelberg (2010). https://doi.org/10.1007/978-3-642-17373-8_23
11. Katsumata, S., Yamada, S.: Group signatures without NIZK: from lattices in the standard model. In: Ishai, Y., Rijmen, V. (eds.) EUROCRYPT 2019. LNCS, vol. 11478, pp. 312–344. Springer, Cham (2019). https://doi.org/10.1007/978-3-030-17659-4_11
12. Libert, B., Ling, S., Nguyen, K., Wang, H.: Zero-knowledge arguments for lattice-based accumulators: logarithmic-size ring signatures and group signatures without trapdoors. In: Fischlin, M., Coron, J.-S. (eds.) EUROCRYPT 2016. LNCS, vol. 9666, pp. 1–31. Springer, Heidelberg (2016). https://doi.org/10.1007/978-3-662-49896-5_1
13. Libert, B., Mouhartem, F., Nguyen, K.: A lattice-based group signature scheme with message-dependent opening. In: Manulis, M., Sadeghi, A.-R., Schneider, S. (eds.) ACNS 2016. LNCS, vol. 9696, pp. 137–155. Springer, Cham (2016). https://doi.org/10.1007/978-3-319-39555-5_8
14. Ling, S., Nguyen, K., Wang, H., Xu, Y.: Lattice-based group signatures: achieving full dynamicity with ease. In: Gollmann, D., Miyaji, A., Kikuchi, H. (eds.) ACNS 2017. LNCS, vol. 10355, pp. 293–312. Springer, Cham (2017). https://doi.org/10.1007/978-3-319-61204-1_15
15. Ling, S., Nguyen, K., Wang, H., Xu, Y.: Constant-size group signatures from lattices. In: Abdalla, M., Dahab, R. (eds.) PKC 2018. LNCS, vol. 10770, pp. 58–88. Springer, Cham (2018). https://doi.org/10.1007/978-3-319-76581-5_3
16. Ling, S., Nguyen, K., Wang, H.: Group signatures from lattices: simpler, tighter, shorter, ring-based. In: Katz, J. (ed.) PKC 2015. LNCS, vol. 9020, pp. 427–449. Springer, Heidelberg (2015). https://doi.org/10.1007/978-3-662-46447-2_19

17. Mohassel, P.: One-time signatures and chameleon hash functions. In: Biryukov, A., Gong, G., Stinson, D.R. (eds.) SAC 2010. LNCS, vol. 6544, pp. 302–319. Springer, Heidelberg (2011). https://doi.org/10.1007/978-3-642-19574-7_21
18. Peikert, C., Shiehian, S.: Noninteractive zero knowledge for np from (plain) learning with errors. In: Boldyreva, A., Micciancio, D. (eds.) CRYPTO 2019. LNCS, vol. 11692, pp. 89–114. Springer, Cham (2019). https://doi.org/10.1007/978-3-030-26948-7_4

An Efficient Blind Signature Scheme Based on SM2 Signature Algorithm

Yudi Zhang[1], Debiao He[1(✉)], Fangguo Zhang[2], Xinyi Huang[3], and Dawei Li[4]

[1] School of Cyber Science and Engineering, Wuhan University, Wuhan, China
zhangyudi007@gmail.com, hedebiao@163.com

[2] School of Data and Computer Science, Sun Yat-sen University, Guangzhou, China
isszhfg@mail.sysu.edu.cn

[3] College of Mathematics and Informatics, Fujian Normal University, Fuzhou, China
xyhuang@fjnu.edu.cn

[4] Ding Xuan Cryptography Testing Co., Ltd., Shenzhen, China
ldw@dxct.org

Abstract. The Chinese government releases the SM2 digital signature algorithm as one part of the Chinese public key crypto standard, and now it has become an international standard algorithm. To protect the privacy of messages, we propose an efficient blind signature scheme based on the SM2 signature algorithm in this paper. We prove that our scheme can satisfy blindness and EUF-CMA (existential unforgeability under chosen message attacks). We implement our scheme using MIRACL Cryptographic SDK, and propose a variant blind signature scheme. Security analysis and experimental evaluation demonstrate that our proposed scheme is practical for real-world applications.

Keywords: SM2 algorithm · Digital signature · Blind signature · Provable security · Implementation

1 Introduction

The digital signature [1–3] plays a key role on the Internet, such as authentication, e-business and cryptocurrency. Digital signatures can provide authentication, integrity and non-repudiation, all of which can make sure the validation of user identity and messages. However, traditional digital signature scheme may cause users' privacy to be leaked. For example, when a user uses e-banking for online transactions, all the transaction information will be returned to the bank. Data breach would occur if the bank collect and leak the data to other parties. Also, in the electronic voting system [4–6], the votes are directly exposed to the administrator. The voters are however not willing to disclose their votes to the administrator. In addition, there are still many privacy breaches of cryptocurrency users. Although mixcoin technique [7] has been proposed and applied, the mixcoin server holds all transaction information. Therefore, how to protect user's privacy has become an urgent problem to be solved.

One of the potential solutions is blind signature, which was first introduced by Chaum [8]. In a blind signature scheme, a signer and a user are involved in

Y. Wu and M. Yung (Eds.): Inscrypt 2020, LNCS 12612, pp. 368–384, 2021.
https://doi.org/10.1007/978-3-030-71852-7_25

the system. The signer can generate a valid signature on the user's message, while the signer can not get any information from the blinded message. Based on the concept of blind signature, many blind signature schemes [9–12] have been proposed. Blind signature has two properties, (1) blindness: signer cannot obtain the original message from the blinded message; (2) unforgeability: the user cannot generate a valid signature without interacting with the signer. Notice that, in the generalized blindness, the signer cannot link any blinded message to its unblinded version, which is also called untraceability.

Recently, He *et al.* [13] proposed a blind signature generation method based on SM2 signature algorithm. However, because He's method [13] employs Paillier encryption algorithm, their scheme is not efficient or practicable. To solve this defect, we propose a novel and lightweight blind signature scheme based on SM2 signature algorithm. In our proposed scheme, the user first blinds the message, then sends the blinded message to the signer. Upon receiving the blinded message, the signer signs on it and returns the blind signature to the user. The user unblinds and verifies the blind signature. If it is valid, then the user outputs the message together with the signature. In addition, our proposed scheme can meet the property of untraceability. Finally, we give a variant of the proposed scheme.

The public key cryptographic algorithm SM2, published by the Chinese State Cryptography Administration Office of Security Commercial Code Administration in 2010, is the Chinese cryptographic public key algorithm standard [14]. Noticeable, ISO/IEC has standardized it in ISO/IEC 14888-3:2016/DAMD 1 [15]. The SM2 algorithm is used in many fields, such as electronic authentication systems, key management systems and applications systems. In our proposed scheme, the signer can generate a valid signature for the user without knowing the original message. Also, the signature can be verified efficiently by the original verification algorithm.

Moreover, we demonstrate that our scheme achieves the blindness property and show the security analysis of our scheme. Finally, we utilize the MIRACL Cryptographic SDK [16] to implement our proposed blind signature scheme on a PC (personal computer) and an Android smartphone. The results show that our scheme is suitable for real-world applications.

1.1 Application Case

Anonymous e-Cash: The user first blinds the e-cash and sends it to the e-bank, then the e-bank returns a blinded signature to the user. Upon receiving the blinded signature, the user unblinds it and sends the payment information to the merchandiser server. Finally, the merchandiser sends the goods or receipt to the user.

Privacy Preserving Cryptocurrency Transactions

1. If a user buys some cryptocurrencies (e.g., Bitcoin, Ethereum and Ripple) by using credit card or PayPal directly, the seller can link the blockchain address to the user's real identity. However, if the user utilizes the blind signature

technique to buy cryptocurrency, it can prevent users' privacy from leaking to sellers.
2. Mixcoin server can employ blind signature technique. The user generates a blind signature of the output address. Therefore, the server cannot link the input addresses to the output addresses.

1.2 Our Contributions

To protect the user's privacy, we propose a novel lightweight blind signature scheme based on SM2 signature algorithm, which yields security and efficiency. Especially, the main contributions of this paper are as follows:

1. First, we design an efficient blind signature scheme based on SM2 signature algorithm.
2. Second, we prove that our scheme can satisfy the property of blindness and existential unforgeability.
3. Finally, we implement our scheme on a PC and a smart phone, the experimental performance shows that our scheme is efficient and convenient for many real-world applications.

1.3 Organization

In Sect. 3, we show the notations and describe the respective building blocks (i.e. SM2 signature algorithm, model and the hash functions). In Sect. 4, we present the detailed algorithms of the proposed blind signature scheme. In Sect. 5, we give the security analysis and prove our scheme achieves the blindness property. In Sect. 6, we implement our proposed scheme under MIRACL cryptographic SDK on Android devices and personal computers (PCs) and evaluate its performance. In Sect. 7, we give a variant scheme of the SM2 blind signature. Section 8 concludes this paper.

2 Related Work

Blind signature was first introduced by Chaum [8] in 1982, which a user can have a message signed without revealing its contents to the signer. Then, blind signature became a practical tool in many applications such as electronic cash and anonymous credentials. However, no formal notion of security has been proved, Pointcheval and Stern [17] proposed a provably secure design for blind signatures, and they first showed the definition of security for blind signatures. Then, Juels *et al.* [18] presented the first complexity-based proof of security for blind signatures. They also showed that both the properties of security and blindness can be defined and satisfied simultaneously. Abe [19] proposed a blind signature scheme which can issue a polynomial number of signatures while only needs three data exchanges. Boldyreva [20] proposed a blind signature scheme which is based on Gap Diffie-Hellman (GDH) group, the construction is simple and it is more efficient than most previous works.

Previous work on blind signature [18] is secure in the standard model in stand model, and it is extremely inefficient. Camenisch *et al.* [21] proposed an efficient blind signature scheme without random oracles. Hazay *et al.* [22] also proposed a scheme for blind signatures without random oracles, which is based on standard cryptographic assumptions, and it is the first to be proven secure in a concurrent setting without random oracles. Fischlin [23] built executable blind signatures schemes, each time a signature is generated, the user and the signer only need to transmit one message each, in addition, they also proposed the definition of universally composable blind signature schemes.

In a universally composable (UC) blind signature functionality, the user needs to commit to the message to be blindly signed. Abe and Ohkubo [24] proposed a framework for UC non-committing blind signatures. Because of lattice operations are more efficient and lattice problems remain hard for quantum adversaries, Rückert [9] constructed a lattice-based blind signature scheme, they showed the way to turn Lyubashevsky's identification scheme into a blind signature scheme.

In recent years, many derivative schemes based on blind signatures have also been proposed. In 2000, Lin and Jan proposed the first proxy blind signature scheme [25]. In the proxy blind signature, a user can require the branch to generate proxy blind signature on behalf of the original signer. Some other proxy blind signature schemes [26,27] have also been put forward. In order to predetermine user's public key by his/her uniquely identifier, some identity-based blind signature schemes [11,28] have been proposed. Group blind signature schemes [29,30] also been studied. The group blind signature scheme combines anonymity properties of both group signature and blind signature, protecting both the message and the signer.

Bonneau *et al.* proposed a Bitcoin mixing protocol proposed which provides strong accountability guarantees [7]. However, in the Mixcoin protocol, the mapping from a user's input to output address is visible to the mixing server. By using the blind signature schemes [8,31], Valenta and Rowan modify the Mixcoin protocol to provide guarantees that the input/output address mapping for any user is kept hidden from the mixing server [32].

3 Preliminaries

In this paper, we use κ for the security parameter. For any polynomial p, if the equation $\mu(\kappa) = O(1/p(\kappa))$ holds, we say that the function $\mu(\kappa)$ is negligible. P.P.T denotes a probabilistic-polynomial time algorithm. $\mathcal{R}$ is a finite set, $a \xleftarrow{r} \mathcal{R}$ denotes that a is selected randomly from $\mathcal{R}$. H and h are two secure hash functions, where $H : \{0,1\}^* \rightarrow \{0,1\}^{256}$, and $h : \{0,1\}^* \rightarrow \mathbb{Z}_n^*$.

3.1 Elliptic Curves Cryptography

In recent decades, elliptic curve cryptography (ECC) has been extensively studied. In 1985, Neal Koblitz and Victor Miller independently proposed using elliptic curves to design public-key cryptographic systems. The advantage of ECC is that to achieve the same level of security, ECC requires a smaller parameters include speed (faster computations) and smaller keys and certificates. In addition, the operations on private key (such as signing and decryption) for ECC are more efficient than RSA and discrete logarithm (DL) private key operations. Therefore, these advantages make ECC widely used, especially on some devices with limited computing resources, such as mobile phones and smart cards.

3.2 Review of SM2 Signature Algorithm

The SM2 signature algorithm includes four sub-algorithms of Setup, Key Generation, Signature Generation and Verification, as follows:

1. Setup: Given the security parameter κ, the administrator executes the following steps:
   (a) Generate an elliptic curve $y^2 = x^3 + ax + b$ over $\mathbb{F}_q$, the parameters of the elliptic curve are (q, a, b, n), where n is a prime number.
   (b) Choose $G \in E(\mathbb{F}_q)$ randomly as a generator, where the order of G is n.
   (c) Set the parameters params $= (q, a, b, n, G)$, and output it.
2. Key Generation: Given the parameters params, the user executes the following steps:
   (a) Choose $x \xleftarrow{r} \mathbb{Z}_n^*$ randomly as the private key.
   (b) Compute $Q = xG$ and set Q as the public key.
   (c) Output the key-pair (x, Q).
3. Signature Generation: Given the parameters params, the message m to be signed and the private key x, the signer executes the following steps:
   (a) Compute $Z = H(ENTL||ID||a||b||G||Y)$, where $ENTL$ is the length of signer's ID.
   (b) Compute $e = h(\bar{a})$, where $\bar{a} = Z||m$.
   (c) Choose $k \xleftarrow{r} \mathbb{Z}_n^*$ randomly, then compute $R = k \cdot G = (r_x, r_y)$.
   (d) Compute $r = r_x + e \mod n$, then check the following equations, if $r = 0$ or $r + k = n$, jump to step 3c, otherwise, go to step 3e.
   (e) Compute $s = (1 + x)^{-1} \cdot (k - rx) \mod n$.
   (f) Set the signature $\sigma = (r, s)$, and output it.
4. Verification: Given the parameters params, the public key $Q = xG$, the message m and the corresponding signature σ, the verifier executes the following steps:
   (a) Compute $Z = H(ENTL||ID||a||b||G||Y)$, where $ENTL$ is the length of signer's ID.
   (b) If $r \notin \mathbb{Z}_n^*$, output 0.
   (c) If $s \notin \mathbb{Z}_n^*$, output 0.
   (d) Set $\bar{a} = Z||m$, compute $e = h(\bar{a})$.
   (e) Compute $t = (r + s) \mod n$, if $t = 0$, terminate the algorithm and output 0, otherwise go to step 4f.
   (f) Compute $(r_x, r_y) = sG + tQ$.
   (g) Compute $R = (e + r_x) \mod n$, if $R \neq r$, the signature is invalid, output 0, otherwise output 1.

3.3 Model of Blind Signature

Following the notion of [8] and [18], we give the detailed model of the blind signature and the blindness property in this subsection. As shown in the Fig. 1, a user and a signer are involved in the blind signature architecture. The signer produces the public parameter and sends it to the user. After that, the user blinds the message m (i.e., e-cash and e-vote). At this step, the message m is converted to a blinded one m', while the blinded message m' does not reveal anything of the original message m. The blinded message m' is sent to the signer. Upon receiving m', the signer signs on it and returns a blind signature σ' to the user. Finally, the device unblinds σ' to obtain the valid signature σ of the original message m.

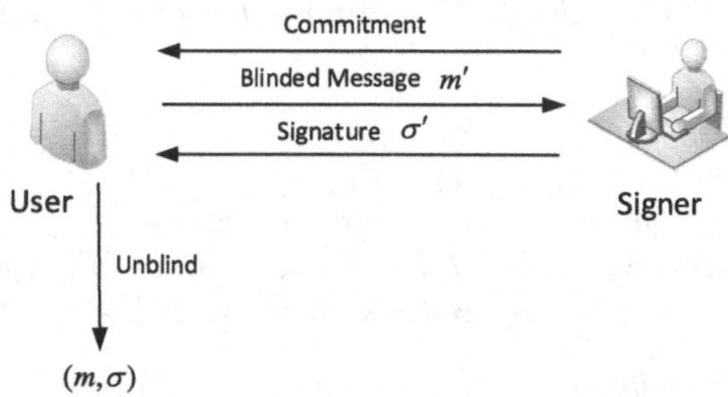

Fig. 1. System model

Definition 1. *Blind Digital Signature: The blind signature scheme consists of the following algorithm: Setup, KeyGen, Blind signature issuing protocol and Verify.*

- Setup: Given the security parameter, the administrator produces the public parameters params, which is published in the system.
- KeyGen: Given the parameters params, the signer generates public-private key pair.
- Blind signature issuing protocol: User and Signer interact with each other. Given params and the message m to be signed, User and Signer engaged in the blind signature generation phase. The generation will cease in a polynomial time. Finally, if the interaction is not completed, Signer outputs not-completed. Otherwise, Signer sends the blind signature to User and outputs completed. After that, User outputs the signature σ of the message m or fail.
- Verify: Given the parameters params, the public key, the original σ, and the message m, the verifier outputs 0 if the signature is invalid. Otherwise, the algorithm outputs 1.

Definition 2. *Blindness Property: Select $b \xleftarrow{r} \{0,1\}$ randomly, where the random number b is kept secret from $\mathcal{A}$, $\mathcal{A}$ is the Signer or a P.P.T algorithm which can control the Signer. $\mathcal{A}$ excutes the following steps with two honest users U_0 and U_1 [8, 18].*

1. $(pk, sk) \leftarrow \mathsf{KeyGen}(1^\kappa)$.
2. $m_0, m_1 \leftarrow \mathcal{A}(1^\kappa, pk, sk)$.
3. $\mathcal{A}$ engages in two parallel interactive protocols, where $\mathcal{A}$ sends m_b to U_0 and m_{1-b} to U_1.
4. If U_0 outputs $\sigma(m_b)$ and U_1 outputs $\sigma(m_{1-b})$, the signature pair $(\sigma(m_b), \sigma(m_{1-b}))$ is given to $\mathcal{A}$, or else, $\perp$ is given to $\mathcal{A}$.
5. $\mathcal{A}$ outputs b', where $b' \in \{0, 1\}$.

If $b' = b$, $\mathcal{A}$ wins the game. In the blind signature scheme, for all P.P.T algorithm $\mathcal{A}$, the maximum probability that $\mathcal{A}$ wins the game is $1/2 + \mu(\kappa)$, where c is a constant.

Definition 3. *Existential Unforgeability under Adaptive Chosen Message Attack: Suppose that there is a challenger $\mathcal{C}$ and an adversary $\mathcal{A}$ playing the following game:*

1. *$\mathcal{C}$ executes KeyGen, then sends pk to $\mathcal{A}$.*
2. *$\mathcal{A}$ sends messages $m_1, m_2, \ldots, m_q$ to $\mathcal{C}$, q is the maximum number of queries. $\mathcal{C}$ replies $\sigma_i = \mathsf{Sign}(m_i, sk)$ to $\mathcal{A}$ for each message.*
3. *Finally, $\mathcal{A}$ outputs and sends the pair (m^*, σ^*) to $\mathcal{C}$. We say the forgery is a valid one, if $m^* \notin m_1, \ldots, m_q$ and $\mathsf{Verify}(m^*, \sigma^*, pk) = 1$.*

If for polynomial bounded q, it is computationally infeasible for $\mathcal{A}$ to output a valid signature, then, the scheme is existentially unforgeable under adaptive chosen message attack (EUF-CMA).

3.4 Collision-Resistant Hash Functions

For any P.P.T adversary $\mathcal{A}$, if the hash function $h : \{0,1\}^* \rightarrow R$ is collision-resistant, then there is a negligible function $\mu(\kappa)$ satisfies that:

$$\Pr[(x, y) \leftarrow \mathcal{A}(1^\kappa, h) : x \neq y, h(x) = h(y)] \leqslant \mu(\kappa).$$

Here, R is the range of the hash function h.

4 The Proposed Blind Signature Scheme

A summary of notations used in our proposed scheme is presented as follows (Table 1).

We show the detailed construction of our proposed scheme in this section. Our proposed scheme consists of the following four algorithms:

1. Setup: Given the security parameter κ, the administrator executes the following steps:
   (a) Generate an elliptic curve $y^2 = x^3 + ax + b$ over $\mathbb{F}_q$, the elliptic curve parameters are (q, a, b, n), where n is a prime number.
   (b) Choose $G \in E(\mathbb{F}_q)$ randomly as a generator, where the order of G is n.
   (c) Set the parameters $\mathsf{params} = (q, a, b, n, G)$ and output params.

Table 1. Notations

Parameter	Meaning
K	Commitment
x	Private key
Q	Public key
α, β	Blind factors
r'	Blinded message
s'	Blinded signature
(r, s)	Original signature

2. Key Generation: Given the parameters params, the Signer executes the following steps:
   (a) Choose $x \xleftarrow{r} \mathbb{Z}_n^*$ randomly as the private key.
   (b) Compute $Q = xG$, set Q as public key.
   (c) Output the key-pair (x, Q).

Signer		User
$k \xleftarrow{r} \mathbb{Z}_n^*$		
Compute $K = kG$		
	$\xrightarrow{K}$	
		$\alpha, \beta \xleftarrow{r} \mathbb{Z}_n^*$
		Compute $K' = \alpha K + \beta G = (r_x, r_y)$
		Compute $r = r_x + e \mod n$
		Compute $r' = \alpha^{-1}(r + \beta)$
	$\xleftarrow{r'}$	
Compute $s' = (1 + x)^{-1}(k - r'x) \mod n$		
	$\xrightarrow{s'}$	
		Compute $s = \alpha \cdot s' + \beta$
		Output (r, s)

Fig. 2. A blind signature scheme.

3. Blind Signature Generation: Given the parameters params and the message m to be signed. User and Signer interact as follows and shown in Fig. 2:
   (a) Committing: The signer selects $k \xleftarrow{r} \mathbb{Z}_n^*$ randomly, computes $K = kG$, then sends K to the user as a commitment.
   (b) Blinding: The user randomly selects two blinding factors $\alpha, \beta \xleftarrow{r} \mathbb{Z}_n^*$, then computes $K' = \alpha K + \beta G = (r_x, r_y)$, $r = r_x + e \mod n$, and $r' = \alpha^{-1}(r + \beta)$, and returns r' to the signer.
   (c) Signing: The signer computes $s' = (1+x)^{-1}(k - r'x) \mod n$, then returns s' to the user.

(d) Unblinding: The user computes $s = \alpha \cdot s' + \beta$, then outputs (r, s) with the corresponding message m.

The unblinded signature is (r, s).

4. Verification: Given the parameters params, the public key Q, and message m with the corresponding signature (r, s). The verifier executes the following steps:
   (a) Compute $Z = H(ENTL||ID||a||b||G||Y)$, where $ENTL$ is the length of signer's ID.
   (b) If $r \notin \mathbb{Z}_n^*$, output 0.
   (c) If $s \notin \mathbb{Z}_n^*$, output 0.
   (d) Set $\bar{a} = Z||m$, compute $e = h(\bar{a})$.
   (e) Compute $t = (r+s) \mod n$, if $t = 0$, terminate the algorithm and output 0, otherwise go to step 4f.
   (f) Compute $(r_x, r_y) = sG + tQ$.
   (g) Compute $R = (e + r_x) \mod n$, if $R \neq r$, the signature is invalid, output 0, otherwise output 1.

In our proposed blind signature generation phase, the User computes $K' = (\alpha \cdot K + \beta \cdot G)$, i.e., $(r_x, r_y) = (\alpha k + \beta)G$. Finally, the User computes the equation that

$$\begin{aligned} s &= \alpha \cdot s' + \beta \\ &= \alpha((1+x)^{-1}(k - r'x) + \beta \\ &= \alpha(1+x)^{-1}(k - \alpha^{-1}(r+\beta)x) + \beta \\ &= (1+x)^{-1}(\alpha k - rx - \beta x) + \beta \\ &= (1+x)^{-1}(\alpha k + \beta - rx) \end{aligned}$$

Compared with the original SM2 signature algorithm, it's obviously to see that $(\alpha k + \beta)$ is same as k in SM2 signature algorithm. Therefore, the blind SM2 signature (r, s) can be verified correctly.

5 Security Analysis

5.1 Mathematical Assumptions

We give the mathematical assumptions in this subsection, which are required in our security proof.

Definition 4. ***Elliptic Curve Discrete Logarithm (DL) Problem:*** *Suppose that $E(\mathbb{F}_q)$ is an elliptic curve over $\mathbb{F}_q$ where $G \in E(\mathbb{F}_q)$. Given a multiple K of G, the elliptic curve DL problem in $E(\mathbb{F}_q)$ is to compute $k \in \mathbb{Z}_n^*$ where $K = kG \in E(\mathbb{F}_q)$. A P.P.T algorithm $\mathcal{A}$ has advantage at least ϵ in solving DL problem in $E(\mathbb{F}_q)$*

$$\Pr\left[\mathcal{A}(G, K) = k : k \in Z_n^*, K = kG\right] \geqslant \epsilon$$

Definition 5. *The elliptic curve DL assumption holds, if no P.P.T algorithm can solve elliptic curve DL problem with a non-negligible advantage.*

5.2 Blindness Property

Theorem 1. *The proposed scheme is blind.*

Proof. Suppose that $\mathcal{A}$ is the Signer or a P.P.T algorithm which can control the Signer. If $\mathcal{A}$ gets $\perp$, then $\mathcal{A}$ wins the game with the probability 0.5, i.e. $\mathcal{A}$ guess b randomly.

$\mathcal{A}$ is assumed to obtain $\sigma_{(m_b)}$ and $\sigma_{(m_{1-b})}$. Let (K_i, s'_i) $(i \in \{0,1\})$ be the data emerging in $\mathcal{A}$'s view during the execution of blind signature generation phase, and (r_0, s_0), (r_1, s_1) are sent to $\mathcal{A}$. Therefore, this is enough to indicate that there are two random factors (α, β) which can map (K_i, s'_i) to (r_j, s_j). We can define that $\alpha = \frac{s_j + r_j}{s'_i + r'_i}$, $\beta = \alpha r'_i - r_j$. We have that:

$$\begin{aligned}
(r_x, r_y) &= s_j G + tQ \\
&= s_j G + r_j Q + s_j Q \\
&= (\alpha(s'_i + r'_i) - r_j)(G + Q) + r_j Q \\
&= \alpha(s'_i + r'_i)(G + Q) - r_j G \\
&= \alpha(s'_i + r'_i)(G + Q) - (\alpha r'_i - \beta)G \\
&= \alpha s'_i(G + Q) + \alpha r'_i Q + \beta G \\
&= \alpha K_i - \alpha r'_i Q + \alpha r'_i Q + \beta G \\
&= \alpha K_i + \beta G
\end{aligned}$$

Therefore,

$$\begin{aligned}
R &= (e + r_x) \mod n \\
&= (e + [\alpha K_i + \beta G]_x) \mod n
\end{aligned}$$

Note that, $[P]_x$ denotes x coordinate of the point P.

5.3 Non-forgeablility

Suppose that there exists a P.P.T adversary $\mathcal{A}$ which may be the user or any other, it holds the system public parameters $\mathsf{params} = (q, a, b, n, G)$. Then $\mathcal{A}$ tries to forge a signature which can pass the verification.

At the beginning, we assume that $\mathcal{A}$ can interact with the signer, therefore K, r' and s' can be viewed by $\mathcal{A}$ in the blind signature generating phase. Since $s' = (1+x)^{-1}(k - r'x) \mod n$. $\mathcal{A}$ knows r'. If $\mathcal{A}$ tries to obtain x from s', he/she must know k. $\mathcal{A}$ knows $K = kG$, it is a DL problem to compute k from K. If DL problem is hard, then $\mathcal{A}$ cannot obtain the private key when he/she interacts with the signer.

Lemma 1. *Assume that h is a uniform and collision-resistant hash function, under adaptively chosen-message attacks in the generic group model, the SM2 signature scheme is existentially unforgeable [33].*

Theorem 2. *If the SM2 signature scheme satisfies EUF-CMA, then our proposed scheme satisfies EUF-CMA.*

Proof. In our proposed scheme, both the signing equation and verifying equation are the same as the SM2 signature scheme. If there exists a P.P.T adversary $\mathcal{A}$ which can produce a signature (r', s') for the given message m, and the forgery can pass the verification algorithm, then for the message m, $\mathcal{A}$ can forge a valid blind signature based on the SM2 signature scheme.

The SM2 signature scheme is EUF-CMA, our proposed blind signature scheme is existentially unforgeable under EUF-CMA attacks.

Remark 1. As mentioned in [34] by Pointcheval and Stern, **one-more signature forgery** is the most powerful attack to the blind signature. However, there are multiple key components in Pointcheval and Stern's scheme, and only one private key is involved in our proposed scheme. Therefore, their theorem cannot be applied to ours.

6 Performance and Experimental Results

In order to implement and analysis the efficiency of our proposed scheme, we utilized the MIRACL Cryptographic SDK. We implement and deploy the proposed scheme on a personal computer (with an AMD Phenom II X6 1100T processor, 16 GB DDR3 RAM and the Microsoft Windows 10 Professional operating system) and a Google Nexus 6 Android phone (with a Qualcomm Snapdragon 805 processor, 3 GB RAM and Android Oreo 8.1.0 operating system). We choose the the elliptic curve in the SM2 algorithm to implement our proposed scheme, that can achieve AES-128 security. In addition, we analyze the run time of each progress in both setup phase and blind signature generation phase.

The experimental results on the PC are shown in Fig. 3. Signer-Step1 denotes the first progress executed by the signer, User-Step1 denotes the first progress executed by the user, after he/she receives the commitment from the signer. Signer-Step2 denotes the progress of blind signature generation which is executed by the signer. User-Step2 denotes the progress of unblinding which is executed by the user. Figure 3 shows the time consuming of each progress in our proposed scheme. Besides, we compared our scheme with the SM2 signature scheme in Table 2. In the Sign algorithm of our proposed scheme, User and the Signer need to interact for three rounds.

The time consuming of each algorithm running on the phone is shown in Fig. 4.

The comparison results of our proposed blind signature scheme and the SM2 signature scheme which are running on the Android phone is shown in Table 3.

We also compared our proposed scheme with He's patent [13]. They use Paillier encryption algorithm to generate an SM2 blind signature. It can be seen from Table 4 that our proposed scheme is far more efficient than [13].

In addition, we evaluate the performance by using the different lengths of messages in both Sign and Verify algorithms. This experiment is running on

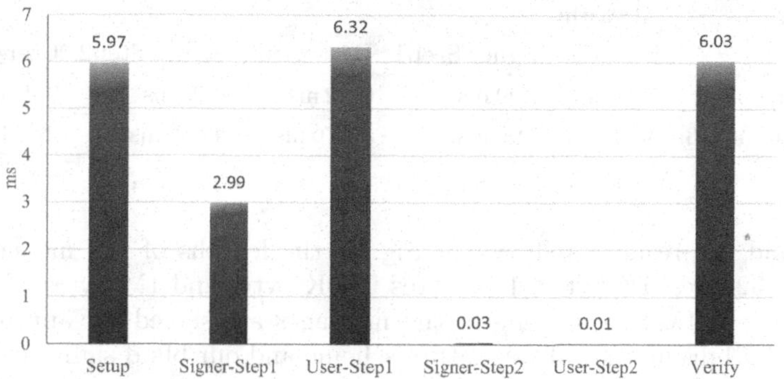

Fig. 3. Time consuming for each algorithm running on PC

Table 2. Running time on PC.

Scheme	Algorithm		
	Setup	Sign	Verify
Original SM2	5.97 ms	3.23 ms	6.03 ms
Blind SM2	5.97 ms	9.35 ms	6.03 ms

Time consuming

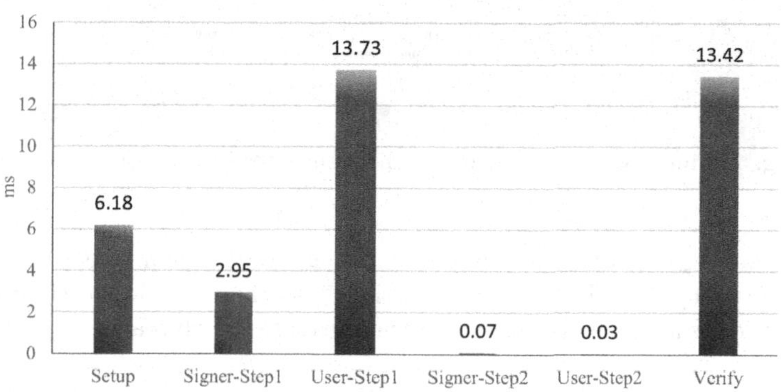

Fig. 4. Time consuming for each algorithm running on phone

Table 3. Running time on phone.

Scheme	Algorithm		
	Setup	Sign	Verify
Original SM2	6.18 s	10.49 ms	13.42 ms
Blind SM2	6.18 ms	16.78 ms	13.42 ms

Table 4. Running time comparison.

Scheme	Algorithm				
	Setup	Signer-Step1	User-Step1	Signer-Step2	User-Step2
Our scheme	5.97 ms	2.99 ms	6.32 ms	0.03 ms	0.01 ms
He's patent [13]	38.38 ms	2.99 ms	31.76 ms	48.87 ms	231.14 ms

the PC and the results is shown in Fig. 5, the lengths of the messages used are 1byte, 32bytes, 1K bytes, 10K bytes, 100K bytes and 1M bytes. Except for the message of 1M-byte in length, the messages are signed for approximately 3.1 ms and 9.1 ms in the SM2 signature scheme and our blind signature scheme, respectively.

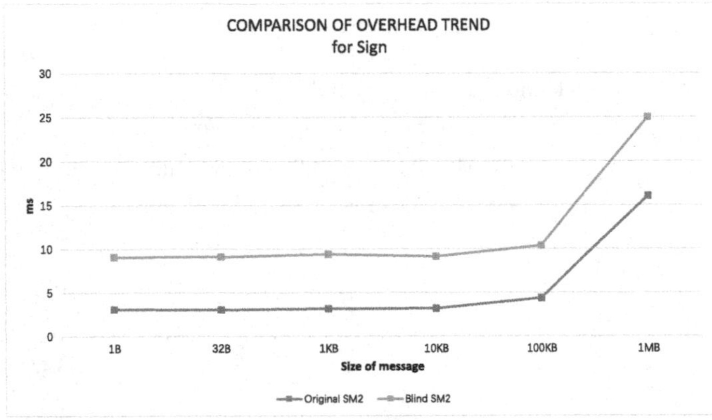

Fig. 5. Time costs for messages of different sizes in the sign algorithm

Since the verification algorithm is same as the original one, we can learn from Fig. 6 that when the message length is less than 1 MB, the time required for verification is about 6 ms, but when the message length reaches 1 MB, it takes 18 ms.

Moreover, we compared our scheme with blind Schnorr signature scheme [35] which was proposed in EUROCRYPT 2020. We implemented the two schemes by using SECP256 curve on a personal computer, the experimental results are show in Fig. 7.

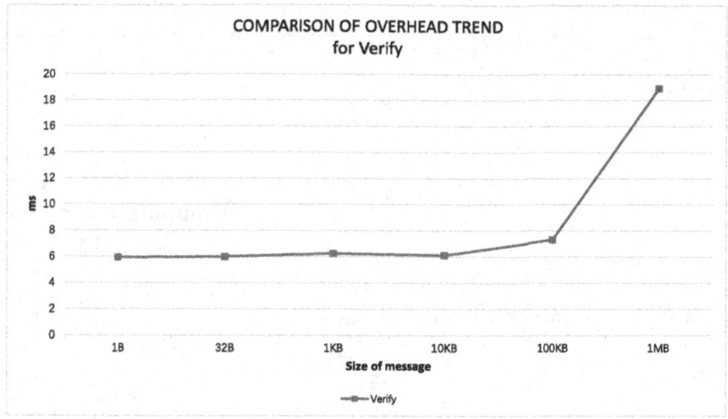

Fig. 6. Time costs for messages of different sizes in the sign algorithm

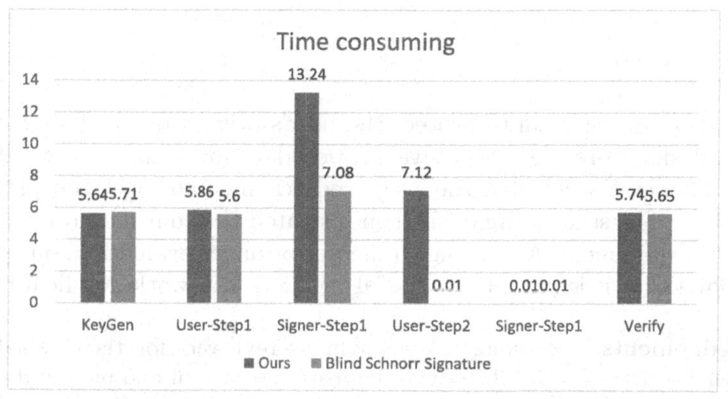

Fig. 7. Comparison between our scheme and [35]

7 Extensions and Discuss

In this section, we slightly change the Blind Signature Generation as follows and shown as in Fig. 8:

1. Committing: The signer selects $k \xleftarrow{r} \mathbb{Z}_n^*$ randomly, computes $K = kG$, then sends K to the user as a commitment.
2. Blinding: The user randomly selects two blinding factors $\alpha, \beta \xleftarrow{r} \mathbb{Z}_n^*$, then computes $K' = \alpha K + \alpha\beta G = (r_x, r_y)$, $r = r_x + e \mod n$, and $r' = \alpha^{-1}r + \beta$, and returns r' to the signer.
3. Signing: The signer computes $s' = (1+x)^{-1}(k - r'x) \mod n$, then returns s' to the user.
4. Unblinding: The user computes $s = \alpha \cdot (s' + \beta)$, then outputs (r, s) with the corresponding message m.

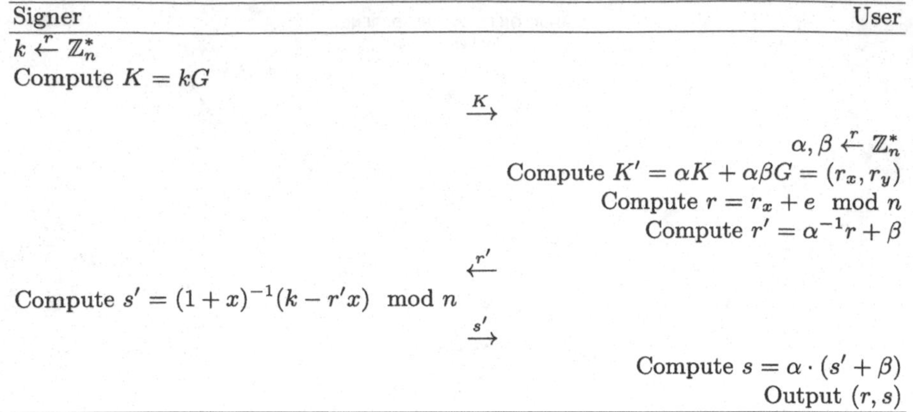

Signer		User
$k \xleftarrow{r} \mathbb{Z}_n^*$		
Compute $K = kG$		
	$\xrightarrow{K}$	
		$\alpha, \beta \xleftarrow{r} \mathbb{Z}_n^*$
		Compute $K' = \alpha K + \alpha\beta G = (r_x, r_y)$
		Compute $r = r_x + e \mod n$
		Compute $r' = \alpha^{-1} r + \beta$
	$\xleftarrow{r'}$	
Compute $s' = (1+x)^{-1}(k - r'x) \mod n$		
	$\xrightarrow{s'}$	
		Compute $s = \alpha \cdot (s' + \beta)$
		Output (r, s)

Fig. 8. The variant SM2 blind signature scheme

8 Conclusion

Blind signature is beneficial to protect the user's privacy on the Internet. Based on the SM2 signature algorithm, we proposed a novel and lightweight blind signature scheme. Specifically, the proposed scheme can meet the property of untraceability. The security analysis demonstrated that our method can achieve the security requirement. According to the performance evaluation, our proposed scheme shows that it is potentially useful in many real-world applications.

Acknowledgements. We thank the anonymous reviewers for their valuable comments and suggestions which helped us to improve the content and presentation of this paper. The work was supported by the National Natural Science Foundation of China (Nos. 61972294, 61932016) and the Opening Project of Guangxi Key Laboratory of Trusted Software (No. kx202001).

References

1. Huang, X., Mu, Y., Susilo, W., Wu, W., Zhou, J., Deng, R.H.: Preserving transparency and accountability in optimistic fair exchange of digital signatures. IEEE Trans. Inf. Forensics Secur. **6**(2), 498–512 (2011)
2. Güneysu, T., Lyubashevsky, V., Pöppelmann, T.: Practical lattice-based cryptography: a signature scheme for embedded systems. In: Prouff, E., Schaumont, P. (eds.) CHES 2012. LNCS, vol. 7428, pp. 530–547. Springer, Heidelberg (2012). https://doi.org/10.1007/978-3-642-33027-8_31
3. Chen, L., Li, J.: Flexible and scalable digital signatures in TPM 2.0. In: Sadeghi, A.-R., Gligor, V.D., Yung, M. (eds.) ACM CCS 2013: 20th Conference on Computer and Communications Security, pp. 37–48. ACM Press, November 2013
4. Huang, Q., Jao, D., Wang, H.J.: Applications of secure electronic voting to automated privacy-preserving troubleshooting. In: Atluri, V., Meadows, C., Juels, A. (eds.) ACM CCS 2005: 12th Conference on Computer and Communications Security, pp. 68–80. ACM Press, November 2005

5. Kremer, S., Ryan, M., Smyth, B.: Election verifiability in electronic voting protocols. In: Gritzalis, D., Preneel, B., Theoharidou, M. (eds.) ESORICS 2010. LNCS, vol. 6345, pp. 389–404. Springer, Heidelberg (2010). https://doi.org/10.1007/978-3-642-15497-3_24
6. Chaidos, P., Cortier, V., Fuchsbauer, G., Galindo, D.: BeleniosRF: a non-interactive receipt-free electronic voting scheme. In: Weippl, E.R., Katzenbeisser, S., Kruegel, C., Myers, A.C., Halevi, S. (eds.) ACM CCS 2016: 23rd Conference on Computer and Communications Security, pp. 1614–1625. ACM Press, October 2016
7. Bonneau, J., Narayanan, A., Miller, A., Clark, J., Kroll, J.A., Felten, E.W.: Mixcoin: anonymity for bitcoin with accountable mixes. In: Christin, N., Safavi-Naini, R. (eds.) FC 2014. LNCS, vol. 8437, pp. 486–504. Springer, Heidelberg (2014). https://doi.org/10.1007/978-3-662-45472-5_31
8. Chaum, D.: Blind signatures for untraceable payments. In: Chaum, D., Rivest, R.L., Sherman, A.T. (eds.) Advances in Cryptology - CRYPTO 1982, pp. 199–203. Plenum Press, New York (1982)
9. Rückert, M.: Lattice-based blind signatures. In: Abe, M. (ed.) ASIACRYPT 2010. LNCS, vol. 6477, pp. 413–430. Springer, Heidelberg (2010). https://doi.org/10.1007/978-3-642-17373-8_24
10. Baldimtsi, F., Lysyanskaya, A.: On the Security of One-Witness Blind Signature Schemes. In: Sako, K., Sarkar, P. (eds.) ASIACRYPT 2013, Part II. LNCS, vol. 8270, pp. 82–99. Springer, Heidelberg (2013). https://doi.org/10.1007/978-3-642-42045-0_5
11. He, D., Chen, J., Zhang, R.: An efficient identity-based blind signature scheme without bilinear pairings. Comput. Electr. Eng. **37**(4), 444–450 (2011)
12. Garg, S., Gupta, D.: Efficient round optimal blind signatures. In: Nguyen, P.Q., Oswald, E. (eds.) EUROCRYPT 2014. LNCS, vol. 8441, pp. 477–495. Springer, Heidelberg (2014). https://doi.org/10.1007/978-3-642-55220-5_27
13. He, D., Zhang, Y., Xie, X., Li, S., Sun, L.: Method and system for generating blind signature, China Patents, 109818730A, 06 March 2019
14. State Cryptography Administration: Public key cryptographic algorithm SM2 based on elliptic curves - part 2: digital signature algorithm (2010). http://www.sca.gov.cn/sca/xwdt/2010-12/17/1002386/files/b791a9f908bb4803875ab6aeeb7b4e03.pdf
15. International Organization for Standardization: ISO/IEC 14888-3:2016/DAmd 1. https://www.iso.org/standard/70631.html. Accessed 2016
16. Miracl: Miracl library (2017). https://www.miracl.com/
17. Pointcheval, D., Stern, J.: Provably secure blind signature schemes. In: Kim, K., Matsumoto, T. (eds.) ASIACRYPT 1996. LNCS, vol. 1163, pp. 252–265. Springer, Heidelberg (1996). https://doi.org/10.1007/BFb0034852
18. Juels, A., Luby, M., Ostrovsky, R.: Security of blind digital signatures. In: Kaliski, B.S. (ed.) CRYPTO 1997. LNCS, vol. 1294, pp. 150–164. Springer, Heidelberg (1997). https://doi.org/10.1007/BFb0052233
19. Abe, M.: A secure three-move blind signature scheme for polynomially many signatures. In: Pfitzmann, B. (ed.) EUROCRYPT 2001. LNCS, vol. 2045, pp. 136–151. Springer, Heidelberg (2001). https://doi.org/10.1007/3-540-44987-6_9
20. Boldyreva, A.: Threshold signatures, multisignatures and blind signatures based on the gap-Diffie-Hellman-group signature scheme. In: Desmedt, Y.G. (ed.) PKC 2003. LNCS, vol. 2567, pp. 31–46. Springer, Heidelberg (2003). https://doi.org/10.1007/3-540-36288-6_3

21. Camenisch, J., Koprowski, M., Warinschi, B.: Efficient blind signatures without random oracles. In: Blundo, C., Cimato, S. (eds.) SCN 2004. LNCS, vol. 3352, pp. 134–148. Springer, Heidelberg (2005). https://doi.org/10.1007/978-3-540-30598-9_10
22. Hazay, C., Katz, J., Koo, C.-Y., Lindell, Y.: Concurrently-secure blind signatures without random oracles or setup assumptions. In: Vadhan, S.P. (ed.) TCC 2007. LNCS, vol. 4392, pp. 323–341. Springer, Heidelberg (2007). https://doi.org/10.1007/978-3-540-70936-7_18
23. Fischlin, M.: Round-optimal composable blind signatures in the common reference string model. In: Dwork, C. (ed.) CRYPTO 2006. LNCS, vol. 4117, pp. 60–77. Springer, Heidelberg (2006). https://doi.org/10.1007/11818175_4
24. Abe, M., Ohkubo, M.: A framework for universally composable non-committing blind signatures. In: Matsui, M. (ed.) ASIACRYPT 2009. LNCS, vol. 5912, pp. 435–450. Springer, Heidelberg (2009). https://doi.org/10.1007/978-3-642-10366-7_26
25. Lin, W., Jan, J.: A security personal learning tools using a proxy blind signature scheme. In: Proceedings of International Conference on Chinese Language Computing, Illinois, USA, pp. 273–277 (2000)
26. Zhang, F., Safavi-Naini, R., Lin, C.-Y.: New proxy signature, proxy blind signature and proxy ring signature schemes from bilinear pairing. Cryptology ePrint Archive, Report 2003/104 (2003). http://eprint.iacr.org/2003/104
27. Awasthi, A.K., Lal, S.: Proxy blind signature scheme. Cryptology ePrint Archive, Report 2003/072 (2003). http://eprint.iacr.org/2003/072
28. Zhang, F., Kim, K.: ID-based blind signature and ring signature from pairings. In: Zheng, Y. (ed.) ASIACRYPT 2002. LNCS, vol. 2501, pp. 533–547. Springer, Heidelberg (2002). https://doi.org/10.1007/3-540-36178-2_33
29. Lysyanskaya, A., Ramzan, Z.: Group blind digital signatures: a scalable solution to electronic cash. In: Hirchfeld, R. (ed.) FC 1998. LNCS, vol. 1465, pp. 184–197. Springer, Heidelberg (1998). https://doi.org/10.1007/BFb0055483
30. Ghadafi, E.: Formalizing group blind signatures and practical constructions without random oracles. In: Boyd, C., Simpson, L. (eds.) ACISP 2013. LNCS, vol. 7959, pp. 330–346. Springer, Heidelberg (2013). https://doi.org/10.1007/978-3-642-39059-3_23
31. Fuchsbauer, G.: Automorphic signatures in bilinear groups and an application to round-optimal blind signatures. Cryptology ePrint Archive, Report 2009/320 (2009). http://eprint.iacr.org/2009/320
32. Valenta, L., Rowan, B.: Blindcoin: blinded, accountable mixes for bitcoin. In: Brenner, M., Christin, N., Johnson, B., Rohloff, K. (eds.) FC 2015. LNCS, vol. 8976, pp. 112–126. Springer, Heidelberg (2015). https://doi.org/10.1007/978-3-662-48051-9_9
33. Zhang, Z., Yang, K., Zhang, J., Chen, C.: Security of the SM2 signature scheme against generalized key substitution attacks. In: Chen, L., Matsuo, S. (eds.) SSR 2015. LNCS, vol. 9497, pp. 140–153. Springer, Cham (2015). https://doi.org/10.1007/978-3-319-27152-1_7
34. Pointcheval, D., Stern, J.: Security arguments for digital signatures and blind signatures. J. Cryptol. **13**(3), 361–396 (2000)
35. Fuchsbauer, G., Plouviez, A., Seurin, Y.: Blind Schnorr signatures and signed ElGamal encryption in the algebraic group model. In: Canteaut, A., Ishai, Y. (eds.) EUROCRYPT 2020. LNCS, vol. 12106, pp. 63–95. Springer, Cham (2020). https://doi.org/10.1007/978-3-030-45724-2_3

A New Efficient Quantum Digital Signature Scheme for Multi-bit Messages

Yukun Wang and Mingqiang Wang(✉)

School of Mathematics, Shandong University, Jinan, China
wangyukun@mail.sdu.edu.cn, wangmingqiang@sdu.edu.cn

Abstract. Quantum digital signatures (QDS) is a cryptography primitive based on quantum mechanics, and has the same role as the classical digital signature. Many novel QDS protocols have been proposed, which can guarantee the information-theoretic security of the signature for a single bit against forging and denying. Recently, T.Y. Wang et al. first proposed a QDS scheme satisfying multi-bit security which based on arbitrary single-bit signature scheme. However, their coding scheme requires $2n + 4$ signature keys to sign a classical n-bit message. In this paper, we propose a more efficient protocol for signing multi-bit message. We need about $1.5n + 7$ signature keys for a n-bit message.

Keywords: Quantum digital signature · High efficiency · Forgery attack

1 Introduction

Digital signature (DS) is a fundamental cryptographic primitive, which can guarantee the non-repudiation, authenticity and transferability of messages. Nevertheless, the security of classical digital signature are based on difficult mathematical problems. With the development of quantum algorithms, these difficult mathematical problems may become easy to solve. Fortunately, Gottesman and Chuang [1] put forward quantum digital signature (QDS), whose security is based on the fundamental principles of quantum mechanics. The early schemes [1–3] require that complex quantum states be prepared in advance, and these states need to be stored in quantum memory, which make these schemes impractical. Then, many new QDS schemes [4–6, 18] without quantum memory are proposed in succession. With the update of quantum technology, some QDS schemes can be implemented on QKD systems [8–15]. The security of signing a single-bit message is unconditionally secure against most existing methods of attack. However, it is not secure to use these schemes directly for multi-bit messages [16] without any preprocessing. A malicious participant can forge a new signature by intercepting part of the legitimate signature. For example, Alice sends a message-signature pair (Don't pay Bob 10$ Sig(Don't) Sig(pay) Sig(Bob) Sig(10$)) to Bob. When Bob receives this message-signature pair, he can get a new valid message-signature pair (Pay bob 10$ Sig(pay) Sig(Bob) Sig(10$)), then sends to

Y. Wu and M. Yung (Eds.): Inscrypt 2020, LNCS 12612, pp. 385–394, 2021.
https://doi.org/10.1007/978-3-030-71852-7_26

Charlie. It is clear that Charlie will accept the signature, which means that Bob successfully forged a valid signature.

Recently, T.Y. Wang et al. [17] has given a solution to the above problems, which is to set a predetermined label for signature and put all the signatures in a sequence. In addition, a special kind of coding of the message is carried out, which makes the truncation attack impossible to implement. However, their scheme requires more than twice as many bits to sign a multi-bit message, which has a great impact on practical efficiency.

Based on the construction framework of [17], we propose a new coding scheme, which increase the efficiency of our scheme by 25% compared with the previous scheme. In our scheme, we encode 0 to 0 and 1 to 01. And then we add a special codeword 11 to the start and 10111 to the end of the codeword sequence. For example, we will encode a message 1010 to 11||01||0||01||0||10111. In T.Y. Wang et al. [17], they encode 0 to 00 and 1 to 01, and add a special codeword 11 at the beginning and end. For example, they will encode a message 1010 to 11|01||00||01||00||11. Obviously, the signature keys needed in [17] for a n bit message are $2n + 4$. But in our scheme, if the message is all 0 bits, then we just need $n + 7$ signature keys for a n bit message which is 50% more efficient than [17]. Generally speaking, the number of 0 bits and 1 bits in the message is roughly the same, and our scheme needs $1.5n + 7$ signature keys, which is 25% more efficient than the previous scheme.

2 An Efficient Scheme

In this section, we give an efficient scheme for signing multi-bit messages which based on the security of signing a single bit. Our proposal includes three stages: the initial stage, the signing state and the verifying stage. There are three parties in our proposal include a signer Alice, a trusted third party (TTP) Joe, who has the ability to judge the validity of signatures and provide a fair judgement in the event of dispute, and several recipients Bod, Charlie, David and so on are also involved in this protocol. Specifically, we will describe our proposal in detail below.

2.1 The Initial Stage

We use $k_i = 0$ or 1 to represent the message bit in the future, $i = 1, 2, 3, \ldots, N$, where the integer N is sufficiently large. For each k_i, Alice generates its signature key S_{k_i} and verification key V_{k_i}. After that, Alice distribute all verification key $\{V_{k_i}\}$, $i = 1, 2, 3, \ldots, N$ to TTP and each recipient. This stage can be completed by any ways in [8–15]. Specially, all signature keys and verification keys should be labeled and sequential, and the signature S_{k_i} is predetermined to sign 0 or 1, which means that if $k_i = 0$, it only can be used to sign bit 0; otherwise, it shall be used to sign bit 1. Besides, the verification key V_{k_i} which TTP and recipient received may be different, which depends on the method used in [8–15]. However each verification key can successfully verify the legitimate signature which generated by the corresponding signature key S_{k_i}. In the following, we no longer distinguish the same kind of verification key and use V_{k_i} to represent it uniformly.

2.2 The Signing Stage

As stated in [17], Alice encodes a message $M = m_1||m_2||\cdots||m_n$, $m_i \in \{0,1\}$, $i = 1,2,\ldots,n$, where $||$ denotes the concatenation between bits, into $\widehat{M}$ using a specific coding rule. For each bit m_i, $i = 1,2,\ldots,n$, if it is 0, Alice encodes it with the codeword 00, otherwise she encodes it with the codeword 01. After that she adds a special codeword 11 to both start and the end of codeword sequence. we use a simple formula to express it as follows:

$$\widehat{M} = 1||1||0||m_1||0||m_2||0||m_3||\cdots||0||m_n||1||1, \tag{1}$$

where n is the length of a classical message in binary. Therefore, the length of $\widehat{M}$ is exactly $2n+4$. Then, she signs $\widehat{M}$ with corresponding signature keys.

In our proposal, we will encodes the bit 0 into 0 and the bit 1 into 01. Furthermore, we add a special codeword 11 to the start and 10111 to the end of the codeword sequence. In this way, the message M is transformed to a bit sequence $\widetilde{M}$. It's easy to see that the length of $\widetilde{M}$ depends on the number of 0 in the message M. Because of our unique coding method, we can't get the exact length of $\widetilde{M}$ as in the scheme above. Without loss of generality, suppose that the length of $\widetilde{M}$ is $n'+7$, $n < n' \leq 2n$, where n is the length of a classical message in binary. The following is the concrete process of our scheme.

1. Bob sends the message M to Alice via a classical authenticated channel.
2. When receiving the message M, Alice encodes it to $\widetilde{M} = \widetilde{m}_1||\widetilde{m}_2||\widetilde{m}_3||\cdots||\widetilde{m}_{n'+2}||\widetilde{m}_{n'+3}||\cdots||\widetilde{m}_{n'+7}$ where $\widetilde{m}_1||\widetilde{m}_2 = 1||1$, $\widetilde{m}_{n'+3}\cdots||\widetilde{m}_{n'+7} = 1||0||1||1||1$ and checks whether the signature keys she had are enough to sign $\widetilde{M}$. If it is not so, she abort.
3. Then Alice chooses $n'+7$ signature keys $S_{k_l+1}, S_{k_l+2}, \ldots, S_{k_l+n'+7}$ in sequence where $k_l + j = \widetilde{m}_j$, $j = 1,2,\ldots,n'+7$. After that, she signs each $\widetilde{m}_j$ with corresponding signature key S_{k_l+j} and the signature of $\widetilde{m}_j$ is denoted as $Sig_{S_{k_l+j}}(\widetilde{m}_j)$. Finally, she sends the message-signature pair $\big(M, Sig(M), l\big)$ to Bob via a classical authenticated channel, where M is the initial message, $l+1$ is the sequence number of the first signature key in the whole, and

$$Sig(M) = Sig_{S_{k_l+1}}(\widetilde{m}_1)||Sig_{S_{k_l+2}}(\widetilde{m}_2)||\cdots||Sig_{S_{k_l+n'+7}}(\widetilde{m}_{n'+7}). \tag{2}$$

4. Bob encodes the message M to $\widetilde{M}$ by the same rule mentioned in 2 when he receives the message-signature pair $\big(M, Sig(M), l\big)$. Then, he checks each signature $Sig_{S_{k_l+j}}(\widetilde{m}_j)$ is legal or not by the corresponding verification key V_{k_l+j}. If every signature $Sig_{S_{k_l+j}}(\widetilde{m}_j)$, $j = 1,2,\ldots,n'+7$ can successfully pass the verification, Bob accepts the message. Otherwise, he rejects it.

2.3 The Verifying Stage

Bob has the right to distribute the received message-signature pair $(M, Sig(M), l)$ to other recipient, such as Charlie, via a classical authenticated channel. Then Charlie can check these message-signature pair by the same way as Bob does in step (4), i.e. if each message-signature pair $(\widetilde{m}_j, Sig_{S_{k_l+j}}(\widetilde{m}_j))(j = 1, 2, \ldots, n'+7)$ matches with the corresponding verification key V_{k_l+j} distributed by Alice in the initial stage, he confirms the legitimacy of message M; otherwise he thinks that the message M does not come from Alice or it has been tampered with.

When any one of the recipient in the protocol has a difference, for example, the singer Alice denies her signature or a recipient doubts the validity of the message-signature pair $(M, Sig(M), l)$, in this case, they send the message-signature pair $(M, Sig(M), l)$ to TTP via a classical authenticated channel. TTP checks the legality of the message-signature pair $(M, Sig(M), l)$ by the same way as Bob does in step (4) of Sect. 2.2 and gives the objective judgement according to the verification results, that means, if the message-signature pair $(M, Sig(M), l)$ pass the verification, he judges the message M come from Alice and $(M, Sig(M), l)$ has not been tampered with; otherwise, he denies that the signature come from Alice.

2.4 Security Analysis

The security of signature includes anti-forgery and undeniable. It has been proved that the signature for a single bit is unconditionally secure in [8–15], that means nobody could forge a valid message-signature pair $(\widetilde{m}_j, Sig_{S_{k_l+j}}(\widetilde{m}_j))$ except with a negligible probability. Obviously, nobody could forge a valid message-signature pair $(M, Sig(M), l)$ by the way of forge a new $(\widetilde{m}'_j, Sig_{S_{k_l+j}}(\widetilde{m}'_j))$ except the signer Alice. On the other hand, the way we construct the protocol creates some new problems. Adversary could recombine the bit-signature pair $(\widetilde{m}_j, Sig_{S_{k_l+j}}(\widetilde{m}_j))$ to forge a valid message-signature pair $(M', Sig(M'), l')$ by using known message-signature pair $(M, Sig(M), l)$. We can prove that an opponent Eve can't form a valid message-signature pair even if he has access to get a lot of valid message-signature pairs $(M_1, Sig(M_1), l_1)$, $(M_2, Sig(M_2), l_2)$, ..., $(M_T, Sig(M_T), l_T)$.

When an opponent Eve wants to forge a message-signature pair, she needs to consider the following three situations. First, the label of verification key for each message bit 0 or 1 is predetermined and sequential, which requires the bit-signature pairs chosen from known message-signature pairs must be also in sequence.

Second, a valid signature

$$Sig(M) = Sig_{S_{k_l+1}}(\widetilde{m}_1)||Sig_{S_{k_l+2}}(\widetilde{m}_2)|| \cdots ||Sig_{S_{k_l+n'+7}}(\widetilde{m}_{n'+7})$$

are tagged with $Sig_{S_{k_l+1}}(1)||Sig_{S_{k_l+2}}(1)$ and $Sig_{S_{k_l+n'+3}}(1)||Sig_{S_{k_l+n'+4}}(0)|| Sig_{S_{k_l+n'+5}}(1)||Sig_{S_{k_l+n'+6}}(1)||Sig_{S_{k_l+n'+7}}(1)$ at the start and the end, i.e., the start of a valid signature $Sig(M)$ must be a signature on the special codeword 11 and the end of a signature must be a signature on the special codeword 10111.

Finally, except the first two and the last five bit signatures in a valid signature $Sig(M)$, all the other bit signatures are consisted of the codewords 0 and 01 in sequence.

In general, if an opponent Eve wants to forge a valid message-signature pair $(M', Sig(M'), l')$ (here the length of the message M' is $\widetilde{n}$) which can pass the verification, she must make the forged signature

$$Sig(M') = Sigs_{k_l'+1}(\widetilde{m}_1')||Sigs_{k_l'+2}(\widetilde{m}_2')||\cdots||Sigs_{k_l'+\widetilde{n}'+7}(\widetilde{m}_{\widetilde{n}'+7}'), \widetilde{n} \leq \widetilde{n}' \leq 2\widetilde{n}$$

satisfy the following three requirements:

1. $\widetilde{m}_1'\widetilde{m}_2' = 11, \widetilde{m}_{\widetilde{n}'+3}'\widetilde{m}_{\widetilde{n}'+4}'\widetilde{m}_{\widetilde{n}'+5}'\widetilde{m}_{\widetilde{n}'+6}'\widetilde{m}_{\widetilde{n}'+7}' = 10111$;
2. $\widetilde{m}_3'\widetilde{m}_4'\cdots\widetilde{m}_{\widetilde{n}'+2}'$ are consisted of the codewords 0 and 01;
3. Each bit-signature pair must pass the verification.

Theorem 1. *It is impossible to forge a valid message-signature pair $(M', Sig(M'), l')$ in our protocol no matter how many valid message-signature pairs $(M_1, Sig(M_1), l_1)$, $(M_2, Sig(M_2), l_2)$, …, $(M_T, Sig(M_T), l_T)$ Eve has access to.*

In order to prove the above theorem, we first prove the following three necessary lemma.

Lemma 1. *Suppose that $C = c_1||c_2||\cdots||c_t, \quad c_i \in \{0, 01\}, i = 1, 2, \ldots, t$, is a bit sequence. then 11 and 10111 $\notin C$.*

Proof. There are only four cases $0||0, 0||01, 01||0, 01||01$ between the concatenation of 0 and 01, which is the basic component of C. Therefore, it is impossible to find a codeword 11 or 10111 in C, no matter how large t is, that is 11 and 10111 $\notin C$.

Lemma 2. *Suppose that $C = 1||1||c_1||c_2||\cdots||c_t||1||0||1||1||1, \quad c_i \in \{0, 01\}, i = 1, 2, \ldots, t$ is a bit sequence, it is impossible to find a sequence $C' = 1||1||c_1'||c_2'||\cdots||c_k'||1||0||1||1||1$ with $c_i' \in \{0, 01\}, i = 1, 2, \ldots, k$ such that $C' \subseteq C$ except $C' = C$. Noted that here all the codewords in C' are in sequence.*

Proof. To find a sequence $C' = 1||1||c_1'||c_2'||\cdots||c_k'||1||0||1||1||1$ with $c_i' \in \{0, 01\}, i = 1, 2, \ldots, k$ such that $C' \subseteq C$, we must find the special codeword 11 and 10111 in the sequence C at first. But, according to Lemma 1, which means that it is impossible to find a codeword sequence $C' = 1||1||c_1'||c_2'||\cdots||c_k'||1||0||1||1||1$ with $c_i' \in \{0, 01\}, i = 1, 2, \ldots, k$ such that $C' \subseteq c_1||c_2||\cdots||c_t$. Besides, the first bit of both the valid codewords 0 and 01 is 0, so we cannot find a new codeword 11 in the sequence $11||c_1||c_2||\cdots||c_t$ except for the primitive codeword 11. When we consider the sequence $c_1||c_2||\cdots||c_t||10111$, if $c_t = 01$ we can find a new codeword 11 in $c_1||c_2||\cdots||01||10111$, but there are no 10111 in this sequence, which means that it is not a valid sequence. Therefore, to find a sequence $C' = 1||1||c'_1||c'_2||\cdots||c'_k||1||0||1||1||1$ with $c'_i \in \{0, 01\}, i = 1, 2, \ldots, k$ such that $C' \subseteq C$, we must choose the first codeword 11 of the sequence C as the start codeword of the sequence C'. Then, the next task is to find codeword 10111 in the sequence $c_1||c_2||\cdots||c_t||1||0||1||1||1$. Through simple analysis, we can see that there is no 10111 in the sequence $c_1||c_2||\cdots||c_t||1||0||1||1||1, c_i \in \{0, 01\}$ except the primitive codeword 10111. Therefore, it is impossible to find a sequence $C' = 1||1||c'_1||c'_2||\cdots||c'_k||1||0||1||1||1$ with $c'_i \in \{0, 01\}, i = 1, 2, \ldots, k$ such that $C' \subseteq C$ except $C' = C$.

Lemma 3. *Suppose that* $C_j = c_1^j||c_2^j||\cdots||c_{n_j}^j, c_1^j = 11, c_{n_j}^j = 10111, c_i^j \in \{0, 01\}, i = 2, 3, \ldots, n_j - 1, j = 1, 2, \ldots, l$, *it is impossible to find a sequence* $C' = c'_1||c'_2||\cdots||c'_{n'}$, *with* $c'_1 = 11, c'_{n'} = 10111, c'_i \in \{0, 01\}, i = 2, 3, \ldots, n' - 1$ *such that* $C' \subseteq C_1||C_2||\cdots||C_l$ *except* $C' = C_j, j = 1, 2, \ldots, l$.

Proof. When $l = 1$, we can reduce Lemma 3 to lemma 2, and the conclusion is obviously right.

When $l = 2$

$$C_1||C_2 = c_1^1||c_2^1||\cdots||c_{n_1-1}^1||c_{n_1}^1||c_1^2||c_2^2||\cdots||c_{n_2-1}^2||c_{n_2}^2.$$

To find a sequence $C' = c'_1||c'_2||\cdots||c'_{n'}$ with $c'_1 = 11, c'_{n'} = 10111, c'_i \in \{0, 01\}, i = 2, 3, \ldots, n' - 1$ such that $C' \subseteq C_1||C_2||\cdots||C_l$, it is necessary to find two new codeword 11 and 10111. By Lemma 2, the new codeword 11 and 10111 can be only found from $c_{n_1-1}^1||c_{n_1}^1||c_1^2$ or $c_{n_2-1}^2||c_{n_2}^2$.

(1) When $c_{n_1-1}^1||c_{n_1}^1||c_1^2 = 0||10111||11$ and $c_{n_2-1}^2||c_{n_2}^2 = 0||10111$, if we choose 11 in the sequence $c_{n_2-1}^2||c_{n_2}^2 = 0||10111$ as the start codeword of the sequence C', there is no end codeword 10111 in the sequence C', so we can only choose new codeword 11 from $c_{n_1-1}^1||c_{n_1}^1||c_1^2 = 0||10111||11$. Nevertheless, if we choose c_1^1 as the start codeword of the sequence C', we can choose $c_{n_1}^1$ as the end codeword, in the case $C' = C_1$; if we choose c_1^1 as the start codeword of the sequence C', we also can choose $c_{n_2}^2$ as the end codeword, i.e., $C' = c'_1||c'_2||\cdots||c'_{n'} = 11||\cdots|||10111||11||101111$, in the case there must exist at least one codeword c'_i such that $c'_i \notin \{0, 01\}$ if we choose the third and fourth bit of $c_{n_1}^1$ as the start codeword of the sequence C', we must choose $c_{n_2}^2$ as the end codeword, i.e., $C' = c'_1||c'_2||\cdots||c'_{n'} = 11||1||11||\cdots|||101111$, in the case there must exist at least one codeword c'_i such that $c'_i \notin \{0, 01\}$; if we choose the fourth and fifth bit of $c_{n_1}^1$ as the start codeword of the sequence C', we must choose $c_{n_2}^2$ as the end codeword, i.e., $C' = c'_1||c'_2||\cdots||c'_{n'} = 11||11||\cdots|||101111$, in the case there must exist at least one codeword c'_i such that $c'_i \notin \{0, 01\}$; if we choose the fifth bit of $c_{n_1}^1$ and the first bit of c_1^2 as the start codeword of the sequence C', we must choose $c_{n_2}^2$ as the end codeword, i.e., $C' = c'_1||c'_2||\cdots||c'_{n'} = 11||1||\cdots|||101111$, in the case there must exist at least one codeword c'_i such that $c'_i \notin \{0, 01\}$; if we choose c_1^2 as the start codeword of the sequence C', we must choose $c_{n_2}^2$ as the end codeword, i.e.,

$C' = C_2$. Therefore, when $c^1_{n_1-1}||c^1_{n_1}||c^2_1 = 0||10111||11$ and $c^2_{n_2-1}||c^2_{n_2} = 0||10111$, it is impossible to find a sequence $C' = c'_1||c'_2||\cdots||c'_{n'}$, with $c'_1 = 11, c'_{n'} = 10111, c'_i \in \{0, 01\}, i = 2, 3, \ldots, n'-1$ such that $C' \subseteq C_1||C_2$ except $C' = C_j, j = 1, 2$.

(2) When $c^1_{n_1-1}||c^1_{n_1}||c^2_1 = 01||10111||11$ and $c^2_{n_2-1}||c^2_{n_2} = 0||10111$, if we choose 11 in the sequence $c^2_{n_2-1}||c^2_{n_2} = 0||10111$ as the start codeword of the sequence C', there is no end codeword 10111 in the sequence C', so we can only choose new codeword 11 from $c^1_{n_1-1}||c^1_{n_1}||c^2_1 = 01||10111||11$. Nevertheless, if we choose c^1_1 as the start codeword of the sequence C', we can choose $c^1_{n_1}$ as the end codeword, in the case $C' = C_1$; if we choose c^1_1 as the start codeword of the sequence C', we can also choose $c^2_{n_2}$ as the end codeword, i.e., $C' = c'_1||c'_2||\cdots||c'_{n'} = 11||\cdots|||10111||11||10111$, in the case there must exist at least one codeword c'_i such that $c'_i \notin \{0, 01\}$ if we choose the last bit of $c^1_{n_1-1}$ and the first bit of $c^1_{n_1}$ as the start codeword of the sequence C', we must choose $c^2_{n_2}$ as the end codeword, i.e., $C' = c'_1||c'_2||\cdots||c'_{n'} = 11||01111||11||\cdots|||10111$, in the case there must exist at least one codeword c'_i such that $c'_i \notin \{0, 01\}$ if we choose the third and fourth bit of $c^1_{n_1}$ as the start codeword of the sequence C', we must choose $c^2_{n_2}$ as the end codeword, i.e., $C' = c'_1||c'_2||\cdots||c'_{n'} = 11||1||11||\cdots|||10111$, in the case there must exist at least one codeword c'_i such that $c'_i \notin \{0, 01\}$; if we choose the fourth and fifth bit of $c^1_{n_1}$ as the start codeword of the sequence C', we must choose $c^2_{n_2}$ as the end codeword, i.e., $C' = c'_1||c'_2||\cdots||c'_{n'} = 11||11||\cdots|||10111$, in the case there must exist at least one codeword c'_i such that $c'_i \notin \{0, 01\}$; if we choose the fifth bit of $c^1_{n_1}$ and the first bit of c^2_1 as the start codeword of the sequence C', we must choose $c^2_{n_2}$ as the end codeword, i.e., $C' = c'_1||c'_2||\cdots||c'_{n'} = 11||1||\cdots|||10111$, in the case there must exist at least one codeword c'_i such that $c'_i \notin \{0, 01\}$; if we choose c^2_1 as the start codeword of the sequence C', we must choose $c^2_{n_2}$ as the end codeword, i.e., $C' = C_2$. Therefore, when $c^1_{n_1-1}||c^1_{n_1}||c^2_1 = 01||10111||11$ and $c^2_{n_2-1}||c^2_{n_2} = 0||10111$, it is impossible to find a sequence $C' = c'_1||c'_2||\cdots||c'_{n'}$, with $c'_1 = 11, c'_{n'} = 10111, c'_i \in \{0, 01\}, i = 2, 3, \ldots, n'-1$ such that $C' \subseteq C_1||C_2$ except $C' = C_j, j = 1, 2$.

(3) When $c^1_{n_1-1}||c^1_{n_1}||c^2_1 = 0||10111||11$ and $c^2_{n_2-1}||c^2_{n_2} = 01||10111$, if we choose 11 in the sequence $c^2_{n_2-1}||c^2_{n_2} = 0||10111$ as the start codeword of the sequence C', there is no end codeword 10111 in the sequence C', so we can only choose new codeword 11 from $c^1_{n_1-1}||c^1_{n_1}||c^2_1 = 0||10111||11$. Nevertheless, if we choose c^1_1 as the start codeword of the sequence C', we can choose $c^1_{n_1}$ as the end codeword, in the case $C' = C_1$; if we choose c^1_1 as the start codeword of the sequence C', we also can choose $c^2_{n_2}$ as the end codeword, i.e., $C' = c'_1||c'_2||\cdots||c'_{n'} = 11||\cdots|||10111||11||101111$, in the case there must exist at least one codeword c'_i such that $c'_i \notin \{0, 01\}$ if we choose the third and fourth bit of $c^1_{n_1}$ as the start codeword of the sequence C', we must choose $c^2_{n_2}$ as the end codeword, i.e., $C' = c'_1||c'_2||\cdots||c'_{n'} = 11||1||11||\cdots|||101111$, in the case there must exist at least one codeword c'_i such that $c'_i \notin \{0, 01\}$; if we choose the fourth and fifth bit of $c^1_{n_1}$ as the start codeword of the sequence C', we must choose

$c^2_{n_2}$ as the end codeword, i.e., $C' = c'_1||c'_2||\cdots||c'_{n'} = 11||11||\cdots|||101111$, in the case there must exist at least one codeword c'_i such that $c'_i \notin \{0, 01\}$; if we choose the fifth bit of $c^1_{n_1}$ and the first bit of c^2_1 as the start codeword of the sequence C', we must choose $c^2_{n_2}$ as the end codeword, i.e., $C' = c'_1||c'_2||\cdots||c'_{n'} = 11||1||\cdots|||101111$, in the case there must exist at least one codeword c'_i such that $c'_i \notin \{0, 01\}$; if we choose c^2_1 as the start codeword of the sequence C', we must choose $c^2_{n_2}$ as the end codeword, i.e., $C' = C_2$. Therefore, when $c^1_{n_1-1}||c^1_{n_1}||c^2_1 = 0||10111||11$ and $c^2_{n_2-1}||c^2_{n_2} = 0||10111$, it is impossible to find a sequence $C' = c'_1||c'_2||\cdots||c'_{n'}$, with $c'_1 = 11, c'_{n'} = 10111, c'_i \in \{0, 01\}, i = 2, 3, \ldots, n'-1$ such that $C' \subseteq C_1||C_2$ except $C' = C_j, j = 1, 2$.

(4) When $c^1_{n_1-1}||c^1_{n_1}||c^2_1 = 01||10111||11$ and $c^2_{n_2-1}||c^2_{n_2} = 01||10111$, if we choose 11 in the sequence $c^2_{n_2-1}||c^2_{n_2} = 01||10111$ as the start codeword of the sequence C', there is no end codeword 10111 in the sequence C', so we can only choose new codeword 11 from $c^1_{n_1-1}||c^1_{n_1}||c^2_1 = 01||10111||11$. Nevertheless, if we choose c^1_1 as the start codeword of the sequence C', we can choose $c^1_{n_1}$ as the end codeword, in the case $C' = C_1$; if we choose c^1_1 as the start codeword of the sequence C', we can also choose $c^2_{n_2}$ as the end codeword, i.e., $C' = c'_1||c'_2||\cdots||c'_{n'} = 11||\cdots|||10111||11||10111$, in the case there must exist at least one codeword c'_i such that $c'_i \notin \{0, 01\}$ if we choose the last bit of $c^1_{n_1-1}$ and the first bit of $c^1_{n_1}$ as the start codeword of the sequence C', we must choose $c^2_{n_2}$ as the end codeword, i.e., $C' = c'_1||c'_2||\cdots||c'_{n'} = 11||01111||11||\cdots|||10111$, in the case there must exist at least one codeword c'_i such that $c'_i \notin \{0, 01\}$ if we choose the third and fourth bit of $c^1_{n_1}$ as the start codeword of the sequence C', we must choose $c^2_{n_2}$ as the end codeword, i.e., $C' = c'_1||c'_2||\cdots||c'_{n'} = 11||1||11||\cdots|||10111$, in the case there must exist at least one codeword c'_i such that $c'_i \notin \{0, 01\}$; if we choose the fourth and fifth bit of $c^1_{n_1}$ as the start codeword of the sequence C', we must choose $c^2_{n_2}$ as the end codeword, i.e., $C' = c'_1||c'_2||\cdots||c'_{n'} = 11||11||\cdots|||10111$, in the case there must exist at least one codeword c'_i such that $c'_i \notin \{0, 01\}$; if we choose the fifth bit of $c^1_{n_1}$ and the first bit of c^2_1 as the start codeword of the sequence C', we must choose $c^2_{n_2}$ as the end codeword, i.e., $C' = c'_1||c'_2||\cdots||c'_{n'} = 11||1||\cdots|||10111$, in the case there must exist at least one codeword c'_i such that $c'_i \notin \{0, 01\}$; if we choose c^2_1 as the start codeword of the sequence C', we must choose $c^2_{n_2}$ as the end codeword, i.e., $C' = C_2$. Therefore, when $c^1_{n_1-1}||c^1_{n_1}||c^2_1 = 01||10111||11$ and $c^2_{n_2-1}||c^2_{n_2} = 0||10111$, it is impossible to find a sequence $C' = c'_1||c'_2||\cdots||c'_{n'}$, with $c'_1 = 11, c'_{n'} = 10111, c'_i \in \{0, 01\}, i = 2, 3, \ldots, n'-1$ such that $C' \subseteq C_1||C_2$ except $C' = C_j, j = 1, 2$.

Therefore, when $l = 2$, the conclusion is also right. Suppose that when $l = n-1$, the conclusion is right, then we consider the case of $l' = n$. Let $C = C_1||C_2||\cdots||C_{l-1}$, assumed by induction method, it is impossible to find a sequence $C' = c'_1||c'_2||\cdots||c'_{n'}$, with $c'_1 = 11, c'_{n'} = 10111, c'_i \in \{0, 01\}, i = 2, 3, \ldots, n'-1$ such that $C' \subseteq C_1||C_2||\cdots||C_{l-1}$ except $C' = C_j, j = 1, 2, \ldots, l-1$. We can see from the above analysis as $l = 2$ that it is impossible to find a sequence $C' = c'_1||c'_2||\cdots||c'_{n'}$, with $c'_1 = 11, c'_{n'} = 10111, c'_i \in \{0, 01\}, i = 2, 3, \ldots, n'-1$ such that $C' \subseteq C||C_l$ except $C' = C_j, j = 1, 2, \ldots, l$.

From Lemma 1, 2 and 3, we can conclude that it is impossible to find a sequence $C' = c'_1||c'_2||\cdots||c'_{n'}$, with $c'_1 = 11, c'_{n'} = 10111, c'_i \in \{0, 01\}, i = 2, 3, \ldots, n'-1$ such that $C' \subseteq C_1||C_2||\cdots||C_l$ except $C' = C_j, j = 1, 2, \ldots, l$, which means that it is impossible to forge a valid message-signature pair $(M', Sig(M'), l')$ no matter how many valid message-signature pairs $(M_1, Sig(M_1), l_1)$, $(M_2, Sig(M_2), l_2)$, ..., $(M_T, Sig(M_T), l_T)$ Eve has access to.

So we can prove that Theorem 1 is true by Lemma 1, Lemma 2, Lemma 3.

Hence, if the single bit signature is unconditionally secure against forging, the protocol we present is also unconditionally secure against forging. Furthermore, there is a TTP in our protocol, which can help the participants to the protocol to verify the validity of the message-signature pairs $(M, Sig(M), l)$ and prevent the denial of a valid message-signature pairs $(M, Sig(M), l)$.

2.5 Efficiency Analysis

In [17], $2n + 4$ signature keys is needed for signing a n bits message. We have improved the encoding of messages so that fewer signature keys are required, which depend on the number of zeros in the message.

Theorem 2. *If there are x $(0 \leq x \leq n)$ 0 bits in a message of length n, then our scheme needs $2n - x + 7$ signature keys.*

Proof. In our scheme, we will encodes the bit 0 into 0 and the bit 1 into 01, so there are $x + 2(n - x) = 2n - x$ codewords for a message of length n with x zeros. Furthermore, we add a special codeword 11 to the start and 10111 to the end of the codeword sequence. So, our scheme needs $2n - x + 7$ signature keys.

3 Conclusion

In this paper, we propose a more efficient proposal for safely singing multi-bit message. Compared with T.Y. Wang et al. [17], which need more than $2n$ signature keys to sign n-bit message, our scheme requires only $n + 7$ to $2n + 7$ signature keys to sign n-bit messages. The number of signature keys we need depends on the number of 0 bits in the message. Specifically, if there are x $(0 \leq x \leq n)$, bits 0 in an n bits message, then $2n - x + 7$ signature keys are required. It is obvious that the more 0 bits in the message, the less signature keys we need, the more efficient our scheme will be. When the message is all bit 0, our scheme has 50% efficiency improvement. Generally speaking, the number of 0,1 bits in a message should be roughly the same, and even so, our scheme still has a big advantage (we just need $1.5n + 7$ signature keys in this case).

Acknowledgements. The authors are supported by National Cryptography Development Fund (Grant No. MMJJ20180210) and National Natural Science Foundation of China (Grant No. 61832012 and No. 61672019).

References

1. Gottesman, D., Chuang, I.: Quantum digital signatures. arXiv:quant-ph/0105032 (2001)
2. Jrn, M.Q.: Quantum pseudosignatures. J. Mod. Opt. **49**, 1269–1276 (2002)
3. Lu, X., Feng, D.G.: Quantum digital signature based on quantum one-way functions. ICACT **1**, 514–517 (2005)
4. Clarke, P.J., Collins, R.J., Dunjko, V., et al.: Experimental demonstration of quantum digital signatures using phase-encoded coherent states of light. Nat. Commun. **3**, 1174 (2012)
5. Dunjko, V., Wallden, P., Andersson, E.: Quantum digital signatures without quantum memory. Phys. Rev. Lett. **112**, 040502 (2014)
6. Wallden, P., Dunjko, V., Kent, A., et al.: Quantum digital signatures with quantum key distribution components. Phys. Rev. A **91**, 042304 (2015)
7. Donaldson, R.J., Collins, R.J., Kleczkowska, K., et al.: Experimental demonstration of kilometer-range quantum digital signatures. Phys. Rev. A **93**(1), 012329 (2016)
8. Collins, R.J., Amiri, R., Fujiwara, M., et al.: Experimental transmission of quantum digital signatures over 90 km of installed optical fiber using a differential phase shift quantum key distribution system. Opt. Lett. **41**(21), 4883–4886 (2016)
9. Yin, H.L., Fu, Y., Liu, H., et al.: Experimental quantum digital signature over 102 km. Phys. Rev. A **95**(3), 032334 (2017)
10. Yin, H.L., Wang, W.L., Tang, Y.L., et al.: Experimental measurement-device-independent quantum digital signatures over a metropolitan network. Phys. Rev. A **95**(4), 042338 (2017)
11. Roberts, G.L., Lucamarini, M., Yuan, Z.L., et al.: Experimental measurement-device-independent quantum digital signatures. Nat. Commun. **8**(1), 1098 (2017)
12. Collins, R.J., Amiri, R., Fujiwara, M., et al.: Experimental demonstration of quantum digital signatures over 43 dB channel loss using differential phase shift quantum key distribution. Sci. Rep. **7**(1), 3235 (2017)
13. Wang, C., Song, X.T., Yin, Z.Q., et al.: Phase-reference-free experiment of measurement-deviceindependent quantum key distribution. Phys. Rev. Lett. **115**(16), 160502 (2015)
14. Yin, H.L., Chen, T.Y., Yu, Z.W., et al.: Measurement-device-independent quantum key distribution over a 404 km optical fiber. Phys. Rev. Lett. **117**(19), 190501 (2016)
15. Wang, C., Yin, Z.Q., Wang, S., Chen, W., Guo, G.C., Han, Z.F.: Measurement-device-independent quantum key distribution robust against environmental disturbances. Optica **4**(9), 1016–1023 (2017)
16. Wang, T.Y., Cai, X.Q., Ren, Y.L., Zhang, R.L.: Security of quantum digital signatures for classical messages. Sci. Rep. **5**, 9231 (2015)
17. Wang, T.-Y., Ma, J.-F., Cai, X.-Q.: The postprocessing of quantum digital signatures. Quantum Inf. Process. **16**(1), 1–10 (2016). https://doi.org/10.1007/s11128-016-1460-3
18. Wang, M.Q., Wang, X., Zhan, T.: An efficient quantum digital signature for classical messages. Quantum Inf. Process. **17**(10), 275 (2018)

Mathematical Fundamental

An Improvement of Multi-exponentiation with Encrypted Bases Argument: Smaller and Faster

Yi Liu[1,2], Qi Wang[1(✉)], and Siu-Ming Yiu[2]

[1] Guangdong Provincial Key Laboratory of Brain-inspired Intelligent Computation, Department of Computer Science and Engineering, Southern University of Science and Technology, Shenzhen 518055, China
liuy7@mail.sustech.edu.cn, wangqi@sustech.edu.cn

[2] Department of Computer Science, The University of Hong Kong, Pokfulam, Hong Kong SAR, China
smyiu@cs.hku.hk

Abstract. A cryptographic primitive, called encryption switching protocol (ESP), has been proposed recently. This two-party protocol enables interactively converting values encrypted under one scheme into another scheme without revealing the plaintexts. Given two additively and multiplicatively homomorphic encryption schemes, parties can now encrypt their data and convert underlying encryption schemes to perform different operations simultaneously. Due to its efficiency, ESP becomes an alternative to fully homomorphic encryption schemes in some privacy-preserving applications.

In this paper, we propose an improvement in ESP. In particular, we consider the multi-exponentiation with encrypted bases argument (MEB) protocol. This protocol is not only the essential component and efficiency bottleneck of ESP, but also has tremendous potential in many applications. For example, it can be used to speed up many intricate cryptographic protocols, such as proof of knowledge of a double logarithm. According to our theoretical analysis and experiments, our proposed MEB protocol has lower communication and computation cost. More precisely, it reduces the communication cost by roughly 29% compared to the original protocol. The computation cost of the verifier is reduced by 19%–42%, depending on the settings of experimental parameters. This improvement is particularly useful for verifiers with weak computing power in some applications. We also provide a formal security proof to confirm the security of the improved MEB protocol.

Keywords: Encryption switching protocols · Paillier encryption · Twin-ciphertext proof · Zero-knowledge

1 Background

Nowadays, data has been widely regarded as a kind of valuable resource. Many solutions have been proposed to preserve the privacy of data during its usage,

Y. Wu and M. Yung (Eds.): Inscrypt 2020, LNCS 12612, pp. 397–414, 2021.
https://doi.org/10.1007/978-3-030-71852-7_27

such as secure multi-party computation (MPC) [9,17,18] and fully homomorphic encryption (FHE) [8]. However, efficiency is still a problem in most cases.

In 2016, Couteau, Peters, and Pointcheval [6] proposed a cryptographic primitive named *encryption switching protocol* (ESP) (for its extension, see [4]), and it was shown that ESP has great potential to achieve many privacy-preserving goals efficiently. In ESP, two parties secretly share the private keys of an additively homomorphic encryption scheme and a multiplicatively homomorphic encryption scheme, such that the two parties can individually encrypt messages, but should cooperate to perform threshold decryption in order to decrypt a ciphertext. Two parties can also work interactively to switch one underlying encryption scheme of a ciphertext to the other without revealing the plaintext. In summary, ESP allows both parties to perform both additions and multiplications on encrypted values to evaluate pre-deterministic circuits securely. It was shown that ESP could be instantiated for generic two-party computation (2PC) protocol [6], and thus ESP is powerful to cover many MPC tasks (see examples in [5]).

To ensure that the encryption switching procedure of ESP is executed correctly in the presence of malicious parties, the authors of [6] introduced a new cryptographic primitive, called *twin-ciphertext proof* (TCP). We call a ciphertext pair $(C_+, C_\times)$ *twin-ciphertext* if the encrypted (or committed) value of the additively homomorphic encryption ciphertext (or commitment) C_+ is equal to the value encrypted in the ciphertext $C_\times$ of multiplicatively homomorphic encryption. In TCP protocol, the prover can *efficiently* prove that a given pair (C_1, C_2) is a twin-ciphertext pair without revealing the encrypted value and corresponding random coins. The main idea of TCP is to generate a random twin-ciphertext pair first, and then show the colinear relation between this random twin-ciphertext pair and the pair (C_1, C_2) to complete the proof. During this approach, the generated random twin-ciphertext pair is consumed. Therefore, to speed up ESP processes, the prover can generate a pool of random twin-ciphertext pairs before executions of ESP and consume them one by one during the ESP executions. We note that this approach is similar to the Beaver triples technique [2].

Although a costly *cut-and-choose* procedure is involved in the generation of random twin-ciphertext pairs, the authors of [6] mentioned that it is possible to batch the executions of TCP. More precisely, by consuming one random twin-ciphertext pair, we are able to prove that some given pairs are all twin-ciphertext pairs simultaneously. This technique can be used to batch the generation of random twin-ciphertext pairs or conduct TCP for many pairs simultaneously. A protocol called *multi-exponentiation with encrypted bases argument* (MEB) is thereby proposed and acts as the underlying basis to batch the executions of TCP. The MEB protocol is designed for additively homomorphic encryption (or commitment) schemes. Informally, given parameters $(\lambda)_{i=1,\ldots,\ell}$ and additively homomorphic encryption ciphertexts $((c_i)_{i=1,\ldots,\ell}, C)$, the MEB protocol allows a prover to prove the knowledge of encrypted values $((m_i)_{i=1,\ldots,\ell}, M)$ and random coins of $((c_i)_{i=1,\ldots,\ell}, C)$, respectively, and the fact that the encrypted value M of C satisfies $M = \prod_{i=1}^{\ell} m_i^{\lambda_i}$, in a zero-knowledge manner. The basic idea of batching TCP executions is to batch the two ciphertexts of all pairs separately in a multi-exponentiation form and execute a TCP for the pair of batched ciphertexts. The MEB protocol is indeed the bottleneck of efficiency for the execution of batch TCP.

TCP, as the direct application of the MEB protocol, is not only the underlying protocol of ESP but also of independent interest. Many commonly used MPC protocols that are expensive in traditional scenarios become very cheap when TCP is involved [6], *e.g.*, proof of knowledge of exponential relation of committed values (for both plain/committed exponent), proof of knowledge of a double logarithm, proof of committed prime, etc. Hence, improvements of the MEB protocol can further enhance the performance of these protocols.

Moreover, MEB can individually play as the underlying protocol of some applications that are typical in commercial and medical areas. For instance, users may wish to evaluate a public function f on an encrypted dataset $(d_i)_{i=1,\ldots,m}$ provided by a data holder, where f is of the form $f = \prod_j (\sum_i a_i d_i)^{\lambda_j}$ with public constant parameters $\{a_1, a_2, \ldots\}$ and $\{\lambda_1, \lambda_2, \ldots\}$. The MEB protocol can thus be used for the data holder to prove the correctness of the encrypted evaluation results without revealing other information of the dataset. Compared with FHE-based solutions, this approach provides a relatively smaller encrypted dataset and is much more efficient for functions with higher depths of multiplication.

In this paper, we provide an improved MEB protocol, in the sense that our protocol is more efficient for both the prover and the verifier, and has lower communication cost than the original MEB protocol in [6]. The same as the original protocol, our MEB protocol is also a public-coin special honest-verifier zero-knowledge (SHVZK) argument of knowledge (see more information in Sect. 2). In general, the argument size of our protocol is roughly 29% smaller than that of the original protocol. Meanwhile, our protocol reduces the computation cost of the verifier by 19%–42% depending on different experimental parameters. The basic idea of our protocol is that we further decompose statements into several conditions and batch them into one proof of a specific relationship to obtain a compact and more efficient protocol (see more details in Sect. 3 and Sect. 4.1).

We summarize the main contributions of this paper in the following.

1. We provide an improvement of the MEB protocol in both argument size and efficiency. To be comparable with the original MEB protocol of [6], we present the construction of our MEB protocol based on Paillier encryption [14]. We remark that MEB protocol for other additively homomorphic schemes, such as Pedersen commitment scheme [15], can be constructed in a similar approach.
2. We provide *proof-of-concept* implementations for both our MEB protocol and the original MEB protocol. We compare the two protocols from the perspectives of theoretical analysis and experiments to verify the improvement of our MEB protocol.

The rest of this paper is organized as follows. In Sect. 2, we introduce some necessary background knowledge. We provide the description of our MEB protocol and the corresponding subprotocols in Sect. 3 and Sect. 4, respectively. Comparisons between our protocol and the original protocol are presented in

Sect. 5 from both theoretical and experimental aspects. We conclude this paper with future work in Sect. 6.

2 Preliminaries

In this paper, we mainly focus on constructing a public-coin SHVZK argument of knowledge and prove its security under standard security definitions (see [12,13] for more information). Note that such a protocol can be compiled to be secure against malicious verifiers with low overhead by many techniques, such as using an equivocal commitment scheme [3] and adopting the Fiat–Shamir heuristic [7].

2.1 Notation

We write $x \leftarrow_\$ S$ for uniformly sampling x from a set S. We use bold letters to represent vectors, *e.g.*, $\boldsymbol{m} = (m_1, \ldots, m_\ell)$ is a vector with ℓ entries. The notation $\boldsymbol{ab}$ denotes the entry-wise product of two vectors $\boldsymbol{a}$ and $\boldsymbol{b}$, *i.e.*, $\boldsymbol{ab} = (a_1 b_1, \ldots, a_\ell b_\ell)$, and the notation $r\boldsymbol{a}$ denotes scalar multiplications, *i.e.*, $r\boldsymbol{a} = (ra_1, \ldots, ra_\ell)$. The notation $||n||$ is used to represent the length of the bit-representation of a given variable n, and the notation $|S|$ denotes the size of a given set S.

We say a function f in variable μ mapping natural numbers to $[0,1]$ is *negligible* if $f(\mu) = \mathcal{O}(\mu^{-c})$ for every constant $c > 0$. We say that $1-f$ is *overwhelming* if f is negligible. In our protocols, we will give a security parameter μ written in unary as input to all parties.

In the following descriptions of protocols, P denotes the prover, and V denotes the verifier.

2.2 Paillier Encryption

Paillier encryption scheme is a public-key additively homomorphic encryption scheme that is semantically secure [10] under the *Decisional Composite Residuosity assumption.* The public key of Paillier encryption scheme is a strong RSA modulus $n = pq$, where p and q are safe primes with the same length. We denote the Paillier encryption algorithm as Enc, and thus encrypting a value m with random coin ρ is represented as $\mathsf{Enc}(m;\rho) = (1+n)^m \rho^n \bmod n^2$. It is easily verified that Paillier encryption scheme is additively homomorphic, such that $\mathsf{Enc}(m_1;\rho_1)\mathsf{Enc}(m_2;\rho_2) = \mathsf{Enc}(m_1+m_2;\rho_1\rho_2)$ and $\mathsf{Enc}(m;\rho)^x = \mathsf{Enc}(xm;\rho^x)$.

2.3 Pedersen Commitment

Pedersen commitment scheme is used as a component of our protocol. Given a strong RSA modulus n, we can expect that there is a reasonably small value $k = \mathcal{O}(\log(n))$, such that $kn+1$ is a prime, and thus find a group $\mathbb{G}$ of order n. Let the commitment key to be $\mathsf{ck} = (g_0, g_1, \ldots, g_\ell, h)$, where $g_0, \ldots, g_\ell, h$ are all generators of $\mathbb{G}$. We denote the Pedersen commitment algorithms for single values as Com_i for $i = 0, \ldots, \ell$. Committing a value m with random coin r by Com_i is via computing $\mathsf{Com}_i(m; r) = g_i^m h^r$. We further denote as Com the general Pedersen commitment for vectors, and committing a vector $\boldsymbol{m}$ with random coin r is to compute $\mathsf{Com}(\boldsymbol{m}; r) = (\prod_{i=1}^{\ell} g_i^{m_i})h^r$. Note that vectors with less than ℓ entries can be committed by setting the remaining entries to 0. In our description here and below, equations of the Pedersen commitment (for both message space and commitment space) implicitly involve modulo operations.

Pedersen commitment is computationally binding under the *discrete logarithm assumption*, such that a non-uniform probabilistic polynomial-time (PPT) adversary cannot find two openings of the same commitment except a negligible probability. The commitment scheme is perfectly hiding, because no matter what value/vector is committed, the commitment is uniformly distributed in $\mathbb{G}$. Clearly, Pedersen commitment scheme is additively homomorphic, such that $\mathsf{Com}(\boldsymbol{m_1}; r_1)\mathsf{Com}(\boldsymbol{m_2}; r_2) = \mathsf{Com}(\boldsymbol{m_1} + \boldsymbol{m_2}; r_1 + r_2)$ and $\mathsf{Com}(\boldsymbol{m}; r)^x = \mathsf{Com}(x\boldsymbol{m}; xr)$.

2.4 The Generalized Schwartz–Zippel Lemma

We will use the following generalized Schwartz–Zippel lemma in this paper.

Lemma 1 (Generalized Schwartz–Zippel). *Let p be a non-zero multivariate polynomial of total degree $d \geq 0$ over a ring $\mathbb{R}$. Let $\mathbb{S} \subseteq \mathbb{R}$ be a finite set with $|\mathbb{S}| \geq d$, such that $\forall a \neq b \in \mathbb{S}$, $a - b \in \mathbb{R}$ is not a zero divisor. Then the probability of $p(x_1, \ldots, x_\ell) = 0$ for randomly chosen $x_1, \ldots, x_\ell \leftarrow_\$ \mathbb{S}$ is at most $\frac{d}{|\mathbb{S}|}$.*

3 Multi-exponentiation with Encrypted Bases Argument

In this section, we give the formal description of MEB protocol, propose the main body of our improved MEB protocol, and prove that our protocol is secure.
Description

- Common Reference String: Pedersen commitment key $\mathsf{ck} = (g_0, g_1, \ldots, g_\ell, h, n)$.
- Word: $\boldsymbol{\lambda} = (\lambda_1, \ldots, \lambda_\ell) \in (\{0,1\}^\kappa)^\ell$, $\ell + 1$ Paillier ciphertexts A and $\boldsymbol{a} = (a_1, \ldots, a_\ell)$. The public key of the Paillier encryption scheme is n, and we denote $\mu = ||n||$. Note that $\ell = \mathcal{O}(\mu^c)$ and $\kappa = \mathcal{O}(\mu^c)$ for a large enough constant c.
- Statement: There are some $(m_i, \rho_i)_{i=1,\ldots,\ell}$ and ρ such that $a_i = \mathsf{Enc}(m_i; \rho_i)$ for all $i = 1, \ldots, \ell$ and $A = \mathsf{Enc}(\prod_{i=1}^{\ell} m_i^{\lambda_i}; \rho)$.
- Witness: ρ, $(m_i, \rho_i)_{i=1,\ldots,\ell}$.

The main idea of this protocol is as follows. First, the prover P provides a list of Pedersen commitments to the verifier V and proves that she knows the openings of commitments, such that each committed value is equal to each encrypted value of $(a_i)_{i=1,\ldots,\ell}$ and A in batches. This approach bridges Paillier encryption and Pedersen commitment schemes. Thus proving the multi-exponentiation relation of these committed values will accordingly impliy the multi-exponentiation relation of encrypted values.

To prove the multi-exponentiation relation of committed values, both parties first can individually write every λ_i as the bit-representation $\lambda_i = \lambda_{i\kappa} \cdots \lambda_{i1}$, and compute the commitment to the vector $\boldsymbol{a_j} = (m_1^{\lambda_{1j}}, \ldots, m_\ell^{\lambda_{\ell j}})$ for $j = 1, \ldots, \kappa$. P then provides V with commitments to vectors

$$\boldsymbol{b_j} = (m_1^{\sum_{\phi=j}^{\kappa} 2^{\phi-j}\lambda_{1\phi}}, \ldots, m_\ell^{\sum_{\phi=j}^{\kappa} 2^{\phi-j}\lambda_{\ell\phi}})$$

and

$$\boldsymbol{c_j} = (m_1^{\sum_{\phi=j}^{\kappa} 2^{\phi-j+1}\lambda_{1\phi}}, \ldots, m_\ell^{\sum_{\phi=j}^{\kappa} 2^{\phi-j+1}\lambda_{\ell\phi}}) .$$

P proves in zero-knowledge that the committed vectors of these given commitments satisfy all equations $\boldsymbol{b_j} = \boldsymbol{a_j}\boldsymbol{c_{j+1}}$ and $\boldsymbol{c_j} = \boldsymbol{b_j}\boldsymbol{b_j}$ in batches. This implicitly indicates that the committed $\boldsymbol{b_1}$ is of the form $\boldsymbol{b_1} = (m_1^{\lambda_1}, \ldots, m_\ell^{\lambda_\ell})$. Finally, P proves to V in zero-knowledge that the product of all entries of the committed $\boldsymbol{b_1}$ is equal to the encrypted value of the Paillier ciphertext A using the corresponding commitment that has been provided in the first step. Following these steps, the statement is proved. The detailed procedure of the protocol is in the following.

Procedure

1. P picks $(r_1, \ldots, r_\ell, r_M) \leftarrow_\$ \mathbb{Z}_n^{\ell+1}$, computes commitments $c_i \leftarrow \mathsf{Com}_i(m_i; r_i)$ for $i = 1, \ldots, \ell$ and $C \leftarrow \mathsf{Com}_0(\prod_{i=1}^{\ell} m_i^{\lambda_i}; r_M)$. Then P sends $(c_i)_{i=1,\ldots,\ell}$ and C to V. V will continue to interact with P if all $c_i \in \mathbb{G}$ and $C \in \mathbb{G}$. Otherwise, V outputs reject.
   Then P proves for each i her knowledge of (m_i, r_i, ρ_i) and the knowledge of $(M = \prod_{i=1}^{\ell} m_i^{\lambda_i}, r_M, \rho)$, such that $c_i = \mathsf{Com}_i(m_i; r_i)$, $a_i = \mathsf{Enc}(m_i; \rho_i)$, $C = \mathsf{Com}_0(M; r_M)$, and $A = \mathsf{Enc}(M; \rho)$, using the batch equality proof introduced in Sect. 4.1. In other words, P proves to V that each committed values of $((c_i)_{i=1,\ldots,\ell}, C)$ is equal to each encrypted values of $((a_i)_{i=1,\ldots,\ell}, A)$.
2. Let $(\lambda_{ij})_{j=1,\ldots,\kappa}$ be the bit decomposition of λ_i, *i.e.*, $\lambda_i = \lambda_{i\kappa} \cdots \lambda_{i1}$. Both parties locally compute general Pedersen commitments

$$c_{a_j} \leftarrow \mathsf{Com}((m_i^{\lambda_{ij}})_{i=1,\ldots,\ell}; \sum_{i=1}^{\ell} \lambda_{ij} r_i)$$

   for $j \in \{1, \ldots, \kappa\}$ from commitments $(c_i)_{i=1,\ldots,\ell}$ via $c_{a_j} = \prod_i c_i^{\lambda_{ij}}$, and set $c_{b_\kappa} \leftarrow c_{a_\kappa}$. We denote the committed vectors of c_{a_j} as $\boldsymbol{a_j} = (m_1^{\lambda_{1j}}, \ldots, m_\ell^{\lambda_{\ell j}})$. P computes for $j \in \{1, \ldots, \kappa - 1\}$

$$c_{b_j} \leftarrow \mathsf{Com}((m_i^{\sum_{\phi=j}^{\kappa} 2^{\phi-j}\lambda_{i\phi}})_{i=1,\ldots,\ell}; r_{b_j})$$

   and for $j \in \{2, \ldots, \kappa\}$

$$c_{c_j} \leftarrow \mathsf{Com}((m_i^{\sum_{\phi=j}^{\kappa} 2^{\phi-j+1}\lambda_{i\phi}})_{i=1,\ldots,\ell}; r_{c_j}) .$$

where all r_{b_j} and r_{c_j} are uniformly sampled from $\mathbb{Z}_n$. We denote the committed vectors of c_{b_j} as $\boldsymbol{b}_j = (m_1^{\sum_{\phi=j}^{\kappa} 2^{\phi-j}\lambda_{1\phi}}, \ldots, m_\ell^{\sum_{\phi=j}^{\kappa} 2^{\phi-j}\lambda_{\ell\phi}})$, and of c_{c_j} as $\boldsymbol{c}_j = (m_1^{\sum_{\phi=j}^{\kappa} 2^{\phi-j+1}\lambda_{1\phi}}, \ldots, m_\ell^{\sum_{\phi=j}^{\kappa} 2^{\phi-j+1}\lambda_{\ell\phi}})$, respectively.
Note that for $j \in \{1, \ldots, \kappa-1\}$,

$$\boldsymbol{b}_j = \boldsymbol{a}_j \boldsymbol{c}_{j+1}\,,$$

and for $j \in \{2, \ldots, \kappa\}$,

$$\boldsymbol{c}_j = \boldsymbol{b}_j \boldsymbol{b}_j\,.$$

P sends $(c_{b_j})_{j=1,\ldots,\kappa-1}$ and $(c_{c_j})_{j=2,\ldots,\kappa}$ to V.

3. If all $c_{b_j} \in \mathbb{G}$ and $c_{c_j} \in \mathbb{G}$, V sends random challenges $x, y \leftarrow_\$ (\mathbb{Z}_n^*)^2$ to P. Otherwise, V outputs reject.
4. Both parties locally compute $c_{a'_j} \leftarrow c_{a_j}^{x^j}$ for $j \in \{1, \ldots, \kappa-1\}$, $c_{b'_j} \leftarrow c_{b_j}^{x^{\kappa+j-2}}$ for $j \in \{2, \ldots, \kappa\}$, $c_d \leftarrow \prod_{j=1}^{\kappa-1} c_{b_j}^{x^j} \prod_{j=2}^{\kappa} c_{c_j}^{x^{\kappa+j-2}}$, and $c_{-1} \leftarrow \mathsf{Com}(-1; 0)$.
Meanwhile, P computes the committed vectors and random coins of $c_{a'_j}$ via $\boldsymbol{a}'_j \leftarrow x^j \boldsymbol{a}_j$ and $r_{a'_j} \leftarrow x^j \sum_{i=1}^{\ell} \lambda_{ij} r_i$, of $c_{b'_j}$ via $\boldsymbol{b}'_j \leftarrow x^{\kappa+j-2} \boldsymbol{b}_j$ and $r_{b'_j} \leftarrow x^{\kappa+j-2} r_{b_j}$, and of c_d via $\boldsymbol{d} \leftarrow \sum_{j=1}^{\kappa-1} x^j \boldsymbol{b}_j + \sum_{j=2}^{\kappa} x^{\kappa+j-2} \boldsymbol{c}_j$ and $r_d \leftarrow \sum_{j=1}^{\kappa-1} x^j r_{b_j} + \sum_{j=2}^{\kappa} x^{\kappa+j-2} r_{c_j}$.
Furthermore, let us define a bilinear operation $*$ for a given variable y as $\boldsymbol{a} * \boldsymbol{b} = \sum_i a_i b_i y^i$.
Then P proves to V the knowledge of $(\boldsymbol{a}'_j, r_{a'_j})_{j=1,\ldots,\kappa-1}$, $(\boldsymbol{b}'_j, r_{b'_j})_{j=2,\ldots,\kappa}$, $(\boldsymbol{c}_j, r_{c_j})_{j=2,\ldots,\kappa}$, $(\boldsymbol{b}_j, r_{b_j})_{j=2,\ldots,\kappa}$, $\boldsymbol{d}, r_d$ such that

$$c_{a'_j} = \mathsf{Com}(\boldsymbol{a}'_j; r_{a'_j})\,, \quad c_{b'_j} = \mathsf{Com}(\boldsymbol{b}'_j; r_{b'_j})\,, \quad c_{c_j} = \mathsf{Com}(\boldsymbol{c}_j; r_{c_j})\,,$$

$$c_{b_j} = \mathsf{Com}(\boldsymbol{b}_j; r_{b_j})\,, \quad c_d = \mathsf{Com}(\boldsymbol{d}; r_d)\,, \quad \sum_{j=1}^{\kappa-1} \boldsymbol{a}'_j * \boldsymbol{c}_{j+1} + \sum_{j=2}^{\kappa} \boldsymbol{b}'_j * \boldsymbol{b}_j - \boldsymbol{1} * \boldsymbol{d} = 0\,.$$

using the zero argument introduced in Sect. 4.2.
5. If the zero argument is rejected, V outputs reject. Otherwise, P proves to V the knowledge of $\boldsymbol{b}_1$, r_{b_1}, $M = \prod_{i=1}^{\ell} m_i^{\lambda_i}$ and r_M, such that

$$c_{b_1} = \mathsf{Com}(\boldsymbol{b}_1; r_{b_1})\,, \quad C = \mathsf{Com}_0(M, r_M)\,, \quad \prod_{i=1}^{\ell} b_{1i} = M$$

using the committed single value product (CSVP) argument introduced in Sect. 4.3.

Theorem 1. *The* MEB *protocol above is a public-coin SHVZK argument of knowledge.*

Proof. The completeness of the protocol first follows from the completeness of the underlying batch equality proof. Then according to the homomorphic property of Pedersen commitment scheme, we can verify that

$$c_{a'_j} = c_{a_j}^{x^j} = \mathsf{Com}((x^j m_i^{\lambda_{ij}})_{i=1,\ldots,\ell}; x^j(\sum_{i=1}^{\ell} \lambda_{ij} r_i)) = \mathsf{Com}(\boldsymbol{a}'_j; r_{\boldsymbol{a}'_j}),$$

$$c_{b'_j} = c_{b_j}^{x^{\kappa+j-2}} = \mathsf{Com}(x^{\kappa+j-2}\boldsymbol{b}_j; x^{\kappa+j-2} r_{\boldsymbol{b}_j}) = \mathsf{Com}(\boldsymbol{b}'_j; r_{\boldsymbol{b}'_j}),$$

and

$$\begin{aligned} c_d &= \prod_{j=1}^{\kappa-1} c_{\boldsymbol{b}_j}^{x^j} \prod_{j=2}^{\kappa} c_{\boldsymbol{c}_j}^{x^{\kappa+j-2}} \\ &= \mathsf{Com}(\sum_{j=1}^{\kappa-1} x^j \boldsymbol{b}_j + \sum_{j=2}^{\kappa} x^{\kappa+j-2} \boldsymbol{c}_j; \sum_{j=1}^{\kappa-1} x^j r_{\boldsymbol{b}_j} + \sum_{j=2}^{\kappa} x^{\kappa+j-2} r_{\boldsymbol{c}_j}) \\ &= \mathsf{Com}(\boldsymbol{d}; r_{\boldsymbol{d}}). \end{aligned}$$

It is easy to verify that $\boldsymbol{b}_j = \boldsymbol{a}_j \boldsymbol{c}_{j+1}$ for $j \in \{1, \ldots, \kappa-1\}$, and $\boldsymbol{c}_j = \boldsymbol{b}_j \boldsymbol{b}_j$ for $j \in \{2, \ldots, \kappa\}$. Thus, we have

$$\begin{aligned} &\sum_{j=1}^{\kappa-1} \boldsymbol{a}'_j \boldsymbol{c}_{j+1} + \sum_{j=2}^{\kappa} \boldsymbol{b}'_j \boldsymbol{b}_j - \boldsymbol{d} \\ &= \sum_{j=1}^{\kappa-1} x^j \boldsymbol{a}_j \boldsymbol{c}_{j+1} + \sum_{j=2}^{\kappa} x^{\kappa+j-2} \boldsymbol{b}_j \boldsymbol{b}_j - \sum_{j=1}^{\kappa-1} x^j \boldsymbol{b}_j - \sum_{j=2}^{\kappa} x^{\kappa+j-2} \boldsymbol{c}_j \\ &= \sum_{j=1}^{\kappa-1} x^j (\boldsymbol{a}_j \boldsymbol{c}_{j+1} - \boldsymbol{b}_j) + \sum_{j=2}^{\kappa} x^{\kappa+j-2} (\boldsymbol{b}_j \boldsymbol{b}_j - \boldsymbol{c}_j) = 0 \end{aligned}$$

Furthermore, given the random y, if $\boldsymbol{ab} = \boldsymbol{c}$, the equation $\boldsymbol{a} * \boldsymbol{b} = \boldsymbol{1} * \boldsymbol{c}$ holds. This shows that

$$\sum_{j=1}^{\kappa-1} \boldsymbol{a}'_j * \boldsymbol{c}_{j+1} + \sum_{j=2}^{\kappa} \boldsymbol{b}'_j * \boldsymbol{b}_j - \boldsymbol{1} * \boldsymbol{d} = 0.$$

Finally, since $b_{1i} = m_i^{\lambda_i}$, the equation $\prod_{i=1}^{\ell} b_{1i} = M$ is always satisfied.

For SHVZK, the simulator $\mathcal{S}$ first picks $(r_1, \ldots, r_\ell, r_M) \leftarrow_\$ \mathbb{Z}_n^{\ell+1}$, computes commitments $c_i \leftarrow \mathsf{Com}_i(0; r_i)$ for $i = 1, \ldots, \ell$ and $C \leftarrow \mathsf{Com}(0; r_M)$. Since Pedersen commitment is prefect hiding, the commitments $(c_i)_{i=1,\ldots,\ell}$ and C have the same distribution as that of the real execution. Then $\mathcal{S}$ runs the SHVZK simulator for the batch equality proof.

Given the challenge x and y, the simulator $\mathcal{S}$ picks $r_{\boldsymbol{b}_j} \leftarrow_\$ \mathbb{Z}_n$ for $j = 1, \ldots, \kappa-1$, and $r_{\boldsymbol{c}_j} \leftarrow \mathbb{Z}_n$ for $j = 2, \ldots, \kappa$, computes commitments $c_{\boldsymbol{b}_j} = \mathsf{Com}(\boldsymbol{0}; r_{\boldsymbol{b}_j})$ and $c_{\boldsymbol{c}_j} = \mathsf{Com}(\boldsymbol{0}; r_{\boldsymbol{c}_j})$, and computes $c_{\boldsymbol{a}_j}$, $c_{\boldsymbol{a}'_j}$, $c_{\boldsymbol{b}'_j}$, $c_{\boldsymbol{d}}$, and c_{-1} as in the real execution. Due to the prefect hiding property of Pedersen commitment scheme, these commitments are perfectly indistinguishable from the real execution. The simulator $\mathcal{S}$ then runs the SHVZK simulators for both the zero argument and the CSVP argument.

Because the distributions of commitments are perfectly indistinguishable from the real execution and the underlying protocols are SHVZK, the simulated transcripts generated by $\mathcal{S}$ are indistinguishable from those of real executions.

Here we show that the protocol is witness-extended emulation. The emulator will run the protocol with a random challenge, and output the resulting transcript. If the argument is rejected, the emulator is done. If the argument is accepted, the emulator will try to extract a witness. The emulator uses witness-extended emulator of the batch equality proof to extract the encrypted values and random coins of Paillier ciphertexts $(a_i)_{i=1,\ldots,\ell}$ and A, and the opening of $(c_i)_{i=1,\ldots,\ell}$ and C that open to the these encrypted values.

Since x and y are randomly choosen, Lemma 1 guarantees that the equation $\sum_{j=1}^{\kappa-1} \boldsymbol{a}'_j * \boldsymbol{c}_{j+1} + \sum_{j=2}^{\kappa} \boldsymbol{b}'_j * \boldsymbol{b}_j - \boldsymbol{1} * \boldsymbol{d} = 0$ holds if $\boldsymbol{b}_j = \boldsymbol{a}_j \boldsymbol{c}_{j+1}$ and $\boldsymbol{c}_j = \boldsymbol{b}_j \boldsymbol{b}_j$, while holds with a negligible probability if there exists one equation that does not hold.

Hence, if the encrypted values of $(a_i)_{i=1,\ldots,\ell}$ and A do not satisfy the statement of MEB, the verifier will output reject with an overwhelming probability based on Lemma 1 and the soundness of the underlying zero argument and CSVP argument. Therefore, the extracted witnesses satisfy the statement with an overwhelming probability, and the soundness of the protocol follows. □

We note that the round complexity of the protocol can be reduced to five rounds. More precisely, the messages sent by the prover in Step 1 and Step 2 could be sent in the same round. Meanwhile, the 3-round batch equality proof and CSVP argument can be executed in parallel from Step 1. In the third round, the batch equality proof and CSVP argument end with the prover answering the challenge messages while the 3-round zero argument protocol starts. Hence the protocol ends in the fifth round, and we obtain a 5-round protocol (see Fig. 1).

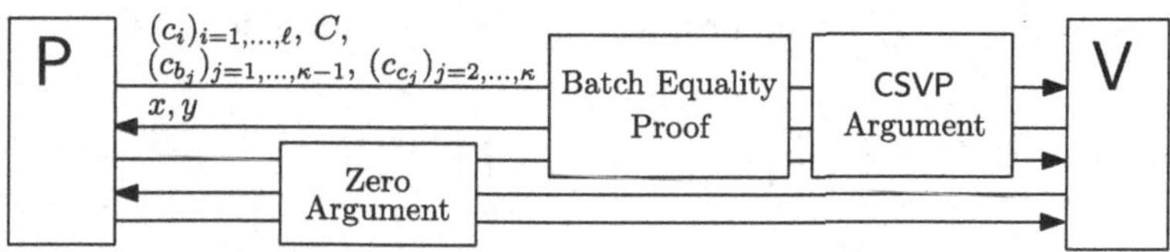

Fig. 1. The procedure of our MEB protocol

4 Subprotocols

In this section, we present the subprotocols mentioned in Sect. 3.

4.1 Batch Equality Proof

Informally, the batch equality proof is for a prover to prove that he knows the encrypted values of a set of Paillier ciphertexts and the openings of a set of Pedersen commitments that can be opened to these encrypted values. We illustrate the batch equality proof in the following.

Description

- Common Reference String: Pedersen commitment key $\mathsf{ck} = (g_0, g_1, \ldots, g_\ell, h, n)$.
- Word: ℓ Pedersen commitments $\boldsymbol{c}$, and ℓ Paillier ciphertexts $\boldsymbol{a}$, where $\ell = \mathcal{O}(\mu^c)$ for a large enough constant c. The public key of the Paillier encryption scheme is n, and we denote $\mu = ||n||$.
- Statement: There exist some $(m_i)_{i=1,\ldots,\ell}$, $(r_i)_{i=1,\ldots,\ell}$, and $(\rho_i)_{i=1,\ldots,\ell}$, such that $c_i = \mathsf{Com}_i(m_i; r_i)$ and $a_i = \mathsf{Enc}(m_i; \rho_i)$ for $i = 1, \ldots, \ell$.
- Witness: $(m_i)_{i=1,\ldots,\ell}$, $(r_i)_{i=1,\ldots,\ell}$, and $(\rho_i)_{i=1,\ldots,\ell}$.

Procedure

1. P picks $\boldsymbol{u} \leftarrow_{\$} (\mathbb{Z}_n)^\ell$, $\boldsymbol{v} \leftarrow_{\$} (\mathbb{Z}_n)^\ell$, $\boldsymbol{w} \leftarrow_{\$} (\mathbb{Z}_n^*)^\ell$, computes $x_i \leftarrow \mathsf{Com}_i(u_i, v_i)$ and $y_i \leftarrow \mathsf{Enc}(u_i; w_i)$ for $i = 1, \ldots, \ell$, and sends $\boldsymbol{x}$, $\boldsymbol{y}$ to V.
2. If all $x_i \in \mathbb{G}$ and $y_i \in \mathbb{Z}_{n^2}^*$, V picks $(d, e) \leftarrow_{\$} (\mathbb{Z}_n^*)^2$, and sends them to P. Otherwise, V outputs reject.
3. P computes $s \leftarrow \sum_{i=1}^{\ell}(v_i+r_i e)d^i \bmod n$, $t_i \leftarrow w_i \rho_i^e \bmod n$, $z_i = u_i + m_i e \bmod n$ for $i = 1, \ldots, \ell$, and sends s, $\boldsymbol{t}$, $\boldsymbol{z}$ to V.
4. V checks whether both $\mathsf{Com}(z_1 d, \ldots, z_\ell d^\ell; s) = \prod_{i=1}^{\ell}(x_i c_i^e)^{d^i}$, $(1+n)^{z_i} t_i^n \equiv y_i a_i^e \bmod n^2$ for $i = 1, \ldots, \ell$ hold and t is relatively prime to n. If all conditions hold, V outputs accept. Otherwise V outputs reject.

Theorem 2. *The batch equality proof above is a public-coin SHVZK proof of knowledge.*

Proof. The completeness of the protocol can be verified as follows.

$$\begin{aligned}\mathsf{Com}(z_1 d, \ldots, z_\ell d^\ell; s) &= \left(\prod_{i=1}^{\ell} g_i^{z_i d^i}\right) h^s = \left(\prod_{i=1}^{\ell} g_i^{(u_i+m_i e)d^i}\right) h^{\sum_{j=1}^{\ell}(v_j+r_j e)d^j} \\ &= \prod_{i=1}^{\ell}(g_i^{u_i d^i} h^{v_i d^i} g_i^{m_i e d^i} h^{r_i e d^i}) = \prod_{i=1}^{\ell}(x_i c_i^e)^{d^i}\end{aligned}$$

$$\begin{aligned}(1+n)^{z_i} t_i^n &\equiv (1+n)^{(u_i+m_i e)}(w_i \rho_i^e)^n \\ &\equiv ((1+n)^{u_i} w_i^n)\,((1+n)^{m_i} \rho_i^n)^e \\ &\equiv y_i a_i^e \bmod n^2\end{aligned}$$

For SHVZK, given e and d, the simulator $\mathcal{S}$ picks $s_i \leftarrow_{\$} \mathbb{Z}_n$, $t_i \leftarrow_{\$} \mathbb{Z}_n^*$, and $z_i \leftarrow_{\$} \mathbb{Z}_n$ for $i = 1, \ldots, \ell$, and computes $s \leftarrow \sum_{i=1}^{\ell} s_i d^i \bmod n$. $\mathcal{S}$ then computes

$x_i \leftarrow g_i^{z_i} h^{s_i} c_i^{-e}$, $y_i \leftarrow (1+n)^{z_i} t_i^n a_i^{-e} \bmod n^2$ for $i = 1, \ldots, \ell$. It is easy to check that the simulated transcript $(\boldsymbol{x}, \boldsymbol{y}, e, d, s, \boldsymbol{t}, \boldsymbol{z})$ is perfectly indistinguishable from the transcript of a real execution.

To prove that the protocol has witness-extended emulation, the emulator runs the protocol with P^*. If the transcript is accepted, it has to extract a witness. We let the emulator rewind the challenge phase to obtain ℓ pairs of accepted transcripts with the same $\boldsymbol{x}$, $\boldsymbol{y}$. Meanwhile, each pair has different random $(d_{(j)})_{j=1,\ldots,\ell}$, and both transcripts in each pair are respectively with different random e and e'. We denote these pairs of accepted transcripts with index $j = 1, \ldots, \ell$ as follows.

$$(\boldsymbol{x}, \boldsymbol{y}, e, d_{(j)}, s_{(j)}, \boldsymbol{t}_{(j)}, \boldsymbol{z}_{(j)}) \qquad (\boldsymbol{x}, \boldsymbol{y}, e', d_{(j)}, s'_{(j)}, \boldsymbol{t}'_{(j)}, \boldsymbol{z}'_{(j)})$$

Note that the witness-extended emulator will make on average 2ℓ arguments, and hence it runs in expected polynomial time.

For each pair of transcripts, we have for $i = 1, \ldots, \ell$ the equations

$$(1+n)^{z_{(j)i}} t_{(j)i}^n \equiv y_i a_i^e \bmod n^2$$

and

$$(1+n)^{z'_{(j)i}} t'^n_{(j)i} \equiv y_i a_i^{e'} \bmod n^2 .$$

Then there should be some $\boldsymbol{m}'$, $\boldsymbol{u}'$, such that

$$z_{(j)i} = u'_i + m'_i e$$

and

$$z'_{(j)i} = u'_i + m'_i e' .$$

The emulator can compute (*e.g.*, via Gaussian Elimination) $\boldsymbol{m}'$ and $\boldsymbol{u}'$, which are encrypted values of $(a_i)_{i=1,\ldots,\ell}$ and $(x_i)_{i=1,\ldots,\ell}$. Due to the fact that Paillier encryption scheme is perfectly binding, the emulator can extract the same $\boldsymbol{m}'$ and $\boldsymbol{u}'$ from every pair of transcripts (and every pair of $(\boldsymbol{z}_{(j)}, \boldsymbol{z}'_{(j)})$ are identical).

Let $\alpha_i \leftarrow a_i(1+n)^{-m'_i} \bmod n^2$. Following the result above, there should be some $\boldsymbol{w}'$ and $\boldsymbol{\rho}'$, such that for $i = 1, \ldots, \ell$,

$$\alpha_i = \rho'^n_i \bmod n^2$$

and for $j = 1, \ldots, \ell$,

$$t^n_{(j)i} \equiv w'_i \rho'^e_i \bmod n^2 , \quad t'^n_{(j)i} \equiv w'_i \rho'^{e'}_i \bmod n^2 .$$

The above first equation indexed by j divided by the second one is equal to

$$(t_{(j)i} t'^{-1}_{(j)i})^n \equiv \rho'^{e-e'}_i \bmod n^2 .$$

Since $e - e'$ is relatively prime to n except a negligible probability, we can find β, γ, such that $n\beta + (e-e')\gamma = 1$. Hence, $\boldsymbol{\rho}'$ can be extracted via

$$\rho'_i = \alpha_i^\beta \left((t_{(j)i} t'^{-1}_{(j)i})^n \right)^\gamma \bmod n^2 ,$$

since we have

$$\alpha_i^\beta \left((t_{(j)i} t'^{-1}_{(j)i})^n \right)^\gamma \equiv \rho_i'^{n\beta} \rho_i'^{(e-e')\gamma} \equiv \rho_i'^{n\beta+(e-e')\gamma} \equiv \rho_i' \bmod n^2 .$$

Therefore, with an overwhelming probability, these (m_i', ρ_i') are the encrypted values and random coins of the ciphertexts $(a_i)_{i=1,\dots,\ell}$.

Now the emulator continues to extract the openings of commitments $(c_i)_{i=1,\dots,\ell}$. There should be some $\boldsymbol{r}'$ and $\boldsymbol{v}'$, such that for $j = 1, \dots, \ell$,

$$c_i = g_i^{m_i'} h^{r_i'} , \quad x_i = g_i^{u_i'} h^{v_i'} .$$

Given a pair of accepted transcripts, we have

$$\mathsf{Com}(z_{(j)1} d_{(j)}, \dots, z_{(j)\ell} d_{(j)}^\ell ; s_{(j)}) = \prod_{i=1}^{\ell} (x_i c_i^e)^{d_{(j)}^i} ,$$

$$\mathsf{Com}(z'_{(j)1} d_{(j)}, \dots, z'_{(j)\ell} d_{(j)}^\ell ; s'_{(j)}) = \prod_{i=1}^{\ell} (x_i c_i^{e'})^{d_{(j)}^i} ,$$

where $\boldsymbol{z}_{(j)} = \boldsymbol{m}' e + \boldsymbol{u}'$ and $\boldsymbol{z}'_{(j)} = \boldsymbol{m}' e' + \boldsymbol{u}'$ according to the prefect binding of Paillier encryption scheme. Thus, it is easy to derive the resulting equations

$$\mathsf{Com}(0, \dots, 0; s_{(j)}) = \prod_{i=1}^{\ell} (x_i c_i^e)^{d^i} g_i^{-z_{(j)1} d_{(j)}^i} = \prod_{i=1}^{\ell} (h^{v_i'} h^{r_i' e})^{d_{(j)}^i}$$

and

$$\mathsf{Com}(0, \dots, 0; s'_{(j)}) = \prod_{i=1}^{\ell} (x_i c_i^{e'})^{d^i} g_i^{-z'_{(j)1} d_{(j)}^i} = \prod_{i=1}^{\ell} (h^{v_i'} h^{r_i' e'})^{d_{(j)}^i} .$$

We can further derive

$$s_{(j)} = \sum_{i=1}^{\ell} (v_i' + r_i' e) d_{(j)}^i \bmod n , \qquad s'_{(j)} = \sum_{i=1}^{\ell} (v_i' + r_i' e') d_{(j)}^i \bmod n .$$

Given ℓ pairs of accepted transcripts, we can easily recover $\boldsymbol{v}'$, $\boldsymbol{r}'$ (*e.g.*, via Gaussian Elimination) with an overwhelming probability. It is easy to verify that these $(m_i', r_i')_{i=1,\dots,\ell}$ and $(u_i', v_i')_{i=1,\dots,\ell}$, are the openings of the commitments $(c_i)_{i=1,\dots,\ell}$ and $(x_i)_{i=1,\dots,\ell}$, respectively.

Hence, the protocol has witness-extended emulation, and the soundness of the protocol follows. □

For the verification step (Step 4), the verifier can pick $f \leftarrow_\$ \mathbb{Z}_n^*$, compute $Z \leftarrow \sum_{i=1}^{\ell} z_i f^i \bmod n$, $T = \prod_{i=1}^{\ell} t_i^{f^i} \bmod n$, and check whether $(1+n)^Z T^n \equiv \prod_{i=1}^{\ell} (y_i a_i^e)^{f^i} \bmod n^2$. If the equation holds, we have $(1+n)^{z_i} t_i^n \equiv y_i a_i^e \bmod n^2$ with an overwhelming probability according to Lemma 1. This could reduce the computation cost of the verification.

4.2 Zero Argument

For completeness, we restate the zero argument introduced in [1] as follows.

Description

- Common Reference String: Pedersen commitment key $\mathsf{ck} = (g_0, g_1, \ldots, g_\ell, h, n)$.
- Word: 2ℓ Pedersen general commitments $(c_{u_i})_{i=1,\ldots,\ell}$, $(c_{v_i})_{i=1,\ldots,\ell}$, a variable y, a bilinear map $*$.
- Statement: There exist some $(\boldsymbol{u_i}, r_{u_i})_{i=1,\ldots,\ell}$, $(\boldsymbol{v_i}, r_{v_i})_{i=1,\ldots,\ell}$, such that $c_{u_i} = \mathsf{Com}(\boldsymbol{u_i}, r_{u_i})$, $c_{v_i} = \mathsf{Com}(\boldsymbol{v_i}, r_{v_i})$ for all $i = 1, \ldots, \ell$, and $\sum_{i=1}^{\ell} \boldsymbol{u_i} * \boldsymbol{v_i} = 0$.
- Witness: $(\boldsymbol{u_i}, r_{u_i})_{i=1,\ldots,\ell}$, $(\boldsymbol{v_i}, r_{v_i})_{i=1,\ldots,\ell}$.

Procedure

1. P picks $(\boldsymbol{u_0}, \boldsymbol{v_{\ell+1}}) \leftarrow_\$ (\mathbb{Z}_n^\ell)^2$, $(r_{u_0}, r_{v_\ell}) \leftarrow_\$ \mathbb{Z}_n^2$, and computes
$$c_{u_0} \leftarrow \mathsf{Com}(\boldsymbol{u_0}; r_{a_0}), \qquad c_{v_{\ell+1}} \leftarrow \mathsf{Com}(\boldsymbol{v_{\ell+1}}; r_{v_{\ell+1}}).$$
Then P computes for $\phi = 0, \ldots, 2\ell$
$$d_\phi \leftarrow \sum_{\substack{0 \leq i \leq \ell, 1 \leq j \leq \ell+1 \\ j=\ell+1-\phi+i}} \boldsymbol{u_i} * \boldsymbol{v_j}.$$
P picks $(r_{d_0}, \ldots, r_{d_{2\ell}}) \leftarrow_\$ \mathbb{Z}_n^{2\ell+1}$, sets $r_{d_{\ell+1}} = 0$, and computes commitments $c_{d_\phi} = \mathsf{Com}_0(d_\phi; r_{d_\phi})$ for $\phi = 0, \ldots, 2\ell$. After the computation, P sends c_{u_0}, $c_{v_{\ell+1}}$, and $(c_{d_\phi})_{\phi=0,\ldots,2\ell}$ to V.
2. V sends $x \leftarrow_\$ \mathbb{Z}_n^*$ to P.
3. P computes
$$\boldsymbol{u} \leftarrow \sum_{i=0}^{\ell} x^i \boldsymbol{u_i} \quad r_u \leftarrow \sum_{i=0}^{\ell} x^i r_{u_i} \quad \boldsymbol{v} \leftarrow \sum_{j=1}^{\ell+1} x^{\ell-j+1} \boldsymbol{v_j} \quad r_v \leftarrow \sum_{j=1}^{\ell+1} x^{\ell+1-j} r_{v_j}$$
$$t \leftarrow \sum_{\phi=0}^{2\ell} x^\phi r_{d_\phi}$$
and sends $\boldsymbol{u}$, r_u, $\boldsymbol{v}$, r_v, t to V.
4. V outputs accept if $c_{u_0} \in \mathbb{G}$, $c_{v_{\ell+1}} \in \mathbb{G}$, $(c_{d_\phi})_{\phi=0,\ldots,2\ell} \in \mathbb{G}^{2\ell+1}$, $c_{d_{\ell+1}} = \mathsf{Com}_0(0; 0)$, $(\boldsymbol{u}, \boldsymbol{v}) \in (\mathbb{Z}_n^\ell)^2$, $(r_u, r_v, t) \in \mathbb{Z}_n^3$, and
$$\prod_{i=0}^{\ell} c_{u_i}^{x^i} = \mathsf{Com}(\boldsymbol{u}; r_u), \quad \prod_{j=1}^{\ell+1} c_{v_j}^{x^{\ell+1-j}} = \mathsf{Com}(\boldsymbol{v}; r_v), \quad \prod_{\phi=0}^{2\ell} c_{d_\phi}^{x^\phi} = \mathsf{Com}_0(\boldsymbol{u} * \boldsymbol{v}; t).$$
Otherwise, V outputs reject.

Theorem 3 ([1]). *The zero argument protocol above is a public-coin SHVZK argument of knowledge.*

4.3 Committed Single Value Product (CSVP) Argument

We restate the committed single value product (CSVP) argument in [11] as follows.

Description

- Common Reference String: Pedersen commitment key $\mathsf{ck} = (g_0, g_1, \ldots, g_\ell, h, n)$.
- Word: A general Pedersen commitment c and a Pedersen commitment C committed by Com_0.
- Statement: There exits some $(\boldsymbol{m}, r)$ and (M, r_M), such that $c = \mathsf{Com}(\boldsymbol{m}; r)$, $C = \mathsf{Com}_0(M; r_M)$, and $M = \prod_{i=1}^{\ell} m_i$.
- Witness: $(\boldsymbol{m}, r)$ and (M, r_M).

Procedure

1. P computes
$$b_1 \leftarrow m_1\,, \quad b_2 \leftarrow m_1 m_2\,, \quad \cdots \quad b_\ell \leftarrow M\,.$$
Then P picks $(d_1, \ldots, d_\ell, r_d, u) \leftarrow_{\$} (\mathbb{Z}_n)^{\ell+2}$, sets $\delta_1 \leftarrow d_1$, $(\delta_2, \ldots, \delta_\ell) \leftarrow_{\$} \mathbb{Z}_n^{\ell-1}$, $(r_\delta, r_\Delta) \leftarrow_{\$} \mathbb{Z}_n^2$, computes
$$c_d \leftarrow \mathsf{Com}(\boldsymbol{d}; r_d)\,, \quad c_\delta \leftarrow \mathsf{Com}(-\delta_1 d_2, \ldots, -\delta_{\ell-1} d_\ell; r_\delta)\,, \quad a \leftarrow \mathsf{Com}_0(\delta_\ell; u)\,,$$
$$c_\Delta \leftarrow \mathsf{Com}(\delta_2 - m_2\delta_1 - b_1 d_2, \ldots, \delta_\ell - m_\ell \delta\ell - 1 - b_{\ell-1} d_\ell; r_\Delta)\,,$$
and sends c_d, c_δ, a, and c_Δ to V.
2. V sends the challenge $x \leftarrow_{\$} \mathbb{Z}_n^*$ to P.
3. P computes
$$m_1' \leftarrow x m_1 + d_1 \quad \cdots, \quad m_\ell' \leftarrow x m_\ell + d_\ell\,, \quad r' \leftarrow x r + r_d\,,$$
$$b_1' \leftarrow x b_1 + \delta_1 \quad \cdots, \quad b_\ell' \leftarrow x b_\ell + \delta_\ell\,, \quad s' \leftarrow x r_\Delta + r_\delta \quad z \leftarrow x r_M + u\,,$$
and sends $m_1', b_1', \ldots, m_\ell', b_\ell', r', s'$, z to V.
4. V outputs accept if all $c_d, c_\delta, c_\Delta \in \mathbb{G}$, $a_1', b_1', \ldots, a_\ell', b_\ell', r', s', z \in \mathbb{Z}_n$ and
$$c^x c_d = \mathsf{Com}(\boldsymbol{m}'; r')\,, \quad c_\Delta^x c_\delta = \mathsf{Com}(x b_2' - b_1' m_2', \ldots, x b_\ell' - b_{\ell-1}' m_n'; s')\,,$$
$$C^x a = \mathsf{Com}_0(b_\ell'; z)\,, \quad b_1' = m_1'\,.$$
Otherwise, V outputs reject.

Theorem 4 ([11]). *The committed single value product (CSVP) argument protocol above is a public-coin SHVZK argument of knowledge.*

5 Evaluation and Comparisons

In this section, we compare our MEB protocol with the original MEB protocol introduced in [6] from both theoretical and experimental aspects. We first analyze the argument size of both protocols and the number of communication rounds required by the protocols. Then, we conduct experiments to compare their running times in different settings of parameters.

5.1 Theoretical Comparison

We denote the length of the bit-representation of the RSA modulus n as μ. Thus, elements in $\mathbb{Z}_n$ and $\mathbb{Z}_n^*$ can be represented by μ bits, and elements in $\mathbb{Z}_{n^2}$ can be represented by 2μ bits. We further denote the length of bit-representation of elements in $\mathbb{G}$ as η, and we can expect that $\eta = \mathcal{O}(\mu)$. The main MEB protocol involves ℓ terms. Table 1 provides the comparison. The argument sizes of subprotocols are calculated according to the parameter settings of the main MEB protocol. For instance, according to Step 1 of the main protocol, the batch equality proof involves $\ell+1$ terms when the main MEB protocol involves ℓ terms.

Table 1. Comparison of argument size and communication rounds

Sub-protocols (Our MEB)	Argument size	Rounds
Batch equality proof	$(4\ell+7)\mu+(\ell+1)\eta$	3
Zero argument	$(2\ell+4)\mu+(4\kappa+1)\eta$	3
CSVP argument	$(2\ell+4)\mu+4\eta$	3
Main MEB argument	$2\mu+(\ell+2\kappa-1)\eta$	5
Overall Comparison:		
Our MEB protocol	$(8\ell+17)\mu+(2\ell+6\kappa+5)\eta$	5
Original MEB protocol [6]	$(12\ell+20)\mu+(2\ell+6\kappa+15)\eta$	5

Table 1 presents the argument size and round complexity of all subprotocols of our protocol together with the overall cost of both our protocol and the original MEB protocol. Both MEB protocols are of 5 rounds, while the size of ours is smaller than that of [6]. Since we can expect that $\eta \approx \mu$, the argument size of our protocol is roughly 29% smaller than that of protocol in [6]. Hence, our protocol has a lower communication cost compared with the original protocol.

5.2 Experimental Results

We provide *proof-of-concept* implementations for both our protocol and the original protocol. The implementations are in `C++` using the `NTL library` [16] for the underlying modular arithmetic. Experiments are carried out on MacBook Air (2018) of macOS 10.15.5 with 1.6 GHz dual-core Intel Core i5, 8 GB of RAM using a single thread. We compare the running times of both protocols using different settings of parameters. Note that the communication cost is given in Sect. 5.1, and we here only measure the running times without the communication time. The results are shown in Table 2.

From Table 2, we can see that our protocol is more efficient for both prover and verifier compared with the original protocol. Our protocol reduces the computation cost of the verifier by 19%–42% depending on different experimental

Table 2. Running time comparison of our MEB protocol and MEB protocol in [6]

μ	ℓ	t	Original MEB protocol [6]			Our MEB protocol		
			Prover	Verifier	Total time	Prover	Verifier	Total time
1024	128	8	1.749 s	0.776 s	2.525 s	1.583 s	0.480 s	2.063 s
1024	256	16	6.272 s	1.787 s	8.059 s	6.112 s	1.453 s	7.565 s
2048	128	8	11.275 s	4.884 s	16.159 s	10.273 s	2.851 s	13.124 s
2048	256	16	38.102 s	11.250 s	49.352 s	36.410 s	8.647 s	45.057 s
2048	512	8	44.506 s	19.507 s	64.013 s	41.636 s	15.824 s	57.460 s

parameters. Especially when $\mu = 2048$, $\ell = 128$ and $t = 8$, the execution time of the verifier in our protocol is 58% of that of the verifier in [6]. Therefore, our protocol saves more computation cost compared with the original protocol. We emphasize that the computation cost of the verifier is critical for many applications. One example is the computation on encrypted datasets as we have mentioned in Sect. 1. In this example, different from the data holder who may serve multiple users and have more computational power, users may use a device with much weaker computational capability. Hence, our improvement in the efficiency of the verifier is significant for this kind of applications.

6 Conclusions and Future Work

In this paper, we provide an improvement of the MEB protocol in both argument size and efficiency. We prove the security of our protocol and demonstrate our improvement from both theoretical and experimental aspects. Since MEB is the bottleneck for batching the executions of TCP and has advantages to be adopted in some applications as mentioned in Sect. 1, our improvement is significant for ESP, TCP-based protocols, and other applications.

Based on our results, future work could be carried out in two main directions. One direction is to further improve the MEB protocol in both communication cost and efficiency. Since we only provide a *proof-of-concept* implementation with *single-thread*, the other direction is to optimize the implementation of the protocol, which may further improve the performance of related cryptographic primitives and protocols.

Acknowledgments. Y. Liu and Q. Wang were partially supported by the National Science Foundation of China under Grant No. 61672015 and Guangdong Provincial Key Laboratory (Grant No. 2020B121201001). Y. Liu and S.-M. Yiu were also partially supported by ITF, Hong Kong (ITS/173/18FP).

References

1. Bayer, S., Groth, J.: Efficient zero-knowledge argument for correctness of a shuffle. In: Pointcheval, D., Johansson, T. (eds.) EUROCRYPT 2012. LNCS, vol. 7237, pp. 263–280. Springer, Heidelberg (2012). https://doi.org/10.1007/978-3-642-29011-4_17
2. Beaver, D.: Precomputing oblivious transfer. In: Coppersmith, D. (ed.) CRYPTO 1995. LNCS, vol. 963, pp. 97–109. Springer, Heidelberg (1995). https://doi.org/10.1007/3-540-44750-4_8
3. Beaver, D.: Adaptive zero knowledge and computational equivocation (extended abstract). In: Miller, G.L. (ed.) Proceedings of the Twenty-Eighth Annual ACM Symposium on the Theory of Computing, Philadelphia, Pennsylvania, USA, 22–24 May 1996, pp. 629–638. ACM (1996)
4. Castagnos, G., Imbert, L., Laguillaumie, F.: Encryption switching protocols revisited: switching modulo p. In: Katz, J., Shacham, H. (eds.) CRYPTO 2017. LNCS, vol. 10401, pp. 255–287. Springer, Cham (2017). https://doi.org/10.1007/978-3-319-63688-7_9
5. Couteau, G., Peters, T., Pointcheval, D.: Secure distributed computation on private inputs. In: Garcia-Alfaro, J., Kranakis, E., Bonfante, G. (eds.) FPS 2015. LNCS, vol. 9482, pp. 14–26. Springer, Cham (2016). https://doi.org/10.1007/978-3-319-30303-1_2
6. Couteau, G., Peters, T., Pointcheval, D.: Encryption switching protocols. In: Robshaw, M., Katz, J. (eds.) CRYPTO 2016. LNCS, vol. 9814, pp. 308–338. Springer, Heidelberg (2016). https://doi.org/10.1007/978-3-662-53018-4_12
7. Fiat, A., Shamir, A.: How to prove yourself: practical solutions to identification and signature problems. In: Odlyzko, A.M. (ed.) CRYPTO 1986. LNCS, vol. 263, pp. 186–194. Springer, Heidelberg (1987). https://doi.org/10.1007/3-540-47721-7_12
8. Gentry, C.: Fully homomorphic encryption using ideal lattices. In: Mitzenmacher, M. (ed.) Proceedings of the 41st Annual ACM Symposium on Theory of Computing, STOC 2009, Bethesda, MD, USA, 31 May–2 June 2009, pp. 169–178. ACM (2009)
9. Goldreich, O., Micali, S., Wigderson, A.: How to play any mental game or A completeness theorem for protocols with honest majority. In: Aho, A.V. (ed.) Proceedings of the 19th Annual ACM Symposium on Theory of Computing, 1987, New York, New York, USA, pp. 218–229. ACM (1987)
10. Goldwasser, S., Micali, S.: Probabilistic encryption. J. Comput. Syst. Sci. **28**(2), 270–299 (1984)
11. Groth, J.: A verifiable secret shuffle of homomorphic encryptions. J. Cryptology **23**(4), 546–579 (2010)
12. Hazay, C., Lindell, Y.: Efficient Secure Two-Party Protocols. ISC. Springer, Heidelberg (2010). https://doi.org/10.1007/978-3-642-14303-8
13. Lindell, Y.: Parallel coin-tossing and constant-round secure two-party computation. J. Cryptology **16**(3), 143–184 (2003)
14. Paillier, P.: Public-key cryptosystems based on composite degree residuosity classes. In: Stern, J. (ed.) EUROCRYPT 1999. LNCS, vol. 1592, pp. 223–238. Springer, Heidelberg (1999). https://doi.org/10.1007/3-540-48910-X_16
15. Pedersen, T.P.: Non-interactive and information-theoretic secure verifiable secret sharing. In: Feigenbaum, J. (ed.) CRYPTO 1991. LNCS, vol. 576, pp. 129–140. Springer, Heidelberg (1992). https://doi.org/10.1007/3-540-46766-1_9
16. Shoup, V.: Ntl: A library for doing number theory. http://www.shoup.net/ntl

17. Yao, A.C.: Protocols for secure computations (extended abstract). In: 23rd Annual Symposium on Foundations of Computer Science, Chicago, Illinois, USA, 3–5 November 1982, pp. 160–164. IEEE Computer Society (1982)
18. Yao, A.C.: How to generate and exchange secrets (extended abstract). In: 27th Annual Symposium on Foundations of Computer Science, Toronto, Canada, 27–29 October 1986. pp. 162–167. IEEE Computer Society (1986)

Number Theoretic Transform: Generalization, Optimization, Concrete Analysis and Applications

Zhichuang Liang[1,3], Shiyu Shen[1], Yuantao Shi[2], Dongni Sun[1], Chongxuan Zhang[2], Guoyun Zhang[2], Yunlei Zhao[1(✉)], and Zhixiang Zhao[4]

[1] School of Computer Science, Fudan University, Shanghai, China
{zcliang19,syshen19,dnsun19,ylzhao}@fudan.edu.cn

[2] School of Mathematical Sciences, Fudan University, Shanghai, China
{shiyt17,cxzhang17,gyzhang17}@fudan.edu.cn

[3] State Key Laboratory of Integrated Services Networks, Xidian University, Xi'an, China

[4] Department of Applied Mathematics, Reading Academy, Nanjing University of Information Science and Technology, Nanjing, China
zhaozhixiang12@126.com

Abstract. Number theoretic transform (NTT) is a basic mathematic operation, and is particularly fundamental to the practical implementations of cryptographic algorithms based on lattices with algebraic structures. In this work, we make a systematic and comprehensive study of NTT and its variants. We first review the NTT technique and the recent advances raised in the implementations of practical lattice-based cryptography. We clarify the relationship of some existing NTT variants, and prove their computational equivalence. We then make the generalizations of NTT, analyze their exact computational complexity, and derive the optimal bounds. Finally, we show the applications of our results to some prominent practical lattice-based algorithms.

Keywords: Number theoretic transform · Practical post-quantum security · Lattice · Key encapsulation mechanism · Applied cryptography · Implementations of cryptosystems

1 Introduction

Multiplications of big integers or polynomials are basic mathematic operations, and are particularly fundamental for practical lattice-based post-quantum cryptography. Most public-key cryptosystems currently in use, based on the hardness of solving (elliptic curve) discrete logarithm or factoring large integers, will

This work is supported in part by National Key Research and Development Program of China under Grant No. 2017YFB0802000, National Natural Science Foundation of China under Grant Nos. 61472084 and U1536205, Shanghai Innovation Action Project under Grant No. 16DZ1100200, Shanghai Science and Technology Development Funds under Grant No. 16JC1400801, and Shandong Provincial Key Research and Development Program of China under Grant Nos. 2017CXGC0701 and 2018CXGC0701.

Y. Wu and M. Yung (Eds.): Inscrypt 2020, LNCS 12612, pp. 415–432, 2021.
https://doi.org/10.1007/978-3-030-71852-7_28

be broken, if large-scale quantum computers are ever built. These cryptosystems are used to implement digital signatures and key establishment, and play a crucial role in ensuring the confidentiality and authenticity of communications on the Internet and other networks. The arrival of such quantum computers is now believed by many scientists to be merely a significant engineering challenge, and is estimated to be within the next two decades or so. Due to this concern, post-quantum cryptography (PQC) was intensively investigated in recent years. It also drove NIST to launch the PQC standardization competition since November 2017. Recently, NIST announced seven finalist algorithms for the third-round competition, in which five algorithms are based on lattices with algebraic structures.

For cryptographic algorithms based on lattices with algebraic structures like the ideal or module lattices, one fundamental and also time-consuming operation is the multiplication of the elements in the polynomial quotient ring $\mathbb{Z}_q[x]/(\Phi(x))$ where $\Phi(x)$ is a cyclotomic polynomial of degree n. Typically, $\Phi(x) = x^n+1$ where n is a power of 2. There are two main approaches to fast polynomial multiplications in this setting: number theoretic transform (NTT) [5,7], and Toom-Cook and Karatsuba based polynomial multiplication methods [6,10,13]. Generally speaking, NTT is the most efficient multiplication method over rings, due to its quasilinear ($O(n \log n)$) time complexity. But the traditional NTT technique puts some restrictions on the modulus and dimension of the underlying ring. On the other hand, Toom-Cook and Karatsuba based polynomial multiplication methods are relatively less efficient in general, but have a wider scope of application parameters. For the five lattice-based algorithms in the third round of NIST PQC standardization, four algorithms use the NTT technique, and only the Saber algorithm [8] uses Toom-Cook and Karatsuba multiplication. Specifically, Saber is based on the *module learning with rounding* (MLWR) problem, and its provable security does not allow to set NTT-friendly parameters.

In this work, we focus on making a systematic study of the NTT technique, and its applications to practical post-quantum cryptography. NTT is a special case of fast Fourier transform (FFT). The origin of FFT can in turn be traced back to discrete Fourier transform (DFT), the idea of which was first developed by Carl Friedrich Gauss in his unpublished work in 1805 [9]. The traditional form of NTT has two major problems in applications. Specifically, it requires $2n|(q-1)$ and n be a power of two. Along with the progress of NIST PQC standardization, many research efforts are made for generalizing the NTT technique in recent years. To relax the requirement on $2n|(q-1)$, the work [15] proposed the "upper dividing" approach referred to as *preprocess-then-NTT* (Pt-NTT), and the work of Kyber [2] used the "bottom cropping" approach that is referred to as *truncated-NTT*(T-NTT in this work for presentation simplicity). The upper dividing (resp., bottom cropping) method was further improved in [16] (resp., [1]) by combining it with the Karatsuba technique [14]. The Karatsuba technique can reduce the number of multiplications at the cost of additional additions. For presentation simplicity, in the rest of this work, by Pt-NTT (resp., T-NTT) we refer to the Karatsuba-aided improved version of Pt-NTT (resp., T-NTT) proposed in [16] (resp., [1]). To our knowledge, the relationship between Pt-NTT

[15,16] and T-NTT [1,2] was not explicitly studied in the literature. Also, the analysis of the exact computational complexity of Pt-NTT in [15,16] was inadequate or incomplete (for example, it lacks the complexity analysis of additions).

To relax the requirement of n being power-of-two, in the work of NTTRU [11], the parameter set of $n = 768 = 3 \cdot 256$ and $q = 7681$ is selected, so that $x^{768} - x^{384} + 1$ can be decomposed into $(x^{384} + 684)(x^{384} - 685)$ in $\mathbb{Z}_q[x]$. Because 684 and 685 are roots of unity in $\mathbb{Z}_q$ in this case, we can use the NTT method to decompose a known polynomial $f(x)$ into cubic polynomials in $\mathbb{Z}_q[x]/(x^{384}+684)$ and $\mathbb{Z}_q[x]/(x^{384} - 685)$ which, at this time, can be multiplied directly. At a high level, NTTRU follows the "bottom cropping" approach of T-NTT but extends to the case of $n = 768$. The NTTRU approach [11] for the case of $n = 768$ was further improved in [1]. On the one hand, the Karatsuba technique [14] was introduced for the cubic polynomial multiplications (actually, polynomial multiplications of degree 5 in [1] with $q = 3457$). On the other hand, q is set to be 3457 instead of 7681 in [1]. Using a smaller q can make the ciphertext more compact and can use smaller noises in randomness sampling. But employing smaller q also brings the following disadvantages:

- The cryptosystems have to use different q's for the case of $n = 768$ and for the case of n being power-of-two (e.g., 512 and 1024);
- The number of NTT layers is changed, and polynomial multiplications of degree 5 are required in the end [1] (rather than cubic as in [11]).

The NTTRU approach [11] and its improved version [1] focus only on the specific case of $n = 768$, and the computational complexity for this special case was not analyzed in [11] and was only demonstrated with computer experiments (rather than mathematical analysis) in [1].

1.1 Our Contributions

In this work we apply Karatsuba technique to Pt-NTT in order to reduce the number of multiplications. Different from [15,16], we calculate the exact and complete computational complexity of Pt-NTT in terms of both additions and multiplications, and derive the optimal computational complexity of Pt-NTT with respect to any fixed (n, q).

Pt-NTT [15,16] follows the upper dividing approach, where $\alpha \geq 0$ upper decompositions are made from the top. On the contrary, T-NTT follows the bottom cropping approach, where $\beta \geq 0$ layers are cropped from the bottom. These two approaches appear to be quite different, and the relationship between them was not explicitly studied in the previous literatures. In this work, we observe that both of them can be represented in the matrix form, based on which we prove that Pt-NTT and T-NTT are actually computationally equivalent.

The upper dividing approach and the bottom cropping approach can accelerate the NTT process individually, by decomposing the polynomials or reducing the layers of decomposition. Based on these clues, we combine the upper dividing approach, the bottom cropping approach, and the Karatsuba technique all together, and propose a new variant of NTT referred to as *hybrid number theoretic transform* (H-NTT for short). In particular, Pt-NTT and T-NTT can be viewed as the special case of H-NTT. We make a complete and comprehensive analysis of the exact computational complexity of H-NTT, and derive its optimal bound w.r.t. any fixed (n, q).

We generalize our NTT techniques to the more general polynomial quotient ring $\mathbb{Z}_q[x]/(\Phi(x))$, where $\Phi(x)$ is the cyclotomic polynomial of degree $n = 3 \cdot 2^m$. Inspired by H-NTT and NTTRU [11], we present a generalized, modular and parallelizable NTT method for the case of $n = 3 \cdot 2^m$, which is referred to as G3-NTT for simplicity. Then we analyze its exact computational complexity and derive its optimal bound. Based on the analysis, we explicitly specify the optimized version of G3-NTT for the case of $n = 768 = 3 \cdot 256$, referred to as P3-NTT, which may arguably be the most important or relevant case in practice. Different from the bottom cropping approach used in NTTRU [11] for the case of $n = 768$, our P3-NTT follows the upper dividing approach leading to better parallelizability and better modularity. Specifically, after dividing the polynomials into three parts from the top, each of the three parts can be independently dealt with in parallel, and enjoys better modularity with the traditional NTT or its variants.

Finally, we apply the NTT techniques proposed in this work to some prominent key encapsulation mechanisms based on lattices with algebraic structures, in particular schemes based on the variants of *learning with errors* (LWE). In this work, we focus on the applications to Kyber [4] and NewHope [12]. Kyber is the prominent KEM scheme based on Module-LWE (MLWE), and is now in the third round of NIST PQC standardization. NewHope is the standing KEM scheme based on Ring-LWE (RLWE), and was one of the candidates in the second round of NIST PQC standardization. Tough NewHope was not moved to the third round, the study and optimization of NewHope still deserve further research exploration.

- For applications to Kyber, we present a new parameter set for Kyber-1024 with our H-NTT technique. The new Kyber-1024 protocol has doubled key size of 512 bits, which can provide more confidence in the target security level in the long run in the post-quantum era and renders us more economic ways to derive longer shared-key in certain application scenarios like future generations of TLS. The H-NTT based implementation of the new Kyber-1024 protocol can reuse the T-NTT codes for Kyber-512 and Kyber-768. In other words, though the parameter set is changed, there is no need for modification of codes of NTT.
- For applications to NewHope, we present a new variant of NewHope, referred to as NewHope-Unified, which sets the same modulus $q = 7681$ for all the three cases of $n \in \{512, 768, 1024\}$. Accordingly, we apply T-NTT, P3-NTT and H-NTT to NewHope-Unified for these three cases respectively. The unified q leads to a trade-off between bandwidth and error probability, and allows more modular, space-efficient and parallelizable implementations.

For all the new protocol variants of Kyber and NewHope proposed in this work, we implement them and provide the performance benchmark.

2 Preliminaries

Let $\Phi_s(x)$ be the s-th cyclotomic polynomial of degree $n = \phi(s)$, where $\phi(s)$ is Euler function. Denote the polynomial ring $\mathbb{Z}_q[x]/(\Phi_s(x))$ by $\mathcal{R}_q$, where q is a prime. Any polynomial $f \in \mathcal{R}_q$ can be written as $f = \sum_{i=0}^{n-1} f_i x^i$, $f = (f_0, f_1, \ldots, f_{n-1})$ or $f = (f_0, f_1, \ldots, f_{n-1})^T$ where $f_i \in \mathbb{Z}_q, i = 0, 1, \ldots, n-1$.

2.1 Karatsuba Technique

Definition 1 (Karatsuba technique) *[14]. Let a, b, c and d be four numbers or polynomials. To compute $s_1 = a \cdot c$, $s_2 = a \cdot d + b \cdot c$ and $s_3 = b \cdot d$, the Karatsuba technique first computes s_1 and s_3, then computes $s_2 = (a+b) \cdot (c+d) - s_1 - s_3$.*

To compute s_1, s_2 and s_3, we initially need 4 multiplications and 1 addition. However, with the Karatsuba technique, we only need to perform 3 multiplications and 4 additions. Thus, the Karatsuba technique can reduce the number of multiplications at the cost of additional additions.

2.2 Number Theoretic Transform

Number theoretic transform (NTT) is a special version of fast Fourier transform (FFT) over a finite field. As for $\mathcal{R}_q = \mathbb{Z}_q[x]/(x^n + 1)$ where n is a power of 2 and q is a prime satisfying $2n|(q-1)$, given $f, g \in \mathcal{R}_q$, to compute $h = fg \in \mathcal{R}_q$ requires ordinary NTT of length $2n$. But it can be turned into NTT of length n, which can be seen below. Let ω be the $2n$-th primitive root of unity in $\mathbb{Z}_q$.

Step 1: $\tilde{f} = (1, \omega, \omega^2, \ldots, \omega^{n-1}) \circ f$, $\tilde{g} = (1, \omega, \omega^2, \ldots, \omega^{n-1}) \circ g$, where "$\circ$" represents the point-wise multiplication of vectors.

Step 2: $\tilde{h} = NTT^{-1}\left(NTT(\tilde{f}) \circ NTT(\tilde{g})\right)$. The forward transformation $\widehat{f} = NTT(\tilde{f})$ is defined by $\widehat{f}_j = \sum_{i=0}^{n-1} \tilde{f}_i \gamma^{ij} \mod q$, $j = 0, 1, \ldots, n-1$, where $\gamma = \omega^2 \mod q$. The inverse transformation $\tilde{f} = NTT^{-1}(\widehat{f})$ is given by $\tilde{f}_i = n^{-1} \sum_{j=0}^{n-1} \widehat{f}_j \gamma^{-ij} \mod q$, $i = 0, 1, \ldots, n-1$. Note that the length of NTT here is n.

Step 3: $h = (1, \omega^{-1}, \omega^{-2}, \ldots, \omega^{-(n-1)}) \circ \tilde{h}$.

Define $\widehat{NTT}(f) = NTT\left((1, \omega, \omega^2, \ldots, \omega^{n-1}) \circ f\right)$ and $\widehat{NTT}^{-1}(\widehat{f}) = (1, \omega^{-1}, \omega^{-2}, \ldots, \omega^{-(n-1)}) \circ NTT^{-1}(\widehat{f})$. It holds that $h = \widehat{NTT}^{-1}\left(\widehat{NTT}(f) \circ \widehat{NTT}(g)\right)$. We can compute $\widehat{NTT}$ by using the FFT trick [3]. The computational complexity in terms of multiplications and additions is listed below. Adding n multiplications in the point-wise multiplication in $\widehat{NTT}$ domain, we obtain the total computational complexity of $\widehat{NTT}$-based polynomial multiplication: $\frac{3}{2}nlogn + 2n$ multiplications and $3nlogn$ additions.

- Multiplications: $T_m(\widehat{NTT}) = \frac{1}{2}nlogn$ and $T_m(\widehat{NTT}^{-1}) = \frac{1}{2}nlogn + n$.
- Additions: $T_a(\widehat{NTT}) = nlogn$ and $T_a(\widehat{NTT}^{-1}) = nlogn$.

However, that explanation cannot explicitly express the real process of $\widehat{NTT}$. There is another explanation based on the Chinese Remainder Theorem (CRT):

$$\mathbb{Z}_q[x]/(x^n+1) \cong \mathbb{Z}_q[x]/(x-\omega) \times \mathbb{Z}_q[x]/(x-\omega^3) \times \cdots \times \mathbb{Z}_q[x]/(x-\omega^{2n-1}) \quad (1)$$

Therefore, we only demand the images of f and g in $\mathbb{Z}_q[x]/(x-\omega^{2i+1})$, $i \in \{0, 1, \cdots, n-1\}$. In fact, if we think of $\widehat{NTT}$ as a special interpolation method, the interpolation points of $\widehat{NTT}$ we may have are $\{\omega, \omega^3, \ldots, \omega^{2n-1}\}$. For presentation simplicity in the proof of equivalence in the subsequent sections, we give the interpolation method in the matrix form.

Definition 2. *Based on the explanation of $\widehat{NTT}$ by CRT, we can think of $\widehat{NTT}$ process as a special form of interpolation. Notice that the process of the interpolation is a linear transformation which can be represented in the matrix form:*

$$\begin{bmatrix} \widehat{f_0} \\ \widehat{f_1} \\ \vdots \\ \widehat{f}_{n-1} \end{bmatrix} = \begin{bmatrix} 1 & \omega & \omega^2 & \cdots & \omega^{n-1} \\ 1 & \omega^3 & \omega^6 & \cdots & \omega^{3(n-1)} \\ \vdots & \vdots & \vdots & \ddots & \vdots \\ 1 & \omega^{2n-1} & \omega^{2(2n-1)} & \cdots & \omega^{(2n-1)(n-1)} \end{bmatrix} \begin{bmatrix} f_0 \\ f_1 \\ \vdots \\ f_{n-1} \end{bmatrix} \quad (2)$$

where we denote the coefficient matrix above by $\mathbf{W_n}$.

3 On the Exact Computational Complexity of Pt-NTT

In this section, we calculate the exact computational complexity of Pt-NTT [15,16] in terms of both multiplications and additions. According to [15,16], as for $\mathcal{R}_q = \mathbb{Z}_q[x]/(x^n+1)$ where n is a power of 2 and q is a prime satisfying $\frac{n}{2^{\alpha-1}} | (q-1)$ for the integer $\alpha \geq 0$, Pt-NTT can have α upper decompositions from the top before the actual NTT progress kicks in. The steps of Pt-NTT in the generalized form are described here.

Step 1: Let $f(x) = \sum_{i=0}^{2^\alpha-1} x^i \widetilde{f}_i(x^{2^\alpha})$ and $g(x) = \sum_{j=0}^{2^\alpha-1} x^j \widetilde{g}_j(x^{2^\alpha})$ be the decompositions of f and g respectively. The degrees of $\widetilde{f}_i(z)$ and $\widetilde{g}_j(z)$ are bounded by $\frac{n}{2^\alpha}$, where $z = x^{2^\alpha}$. To compute $h(x) \equiv f(x)g(x) \mod (x^n+1)$, we write $h(x) = \sum_{i=0}^{2^\alpha-1} x^i \widetilde{h}_i(x^{2^\alpha})$.

Step 2: For $i = 0, 1, \ldots, 2^\alpha - 1$, we have

$$\begin{aligned} \widetilde{h}_i(z) &= \sum_{l=0}^{i} \widetilde{f}_l(z)\widetilde{g}_{i-l}(z) + \sum_{l=i+1}^{2^\alpha-1} z\widetilde{f}_l(z)\widetilde{g}_{2^\alpha+i-l}(z) \\ &= \widehat{NTT}^{-1}\left(\sum_{l=0}^{i} \widehat{NTT}(\widetilde{f}_l(z)) \circ \widehat{NTT}(\widetilde{g}_{i-l}(z)) + \sum_{l=i+1}^{2^\alpha-1} \widehat{NTT}(z) \circ \widehat{NTT}(\widetilde{f}_l(z)) \circ \widehat{NTT}(\widetilde{g}_{2^\alpha+i-l}(z))\right). \end{aligned}$$

Step 3: Compute $h(x) = \sum_{i=0}^{2^\alpha - 1} x^i \widetilde{h}_i(x^{2^\alpha})$.

In Step 2, by applying the Karatsuba technique, for any $i \neq j$ we have $\widehat{NTT}(\widetilde{f}_i) \circ \widehat{NTT}(\widetilde{g}_j) + \widehat{NTT}(\widetilde{f}_j) \circ \widehat{NTT}(\widetilde{g}_i) = (\widehat{NTT}(\widetilde{f}_i) + \widehat{NTT}(\widetilde{f}_j)) \circ (\widehat{NTT}(\widetilde{g}_i) + \widehat{NTT}(\widetilde{g}_j)) - \widehat{NTT}(\widetilde{f}_i) \circ \widehat{NTT}(\widetilde{g}_i) - \widehat{NTT}(\widetilde{f}_j) \circ \widehat{NTT}(\widetilde{g}_j)$.

From the above description, the operations that Pt-NTT [16] needs to compute in total are listed:

- $2^{\alpha+1}$ $\widehat{NTT}$s. Every $\widehat{NTT}$ requires $\frac{n}{2^{\alpha+1}} log \frac{n}{2^\alpha}$ multiplications and $\frac{n}{2^\alpha} log \frac{n}{2^\alpha}$ additions.
- 2^α $\widehat{NTT}^{-1}$s. Every $\widehat{NTT}^{-1}$ requires $\frac{n}{2^{\alpha+1}} log \frac{n}{2^\alpha} + \frac{n}{2^\alpha}$ multiplications and $\frac{n}{2^\alpha} log \frac{n}{2^\alpha}$ additions.
- $3 \cdot 2^{2\alpha-2} + 2^{\alpha-1}$ point-wise multiplications of vectors. Every point-wise multiplication of vectors requires $\frac{n}{2^\alpha}$ multiplications.
- $2^{2\alpha+1} + 2^{2\alpha-1} - 5 \cdot 2^{\alpha-1}$ additions of vectors. Every addition of vectors requires $\frac{n}{2^\alpha}$ additions.

Finally, we obtain the exact computational complexity of Pt-NTT in its generalized form:

- Multiplications:
$$T_m(\text{Pt-NTT}) = \begin{cases} \frac{3}{2} nlogn + (3 \cdot 2^{\alpha-2} + \frac{3}{2} - \frac{3\alpha}{2})n, \alpha \geq 1. \\ \frac{3}{2} nlogn + 2n, \alpha = 0 \text{ (i.e., Pt-NTT degenerates to } \widehat{NTT}). \end{cases}$$
- Additions: $T_a(\text{Pt-NTT}) = 3nlogn + (5 \cdot 2^{\alpha-1} - \frac{5}{2} - 3\alpha)n$.

By mathematical analysis, we can conclude that the computational complexity of Pt-NTT reaches its optimization when $\alpha = 1$ w.r.t. the fixed (n, q): $\frac{3}{2} nlogn + \frac{3}{2} n$ multiplications and $3nlogn - \frac{1}{2} n$ additions. In comparison, the computational complexity analysis of Pt-NTT in [16] is incomplete and incorrect. On the one hand, the complexity of additions was not analyzed in [16]. On the other hand, the complexity of multiplications was incorrectly concluded to be $T(n) = 3n \log n + (3 \cdot 2^{\alpha-2} - 3\alpha + \frac{1}{2})n$ in [16].

4 On the Computational Equivalence of Pt-NTT and T-NTT

Pt-NTT [15,16] follows the upper dividing approach, where α upper decompositions are made from the top. On the contrary, T-NTT follows the bottom cropping approach, where β layers are cropped from the bottom. To the best of our knowledge, the relationship between Pt-NTT and T-NTT was not explicitly studied in the previous literatures. In this section, we show that they are actually computationally equivalent.

For ease of understanding, we consider the special case of Pt-NTT, i.e., $\alpha = 1$. We have $f = f_e + x f_o$ and $g = g_e + x g_o$, i.e.,

$$\begin{cases} f = f_0 + f_1 x + \ldots + f_{n-1} x^{n-1} \\ f_e = f_0 + f_2 y + \ldots + f_{n-2} y^{\frac{n}{2}-1} \\ f_o = f_1 + f_3 y + \ldots + f_{n-1} y^{\frac{n}{2}-1} \end{cases}, \begin{cases} g = g_0 + g_1 x + \ldots + g_{n-1} x^{n-1} \\ g_e = g_0 + g_2 y + \ldots + g_{n-2} y^{\frac{n}{2}-1} \\ g_o = g_1 + g_3 y + \ldots + g_{n-1} y^{\frac{n}{2}-1} \end{cases} \quad (3)$$

where we define $y = x^2$. We can obtain $h = fg = h_e + xh_o$, where $h_e = f_e g_e + x^2 f_o g_o$ and $h_o = f_o g_e + f_e g_o$.

As for T-NTT with $\beta = 1$, from [2] we know it can be explained by CRT:

$$\mathbb{Z}_q[x]/(x^n+1) \cong \mathbb{Z}_q[x]/(x^2-\omega) \times \mathbb{Z}_q[x]/(x^2-\omega^3) \times \cdots \times \mathbb{Z}_q[x]/(x^2-\omega^{n-1}) \tag{4}$$

where ω is the n-th primitive root of unity in $\mathbb{Z}_q$. Based on formula (4) above which is similar to formula (1), T-NTT with $\beta = 1$ can be considered as a special form of interpolation. Similar to Definition 2 and formula (2), we can give its matrix form here:

$$\begin{bmatrix} \widehat{f_0}+\widehat{f_1}x \\ \widehat{f_2}+\widehat{f_3}x \\ \vdots \\ \widehat{f_{n-2}}+\widehat{f_{n-1}}x \end{bmatrix} = \mathbf{W}_{\frac{n}{2}} \begin{bmatrix} f_0+f_1x \\ f_2+f_3x \\ \vdots \\ f_{n-2}+f_{n-1}x \end{bmatrix}, \text{ i.e., } \begin{bmatrix} \widehat{f_0} \\ \widehat{f_2} \\ \vdots \\ \widehat{f_{n-2}} \end{bmatrix} + x \begin{bmatrix} \widehat{f_1} \\ \widehat{f_3} \\ \vdots \\ \widehat{f_{n-1}} \end{bmatrix} = \mathbf{W}_{\frac{n}{2}} \begin{bmatrix} f_0 \\ f_2 \\ \vdots \\ f_{n-2} \end{bmatrix} + x\mathbf{W}_{\frac{n}{2}} \begin{bmatrix} f_1 \\ f_3 \\ \vdots \\ f_{n-1} \end{bmatrix}$$

$$\text{which implies } \begin{bmatrix} \widehat{f_0} \\ \widehat{f_2} \\ \vdots \\ \widehat{f_{n-2}} \end{bmatrix} = \mathbf{W}_{\frac{n}{2}} \begin{bmatrix} f_0 \\ f_2 \\ \vdots \\ f_{n-2} \end{bmatrix} \text{ and } \begin{bmatrix} \widehat{f_1} \\ \widehat{f_3} \\ \vdots \\ \widehat{f_{n-1}} \end{bmatrix} = \mathbf{W}_{\frac{n}{2}} \begin{bmatrix} f_1 \\ f_3 \\ \vdots \\ f_{n-1} \end{bmatrix}.$$

Note that $\mathbf{W}_{\frac{n}{2}} \begin{bmatrix} f_0 \\ f_2 \\ \vdots \\ f_{n-2} \end{bmatrix}$ and $\mathbf{W}_{\frac{n}{2}} \begin{bmatrix} f_1 \\ f_3 \\ \vdots \\ f_{n-1} \end{bmatrix}$ are actually $\widehat{NTT}(f_e)$ and $\widehat{NTT}(f_o)$ respectively, which are the terms obtained from the process of Pt-NTT with $\alpha = 1$.

The point-wise multiplication of $\begin{bmatrix} \widehat{f_0}+\widehat{f_1}x \\ \widehat{f_2}+\widehat{f_3}x \\ \vdots \\ \widehat{f_{n-2}}+\widehat{f_{n-1}}x \end{bmatrix}$ and $\begin{bmatrix} \widehat{g_0}+\widehat{g_1}x \\ \widehat{g_2}+\widehat{g_3}x \\ \vdots \\ \widehat{g_{n-2}}+\widehat{g_{n-1}}x \end{bmatrix}$ is equivalent to

$$\begin{bmatrix} \widehat{f_0} \\ \widehat{f_2} \\ \vdots \\ \widehat{f_{n-2}} \end{bmatrix} \circ \begin{bmatrix} \widehat{g_0} \\ \widehat{g_2} \\ \vdots \\ \widehat{g_{n-2}} \end{bmatrix} + x^2 \begin{bmatrix} \widehat{f_1} \\ \widehat{f_3} \\ \vdots \\ \widehat{f_{n-1}} \end{bmatrix} \circ \begin{bmatrix} \widehat{g_1} \\ \widehat{g_3} \\ \vdots \\ \widehat{g_{n-1}} \end{bmatrix} + x \left(\begin{bmatrix} \widehat{f_1} \\ \widehat{f_3} \\ \vdots \\ \widehat{f_{n-1}} \end{bmatrix} \circ \begin{bmatrix} \widehat{g_0} \\ \widehat{g_2} \\ \vdots \\ \widehat{g_{n-2}} \end{bmatrix} + \begin{bmatrix} \widehat{f_0} \\ \widehat{f_2} \\ \vdots \\ \widehat{f_{n-2}} \end{bmatrix} \circ \begin{bmatrix} \widehat{g_1} \\ \widehat{g_3} \\ \vdots \\ \widehat{g_{n-1}} \end{bmatrix} \right).$$

Here, x^2 is actually a vector, going as $(\omega, \omega^3, \cdots, \omega^{n-1})^T$. And similar to $\widehat{NTT}(y)$ in Pt-NTT, the process of x^2 is point-wise multiplication. Therefore, T-NTT$(f)\circ$T-NTT$(g) = \widehat{NTT}(f_e)\circ\widehat{NTT}(g_e)+\widehat{NTT}(y)\circ\widehat{NTT}(f_o)\circ\widehat{NTT}(g_o)+x(\widehat{NTT}(f_e)\circ\widehat{NTT}(g_o)+\widehat{NTT}(f_o)\circ\widehat{NTT}(g_e))$. So we can see that Pt-NTT with $\alpha = 1$ has the same computing process as T-NTT with $\beta = 1$.

Given $f \in \mathbb{Z}_q[x]/(x^n+1)$ where n is a power of 2 and q is a prime satisfying $\frac{n}{2^{\beta-1}}|(q-1)$ for the integer $\beta \geq 0$, we give the generalized form of T-NTT(f):

$$\text{T-NTT}(f) = \begin{bmatrix} \hat{f}_0 + \hat{f}_1 x + \ldots + \hat{f}_{2^\beta-1} x^{2^\beta-1} \\ \hat{f}_{2^\beta} + \hat{f}_{2^\beta+1} x + \ldots + \hat{f}_{2^{\beta+1}-1} x^{2^\beta-1} \\ \vdots \\ \hat{f}_{n-2^\beta} + \hat{f}_{n+1-2^\beta} x + \ldots + \hat{f}_{n-1} x^{2^\beta-1} \end{bmatrix} = \mathbf{W}_{\frac{\mathbf{n}}{\mathbf{2^\beta}}} \begin{bmatrix} f_0 + f_1 x + \ldots + f_{2^\beta-1} x^{2^\beta-1} \\ f_{2^\beta} + f_{2^\beta+1} x + \ldots + f_{2^{\beta+1}-1} x^{2^\beta-1} \\ \vdots \\ f_{n-2^\beta} + f_{n+1-2^\beta} x + \ldots + f_{n-1} x^{2^\beta-1} \end{bmatrix}$$

Applying the method similar to the above analysis for $\alpha = \beta = 1$, we can get the computational equivalence between Pt-NTT and T-NTT for any $\alpha = \beta$. Thus, the computational complexity of T-NTT can be derived from that of Pt-NTT.

- Multiplications:
  $$T_m(\text{T-NTT}) = \begin{cases} \frac{3}{2}nlogn + (3 \cdot 2^{\beta-2} + \frac{3}{2} - \frac{3\beta}{2})n, \beta \geq 1. \\ \frac{3}{2}nlogn + 2n, \beta = 0 \text{ (i.e., T-NTT degenerates to } \widehat{NTT}). \end{cases}$$
- Additions: $T_a(\text{T-NTT}) = 3nlogn + (5 \cdot 2^{\beta-1} - \frac{5}{2} - 3\beta)n$.

5 Hybrid Number Theoretic Transform (H-NTT)

Pt-NTT [16] accelerates the computing process by decomposing the polynomial ahead of other procedures, while T-NTT aims at promoting the efficiency by reducing the layers of decomposing from the bottom. From the computational complexity analysis of Pt-NTT and T-NTT, we can see that each of Pt-NTT and T-NTT has certain computational advantage over the traditional NTT on its own. This motivates us to examine whether more efficient NTT algorithms can be achieved by combining them both. This brings the introduction of hybrid number theoretic transform (H-NTT). The purpose of the H-NTT is to calculate $h = fg$ more efficiently and more modularly, as we shall see with the applications to the implementations of latticed-based cryptographic algorithms.

We refer to H-NTT(n, α, β) as the H-NTT process with α upper decompositions from the top and β layers cropped from the bottom. As mentioned in Sect. 2, we operate it on $\mathbb{Z}_q[x]/(x^n+1)$, where n is a power of 2 and q is a prime satisfying $\frac{n}{2^{\alpha+\beta-1}}|(q-1)$. The H-NTT process is specified and discussed below.

Step 1: Similar to Pt-NTT, we first decompose the original polynomials: $f(x) = \sum_{i=0}^{2^\alpha-1} x^i \widetilde{f}_i(x^{2^\alpha})$ and $g(x) = \sum_{j=0}^{2^\alpha-1} x^j \widetilde{g}_j(x^{2^\alpha})$. The degrees of $\widetilde{f}_i(z)$ and $\widetilde{g}_j(z)$ are bounded by $\frac{n}{2^\alpha}$, where $z = x^{2^\alpha}$. To compute $h(x) \equiv f(x)g(x) \mod (x^n + 1)$, we write $h(x) = \sum_{i=0}^{2^\alpha-1} x^i \widetilde{h}_i(x^{2^\alpha})$.

Step 2: Then we compute $\widetilde{h}_i(z)$ in $\mathbb{Z}_q[z]/(z^{\frac{n}{2^\alpha}}+1)$. For $i = 0, 1, \ldots, 2^\alpha - 1$, we have

$$\widetilde{h}_i(z) = \sum_{l=0}^{i} \widetilde{f}_l(z)\widetilde{g}_{i-l}(z) + \sum_{l=i+1}^{2^\alpha-1} z\widetilde{f}_l(z)\widetilde{g}_{2^\alpha+i-l}(z)$$

$$= \text{T-NTT}^{-1}\left(\sum_{l=0}^{i} \text{T-NTT}(\widetilde{f}_l) \circ \text{T-NTT}(\widetilde{g}_{i-l}) + \sum_{l=i+1}^{2^\alpha-1} \text{T-NTT}(z) \circ \text{T-NTT}(\widetilde{f}_l) \circ \text{T-NTT}(\widetilde{g}_{2^\alpha+i-l})\right).$$

In Step 2, β layers are cropped from the bottom in T-NTT. By applying the Karatsuba technique, for any $i \neq j$ we have $\text{T-NTT}(\widetilde{f}_i) \circ \text{T-NTT}(\widetilde{g}_j) + \text{T-NTT}(\widetilde{f}_j) \circ \text{T-NTT}(\widetilde{g}_i) = (\text{T-NTT}(\widetilde{f}_i) + \text{T-NTT}(\widetilde{f}_j)) \circ (\text{T-NTT}(\widetilde{g}_i) + \text{T-NTT}(\widetilde{g}_j)) - \text{T-NTT}(\widetilde{f}_i) \circ \text{T-NTT}(\widetilde{g}_i) - \text{T-NTT}(\widetilde{f}_j) \circ \text{T-NTT}(\widetilde{g}_j)$.

There are a few points that require our attention:

- The "$\circ$" operator in "$\text{T-NTT}(\widetilde{f}_i) \circ \text{T-NTT}(\widetilde{g}_j)$" means the point-wise multiplication of polynomial vectors.
- $\text{T-NTT}(z) = (z, z, \ldots, z)$, including $\frac{n}{2^{\alpha+\beta}}$ z's in total.
- Though the "$\circ$" operator in "$\text{T-NTT}(z)\ \circ$" means the point-wise multiplication of polynomial vectors, we actually need to process only $\frac{n}{2^{\alpha+\beta}}$ multiplications. As a matter of fact, we can call "$\circ$" the point-wise multiplication of vectors.

Step 3: $h(x) = \sum_{i=0}^{2^\alpha-1} x^i \widetilde{h}_i(x^{2^\alpha})$.

Observe that, in Step 1 and Step 3, we are simply doing splitting and combining of lists. Consequently, these two steps are not taken into account for calculating the complexity in terms of multiplications and additions.

In Step 2, the computational complexity can be calculated as follows: $2^{\alpha+1}$ T-NTTs, 2^α $\text{T-NTT}^{-1}s$, $2^{2\alpha-1} + 2^{\alpha-1}$ point-wise multiplications of polynomial vectors, $2^{2\alpha-2}$ point-wise multiplications of vectors, and $2^{2\alpha+1} + 2^{2\alpha-1} - 5 \cdot 2^{\alpha-1}$ additions of polynomials. Each of these processes requires different numbers of multiplications and additions:

- Every T-NTT requires $\frac{n}{2^{\alpha+1}}(log\frac{n}{2^\alpha} - \beta)$ multiplications and $\frac{n}{2^\alpha}(log\frac{n}{2^\alpha} - \beta)$ additions.
- Every T-NTT^{-1} requires $\frac{n}{2^{\alpha+1}}(log\frac{n}{2^\alpha} - \beta)$ multiplications and $\frac{n}{2^\alpha}(log\frac{n}{2^\alpha} - \beta)$ additions.
- Every point-wise multiplications of polynomial vectors requires $(3 \cdot 2^{(\beta-2)} + \frac{1}{2}) \cdot \frac{n}{2^\alpha}$ multiplications and $(5 \cdot 2^{(\beta-1)} - \frac{5}{2}) \cdot \frac{n}{2^\alpha}$ additions.
- Every point-wise multiplication of vectors requires $\frac{n}{2^{\alpha+\beta}}$ multiplications.
- Every addition of polynomials requires $\frac{n}{2^\alpha}$ additions.

Finally, by combining all the multiplications and additions listed above, we obtain the computational complexity of H-NTT in its generalized form:

- Multiplications: $T_m(\text{H-NTT}) = \frac{3}{2}nlogn + (3 \cdot 2^{\alpha+\beta-3} + 2^{\alpha-2} + 3 \cdot 2^{\beta-3} + 2^{\alpha-\beta-2} - \frac{3}{2}(\alpha+\beta) + \frac{5}{4})n$.
- Additions: $T_a(\text{H-NTT}) = 3nlogn + (5 \cdot 2^{\alpha+\beta-2} + 5 \cdot 2^{\beta-2} + 5 \cdot 2^{\alpha-2} - 3 \cdot (\alpha + \beta) - \frac{15}{4})n$.

By mathematical analysis, we can conclude that the computational complexity of H-NTT can reach its optimization when $\alpha = \beta = 1$, which contains $\frac{3}{2}nlogn + \frac{5}{4}n$ multiplications and $3nlogn + \frac{1}{4}n$ additions. Recall that Pt-NTT (resp., T-NTT) reaches its optimization when $\alpha = 1$ (resp., $\beta = 1$): $\frac{3}{2}nlogn + \frac{3}{2}n$ multiplications and $3nlogn - \frac{1}{2}n$ additions.

6 G3-NTT and P3-NTT

In this section, in the spirit of H-NTT, we present generalized, parallelizable and modular NTT algorithms for the case of $n = 3 \cdot 2^m$ for any integer $m \geq 0$. We can check that $\Phi_s(x) = x^{3 \cdot 2^m} - x^{3 \cdot 2^{m-1}} + 1$ is the s-th cyclotomic polynomial of degree $n = 3 \cdot 2^m$ where $s = 3^2 \cdot 2^m$ satisfying $n = \phi(s)$. In the subsequent discussions, we will consider the polynomial multiplications in $\mathcal{R}_q = \mathbb{Z}_q[x]/(\Phi_s(x)) = \mathbb{Z}_q[x]/(x^{3 \cdot 2^m} - x^{3 \cdot 2^{m-1}} + 1)$ where q is a prime (more on this point later).

We first present the generalized form of NTT for this case, which is referred to as G3-NTT for simplicity, analyze its computational complexity and derive its optimality. Then, we present the special and optimal version of G3-NTT for the most important case of $n = 768 = 3 \cdot 256$, which is referred to as P3-NTT. We first present the procedures of G3-NTT for the general case of $n = 3 \cdot 2^m$, referred to as G3-NTT($n = 3 \cdot 2^m, \alpha, \beta$) where $3 \cdot 2^\alpha$ parts are generated from the top and β layers are cropped from the bottom in T-NTT.

Step 1: Given $f, g \in \mathcal{R}_q$, we divide the original polynomials into $3 \cdot 2^\alpha$ parts: $f(x) = \sum_{i=0}^{3 \cdot 2^\alpha - 1} x^i \widetilde{f}_i(x^{3 \cdot 2^\alpha})$ and $g(x) = \sum_{j=0}^{3 \cdot 2^\alpha - 1} x^j \widetilde{g}_j(x^{3 \cdot 2^\alpha})$. The degrees of $\widetilde{f}_i(z)$ and $\widetilde{g}_j(z)$ are bounded by $\frac{n}{3 \cdot 2^\alpha}$, where $z = x^{3 \cdot 2^\alpha}$. To compute $h = fg \in \mathcal{R}_q$, we write $h(x) = \sum_{i=0}^{3 \cdot 2^\alpha - 1} x^i \widetilde{h}_i(x^{3 \cdot 2^\alpha})$.

Step 2: Compute $\widetilde{h}_i(z)$ in $\mathbb{Z}_q[z]/(z^{\frac{n}{3 \cdot 2^\alpha}} - z^{\frac{n}{3 \cdot 2^{\alpha+1}}} + 1)$. For $i = 0, 1, \ldots, 3 \cdot 2^\alpha - 1$, we have

$$\widetilde{h}_i(z) = \sum_{l=0}^{i} \widetilde{f}_l(z)\widetilde{g}_{i-l}(z) + \sum_{l=i+1}^{3 \cdot 2^\alpha - 1} z\widetilde{f}_l(z)\widetilde{g}_{3 \cdot 2^\alpha + i - l}(z)$$

$$= \text{T-NTT}^{-1}\left(\sum_{l=0}^{i} \text{T-NTT}(\widetilde{f}_l) \circ \text{T-NTT}(\widetilde{g}_{i-l}) + \sum_{l=i+1}^{3 \cdot 2^\alpha - 1} \text{T-NTT}(z) \circ \text{T-NTT}(\widetilde{f}_l) \circ \text{T-NTT}(\widetilde{g}_{3 \cdot 2^\alpha + i - l})\right).$$

In Step 2, for any $i \neq j$ we have $\text{T-NTT}(\widetilde{f}_i) \circ \text{T-NTT}(\widetilde{g}_j) + \text{T-NTT}(\widetilde{f}_j) \circ \text{T-NTT}(\widetilde{g}_i) = (\text{T-NTT}(\widetilde{f}_i) + \text{T-NTT}(\widetilde{f}_j)) \circ (\text{T-NTT}(\widetilde{g}_i) + \text{T-NTT}(\widetilde{g}_j)) - \text{T-NTT}(\widetilde{f}_i) \circ \text{T-NTT}(\widetilde{g}_i) - \text{T-NTT}(\widetilde{f}_j) \circ \text{T-NTT}(\widetilde{g}_j)$.

Some notes are in place:

- $\text{T-NTT}(z) = (z, z, \ldots, z)$, including $\frac{n}{3 \cdot 2^{\alpha+\beta}}$ z's in total.
- The operator "$\circ$" in "$\text{T-NTT}(z) \circ$" only needs $\frac{n}{3 \cdot 2^{\alpha+\beta}}$ multiplications.

Step 3: $h(x) = \sum_{i=0}^{3 \cdot 2^\alpha - 1} x^i \widetilde{h}_i(x^{3 \cdot 2^\alpha})$.

According to the analysis above, the computational complexity of G3-NTT($n = 3 \cdot 2^m, \alpha, \beta$) can be calculated as follow. We categorize the analysis into several distinct cases, according to whether α or β is assigned to be 0 or not.

Case 1: $\alpha = 0, \beta \geq 1$,
- Multiplications: T_m(G3-NTT) $= \frac{3}{2}nlogn + (3 \cdot 2^{\beta-1} + 2 + \frac{1}{3}2^{-\beta+1} - \frac{3}{2}log3 - \frac{3}{2}\beta)n$.
- Additions: T_a(G3-NTT) $= 3nlogn + (5 \cdot 2^{\beta} + 1 - 3log3 - 3\beta)n$.

Case 2: $\alpha \geq 1, \beta = 0$,
- Multiplications: T_m(G3-NTT) $= \frac{3}{2}nlogn + (9 \cdot 2^{\alpha-2} + \frac{3}{2} - \frac{3}{2}log3 - \frac{3}{2}\alpha)n$.
- Additions: T_a(G3-NTT) $= 3nlogn + (15 \cdot 2^{\alpha-2} - \frac{3}{2} - 3log3 - 3\alpha)n$.

Case 3: $\alpha \geq 1, \beta \geq 1$,
- Multiplications: T_m(G3-NTT) $= \frac{3}{2}nlogn + (9 \cdot 2^{\alpha+\beta-3} + 3 \cdot 2^{\alpha-2} + 3 \cdot 2^{\beta-3} + 3 \cdot 2^{\alpha-\beta-2} + \frac{5}{4} - \frac{3}{2}log3 - \frac{3}{2}(\alpha+\beta))n$.
- Additions: T_a(G3-NTT) $= 3nlogn + (15 \cdot 2^{\alpha+\beta-2} - 5 \cdot 2^{\beta-2} - 3(\alpha+\beta) - 3log3 - \frac{11}{4})n$.

Case 4: $\alpha = 0, \beta = 0$,
- Multiplications: T_m(G3-NTT) $= \frac{3}{2}nlogn + (\frac{11}{3} - \frac{3}{2}log3)n$.
- Additions: T_a(G3-NTT) $= 3nlogn + (6 - 3log3)n$.

From the discussion above, we can see that when (n, q) is fixed, the computational complexity of G3-NTT($n = 3 \cdot 2^m, \alpha, \beta$) reaches the minimum value when $\alpha = \beta = 0$. We show more interest in this case, i.e., G3-NTT($n = 3 \cdot 2^m, \alpha = 0, \beta = 0$), and more details about this optimized case of G3-NTT are given below.

With $\alpha = \beta = 0$ in G3-NTT, considering $s = 3^2 \cdot 2^m$ and $n = 3 \cdot 2^m$, we only require $q \equiv 1 \mod 3 \cdot 2^m$. Let ω be the $3 \cdot 2^m$-th primitive root of unity in $\mathbb{Z}_q$ here. Define $y = x^3$. We have $\mathbb{Z}_q[x]/(\Phi_s(x)) = \mathbb{Z}_q[y]/(y^{2^m} - y^{2^{m-1}} + 1) \sqcup x\mathbb{Z}_q[y]/(y^{2^m} - y^{2^{m-1}} + 1) \sqcup x^2\mathbb{Z}_q[y]/(y^{2^m} - y^{2^{m-1}} + 1)$ where $\mathbb{Z}_q[y]/(y^{2^m} - y^{2^{m-1}} + 1) \cong \mathbb{Z}_q[y]/(y^{2^{m-1}} - \omega^{2^{m-1}}) \times \mathbb{Z}_q[y]/(y^{2^{m-1}} - \omega^{5 \cdot 2^{m-1}})$. Then, we apply T-NTT(with $\beta = 0$) in both $\mathbb{Z}_q[y]/(y^{2^{m-1}} - \omega^{2^{m-1}})$ and $\mathbb{Z}_q[y]/(y^{2^{m-1}} - \omega^{5 \cdot 2^{m-1}})$.

Note that $f, g \in \mathcal{R}_q$ are divided into 3 parts respectively, i.e., $f = f_0 + xf_1 + x^2 f_2$ and $g = g_0 + xg_1 + x^2 g_2$. To compute $h = fg \in \mathcal{R}_q$, we concretely write $h = h_0 + xh_1 + x^2 h_2$. By applying the Karatsuba technique, we get $h_0 = f_0g_0 + [(f_1+f_2)(g_1+g_2) - f_1g_1 - f_2g_2]y$, $h_1 = (f_0+f_1)(g_0+g_1) - f_1g_1 - f_0g_0 + yf_2g_2$ and $h_2 = (f_0 + f_2)(g_0 + g_2) - f_2g_2 - f_0g_0 + f_1g_1$.

In applications of lattice-based cryptography, the dimension n of polynomials usually dominates the bandwidth and security in some schemes. The case of $n = 768 = 3 \cdot 256$ (i.e., $m = 8$ and $s = 3^2 \cdot 256$) may arguably be the most important or relevant case in reality. Consequently, we explicitly specify the special (optimized) case of G3-NTT: G3-NTT($n = 768, \alpha = 0, \beta = 0$), which is referred to as P3-NTT. We can obtain the cyclotomic polynomial of degree $n = 768$: $\Phi_s(x) = x^{768} - x^{384} + 1$, which implies $\mathcal{R}_q = \mathbb{Z}_q[x]/(x^{768} - x^{384} + 1)$ where q is a prime only satisfying $q \equiv 1 \mod 768$. That is, ω is set to be the 768-th primitive root of unity in $\mathbb{Z}_q$.

The calculation process of P3-NTT is the same as that of G3-NTT($n = 3 \cdot 2^m, \alpha = 0, \beta = 0$) by simply fixing $m = 8$. We give the concrete computational complexity of P3-NTT, by setting $n = 768$ and $\alpha = \beta = 0$ in the analysis of G3-NTT. Obviously, the computational complexity of P3-NTT reaches the minimum value because of $\alpha = \beta = 0$.

- Multiplications: $T_m(\text{P3-NTT}) = \frac{3}{2}nlogn + (\frac{11}{3} - \frac{3}{2}log3)n$.
- Additions: $T_a(\text{P3-NTT}) = 3nlogn + (6 - 3log3)n$.

7 Applications to Kyber and NewHope

In this section, we apply the NTT techniques proposed in this work to Kyber [4] and NewHope [12]. Kyber is the prominent KEM scheme based on MLWE, and is now in the third round of NIST PQC standardization. NewHope is the standing KEM scheme based on RLWE, and was one of the candidates in the second round of NIST PQC standardization. Tough NewHope was not moved to the third round, the study and optimization of NewHope still deserve further research exploration.

Let $\mathcal{R}$ and $\mathcal{R}_q$ (restated) denote the rings $\mathbb{Z}[x]/(x^n+1)$ and $\mathbb{Z}_q[x]/(x^n+1)$, respectively. Denote by $S_\eta \subseteq \mathcal{R}^k$ the set of elements $w \in \mathcal{R}^k$ such that $||w||_\infty \leq \eta$, where $k \geq 0$ is an integer. Roughly speaking, the Module-LWE (MLWE) problem states that given $\mathbf{A} \leftarrow \mathcal{R}_q^{k\times k}$ and $\mathbf{b} := \mathbf{As} + \mathbf{e}$ where $\mathbf{s}, \mathbf{e} \leftarrow S_\eta$, no efficient algorithm can recover $\mathbf{s}$ with non-negligible probability. Kyber sets $n = 256$, $q = 3329$ and $\eta = 2$, and provides three sets of parameters, referred to as Kyber-512, Kyber-768 and Kyber-1024 respectively, which correspond to $k = 2, 3$ and 4 respectively. The Ring-LWE (RLWE) problem can be viewed as a special case of MLWE with $k = 1$. NewHope sets $q = 12289$, $\eta = 8$ and $k = 1$, and provides two sets of parameters, referred to as NewHope-512 and NewHope-1024, which correspond to $n = 512$ and $n = 1024$ respectively.

7.1 Application to Kyber

We focus on the Kyber-1024 parameter set, which aims at about 230-bit post-quantum security but with 256-bit shared-key to be encapsulated. In this work, we provide a new set of parameters for Kyber-1024: $n = 512$, $k = 2$ (and the same $q = 3329$ and $\eta = 2$), which is summarized in Table 1 (page 12). In comparison with the parameter set in [4], at the same level of security and error probability the new Kyber-1024 parameter set has doubled key size (say, 512 bits). Here, we would like to highlight the importance and desirability of larger shared-key size.

- Doubling the shared-key size means more powerful and economic ability of key transportation, at the same level of security. For applications that require a 512-bit shared-key, we may run Kyber-1024 twice. In this case, running our new Kyber-1024 is much more efficient both in computation and in bandwidth, though the size of public key and that of ciphertext of the new Kyber-1024 are relatively larger on their own.
- Doubling the shared-key size is important for the targeted security level against Grover's search algorithm, and against the possibility of more sophisticated quantum cryptanalysis in the long run. Note that for Kyber-1024, its target security level is about 230-bit post-quantum security. Even if the underlying MLWE problem provides this level of hardness, the 256-bit shared-key

may not. Though the standardization of post-quantum symmetric key cryptography is not considered yet, it is expected that the key size will increase to remain the same security level in the post-quantum era.
- Larger key size is indeed needed in many cryptographic standards. For example, according to different security levels (specifically, 128, 192, 256-bit security), in TLS 1.3 it mandates three options for the master secrecy size: 256, 384 and 512, by employing the secp256r1, secp384r1 and secp512r1 curves respectively.

We apply our H-NTT technique with $\alpha = \beta = 1$ to the new Kyber-1024 protocol. We note that the new Kyber-1024 protocol implementation can reuse the NTT codes of Kyber-512 (for $n = 256$ and $k = 2$) and those of Kyber-768 (for $n = 256$ and $k = 3$). Specifically, Kyber-512 and Kyber-768 use T-NTT that is a 7-level 256-point NTT. In this work, each polynomial used in the new Kyber-1024 protocol is of degree 512, and is divided into two parts of degree 256 which can then utilize the 7-level 256-point T-NTT used in Kyber-512 and Kyber-768. Our H-NTT based implementation of the new Kyber-1024 protocol reuses the codes of T-NTT employed in the implementations of Kyber-512 and Kyber-768. In this sense, our H-NTT is compatible with the initial T-NTT utilized in Kyber, since the initial codes of T-NTT can be reused as a sub-procedure in H-NTT. In other words, though the parameter set is changed, there is no need for modification of codes of NTT. As a consequence, our method can save the code size of NTT and can improve computational efficiency.

Table 1. Parameter sets for Kyber-1024. Here, $|K|$ refers to the size of the key to be encapsulated; $|pk|$ (resp., $|ct|$) refers to the size of public key (resp., ciphertext) in bytes; pq-sec refers to the post-quantum bit security; *err* refers to the error probability.

Schemes		n	k	q	η	$\|K\|$	$(\|pk\|, \|ct\|)$	pq-sec	err
Kyber-1024	[2]	256	4	3329	2	256	(1568,1568)	230	2^{-174}
	(Ours)	512	2	3329	2	512	(1600,1728)	230	2^{-174}

7.2 Application to NewHope

NewHope in [12] sets $q = 12289$ and $\eta = 8$, and provides two sets of parameters, referred to as NewHope-512 and NewHope-1024, which correspond to $n = 512$ and $n = 1024$ respectively. Recently, the work [1] provides its variant: NewHope-Compact, which provides three sets of parameters referred to as NewHope-Compact-512, NewHope-Compact-768 and NewHope-Compact-1024 respectively. Both NewHope-Compact-512 and NewHope-Compact-1024 set $q = 3329$, similar to Kyber. But NewHope-Compact-768 sets $q = 3457$ for the case of $n = 768$ by employing an improved version of the NTTRU approach [11].

In this work, we present a new variant of NewHope, referred to as NewHope-Unified for simplicity, which sets the same modulus $q = 7681$ (as well as the same $\eta = 4$) for all the three cases of $n \in \{512, 768, 1024\}$. The parameters for NewHope-Unified are given in Table 2 (page 13). For the three cases of $n = 512, 768$ and 1024 of NewHope-Unified, we apply T-NTT (with $\beta = 1$), P3-NTT, and H-NTT (with $\alpha = \beta = 1$) respectively. Accordingly, their moduli q's should satisfy $q \equiv 1 \mod 512$, $q \equiv 1 \mod 768$, and $q \equiv 1 \mod 512$ respectively. The smallest modulus q meeting these conditions is 7681. Note that H-NTT for NewHope-Unified-1024 can reuse the codes of T-NTT for NewHope-Unified-512. Specifically, the T-NTT used by NewHope-Unified-512 is an 8-level 512-point NTT. The polynomials used in NewHope-Unified-1024 are of degree 1024 and are divided into two parts of degree 512, which can then reuse the T-NTT codes for NewHope-Unified-512. For NewHope-Unified-768, we apply the P3-NTT technique developed in this work. It divides the polynomial of degree 768 into three parts of degree 256, and the NTT process of each part can be performed independently in parallel.

As shown in Table 3 (page 14), NewHope-Unified provides a trade-off between bandwidth and error probability. Specifically, it has lower sizes of ciphertexts and public/secret keys than that of NewHope, and has lower error probability than that of NewHope-Compact for the cases of $n = 512$ and $n = 768$. Finally, we highlight some advantages of employing the unified modulus $q = 7681$ for all the three cases of $n \in \{512, 768, 1024\}$:

- It allows more modular implementations, and simplifies implementation complexity. For example, the same modular reduction can be used for all the three cases.
- It allows more space-efficient implementations. Specifically, two tables *omega* and *omega_inv* are needed in NTTs. However, the contents of the tables vary with q. If q is not unified, we need more tables to store the pre-computed values of ω^i and ω^{-i}. In our implementation, we keep $q = 7681$ unified for different n's, so the storage of these pre-computed tables, as well as the size of the program codes, can be reduced.

Table 2. Parameter sets of NewHope-Unified

Schemes	n	q	ω	η
NewHope-Unified-512	512	7681	62	4
NewHope-Unified-768	768	7681	20	4
NewHope-Unified-1024	1024	7681	62	4

7.3 Implementation and Benchmark

We implement the algorithms and run the benchmark in reference C implementations on Intel(R) Core(TM) i7-9700k CPU @ 3.60 GHz, with HyperThreading off. The codes are compiled with the option -mavx2 -maes -mbmi2 -mpopcnt -O3 -Wall -Wextra -Wpedantic -Wmissing-prototypes -Wredundant-decls -fPIC -std=c99. We run KeyGen, Encaps and Decaps for 1000 times respectively. The averages of CPU cycle counts are given in Table 4 (page 15) for Kyber and Table 5 (page 15) for NewHope (and its variants) respectively. Here, we highlight some points of the implementations.

Table 3. Comparison of NewHope, NewHope-Compact and NewHope-Unified. Here, $|pk|$, $|sk|$ and $|ct|$ refer to the size of public key, secret key and ciphertext in bytes respectively; pq-sec refers to the post-quantum bit security; *err* refers to the error probability.

Schemes	n	q	err	pq-sec	$\lvert pk\rvert$	$\lvert sk\rvert$	$\lvert ct\rvert$
NewHope	512	12289	2^{-213}	101	928	1888	1120
	1024	12289	2^{-216}	233	1824	3680	2208
NewHope-Compact	512	3329	2^{-256}	100	800	1632	992
	768	3457	2^{-170}	163	1184	2400	1568
	1024	3329	2^{-181}	230	1568	3168	2080
NewHope-Unified(Ours)	512	7681	2^{-300}	98	864	1760	1056
	768	7681	2^{-229}	161	1280	2592	1568
	1024	7681	2^{-176}	227	1696	3424	2080

Butterfly Operation. Note that Cooley-Tukey butterfly takes input in the normal order and outputs in the bit-reversed order, while Gentleman-Sande butterfly takes input in the bit-reversed order and outputs in the normal order. With this observation, unlike the implementation of NewHope [12], our implementation uses Cooley-Tukey butterfly in forward NTT and Gentleman-Sande butterfly in NTT^{-1} for various n's, in order to save a bit-reversal operation. Otherwise, if Gentleman-Sande butterfly is used in both forward NTT and NTT^{-1}, we need an extra bit-reversal firstly.

Barrett Reduction and Lazy Reduction. For Barrett reduction, the range of its input value a is $-\frac{t}{2} \leq a < \frac{t}{2}$ where $t = 2^{16}$ in this work, and the range of its output is $r = a \mod q$. Therefore, the coefficients of the polynomial can be added or subtracted up to 3 times for the case of $q = 7681$, without exceeding the input range of Barrett reduction. Thus, we do not need to perform modular reduction after every addition or subtraction. Instead, we can perform it only after every three additions or subtractions. This lazy reduction technique allows us to greatly reduce the number of reductions.

Montgomery Reduction. For Montgomery reduction, its input value a is a 32-bit integer ranging from $-\frac{t}{2}q$ to $\frac{t}{2}q$ where $t = 2^{16}$. The range of its output is $-q < r < q$ where $r = t^{-1}a \mod q$. This algorithm is used to keep the product of two polynomial coefficients in the Montgomery domain. Actually, the product of two polynomial coefficients is in the range of input of Montgomery reduction.

Sampling and Noise. Our parameter sets allow much faster sampling of secret and noise polynomials. Usually, they are sampled by centered binomial distribution ψ_η, which can be computed with $\sum_{i=1}^{\eta}(a_i - b_i)$ where the bits a_i and b_i are chosen uniformly at random from $\{0,1\}$. In this work, we sample them by ψ_4 when implementing NewHope-Unified. On each call, **SHAKE256** generates 128 bytes, every byte of which can be used to construct one coefficient according to ψ_4. That is, we can sample 128 coefficients on each call. To generate all coefficients of polynomials in $\mathcal{R}_q$, **SHAKE256** has to be called 4, 6 and 8 times respectively for $n = 512, 768$ and 1024 in NewHope-Unified. As for the implementation of our new Kyber-1024 protocol, we use the same ψ_2 as in the original Kyber-1024 implementation [2].

Table 4. Cycle counts of Kyber-1024

Schemes		KeyGen	Encaps	Decaps
Kyber-1024	[2]	65145	109851	89781
	(Ours)	36772	49113	45976

Table 5. Cycle counts of NewHope, NewHope-Compact and NewHope-Unified

Schemes	n	KeyGen	Encaps	Decaps
NewHope	512	85177	123058	144323
	1024	163756	245402	278182
NewHope-Compact	512	49699	93731	119334
	768	76434	187455	195533
	1024	107655	204469	241979
NewHope-Unified(Ours)	512	77438	112867	129657
	768	147917	233193	252238
	1024	104402	210770	224403

References

1. Alkım, E., Bilgin, Y.A., Cenk, M.: Compact and simple RLWE based key encapsulation mechanism. In: Schwabe, P., Thériault, N. (eds.) LATINCRYPT 2019. LNCS, vol. 11774, pp. 237–256. Springer, Cham (2019). https://doi.org/10.1007/978-3-030-30530-7_12
2. Avanzi, R., et al.: Cyrystals-kyber: algorithm specifications and supporting documentation (version 2.0). NIST Post-Quantum Cryptography Standardization Process (2019)
3. Bernstein, D.J.: Multidigit multiplication for mathematicians (2001)
4. Bos, J.W., et al.: CRYSTALS - Kyber: a CCA-secure module-lattice-based KEM. In: EuroS&P 2018, pp. 353–367. IEEE (2018)
5. Cohen, H.: A Course in Computational Algebraic Number Theory. Graduate Texts in Mathematics. Springer, Heidelberg (1993). https://doi.org/10.1007/978-3-662-02945-9
6. Cook, S.A., Aanderaa, S.O.: On the minimum computation time of functions. Trans. Am. Math. Soc. **142**, 291–314 (1969)
7. Cooly, J.W., Tukey, J.W.: An algorithm for the machine calculation of complex fourier series. Math. Comput. **19**(90), 297–301 (1965)
8. D'Anvers, J.-P., Karmakar, A., Sinha Roy, S., Vercauteren, F.: Saber: module-LWR based key exchange, CPA-secure encryption and CCA-secure KEM. In: Joux, A., Nitaj, A., Rachidi, T. (eds.) AFRICACRYPT 2018. LNCS, vol. 10831, pp. 282–305. Springer, Cham (2018). https://doi.org/10.1007/978-3-319-89339-6_16
9. Gauss, C.F.: Theoria interpolationis methodo nova tractata (1805)
10. Karatsuba, A.A., Ofman, Y.P.: Multiplication of many-digital numbers by automatic computers. In: Doklady Akademii Nauk, vol. 145, pp. 293–294. Russian Academy of Sciences (1962)
11. Lyubashevsky, V., Seiler, G.: NTTRU: truly fast NTRU using NTT. IACR Trans. Cryptogr. Hardw. Embed. Syst. **2019**(3), 180–201 (2019)
12. Pöppelmann, T., Alkim, E., Ducas, L., Schwabe, P.: Newhope: algorithm specifications and supporting documentation (version 1.0.3). NIST Post-Quantum Cryptography Standardization Process (2019)
13. Toom, A.L.: The complexity of a scheme of functional elements realizing the multiplication of integers. Dokl. Akad. Nauk SSSR **3**(3), 496–498 (1963)
14. Weimerskirch, A., Paar, C.: Generalizations of the karatsuba algorithm for efficient implementations. IACR Cryptology ePrint Archive 2006:224 (2006)
15. Zhou, S., Xue, H., Zhang, D., Wang, K., Lu, X., Li, B., He, J.: Preprocess-then-NTT technique and its applications to Kyber and NewHope. In: Guo, F., Huang, X., Yung, M. (eds.) Inscrypt 2018. LNCS, vol. 11449, pp. 117–137. Springer, Cham (2019). https://doi.org/10.1007/978-3-030-14234-6_7
16. Zhu, Y., Liu, Z., Pan, Y.: When NTT meets Karatsuba: preprocess-then-NTT technique revisited. IACR Cryptology ePrint Archive 2019:1079 (2019)

On Galois NFSRs Equivalent to Fibonacci Ones

Jianghua Zhong[1(✉)], Yingyin Pan[1,2], and Dongdai Lin[1]

[1] State Key Laboratory of Information Security, Institute of Information Engineering, Chinese Academy of Sciences, Beijing 100093, China
{zhongjianghua,panyingyin,ddlin}@iie.ac.cn
[2] School of Cyber Security, University of Chinese Academy of Sciences, Beijing 100049, China

Abstract. Nonlinear feedback shift registers (NFSRs) are used in many stream ciphers as their main building blocks. According to implementation configurations, NFSRs are generally classified as Fibonacci NFSRs and Galois NFSRs. Compared to Fibonacci NFSRs, Galois NFSRs have potentially shorter propagation time and higher throughput. Moreover, if a Galois NFSR is equivalent to a Fibonacci NFSR in the sense that they have the same set of output sequences, then this particular Galois NFSR can overcome some drawbacks of a general one, and therefore may improve the security of NFSR-based stream ciphers. Previous work has found some types of Galois NFSRs equivalent to Fibonacci NFSRs, and has shown many Galois NFSRs equivalent to a given Fibonacci NFSR with the same stage number. This paper gives another type of Galois NFSRs equivalent to a given Fibonacci NFSR, in which their all corresponding states have either equal or complementary components at the same positions. As an application of this result, the paper shows that the stream ciphers Grain, Trivium and Acorn have used the NFSRs with the lowest cost of hardware implementation among their own equivalent Galois NFSRs of this type. The paper also enumerates the Galois NFSRs equivalent to a given Fibonacci NFSR with the same stage number. Moreover, it reveals some common characterizations of Galois NFSRs that are equivalent to Fibonacci ones from the perspectives of their stage number and feedback functions, helpful to the design of stream ciphers.

Keywords: Shift register · Stream cipher · Equivalence

1 Introduction

Nonlinear feedback shift registers (NFSRs) have been used as the main building blocks in many stream ciphers, such as the finalists of Grain [1] and Trivium [2] in the eSTREAM project, and the finalist of Acorn [3] in the CAESAR competition. An NFSR can be generally implemented in Fibonacci or Galois configuration. In Fibonacci configuration, the feedback of an NFSR is only applied to the last

Y. Wu and M. Yung (Eds.): Inscrypt 2020, LNCS 12612, pp. 433–449, 2021.
https://doi.org/10.1007/978-3-030-71852-7_29

bit, while in the Galois configuration, the feedback can be applied to every bit. NFSRs in Fibonacci configuration are called Fibonacci NFSRs, and those in Galois configuration are called Galois NFSRs. Compared to Fibonacci NFSRs, Galois NFSRs have potentially shorter propagation time and higher throughput [4]. Actually, the foregoing stream ciphers have all used the Galois NFSRs.

Two NFSRs are said to be equivalent if their sets of output sequences are equal. So far, some work has been done on the equivalence of NFSRs. First, for the equivalence between Galois NFSRs, a Galois NFSR in which the feedback function of the i-th bit satisfies $f_i(X_1, X_2, \ldots, X_n) = X_{(i+1) \bmod n} \oplus g_i(X_1, \ldots, X_i, X_{i+2}, \ldots, X_n)$ was found equivalent to a class of Galois NFSRs [5]. In addition, as particular Galois NFRSRs, cascade connections of two NFSRs were characterized from the perspective of feedback functions if they are equivalent [6]. Second, for the equivalence between Galois NFSRs and Fibonacci ones, on one hand, it was found that any given Fibonacci NFSR can be equivalent to "uniform" Galois NFSRs with the same stage number [4] and their initial states were matched [7]; moreover, experiments verified Galois NFSRs capable of improving throughput and reducing areas, compared to their equivalent Fibonacci NFSRs [4]. On the other hand, "lower triangular" Galois NFSRs [8] and cascade connections of two NFSRs [9] were revealed equivalent to Fibonacci NFSRs, which in fact are some *sufficient conditions* for Galois NFSRs equivalent to Fibonacci NFSRs.

If a Galois NFSR is equivalent to a Fibonacci one, then this particular Galois NFSR overcomes some drawbacks of a general one. Those drawbacks include the output sequence of a general Galois NFSR having a period shorter than the length of the longest cyclic sequence of its consecutive states, and a general n-stage Galois NFSR with period $2^n - 1$ unsatisfying the first and second randomness postulates of Golomb [4]. Such overcome drawbacks may improve the security of NFSR-based stream ciphers. However, not all types of Galois NFSRs equivalent to Fibonacci ones have been found, and *how many* Galois NFSRs equivalent to a given Fibonacci NFSR is unclear, either. Moreover, it is still unknown what *necessary conditions* are for the Galois NFSRs equivalent to Fibonacci NFSRs? In other words, what are common characterizations of Galois NFSRs equivalent to Fibonacci ones? These are what the paper addresses.

An NFSR has the same mathematical model as a Boolean network, which is a finite automaton evolving through Boolean functions. Boolean networks haven been well developed in the community of systems and control [10] via a powerful tool of semi-tensor product [11]. As the literature [12–15], this paper views NFSRs as Boolean networks, and uses the developed theory of Boolean networks therein to analyze the cryptographical properties of NFSRs.

Contribution. The paper first gives a new type of Galois NFSRs equivalent to a given Fibonacci NFSR, in which their all corresponding states have either equal or complementary components at the same positions. As an application of this result, the paper shows that the stream ciphers Grain, Trivium and Acorn have used the NFSRs with the lowest cost of hardware implementation among their own equivalent Galois NFSRs of this type. The paper then enumerates

n-stage Galois NFSRs equivalent to a given n-stage Fibonacci NFSR. Finally, it reveals some common characterizations of Galois NFSRs that are equivalent to Fibonacci ones from the perspectives of their stage number and feedback functions. All these are helpful to the design of NFSR-based stream ciphers.

Organization. The paper is organized as follows. Section 2 presents some preliminaries. Section 3 is our main results. The paper concludes in Sect. 4.

2 Preliminaries

In this section, we first introduce some notations used throughout the paper. We then review some concepts on Boolean functions and semi-tensor product. Finally, we revisit the linear system representation of Boolean networks.

2.1 Notations

- $\mathbb{F}_2$: binary field.
- $\mathbb{F}_2^n$: n-dimensional vector space over $\mathbb{F}_2$.
- $\mathbb{N}$: set of nonnegative integers.
- I_n: identity matrix of dimension n.
- δ_n^i: the i-th column of the matrix I_n with $i \in \{1, 2, \ldots, n\}$.
- Δ_n: set of all columns of the matrix I_n.
- $\mathcal{L}_{n\times m}$: set of $n \times m$ matrices, whose columns belong to Δ_n. If $L \in \mathcal{L}_{n\times m}$, then $L = [\delta_n^{i_1}\ \delta_n^{i_2}\ \cdots\ \delta_n^{i_m}]$, and its transpose $L^T = [(\delta_n^{i_1})^T\ (\delta_n^{i_2})^T\ \cdots\ (\delta_n^{i_m})^T]^T$. For simplicity, we write L and L^T in compact forms, as $L = \delta_n[i_1\ i_2\ \cdots\ i_m]$ and $L^T = \delta_n[i_1\ i_2\ \cdots\ i_m]^T$.
- $\mathrm{Col}_j(A)$: the j-th column of a matrix A.
- $N!$: factorial of a positive integer N.
- $\otimes$ and $\ltimes$: Kronecker product and semi-tensor product, respectively.
- $+$, $-$ and $\times$: ordinary addition, subtraction and multiplication in the real field, respectively.
- $\oplus$ and $\odot$: addition and multiplication modulo 2 over $\mathbb{F}_2$, respectively.

2.2 Boolean Function

An n-variable Boolean function f is a mapping from $\mathbb{F}_2^n$ to $\mathbb{F}_2$. Let i be the decimal number corresponding to the binary $(i_1, i_2, \ldots, i_n)$ via the mapping $i = i_1 2^{n-1} + i_2 2^{n-2} + \cdots + i_n$. Then i ranges from 0 to $2^n - 1$. For the simplicity, we denote $f(i) = f(i_1, i_2, \ldots, i_n)$. Then the binary string $[f(2^n-1), f(2^n-2), \ldots, f(0)]$ is called the truth table of f, arranged in the *reverse alphabet order.* The matrix

$$F = \begin{bmatrix} f(2^n-1) & f(2^n-2) & \cdots & f(0) \\ 1-f(2^n-1) & 1-f(2^n-2) & \cdots & 1-f(0) \end{bmatrix},$$

is called the *structure matrix* of f [10,16]. The function $\mathbf{f} = [f_1\ \ f_2\ \ldots\ f_n]^T$ is a *vectorial function* if f_is are Boolean functions for all $i = 1, 2, \ldots, n$.

The *Hamming weight* of a binary string α of finite length is the number of ones in α, denoted by $\mathrm{wt}(\alpha)$. The Hamming weight of a Boolean function f, denoted by $\mathrm{wt}(f)$, is the Hamming weight of its truth table. The Hamming weight is one of the most basic properties of a Boolean function, and is a crucial criterion in cryptography [17]. If an n-variable Boolean function f has the Hamming weight $\mathrm{wt}(f) = 2^{n-1}$, then the Boolean function f is said to be *balanced.* An n-variable Boolean function f is said to be *linear* with respect to the variable X_i if $f(X_1, X_2, \ldots, X_n) = X_i \oplus \tilde{f}(X_1, X_2, \ldots, X_{i-1}, X_{i+1}, \ldots, X_n)$ for some i satisfying $1 \leq i \leq n$. If a Boolean function f is linear with respect to some variable, then it is balanced.

2.3 Semi-tensor Product

Definition 1 ([18]). *Let $A = (a_{ij})$ and B be matrices of dimensions $n \times m$ and $p \times q$, respectively. The Kronecker product of A and B, is defined as an $np \times mq$ matrix, given by*

$$A \otimes B = \begin{bmatrix} a_{11}B & a_{12}B & \cdots & a_{1m}B \\ a_{21}B & a_{22}B & \cdots & a_{2m}B \\ \vdots & \vdots & & \vdots \\ a_{n1}B & a_{n2}B & \cdots & a_{nm}B \end{bmatrix}.$$

Definition 2 ([11]). *For an $n \times m$ matrix A and a $p \times q$ matrix B, let α be the least common multiple of m and p. The (left) semi-tensor product of A and B is defined as an $\frac{n\alpha}{m} \times \frac{q\alpha}{p}$ matrix, given by*

$$A \ltimes B = (A \otimes I_{\frac{\alpha}{m}})(B \otimes I_{\frac{\alpha}{p}}),$$

where $\otimes$ represents the Kronecker product.

Clearly, in Definition 2 if $m = p$, then the semi-tensor product $A \ltimes B$ is reduced to the conventional matrix product AB. In fact, the semi-tensor product is a generalization of the conventional matrix product, but it retains all major properties of the conventional matrix product, such as the associative law and the distributive law [11].

Lemma 1 ([11]). *Let $\mathbf{X}$ and $\mathbf{Y}$ be two column vectors of dimensions m and n, respectively. Then $\mathbf{X} \ltimes \mathbf{Y} = \mathbf{X} \otimes \mathbf{Y}$.*

2.4 Linear System Representation of Boolean Networks

In general, a Boolean network with n nodes can be described as a nonlinear system:

$$\mathbf{X}(t+1) = \mathbf{g}(\mathbf{X}(t)),\ t \in \mathbb{N}, \tag{1}$$

where $\mathbf{X} = [X_1 \ \ X_2 \ \ \cdots \ \ X_n]^T \in \mathbb{F}_2^n$ is the state, and the vectorial function $\mathbf{g} = [g_1 \ \ g_2 \ \ldots \ g_n]^T$ is the state transition function.

Lemma 2 **([10]).** *Let* $\mathbf{x} = [X_1 \;\; X_1 \oplus 1]^T \ltimes [X_2 \;\; X_2 \oplus 1]^T \ltimes \cdots \ltimes [X_n \;\; X_n \oplus 1]^T$ *with* $X_i \in \mathbb{F}_2$, $i = 1, 2, \ldots, n$. *Then* $\mathbf{x} \in \Delta_{2^n}$. *Moreover, the state* $\mathbf{X} = [X_1 \;\; X_2 \;\; \cdots \;\; X_n]^T \in \mathbb{F}_2^n$ *and the state* $\mathbf{x} = \delta_{2^n}^j \in \Delta_{2^n}$ *with* $j = 2^n - (2^{n-1}X_1 + 2^{n-2}X_2 + \cdots + X_n)$ *are one-to-one correspondent.*

Lemma 3 **([10]).** *The nonlinear system (1) representing a Boolean network can be equivalently expressed as the linear system:*

$$\mathbf{x}(t+1) = L\mathbf{x}(t), \; t \in \mathbb{N}, \tag{2}$$

where $\mathbf{x} \in \Delta_{2^n}$ *is the state, and* $L \in \mathcal{L}_{2^n \times 2^n}$ *is the state transition matrix, satisfying*

$$Col_j(L) = Col_j(G_1) \otimes Col_j(G_2) \otimes \cdots \otimes Col_j(G_n), \; j = 1, 2, \ldots, 2^n, \tag{3}$$

with the structure matrix G_i *of the i-th component* g_i *of the vectorial function* $\mathbf{g}$ *in (1) for any* $i \in \{1, 2, \ldots, n\}$.

2.5 Nonlinear Feedback Shift Registers

Galois and Fibonacci NFSRs. Figure 1(a) gives the diagram of an n-stage Galois NFSR, in which each small square represents a binary storage device, also called *bit*. Each i-th bit has a feedback function f_i. All these feedback functions $f_1, f_2, \ldots, f_n$ form the feedback $\mathbf{f} = [f_1 \;\; f_2 \;\; \ldots \;\; f_n]^T$ of the Galois NFSR. At each periodic interval determined by a master clock, the content of each bit is updated by the value of its feedback function at the previous contents of all bits. The n-stage Galois NFSR can be described as the following system:

$$\begin{cases} X_1(t+1) = f_1(X_1, X_2, \ldots, X_n), \\ X_2(t+1) = f_2(X_1, X_2, \ldots, X_n), \\ \quad \vdots \\ X_n(t+1) = f_n(X_1, X_2, \ldots, X_n), \end{cases} \tag{4}$$

where $t \in \mathbb{N}$ represents time instant. The content of the first bit is used as the output of the Galois NFSR.

In particular, if there is only shift between neighboring bits for the first $n-1$ bits, that is, $f_i(X_1, X_2, \ldots, X_n) = X_{i+1}$ for all $i = 1, 2, \ldots, n-1$, then the n-stage Galois NFSR is reduced to an n-stage Fibonacci NFSR. Figure 1(b) shows the diagram of an n-stage Fibonacci NFSR, in which the Boolean function f is called the feedback function of the Fibonacci NFSR. A Fibonacci NFSR is *nonsingular* if and only if its feedback function f is nonsingular, that is, $f(X_1, X_2, \ldots, X_n) = X_1 \oplus \tilde{f}(X_1, X_2, \ldots, X_n)$ [19].

Lemma 4 **([13]).** *An n-stage Fibonacci NFSR with a feedback function f can be represented by a linear system:*

$$\mathbf{x}(t+1) = L_f\mathbf{x}(t), \; t \in N,$$

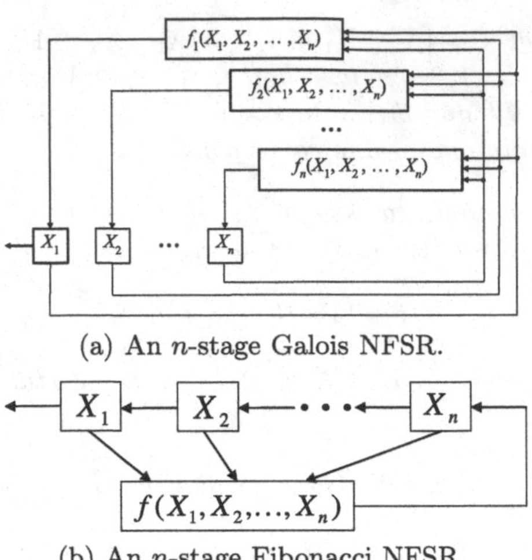

(a) An n-stage Galois NFSR.

(b) An n-stage Fibonacci NFSR.

Fig. 1. Galois and Fibonacci NFSRs.

where $x \in \Delta_{2^n}$ *is the state,* $L_f = \delta_{2^n}[\eta_1 \ \ \eta_2 \ \ \ldots \ \ \eta_{2^n}] \in \mathcal{L}_{2^n \times 2^n}$ *is the state transition matrix, satisfying*

$$\begin{cases} \eta_{2^{n-1}+i} = 2i - f(2^{n-1} - i), \\ \eta_i = 2i - f(2^n - i), \ i = 1, 2, \ldots, 2^{n-1}. \end{cases}$$

Moreover, the Fibonacci NFSR is nonsingular if and only if its state transition matrix L_f *is nonsingular.*

State Diagram of NFSRs. The *state diagram* of an n-stage NFSR is a directed graph consisting of 2^n nodes and 2^n edges, in which each node represents a state of the NFSR, and each edge represents a transition between states. An edge from state $\mathbf{X}$ to state $\mathbf{Y}$ means that the state $\mathbf{X}$ is updated to the state $\mathbf{Y}$. $\mathbf{X}$ is called a *predecessor* of $\mathbf{Y}$, and $\mathbf{Y}$ is called the *successor* of $\mathbf{X}$. A sequence of p distinct states, $\mathbf{X}_1, \mathbf{X}_2, \ldots, \mathbf{X}_p$, is called a *cycle of length* p if $\mathbf{X}_1$ is the successor of $\mathbf{X}_p$, and $\mathbf{X}_{i+1}$ is a successor of $\mathbf{X}_i$ for any $i \in \{1, 2, \ldots, p-1\}$.

Let $G = (V, A)$ and $\bar{G} = (\bar{V}, \bar{A})$ be the state diagrams of two n-stage NFSRs, where V and $\bar{V}$ are their sets of states, while A and $\bar{A}$ are their sets of edges. G and $\bar{G}$ are said to be *isomorphic* if there exists a bijection mapping $\varphi : V \to \bar{V}$ such that for any edge $E \in A$ from state $\mathbf{X}$ to state $\mathbf{Y}$, there exists an edge $\bar{E} \in \bar{A}$ from $\varphi(\mathbf{X})$ to $\varphi(\mathbf{Y})$.

Lemma 5 ([20]). *Let* $y(t) = g(\mathbf{X}(t))$*, where* $\mathbf{X}$ *is the state of a Galois NFSR, and* g *is a Boolean function, and* t *represents the time instant. Then the period of the sequence* $(y(t))_{t \geq 0}$ *is a factor of the period of the state sequence* $(\mathbf{X}(t))_{t \geq 0}$.

Lemma 6 ([21]). *If an* n*-stage Fibonacci NFSR and an* n*-stage Galois NFSR are equivalent, then their state diagrams are isomorphic.*

3 Main Results

In this section, we will reveal some characterizations of Galois NFSRs that are equivalent to Fibonacci NFSRs from the point of view of their stage number and feedback functions.

Lemma 7. *An n-stage Galois NFSR with feedback* $\mathbf{f} = [f_1 \ f_2 \ \dots \ f_n]^T$ *can be equivalently expressed as a linear system:*

$$\mathbf{x}(t+1) = L_g \mathbf{x}(t), \ t \in \mathbb{N},$$

where $\mathbf{x} \in \Delta_{2^n}$ *is the state, and* $L_g = \delta_{2^n}[\zeta_1 \ \zeta_2 \ \dots \ \zeta_{2^n}] \in \mathcal{L}_{2^n \times 2^n}$ *is the state transition matrix, satisfying*

$$\zeta_i = 2^n - 2^{n-1} f_1(2^n - i) - 2^{n-2} f_2(2^n - i) - \cdots - 2 f_{n-1}(2^n - i) - f_n(2^n - i), \ i = 1, 2, \dots, 2^n.$$

Proof. View the Galois NFSR as a Boolean network. Then the result follows from Lemmas 1, 2 and 3. □

Theorem 1. *If a Galois NFSR is equivalent to a Fibonacci NFSR, then its stage number is no less than that of the Fibonacci NFSR.*

Proof. If a Galois NFSR is equivalent to a Fibonacci NFSR, then they have the same set of output sequences. Thus, their corresponding output sequences have the same period. According to Lemma 5, we know that the output sequence of a Galois NFSR has a period dividing into the cycle length of its consecutive states. It implies that a Galois NFSR possibly needs more states than its equivalent Fibonacci NFSR to generate the same output sequence. The possible requirement of more states induces possibly greater stage number. □

From Theorem 1, we know that from the economical perspective of the hardware implementation cost, we can only consider the equivalent Galois NFSR with stage number equal to that of a given Fibonacci NFSR.

Lemma 8. *An n-stage Galois NFSR represented by System* $\mathbf{X}(t+1) = F(\mathbf{X}(t))$ *with state* $\mathbf{X} \in \mathbb{F}_2^n$ *is equivalent to an n-stage Fibonacci NFSR represented by System* $\mathbf{Y}(t+1) = H(\mathbf{Y}(t))$ *with state* $\mathbf{Y} \in \mathbb{F}_2^n$*, if and only if there exists a bijective mapping* $\varphi : \mathbf{X} \mapsto \mathbf{Y}$ *such that* $\varphi(F(\mathbf{X})) = H(\varphi(\mathbf{X}))$ *and* $[1 \ 0 \ \cdots \ 0]\varphi(\mathbf{X}) = [1 \ 0 \ \cdots \ 0]\mathbf{X}$ *for all* $\mathbf{X} \in \mathbb{F}_2^n$.

Proof. Necessity: Clearly, for each $\mathbf{X} \in \mathbb{F}_2^n$, there exists an edge from state $\mathbf{X}$ to state $F(\mathbf{X})$ in the state diagram of the Galois NFSR. Similarly, for each state $\mathbf{Y} \in \mathbb{F}_2^n$, there exists an edge from state $\mathbf{Y}$ to state $H(\mathbf{Y})$ in the state diagram of the Fibonacci NFSR. If a Galois NFSR is equivalent to a Fibonacci NFSR, then according to Lemma 6, their state diagrams are isomorphic, which is equivalent to that there exists a bijective mapping $\varphi : \mathbf{X} \mapsto \mathbf{Y}$ such that $\varphi(F(\mathbf{X})) = H(\mathbf{Y}) = H(\varphi(\mathbf{X}))$ for each $\mathbf{X} \in \mathbb{F}_2^n$. Moreover, since the output of an NFSR is the content of the first bit, each state $\mathbf{X}$ and its correspondingly transformed state $\mathbf{Y}$ have the same first component, which is equivalent to $[1\ 0\ \cdots\ 0]\varphi(\mathbf{X}) = [1\ 0\ \cdots\ 0]\mathbf{X}$ for each $\mathbf{X} \in \mathbb{F}_2^n$.

Sufficiency: If there exists a bijective mapping $\varphi : \mathbf{X} \mapsto \mathbf{Y}$ such that $\varphi(F(\mathbf{X})) = H(\varphi(\mathbf{X}))$ and $[1\ 0\ \cdots\ 0]\varphi(\mathbf{X}) = [1\ 0\ \cdots\ 0]\mathbf{X}$ for all $\mathbf{X} \in \mathbb{F}_2^n$, then according to the necessity proof, the state diagrams of the Galois NFSR and the Fibonacci NFSR are isomorphic, and each state and its correspondingly transformed state have the same first component. Hence, the Galois NFSR and the Fibonacci NFSR have the same set of output sequences. Therefore, they are equivalent. □

Lemma 8 shows that an n-stage Galois NFSR equivalent to an n-stage Fibonacci NFSR means their corresponding states mapped by a bijection have the same first component. Each pair of corresponding states is called *equivalent states.* The following result gives a type of Galois NFSRs, which are equivalent to a given Fibonacci NFSR, and all pairs of equivalent states have either equal or complementary components at the same positions.

Theorem 2. *An n-stage Fibonacci NFSR with a feedback function f is equivalent to an n-stage Galois NFSR with a feedback $\mathbf{f} = [f_1\ \ f_2\ \ldots\ f_n]^T$, in which for some positive integers $k_1, k_2 \ldots, k_r$ satisfying $1 < k_1 < k_2 < \cdots < k_r \le n$, the f_ks are expressed as:*

$$\begin{cases} f_k = X_{k+1}, & \text{if } 1 \le k \le k_1 - 2, \\ & \quad \text{or } k_i + 1 \le k \le k_{i+1} - 2, \\ & \quad \text{or } k = k_i = k_{i+1} - 1,\ i = 1, 2, \ldots, r-1, \\ f_k = X_{k+1} \oplus 1, & \text{if } 1 \le k = k_1 - 1, \\ & \quad \text{or } k_i + 1 \le k = k_{i+1} - 1, \\ & \quad \text{or } k_i = k \le k_{i+1} - 2, i = 1, 2, \ldots, r-1, \\ f_n = f(Y_1, Y_2, \ldots, Y_n), & \text{if } k_r < n, \\ f_n = f(Y_1, Y_2, \ldots, Y_n) \oplus 1, & \text{if } k_r = n, \end{cases} \tag{5}$$

where the variables $Y_1, Y_2, \ldots, Y_n$ satisfy

$$\begin{cases} Y_k = X_k \oplus 1, & \text{if } k = k_1, k_2, \ldots, k_r, \\ Y_k = X_k, & \text{otherwise.} \end{cases} \tag{6}$$

Moreover, each pair of their equivalent states $\mathbf{X} = [X_1\ \ X_2\ \ldots\ X_n]^T$ and $\mathbf{Y} = [Y_1\ \ Y_2\ \ldots\ Y_n]^T$, respectively, of the Galois NFSR and of the Fibonacci NFSR, satisfies Eq. (6).

Proof. Let φ be a mapping from states $\mathbf{X}$s of the Galois NFSR to the states $\mathbf{Y}$s of the Fibonacci NFSR, satisfying Eq. (6). We can easily see that φ is a bijective mapping, and preserves the first component of $\mathbf{X}$. Thus, according to Lemma 8, the Galois NFSR and the Fibonacci NFSR are equivalent. On the other hand, note that the Fibonacci NFSR with a feedback function f can be expressed as

$$\begin{cases} Y_k(t+1) = Y_{k+1}(t), k = 1, 2, \ldots, n-1, \\ Y_n(t+1) = f(Y_1(t), Y_2(t), \ldots, Y_n(t)). \end{cases}$$

Under the mapping φ, the above equation is transformed into the equation $X_k(t+1) = f_k(X_1(t), X_2(t), \ldots, X_n(t))$ for all $k = 1, 2, \ldots, n$, where f_ks satisfy Eq. (5). □

The Galois NFSR with feedback $\mathbf{f} = [f_1 \; f_2 \; \ldots \; f_n]^T$ satisfying Eq. (5) belongs to the class of "lower triangular" Galois NFSRs, shown equivalent to a Fibonacci NFSR in [8]. However, for this particular "lower triangular" Galois NFSR, its equivalent Fibonacci NFSR has the feedback function just being the function appearing in the n-th bit of the Galois NFSR, and their equivalent states have either equal or complementary components at the same positions.

Compared to the given Fibonacci NFSR, its equivalent Galois NFSR with a feedback $\mathbf{f} = [f_1 \; f_2 \; \ldots \; f_n]^T$ satisfying Eq. (5) may lower the hardware implementation cost. We give a simple example below as an illustration.

Example 1. *For a 4-stage Fibonacci NFSR with a feedback function* $f = Y_2Y_3Y_4 \oplus Y_2Y_3 \oplus Y_2Y_4 \oplus Y_3Y_4 \oplus Y_1 \oplus Y_3 \oplus Y_4 \oplus 1$, *via a mapping* $\varphi : \mathbf{Y} = [Y_1 \; Y_2 \; Y_3 \; Y_4]^T \rightarrow \mathbf{X} = [X_1 \; X_2 \; X_3 \; X_4]^T$ *with*

$$X_1 = Y_1, X_2 = Y_2 \oplus 1, X_3 = Y_3 \oplus 1, X_4 = Y_4 \oplus 1, \tag{7}$$

it is transformed into a 4-stage Galois NFSR with a feedback $\mathbf{f} = [f_1 \; f_2 \; f_3 \; f_4]^T$ *satisfying* $f_1 = X_2 \oplus 1, f_2 = X_3, f_3 = X_4, f_4 = X_2X_3X_4 \oplus X_1 \oplus X_2$.

φ defined above is obviously a bijective mapping, and preserves the first components of all states. Thus, according to Theorem 2, both NFSRs are equivalent, and each pair of their equivalent states $\mathbf{X} = [X_1 \; X_2 \; X_3 \; X_4]^T$ *and* $\mathbf{Y} = [Y_1 \; Y_2 \; Y_3 \; Y_4]$ *satisfies Eq. (7). All these are consistent with the facts in Fig. 2, which describes their state diagrams.*

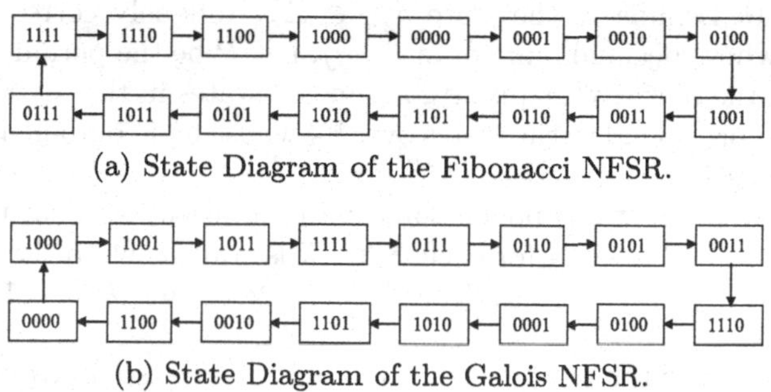

Fig. 2. State diagrams of two NFSRs in Example 1.

The feedback function f_1 to the first bit of the equivalent Galois NFSR has one more constant term than that of the Fibonacci NFSR, while the feedback functions f_2 and f_3 to the second and third bits of the Galois NFSR are the same as those of the Fibonacci NFSR. However, the feedback function f to the fourth bit of the Fibonacci NFSR has three more quadratic terms and one more *linear term and one more constant term than the feedback function f_4 to the fourth bit of the Galois NFSR. All these imply that the equivalent Galois NFSR has lower cost of hardware implementation than its equivalent Fibonacci NFSR.*

Example 2. *As an application of Theorem 2, we consider the stream ciphers Grain, Trivium and Acorn. Notably, if the Galois NFSR resulted from Theorem 2 lowers the cost of hardware implementation than its equivalent Fibonacci NFSR, then the feedback function of the Fibonacci NFSR has some terms being the factors of some other terms with greater degree. In the stream ciphers Grain, Trivium and Acorn, no bit appears more than once in the feedback functions of their separate Fibonacci NFSRs and therefore, these stream ciphers have used the NFSRs with the lowest cost of hardware implementation among their own equivalent Galois NFSRs resulted from Theorem 2.*

Proposition 1. *An n-stage Galois NFSR represented by System $\mathbf{x}(t+1) = L_g\mathbf{x}(t)$ with state $\mathbf{x} \in \Delta_{2^n}$ is equivalent to an n-stage Fibonacci NFSR represented by System $\mathbf{y}(t+1) = L_f\mathbf{y}(t)$ with state $\mathbf{y} \in \Delta_{2^n}$, if and only if there exists a transformation $\mathbf{y} = P\mathbf{x}$ with permutation matrix $P = \delta_{2^n}[j_1\ j_2\ \cdots\ j_{2^n}]$ satisfying $1 \le j_i \le 2^{n-1}$ and $2^{n-1}+1 \le j_{2^{n-1}+i} \le 2^n$ for all $i = 1, 2, \ldots, 2^{n-1}$, such that $L_g = P^{-1}L_fP$.*

Proof. Let the system $\mathbf{x}(t+1) = L_g\mathbf{x}(t)$ with $\mathbf{x} \in \Delta_{2^n}$ be equivalently expressed as $\mathbf{X}(t+1) = F(\mathbf{X}(t))$ with $\mathbf{X} \in \mathbb{F}_2^n$, and let $\mathbf{y}(t+1) = L_f\mathbf{y}(t)$ with $\mathbf{y} \in \Delta_{2^n}$ be equivalently expressed as $\mathbf{Y}(t+1) = H(\mathbf{Y}(t))$ with $\mathbf{Y} \in \mathbb{F}_2^n$. According to Lemma 8, the Galois NFSR is equivalent to the Fibonacci NFSR if and only if there exists a bijective mapping $\varphi : \mathbf{X} \mapsto \mathbf{Y}$ such that $\varphi(F(\mathbf{X})) = H(\varphi(\mathbf{X}))$ and $[1\ 0\ \cdots\ 0]\varphi(\mathbf{X}) = [1\ 0\ \cdots\ 0]\mathbf{X}$ for all $\mathbf{X} \in \mathbb{F}_2^n$.

According to Lemma 2, the state $\delta_{2^n}^j \in \Delta_{2^n}$ uniquely corresponds to the state over $\mathbb{F}_2^n$ whose decimal number is $2^n - j$. Let P be the permutation matrix determined by the bijective mapping φ. Since all states in the set $S_1 = \{\delta_{2^n}^j | j = 1, 2, \ldots, 2^{n-1}\}$ correspond to the states over $\mathbb{F}_2^n$ whose first components are 1, and all states in the set $S_2 = \{\delta_{2^n}^j | j = 2^{n-1}+1, 2^{n-1}+2, \ldots, 2^n\}$ correspond to the states over $\mathbb{F}_2^n$ whose first components are 0, we can easily see that the condition $[1\ 0\ \cdots 0]\varphi(\mathbf{X}) = [1\ 0\ \cdots 0]\mathbf{X}$ for each $\mathbf{X} \in \mathbb{F}_2^n$ is equivalent to the permutation matrix $P = \delta_{2^n}[j_1\ j_2\ \cdots\ j_{2^n}]$ satisfying $1 \le j_i \le 2^{n-1}$ and $2^{n-1}+1 \le j_{2^{n-1}+i} \le 2^n$ for all $i = 1, 2, \ldots, 2^{n-1}$.

In addition, under the transformation $\mathbf{y} = P\mathbf{x}$, the system $\mathbf{x}(t+1) = L_g\mathbf{x}(t)$ is clearly transformed to the system $\mathbf{y}(t+1) = L_f\mathbf{y}(t)$; moreover, L_g and L_f satisfy $L_g = P^{-1}L_fP$. Therefore, the result follows. □

Theorem 3. *The number of n-stage Galois NFSRs that are equivalent to a given n-stage Fibonacci NFSR is $(2^{n-1}!)^2$.*

Proof. Let an n-stage Galois NFSR be represented by $\mathbf{x}(t+1) = L_g\mathbf{x}(t)$ with $\mathbf{x} \in \Delta_{2^n}$, and let an n-stage Fibonacci NFSR be represented by $\mathbf{y}(t+1) = L_f\mathbf{y}(t)$ with $\mathbf{y} \in \Delta_{2^n}$. Then, according to Proposition 1, an n-stage Galois NFSRs is equivalent to an n-stage Fibonacci NFSR if and only if there exists a transformation $\mathbf{x} = P^{-1}\mathbf{y}$ with permutation matrix $P = \delta_{2^n}[j_1 \ j_2 \ \dots \ j_{2^n}]$ satisfying $1 \le j_i \le 2^{n-1}$ and $2^{n-1}+1 \le j_{2^{n-1}+i} \le 2^n$ for all $i = 1, 2, \dots, 2^{n-1}$, such that $L_g = P^{-1}L_f P$. Clearly, there are $(2^{n-1}!)^2$ possible forms of such permutation matrix P, since $(j_1, j_2, \dots, j_{2^{n-1}})$ can be any permutation of $(1, 2, \dots, 2^{n-1})$, and $(j_{2^{n-1}+1}, j_{2^{n-1}+2}, \dots, j_{2^n})$ can any permutation of $(2^{n-1}+1, 2^{n-1}+2, \dots, 2^n)$, and the total number of permutations of $(j_1, j_2, \dots, j_{2^{n-1}})$ (or $(j_{2^{n-1}+1}, j_{2^{n-1}+2}, \dots, j_{2^n})$) is $2^{n-1}!$. Hence, there are $(2^{n-1}!)^2$ possible P^{-1}s. Moreover, different transformation $\mathbf{x} = P^{-1}\mathbf{y}$ results in different state diagram of a Galois NFSR and therefore, results in different Galois NFSR. Thus, the result follows. □

Theorem 4. *If an n-stage Galois NFSR with feedback $\mathbf{f} = [f_1 \ f_2 \ \dots \ f_n]^T$ is equivalent to an n-stage Fibonacci NFSR, then for any $i_0 \in \mathcal{I} = \{0, 1, \dots, 2^n - 1\}$, there is at most one $i_1 \in \mathcal{I}$ such that $f_k(i_1) = f_k(i_0)$ for all $k = 1, 2, \dots, n$. Moreover,*

1. *if $i_0 \in \mathcal{I}_0 = \{0, 1, \dots, 2^{n-1} - 1\}$, then $i_1 \in \mathcal{I}_1 = \{2^{n-1}, 2^{n-1} + 1, \dots, 2^n - 1\}$;*
2. *if $i_0 \in \mathcal{I}_1$, then $i_1 \in \mathcal{I}_0$;*
3. *if the Fibonacci NFSR is nonsingular, then such above i_1 does not exist.*

Proof. For any $i_0 \in \mathcal{I} = \{0, 1, \dots, 2^n - 1\}$, let $\mathbf{X}_0 = [X_1 \ X_2 \ \dots \ X_n]^T$ be a state of an n-stage Galois NFSR, corresponding to the decimal number i_0. Accordingly, let $\mathbf{X}_1 = [X_1 \oplus 1 \ X_2 \ \dots \ X_n]^T$ be a state of the Galois NFSR, corresponding to the decimal number i_1. Then, it is easy to see that if $i_0 \in \mathcal{I}_0$, then $i_1 \in \mathcal{I}_1$, and that if $i_0 \in \mathcal{I}_1$, then $i_1 \in \mathcal{I}_0$.

If the n-stage Galois NFSR is equivalent to an n-stage Fibonacci NFSR, then from Lemma 8, we know that there exists a bijective mapping $\varphi : \mathbf{X}_r \mapsto \mathbf{Y}_r$ with $r = 0, 1$, and $\mathbf{Y}_r$ being the states of Fibonacci NFSR; moreover, the equivalent states $\mathbf{X}_r$ and $\mathbf{Y}_r$ have the same first component.

For the state $\mathbf{Y}_0 = [Y_1 \ Y_2 \ \dots \ Y_n]^T$ of the Fibonacci NFSR, there exists at most another state $\mathbf{Y}_1 = [Y_1 \oplus 1 \ Y_2 \ \dots \ Y_n]^T$ such that $\mathbf{Y}_1$ has the same successor as $\mathbf{Y}_0$. If the Fibonacci NFSR is nonsingular, then such a $\mathbf{Y}_1$ does not exist. If the Galois NFSR is equivalent to the Fibonacci NFSR, then according to Lemma 6, their state diagrams are isomorphic. Thus, the state $\mathbf{X}_0$ of the Galois NFSR has at most another $\mathbf{X}_1$ such that $\mathbf{X}_1$ has the same successor as $\mathbf{X}_0$. If the Fibonacci NFSR is nonsingular, then such an $\mathbf{X}_1$ does not exist. Notably, if $\mathbf{X}_0$ and $\mathbf{X}_1$ have the same successor, then $\mathbf{f}(\mathbf{X}_0) = \mathbf{f}(\mathbf{X}_1)$, which implies $f_k(i_0) = f_k(i_1)$ for all $k = 1, 2, \dots, n$. □

Theorem 5. *If an n-stage Galois NFSR with feedback $\mathbf{f} = [f_1 \ f_2 \ \dots \ f_n]^T$ is equivalent to an n-stage Fibonacci NFSR, then $wt([f_1(2^n - 1), f_1(2^n - 2), \dots, f_1(2^{n-1})]) = wt([f_1(2^{n-1} - 1), f_1(2^{n-1} - 2), \dots, f_1(0)]) = 2^{n-2}$.*

Proof. If an n-stage Galois NFSR is equivalent to an n-stage Fibonacci NFSR, then according to Proposition 1, there exists a permutation matrix $P = \delta_{2^n}[j_1 \ j_2 \ \dots \ j_{2^n}]$ satisfying $1 \le j_i \le 2^{n-1}$ and $2^{n-1}+1 \le j_{2^{n-1}+i} \le 2^n$ for all $i = 1, 2, \ldots, 2^{n-1}$, such that $L_g = P^{-1} L_f P$, where L_g and L_f are the state transition matrices of the Galois NFSR and the Fibonacci NFSR, respectively. Let $L_f = \delta_{2^n}[\eta_1 \ \eta_2 \ \ldots \ \eta_{2^n}]$, and $L_g = \delta_{2^n}[\zeta_1 \ \zeta_2 \ \ldots \ \zeta_{2^n}]$. Hence,

$$\begin{aligned} L_g = P^{-1} L_f P &= P^T \delta_{2^n}[\eta_1 \ \eta_2 \ \ldots \ \eta_{2^n}] \delta_{2^n}[j_1 \ j_2 \ \ldots \ j_{2^n}] \\ &= \delta_{2^n}[j_1 \ j_2 \ \ldots \ j_{2^n}]^T \delta_{2^n}[\eta_{j_1} \ \eta_{j_2} \ \ldots \ \eta_{2^n}], \end{aligned}$$

which yields $\delta_{2^n}^{\zeta_i} = \delta_{2^n}[j_1 \ j_2 \ \ldots \ j_{2^n}]^T \delta_{2^n}^{\eta_{j_i}}$, $i = 1, 2, \ldots, 2^n$, that is,

$$[0 \cdots 0 \ \underset{\zeta_i\text{-th}}{1} \ 0 \cdots 0]^T = \delta_{2^n}[j_1 \ j_2 \ \ldots \ j_{2^n}]^T [0 \cdots 0 \ \underset{\eta_{j_i}\text{-th}}{1} \ 0 \cdots 0]^T. \tag{8}$$

From Eq. (8), we can easily see that the column vector $[0 \cdots 0 \ \underset{\zeta_i\text{-th}}{1} \ 0 \cdots 0]^T$ is just a row permutation of $[0 \cdots 0 \ \underset{\eta_{j_i}\text{-th}}{1} \ 0 \cdots 0]^T$ via the permutation $(j_1 \ j_2 \ldots j_{2^n})$. Since $1 \le j_i \le 2^{n-1}$ and $2^{n-1}+1 \le j_{2^{n-1}+i} \le 2^n$ for all $i = 1, 2, \ldots, 2^{n-1}$, we can infer that if $1 \le \eta_i \le 2^{n-1}$, then $1 \le \eta_{j_i} \le 2^{n-1}$ and thereby $1 \le \zeta_i \le 2^{n-1}$, and that if $2^{n-1}+1 \le \eta_i \le 2^n$, then $2^{n-1}+1 \le \eta_{j_i} \le 2^n$ and therefore $2^{n-1}+1 \le \zeta_i \le 2^n$.

According to Lemma 4, for all $i = 1, 2, \ldots, 2^{n-1}$ (resp., for all $i = 2^{n-1}+1, 2^{n-1}+2, \ldots, 2^n$), there are 2^{n-2} η_is satisfying $1 \le \eta_i \le 2^{n-1}$, and 2^{n-2} η_is satisfying $2^{n-1}+1 \le \eta_i \le 2^n$. Hence, for all $i = 1, 2, \ldots, 2^{n-1}$ (resp., for all $i = 2^{n-1}+1, 2^{n-1}+2, \ldots, 2^n$), there are 2^{n-2} ζ_is satisfying $1 \le \zeta_i \le 2^{n-1}$, and 2^{n-2} ζ_is satisfying $2^{n-1}+1 \le \zeta_i \le 2^n$. From Lemma 7, we know

$$\zeta_i = 2^n - 2^{n-1} f_1(2^n - i) - 2^{n-2} f_2(2^n - i) - \cdots - f_n(2^n - i), \ i = 1, 2, \ldots, 2^n.$$

Thus, we can easily compute that $1 \le \zeta_i \le 2^{n-1}$ yields $f_1(2^n - i) = 1$, and that $2^{n-1}+1 \le \zeta_i \le 2^n$ yields $f_1(2^n - i) = 0$. Therefore, there are 2^{n-2} ones in the $[f_1(2^n-1), f_1(2^n-2), \ldots, f_1(2^{n-1})]$, and there are also 2^{n-2} ones in the $[f_1(2^{n-1}-1), f_1(2^{n-1}-2), \ldots, f_1(0)]$. □

Theorem 5 reveals a necessary condition for the feedback function of the first bit of a Galois NFSR equivalent to a Fibonacci one. Note that in general there is a shift between the adjacent bits for a shift register. In the following, we give a feedback function for the first bit of a Galois NFSR, which satisfies the necessary condition in Theorem 5, as well as satisfies the shift condition of a shift register.

Proposition 2. *The Boolean function* $f(X_1, X_2, \ldots, X_n) = X_2 \oplus g(X_3, \ldots, X_n)$ *satisfies*

$$wt([f(2^n-1), f(2^n-2), \ldots, f(2^{n-1})]) = wt([f(2^{n-1}-1), f(2^{n-1}-2), \ldots, f(0)]) = 2^{n-2}.$$

Proof. Set $Y_i = X_{i+1}$, $i = 1, 2, \ldots, n-1$, and set $h = f$. Then $h(Y_1, Y_2, \ldots, Y_{n-1}) = Y_1 \oplus g(Y_2, Y_3, \ldots, Y_{n-1})$. Clearly, h is an $(n-1)$-variable function and is linear with respect to the variable Y_1. Hence, h is balanced, and thereby $\mathrm{wt}(h) = 2^{n-2}$.

On the other hand, note that $f(2^n-1), f(2^n-2), \ldots, f(2^{n-1})$ are the possible values of $f(1, X_2, \ldots, X_n)$, while $f(2^{n-1}-1), f(2^{n-1}-2), \ldots, f(0)$ are the possible values of $f(0, X_2, \ldots, X_n)$. Together considering $f(1, X_2, \ldots, X_n) = f(0, X_2, \ldots, X_n)$ for all $[X_2\ X_3\ \ldots\ X_n]^T \in \mathbb{F}_2^{n-1}$, we have $f(2^n - i) = f(2^{n-1} - i)$ for all $i = 1, 2, \ldots, 2^{n-1}$. Thus, $\mathrm{wt}([f(2^n - 1), f(2^n - 2), \ldots, f(2^{n-1})]) = \mathrm{wt}(h) = 2^{n-2}$, and $\mathrm{wt}([f(2^{n-1} - 1), f(2^{n-1} - 2), \ldots, f(0)]) = \mathrm{wt}(h) = 2^{n-2}$ as well. □

Proposition 2 gives a class of Boolean functions that satisfies the necessary condition in Theorem 5, but is not relative to the first bit variable X_1. In the following, we give another class of Boolean functions, which satisfies the necessary condition in Theorem 5, as well as is relative to the first bit variable X_1.

Proposition 3. *The Boolean function* $f(X_1, X_2, \ldots, X_n) = X_1 \oplus X_2 \oplus g(X_3, \ldots, X_n)$ *satisfies* $wt([f(2^n - 1), f(2^n - 2), \ldots, f(2^{n-1})]) = wt([f(2^{n-1} - 1), f(2^{n-1} - 2), \ldots, f(0)]) = 2^{n-2}$.

Proof. Let $h_1(X_1, X_2, \ldots, X_n) = X_1$, and let $h_2(X_1, X_2, \ldots, X_n) = X_2 \oplus g(X_3, \ldots, X_n)$. Then, $f = h_1 \oplus h_2$. On one hand, clearly, the left part of the truth table of h_1, arranged in the alphabet order, is $[1, 1, \ldots, 1]$ and its weight is 2^{n-1}, while the right half part of h_1 is $[0, 0, \ldots, 0]$ and its weight is 0. On the other hand, according to Proposition 2, the weight of the left part of the truth table of h_2 is 2^{n-2}, and the weight of its left half part is 2^{n-2} as well. Therefore, the weight of the left half part of the truth table of f is $2^{n-1} - 2^{n-2} = 2^{n-2}$, and the weight of its right half part is $0 + 2^{n-2} = 2^{n-2}$. □

Example 3. *Consider a 4-stage Galois NFSR given in [4], whose feedback* $\mathbf{f} = [f_1\ \ f_2\ \ f_3\ \ f_4]^T$ *satisfies* $f_1 = X_1 \oplus X_2, f_2 = X_3, f_3 = X_4, f_4 = X_1 \oplus X_3X_4$. *This Galois NFSR is equivalent to a 4-stage Fibonacci NFSR [4], whose feedback function is* $f = X_1 \oplus X_3 \oplus X_4 \oplus X_2X_3 \oplus X_2X_4 \oplus X_3X_4$ *[8]. On one hand, by direct computation, we know that the truth table of* f_1*, arranged in the alphabet order, is* $[0, 0, 0, 0, 1, 1, 1, 1, 1, 1, 1, 1, 0, 0, 0, 0]$. *Clearly, both left and right half parts of the truth table have the Hamming weight 4, which is consistent with the result in Theorem 5. On the other hand, this Boolean function* f_1 *is a particular form of* f *in Proposition 3. According to Proposition 3, both the left half part and the right half part of the truth table of* f_1 *are 4, consistent with the above fact.*

Example 4. *Consider a 4-stage Galois NFSR with feedback* $\mathbf{f} = [f_1\ \ f_2\ \ f_3\ \ f_4]^T$ *given in [4], where* $f_1 = X_2 \oplus X_1X_2, f_2 = X_3 \oplus X_1 \oplus X_1X_3 \oplus X_1X_2X_3, f_3 = X_4 \oplus X_1 \oplus X_2 \oplus X_3 \oplus X_1X_3 \oplus X_2X_3, f_4 = X_1 \oplus X_2X_4$. *It was found not equivalent to Fibonacci NFSRs [4]. In fact, we can directly compute that the truth table of* f_1*, arranged in the alphabet order, is* $[0, 0, 0, 0, 0, 0, 0, 0, 1, 1, 1, 1, 0, 0, 0, 0]$. *It is seen that the left half part of the truth table is* $[0, 0, 0, 0, 0, 0, 0, 0]$, *whose Hamming weight is 0, not 4. According to Theorem 5, this Galois NFSR must not be equivalent to a 4-stage Fibonacci NFSR, consistent with the fact found in [4].*

Theorem 6. *If an* n*-stage Galois NFSR with feedback* $\mathbf{f} = [f_1\ \ f_2\ \ \ldots\ \ f_n]^T$ *is equivalent to an* n*-stage Fibonacci NFSR, then* $wt(f_k) = 2^{n-1}$ *for all* $k = 1, 2, \ldots, n-1$. *Moreover, if the Fibonacci NFSR is nonsingular, then* $wt(f_n) = 2^{n-1}$.

Proof. If an n-stage Galois NFSR with feedback $\mathbf{f} = [f_1 \ f_2 \ \dots \ f_n]^T$ is equivalent to an n-stage Fibonacci NFSR, then according to Theorem 5, we know that $\mathrm{wt}([f_1(2^n-1), f_1(2^n-2), \dots, f_1(2^{n-1})]) = \mathrm{wt}([f_1(2^{n-1}-1), f_1(2^{n-1}-2), \dots, f_1(0)]) = 2^{n-2}$. Since the Hamming weight of a Boolean function is the Hamming weight of its truth table, we have $\mathrm{wt}(f_1) = 2^{n-2}+2^{n-2} = 2^{n-1}$. Thus, the result holds for f_1. Next, we show the result is valid for $f_2, f_3, \dots, f_{n-1}$.

Let $L_g = \delta_{2^n}[\zeta_1 \ \zeta_2 \ \dots \ \zeta_{2^n}]$ and $L_f = \delta_{2^n}[\eta_1 \ \eta_2 \ \dots \ \eta_{2^n}]$ be the state transition matrices of the Galois NFSR and its equivalent Fibonacci NFSR, respectively, and let $P = \delta_{2^n}[j_1 \ j_2 \ \dots \ j_{2^n}]$ be the permutation matrix determined by the bijective mapping between the state diagrams of both equivalent NFSRs, satisfying $1 \le j_i \le 2^{n-1}$ and $2^{n-1}+1 \le j_{2^{n-1}+i} \le 2^n$ for all $i = 1, 2, \dots, 2^{n-1}$. According to the proof of Theorem 5, we know that, 1) if $1 \le \eta_{j_i} \le 2^{n-1}$, then $1 \le \zeta_i \le 2^{n-1}$; 2) if $2^{n-1}+ \le \eta_{j_i} \le 2^n$, then $2^{n-1}+1 \le \zeta_i \le 2^n$.

We equally divide $N = \{1, 2, \dots, 2^n\}$ into four subsets, $N_{11} = \{1, 2, \dots, 2^{n-2}\}$, $N_{12} = \{2^{n-2}+1, 2^{n-2}+2, \dots, 2^{n-1}\}$, $N_{21} = \{2^{n-1}+1, 2^{n-1}+2, \dots, 2^{n-1}+2^{n-2}\}$, and $N_{22} = \{2^{n-1}+2^{n-2}+1, 2^{n-1}+2^{n-2}+2, \dots, 2^n\}$. According to Lemma 4, we can infer that, among $\eta_1, \eta_2, \dots, \eta_{2^n}$, there are 2^{n-2} η_{j_i}s taking values from each N_{kl} with $k, l = 1, 2$. Hence, in the state transition matrix $L_g = \delta_{2^n}[\zeta_1 \ \zeta_2 \ \dots \ \zeta_{2^n}]$ of the Galois NFSR, we can deduce that, among $\zeta_1, \zeta_2, \dots, \zeta_{2^n}$, there are also 2^{n-2} ζ_{j_i}s taking values from each N_{kl} with $k, l = 1, 2$.

From Lemma 7, we know

$$\zeta_i = 2^n - 2^{n-1}f_1(2^n-i) - 2^{n-2}f_2(2^n-i) - \dots - 2f_{n-1}(2^n-i) - f_n(2^n-i), \ i = 1, 2, \dots, 2^n. \tag{9}$$

According to the above equation, we can easily compute that

1. if $1 \le \zeta_i \le 2^{n-2}$, then $f_2(2^n-i) = 1$,
2. if $2^{n-2}+1 \le \zeta_i \le 2^{n-1}$, then $f_2(2^n-i) = 0$,
3. if $2^{n-1}+1 \le \zeta_i \le 2^{n-1}+2^{n-2}$, then $f_2(2^n-i) = 1$,
4. if $2^{n-1}+2^{n-2}+1 \le \zeta_i \le 2^n$, then $f_2(2^n-i) = 0$.

Therefore, there are totally 2^{n-1} ones in the truth table $[f_2(2^n-1), f_2(2^n-2), \dots, f_2(0)]$ of f_2. Thus, $\mathrm{wt}(f_2) = 2^{n-1}$. For the case of $3 \le k \le n-1$, we equally divide $N = \{1, 2, \dots, 2^n\}$ into 2^k subsets, and we can prove $\mathrm{wt}(f_k) = 2^{n-1}$ in a similar way.

Furthermore, if the Fibonacci NFSR is nonsingular, then according to Lemma 4, its state transition matrix L_f is nonsingular. According to Proposition 1, the state transition matrix $L_g = \delta_{2^n}[\zeta_1 \ \zeta_2 \ \dots \ \zeta_{2^n}]$ of the Galois NFSR is nonsingular as well, which implies that $\zeta_1, \zeta_2, \dots, \zeta_{2^n}$ are pairwise distinct, and that they take all possible values of $1, 2, \dots, 2^n$. Hence, among $\zeta_1, \zeta_2, \dots, \zeta_{2^n}$, there are 2^{n-1} odd ζ_is and there are also 2^{n-1} even ζ_is. According to Eq. (9), we can easily see that ζ_i is odd if and only if $f_n(2^n-i) = 1$, and that ζ_i is even if and only if $f_n(2^n-i) = 0$. Thereby, there are 2^{n-1} ones in the truth table $[f_n(2^n-1), f_n(2^n-2), \dots, f_n(0)]$ of f_n. Thus, $\mathrm{wt}(f_n) = 2^{n-1}$. □

Corollary 1. *If an n-stage Galois NFSR with feedback* $\mathbf{f} = [f_1 \; f_2 \; \dots \; f_n]^T$ *is equivalent to an n-stage nonsingular Fibonacci NFSR, then* $wt(f_k) = 2^{n-1}$ *for all* $k = 1, 2, \dots, n$.

Example 5. *Consider a cascade connection of an m-stage NFSR1 into an n-stage NFSR2. It is a particular* $(m+n)$*-stage Galois NFSR with feedback* $\mathbf{f} = [f_1 \; f_2 \; \dots \; f_{m+n}]^T$, *where*

$$\begin{cases} f_i = X_{i+1}, \; i = 1, 2, \dots, n-1, \\ f_n = Y_1 \oplus g(X_1, X_2, \dots, X_n), \\ f_{n+l} = Y_{l+1}, \; l = 1, 2, \dots, m-1, \\ f_{n+m} = h(Y_1, Y_2, \dots, Y_m). \end{cases}$$

It is equivalent to an $(n+m)$*-stage Fibonacci NFSR [9], and it is nonsingular if and only if g and h are nonsingular [21].*

On one hand, f_i *with* $i = 1, 2, \dots, m+n-1$ *are linear with respect to some variables and thereby,* $wt(f_k) = 2^{n-1}$. *If the Fibonacci NFSR is nonsingular, then the cascade connection is nonsingular, and thereby h is nonsingular, that is,* $h(Y_1, Y_2, \dots, Y_m) = Y_1 \oplus \bar{h}(Y_2, Y_3, \dots, Y_m)$. *In this case, h is linear with respect to the variable* Y_1 *and therefore,* $wt(f_{n+m}) = 2^{n-1}$.

On the other hand, since this particular Galois NFSR is equivalent to a Fibonacci NFSR, according to Theorem 6, we know that $wt(f_i) = 2^{n-1}$ *for all* $i = 1, 2, \dots, m+n-1$. *If the Fibonacci NFSR is nonsingular, then* $wt(f_{m+n}) = 2^{n-1}$. *All these are consistent with the facts mentioned before.*

Theorems 5 and 6 give some necessary conditions for an n-stage Galois NFSR equivalent to an n-stage Fibonacci NFSR. It is worth pointing out that they are not sufficient conditions. Take a 4-stage Galois NFSR as an example, whose feedback $\mathbf{f} = [f_1 \; f_2 \; f_3 \; f_4]^T$ satisfies

$$\begin{cases} f_1 = X_2 \oplus X_3 X_4, \\ f_2 = X_3 \oplus X_1 X_2 X_4, \\ f_3 = X_4 \oplus X_1 X_3 \oplus X_2 X_3, \\ f_4 = X_1 \oplus X_2 X_4. \end{cases}$$

Clearly, here f_1, f_2 and f_3 are linear with respect to the variables X_2, X_3 and X_4, respectively. Thus, $\mathrm{wt}(f_k) = 8$ with $k = 1, 2, 3$, satisfying the necessary condition in Theorem 6. Moreover, we can easily compute that f_1 has its truth table $[0,1,1,1,1,0,0,0,0,1,1,1,1,0,0,0]$, arranged in the reverse alphabet order. The left half part of this truth table is $[0,1,1,1,1,0,0,0]$, and its right half part is $[0,1,1,1,1,0,0,0]$ as well. We can seen both parts have the Hamming weight 4, satisfying the necessary condition in Theorem 5. On the other hand, it is easily seen that the state $[1 \; 1 \; 1 \; 0]^T$ of the Galois NFSR has three predecessors, $[0 \; 0 \; 1 \; 1]^T$, $[0 \; 1 \; 1 \; 0]^T$ and $[1 \; 1 \; 0 \; 1]^T$. If this 4-stage Galois NFSR is equivalent to a 4-stage Fibonacci NFSR, then according to Lemma 6, their state diagrams are isomorphic. Thereby, in the state diagram of the Fibonacci NFSR, there is a state having three predecessors, which is in contradiction with the fact that any state of a Fibonacci NFSR has at most two predecessors. Therefore, this 4-stage Galois NFSR is not equivalent to a 4-stage Fibonacci NFSR, even through it satisfies the necessary conditions in Theorems 5 and 6.

4 Conclusion

This paper considered the Galois NFSRs equivalent to Fibonacci ones. First, it gave a new type of Galois NFSRs equivalent to a given Fibonacci NFSR, in which their corresponding states have either equal or complementary components at the same positions. As an application of this result, the paper showed that the stream ciphers Grain, Trivium and Acorn have used the NFSRs with the lowest cost of hardware implementation among their own equivalent Galois NFSRs of this type. Second, the paper enumerated n-stage Galois NFSRs equivalent to a given n-stage Fibonacci NFSR. Third, it revealed some common characterizations of Galois NFSRs equivalent to Fibonacci ones from the perspectives of their stage number and feedback functions. In future work, it is interesting to find more types and more common features of Galois NFSRs equivalent to Fibonacci ones.

Acknowledgments. This work was supported by the National Natural Science Foundation of China under Grant Nos. 61772029 and 61872359.

References

1. Hell M., Johansson T., Meier W.: Grain-a stream cipher for constrained environments. eSTREAM, ECRYPT Stream Cipher Project, London, U.K., Technical report, 2005/010 (2005)
2. Cannière De C., Preneel B.: Trivium Specifications. eSTREAM, ECRYPT Stream Cipher Project, London, U.K., Technical report, 2005/030 (2005)
3. Wu, H.: ACORN: A lightweight authenticated cipher (v3). Submission to CAESAR (2016). http://competitions.cr.yp.to/round3/acornv3.pdf
4. Dubrova, E.: A transformation from the Fibonacci to the Galois NLFSRs. IEEE Trans. Inf. Theory **55**(11), 5263–5271 (2009)
5. Dubrova, E.: An equivalence-preserving transformation of shift registers. In: Schmidt, K.-U., Winterhof, A. (eds.) SETA 2014. LNCS, vol. 8865, pp. 187–199. Springer, Cham (2014). https://doi.org/10.1007/978-3-319-12325-7_16
6. Zhong, J.: On equivalence of cascade connections of two nonlinear feedback shift registers. Comput. J. **62**(12), 1793–1804 (2019)
7. Dubrova, E.: Finding matching initial states for equivalent NLFSRs in the Fibonacci and the Galois configurations. IEEE Trans. Inf. Theory **56**(6), 2961–2966 (2010)
8. Lin Z.: The transformation from the Galois NLFSR to the Fibonacci configuration. In: EI-DWT 2013, pp. 335–339. IEEE Press, Piscataway (2013)
9. Mykkeltveit, J., Siu, M.-K., Ton, P.: On the cylcle structure of some nonlinear shift register sequences. Inf. Control **43**, 202–215 (1979)
10. Cheng, D., Qi, H., Li, Z.: Analysis and Control of Boolean Networks. Springer, London (2011). https://doi.org/10.1007/978-0-85729-097-7

11. Cheng, D., Qi, H., Zhao, Y.: An Introduction to Semi-Tensor Product of Matrices and Its Applications. World Scientific Publishing Company, Singapore (2012)
12. Zhao, D.W., Peng, H.P., Li, L.X., Hui, S.L., Yang, Y.X.: Novel way to research nonlinear feedback shift register. Sci. China Inf. Sci. **57**(9), 1–14 (2014). https://doi.org/10.1007/s11432-013-5058-4
13. Zhong, J., Lin, D.: A new linearization method of nonlinear feedback shift registers. J. Comput. Syst. Sci. **81**(4), 783–796 (2015)
14. Zhong, J., Lin, D.: Driven stability of nonlinear feedback shift registers. IEEE Trans. Commun. **64**(6), 2274–2284 (2016)
15. Zhong, J., Lin, D.: On minimum period of nonlinear feedback shift registers in Grain-like structure. IEEE Trans. Inf. Theory **64**(99), 6429–6442 (2018)
16. Qi, H., Cheng, D.: Logic and logic-based control. J. Control Theory Appl. **6**(1), 123–133 (2008)
17. Barbier, M., Cheballah, H., Le Bars, J.-M.: On the computation of the Möbius transform. Theor. Comput. Sci. **809**, 171–188 (2020)
18. Roger, A.H., Johnson, C.R.: Topics in Matrix Analysis. Cambridge University Press, Cambridge (1991)
19. Golomb, S.W.: Shift Register Sequences. Holden-Day, Laguna Hills (1967)
20. Kalouptsidis, N., Limniotis, K.: Nonlinear span, minimal realizations of sequences over finite fields and de Brujin generators. In: ISITA 2004, pp. 794–799. IEEE Press, Piscataway (2004)
21. Zhong, J., Lin, D.: Decomposition of nonlinear feedback shift registers based on Boolean networks. Sci. China Inf. Sci. **62**(3), 1–3 (2019). https://doi.org/10.1007/s11432-017-9460-4

Symmetric Cipher

Bagua: A NFSR-Based Stream Cipher Constructed Following Confusion and Diffusion Principles

Lin Tan(✉), Xuanyong Zhu, and Wenfeng Qi

PLA Strategic Support Force Information Engineering University, Zhengzhou, China
tanlin100@163.com, xuanyong.zhu@263.net, wenfeng.qi@263.net

Abstract. Confusion and diffusion are important design principles in block ciphers. The famous structures in block ciphers such as SPN, Feistel and Misty are proposed based on them and towards provable security against differential and linear cryptanalyses. There is few structure based on the two principles in stream ciphers except for Trivium. In this paper, we generalize the design ideas of Trivium to propose a new construction of Galois structure nonlinear feedback shift registers based on confusion and diffusion principles. As an application of this construction, a stream cipher named Bagua is proposed, which is a hardware-oriented primitive of 128-bit initialization vector and 128-bit or 256-bit key. It can be implemented in parallel up to 32 iterations at once, and the maximum throughout can be up to 8 Gbps. One can choose the parallel degree in implementation according to the requirement of throughput and hardware overhead in different application environments. Its resistances against differential and linear cryptanalyses are estimated theoretically and experimentally.

Keywords: Stream ciphers · Nonlinear feedback shift registers · Trivium · Confusion · Diffusion

1 Introduction

In the field of symmetric cryptography, block ciphers seem more popular than stream ciphers. Even in some cryptographic applications stream ciphers have been replaced by block ciphers. For example, in IEEE 802.11 standard wired equivalent privacy (WEP) the stream cipher RC4 [1] has been replaced by AES [2]. The main reason is that the security of block ciphers seems to be better understood and many famous structures in block ciphers such as SPN, Feistel, Misty and Lai-Massey have been studied well in theorem. There is much less the case for stream ciphers. Another reason is that many block ciphers can be lightweight and efficient, which are ever advantages of steam ciphers, such as PRESENT [4], KATAN and KTANTAN [5], HIGHT [20] and LBlock [21]. This poses challenges for stream ciphers to develop simpler and reliable design criteria or structures.

Y. Wu and M. Yung (Eds.): Inscrypt 2020, LNCS 12612, pp. 453–465, 2021.
https://doi.org/10.1007/978-3-030-71852-7_30

Confusion and diffusion are the cryptography design principles early proposed by Shannon [22], which have been applied successfully to design modern block ciphers. Differential cryptanalysis and linear cryptanalysis are the two most powerful known attacks on block ciphers. The famous SPN, Feistel and Misty block cipher structures are designed based on the confusion and diffusion principles, and they can be evaluated towards provable security [6] or practical security [9] against differential and linear cryptanalyses. For provable security of a cipher, the low bounds of the maximum differential probability [7] and linear hull probability [8] are used to evaluate the resistance against differential and linear cryptanalyses. The practical security of a cipher concentrates on the differential characteristic and linear characteristic probabilities, which usually are reduced to compute the lower bound on the number of active S-boxes. The provable security against differential and linear cryptanalyses were studied for Feistel structure [6,7] and for SPN structure [10–12], while Misty structure [13] was proposed towards provable security.

Linear feedback shift registers (LFSRs) were the most popular building blocks used to design stream ciphers [3], for they have very good statistical properties, efficient implementations, and well-studied algebraic structures. However, it is found that stream ciphers based on LFSRs are susceptible to algebraic attacks and correlation attacks. As an alternative, many stream ciphers use nonlinear feedback shift registers (NFSRs), such as Trivium [14], Grain [15], MICKEY [16], and Fountain [24]. Besides, NFSRs are also used in block ciphers (see Keeloq [17] and GF-NLFSR [23]) and hash functions (see Quark [18]). Trivium is a stream cipher based on the design principles of block ciphers [19], which is one of the eSTREAM hardware-oriented finalists and an International Standard under ISO/IEC 29192-3:2012. It is a bit-oriented design according to SPN structure of block ciphers, where substitution layer consists of three 2-bit products and permutation layer is realized by the feedforward and feedback of shift registers. In this paper, we generalize the design ideas of Trivium and propose a new construction of Galois-NFSR based on confusion and diffusion principles. As an application of this construction, a stream cipher named Bagua is proposed, which is a hardware-oriented primitive of 128-bit initialization vector and 128-bit or 256-bit key. It can be implemented in parallel up to 32 iterations at once.

The rest of this paper is organized as follows. In Sect. 2, we review the model of Galois feedback shift register and some definitions. A new construction of Galois-NFSR is proposed in Sect. 3. Bagua, a stream cipher based on this construction is described in Sect. 4 and the security analysis follows in Sect. 5. We close the paper with the conclusions.

2 Preliminaries

2.1 Feedback Shift Register

Feedback shift register (FSR) is the main component used in the design of pseudorandom numbers generator and stream cipher. An n-stage Galois-FSR consists of n registers and n feedback functions, while Fibonacci-FSR is the special case of Galois-FSR and has only a feedback function. The structure of an n-stage Galois-FSR is shown in Fig. 1, where the register x_i is updated by the i-th feedback function $f_i(x_1, x_2, ..., x_n)$, $i = 1, 2, ..., n$. The output sequence is usually some register or a simple function of the FSR's state. If all feedback functions are linear, then the FSR is called linear feedback shift register, else it is called nonlinear feedback shift register.

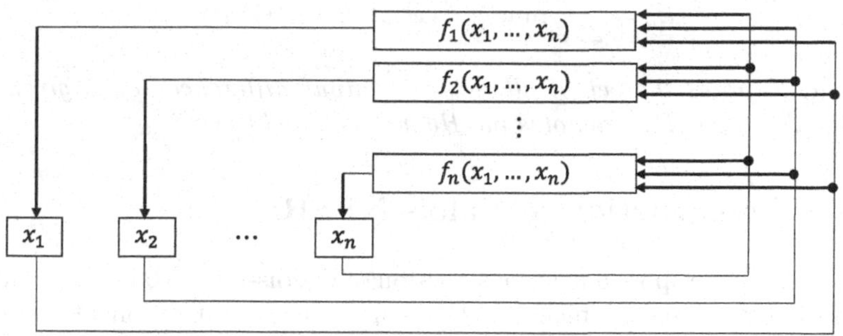

Fig. 1. Structure of n-stage Galois-FSR

2.2 Definitions

Definition 1. *Let S be an $n \times n$ S-box. For any given $\Delta x, \Delta y, \Gamma x, \Gamma y \in F_2^n$, the differential and linear approximation probabilities of S are defined as*

$$DP^S(\Delta x \to \Delta y) = \frac{\#\{x \in F_2^n | S(x) + S(x + \Delta x) = \Delta y\}}{2^n},$$

$$LP^S(\Gamma y \to \Gamma x) = \left(2 \times \frac{\#\{x \in F_2^n | x \cdot \Gamma x = S(x) \cdot \Gamma y\}}{2^n} - 1\right)^2.$$

Definition 2. *Let S be an $n \times n$ S-box. The maximum differential and linear approximation probabilities of S are defined as*

$$MDP^S = \max_{\Delta x \neq 0, \Delta y} DP^S(\Delta x \to \Delta y),$$

$$MLP^S = \max_{\Gamma x, \Gamma y \neq 0} LP^S(\Gamma y \to \Gamma x).$$

Definition 3. *A differential active S-box is defined as an S-box given a nonzero input difference, while a linear active S-box is defined as an S-box given a nonzero output mask value.*

If all differential or linear characteristics of a cipher involve at least k differential or linear active S-boxes, we can derive the upper bound $(MDP^S)^k$ and $(MLP^S)^k$ of the maximum differential and linear characteristic probabilities which are used to evaluate the practical security against differential and linear cryptanalysis. In SPN structure ciphers, the differential and linear branch numbers of diffusion layer are used to compute the number of differential and linear active S-boxes. In the following we also give the definition of differential branch number for an S-box.

Definition 4. *Let S be an $n \times n$ S-box. The differential branch number B_d of S is defined as:*

$$B_d = \min_{\Delta x \neq 0, \Delta y \in C_{\Delta x}} (H(\Delta x) + H(\Delta y)),$$

where $C_{\Delta x}$ denotes the set of all possible output differences of S given input difference Δx, and $H(x)$ denotes the Hamming weight of x.

3 New Construction of Galois-NFSR

In this section we propose a new construction of Galois-NFSR based on confusion and diffusion principles, which can be seen as a generalization of the design of Trivium, see Fig. 2. This construction consists of three components: FSRs, confusion layer and diffusion layer. The FSRs part contains eight feedback shift registers with different length. The confusion layer is a 8-bit input and 8-bit output S-box as in block ciphers. The diffusion layer consists of eight linear boolean functions instead of the permutation matrix in SPN structure block ciphers.

Denote the eight FSRs by FSR_i and their lengths by $n_i, i = 1, 2, ..., 8$. Denote eight linear boolean functions in diffusion layer by f_i and the output bits of S-box by $w_i, i = 1, 2, ..., 8$. Denote the state of FSR_i by $FSR_i[n_i], FSR_i[n_i - 1], ..., FSR_i[1], i = 1, 2, ..., 8$. In the work stage of this construction the states of FSR_i are updated for per iteration as follows

$$\begin{aligned} FSR_i[j] &= FSR_i[j+1], \quad 1 \leq j \leq n_i - 1, \\ FSR_i[n_i] &= w_i + f_i. \end{aligned}$$

For each FSR the feedback tap is updated by one output bit of confusion layer XORing with one output bit of diffusion layer, while the other registers are updated by shift. The eight bits input of S-box come from eight FSRs respectively. It can be written by

$$(w_1, w_2, ..., w_8) = \text{S-box}(FSR_1[t_1], FSR_2[t_2], ..., FSR_8[t_8])$$

where $1 \leq t_i \leq n_i, i = 1, 2, ..., 8$. We suggest that the positions in FSRs selected as the input of S-box should follow the two principles:

(1) The position t_i selected in FSR_i should be close to the register $FSR_i[n_i]$ such that the feedback update of FSR_i can enter into S-box as soon as possible.
(2) The distances $n_i - t_i, i = 1, 2, ..., 8$, should be different so as to avoid two feedback bits of FSRs entering into S-box at the same time.

The eight linear boolean functions in diffusion layer are expressed by

$$f_i = FSR_i[1] + FSR_i[k_i] + FSR_{[i+1]}[u_i] + FSR_{[i+4]}[v_i],$$

where $1 < k_i < n_i, 1 < u_i < n_{[i+1]}, 1 < v_i < n_{[i+4]}, i = 1, 2, ..., 8$. The subscripts $[i+1]$ and $[i+4]$ denote $i+1$ and $i+4$ modulo 8 respectively, and the representative elements modulo 8 are $\{1, 2, ..., 8\}$. For the 4 bits input of f_i, there two taps are selected in FSR_i and another two taps are selected in the neighbors $FSR_{[i+1]}$ and $FSR_{[i+4]}$ respectively. We also suggest that the positions k_i in FSR_i, u_i in $FSR_{[i+1]}$, and v_i in $FSR_{[i+4]}$ selected as the input of f_i should follow the two principles:

(1) The distances $n_i - k_i, n_{[i+1]} - u_i$ and $n_{[i+4]} - v_i, i = 1, 2, ..., 8$, are different.
(2) The positions selected distribute as uniform as possible in the eight FSRs.

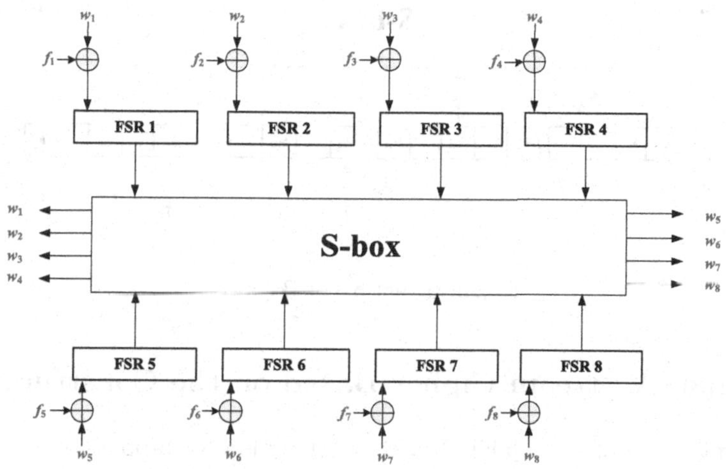

Fig. 2. New construction of Galois-NFSR

Theorem 1. *Let l be the longest distance in $n_i - t_i, i = 1, 2, ..., 8$. Then there exists a positive integer N, after N iterations the differential characteristic of the construction in any l iterations has d active S-boxes at least, where d is the differential branch number of S-box.*

Proof. For any input difference of this construction, there must be a positive integer N such that the difference in any register of eight FSRs is unknown after N iterations. The minimal value of N can be searched by computer program. Since the distances $n_i - t_i, i = 1, 2, ..., 8$, are different, the input bits of S-box come from the feedbacks at eight different times. In other words, the output bits of S-box will enter into S-boxs at eight different times. Since l is the longest distance in $n_i - t_i, i = 1, 2, ..., 8$, all output bits of S-box will be involved in S-box again respectively after l iterations. Thus any differential characteristic of this construction after l iterations has d active S-boxes at least, where d is the differential branch number of S-box.

Theorem 1 can be used to evaluate the number of rounds in the initialization stage of a stream cipher based on this construction to resist differential cryptanalysis. The number of active S-boxes in the linear characteristics is determined by the detail of the eight linear boolean functions in diffusion layer, while there are some results in this aspect for the design of Trivium in [19].

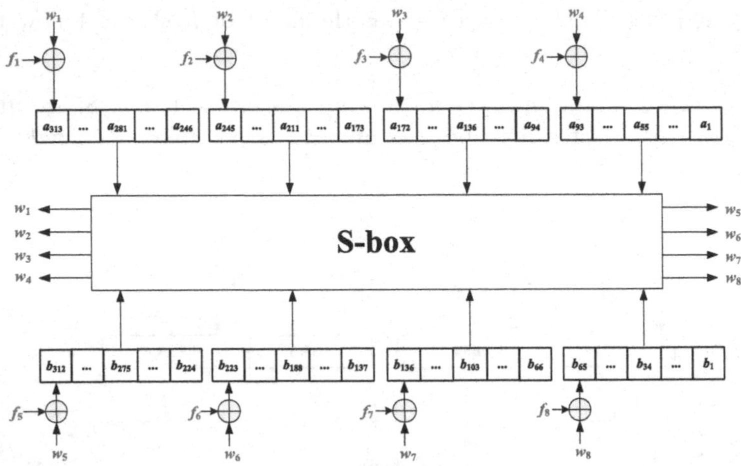

Fig. 3. Structure of Bagua

4 Bagua: A Stream Cipher Based on the Construction

As an application of this Galois-NFSR construction we propose a synchronous stream cipher called Bagua in this section. Bagua is a hardware-oriented primitive of 128-bit initialization vector and 128-bit or 256-bit key. It can be implemented in parallel up to 32 iterations at once. One can choose the parallel degree in implementation according to the requirement of throughput and hardware overhead in different application environments.

4.1 Description of Bagua

The structure of Bagua is shown in Fig. 3. The lengths of eight FSRs are 68, 73, 79, 93, 89, 87, 71 and 65 respectively. Denote the registers in the first four FSRs by $a_{313}, a_{312}, ..., a_1$ and the registers in the latter four FSRs by $b_{312}, b_{311}, ..., b_1$. The states of FSRs are updated per iteration as follows

$$\begin{aligned}
FSR_1 &: (a_{313}, a_{312}, ..., a_{246}) \leftarrow (f_1 + w_1, a_{313}, ..., a_{247}),\\
FSR_2 &: (a_{245}, a_{241}, ..., a_{173}) \leftarrow (f_2 + w_2, a_{245}, ..., a_{174}),\\
FSR_3 &: (a_{172}, a_{171}, ..., a_{94}) \leftarrow (f_3 + w_3, a_{172}, ..., a_{95}),\\
FSR_4 &: (a_{93}, a_{92}, ..., a_1) \leftarrow (f_4 + w_4, a_{93}, ..., a_2),\\
FSR_5 &: (b_{312}, b_{311}, ..., b_{224}) \leftarrow (f_5 + w_5, b_{312}, ..., b_{225}),\\
FSR_6 &: (b_{223}, b_{222}, ..., b_{137}) \leftarrow (f_6 + w_6, b_{223}, ..., b_{138}),\\
FSR_7 &: (b_{136}, b_{135}, ..., b_{66}) \leftarrow (f_7 + w_7, b_{136}, ..., b_{67}),\\
FSR_8 &: (b_{65}, b_{64}, ..., b_1) \leftarrow (f_8 + w_8, b_{65}, ..., b_2).
\end{aligned}$$

The update of whole Galois-NFSR is a reversible transformation. The eight linear boolean functions in the diffusion layer are

$$\begin{aligned}
f_1 &= a_{246} + a_{263} + a_{212} + b_{277},\\
f_2 &= a_{173} + a_{192} + a_{139} + b_{192},\\
f_3 &= a_{94} + a_{115} + a_{60} + b_{102},\\
f_4 &= a_1 + a_{28} + b_{281} + b_{32},\\
f_5 &= b_{224} + b_{250} + b_{185} + a_{277},\\
f_6 &= b_{137} + b_{162} + b_{98} + a_{205},\\
f_7 &= b_{66} + b_{85} + b_{27} + a_{128},\\
f_8 &= b_1 + b_{17} + b_{272} + a_{62}.
\end{aligned}$$

The confusion layer is an 8×8 reversible S-box and is written by

$$(w_1, w_2, ..., w_8) = \text{S-box}(a_{281}, a_{211}, a_{136}, a_{55}, b_{275}, b_{188}, b_{103}, b_{34}).$$

The Design of S-box. For hardware implementation efficiency, the 8-bit S-box is designed by SPS structure consisting of four different 4-bit S-boxes and a lightweight linear transformation, see Fig. 4. The four 4-bit S-boxes are not affine equivalent and have the optimal differential and linear properties in all 4-bit S-boxes. That is, for each S-boxes both the maximum differential probability and the maximum linear approximation probability are 2^{-2}. The actions of the four 4-bit S-boxes in hexadecimal notation are given in the following table.

x	0	1	2	3	4	5	6	7	8	9	A	B	C	D	E	F
$S_1[x]$	B	F	3	2	A	C	9	1	6	7	8	0	E	5	D	4
$S_2[x]$	1	D	F	0	E	8	2	B	7	4	C	A	9	3	5	6
$S_3[x]$	7	4	A	9	1	F	B	0	C	3	2	6	8	E	D	5
$S_4[x]$	E	9	F	0	D	4	A	B	1	2	8	3	7	6	C	5

Let (x_1, x_2, x_3, x_4) be the input of 4-bit S-box, and (y_1, y_2, y_3, y_4) be its output. Then

$$y_1 + 2y_2 + 2^2y_3 + 2^3y_4 = S_i[x_1 + 2x_2 + 2^2x_3 + 2^3x_4], \quad i = 1, 2, 3, 4.$$

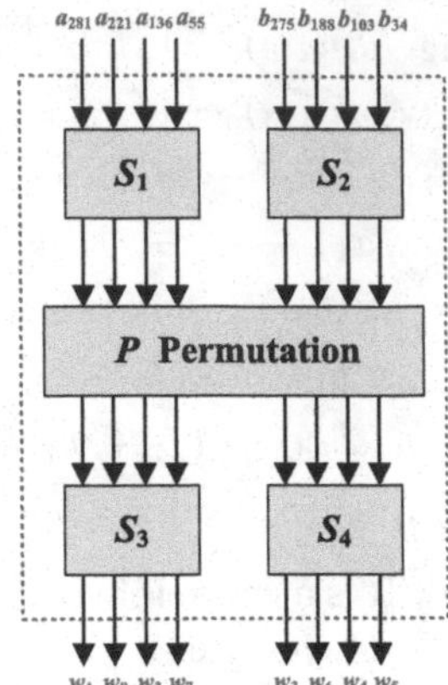

Fig. 4. S-box

The input of S_1 is $(a_{281}, a_{211}, a_{136}, a_{55})$ and the input of S_2 is $(b_{275}, b_{188}, b_{103}, b_{34})$. The output of S_3 is assigned to (w_1, w_8, w_2, w_7) and the output of S_4 is assigned to (w_3, w_6, w_4, w_5). The linear transformation can be represented by $P(x) = P \cdot x$, where P is the following 8×8 matrix

$$P = \begin{bmatrix} 0\,1\,0\,0\,1\,0\,0\,1 \\ 1\,0\,0\,0\,1\,1\,0\,0 \\ 0\,0\,1\,0\,0\,1\,1\,0 \\ 0\,0\,0\,1\,0\,0\,1\,1 \\ 0\,0\,1\,1\,0\,1\,0\,0 \\ 1\,0\,1\,0\,0\,0\,1\,0 \\ 0\,1\,0\,1\,0\,0\,0\,1 \\ 0\,1\,1\,0\,1\,0\,0\,0 \end{bmatrix}.$$

For the whole 8-bit S-box in Bagua, the maximum differential probability is $\frac{7}{128}$ and the maximum linear approximation probability is 2^{-4}. If we treat S-box as an 8-bit input and 8-bit output vector boolean function, the algebraic degree of component functions all are 6 and the number of monomials in the ANFs are 91, 98, 103, 99, 99, 96, 114 and 110 respectively.

4.2 Initialization and Output

Bagua has 128-bit initialization vector IV and supports key of lengths 128 or 256 bits. In order to unify the key loading, for the case of 128-bit key we copy it to obtain a 256-bit tuple. Denote $Key = (k_0, k_1, ..., k_{255})$ and $IV = (iv_0, iv_1, ..., iv_{127})$. Then the Key and IV are loaded as following

$$FSR_1 : (a_{313}, a_{312}, ..., a_{246}) = (1, 0, ..., 0, k_0, ..., k_{51}),$$
$$FSR_2 : (a_{245}, a_{241}, ..., a_{173}) = (1, 0, ..., 0, k_{52}, ..., k_{103}),$$
$$FSR_3 : (a_{172}, a_{171}, ..., a_{94}) = (1, 0, ..., 0, k_{104}, ..., k_{155}),$$
$$FSR_4 : (a_{93}, a_{92}, ..., a_1) = (1, 0, ..., 0, k_{156}, ..., k_{207}),$$
$$FSR_5 : (b_{312}, b_{311}, ..., b_{224}) = (1, 0, ..., 0, k_{208}, ..., k_{255}),$$
$$FSR_6 : (b_{223}, b_{222}, ..., b_{137}) = (1, 0, ..., 0, iv_0, ..., iv_{55}),$$
$$FSR_7 : (b_{136}, b_{135}, ..., b_{66}) = (1, 0, ..., 0, iv_{56}, ..., iv_{95}),$$
$$FSR_8 : (b_{65}, b_{64}, ..., b_1) = (1, 0, ..., 0, iv_{96}, ..., iv_{127}).$$

The constant vectors $1, 0, ..., 0$ are filled in the eight FSRs to avoid sliding attack, where the lengths of constant vectors are 16, 21, 27, 41, 41, 31, 31 and 33 respectively. After key and initialization vector loading Bagua runs 960 iterations without output for 128-bit key, while running 1600 iterations without output for 256-bit key. After initialization it enters into the stage of generating sequence. One bit is generated per iteration, which is a simple function of the output bits of diffusion layer as following

$$output = f_1 \times f_7 + f_3 \times f_5 + f_2 + f_4 + f_6 + f_8.$$

4.3 Hardware Performance

Bagua allows parallel implementation up to 32 iterations at once. One can choose the parallel degree in implementation according to the requirement of throughput and hardware overhead in different application environments. The area requirements of Bagua implemented in ASIC under different parallel degree are evaluated in Table 1, where the most economical implementation needs about 3905 gates. We also evaluate the performance of Bagua in FPGA implementation using Verilog HDL simulation, see Table 2. It shows that the maximum throughout can be up to 8 Gbps in 32-iteration parallel implementation.

Table 1. Area (GE) requirement of ASIC implementation

Parallel degree	FSRs	S-box	Other	Sum
1	3750	116	39	3905
4	3750	464	156	4370
8	3750	928	312	4990
16	3750	1856	624	6230
32	3750	3712	1248	8710

Table 2. The performance in FPGA implementation

Parallel degree	Area (LE)	Peak frequency (MHz)	Throughput (Gbps)
1	1104	329.6	0.329
8	1465	299.58	2.397
16	2101	256.34	4.101
32	2554	250.13	8.004

5 Security Analysis

We have tested the pseudo-randomness of the output sequences using the NIST's suit sts-2.1.2 for Bagua-128 and Bagua-256. For the three cases of all-zero Key and IV, all-one Key and IV, and random Key and IV, all tests are passed. In the following we mainly evaluate the security of Bagua against linear, differential and algebraic cryptanalyses.

5.1 Linear Cryptanalysis

In order to evaluate the resistance of Bagua against linear cryptanalysis, we estimate the lower bound on the number of active S-boxes in the linear characteristics. Since the eight linear functions in this construction can provide good diffusivity, the larger the Hamming weight of the input linear mask, the more active S-box will be involved in the linear characteristic. So we consider all one-bit input masks of the initial state of FSRs, then estimate the lower bounds on the number of active S-boxes per 50 iterations in the stage of initialization by computer program. When the bit of input mask is selected in one of the positions $a_{93}, a_{172}, a_{245}, a_{313}, b_{65}, b_{136}, b_{223}, b_{312}$, one could find the linear characteristic with less active S-boxes. For the eight kinds of input masks, Table 3 presents the growth of the estimating number of active S-boxes along with the iteration rounds. It shows that the minimal number of active S-boxes after 350 rounds is 128 in all considered linear characteristics. Since the maximum linear approximation probability of S-box is 2^{-4} and the output sequence is a quadratic function of internal state, Bagua is practical secure against linear cryptanalysis.

5.2 Differential Cryptanalysis

For any one-bit input difference of Bagua, the longest path of the difference entering into S-box has 65 iterations and the differences in all registers will be unknown after 247 iterations. The longest distance between feedback taps and positions selected as the input of S-box in FSRs is 38, that is, $\max_{1\leq i\leq 8}\{n_i - t_i\} = 38$. Since S-box is reversible, its differential branch number is 2 at least. By Theorem 1, we know that after 960 iterations any differential characteristic of Bagua has at least $2 \cdot \lfloor \frac{960-247}{38} \rfloor = 36$ active S-boxes, while after

Table 3. Number of active S-boxes with different rounds for 8 input masks

Rounds	100	150	200	250	300	350	400	450	500	550	600	650	700	750
a_{93}	1	6	22	54	98	146	196	246	294	344	393	443	493	541
a_{172}	2	14	53	100	149	198	247	296	344	393	443	493	543	592
a_{245}	2	14	46	90	136	184	234	284	333	383	433	483	533	583
a_{313}	2	18	55	100	149	199	248	298	348	397	446	496	546	596
b_{65}	2	5	15	39	81	128	177	227	276	326	376	425	475	525
b_{136}	3	20	54	99	147	195	243	292	341	391	441	491	540	590
b_{223}	1	7	37	82	130	179	229	279	328	377	427	476	526	576
b_{312}	1	8	36	77	125	174	224	272	321	371	421	471	520	569

1600 iterations any differential characteristic has at least $2 \cdot \lfloor \frac{1600-247}{38} \rfloor = 70$ active S-boxes. Note that the maximum differential probability of S-box is $\frac{7}{128}$. Then for 960 rounds initialization the differential characteristic probability is less than $(\frac{7}{128})^{36} \approx 2^{-150.9}$ and for 1600 rounds initialization the differential characteristic probability is less than $(\frac{7}{128})^{70} \approx 2^{-293}$. It shows Bagua is practical secure against differential cryptanalysis.

5.3 Algebraic Cryptanalysis

The general idea of algebraic attack is to treat the encryption algorithm as an over-defined system of algebraic equations. Then the secret key or the internal state at certain time interval can be recovered by solving this system of multivariate algebraic equations. In Bagua algorithm, for each output bit of S-box the algebraic degree is 6 and the number of monomials in their algebraic normal forms are $91, 98, 103, 99, 99, 96, 114$ and 110 respectively. If we set the internal state at some time interval as variables to construct equations using output sequence, after 119 iterations each equation will involve all 625 variables and the algebraic degree is too high. It is impossible to solve this kind of equations using some known methods, such as linearization, XL, XSL and Gröbner basis methods. As far as we know no method has been found to control the number of variables and the degree of equations.

6 Conclusions

In this paper, we propose a new construction of Galois-NFSR based on Shannon's confusion and diffusion design principles. As an application of this construction, we propose a hardware-oriented stream cipher named Bagua, which has 128-bit initialization vector and 128-bit or 256-bit key. It can be implemented in parallel up to 32 iterations at once, and the most economical implementation needs about 3905 gates. The simulation evaluation of Bagua in FPGA implementation shows that the maximum throughout can be up to 8 Gbps in 32-iteration parallel implementation. We analyze its resistances against differential and linear cryptanalyses theoretically and experimentally. More cryptanalyses on Bagua and researches on the provable security for the Galois-NFSR construction are expected in the future.

Acknowledgements. The authors are grateful to the anonymous reviewers for their helpful comments and suggestions. This work was supported by the National Cryptography Development Fund of China under grant numbers MMJJ20170103 and MMJJ20180204, and the National Natural Science Foundations of China under grant number 61521003.

References

1. Schneier, B.: Applied Cryptography: Protocols, Algorithms, and Source Code in C, 2nd edn. Wiley, New York (1996)
2. Daemen, J., Rijmen, V.: The Design of Rijndael: AES - The Advanced Encryption Standard. Information Security and Cryptography. Springer, Heidelberg (2002). https://doi.org/10.1007/978-3-662-04722-4
3. Lidl, R., Niederreiter, H.: Introduction to Finite Fields and Their Applications, Revised edn. Cambridge University Press, Cambridge (1994)
4. Bogdanov, A., et al.: PRESENT: an ultra-lightweight block cipher. In: Paillier, P., Verbauwhede, I. (eds.) CHES 2007. LNCS, vol. 4727, pp. 450–466. Springer, Heidelberg (2007). https://doi.org/10.1007/978-3-540-74735-2_31
5. De Cannière, C., Dunkelman, O., Knežević, M.: KATAN and KTANTAN—a family of small and efficient hardware-oriented block ciphers. In: Clavier, C., Gaj, K. (eds.) CHES 2009. LNCS, vol. 5747, pp. 272–288. Springer, Heidelberg (2009). https://doi.org/10.1007/978-3-642-04138-9_20
6. Nyberg, K., Knudsen, L.R.: Provable security against a differential attack. J. Cryptol. **8**(1), 27–37 (1995). https://doi.org/10.1007/BF00204800
7. Lai, X., Massey, J.L., Murphy, S.: Markov ciphers and differential cryptanalysis. In: Davies, D.W. (ed.) EUROCRYPT 1991. LNCS, vol. 547, pp. 17–38. Springer, Heidelberg (1991). https://doi.org/10.1007/3-540-46416-6_2
8. Nyberg, K.: Linear approximation of block ciphers. In: De Santis, A. (ed.) EUROCRYPT 1994. LNCS, vol. 950, pp. 439–444. Springer, Heidelberg (1995). https://doi.org/10.1007/BFb0053460
9. Knudsen, L.R.: Practically secure Feistel ciphers. In: Anderson, R. (ed.) FSE 1993. LNCS, vol. 809, pp. 211–221. Springer, Heidelberg (1994). https://doi.org/10.1007/3-540-58108-1_26
10. Hong, S., Lee, S., Lim, J., Sung, J., Cheon, D., Cho, I.: Provable security against differential and linear cryptanalysis for the SPN structure. In: Goos, G., Hartmanis, J., van Leeuwen, J., Schneier, B. (eds.) FSE 2000. LNCS, vol. 1978, pp. 273–283. Springer, Heidelberg (2001). https://doi.org/10.1007/3-540-44706-7_19
11. Kang, J.S., Hong, S., Lee, S., Yi, O., Park, C., Lim, J.: Practical and provable security against differential and linear cryptanalysis for substitution-permutation networks. ETRI J. **23**(4), 158–167 (2001)
12. Park, S., Sung, S.H., Lee, S., Lim, J.: Improving the upper bound on the maximum differential and the maximum linear hull probability for SPN structures and AES. In: Johansson, T. (ed.) FSE 2003. LNCS, vol. 2887, pp. 247–260. Springer, Heidelberg (2003). https://doi.org/10.1007/978-3-540-39887-5_19

13. Matsui, M.: New structure of block ciphers with provable security against differential and linear cryptanalysis. In: Gollmann, D. (ed.) FSE 1996. LNCS, vol. 1039, pp. 205–218. Springer, Heidelberg (1996). https://doi.org/10.1007/3-540-60865-6_54
14. De Cannière, C., Preneel, B.: TRIVIUM. In: Robshaw, M., Billet, O. (eds.) New Stream Cipher Designs. LNCS, vol. 4986, pp. 244–266. Springer, Heidelberg (2008). https://doi.org/10.1007/978-3-540-68351-3_18
15. Hell, M., Johansson, T., Maximov, A., Meier, W.: The grain family of stream ciphers. In: Robshaw, M., Billet, O. (eds.) New Stream Cipher Designs. LNCS, vol. 4986, pp. 179–190. Springer, Heidelberg (2008). https://doi.org/10.1007/978-3-540-68351-3_14
16. Babbage, S., Dodd, M.: The MICKEY stream ciphers. In: Robshaw, M., Billet, O. (eds.) New Stream Cipher Designs. LNCS, vol. 4986, pp. 191–209. Springer, Heidelberg (2008). https://doi.org/10.1007/978-3-540-68351-3_15
17. Aerts, W., et al.: A practical attack on KeeLoq. J. Cryptol. **25**(1), 136–157 (2010). https://doi.org/10.1007/s00145-010-9091-9
18. Aumasson, J.-P., Henzen, L., Meier, W., Naya-Plasencia, M.: QUARK: a lightweight hash. J. Cryptol. **26**(2), 313–339 (2012). https://doi.org/10.1007/s00145-012-9125-6
19. De Cannière, C.: TRIVIUM: a stream cipher construction inspired by block cipher design principles. In: Katsikas, S.K., López, J., Backes, M., Gritzalis, S., Preneel, B. (eds.) ISC 2006. LNCS, vol. 4176, pp. 171–186. Springer, Heidelberg (2006). https://doi.org/10.1007/11836810_13
20. Hong, D., et al.: HIGHT: a new block cipher suitable for low-resource device. In: Goubin, L., Matsui, M. (eds.) CHES 2006. LNCS, vol. 4249, pp. 46–59. Springer, Heidelberg (2006). https://doi.org/10.1007/11894063_4
21. Wu, W., Zhang, L.: LBlock: a lightweight block cipher. In: Lopez, J., Tsudik, G. (eds.) ACNS 2011. LNCS, vol. 6715, pp. 327–344. Springer, Heidelberg (2011). https://doi.org/10.1007/978-3-642-21554-4_19
22. Shannon, C.E.: Communication theory of secrecy systems. Bell Syst. Tech. J. **28**, 657–715 (1949)
23. Choy, J., Chew, G., Khoo, K., Yap, H.: Cryptographic properties and application of a generalized unbalanced Feistel network structure. In: Boyd, C., González Nieto, J. (eds.) ACISP 2009. LNCS, vol. 5594, pp. 73–89. Springer, Heidelberg (2009). https://doi.org/10.1007/978-3-642-02620-1_6
24. Zhang, B.: Fountain: a lightweight authenticated cipher. In: The First-Round Candidates of NIST Lightweight Cryptography (2019)

Provable Related-Key Security of Contracting Feistel Networks

Wenqi Yu[1,2], Yuqing Zhao[1,2], and Chun Guo[1,2,3,4](✉)

[1] School of Cyber Science and Technology, Shandong University, Qingdao, Shandong, China
{wenqiyu,yqzhao}@mail.sdu.edu.cn, chun.guo@sdu.edu.cn
[2] Key Laboratory of Cryptologic Technology and Information Security of Ministry of Education, Shandong University, Qingdao 266237, Shandong, China
[3] Shandong Institute of Blockchain, Jinan, China
[4] State Key Laboratory of Information Security, Institute of Information Engineering, Chinese Academy of Sciences, Beijing 100093, China

Abstract. We continue the line of works constructing related-key secure PRFs (Bellare and Cash, CRYPTO 2010) and PRPs (Barbosa and Farshim, FSE 2014). In detail, we consider generalized Feistel networks using *contracting round functions* from $\{0,1\}^m$ to $\{0,1\}^n$, and explore conditions that are sufficient for such Contracting Feistel Networks (CFNs) to achieve security up to $2^{n/2}$ adversarial queries. As results, we show that provable related-key security is achieved with $\lceil \frac{m}{n} \rceil + 3$ rounds, as long as the CFN uses two independent main keys K_1, K_2 in all the rounds in a close-to-alternating manner. Our results provide new approaches to construct related-key secure variable-input-length block ciphers from related-key secure variable-input-length PRFs.

Keywords: Block cipher · Contracting feistel networks · Related-key attack · CCA-security · H-coefficient technique

1 Introduction

Feistel Networks. A plenty of modern block ciphers consist of iterative applications of a simple Feistel permutation, which maps $(A, B) \in \{0,1\}^n \times \{0,1\}^n$ to $(B, A \oplus F_K(B))$ for a domain-preserving *round function* $F : \mathcal{K} \times \{0,1\}^n \to \{0,1\}^n$. The most popular instance is likely the Data Encryption Standard (DES) [16]. This popularity has motivated a number of works investigating such *Feistel networks*.

A popular approach to analyzing the security of Feistel networks, pioneered by Luby and Rackoff [23], is to model the round function F_K as a secret random function. This allows proving its information theoretic indistinguishability, i.e., any *distinguisher* should not be able to distinguish the Feistel network from a random permutation on $2n$-bit strings. With this model, Luby and Rackoff

W. Yu and Y. Zhao are co-first authors of the article.

Y. Wu and M. Yung (Eds.): Inscrypt 2020, LNCS 12612, pp. 466–490, 2021.
https://doi.org/10.1007/978-3-030-71852-7_31

proved the security for 4 rounds Feistel networks, following which a long series of work has established either better security bounds [19,28] or reduced construction complexity [26,32].

Contracting Feistel Networks. The above classical Feistel networks could be generalized in various manners. In this paper, we consider replacing the domain-preserving round function F by contracting ones. Concretely, assuming using a contracting function $F : \mathcal{K} \times \{0,1\}^{kn+r} \to \{0,1\}^n$, where $k \in \{1,...\}$ is a positive integer and $0 \leq r \leq n-1$, then a contracting Feistel permutation maps $(A, B) \in \{0,1\}^n \times \{0,1\}^{kn+r}$ to $(B, A \oplus F_K(B))$. Note this yields a permutation on $\{0,1\}^{(k+1)n+r}$. The idea dates back to [33], with real instances BEAR and LION [2] and later the Chinese standard SMS4 [13]. Such Contracting Feistels Networks (CFNs) appear particularly useful in motivating ultra-lightweight block ciphers [35] and full-domain secure encryption [25]. Moreover, with Variable-Input-Length (VIL) PRFs (though not necessarily domain-preserving), it also gives rise to wide cryptographic permutations [17].

Information theoretic security of GFNs could be analyzed similarly to classical Feistel, with various "birthday-bound" results showed in [2,7,11,24,25,27,37] and "beyond-birthday-bound" results found in [19,30]. It has been proved that, with a sufficient number of rounds, CFNs are CCA-secure up to $2^{(kn+r)(1-\varepsilon)}$ adversarial queries for any $\varepsilon > 0$ [19,34].

Our Question. Despite the asymptotically optimal provable bounds, CFNs remain far less understood regarding security beyond the classical PRP or SPRP notions. In this regime, the arguably most important model is security against the so-called *Related-Key Attacks* (RKAs) that were independently introduced by Biham [8] and Knudsen [21] in early 1990s. Such attacks concentrate on multiple secret keys satisfying some adversary-chosen relations, the presence of which may be the consequence of a protocol-level key update [20] or tampering [3]. Compared to the classical "single-key" setting, the increased adversarial power enables very efficient attacks against quite a number of block ciphers [9,10,14].

In light of such influential results, Bellare and Kohno [6] initiated the theoretical treatment of security under related-key attacks by proposing definitions for RKA secure pseudorandom functions (PRFs) and pseudorandom permutations (PRPs), formalizing the adversarial goal as distinguishing the cipher oracles with related-keys from independent random functions or permutations, and presenting possibility and impossibility results for these primitives. Since then, follow up works have established various important positive results for provably RKA secure constructions of complex cryptographic primitives [1,4,5,18]. Particularly relevant to us, Barbosa and Farshim established RKA security for 4 rounds balanced Feistel networks with two master keys K_1 and K_2 alternatively used in each round [4], and Guo established RKA security for the so-called Feistel-2 or key-alternating Feistel ciphers [18].

Our Results. This paper considers the RKA security of contracting Feistel networks built upon a round function $F : \mathcal{K} \times \{0,1\}^{kn+r} \to \{0,1\}^n$. As observed in the context of balanced Feistel networks [4,6], to achieve RKA security, the round keys have to be somewhat correlated. Thus, the first step is to pinpoint a plausible key assignment. Motivated by the 4 rounds result in [4], we consider assigning two κ-bit master keys K_1, K_2 to all the rounds alternatively, which appears a quite natural idea. However, note that an odd number of Feistel rounds with such alternated key assignment yields an involution, which is clearly insecure as a block cipher. This means some "interference" is necessary, which gives rise to the following key assignment scheme:

- When the number t of rounds of the candidate CFN is even, the two master keys K_1 and K_2 are alternatively used in each round. I.e., the round keys are of the form $K_1, K_2, K_1, K_2, ...$
- When the number t of rounds of the candidate CFN is odd, the two master keys K_1 and K_2 are alternatively used in the 4-th to the t-th rounds, while the round keys in the first three rounds are K_1, K_2, K_2. I.e., the round keys are of the form $K_1, K_2, K_2, K_1, K_2, ...$

We remark that the key assignment $K_1, K_2, K_1, K_2, ..., K_2, K_2$ can also be used when the rounds of CFN is odd, however, due to the page limits, we do not provide a detailed proof. With above key assignment scheme using the round function $F : \mathcal{K} \times \{0,1\}^{kn+r} \to \{0,1\}^n$, we show that $k+4$ rounds are sufficient for RKA security up to $2^{n/2}$ adversarial queries, establishing the classical birthday-bound security. As shown in [31, Table 4], for contracting Feistel networks using the round function $F : \mathcal{K} \times \{0,1\}^{kn+r} \to \{0,1\}^n$, $k+3$ rounds are necessary for provable CPA security even in the single-key setting. By this, the round complexity of our results is quite close to optimal (though we leave tightening as an open problem).

CFNs are valuable due to the compatibility with "irregular" round functions. For example, one of the RKA secure PRF candidates constructed in [5] maps n-bit strings to elements in a group of prime order. Depending on the concrete parameters, it may not be efficient (even possible) to truncate such a PRF to a domain-preserving PRF. CFNs offer a more "direct" approach to construct RKA secure PRPs from such PRFs. Moreover, with RKA secure VIL PRFs, our results provide new approaches to construct related-key secure variable-input-length block ciphers from related-key secure PRFs, which may find applications in the context of, e.g., non-malleable codes for VIL messages [15, Sect. 6], and wide tweakable block ciphers [22].

Related Work. Contracting Feistel networks have been analyzed regarding provable CCA security [19,34,36] and generic attacks [31]. The CCA result in [19,34] was established via the cascade of NCPA secure networks, and thus the round complexities are much larger than ours. The CCA result in [36] was established via a dedicated analysis, and has the same round complexities as ours, though we are in the stronger RKA setting. Finally, provable related-key security of classical balanced Feistel networks has been investigated [4,18], which, as mentioned, also serves a part of our motivation.

Organization. We serve necessary notations and definitions in Sect. 2. Then, as a warm up, in Sect. 3 we analyze the simplest setting of 5 rounds in detail.

We serve the analysis of 6 rounds as another instructive example, which is however deferred to Appendix A due to page limits. After that, we present our main result in Sect. 4. We finally conclude in Sect. 5.

2 Preliminaries

For $X \in \{0,1\}^m$, we denote by $X[a,b]$ the string consisting of the $b-a+1$ bits between the a-th position and the b-th position. The t-round contracting Feistel construction using a vector of round keys $\mathbf{K} = (K_1, ..., K_t)$ is defined as

$$\mathsf{CFN}_{\mathbf{K}}^{F^{kn+r,n},t}(X) := \Psi^{F_{K_t}^{kn+r,n}} \circ ... \circ \Psi^{F_{K_1}^{kn+r,n}}(X).$$

For such a round key vector $\mathbf{K} = (K_1, ..., K_t)$, we denote by $\mathbf{K}[i]$ the i-th round key K_i. Then, for $X \in \{0,1\}^{(k+1)n+r}$, a contracting Feistel round using the key K_i is defined as (see Fig. 1)

$$\Psi^{F_{K_i}^{kn+r,n}}(X_i) := X_i[n+1,(k+1)n+r] \| F_{K_i}^{kn+r,n}(X_i[n+1,(k+1)n+r]) \oplus X_i[1,n].$$

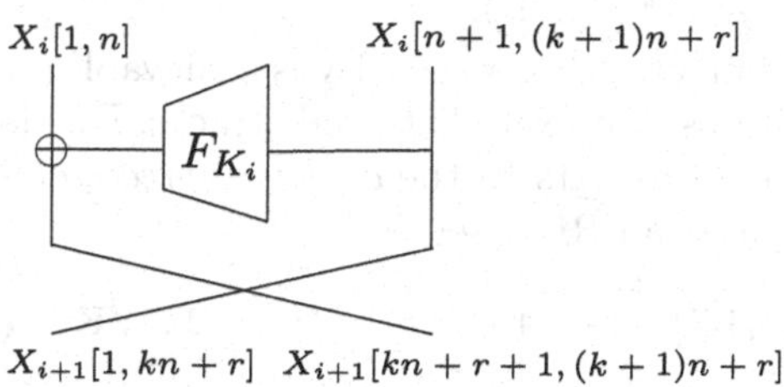

Fig. 1. The i-th round of $\mathsf{CFN}_{\mathbf{K}}^{F^{kn+r,n}}$, and our notations.

2.1 (Multi-key) RKA Security

The RKA security notion is parameterized by a so-called related-key deriving (RKD) sets. Formally, an n-ary RKD set Φ consists of RKD functions ϕ mapping an n-tuple of keys in some key space $\mathcal{K}^n$ to a new key in $\mathcal{K}$, i.e., $\phi : \mathcal{K}^n \to \mathcal{K}$.

Let $F : \mathcal{K} \times \{0,1\}^m \to \{0,1\}^n$ be a keyed function, and fix a key $K \in \mathcal{K}$. We define the Φ-restricted related-key oracle $\mathsf{RK}[F_K]$, which takes a RKD function $\phi \in \Phi$ and an input $X \in \{0,1\}^m$ as input, and returns $\mathsf{RK}[F_K](\phi, X) := F_{\phi(K)}(X)$. Then, we consider a Φ-restricted related-key adversary D which has access to u related-key oracles instantiated with either F or a random function $\mathsf{RF} : \mathcal{K} \times \{0,1\}^m \to \{0,1\}^n$, and must distinguish between two worlds as follows:

- the "real" world, where it interacts with $\mathsf{RK}[F_{K_1}], ..., \mathsf{RK}[F_{K_u}]$, and $K_1, ..., K_u$ are randomly and independently drawn;

– the "ideal" world, where it interacts with $\mathsf{RK}[\mathsf{RF}_{K_1}], ..., \mathsf{RK}[\mathsf{RF}_{K_u}]$, and $K_1, ..., K_u$ are randomly and independently drawn.

The adversary is adaptive. Note that in the ideal world, each oracle $\mathsf{RK}[\mathsf{RF}_{K_i}]$ essentially implements an independent random function for each related-key $\phi(K_i)$. Formally, D's distinguishing advantage on F is defined as

$$\mathbf{Adv}_F^{\Phi\text{-rka}[u]}(D) := \Big|\Pr_{\mathsf{RF},K_1,...,K_u}\big[D^{\mathsf{RK}[\mathsf{RF}_{K_1}],\mathsf{RK}[\mathsf{RF}_{K_1}]^{-1},...,\mathsf{RK}[\mathsf{RF}_{K_u}],\mathsf{RK}[\mathsf{RF}_{K_u}]^{-1}} = 1\big] - \Pr_{K_1,...,K_u}\big[D^{\mathsf{RK}[F_{K_1}],\mathsf{RK}[F_{K_1}]^{-1},...,\mathsf{RK}[F_{K_u}],\mathsf{RK}[F_{K_u}]^{-1}} = 1\big]\Big|.$$

It was proved that, under some natural restrictions on RKD sets, the single-key and multi-key RKA security notions are equivalent. We refer to [4] for details.

Similarly, a block cipher $E : \mathcal{K} \times \{0,1\}^m \to \{0,1\}^m$ shall be indistinguishable from an ideal cipher. For this we will only consider the single-key setting. Formally, D's distinguishing advantage on E is defined as

$$\mathbf{Adv}_E^{\Phi\text{-rka}[1]}(D) := \Big|\Pr_{\mathsf{IC},K}\big[D^{\mathsf{RK}[\mathsf{IC}_K],\mathsf{RK}[\mathsf{IC}_K]^{-1}} = 1\big] - \Pr_K\big[D^{\mathsf{RK}[E_K],\mathsf{RK}[E_K]^{-1}}\big]\Big|,$$

where $\mathsf{RK}[E_K]^{-1}(\phi, Y) := E^{-1}_{\phi(K)}(Y)$.

As already noticed in [6], Φ-RKA security is achievable only if the RKD set Φ satisfies certain conditions that exclude trivial attacks. For this, we follow [4] and characterize three properties. Firstly, the *output unpredictability (UP)* advantage of an adversary $\mathcal{A}$ against an RKD set Φ is

$$\mathbf{Adv}_\Phi^{\mathsf{up}}(\mathcal{A}) := \Pr\big[\exists(\phi, \mathbf{K}^*) \in \mathsf{L}_1 \times \mathsf{L}_2 \quad \text{s.t.} \quad \phi(\mathbf{K}) = \mathbf{K}^* : \mathbf{K} \leftarrow_\$ \mathcal{K}; (\mathsf{L}_1, \mathsf{L}_2) \leftarrow \mathcal{A}\big].$$

Secondly, the *claw-freeness* (CF) advantage of an adversary $\mathcal{A}$ against an RKD set Φ is

$$\mathbf{Adv}_\Phi^{\mathsf{cf}}(\mathcal{A}) := \Pr\big[\exists\phi_1, \phi_2 \in \mathsf{L} \quad \text{s.t.} \quad \phi_1(\mathbf{K}) = \phi_2(\mathbf{K}) \wedge \phi_1 \neq \phi_2 : \mathbf{K} \leftarrow_\$ \mathcal{K}; \mathsf{L} \leftarrow \mathcal{A}\big].$$

Finally, the *switch-freeness* (SF) advantage of an adversary $\mathcal{A}$ against an RKD set Φ is

$$\mathbf{Adv}_\Phi^{\mathsf{sf}}(\mathcal{A}) := \Pr\big[(\exists\phi_1, \phi_2 \in \mathsf{L})(\exists i \neq j \in \{1, ..., t\}) \quad \phi_1(\mathbf{K})[i] = \phi_2(\mathbf{K})[j] : \mathbf{K} \leftarrow_\$ \mathcal{K}; \mathsf{L} \leftarrow \mathcal{A}\big].$$

We require the three advantages to be sufficiently small. The necessity of UP and CF has already been noticed in [6]: if $\mathcal{A}$ is able to figure out $\phi \in \Phi$ such that $\phi(K) = c$ for some constant c or $\phi(K) = \phi'(K)$ for some $\phi' \neq \phi$, then distinguishing is always possible by comparing $\mathsf{RK}[E_K](\phi, X)$ with $E_c(X)$ or with $\mathsf{RK}[E_K](\phi', X)$ respectively.

2.2 The H-coefficient Technique

The core step of our proofs consists of analyzing information theoretic indistinguishability of CFNs built upon random round functions, which will employ the H-coefficient technique [12,29]. To this end, we assume deterministic a distinguisher that has unbounded computation power, and we summarize the information gathered by the distinguisher in a tuple

$$\mathcal{Q} = ((\phi_1, X_1, Y_1), \ldots, (\phi_{q_e}, X_{q_e}, Y_{q_e}))$$

called the *transcript*, meaning that the j-th query was either a forward query (ϕ_j, X_j) with answer Y_j, or a backward query (ϕ_j, Y_j) with answer X_j.

To simplify the arguments (in particular, the definition of "bad transcripts"), we reveal the key K to the distinguisher at the end of the interaction. This is wlog since D is free to ignore this additional information to compute its output bit. Formally, we append K to τ and obtain what we call the *transcript* $\tau = (\mathcal{Q}, K)$ of the attack. With respect to some fixed distinguisher D, a transcript τ is said *attainable*, if there exists oracles IC such that the interaction of D with the ideal world $\mathsf{RK}[\mathsf{IC}_K]$ yields $\mathcal{Q}$. We denote $\mathcal{T}$ the set of attainable transcripts. In all the following, we denote T_{re}, resp. T_{id}, the probability distribution of the transcript τ induced by the real world, resp. the ideal world (note that these two probability distributions depend on the distinguisher). By extension, we use the same notation for a random variable distributed according to each distribution.

Given a transcript $\mathcal{Q}$, a block cipher E, and a key $K \in \mathcal{K}$, we say the related-key oracle $\mathsf{RK}[E_K]$ *extends* $\mathcal{Q}$, denoted $\mathsf{RK}[E_K] \vdash \mathcal{Q}$, if $E_{\phi(K)}(X) = Y$ for all $(\phi, X, Y) \in \mathcal{Q}$. It is easy to see that for any attainable transcript $\tau = (\mathcal{Q}, K)$, the interaction of the distinguisher with oracles $\mathsf{RK}[E_K]$ produces $(\mathcal{Q}, K)$ if and only if K is sampled in the interaction and $\mathsf{RK}[E_K] \vdash \tau$.

With all the above definitions, the main lemma of H-coefficient technique is as follows (see [12]).

Lemma 1. *Fix a distinguisher D. Let $\mathcal{T} = \mathcal{T}_{good} \cup \mathcal{T}_{bad}$ be a partition of the set of attainable transcripts $\mathcal{T}$. Assume that there exists ε_1 such that for any $\tau \in \mathcal{T}_{good}$, one has*

$$\frac{\Pr[T_{re} = \tau]}{\Pr[T_{id} = \tau]} \geq 1 - \varepsilon_1,$$

and that there exists ε_2 such that $\Pr[T_{id} \in \mathcal{T}_{bad}] \leq \varepsilon_2$. Then $\mathbf{Adv}(D) \leq \varepsilon_1 + \varepsilon_2$.

3 Security Proof for $\mathsf{CFN}^{F^{2n,n}}$

In this section, we prove RKA-CCA security for $\mathsf{CFN}^{F^{2n,n}}$, i.e., the simplest case of $k = 2$. According to [31, Table 4], 5 rounds are needed for $\mathsf{CFN}^{F^{2n,n}}$. As mentioned in the Introduction, we consider the key assignment $\mathbf{K} = (K_1, K_2, K_2, K_1, K_2)$.

Theorem 1. *For any distinguisher D making at most q queries to $RK[\mathsf{CFN}_{\mathbf{K}}^{F^{2n,n},5}]$ and $RK[\mathsf{CFN}_{\mathbf{K}}^{F^{2n,n},5}]^{-1}$ in total, where $\mathbf{K} = (K_1, K_2, K_2, K_1, K_2)$, it holds*

$$\mathbf{Adv}_{\mathsf{CFN}^{F^{2n,n},5}}^{\Phi\text{-}rka[1]}(D) \leq \mathbf{Adv}_{F^{2n,n}}^{\Phi\text{-}rka[2]}(D) + \mathbf{Adv}_{\Phi}^{cf}(D) + \mathbf{Adv}_{\Phi}^{sf}(D) + \frac{7q^2}{2^n} + \frac{q^2}{2^{3n}}.$$

The bound appears independent of the unpredictability advantage $\mathbf{Adv}_{\Phi}^{\mathsf{up}}(D)$. Though, $\mathbf{Adv}_{\Phi}^{\mathsf{up}}(D)$ shall be small in order to ensure that $\mathbf{Adv}_{F^{2n,n}}^{\Phi\text{-rka}[2]}(D)$ is sufficiently small.

Outline of the Proof. As the first step, we replace the keyed function $F^{2n,n}$ with a random function $\mathsf{RF}^{2n,n} : \mathcal{K} \times \{0,1\}^{2n} \to \{0,1\}^n$. As two independent keys K_1 and K_2 are involved, a standard hybrid argument yields

$$\left|\mathbf{Adv}_{\mathsf{CFN}^{F^{2n,n},5}}^{\Phi\text{-rka}[1]}(D) - \mathbf{Adv}_{\mathsf{CFN}^{\mathsf{RF}^{2n,n},5}}^{\Phi\text{-rka}[1]}(D)\right| \leq \mathbf{Adv}_{F^{2n,n}}^{\Phi\text{-rka}[2]}(D).$$

The core step is to analyze $\mathbf{Adv}_{\mathsf{CFN}^{\mathsf{RF}^{2n,n},5}}^{\Phi\text{-rka}[1]}(D)$ for the random CFN, which, as mentioned, will employ the H-coefficient technique. We will define bad transcripts and upper bound their probability in ideal world, and then show that the probabilities to obtain any good transcript in the real word and the ideal world are sufficiently close.

As notations, we denote $X_{i,j}[s,t]$, where i refers to the input of the i-th round in the forward inquiry, j is the j-th inquiry of the adversary to the Oracle, s is the starting bit position and t is the ending bit position. In this article, we divide them into n bits, we have

$$X[1,(k+1)n+r] = X[1,n] \| X[n+1,2n] \| \ldots\ldots \| X[(k+1)n+1,(k+1)n+r].$$

3.1 Bad Transcripts

In this subsection, we define bad transcripts, which capture either a claw or a switch exists in $\mathbf{K}$.

Definition 1. *An attainable transcript $\tau = (\mathcal{Q}, \boldsymbol{K})$ is bad, if the condition $EV^{\mathsf{cf}} \vee EV^{\mathsf{sf}}$, which means either a claw or a switch exists in $\boldsymbol{K}$, is fulfilled. Otherwise we say τ is good.*

It is clear that

$$\Pr[T_{id} \in \mathcal{T}_{bad}] = \Pr[\mathrm{EV}^{\mathsf{cf}} \vee \mathrm{EV}^{\mathsf{sf}}] \leq \mathbf{Adv}_{\Phi}^{\mathsf{cf}}(D) + \mathbf{Adv}_{\Phi}^{\mathsf{sf}}(D). \quad (1)$$

3.2 Analyzing Good Transcripts

Bad Predicate. We define a "bad predicate" $\mathsf{Bad}(\mathsf{RF}^{2n,n})$ on the ideal keyed function $\mathsf{RF}^{2n,n}$, such that once $\mathsf{Bad}(\mathsf{RF}^{2n,n})$ is not fulfilled, the event $T_{id} = \tau$ is equivalent to $\mathsf{RF}^{2n,n}$ satisfying $3q$ new and distinct equations. Since the keys of the 2nd and 3rd rounds are the same, we need to ensure that for these two rounds, there exists $2q$ different equations for q queries. At the same time, it is necessary to ensure that the input of the fourth round is collision free. And then, K_1^{bad} leads to $\mathsf{RF}_{K_2}^{2n,n}$ input collisions and K_2^{bad} causes $\mathsf{RF}_{K_1}^{2n,n}$ input collisions. Formally, the specific definition and probability analysis are as follows.

Definition 2. *Given a function* $\mathsf{RF}^{2n,n}$*, the predicate* $\mathsf{Bad}(\mathsf{RF}^{2n,n})$ *is fulfilled, if either of the conditions "K_1 is bad" and "K_2 is bad" is fulfilled.*

- *The condition "K_1 is bad" consists of five subconditions as follows.*
  (B-1) there exists i and j such that $X_{2,i}[n+1,3n] = X_{2,j}[n+1,3n], (i \neq j)$.
  (B-2) there exists i and j such that $X_{2,i}[n+1,3n] = X_{3,j}[n+1,3n]$.
  (B-3) there exists i and j such that $X_{2,i}[n+1,3n] = X_{5,j}[n+1,3n]$.
  (B-4) there exists i and j such that $X_{3,i}[n+1,3n] = X_{3,j}[n+1,3n]], (i \neq j)$.
  (B-5) there exists i and j such that $X_{3,i}[n+1,3n] = X_{5,j}[n+1,3n]$.
- *The condition "K_2 is bad" consists of two subconditions as follows.*
  (B-6) there exists i and j such that $X_{4,i}[n+1,3n] = X_{1,j}[n+1,3n]$.
  (B-7) there exists i and j such that $X_{4,i}[n+1,3n] = X_{4,j}[n+1,3n], (i \neq j)$.

Otherwise we say τ is good.

Below we analyze the conditions in turn.

"K_1 IS BAD". Now we analyze the situation of K_1^{bad}. Firstly, we pay attention to (B-1).

1. Case $\phi^{(i)} \neq \phi^{(j)}$.
   We have $(K_{1,i}, K_{2,i}) \neq (K_{1,j}, K_{2,j})$ and consider the following situations.
   (a) When $K_{1,i} \neq K_{1,j}$, we consider $K_{2,i}$ and $K_{2,j}$. If $K_{2,i} \neq K_{2,j}$, then we have the key assignments like $(K_1, K_2, K_2, K_1, K_2)$ and $(K_3, K_4, K_4, K_3, K_4)$, we need not to care the collision of the inputs in here. If $K_{2,i} = K_{2,j}$, then we have the key assignments like $(K_1, K_2, K_2, K_1, K_2)$ and $(K_3, K_2, K_2, K_3, K_2)$, the probability of $X_{2,i}[n+1,3n] = X_{2,j}[n+1,3n]$ is up to $1/2^n$.
   (b) When $K_{1,i} = K_{1,j}$, due to the claw-freeness, we can know that $K_{2,i} \neq K_{2,j}$, then we have the key assignments like $(K_1, K_2, K_2, K_1, K_2)$ and $(K_1, K_4, K_4, K_1, K_4)$, we do not need to care the collision of the inputs in here.
2. Case $\phi^{(i)} = \phi^{(j)}$.
   (a) When $X_{1,i}[2n+1,3n] \neq X_{1,j}[2n+1,3n]$, there is definitely no collision.
   (b) When $X_{1,i}[2n+1,3n] = X_{1,j}[2n+1,3n]$. Under this condition, we consider $X_{1,i}[n+1,2n] = X_{1,j}[n+1,2n]$. Because of $X_{1,i}[1,n] \neq X_{1,j}[1,n]$, we can know that $X_{2,i}[2n+1,3n] \neq X_{2,j}[2n+1,3n]$.
   (c) When $X_{1,i}[2n+1,3n] = X_{1,j}[2n+1,3n]$. Under this condition, due to the contracting Feistel construction we know $X_2[n+1,2n] = X_1[2n+1,3n]$, we consider $X_{1,i}[n+1,2n] \neq X_{1,j}[n+1,2n]$, the probability of $X_{2,i}[2n+1,3n] = X_{2,j}[2n+1,3n]$ is up to $1/2^n$.

Further, the probability of (B-1) is

$$\Pr\left[X_{2,i}[n+1,3n] = X_{2,j}[n+1,3n]\right] \leq \frac{1}{2^n}.$$

Secondly, we think about (B-2), (B-3), (B-5). This is a random collision for each of them, so we have the probabilities

$$\Pr\left[X_{2,i}[n+1,3n] = X_{3,j}[n+1,3n]\right] = \frac{1}{2^{2n}},$$
$$\Pr\left[X_{2,i}[n+1,3n] = X_{5,j}[n+1,3n]\right] = \frac{1}{2^{2n}},$$
$$\Pr\left[X_{3,i}[n+1,3n] = X_{5,j}[n+1,3n]\right] = \frac{1}{2^{2n}}.$$

Finally, we pay attention to (B-4).

1. Case $\phi^{(i)} \neq \phi^{(j)}$.
   We have $(K_{1,i}, K_{2,i}) \neq (K_{1,j}, K_{2,j})$ and consider two sub-case.
   (a) Case $K_{1,i} \neq K_{1,j}$.
   If $K_{2,i} \neq K_{2,j}$, we need not to care the collision of the inputs in here. If $K_{2,i} = K_{2,j}$, the probability of $X_{3,i}[n+1,3n] = X_{3,j}[n+1,3n]$ is up to $1/2^n$.
   (b) Case $K_{1,i} = K_{1,j}$.
   Due to the claw-freeness, we can know $K_{2,i} \neq K_{2,j}$. So we do not need to care the collision of the inputs in here.
2. Case $\phi^{(i)} = \phi^{(j)}$.
   (a) When $X_{1,i}[1,n] \neq X_{1,j}[1,n]$.
   (a-1) If $X_{1,i}[n+1,2n] = X_{1,j}[n+1,2n]$, $X_{1,i}[2n+1,3n] = X_{1,j}[2n+1,3n]$, there is definitely no collision.
   (a-2) If $X_{1,i}[n+1,2n] = X_{1,j}[n+1,2n]$, $X_{1,i}[2n+1,3n] \neq X_{1,j}[2n+1,3n]$, we have the probability $\Pr[X_{3,i}[n+1,2n] = X_{3,j}[n+1,2n]] \leq 1/2^n$ and due to the character of the contracting function, we have the probability $\Pr[X_{3,i}[2n+1,3n] = X_{3,j}[2n+1,3n]] = 1/2^n$, so the probability of $X_{3,i}[n+1,3n] = X_{3,j}[n+1,3n]$ is $1/2^{2n}$.
   (a-3) If $X_{1,i}[n+1,2n] \neq X_{1,j}[n+1,2n]$, $X_{1,i}[2n+1,3n] = X_{1,j}[2n+1,3n]$, then we get $\Pr[X_{2,i}[2n+1,3n] = X_{2,j}[2n+1,3n]] \leq 1/2^n$. When $X_{2,i}[2n+1,3n] = X_{2,j}[2n+1,3n]$, because of $X_{2,i}[1,n] \neq X_{2,j}[1,n]$, there is no collision. When $X_{2,i}[2n+1,3n] \neq X_{2,j}[2n+1,3n]$, because of $X_{3,i}[n+1,2n] \neq X_{3,j}[n+1,2n]$, there is also no collision.
   (a-4) If $X_{1,i}[n+1,2n] \neq X_{1,j}[n+1,2n]$, $X_{1,i}[2n+1,3n] \neq X_{1,j}[2n+1,3n]$, $\Pr[X_{3,i}[n+1,3n] = X_{3,j}[n+1,3n]] \leq 1/2^{2n}$.
   (b) When $X_{1,i}[1,n] = X_{1,j}[1,n]$.
   (b-1) If $X_{1,i}[n+1,2n] = X_{1,j}[n+1,2n]$, $X_{1,i}[2n+1,3n] = X_{1,j}[2n+1,3n]$, we suppose the adversary does not query like that.
   (b-2) If $X_{1,i}[n+1,2n] = X_{1,j}[n+1,2n]$, $X_{1,i}[2n+1,3n] \neq X_{1,j}[2n+1,3n]$, we have the probabilities $\Pr[X_{3,i}[n+1,2n] = X_{3,j}[n+1,2n]] = 1/2^n$ and $\Pr[X_{3,i}[2n+1,3n] = X_{3,j}[2n+1,3n]] = 1/2^n$. So the probability of

$X_{3,i}[n+1,3n] = X_{3,j}[n+1,3n]$ is $1/2^{2n}$.
(b-3) If $X_{1,i}[n+1,2n] \neq X_{1,j}[n+1,2n]$, $X_{1,i}[2n+1,3n] = X_{1,j}[2n+1,3n]$, then we can get $\Pr[X_{2,i}[2n+1,3n] = X_{2,j}[2n+1,3n]] = 1/2^n$.
When $X_{2,i}[2n+1,3n] = X_{2,j}[2n+1,3n]$, because of $X_{2,i}[1,n] \neq X_{2,j}[1,n]$, there is no collision. When $X_{2,i}[2n+1,3n] \neq X_{2,j}[2n+1,3n]$, because of $X_{3,i}[n+1,2n] \neq X_{3,j}[n+1,2n]$, there is also no collision.
(b-4) If $X_{1,i}[n+1,2n] \neq X_{1,j}[n+1,2n]$, $X_{1,i}[2n+1,3n] \neq X_{1,j}[2n+1,3n]$, we can get the probability is $\Pr[X_{3,i}[n+1,3n] = X_{3,j}[n+1,3n]] = 1/2^{2n}$.

So the probability of (B-4) is

$$\Pr\Big[X_{3,i}[n+1,3n] = X_{3,j}[n+1,3n]\Big] \leq \frac{1}{2^n}.$$

In all,

$$\Pr\big[K_1 \text{ is bad} \mid \neg(\mathsf{EV}^{\mathsf{cf}} \vee \mathsf{EV}^{\mathsf{sf}})\big] \leq \frac{5q^2}{2^n}. \tag{2}$$

"K_2 IS BAD". Firstly, we pay attention to (B-6). This is a random collision, so we have the probability

$$\Pr\Big[X_{4,i}[n+1,3n] = X_{1,j}[n+1,3n]\Big] = \frac{1}{2^{2n}}.$$

Secondly, we think about (B-7). The detailed analysis is as follows.

1. Case $\phi^{(i)} \neq \phi^{(j)}$.
   We have $(K_{1,i}, K_{2,i}) \neq (K_{1,j}, K_{2,j})$ and consider the following situations.
   (a) When $K_{2,i} \neq K_{2,j}$, we consider $K_{1,i}$ and $K_{1,j}$. If $K_{1,i} \neq K_{1,j}$, we need not to care the collision of the inputs in here. If $K_{1,i} = K_{1,j}$, the probability of the collision of $X_4[n+1,3n]$ is up to $1/2^n$.
   (b) When $K_{2,i} = K_{2,j}$, due to the claw-freeness, we can know that $K_{1,i} \neq K_{1,j}$, we do not need to care the collision of the inputs in here.
2. Case $\phi^{(i)} = \phi^{(j)}$.
   (a) If $X_{6,i}[n+1,2n] \neq X_{6,j}[n+1,2n]$. There is definitely no collision.
   (b) If $X_{6,i}[n+1,2n] = X_{6,j}[n+1,2n]$. Under this condition, we consider $X_{6,i}[2n+1,3n] = X_{6,j}[2n+1,3n]$. Because of the difference of $X_6[1,n]$, we can know $X_{4,i}[n+1,2n] \neq X_{4,j}[n+1,2n]$, so there is no collision.
   (c) If $X_{6,i}[n+1,2n] = X_{6,j}[n+1,2n]$. Under this condition, we consider $X_{6,i}[2n+1,3n] \neq X_{6,j}[2n+1,3n]$ and we can get the probability $\Pr[X_{4,i}[n+1,2n] = X_{4,j}[n+1,2n]] = 1/2^n$.

Further, the probability of (B-7) is

$$\Pr\Big[X_{4,i}[n+1,3n] = X_{4,j}[n+1,3n]\Big] \leq \frac{1}{2^n}.$$

In all,

$$\Pr\left[K_2 \text{ is bad} \mid \neg(\mathrm{EV}^{\mathsf{cf}} \vee \mathrm{EV}^{\mathsf{sf}})\right] \leq \frac{2q^2}{2^n}. \tag{3}$$

Gathering Eqs. (2) and (3), we reach

$$\Pr\left[\mathsf{Bad}(\mathsf{RF}^{2n,n})\right] \leq \frac{7q^2}{2^n}. \tag{4}$$

Completing the Proof. For the remaining, we fix a good transcript $\tau = (\mathcal{Q}, K)$, where $\mathcal{Q} = (\phi_i, X_{1,i}[1,3n], X_{6,i}[1,3n])_{i=1,\ldots,q}$.

First, we classify RKD functions ϕ_i, suppose that the quantity of ϕ_i is α, which are denoted $\phi^{(1)}, \phi^{(2)}, \cdots, \phi^{(\alpha)}$ respectively. $\mathcal{Q}_i (i = 1, \ldots, \alpha)$ are denoted a set of transcripts with RKD functions ϕ_i. In detail, for $i = 1, \ldots, \alpha$, define

$$\mathcal{Q}_i = \left\{(\phi^{(i)}, X_{1i}[1,3n], X_{6i}[1,3n]), \ldots, (\phi^{(i)}, X_{1q_i}[1,3n], X_{6q_i}[1,3n])\right\},$$

where $\mathcal{Q}_i$ has q_i different inputs. Suppose that $\phi^{(1)}, \phi^{(2)}, \cdots, \phi^{(\alpha)}$ can derive β different K_1: $K_1^{(1)}$, $K_1^{(2)}$, ..., $K_1^{(\beta)} (\beta \leq \alpha)$. Suppose that q queries to Related-Key Oracle constitute of $q_1^*, \ldots, q_\beta^*$ inputs separately in $K_1^{(1)}$, $K_1^{(2)}$, ..., $K_1^{(\beta)}$.

The probability to obtain τ in ideal word is

$$\Pr[T_{id} = \tau] = \left(\frac{1}{|\mathcal{K}|}\right) \prod_{i=0}^{\alpha} \frac{1}{(2^{3n})_{q_i}} \leq \left(\frac{1}{|\mathcal{K}|}\right) \left(2^{3n} - q\right)^{-q}.$$

On the other hand, the probability to obtain τ in the real world is

$$\begin{aligned}
\Pr[T_{re} = \tau] &= \Pr\left[\mathsf{RK}[\mathsf{CFN}_K^{\mathsf{RF}^{2n,n},5}] \vdash \mathcal{Q}\right] \cdot \Pr_{K^*}[K^* = K] \\
&\geq \left(\frac{1}{|\mathcal{K}|}\right) \cdot \Pr\left[\mathsf{RK}[\mathsf{CFN}_K^{\mathsf{RF}^{2n,n},5}] \vdash \mathcal{Q} \wedge \neg\mathsf{Bad}(\mathsf{RF}^{2n,n})\right] \\
&= \left(\frac{1}{|\mathcal{K}|}\right) \cdot \left(1 - \Pr\left[\mathsf{Bad}(\mathsf{RF}^{2n,n})\right]\right) \cdot \Pr\left[\mathsf{RK}[\mathsf{CFN}_K^{\mathsf{RF}^{2n,n},5}] \vdash \mathcal{Q} \mid \neg\mathsf{Bad}(\mathsf{RF}^{2n,n})\right].
\end{aligned}$$

It can be seen that the event $\mathsf{RK}[\mathsf{CFN}_K^{\mathsf{RF}^{2n,n},5}] \vdash \mathcal{Q}$ is equivalent to the event that $\mathsf{RF}^{2n,n}$ satisfies $3q$ equations, i.e., for $i = 1, ..., q$,

$$\begin{aligned}
\mathsf{RF}_{K_2}^{2n,n}(X_{2i}[n+1,3n]) &= X_{2i}[1,n] \oplus X_{3i}[2n+1,3n], \\
\mathsf{RF}_{K_2}^{2n,n}(X_{3i}[n+1,3n]) &= X_{3i}[1,n] \oplus X_{4i}[2n+1,3n], \\
\mathsf{RF}_{K_1}^{2n,n}(X_{4i}[n+1,3n]) &= X_{4i}[1,n] \oplus X_{5i}[2n+1,3n].
\end{aligned}$$

Therefore, we have the probability

$$\begin{aligned}
&\Pr\big[\mathsf{RK}[\mathsf{CFN}_K^{\mathsf{RF}^{2n,n},5}] \vdash \mathcal{Q} \mid \neg\mathsf{Bad}(\mathsf{RF}^{2n,n})\big] \\
&= \prod_{i=1}^{q} \Big(\Pr\big[\mathsf{RF}_{K_2}^{2n,n}(X_{2i}[n+1,3n]) = X_{2i}[1,n] \oplus X_{3i}[2n+1,3n]\big] \\
&\quad \times \Pr\big[\mathsf{RF}_{K_2}^{2n,n}(X_{3i}[n+1,3n]) = X_{3i}[1,n] \oplus X_{4i}[2n+1,3n]\big] \\
&\quad \times \Pr\big[\mathsf{RF}_{K_1}^{2n,n}(X_{4i}[n+1,3n]) = X_{4i}[1,n] \oplus X_{5i}[2n+1,3n]\big] \Big) \\
&= \Big(\frac{1}{2^n}\Big)^{3q}.
\end{aligned}$$

The probability that a random function fulfilling each of $3q$ equations is $1/2^n$. In all, using Eq. (4), we have

$$\begin{aligned}
&\frac{\Pr[T_{re} = \tau]}{\Pr[T_{id} = \tau]} \\
&\geq \Big(1 - \Pr\big[\mathsf{Bad}(\mathsf{RF}^{2n,n})\big]\Big) \cdot \Pr\big[\mathsf{RK}[\mathsf{CFN}_K^{\mathsf{RF}^{2n,n},5}] \vdash \mathcal{Q} \mid \neg\mathsf{Bad}(\mathsf{RF}^{2n,n})\big] \Big/ \prod_{i=0}^{\alpha} \frac{1}{(2^{3n})_{q_i}} \\
&\geq \Big(1 - \frac{7q^2}{2^n}\Big) \times \Big(\frac{1}{2^{3n}}\Big)^q \times (2^{3n} - q)^q \\
&\geq 1 - \Big(\frac{7q^2}{2^n} + \frac{q^2}{2^{3n}}\Big).
\end{aligned} \tag{5}$$

Gathering Eqs. (1) and (5), and using Lemma 1, we complete the proof of Theorem 1.

3.3 The Case of $\mathsf{CFN}^{F^{3n,n}}$

By [31, Table 4], 6 rounds are needed for $\mathsf{CFN}^{F^{3n,n}}$, and we consider the alternating key assignment.

Theorem 2. *For any distinguisher D making at most q queries to $\mathsf{RK}[\mathsf{CFN}_{\mathbf{K}}^{F^{3n,n},6}]$ and $\mathsf{RK}[\mathsf{CFN}_{\mathbf{K}}^{F^{3n,n},6}]^{-1}$ in total, where $\mathbf{K} = (K_1, K_2, K_1, K_2, K_1, K_2)$, it holds*

$$\mathbf{Adv}_{\mathsf{CFN}^{F^{3n,n}},6}^{\Phi\text{-}rka[1]}(D) \leq \mathbf{Adv}_{F^{3n,n}}^{\Phi\text{-}rka[2]}(D) + \mathbf{Adv}_{\Phi}^{sf}(D) + \mathbf{Adv}_{\Phi}^{cf}(D) + \frac{10q^2}{2^n} + \frac{q^2}{2^{4n}}.$$

The proof resembles that of Theorem 1 and is deferred to Appendix A.

4 Security Proof for General $\mathsf{CFN}^{F^{kn+r,n}}$

After the above warm-up, we now proceed to establish security for CFNs using round function $F^{kn+r,n}$ for general k and r and $k{+}4$ rounds. Due to the deviation in key assignments, below we first consider the case of $k + 4$ odd in Sect. 4.1, and then the case of $k + 4$ even in Sect. 4.2.

4.1 $k+4$ is Odd

As mentioned in the Introduction, for odd number of rounds, we consider using K_1, K_2, K_2 in the first three rounds, and then alternate the remaining.

Theorem 3. *For any distinguisher D making q queries to* $\mathsf{RK}[\mathsf{CFN}_{\boldsymbol{K}}^{F^{kn+r,n},k+4}]$ *and* $\mathsf{RK}[\mathsf{CFN}_{\boldsymbol{K}}^{F^{kn+r,n},k+4}]^{-1}$ *in total, where* $\boldsymbol{K} = (K_1, K_2, K_2, K_1, K_2, \ldots, K_1, K_2)$, *it holds*

$$\mathbf{Adv}^{\Phi\text{-}rka[1]}_{\mathsf{CFN}^{F^{kn+r,n},k+4}}(D) \leq \mathbf{Adv}^{\Phi\text{-}rka[2]}_{F^{kn+r,n}}(D) + \mathbf{Adv}^{cf}_{\Phi}(D) + \mathbf{Adv}^{sf}_{\Phi}(D) + \frac{(k^2+10k+17)q^2}{2^{n+2}} + \frac{q^2}{2^{(k+1)n+r}}. \quad (6)$$

Similarly to Sect. 3, we (could) focus on analyzing $\mathbf{Adv}^{\Phi\text{-rka}[1]}_{\mathsf{CFN}^{\mathsf{RF}^{kn+r,n},k+4}}(D)$ for the random CFN, which follows the general flow in Sect. 3.

Definition 3 (Bad Transcripts for $k+4$ odd). *An attainable transcript* $\tau = (\mathcal{Q}, \boldsymbol{K})$ *is bad, if the condition* $EV^{\mathsf{cf}} \vee EV^{\mathsf{sf}}$, *which means either a claw or a switch exists in* $\boldsymbol{K}$, *is fulfilled. Otherwise we say* τ *is good.*

It is clear that

$$\Pr[T_{id} \in \mathcal{T}_{bad}] = \Pr[\mathrm{EV}^{\mathsf{cf}} \vee \mathrm{EV}^{\mathsf{sf}}] \leq \mathbf{Adv}^{\mathsf{cf}}_{\Phi}(D) + \mathbf{Adv}^{\mathsf{sf}}_{\Phi}(D). \quad (7)$$

Bad Predicate. We define a "bad predicate" $\mathsf{Bad}(\mathsf{RF}^{kn+r,n})$ on the ideal keyed function $\mathsf{RF}^{kn+r,n}$, such that once $\mathsf{Bad}(\mathsf{RF}^{kn+r,n})$ is not fulfilled, the event $T_{id} = \tau$ is equivalent to $\mathsf{RF}^{kn+r,n}$ satisfying $(k+2)q$ new and distinct equations. Since the keys of the 2nd round, the 3rd round and the remaining odd rounds are K_2, while the keys of the even rounds are K_1, we need to ensure that for these middle $k+2$ rounds, there exists $(k+2)q$ different equations.

To facilitate, for any $\mathsf{RF}^{kn+r,n}$ and every $(\phi_i, X_i, Y_i) \in \mathcal{Q}$, we define $X_{1,i} := X_i, X_{k+4,i} := Y_i$, and define the "induced intermediate values" as follows.

$$X_{2,i} := \Psi^{\mathsf{RF}^{kn+r,n}_{K_1}}(X_{1,i}), \quad X_{k+3,i} := \left(\Psi^{\mathsf{RF}^{kn+r,n}_{K_2}}\right)^{-1}(X_{k+4,i}).$$

Note that the 2nd round intermediate value $X_{2,i}$ is derived along the "forward direction", while the $(k+3)$-th round intermediate value $X_{k+3,i}$ is derived along the "backward direction". And then, K_1^{bad} leads to $\mathsf{RF}^{kn+r,n}_{K_2}$ input collisions and K_2^{bad} causes $\mathsf{RF}^{kn+r,n}_{K_1}$ input collisions. Formally, the specific definition and probability analysis are as follows.

Definition 4. *Given a function* $\mathsf{RF}^{kn+r,n}$, *the predicate* $\mathsf{Bad}(\mathsf{RF}^{kn+r,n})$ *is fulfilled, if either of the conditions "K_1 is bad" and "K_2 is bad" is fulfilled.*

- *The condition "K_1 is bad" consists of* $\frac{k^2+12k+27}{8}$ *subconditions as follows.*
  (B-1) there exists i and j such that
  $X_{2,i}[n+1, (k+1)n+r] = X_{2,j}[n+1, (k+1)n+r], (i \neq j)$.

(B-2) there exists i and j such that
$X_{2,i}[n+1,(k+1)n+r] = X_{3,j}[n+1,(k+1)n+r]$.

$\vdots \quad \vdots \quad \vdots$

(B-$\frac{k+5}{2}$) there exists i and j such that
$X_{2,i}[n+1,(k+1)n+r] = X_{k+4,j}[n+1,(k+1)n+r]$.
(B-$\frac{k+7}{2}$) there exists i and j such that
$X_{3,i}[n+1,(k+1)n+r] = X_{3,j}[n+1,(k+1)n+r], (i \neq j)$.
(B-$\frac{k+9}{2}$) there exists i and j such that
$X_{3,i}[n+1,(k+1)n+r] = X_{5,j}[n+1,(k+1)n+r]$.

$\vdots \quad \vdots \quad \vdots$

(B-$k+4$) there exists i and j such that
$X_{3,i}[n+1,(k+1)n+r] = X_{k+4,j}[n+1,(k+1)n+r]$

$\vdots \quad \vdots \quad \vdots$

(B-$\frac{k^2+12k+19}{8}$) there exists i and j such that
$X_{k+2,i}[n+1,(k+1)n+r] = X_{k+2,j}[n+1,(k+1)n+r]$.
(B-$\frac{k^2+12k+27}{8}$) there exists i and j such that
$X_{k+2,i}[n+1,(k+1)n+r] = X_{k+4,j}[n+1,(k+1)n+r]$.

– *The condition "K_2 is bad" consists of $\frac{k^2+8k+7}{8}$ subconditions as follows.*
(B-$\frac{k^2+12k+35}{8}$) there exists i and j such that
$X_{k+3,i}[n+1,(k+1)n+r] = X_{k+3,j}[n+1,(k+1)n+r], (i \neq j)$.
(B-$\frac{k^2+12k+43}{8}$) there exists i and j such that
$X_{k+3,i}[n+1,(k+1)n+r] = X_{k+1,j}[n+1,(k+1)n+r]$.

$\vdots \quad \vdots \quad \vdots$

(B-$\frac{k^2+16k+39}{8}$) there exists i and j such that
$X_{k+3,i}[n+1,(k+1)n+r] = X_{1,j}[n+1,(k+1)n+r]$.
(B-$\frac{k^2+16k+47}{8}$) there exists i and j such that
$X_{k+1,i}[n+1,(k+1)n+r] = X_{k+1,j}[n+1,(k+1)n+r], (i \neq j)$.
(B-$\frac{k^2+16k+55}{8}$) there exists i and j such that
$X_{k+1,i}[n+1,(k+1)n+r] = X_{k-1,j}[n+1,(k+1)n+r]$.

$\vdots \quad \vdots \quad \vdots$

(B-$\frac{k^2+20k+43}{8}$) there exists i and j such that
$X_{k+1,i}[n+1,(k+1)n+r] = X_{1,j}[n+1,(k+1)n+r]$.

$\vdots \quad \vdots \quad \vdots$

(B-$\frac{k^2+10k+13}{4}$) there exists i and j such that
$X_{4,i}[n+1,(k+1)n+r] = X_{4,j}[n+1,(k+1)n+r]$.
(B-$\frac{k^2+10k+17}{4}$) there exists i and j such that
$X_{4,i}[n+1,(k+1)n+r] = X_{1,j}[n+1,(k+1)n+r]$.

Otherwise we say τ is good.

Similarly to Sect. 3.2, we expand the probability of each $(B-i)$ to $1/2^n$ and obtain

$$\Pr\left[K_1 \text{ is bad} \mid \neg(\mathrm{EV}^{\mathsf{cf}} \vee \mathrm{EV}^{\mathsf{sf}})\right] \leq \frac{(k^2+12k+27)q^2}{8\cdot 2^n},$$
$$\Pr\left[K_2 \text{ is bad} \mid \neg(\mathrm{EV}^{\mathsf{cf}} \vee \mathrm{EV}^{\mathsf{sf}})\right] \leq \frac{(k^2+8k+7)q^2}{8\cdot 2^n}.$$

And we reach

$$\Pr\left[\mathsf{Bad}(\mathsf{RF}^{kn+r,n})\right] \leq \frac{(k^2+10k+17)q^2}{2^{n+2}}. \tag{8}$$

Completing the Proof. For the remaining, we fix a good transcript $\tau = (\mathcal{Q}, K)$, where $\mathcal{Q} = (\phi_i, X_{1,i}[1,(k+1)n+r], X_{k+5,i}[1,(k+1)n+r])_{i=1,\ldots,q}$.

First, we classify RKD functions ϕ_i, suppose that the quantity of ϕ_i is α, which are denoted $\phi^{(1)}, \phi^{(2)}, \cdots, \phi^{(\alpha)}$ respectively. $\mathcal{Q}_i(\ i=1,\ldots,\alpha)$ are denoted a set of transcripts with RKD functions ϕ_i. In detail, for $i=1,\ldots,\alpha$, define

$$\begin{aligned}\mathcal{Q}_i =& \{(\phi^{(i)}, X_{1i}[1,(k+1)n+r], X_{(k+5)i}[1,(k+1)n+r]),\\ &\ldots,(\phi^{(i)}, X_{1q_i}[1,(k+1)n+r], X_{(k+5)q_i}[1,(k+1)n+r])\},\end{aligned}$$

where $\mathcal{Q}_i$ has q_i different inputs. Suppose that $\phi^{(1)}, \phi^{(2)}, \cdots, \phi^{(\alpha)}$ can derive β different K_1: $K_1^{(1)}$, $K_1^{(2)}$, ..., $K_1^{(\beta)}(\beta \leq \alpha)$. Suppose that q queries to Related-Key Oracle constitute of $q_1^*, \ldots, q_\beta^*$ inputs separately in $K_1^{(1)}$, $K_1^{(2)}$, ..., $K_1^{(\beta)}$. The probability to obtain τ in ideal word is

$$\Pr[T_{id}=\tau] = \left(\frac{1}{|\mathcal{K}|}\right)\prod_{i=0}^{\alpha}\frac{1}{(2^{(k+1)n+r})_{q_i}} \leq \left(\frac{1}{|\mathcal{K}|}\right)\left(2^{(k+1)n+r}-q\right)^{-q}.$$

In a similar vein to Sect. 3, the probability in real world is

$$\begin{aligned}\Pr[T_{re}=\tau] &= \Pr\left[\mathsf{RK}[\mathsf{CFN}_K^{\mathsf{RF}^{kn+r,n},k+4}] \vdash \mathcal{Q}\right]\cdot \Pr_{K^*}[K^*=K]\\ &\geq \left(\frac{1}{|\mathcal{K}|}\right)\cdot \Pr\left[\mathsf{RK}[\mathsf{CFN}_K^{\mathsf{RF}^{kn+r,n},k+4}] \vdash \mathcal{Q} \wedge \neg\mathsf{Bad}(\mathsf{RF}^{kn+r,n})\right]\\ &= \left(\frac{1}{|\mathcal{K}|}\right)\cdot \Pr\left[\mathsf{RK}[\mathsf{CFN}_K^{\mathsf{RF}^{kn+r,n},k+4}] \vdash \mathcal{Q} \mid \neg\mathsf{Bad}(\mathsf{RF}^{kn+r,n})\right]\\ &\quad\cdot\left(1-\Pr\left[\mathsf{Bad}(\mathsf{RF}^{kn+r,n})\right]\right).\end{aligned}$$

It can be seen that the event $\mathsf{RK}[\mathsf{CFN}_K^{\mathsf{RF}^{kn+r,n},k+4}] \vdash \mathcal{Q}$ is equivalent to the event that $\mathsf{RF}^{kn+r,n}$ satisfies $(k+2)q$ equations, i.e., for $i = 1, ..., q$,

$$\begin{aligned}
\mathsf{RF}_{K_2}^{kn+r,n}(X_{2i}[n+1,(k+1)n+r]) &= X_{2i}[1,n-r] \oplus X_{(k+4)i}[kn+2r+1,(k+1)n+r] \\
&\quad \oplus \mathsf{RF}_{K_1}^{kn+r,n}(X_{(k+4)i}[1,kn+r])[r+1,n] \| X_{2i}[n-r+1,n] \oplus X_{(k+4)i}[1,r] \\
\mathsf{RF}_{K_2}^{kn+r,n}(X_{3i}[n+1,(k+1)n+r]) &= X_{3i}[1,n] \oplus X_{4i}[kn+r,(k+1)n+r], \\
&\vdots \\
\mathsf{RF}_{K_2}^{kn+r,n}(X_{(k+2)i}[n+1,(k+1)n+r]) &= X_{(k+2)i}[1,n] \oplus X_{(k+3)i}[kn+r,(k+1)n+r], \\
\mathsf{RF}_{K_1}^{kn+r,n}(X_{(k+4)i}[1,kn+r])[1,r] &= X_{2i}[(k+1)n+1,(k+1)n+r] \\
&\quad \oplus X_{(k+4)i}[kn+r+1,kn+2r].
\end{aligned}$$

We remark that the last equality is only on r output bits of $\mathsf{RF}_{K_1}^{kn+r,n}(X_{(k+4)i}[1,kn+r])$. This turns out crucial for the calculations. In detail, these indicate

$$\begin{aligned}
&\Pr\left[\mathsf{RK}[\mathsf{CFN}_K^{\mathsf{RF}^{kn+r,n},k+4}] \vdash \mathcal{Q} \mid \neg\mathsf{Bad}(\mathsf{RF}^{kn+r,n})\right] \\
&= \prod_{i=1}^{q}\Big(\Pr\big[\mathsf{RF}_{K_2}^{kn+r,n}(X_{2i}[n+1,(k+1)n+r]) = X_{2i}[1,n-r] \oplus X_{(k+4)i}[kn+2r+1, \\
&\qquad (k+1)n+r] \oplus \mathsf{RF}_{K_1}^{kn+r,n}(X_{(k+4)i}[1,kn+r])[r+1,n] \\
&\qquad \| X_{2i}[n-r+1,n] \oplus X_{(k+4)i}[1,r]\big] \\
&\quad \times \Pr\big[\mathsf{RF}_{K_2}^{kn+r,n}(X_{3i}[n+1,(k+1)n+r]) = X_{3i}[1,n] \oplus X_{4i}[kn+r,(k+1)n+r]\big] \\
&\qquad \vdots \\
&\quad \times \Pr\big[\mathsf{RF}_{K_2}^{kn+r,n}(X_{(k+2)i}[n+1,(k+1)n+r]) = X_{(k+2)i}[1,n] \oplus X_{(k+3)i}[kn+r, \\
&\qquad (k+1)n+r]\big] \\
&\quad \times \Pr\big[\mathsf{RF}_{K_1}^{kn+r,n}(X_{(k+4)i}[1,kn+r])[1,r] = X_{2i}[(k+1)n+1,(k+1)n+r] \\
&\qquad \oplus X_{(k+4)i}[kn+r+1,kn+2r]\big]\Big) \\
&= \left(\frac{1}{2^{(k+1)n}}\right)^q \left(\frac{1}{2^r}\right)^q.
\end{aligned}$$

We remark that, the equation on $\mathsf{RF}_{K_2}^{kn+r,n}(X_{2i}[n+1,(k+1)n+r])$ depends on the function value $\mathsf{RF}_{K_1}^{kn+r,n}(X_{(k+4)i}[1,kn+r])[r+1,n]$. Though, this won't affect the distribution of $\mathsf{RF}_{K_1}^{kn+r,n}(X_{(k+4)i}[1,kn+r])[1,r]$, as the two parts $\mathsf{RF}_{K_1}^{kn+r,n}(X_{(k+4)i}[1,kn+r])[r+1,n]$ and $\mathsf{RF}_{K_1}^{kn+r,n}(X_{(k+4)i}[1,kn+r])[1,r]$ are independent. In all, using Eq. (8), we have

$$\begin{aligned}
&\frac{\Pr[T_{re}=\tau]}{\Pr[T_{id}=\tau]}\\
&\geq \frac{\Big(1-\Pr\big[\mathsf{Bad}(\mathsf{RF}^{kn+r,n})\big]\Big)\cdot\Pr\big[\mathsf{RK}[\mathsf{CFN}_K^{\mathsf{RF}^{kn+r,n},k+4}]\vdash\mathcal{Q}\mid\neg\mathsf{Bad}(\mathsf{RF}^{kn+r,n})\big]}{\prod_{i=0}^{\alpha}\frac{1}{(2^{(k+1)n+r})_{q_i}}}\\
&\geq \frac{\Big(1-\frac{(k^2+10k+17)q^2}{2^{n+2}}\Big)\times\Big(\frac{1}{2^{(k+1)n+r}}\Big)^q}{(2^{(k+1)n+r}-q)^{-q}}\\
&\geq 1-\Big(\frac{(k^2+10k+17)q^2}{2^{n+2}}+\frac{q^2}{2^{(k+1)n+r}}\Big).
\end{aligned} \tag{9}$$

Gathering Eqs. (7) and (9) yields Eq. (6).

4.2 $k+4$ is Even

For even number of rounds, we consider the alternating key assignment.

Theorem 4. *For any distinguisher D making at most q queries to RK $[\mathsf{CFN}_{\mathbf{K}}^{F^{kn+r,n},k+4}]$ and RK$[\mathsf{CFN}_{\mathbf{K}}^{F^{kn+r,n},k+4}]^{-1}$ in total, where $\boldsymbol{K}=(K_1,K_2,K_1,K_2,\ldots)$, it holds*

$$\mathbf{Adv}^{\Phi\text{-}rka[1]}_{\mathsf{CFN}^{F^{kn+r,n},k+4}}(D)\leq \mathbf{Adv}^{\Phi\text{-}rka[2]}_{F^{kn+r,n}}(D)+\mathbf{Adv}^{cf}_{\Phi}(D)+\mathbf{Adv}^{sf}_{\Phi}(D)+\frac{(k^2+10k+16)q^2}{2^{n+2}}+\frac{q^2}{2^{(k+1)n+r}}. \tag{10}$$

We also focus on analyzing $\mathbf{Adv}^{\Phi\text{-rka}[1]}_{\mathsf{CFN}^{\mathsf{RF}^{kn+r,n},k+4}}(D)$.

Definition 5 (Bad Transcripts for $k+4$ even). *An attainable transcript $\tau=(\mathcal{Q},\boldsymbol{K})$ is bad, if the condition $EV^{\mathsf{cf}}\vee EV^{\mathsf{sf}}$, which means either a claw or a switch exists in $\boldsymbol{K}$, is fulfilled. Otherwise we say τ is good.*

It is clear that

$$\Pr\big[T_{id}\in\mathcal{T}_{bad}\big]=\Pr\big[\mathrm{EV}^{\mathsf{cf}}\vee\mathrm{EV}^{\mathsf{sf}}\big]\leq\mathbf{Adv}^{\mathsf{cf}}_{\Phi}(D)+\mathbf{Adv}^{\mathsf{sf}}_{\Phi}(D). \tag{11}$$

Bad Predicate. We define a "bad predicate" $\mathsf{Bad}(\mathsf{RF}^{kn+r,n})$ on the ideal keyed function $\mathsf{RF}^{kn+r,n}$, such that once $\mathsf{Bad}(\mathsf{RF}^{kn+r,n})$ is not fulfilled, the event $T_{id}=\tau$ is equivalent to $\mathsf{RF}^{kn+r,n}$ satisfying $(k+2)q$ new and distinct equations. Since the keys of the even rounds are are K_2, while the keys of the odd rounds are K_1, we need to ensure that for these middle $k+2$ rounds, there exists $(k+2)q$ different equations. The specific definition and probability analysis are as follows.

Definition 6. *Given a function* $\mathsf{RF}^{kn+r,n}$*, the predicate* $\mathsf{Bad}(\mathsf{RF}^{kn+r,n})$ *is fulfilled, if either of the conditions "*K_1 *is bad" and "*K_2 *is bad" is fulfilled.*

- *The condition "*K_1 *is bad" consists of* $\frac{k^2+10k+16}{8}$ *subconditions as follows.*
  (B-1) there exists i *and* j *such that*
  $X_{2,i}[n+1,(k+1)n+r] = X_{2,j}[n+1,(k+1)n+r], (i \neq j)$.
  (B-2) there exists i *and* j *such that*
  $X_{2,i}[n+1,(k+1)n+r] = X_{4,j}[n+1,(k+1)n+r]$.

  $\vdots \quad \vdots \quad \vdots$

  (B-$\frac{k+4}{2}$*) there exists* i *and* j *such that*
  $X_{2,i}[n+1,(k+1)n+r] = X_{k+4,j}[n+1,(k+1)n+r]$.
  (B-$\frac{k+6}{2}$*) there exists* i *and* j *such that*
  $X_{4,i}[n+1,(k+1)n+r] = X_{4,j}[n+1,(k+1)n+r], (i \neq j)$.
  (B-$\frac{k+8}{2}$*) there exists* i *and* j *such that*
  $X_{4,i}[n+1,(k+1)n+r] = X_{6,j}[n+1,(k+1)n+r]$.

  $\vdots \quad \vdots \quad \vdots$

  (B-k + 3) there exists i *and* j *such that*
  $X_{4,i}[n+1,(k+1)n+r] = X_{k+4,j}[n+1,(k+1)n+r]$.

  $\vdots \quad \vdots \quad \vdots$

  (B-$\frac{k^2+10k+8}{8}$*) there exists* i *and* j *such that*
  $X_{k+2,i}[n+1,(k+1)n+r] = X_{k+2,j}[n+1,(k+1)n+r]$.
  (B-$\frac{k^2+10k+16}{8}$*) there exists* i *and* j *such that*
  $X_{k+2,i}[n+1,(k+1)n+r] = X_{k+4,j}[n+1,(k+1)n+r]$.
- *The condition "*K_2 *is bad" consists of* $\frac{k^2+10k+16}{8}$ *subconditions as follows.*
  (B-$\frac{k^2+10k+24}{8}$*) there exists* i *and* j *such that*
  $X_{k+3,i}[n+1,(k+1)n+r] = X_{k+3,j}[n+1,(k+1)n+r], (i \neq j)$.
  (B-$\frac{k^2+10k+32}{8}$*) there exists* i *and* j *such that*
  $X_{k+3,i}[n+1,(k+1)n+r] = X_{k+1,j}[n+1,(k+1)n+r]$.

  $\vdots \quad \vdots \quad \vdots$

  (B-$\frac{k^2+14k+32}{8}$*) there exists* i *and* j *such that*
  $X_{k+3,i}[n+1,(k+1)n+r] = X_{1,j}[n+1,(k+1)n+r]$.
  (B-$\frac{k^2+14k+40}{8}$*) there exists* i *and* j *such that*
  $X_{k+1,i}[n+1,(k+1)n+r] = X_{k+1,j}[n+1,(k+1)n+r], (i \neq j)$.
  (B-$\frac{k^2+14k+48}{8}$*) there exists* i *and* j *such that*
  $X_{k+1,i}[n+1,(k+1)n+r] = X_{k-1,j}[n+1,(k+1)n+r]$.

  $\vdots \quad \vdots \quad \vdots$

  (B-$\frac{k^2+18k+40}{8}$*) there exists* i *and* j *such that*
  $X_{k+1,i}[n+1,(k+1)n+r] = X_{1,j}[n+1,(k+1)n+r]$.

  $\vdots \quad \vdots \quad \vdots$

  (B-$\frac{k^2+10k+12}{4}$*) there exists* i *and* j *such that*
  $X_{3,i}[n+1,(k+1)n+r] = X_{3,j}[n+1,(k+1)n+r]$.

(B-$\frac{k^2+10k+16}{4}$) *there exists* i *and* j *such that*
$X_{3,i}[n+1,(k+1)n+r] = X_{1,j}[n+1,(k+1)n+r]$.

Otherwise we say τ *is good.*

Similarly to Sect. 3.2, we expand the probability of each $(B-i)$ to $1/2^n$ and obtain

$$\Pr\big[K_1 \text{ is bad} \mid \neg(\mathsf{EV}^{\mathsf{cf}} \vee \mathsf{EV}^{\mathsf{sf}})\big] \leq \frac{(k^2+10k+16)q^2}{8 \cdot 2^n},$$
$$\Pr\big[K_2 \text{ is bad} \mid \neg(\mathsf{EV}^{\mathsf{cf}} \vee \mathsf{EV}^{\mathsf{sf}})\big] \leq \frac{(k^2+10k+16)q^2}{8 \cdot 2^n}.$$

And we reach

$$\Pr\big[\mathsf{Bad}(\mathsf{RF}^{kn+r,n})\big] \leq \frac{(k^2+10k+16)q^2}{2^{n+2}}. \tag{12}$$

Completing the Proof. For the remaining, we fix a good transcript $\tau = (\mathcal{Q}, K)$, where $\mathcal{Q} = (\phi_i, X_{1,i}[1,(k+1)n+r], X_{k+5,i}[1,(k+1)n+r])_{i=1,\ldots,q}$.

First, we classify RKD functions ϕ_i, suppose that the quantity of ϕ_i is α, which are denoted $\phi^{(1)}, \phi^{(2)}, \cdots, \phi^{(\alpha)}$ respectively. $\mathcal{Q}_i(\ i=1,\ldots,\alpha)$ are denoted a set of transcripts with RKD functions ϕ_i. For $i=1,\ldots,\alpha$, define

$$\begin{aligned}\mathcal{Q}_i =& \big\{(\phi^{(i)}, X_{1i}[1,(k+1)n+r], X_{(k+5)i}[1,(k+1)n+r]),\\ &\ldots,(\phi^{(i)}, X_{1q_i}[1,(k+1)n+r], X_{(k+5)q_i}[1,(k+1)n+r])\big\},\end{aligned}$$

where $\mathcal{Q}_i$ has q_i different inputs. Suppose that $\phi^{(1)}, \phi^{(2)}, \cdots, \phi^{(\alpha)}$ can derive β different K_1: $K_1^{(1)}$, $K_1^{(2)}$, ..., $K_1^{(\beta)} (\beta \leq \alpha)$. Suppose that q queries to Related-Key Oracle constitute of $q_1^*, \ldots, q_\beta^*$ inputs separately in $K_1^{(1)}$, $K_1^{(2)}$, ..., $K_1^{(\beta)}$. The probability to obtain τ in ideal word is

$$\Pr[T_{id} = \tau] = \left(\frac{1}{|\mathcal{K}|}\right) \prod_{i=0}^{\alpha} \frac{1}{(2^{(k+1)n+r})_{q_i}} \leq \left(\frac{1}{|\mathcal{K}|}\right)\left(2^{(k+1)n+r} - q\right)^{-q}.$$

In a similar vein to Sect. 4.1, the probability in real world is

$$\Pr[T_{re} = \tau] \geq \left(\frac{1}{|\mathcal{K}|}\right) \cdot \Pr\big[\mathsf{RK}[\mathsf{CFN}_K^{\mathsf{RF}^{kn+r,n},k+4}] \vdash \mathcal{Q} \mid \neg\mathsf{Bad}(\mathsf{RF}^{kn+r,n})\big].$$

It can be seen that the event $\mathsf{RK}[\mathsf{CFN}_K^{\mathsf{RF}^{kn+r,n},k+4}] \vdash \mathcal{Q}$ is equivalent to the event that $\mathsf{RF}^{kn+r,n}$ satisfies $(k+2)q$ equations, i.e., for $i=1,...,q$. Similarly to Sect. 4.1, $\mathsf{RF}_{K_2}^{kn+r,n}(X_{2i}[n+1,(k+1)n+r])$ depends on the function value $\mathsf{RF}_{K_1}^{kn+r,n}(X_{(k+4)i}[1,kn+r])[r+1,n]$. Therefore we directly appeal to the result, we have the probability

$$\Pr\big[\mathsf{RK}[\mathsf{CFN}_K^{\mathsf{RF}^{kn+r,n},k+4}] \vdash \mathcal{Q} \mid \neg\mathsf{Bad}(\mathsf{RF}^{kn+r,n})\big] = \left(\frac{1}{2^{(k+1)n+r}}\right)^q.$$

In all, using Eq. (12), we have

$$\frac{\Pr[T_{re}=\tau]}{\Pr[T_{id}=\tau]}$$
$$\geq \frac{\Big(1-\Pr\big[\mathsf{Bad}(\mathsf{RF}^{kn+r,n})\big]\Big)\cdot\Pr\big[\mathsf{RK}[\mathsf{CFN}_K^{\mathsf{RF}^{kn+r,n},k+4}]\vdash\mathcal{Q}\mid\neg\mathsf{Bad}(\mathsf{RF}^{kn+r,n})\big]}{\prod_{i=0}^{\alpha}\frac{1}{(2^{(k+1)n+r})_{q_i}}}$$
$$\geq \frac{\left(1-\frac{(k^2+10k+16)q^2}{2^{n+2}}\right)\times\left(\frac{1}{2^{(k+1)n+r}}\right)^q}{(2^{(k+1)n+r}-q)^{-q}}$$
$$\geq 1-\left(\frac{(k^2+10k+16)q^2}{2^{n+2}}+\frac{q^2}{2^{(k+1)n+r}}\right). \tag{13}$$

Gathering Eqs. (11) and (13) eventually establishes Eqs. (10).

5 Conclusion

We study related-key security of generalized Feistel networks using contracting round functions. Assuming using contracting round functions from $\{0,1\}^m$ to $\{0,1\}^n$, and using two independent main keys K_1, K_2 in all the rounds in a close-to-alternating manner, we prove birthday-bound security at $\lceil\frac{m}{n}\rceil+3$ rounds. The result provides new constructions for related-key secure variable-input-length block ciphers and wide tweakable block ciphers.

Acknowledgements. We sincerely thank the reviewers of Inscrypt 2020 for their invaluable comments that help improving the quality of this paper. This work was partly supported by the Program of Qilu Young Scholars (Grant No. 61580089963177) of Shandong University.

A Security Proof for $\mathsf{CFN}^{F^{3n,n}}$

The main flow quite resembles Sect. 3. In detail, we first replace the keyed function $F^{3n,n}$ with an random function $\mathsf{RF}^{3n,n}:\mathcal{K}\times\{0,1\}^{3n}\rightarrow\{0,1\}^n$ and obtain the random CFN $\mathsf{CFN}^{\mathsf{RF}^{3n,n}}$ with a security gap at most $\mathbf{Adv}_{F^{3n,n}}^{\Phi\text{-rka}[2]}(D)$. This allows us to focus on analyzing $\mathbf{Adv}_{\mathsf{CFN}^{\mathsf{RF}^{3n,n}},6}^{\Phi\text{-rka}[1]}(D)$ below.

A.1 Bad Transcripts

Definition 7. *An attainable transcript* $\tau=(\mathcal{Q},\boldsymbol{K})$ *is bad, if the condition* $EV^{\mathsf{cf}}\vee EV^{\mathsf{sf}}$*, which means either a claw or a switch exists in* $\boldsymbol{K}$*, is fulfilled. Otherwise we say* τ *is good.*

It is clear that

$$\Pr\big[T_{id}\in\mathcal{T}_{bad}\big]=\Pr\big[\mathrm{EV}^{\mathsf{cf}}\vee\mathrm{EV}^{\mathsf{sf}}\big]\leq\mathbf{Adv}_{\Phi}^{\mathsf{cf}}(D)+\mathbf{Adv}_{\Phi}^{\mathsf{sf}}(D). \tag{14}$$

A.2 Analyzing Good Transcripts

Bad Predicate. We define a "bad predicate" $\mathsf{Bad}(\mathsf{RF}^{3n,n})$ on the ideal keyed function $\mathsf{RF}^{3n,n}$, such that once $\mathsf{Bad}(\mathsf{RF}^{3n,n})$ is not fulfilled, the event $T_{id} = \tau$ is equivalent to $\mathsf{RF}^{3n,n}$ satisfying $4q$ new and distinct equations. Since the keys of the 2nd and 4th rounds are same, while the keys of the 3rd and 5th rounds are also same, we need to ensure that for these four rounds, there exists $4q$ different equations. And then K_1^{bad} leads to $\mathsf{RF}_{K_2}^{3n,n}$ input collisions and K_2^{bad} causes $\mathsf{RF}_{K_1}^{3n,n}$ input collisions. Formally, the specific definition and probability analysis are as follows.

Definition 8. *Given a function* $\mathsf{RF}^{3n,n}$, *the predicate* $\mathsf{Bad}(\mathsf{RF}^{3n,n})$ *is fulfilled, if either of the conditions "K_1 is bad" and "K_2 is bad" is fulfilled.*

- *The condition "K_1 is bad" consists of five subconditions as follows.*
  (B-1) there exists i *and* j *such that* $X_{2,i}[n+1,4n] = X_{2,j}[n+1,4n], (i \neq j)$.
  (B-2) there exists i *and* j *such that* $X_{2,i}[n+1,4n] = X_{4,j}[n+1,4n]$.
  (B-3) there exists i *and* j *such that* $X_{2,i}[n+1,4n] = X_{6,j}[n+1,4n]$.
  (B-4) there exists i *and* j *such that* $X_{4,i}[n+1,4n] = X_{4,j}[n+1,4n], (i \neq j)$.
  (B-5) there exists i *and* j *such that* $X_{4,i}[n+1,4n] = X_{6,j}[n+1,4n]$.
- *The condition "K_2 is bad" consists of five subconditions as follows.*
  (B-6) there exists i *and* j *such that* $X_{5,i}[n+1,4n] = X_{5,j}[n+1,4n], (i \neq j)$.
  (B-7) there exists i *and* j *such that* $X_{5,i}[n+1,4n] = X_{3,j}[n+1,4n]$.
  (B-8) there exists i *and* j *such that* $X_{5,i}[n+1,4n] = X_{1,j}[n+1,4n]$.
  (B-9) there exists i *and* j *such that* $X_{3,i}[n+1,4n] = X_{3,j}[n+1,4n], (i \neq j)$.
  (B-10) there exists i *and* j *such that* $X_{3,i}[n+1,4n] = X_{1,j}[n+1,4n]$.

Otherwise we say τ *is good.*

Similarly to Sect. 3.2, we expand the probability of each $(B-i)$ to $1/2^n$ and obtain

$$\Pr\left[K_1 \text{ is bad} \mid \neg(\mathrm{EV}^{\mathsf{cf}} \vee \mathrm{EV}^{\mathsf{sf}})\right] \leq \frac{5q^2}{2^n},$$

$$\Pr\left[K_2 \text{ is bad} \mid \neg(\mathrm{EV}^{\mathsf{cf}} \vee \mathrm{EV}^{\mathsf{sf}})\right] \leq \frac{5q^2}{2^n}.$$

And we reach,

$$\Pr\left[\mathsf{Bad}(\mathsf{RF}^{3n,n})\right] \leq \frac{10q^2}{2^n}. \tag{15}$$

Completing the Proof. For the remaining, we fix a good transcript $\tau = (\mathcal{Q}, K)$, where $\mathcal{Q} = (\phi_i, X_{1,i}[1,4n], X_{7,i}[1,4n])_{i=1,\ldots,q}$.

First, we classify RKD functions ϕ_i, suppose that the quantity of ϕ_i is α, which are denoted $\phi^{(1)}, \phi^{(2)}, \cdots, \phi^{(\alpha)}$ respectively. $\mathcal{Q}_i(\ i = 1, \ldots, \alpha)$ are denoted a set of transcripts with RKD functions ϕ_i. For $i = 1, \ldots, \alpha$, define

$$\mathcal{Q}_i = \left\{(\phi^{(i)}, X_{1i}[1,4n], X_{7i}[1,4n]), \ldots, (\phi^{(i)}, X_{1q_i}[1,4n], X_{7q_i}[1,4n])\right\},$$

where $\mathcal{Q}_i$ has q_i different inputs. Suppose that $\phi^{(1)}, \phi^{(2)}, \cdots, \phi^{(\alpha)}$ can derive β different K_1: $K_1^{(1)}$, $K_1^{(2)}$, ..., $K_1^{(\beta)}$ $(\beta \leq \alpha)$. Suppose that q queries to Related-Key Oracle constitute of $q_1^*, \cdots, q_\beta^*$ inputs separately in $K_1^{(1)}$, $K_1^{(2)}$, ..., $K_1^{(\beta)}$. The probability to obtain τ in ideal word is

$$\Pr[T_{id} = \tau] = \left(\frac{1}{|\mathcal{K}|}\right) \prod_{i=0}^{\alpha} \frac{1}{(2^{4n})_{q_i}} \leq \left(\frac{1}{|\mathcal{K}|}\right)\left(2^{4n} - q\right)^{-q}.$$

In a similar vein to Sect. 3.2, the probability in real world is

$$\begin{aligned}
&\Pr[T_{re} = \tau] = \Pr\left[\mathsf{RK}[\mathsf{CFN}_K^{\mathsf{RF}^{3n,n},6}] \vdash \mathcal{Q}\right] \cdot \Pr_{K^*}[K^* = K] \\
&= \left(\frac{1}{|\mathcal{K}|}\right) \cdot \left(1 - \Pr\left[\mathsf{Bad}(\mathsf{RF}^{3n,n})\right]\right) \cdot \Pr\left[\mathsf{RK}[\mathsf{CFN}_K^{\mathsf{RF}^{3n,n},6}] \vdash \mathcal{Q} \mid \neg\mathsf{Bad}(\mathsf{RF}^{3n,n})\right].
\end{aligned}$$

It can be seen that the event $\mathsf{RK}[\mathsf{CFN}_K^{\mathsf{RF}^{3n,n},6}] \vdash \mathcal{Q}$ is equivalent to the event that $\mathsf{RF}^{3n,n}$ satisfies $4q$ equations for the 2rd round to the 5th round, i.e., for $i = 1, ..., q$,

$$\begin{aligned}
\mathsf{RF}_{K_2}^{3n,n}(X_{2i}[n+1, 4n]) &= X_{2i}[1, n] \oplus X_{3i}[3n+1, 4n], \\
\mathsf{RF}_{K_1}^{3n,n}(X_{3i}[n+1, 4n]) &= X_{3i}[1, n] \oplus X_{4i}[3n+1, 4n], \\
\mathsf{RF}_{K_2}^{3n,n}(X_{4i}[n+1, 4n]) &= X_{4i}[1, n] \oplus X_{5i}[3n+1, 4n], \\
\mathsf{RF}_{K_1}^{3n,n}(X_{5i}[n+1, 4n]) &= X_{5i}[1, n] \oplus X_{6i}[3n+1, 4n].
\end{aligned}$$

Therefore, we have the probability

$$\begin{aligned}
&\Pr\left[\mathsf{RK}[\mathsf{CFN}_K^{\mathsf{RF}^{3n,n},6}] \vdash \mathcal{Q} \mid \neg\mathsf{Bad}(\mathsf{RF}^{3n,n})\right] \\
&= \prod_{i=1}^{q} \Bigg(\Pr\left[\mathsf{RF}_{K_2}^{3n,n}(X_{2i}[n+1, 4n]) = X_{2i}[1, n] \oplus X_{3i}[3n+1, 4n]\right] \\
&\quad \times \Pr\left[\mathsf{RF}_{K_1}^{3n,n}(X_{3i}[n+1, 4n]) = X_{3i}[1, n] \oplus X_{4i}[3n+1, 4n]\right] \\
&\quad \times \Pr\left[\mathsf{RF}_{K_2}^{3n,n}(X_{4i}[n+1, 4n]) = X_{4i}[1, n] \oplus X_{5i}[3n+1, 4n]\right] \\
&\quad \times \Pr\left[\mathsf{RF}_{K_1}^{3n,n}(X_{5i}[n+1, 4n]) = X_{5i}[1, n] \oplus X_{6i}[3n+1, 4n]\right]\Bigg) \\
&= \left(\frac{1}{2^n}\right)^{4q}.
\end{aligned}$$

In all, using Eq. (15), we have

$$\begin{aligned}
&\frac{\Pr[T_{re} = \tau]}{\Pr[T_{id} = \tau]} \\
&\geq \left(1 - \Pr\left[\mathsf{Bad}(\mathsf{RF}^{3n,n})\right]\right) \cdot \Pr\left[\mathsf{RK}[\mathsf{CFN}_K^{\mathsf{RF}^{3n,n},6}] \vdash \mathcal{Q} \mid \neg\mathsf{Bad}(\mathsf{RF}^{3n,n})\right] \Big/ \prod_{i=0}^{\alpha} \frac{1}{(2^{4n})_{q_i}} \\
&\geq \left(1 - \frac{10q^2}{2^n}\right) \times \left(\frac{1}{2^{4n}}\right)^q \times (2^{4n} - q)^q \\
&\geq 1 - \left(\frac{10q^2}{2^n} + \frac{q^2}{2^{4n}}\right). \qquad (16)
\end{aligned}$$

Gathering Eq. (14) and (16), and using Lemma 1, we complete the proof of Theorem 2.

References

1. Abdalla, M., Benhamouda, F., Passelègue, A., Paterson, K.G.: Related-key security for pseudorandom functions beyond the linear barrier. In: Garay, J.A., Gennaro, R. (eds.) CRYPTO 2014, Part I. LNCS, vol. 8616, pp. 77–94. Springer, Heidelberg (2014). https://doi.org/10.1007/978-3-662-44371-2_5
2. Anderson, R., Biham, E.: Two practical and provably secure block ciphers: BEAR and LION. In: Gollmann, D. (ed.) FSE 1996. LNCS, vol. 1039, pp. 113–120. Springer, Heidelberg (1996). https://doi.org/10.1007/3-540-60865-6_48
3. Anderson, R., Kuhn, M.: Low cost attacks on tamper resistant devices. In: Christianson, B., Crispo, B., Lomas, M., Roe, M. (eds.) Security Protocols 1997. LNCS, vol. 1361, pp. 125–136. Springer, Heidelberg (1998). https://doi.org/10.1007/BFb0028165
4. Barbosa, M., Farshim, P.: The related-key analysis of Feistel constructions. In: Cid, C., Rechberger, C. (eds.) FSE 2014. LNCS, vol. 8540, pp. 265–284. Springer, Heidelberg (2015). https://doi.org/10.1007/978-3-662-46706-0_14
5. Bellare, M., Cash, D.: Pseudorandom functions and permutations provably secure against related-key attacks. In: Rabin, T. (ed.) CRYPTO 2010. LNCS, vol. 6223, pp. 666–684. Springer, Heidelberg (2010). https://doi.org/10.1007/978-3-642-14623-7_36
6. Bellare, M., Kohno, T.: A theoretical treatment of related-key attacks: RKA-PRPs, RKA-PRFs, and applications. In: Biham, E. (ed.) EUROCRYPT 2003. LNCS, vol. 2656, pp. 491–506. Springer, Heidelberg (2003). https://doi.org/10.1007/3-540-39200-9_31
7. Bellare, M., Ristenpart, T., Rogaway, P., Stegers, T.: Format-preserving encryption. In: Jacobson, M.J., Rijmen, V., Safavi-Naini, R. (eds.) SAC 2009. LNCS, vol. 5867, pp. 295–312. Springer, Heidelberg (2009). https://doi.org/10.1007/978-3-642-05445-7_19
8. Biham, E.: New types of cryptanalytic attacks using related keys. J. Cryptol. **7**(4), 229–246 (1994). https://doi.org/10.1007/BF00203965
9. Biryukov, A., Khovratovich, D.: Related-key cryptanalysis of the full AES-192 and AES-256. In: Matsui, M. (ed.) ASIACRYPT 2009. LNCS, vol. 5912, pp. 1–18. Springer, Heidelberg (2009). https://doi.org/10.1007/978-3-642-10366-7_1

10. Biryukov, A., Khovratovich, D., Nikolić, I.: Distinguisher and related-key attack on the full AES-256. In: Halevi, S. (ed.) CRYPTO 2009. LNCS, vol. 5677, pp. 231–249. Springer, Heidelberg (2009). https://doi.org/10.1007/978-3-642-03356-8_14
11. Black, J., Rogaway, P.: Ciphers with arbitrary finite domains. In: Preneel, B. (ed.) CT-RSA 2002. LNCS, vol. 2271, pp. 114–130. Springer, Heidelberg (2002). https://doi.org/10.1007/3-540-45760-7_9
12. Chen, S., Steinberger, J.: Tight security bounds for key-alternating ciphers. In: Nguyen, P.Q., Oswald, E. (eds.) EUROCRYPT 2014. LNCS, vol. 8441, pp. 327–350. Springer, Heidelberg (2014). https://doi.org/10.1007/978-3-642-55220-5_19
13. Diffie, W., (translators), Ledin, G.: SMS4 encryption algorithm for wireless networks. Cryptology ePrint Archive, Report 2008/329 (2008). http://eprint.iacr.org/2008/329
14. Dunkelman, O., Keller, N., Shamir, A.: A practical-time related-key attack on the KASUMI cryptosystem used in GSM and 3G telephony. J. Cryptol. **27**(4), 824–849 (2014)
15. Fehr, S., Karpman, P., Mennink, B.: Short non-malleable codes from related-key secure block ciphers. IACR Trans. Symm. Cryptol. **2018**(1), 336–352 (2018)
16. Feistel, H., Notz, W.A., Smith, J.L.: Some cryptographic techniques for machine-to-machine data communications. Proc. IEEE **63**(11), 1545–1554 (1975)
17. Gueron, S., Mouha, N.: Simpira v2: a family of efficient permutations using the AES round function. In: Cheon, J.H., Takagi, T. (eds.) ASIACRYPT 2016. LNCS, vol. 10031, pp. 95–125. Springer, Heidelberg (2016). https://doi.org/10.1007/978-3-662-53887-6_4
18. Guo, C.: Understanding the related-key security of feistel ciphers from a provable perspective. IEEE Trans. Inf. Theory **65**(8), 5260–5280 (2019). https://doi.org/10.1109/TIT.2019.2903796
19. Hoang, V.T., Rogaway, P.: On generalized Feistel networks. In: Rabin, T. (ed.) CRYPTO 2010. LNCS, vol. 6223, pp. 613–630. Springer, Heidelberg (2010). https://doi.org/10.1007/978-3-642-14623-7_33
20. Iwata, T., Kohno, T.: New security proofs for the 3GPP confidentiality and integrity algorithms. In: Roy, B., Meier, W. (eds.) FSE 2004. LNCS, vol. 3017, pp. 427–445. Springer, Heidelberg (2004). https://doi.org/10.1007/978-3-540-25937-4_27
21. Knudsen, L.R.: Cryptanalysis of LOKI 91. In: Seberry, J., Zheng, Y. (eds.) AUSCRYPT 1992. LNCS, vol. 718, pp. 196–208. Springer, Heidelberg (1993). https://doi.org/10.1007/3-540-57220-1_62
22. Liskov, M., Rivest, R.L., Wagner, D.: Tweakable block ciphers. J. Cryptol. **24**(3), 588–613 (2011)
23. Luby, M., Rackoff, C.: How to construct pseudorandom permutations from pseudorandom functions. SIAM J. Comput. **17**(2), 373–386 (1988)
24. Lucks, S.: Faster Luby-Rackoff ciphers. In: Gollmann, D. (ed.) FSE 1996. LNCS, vol. 1039, pp. 189–203. Springer, Heidelberg (1996). https://doi.org/10.1007/3-540-60865-6_53
25. Morris, B., Rogaway, P., Stegers, T.: How to encipher messages on a small domain. In: Halevi, S. (ed.) CRYPTO 2009. LNCS, vol. 5677, pp. 286–302. Springer, Heidelberg (2009). https://doi.org/10.1007/978-3-642-03356-8_17
26. Nandi, M.: On the optimality of non-linear computations of length-preserving encryption schemes. In: Iwata, T., Cheon, J.H. (eds.) ASIACRYPT 2015. LNCS, vol. 9453, pp. 113–133. Springer, Heidelberg (2015). https://doi.org/10.1007/978-3-662-48800-3_5

27. Naor, M., Reingold, O.: On the construction of pseudorandom permutations: Luby-Rackoff revisited. J. Cryptol. **12**(1), 29–66 (1999)
28. Patarin, J.: Security of random Feistel schemes with 5 or more rounds. In: Franklin, M. (ed.) CRYPTO 2004. LNCS, vol. 3152, pp. 106–122. Springer, Heidelberg (2004). https://doi.org/10.1007/978-3-540-28628-8_7
29. Patarin, J.: The "coefficients H" technique. In: Avanzi, R.M., Keliher, L., Sica, F. (eds.) SAC 2008. LNCS, vol. 5381, pp. 328–345. Springer, Heidelberg (2009). https://doi.org/10.1007/978-3-642-04159-4_21
30. Patarin, J.: Security of balanced and unbalanced Feistel schemes with linear non equalities. Cryptology ePrint Archive, Report 2010/293 (2010). http://eprint.iacr.org/2010/293
31. Patarin, J., Nachef, V., Berbain, C.: Generic attacks on unbalanced Feistel schemes with contracting functions. In: Lai, X., Chen, K. (eds.) ASIACRYPT 2006. LNCS, vol. 4284, pp. 396–411. Springer, Heidelberg (2006). https://doi.org/10.1007/11935230_26
32. Sadeghiyan, B., Pieprzyk, J.: A construction for super pseudorandom permutations from a single pseudorandom function. In: Rueppel, R.A. (ed.) EUROCRYPT 1992. LNCS, vol. 658, pp. 267–284. Springer, Heidelberg (1993). https://doi.org/10.1007/3-540-47555-9_23
33. Schneier, B., Kelsey, J.: Unbalanced Feistel networks and block cipher design. In: Gollmann, D. (ed.) FSE 1996. LNCS, vol. 1039, pp. 121–144. Springer, Heidelberg (1996). https://doi.org/10.1007/3-540-60865-6_49
34. Shen, Y., Guo, C., Wang, L.: Improved security bounds for generalized Feistel networks. IACR Trans. Symmetric Cryptol. **2020**(1), 425–457 (2020). https://doi.org/10.13154/tosc.v2020.i1.425-457
35. Shibutani, K., Isobe, T., Hiwatari, H., Mitsuda, A., Akishita, T., Shirai, T.: *Piccolo*: an ultra-lightweight blockcipher. In: Preneel, B., Takagi, T. (eds.) CHES 2011. LNCS, vol. 6917, pp. 342–357. Springer, Heidelberg (2011). https://doi.org/10.1007/978-3-642-23951-9_23
36. Zhang, L., Wu, W.: Pseudorandomness and super pseudorandomness on the unbalanced Feistel networks with contracting functions. Chin. J. Comput. **32**(7), 1320–1330 (2009). Clarified via personal communication
37. Zheng, Y., Matsumoto, T., Imai, H.: On the construction of block ciphers provably secure and not relying on any unproved hypotheses. In: Brassard, G. (ed.) CRYPTO 1989. LNCS, vol. 435, pp. 461–480. Springer, New York (1990). https://doi.org/10.1007/0-387-34805-0_42

Revisiting Construction of Online Cipher in Hash-ECB-Hash Structure

Gang Liu[1,2], Peng Wang[1,2(✉)], Rong Wei[3], and Dingfeng Ye[1,2]

[1] SKLOIS, Institute of Information Engineering, CAS, Beijing, China
{liugang,wpeng,yedingfeng}@iie.ac.cn
[2] School of Cyber Security, University of Chinese Academy of Sciences, Beijing, China
[3] Beijing Satellite Information Engineer Institute, Beijing, China

Abstract. Online cipher is an important primitive in many cryptographic schemes, such as authenticated encryption schemes. Considering performance and security, the Hash-ECB-Hash (HEH) structure provides a potential way to construct parallelizable and CCA secure online cipher. In this paper, we start from the online cipher POE which is the only instantiation of Hash-ECB-Hash structure in the literature. However, the AXU property of hash function in the hash layer cannot guarantee the security of POE. Then we propose a new concept of online universal hash function (OUHF) for the hash layer and prove that the Hash-ECB-Hash structure is CCA secure, if the hash layer is online almost universal (OAU) hash function and the underlying block cipher is CCA secure. We also give several concrete constructions of OAU.

Keywords: Online cipher · POE · Hash-ECB-Hash · Online universal hash function

1 Introduction

Security is widely applied in daily scenarios such as live broadcasts, stock trading system, which puts forward more online requirements for ciphers. These applications require high performance and low latency but the emerging memory-restricted devices can only handle a small segmented data at a time. The security and efficiency of online data processing becomes more important.

Online Cipher (OC). The concept of online cipher was proposed by Bellare et al. [4] in 2001, which is a cryptographic primitive that enciphers data blocks in an online way. There are a lot of online authenticated encryption schemes based on online ciphers, such as McOE [13], POET [1], COPA [3], ELmD [11], COLM [2].

Online ciphers can be constructed from block ciphers, tweakable block ciphers or permutations combined with universal hash functions (UHFs). They can be sequential or non-sequential. The non-sequential designs usually adopt multi-layer structure, including the 4-round Feistel structure in OleF [6], the Encrypt-Mix-Encrypt (EME) structure in COPA [3], ELmD [11] and COLM [2], and

Y. Wu and M. Yung (Eds.): Inscrypt 2020, LNCS 12612, pp. 491–503, 2021.
https://doi.org/10.1007/978-3-030-71852-7_32

the Hash-ECB-Hash (HEH) structure in POE [1]. Multi-layer structure implies potentially parallel computing. The first structure processes each block with 4-round Feistel, achieving CCA security, but the block-length is twice that of the round function. The EME is only CPA secure [10]. The HEH structure firstly processes the blocks using UHFs, then encrypts the blocks using ECB mode, and finally processes the blocks using UHFs again. The UHF [9], which has great advantage at efficiency, is widely used in cryptographic schemes, including message authentication codes (MACs) [7,12,15,25], tweakable enciphering schemes [14,24] and authenticated encryption schemes [17,20]. See Table 1 for more details about existing online ciphers.

Table 1. Categories and security of online ciphers.

	Sequential	Non-sequential
CPA-secure	HCBC1 [4], TC1 [21]	COPE (in COPA) [3], online ciphers in ELmD [11] /COLM [2]
CCA-secure	HCBC2 [4], MCBC [18], MHCBC [18], TC2 [21], TC3 [21], XTC [16]	OleF [6], POE (in POET) [1]

The Flaw in Instantiation of Hash-ECB-Hash Structure. So far the only instantiation of HEH structure is the online cipher POE which is used in the authenticated encryption scheme POET [1]. Unfortunately, Nandi [19] proposed a successful distinguishing attack against POE by making only one encryption query when the underlying UHF is chosen as a special one. Therefore the security precondition is not reasonable and the security proof of POE has flaws.

Motivations. For fast implementation and security, an ideal online cipher should be both non-sequential and CCA-secure. The HEH structure gives a potential way to satisfy the both conditions. Therefore POE is a good starting point. *We want to make it clear what on earth is wrong with the design of POE.* We notice that POE uses a UHF f with almost XOR universal (AXU) property in the CFB mode as the hash layer denoted as CFB$[f]$, and the AXU property of f may not guarantee the security of HEH structure according to the work of Nandi [19]. *One question is what property of f can guarantee the security of POE?* Other than CFB mode, there are many other modes to construct the hash layer. A more general question is *what property of the whole hash layer can guarantee the security of HEH structure?*

Our Contributions. 1) We analyze the structure of POE. In order to thwart the attacks to POE, the output-collision probability of the component function of the hash layer should be negligible. 2) We extend the classic concept of UHF into online one and define the concept of online universal hash function (OUHF), including online almost universal (OAU) and online almost XOR universal (OAXU) hash function. The CFB mode in POE using a uniform random involution function or a Galois-Field multiplication function is not OAU. 3) We give concrete constructions of online universal hash function based on uniform random function, including the CFB and CBC modes. We also give a construction, named MCFB, based on finite field multiplication function. 4) We prove that HEH is CCA secure, if the hash layer is an online almost universal (OAU) hash function and the block cipher is a pseudorandom permutation against chosen ciphertext attack (PRP-CCA).

2 Preliminaries

Notations. Let $\{0,1\}^n$ be all n-bit strings and $\{0,1\}^{n*}$ be all strings whose bit length is the multiple of n excluding empty string ϵ. The bit length of string M is written as $|M|$. A string $X \in \{0,1\}^{n*}$ can be divided into n-bit blocks, and its block-length is written as $|X|_n$. If $|X|_n = m$, its i-th block is denoted as $X[i]$, then $X = (X[1], \cdots, X[m])$. Continuous blocks from the i-th to j-th $(1 \leq i < j \leq m)$ block of X are denoted as $X[i..j] = (X[i], X[i+1], \cdots, X[j])$. The longest common n-prefix of $X, Y \in \{0,1\}^{n*}$, denoted as $LCP_n(X,Y)$, is the longest string $Z \in \{0,1\}^{n*}$ so that $Z = X[1..i] = Y[1..i]$ and $X[i+1] \neq Y[i+1]$, where $i \leq |X|_n, i \leq |Y|_n$. The length of longest common n-prefix written as $LLCP_n(X,Y)$ is the block-length of the longest common n-prefix, that is $LLCP_n(X,Y) = |Z|_n$. Specially, $LCP_n(X,X) = X$ and $LLCP_n(X,X) = |X|_n$.

Generally, the symbol of multiplication operation $\cdot$ can be omitted without confusion, i.e. $KX = K \cdot X$. K^i denotes the product of K for i times. $\mathcal{S}_1 \times \mathcal{S}_2$ denotes the Cartesian product of two sets $\mathcal{S}_1$ and $\mathcal{S}_2$. $s \stackrel{\$}{\leftarrow} \mathcal{S}$ denotes choosing a uniform random element s from the set $\mathcal{S}$.

Let $A^{\mathcal{O}} \Rightarrow 1$ denote an adversary A that asks queries to one or more oracles $\mathcal{O}$ and outputs a bit 1. Without loss of generality, adversaries never ask a query for which the answer is trivially known, e.g. an adversary never repeats the query to a deterministic oracle and never asks an answer derived from the encryption oracle to the decryption oracle, and so forth.

Online Function and Online Permutation. $G : \{0,1\}^{n*} \rightarrow \{0,1\}^{n*}$ is an online function if G is length-preserving, i.e. m-block input $X = (X[1], X[2], \cdots, X[m])$ is mapped to m-block output $Y = (Y[1], Y[2], \cdots, Y[m])$, where $|X[i]| = |Y[i]| = n$, $i = 1, 2, \cdots, m$, and every output block $Y[i]$ only depends on $X[1..i]$, i.e. there exists a variable-input-length (VIL) function $G^c : \{0,1\}^{n*} \rightarrow \{0,1\}^n$ which is called component function, such that $Y[i] = G^c(X[1..i])$. The component function only outputs the last output block of the online function. Therefore $G(X) = (G^c(X[1]), \cdots, G^c(X[1..m]))$, $i = 1, 2, \cdots$. For example, Xor defined by $Xor^c(X[1..i]) = \bigoplus_{j=1}^{i} X[i]$, $i = 1, 2, \cdots$ is an online function.

Furthermore any practical online function should be computed efficiently in an online way. E.g. $Xor(X[1..m]) = Y[1..m] : S = S \oplus X[i]$, $Y[i] = S$, for $i = 1, 2, \cdots, m$, where $S \in \{0,1\}^n$ is a state maintained during the online computing and initialized as 0. Therefore we can describe an online function by the original multiple-block-input and multiple-block-input function, its component function, or its online computation procedure.

When G is invertible, in other words for any $X[1..i-1] \in \{0,1\}^{n(i-1)}$, $G^c(X[1..i-1],\cdot)$, $i=1,2,\cdots$, are all permutations on $\{0,1\}^n$, we say that G is an online permutation, where $G^c(X[1..0],\cdot) = G^c(\cdot)$. The inverse of G is written as G^{-1}, then G^{-1} is also an online permutation, and $(G^{-1})^c(Y[1..i-1],\cdot)$ is the inverse of $G^c(X[1..i-1],\cdot)$ if $Y[1..i-1] = G(X[1..i-1])$, $i=2,3,\cdots$. As an example, Xor is also an online permutation.

If G is an online permutation, $X, X' \in \{0,1\}^{n*}$ and $LLCP_n(X,X') = l$, then $LLCP_n(G(X),G(X')) = LLCP_n(G^{-1}(X),G^{-1}(X')) = l$. We call it longest common prefix preserving property (LCPP property).

Block Cipher and Online Cipher. $E : \mathcal{K} \times \{0,1\}^n \rightarrow \{0,1\}^n$ is a block cipher if $\mathcal{K}$ is a key space and $E(K,\cdot)$ is a permutation on $\{0,1\}^n$ for any $K \in \mathcal{K}$. We often write the key as a subscript: $E_K(\cdot) = E(K,\cdot)$. The inverse of E_K is denoted as D_K. $OC : \mathcal{K} \times \{0,1\}^{n*} \rightarrow \{0,1\}^{n*}$ is an online cipher if $\mathcal{K}$ is a key space and OC_K is an online permutation for any $K \in \mathcal{K}$. Generally $F : \mathcal{K} \times \{0,1\}^m \rightarrow \{0,1\}^n$ is a keyed function where $\mathcal{K}$ is a key space.

When we use a block cipher, an online cipher or a general keyed function, the key is uniform random: $K \xleftarrow{\$} \mathcal{K}$, so that a random permutation, an online random permutation or a random function is chosen. Let $\mathrm{Perm}(n)$ be a set of all permutations on $\{0,1\}^n$. A uniform random permutation (URP) is $\pi \xleftarrow{\$} \mathrm{Perm}(n)$. Let $\mathrm{OPerm}(n)$ be a set of all online permutations on $\{0,1\}^{n*}$. An online uniform random permutation (OURP) is $\rho \xleftarrow{\$} \mathrm{OPerm}(n)$. Let $\mathrm{Func}(m,n)$ be a set of all functions from $\{0,1\}^m$ to $\{0,1\}^n$. When $m = n$ we denote it as $\mathrm{Func}(n)$. A uniform random function (URF) is $f \xleftarrow{\$} \mathrm{Func}(m,n)$.

The security of block cipher, online cipher or keyed function is defined as indistinguishability from the corresponding uniform random object.

Definition 1 (PRP-CPA, PRP-CCA, OPRP-CPA, OPRP-CCA, PRF). *$E : \mathcal{K} \times \{0,1\}^n \rightarrow \{0,1\}^n$ is a block cipher, $OC : \mathcal{K} \times \{0,1\}^{n*} \rightarrow \{0,1\}^{n*}$ is an online cipher and $F : \mathcal{K} \times \{0,1\}^m \rightarrow \{0,1\}^n$ is a keyed function. The distinguishing advantages of the adversary A are defined as follows:*

$$\begin{aligned}
\mathbf{Adv}_E^{\text{prp-cpa}}(A) &= \Pr[A^{E_K} \Rightarrow 1] - \Pr[A^{\pi} \Rightarrow 1],\\
\mathbf{Adv}_E^{\text{prp-cca}}(A) &= \Pr[A^{E_K,D_K} \Rightarrow 1] - \Pr[A^{\pi,\pi^{-1}} \Rightarrow 1],\\
\mathbf{Adv}_{OC}^{\text{oprp-cpa}}(A) &= \Pr[A^{OC_K} \Rightarrow 1] - \Pr[A^{\rho} \Rightarrow 1],\\
\mathbf{Adv}_{OC}^{\text{oprp-cca}}(A) &= \Pr[A^{OC_K,OC_K^{-1}} \Rightarrow 1] - \Pr[A^{\rho,\rho^{-1}} \Rightarrow 1],\\
\mathbf{Adv}_F^{\text{prf}}(A) &= \Pr[A^{F_K} \Rightarrow 1] - \Pr[A^{f} \Rightarrow 1].
\end{aligned}$$

Here PRP-CPA, PRP-CCA, OPRP-CPA, OPRP-CCA and PRF are acronyms of pseudorandom permutation against chosen plaintext attack, pseudorandom permutation against chosen ciphertext attack, online pseudorandom permutation against chosen plaintext attack, online pseudorandom permutation against chosen ciphertext attack and pseudorandom function respectively. In the following, we write the maximal advantage of A with resources at most $\mathcal{R}$ as

$\mathbf{Adv}_{\Pi}^{\text{xxx}}(\mathcal{R}) = max_A\{\mathbf{Adv}_{\Pi}^{\text{xxx}}(A)\}$. The resources include the total number of oracle queries q and the total block-length of those queries σ and the running time t, etc. When $\mathbf{Adv}_{\Pi}^{\text{xxx}}(\mathcal{R})$ is negligible, we say that Π is a xxx.

Switching Lemma. When querying a block cipher which is idealized as a URP, it behaves like a URF, which always returns uniform random values. It is known as PRP/PRF switching lemma [5]. The distinguishing advantage is bounded by $q(q-1)/2^{n+1}$, where q is the number of queries.

Analogously, we have OPRP/OPRF switching lemma [4]: An online uniform random permutation (OURP) approximately replies to queries with random block values unless constrained by LCPP property. In other words, during the querying to the encryption oracle and the decryption oracle, there exists a transcript recording plaintext-ciphertext pairs. For any query of Z to the encryption/decryption oracle, find the maximal longest common prefix of Z and the plaintext/ciphertext records, and output the corresponding ciphertext/plaintext prefix and uniform random blocks for the remaining blocks.

Lemma 1 (OPRP/OPRF Switching Lemma [4]**).** *Let A be an adversary making oracle queries totalling at most σ blocks. Then,*

$$\Pr[A^{\rho,\rho^{-1}} \Rightarrow 1] - \Pr[A^{g,g'} \Rightarrow 1] \leq \sigma(\sigma-1)/2^{n+1},$$

where $\rho \stackrel{\$}{\leftarrow} \mathrm{OPerm}(n)$, and g and g' reply to queries with uniform random block values unless constrained by LCPP property.

Universal Hash Functions (UHF). Two commonly used UHFs are almost-universal (AU) and almost-XOR-universal (AXU) hash function [23]. The output-collision probability for any two different inputs of AU is negligible. The output-differential probability for any two different inputs of AXU is negligible. Clearly, if H is δ-AXU, it is also δ-AU. If $H : \mathcal{K} \times \mathcal{D} \to \{0,1\}^n$ is δ-AXU, then $H' : \mathcal{K} \times \mathcal{D} \times \{0,1\}^n \to \{0,1\}^n$ defined as $H'_K(X, X') = H_K(X) \oplus X'$ is δ-AU. The AU is often used to extend the input length of a PRF. The composition of a PRF and an AU is still a PRF.

Lemma 2 (PRF(AU) = PRF [22]**).** *$F : \mathcal{K} \times \{0,1\}^n \to \{0,1\}^m$ is a keyed function and $H : \mathcal{K}' \times \mathcal{D} \to \{0,1\}^n$ is a δ-AU hash function. The composition of F and H is defined as $FH_{K_1,K_2}(X) = F_{K_1}(H_{K_2}(X))$. For any PRF-adversary A against FH that asks q queries, then there exists a PRF-adversary B against F that asks q queries in approximately the same time as A, such that*

$$\mathbf{Adv}_{FH}^{\text{prf}}(A) \leq \mathbf{Adv}_{F}^{\text{prf}}(B) + q^2\delta/2.$$

3 Analysis of POE

The Structure of POE. POE (Pipelineable On-line Encryption) [1] proposed by Abed etc. in 2014 is an online cipher using HEH structure, which is the core of authenticated encryption scheme POET. POET was published with POE in

FSE 2014 and also submitted to CAESAR competition, ending up as one of second-round candidates due to Nandi's attack [19].

All three layers of POE are keyed online permutations. The first layer is a hash layer which is a CFB mode based on a universal hash function $F : \mathcal{K} \times \{0,1\}^n \rightarrow \{0,1\}^n$. The middle layer is an ECB mode based on a block cipher E. The third layer is also a hash layer which is the inverse of the CFB mode using F but with a different key. See Fig. 1.

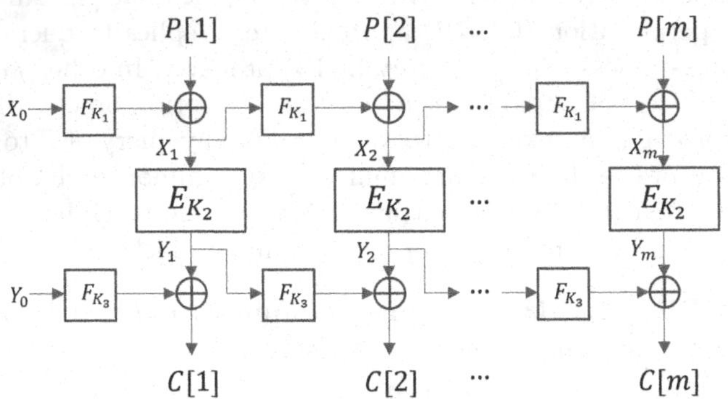

Fig. 1. Online cipher P.OE, where X_0 and Y_0 are two constants used as fixed IVs

More specifically, the encryption of POE is as follows:
Input: $P = (P[1], P[2], \cdots, P[m])$.

1) The first layer CFB$[F_{K_1}]$: $X_i = F_{K_1}(X_{i-1}) \oplus P[i]$ for $i = 1, 2, \cdots, m$, and X_0 is a constant.
2) The second layer ECB$[E_{K_2}]$: $Y_i = E_{K_2}(X_i)$ for $i = 1, 2, \cdots, m$.
3) The third layer CFB$^{-1}[F_{K_3}]$: $C[i] = F_{K_3}(Y_{i-1}) \oplus Y_i$ for $i = 1, 2, \cdots, m$, and Y_0 is a constant. Output: $C = (C[1], C[2], \cdots, C[m])$.

So we can denote POE as CFB$[F_{K_1}]$-ECB$[E_{K_2}]$-CFB$^{-1}[F_{K_3}]$.

The AXU Property is Not Enough. POE was claimed to be an OPRP-CCA if F is an AXU hash function and E is a PRP-CCA. But in fact, POE is not even an OPRP-CPA if F is instantiated as some special AXU hash functions.

If find two different $(P[1], P[2], \cdots, P[i])$ and $(P'[1], P'[2], \cdots, P'[j])$ so that

$$\mathrm{CFB}[F_{K_1}]^c(P[1], P[2], \cdots, P[i]) = \mathrm{CFB}[F_{K_1}]^c(P'[1], P'[2], \cdots, P'[j]),$$

then for any $Y \in \{0,1\}^n$,

$$\mathrm{CFB}[F_{K_1}]^c(P[1], P[2], \cdots, P[i], Y) = \mathrm{CFB}[F_{K_1}]^c(P'[1], P'[2], \cdots, P'[j], Y).$$

In the third layer of CFB$^{-1}[F_{K_3}]$ each output block only depends on two input blocks, i.e. the current and the previous ones. Therefore for any $Y \in \{0,1\}^n$,

$$\mathrm{POE}^c(P[1], P[2], \cdots, P[i], Y) = \mathrm{POE}^c(P'[1], P'[2], \cdots, P'[j], Y).$$

An adversary can query $(P[1], P[2], \cdots, P[i], Y)$ and $(P'[1], P'[2], \cdots, P'[j], Y)$ to the oracles. If the two last output blocks are identical, the adversary outputs 1, otherwise 0. The distinguishing advantage is $1 - 2^{-n}$. So the crux of the attack to POE is to find an output-collision for the component function of hash layer.

In the following we show that some special AXU hash functions will make the above attack happen. The AXU hash functions are derived from Nandi's paper [19], but rearranged under the output-collision property of the hash layer.

The first instantiation is a uniform random involution function θ on $\{0,1\}^n$. It is easy to verify that θ is a $2/(2^n - 2)$-AXU hash function. Because $\theta(\theta(X)) = X$ for any $X \in \{0,1\}^n$, we have that $\text{CFB}[\theta]^c(X) = \text{CFB}[\theta]^c(X, 0, 0)$, for any $X \in \{0,1\}^n$. The second is a finite field multiplication function $F_K(X) = KX$, where $K, X \in \{0,1\}^n$ and KX is the finite field multiplication of K and X. Assume that $X_0 = 0$, then $\text{CFB}[F_K]^c(X) = \text{CFB}[F_K]^c(0, X)$, for any $X \in \{0,1\}^n$.

From the above analysis, we know that the AXU property of F in POE may not guarantee the security of $\text{CFB}[F_{K_1}]\text{-ECB}[E_{K_2}]\text{-CFB}^{-1}[F_{K_3}]$. One question is which property of F can guarantee the security of CFB-ECB-CFB^{-1} structure? The CFB mode is only one way to construct the hash layer. As a general online function, what property of the hash layer can insure the security of HEH structure? We need a new concept of online universal hash function (OUHF).

4 Definitions of Online Universal Hash Function

OAU and OAXU. In order to thwart the attacks to POE, the output collision probability of the component function should be negligible. Corresponding to the definitions of AU and AXU hash functions, we propose concepts of online almost universal (OAU) and online almost XOR universal (OAXU) hash functions, defined by properties of their component functions.

The output-collision probability of OAU's component function is negligible. The output-differential probability of OAXU's component function is negligible.

Definition 2 (OAU). *$G : \mathcal{K} \times \{0,1\}^{n*} \rightarrow \{0,1\}^{n*}$ is a keyed online function. G is δ-online-almost-universal (δ-OAU) hash function, if its component function G^c is δ-almost-universal (δ-AU) hash function and δ is negligible, in other words, for any $X, X' \in \{0,1\}^{n*}$, $X \neq X'$,*

$$\Pr[K \xleftarrow{\$} \mathcal{K} : G_K^c(X) = G_K^c(X')] \leq \delta.$$

Definition 3 (OAXU). *$G : \mathcal{K} \times \{0,1\}^{n*} \rightarrow \{0,1\}^{n*}$ is a keyed online function. G is δ-online-almost-XOR-universal (δ-OAXU) hash function, if its component function G^c is δ-almost-XOR-universal (δ-AXU) hash function and δ is negligible, in other words, for any $X, X' \in \{0,1\}^{n*}$, $X \neq X'$, and any $Y \in \{0,1\}^n$,*

$$\Pr[K \xleftarrow{\$} \mathcal{K} : G_K^c(X) \oplus G_K^c(X') = Y] \leq \delta.$$

δ-OAU is a special case of δ-OAXU when $Y = 0$.

In Sect. 3 we show that the CFB mode using some special AXU, including uniform random involution function and multiplication function, is not OAU.

The concept of OUHF can been viewed as the online version of blockwise UHF in [14], which was proposed to construct a tweakable enciphering scheme TET. The hash layer in TET is not online, because each output block depends on all input blocks.

By the analysis of POE in Sect. 3, if we find $X \neq X' \in \{0,1\}^{n*}$, such that $\mathrm{CFB}^c(X) = \mathrm{CFB}^c(X')$ with high probability such as p, we can distinguish POE from the OURP with the advantage of $p - 2^{-n}$. The OAU property of hash layer can prevent us from carrying out such an attack. Furthermore, in Sect. 6 we prove that when the hash layer is OAU and the block cipher is a PRP-CCA, the HEH structure is an OPRP-CCA. Therefore the OAU property of the hash layer is exactly what we need to insure the security of HEH structure. In the following, we focus on the constructions of online function with OAU property.

5 Constructions of OUHF Using OAU

The hash layer of POE [1] is the CFB mode. Although when f is a uniform random involution function or a multiplication function, CFB[f] is not OAU. Actually when f is a uniform random function, CFB[f] is OAU. So whether the hash layer is OAU or not depends on the strength of underlying function.

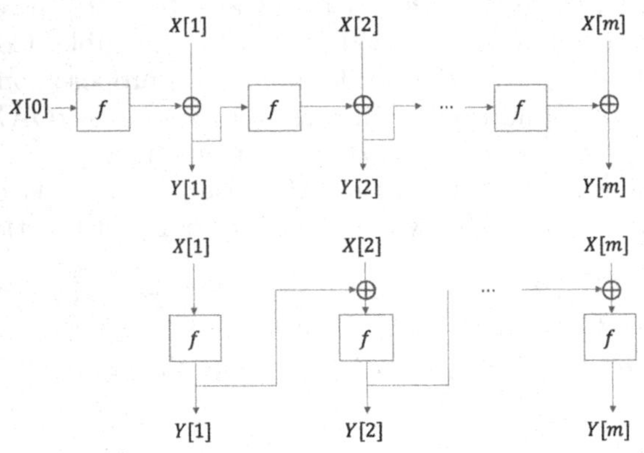

Fig. 2. CFB[f] (above) and CBC[f] (below).

The CFB/CBC Mode Using URF is OAU. The CFB mode and the CBC mode are illustrated in Fig. 2 and listed below.

- The CFB mode. $\mathrm{CFB}[f](X[1..m]) = Y[1..m]$: $Y[i] = f(Y[i-1]) \oplus X[i]$ for $i = 1, 2, \cdots, m$, where $Y[0]$ is a constant and $f \xleftarrow{\$} \mathrm{Func}(n)$.

- The CBC mode. $\mathrm{CBC}[f](X[1..m]) = Y[1..m]$: $Y[i] = f(Y[i-1] \oplus X[i])$ for $i = 1, 2, \cdots, m$, where $Y[0] = 0$ and $f \xleftarrow{\$} \mathrm{Func}(n)$.

According to Lemma 3 in [8], CBC-MAC is AU. When $f \xleftarrow{\$} Func(n)$, $\mathrm{CBC}[f]^c$ is exactly CBC-MAC$[f]$ in [8], thus $\mathrm{CBC}[f]$ is OAU. The relationship between $\mathrm{CBC}[f]$ and $\mathrm{CFB}[f]$ is $f(\mathrm{CFB}[f]^c(X[1..m])) = \mathrm{CBC}[f]^c(X[0], X[1..m])$.

For $X \neq X' \in \{0,1\}^{n*}$, $\mathrm{CFB}[f]^c(X) = \mathrm{CFB}[f]^c(X')$ implies $f(\mathrm{CFB}[f]^c(X)) = f(\mathrm{CFB}[f]^c(X'))$, i.e. $\mathrm{CBC}[f]^c(X[0], X) = \mathrm{CBC}[f]^c(X[0], X')$. So that

$$\Pr[\mathrm{CFB}[f]^c(X) = \mathrm{CFB}[f]^c(X')] \leq \Pr[\mathrm{CBC}[f]^c(X[0], X) = \mathrm{CBC}[f]^c(X[0], X')].$$

Thus $\mathrm{CFB}[f]$ is also OAU.

According to PRP/PRF switching lemma, f can be instantiated by a block cipher, meaning three calls to block cipher for each block data process in the HEH structure. It is overweight for some applications. Universal hash function is a more lightweight function than block cipher. Although Sect. 3 shows that, for multiplication function $F_K(X) = KX$, $\mathrm{CFB}[F_K]$ is not OAU, it is still valuable to construct OAU hash functions using universal hash functions such as F_K.

Multiplication Function Based Construction. We notice $\mathrm{CFB}[F_K]^c(X[1..m]) = X[1]K^{m-1} \oplus X[2]K^{m-2} \oplus \cdots \oplus X[m]$ is a classic polynomial evaluation function used in GCM [17], HCTR [24], etc. Although $\mathrm{CFB}[F_K]^c$ is not AU on $\{0,1\}^{n*}$, it is AU on $\{0,1\}^{nd}$ for any fixed integer d.

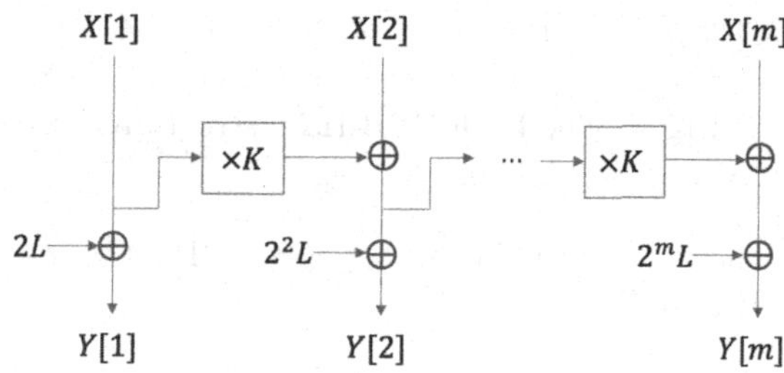

Fig. 3. $\mathrm{MCFB}[F_K]$.

In order to preserve OAU property for variable-input-length data, we XOR 2^iL, $i = 1, 2, \cdots$, to the output blocks of $\mathrm{CFB}[F_K]$, where $2 = 0^{n-2}10$ and $L \xleftarrow{\$} \{0,1\}^n$ is a secret key, as illustrated in Fig. 3. We denote such mode as MCFB (masked CFB). The component function $\mathrm{MCFB}[F_K]^c(X[1..m]) = X[1]K^{m-1} \oplus X[2]K^{m-2} \oplus \cdots \oplus X[m] \oplus 2^m L$.

Suppose that $X, X' \in \{0,1\}^{n*}$, $X \neq X'$, $|X|_n = m$, $|X'|_n = m'$. If $m = m'$, $\mathrm{MCFB}^c(X) \oplus \mathrm{MCFB}^c(X')$ is a none-zero polynomial in K with degree of at most $(m-1)$. So it has at most $(m-1)$ roots in finite field and the output-collision probability of $\mathrm{MCFB}[F_K]^c$ is bounded by $(m-1)/2^n$. If $m \neq m'$,

$\mathrm{MCFB}^c(X) \oplus \mathrm{MCFB}^c(X')$ has a monomial of $(2^m \oplus 2^{m'})L$, so the output-collision probability is $1/2^n$. Therefore $\mathrm{MCFB}[F_K]$ is OAU.

Compared with $\mathrm{CFB}[F_K]$, the extra computations $2^i L$ in $\mathrm{MCFB}[F_K]$ are trivial, costing one shift and one XOR operations for each mask [20].

6 Security of Hash-ECB-Hash Structure

A general HEH structure is illustrated in Fig. 4: the first layer is a keyed online permutation $G : \mathcal{K} \times \{0,1\}^{n*} \to \{0,1\}^{n*}$; the second layer is ECB mode with a block cipher $E : \mathcal{K}' \times \{0,1\}^n \to \{0,1\}^n$; the third layer is the inverse of G; each layer uses an independent key. The structure is denoted as $\mathrm{HEH}[G, E]$. The encryption and decryption of $\mathrm{HEH}[G, E]$ are denoted as $\mathcal{E}[G, E]$ and $\mathcal{D}[G, D]$.

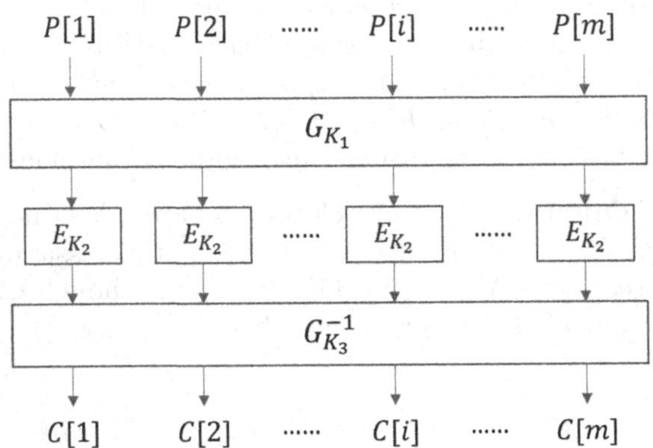

Fig. 4. The Hash-ECB-Hash structure.

We prove that when G is an OAU and E is a PRP-CCA, the HEH structure $\mathrm{HEH}[G, E]$ is an OPRP-CCA.

Theorem 1. *In HEH[G, E], if G is δ-OAU, then for any OPRP-CCA-adversary A against HEH[G, E] making oracle queries totalling σ blocks, there exists a PRP-CCA-adversary B against E that asks σ queries in approximately the same time as A, such that*

$$\mathbf{Adv}^{\text{oprp-cca}}_{\mathrm{HEH}[G,E]}(A) \leq \mathbf{Adv}^{\text{prp-cca}}_{E}(B) + \sigma^2/2^n + \sigma^2\delta.$$

Proof. The goal is to prove the indistinguishability between two oracle pairs: $(\mathcal{E}[G, E], \mathcal{D}[G, D])$ and (ρ, ρ^{-1}), where $\rho \xleftarrow{\$} \mathrm{OPerm}(n)$. We add three oracle pairs, as shown by Fig. 5. We only need to prove the indistinguishability between the adjacent pairs, then using the hybrid technique to fulfill the proof.

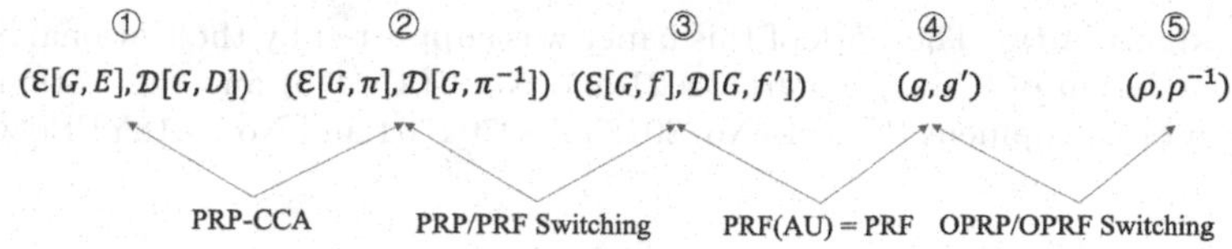

Fig. 5. Roadmap of the proof.

① - ②: $(\mathcal{E}[G,E],\mathcal{D}[G,D])$ and $(\mathcal{E}[G,\pi],\mathcal{D}[G,\pi^{-1}])$, where $\pi \xleftarrow{\$} \text{Perm}(n)$. If we replace (E_{K_2}, D_{K_2}) in the first oracle pair by (π, π^{-1}), we get the second pair. Adversary B simulates the query process of A, and returns what A returns, then

$$\Pr[A^{\mathcal{E}[G,E],\mathcal{D}[G,D]} \Rightarrow 1] - \Pr[A^{\mathcal{E}[G,\pi],\mathcal{D}[G,\pi^{-1}]} \Rightarrow 1] = \mathbf{Adv}_E^{\text{prp-cca}}(B). \quad (1)$$

② - ③: $(\mathcal{E}[G,\pi],\mathcal{D}[G,\pi^{-1}])$ and $(\mathcal{E}[G,f],\mathcal{D}[G,f'])$, where $f, f' \xleftarrow{\$} \text{Func}(n)$. f and f' reply queries with random block values. Using PRP/PRF switching lemma,

$$\Pr[A^{\mathcal{E}[G,\pi],\mathcal{D}[G,\pi^{-1}]} \Rightarrow 1] - \Pr[A^{\mathcal{E}[G,f],\mathcal{D}[G,f']} \Rightarrow 1] \le \sigma(\sigma-1)/2^{n+1}. \quad (2)$$

③ - ④: $(\mathcal{E}[G,f],\mathcal{D}[G,f'])$ and (g,g'), where (g,g') replies to queries with random block values unless constrained by LCPP property. The component function of the first two layers of the encryption oracle is $f(G_{K_1}^c(X))$, which is the composition of a uniform random function and an AU hash function. By Lemma 2 (PRF(AU) = PRF) [22], it is a PRF. The third layer is an independent online permutation, so the component function of $\mathcal{E}[G,f]$ is a PRF. By the same logic, the component function of $\mathcal{D}[G,f']$ is also a PRF. More specifically,

$$\Pr[A^{\mathcal{E}[G,f],\mathcal{D}[G,f']} \Rightarrow 1] - \Pr[A^{g,g'} \Rightarrow 1] \le \sigma^2\delta. \quad (3)$$

④ - ⑤: (g,g') and (ρ,ρ^{-1}). According to OPRP/OPRF switching lemma [4],

$$\Pr[A^{g,g'} \Rightarrow 1] - \Pr[A^{\rho,\rho^{-1}} \Rightarrow 1] \le \sigma(\sigma-1)/2^{n+1}. \quad (4)$$

Combining (1), (2), (3) and (4), we have that

$$\begin{aligned}\mathbf{Adv}_{\text{HEH}[G,E]}^{\text{oprp-cca}}(A) &= \Pr[A^{\mathcal{E}[G,E],\mathcal{D}[G,D]} \Rightarrow 1] - \Pr[A^{\rho,\rho^{-1}} \Rightarrow 1] \\ &\le \mathbf{Adv}_E^{\text{prp-cca}}(B) + \sigma^2/2^n + \sigma^2\delta.\end{aligned}$$

7 Conclusions

By analysis of POE, the only instantiation of HEH structure in online cipher, we extend the classic concepts of UHF into online ones and define the concepts of online UHF. We prove that HEH is CCA secure, if the hash layer is OAU and the block cipher is CCA secure. We give concrete constructions of OAU hash functions, including the CFB and CBC modes based on URF, and the MCFB mode based on multiplication function. The HEH structure provides a general method to construct parallelizable and CCA secure online cipher, which is the core of many online authenticated encryption schemes.

Acknowledgements. The work of this paper was supported by the National Natural Science Foundation of China (No. 61732021 and No. 61472415) and the National Key Research and Development Project (No. 2018YFA0704704 and No. 2018YFB0803801).

References

1. Abed, F., et al.: Pipelineable on-line encryption. In: Cid, C., Rechberger, C. (eds.) FSE 2014. LNCS, vol. 8540, pp. 205–223. Springer, Heidelberg (2015). https://doi.org/10.1007/978-3-662-46706-0_11
2. Andreeva, E., et al.: COLM v1. submission to the CAESAR competition (2016). https://competitions.cr.yp.to/round3/colmv1.pdf
3. Andreeva, E., Bogdanov, A., Luykx, A., Mennink, B., Tischhauser, E., Yasuda, K.: Parallelizable and authenticated online ciphers. In: Sako, K., Sarkar, P. (eds.) ASIACRYPT 2013. LNCS, vol. 8269, pp. 424–443. Springer, Heidelberg (2013). https://doi.org/10.1007/978-3-642-42033-7_22
4. Bellare, M., Boldyreva, A., Knudsen, L., Namprempre, C.: Online ciphers and the hash-CBC construction. In: Kilian, J. (ed.) CRYPTO 2001. LNCS, vol. 2139, pp. 292–309. Springer, Heidelberg (2001). https://doi.org/10.1007/3-540-44647-8_18
5. Bellare, M., Rogaway, P.: The security of triple encryption and a framework for code-based game-playing proofs. In: Vaudenay, S. (ed.) EUROCRYPT 2006. LNCS, vol. 4004, pp. 409–426. Springer, Heidelberg (2006). https://doi.org/10.1007/11761679_25
6. Bhaumik, R., Nandi, M.: OleF: an inverse-free online cipher. an online SPRP with an optimal inverse-free construction. IACR Trans. Symmetric Cryptol. **2016**(2), 30–51 (2016). https://doi.org/10.13154/tosc.v2016.i2.30-51
7. Black, J., Halevi, S., Krawczyk, H., Krovetz, T., Rogaway, P.: UMAC: fast and secure message authentication. In: Wiener, M. (ed.) CRYPTO 1999. LNCS, vol. 1666, pp. 216–233. Springer, Heidelberg (1999). https://doi.org/10.1007/3-540-48405-1_14
8. Black, J., Rogaway, P.: CBC MACs for arbitrary-length messages: the three-key constructions. In: Bellare, M. (ed.) CRYPTO 2000. LNCS, vol. 1880, pp. 197–215. Springer, Heidelberg (2000). https://doi.org/10.1007/3-540-44598-6_12
9. Carter, L., Wegman, M.N.: Universal classes of hash functions. J. Comput. Syst. Sci. **18**(2), 143–154 (1979). https://doi.org/10.1016/0022-0000(79)90044-8
10. Datta, N., Luykx, A., Mennink, B., Nandi, M.: Understanding RUP integrity of COLM. IACR Trans. Symmetric Cryptol. **2017**(2), 143–161 (2017)
11. Datta, N., Nandi, M.: ELmD v2.0. submission to the CAESAR competition (2015). https://competitions.cr.yp.to/round2/elmdv20.pdf
12. Etzel, M., Patel, S., Ramzan, Z.: Square hash: fast message authentication via optimized universal hash functions. In: Wiener, M. (ed.) CRYPTO 1999. LNCS, vol. 1666, pp. 234–251. Springer, Heidelberg (1999). https://doi.org/10.1007/3-540-48405-1_15
13. Fleischmann, E., Forler, C., Lucks, S.: McOE: a family of almost foolproof on-line authenticated encryption schemes. In: Canteaut, A. (ed.) FSE 2012. LNCS, vol. 7549, pp. 196–215. Springer, Heidelberg (2012). https://doi.org/10.1007/978-3-642-34047-5_12
14. Halevi, S.: Invertible universal hashing and the TET encryption mode. In: Menezes, A. (ed.) CRYPTO 2007. LNCS, vol. 4622, pp. 412–429. Springer, Heidelberg (2007). https://doi.org/10.1007/978-3-540-74143-5_23

15. Halevi, S., Krawczyk, H.: MMH: Software message authentication in the Gbit/second rates. In: Biham, E. (ed.) FSE 1997. LNCS, vol. 1267, pp. 172–189. Springer, Heidelberg (1997). https://doi.org/10.1007/BFb0052345
16. Jha, A., Nandi, M.: On rate-1 and beyond-the-birthday bound secure online ciphers using tweakable block ciphers. Crypt. Commun. **10**(5), 731–753 (2018). https://doi.org/10.1007/s12095-017-0275-0
17. McGrew, D.A., Viega, J.: The security and performance of the Galois/Counter Mode (GCM) of operation. In: Canteaut, A., Viswanathan, K. (eds.) INDOCRYPT 2004. LNCS, vol. 3348, pp. 343–355. Springer, Heidelberg (2004). https://doi.org/10.1007/978-3-540-30556-9_27
18. Nandi, M.: Two new efficient CCA-secure online ciphers: MHCBC and MCBC. In: Chowdhury, D.R., Rijmen, V., Das, A. (eds.) INDOCRYPT 2008. LNCS, vol. 5365, pp. 350–362. Springer, Heidelberg (2008). https://doi.org/10.1007/978-3-540-89754-5_27
19. Nandi, M.: Forging attacks on two authenticated encryption schemes COBRA and POET. In: Sarkar, P., Iwata, T. (eds.) ASIACRYPT 2014. LNCS, vol. 8873, pp. 126–140. Springer, Heidelberg (2014). https://doi.org/10.1007/978-3-662-45611-8_7
20. Rogaway, P.: Efficient instantiations of tweakable blockciphers and refinements to modes OCB and PMAC. In: Lee, P.J. (ed.) ASIACRYPT 2004. LNCS, vol. 3329, pp. 16–31. Springer, Heidelberg (2004). https://doi.org/10.1007/978-3-540-30539-2_2
21. Rogaway, P., Zhang, H.: Online ciphers from tweakable blockciphers. In: Kiayias, A. (ed.) CT-RSA 2011. LNCS, vol. 6558, pp. 237–249. Springer, Heidelberg (2011). https://doi.org/10.1007/978-3-642-19074-2_16
22. Shoup, V.: Sequences of games: a tool for taming complexity in security proofs. IACR Cryptol. ePrint Arch. 2004/332 (2004). https://ia.cr/2004/332
23. Stinson, D.R.: Universal hashing and authentication codes. In: Feigenbaum, J. (ed.) CRYPTO 1991. LNCS, vol. 576, pp. 74–85. Springer, Heidelberg (1992). https://doi.org/10.1007/3-540-46766-1_5
24. Wang, P., Feng, D., Wu, W.: HCTR: a variable-input-length enciphering mode. In: Feng, D., Lin, D., Yung, M. (eds.) CISC 2005. LNCS, vol. 3822, pp. 175–188. Springer, Heidelberg (2005). https://doi.org/10.1007/11599548_15
25. Wegman, M.N., Carter, L.: New hash functions and their use in authentication and set equality. J. Comput. Syst. Sci. **22**(3), 265–279 (1981)

Author Index

Printed in the United States
by Baker & Taylor Publisher Services